Cowlitz Dictionary
and
Grammatical Sketch

UM

Occasional Papers in Linguistics No. 18, 2004

Cowlitz Dictionary
and
Grammatical Sketch

M. Dale Kinkade

First Published December 2004

UMOPL — A series dedicated to the study
of the Native languages of the Northwest.

SERIES EDITORS
Anthony Mattina, University of Montana (anthony.mattina@umontana.edu)
Timothy Montler, University of North Texas (montler@unt.edu)

Address all correspondence to:
UMOPL — Linguistics Laboratory
The University of Montana
Missoula, MT 59812
USA

Library of Congress Cataloging-in-Publication Data

Kinkade, M. Dale (Marvin Dale), 1933-
Cowlitz dictionary and grammatical sketch / M. Dale Kinkade.
p. cm. -- (University of Montana occasional papers in linguistics ; no. 18)
In English and Cowlitz.
Includes bibliographical references.

ISBN 1-879763-18-4 (alk. paper)

1. Cowlitz language--Dictionaries--English. 2. Cowlitz language--Grammar.
3. English language--Dictionaries--Cowlitz. I. Title. II. Occasional papers
in linguistics (Missoula, Mont.); no. 18.

PM982.Z5K55 2004

497'.94--dc22

2004024853

CONTENTS

This dictionary of the Cowlitz language is an imperfect document, but collecting the data for it was a true salvage effort. I had been told for some time that this language had not been spoken since the 1940s, and I accepted that, but hoped that manuscript materials recording the language collected by Thelma Adamson in 1926 and 1927 would turn up. The latter, if they still exist, have not been located. But in 1967 I decided to make sure to my own satisfaction that the language was extinct. I spoke to officials and elders of the Cowlitz tribe, who lived in the Longview-Kelso area, and other places in southwestern Washington State. I did locate one woman in South Kelso who had a very limited knowledge of the language, but I did not pursue work with her. I also asked about descendants of the Cowlitz from whom Adamson had collected texts, on the off chance that one of them might know the language. This paid off. Adamson had collected a few texts from Mrs. Frances Northover, who everyone told me lived on the Yakima Reservation in Eastern Washington, well out of Cowlitz territory. It was suggested that I speak with Kay Merritt, a granddaughter of Mrs. Northover, who worked at the Yakima County Sheriff's office in Yakima. When I found her, she assured me that her two aunts living in the area both spoke Cowlitz, and that she was sure it was Lower Cowlitz, the language I was looking for. Furthermore, she said that her grandmother had lived until 1960, and that another aunt, who had taken care of Mrs. Northover, had died only the year before (i.e. 1966). I was still skeptical, because of the confusion of Lower Cowlitz, a Salish language, and Upper Cowlitz, a dialect of Sahaptin (and also known as Taitnapam). It was more likely that there would be speakers of Upper Cowlitz. I next contacted one of Mrs. Merritt's aunts, Mrs. Lucy James, who lived in Yakima. She assured me that she spoke Cowlitz, and when I asked her the native name for the language, she said "sx̣ʼpúlmixq", and that made it clear that this was the Salish Cowlitz. She was quite willing to work with me, as was her younger sister, Emma Mesplie, who lived a few miles further south, on the Yakima Indian Reservation. Erik Beukenkamp, a graduate student from The University of Kansas came out to assist me, and we spent that summer collecting Cowlitz language material. Mrs. James had lived away from Cowlitz speakers for many years, but nevertheless remembered much of the language. Neither sister had a perfect memory of the language, and could not recall a number of vocabulary items (particularly placenames and words relating to fauna and flora). They knew no traditional texts, but it was possible to collect a very limited number of short historical narratives from them, and some conversation between them. The latter was difficult, because they kept lapsing into English.

It was possible to proceed rapidly with elicitation, because Cowlitz proved to be very much like Upper Chehalis, with which I had considerable acquaintance, and it was possible to avoid dead ends, and to ask relevant grammatical constructions. Although there are many gaps in these data, they are presented here as collected, even though some phrases appear to have been made up on the spot. Comparison with data collected in the 19th and early 20th centuries show that data collected from Mrs. James and Mrs. Mesplie are genuine and reliable Cowlitz.

A number of people and organizations deserve special thanks for making this dictionary possible. First and foremost, I thank Mrs. James and Mrs. Mesplie, two very kind and charming ladies who gave generously of their time in order to make this record of their language possible. Their niece, Kay Merritt, was helpful throughout in encouraging me and helping with some translations (she has a passive knowledge of the language learned from her grandmother, who raised her). I also thank Erik Beukenkamp, who was an invaluable assistant in recording the Cowlitz material in the summer of 1967. Thanks also to Henry Davis and Lisa Matthewson, who read an initial draft of the grammatical sketch; they made extensive comments and suggestions which have helped to make it a more useful document. Throughout my work on this language, I have received much moral and intellectual support and advice from fellow scholars, particularly L. C. and M. T. Thompson and A. H. Kuipers. The latter kindly persuaded the Nederlandse Organisatie voor Zuiver Wetenschappelijk Onderzoek to provide me with a grant to spend a few months in Holland so that I could work with Dr. Kuipers, and which enabled me to make much progress on this dictionary. I also want to thank Brian Compton who helped identify flora and fauna, Paul Kroeber and Bill Seaburg who helped proofread the manuscript, and Tony Mattina who helped with his steady encouragement to get the thing done. Finally, I wish to acknowledge the financial support provided over the years by the National Science Foundation, The University of Kansas, the University of British Columbia, and the Nederlandse Organisatie voor Zuiver Wetenschappelijk Onderzoek.

Cowlitz is a Salishan language formerly spoken in southwestern Washington along the Cowlitz River from near its confluence with the Columbia nearly up to the present-day community of Mossy Rock. Their upriver neighbors were the Taitnapam (sometimes called the Upper Cowlitz), a Sahaptin-speaking group, and their southern neighbors were the Cathlamet Chinooks. To the north were the Upper Chehalis, who spoke a language quite similar to Cowlitz. The name Cowlitz (/káwlic/) apparently referred primarily to the river; the origin of the name is unknown. The Cowlitz called themselves sƛpúlmx meaning something like 'the lower people' or 'the people below'. The language was apparently quite homogeneous, and no dialect variations are known to have existed. However, Cowlitz may have shaded off into Upper Chehalis, particularly along the south fork of the Chehalis River.

Materials for this dictionary were compiled from data tape recorded and transcribed with the help of Erik Beukenkamp in the summer of 1967 from Mrs. Lucy James of Yakima, Washington and Mrs. Emma Mesplie, of Brownstown, Washington. Mrs. James was then 81, and Mrs. Mesplie was 77. These two sisters were, along with Mrs. Susan Olney, the only known surviving persons with a knowledge of more than a handful of words of Cowlitz. All are now deceased. I was unable to work with Mrs. Olney because of her poor health.

Mrs. James was born at Cowlitz Prairie in October 1887, Mrs. Mesplie near Toledo in December 1894. The family moved to the Yakima Reservation about 1895 and lived in the Simcoe Valley. Both daughters attended school for a few years at Fort Simcoe. There were also two older sisters and a brother. Their mother, Frances Northover was raised by an uncle who spoke Cowlitz; she died in 1963 at the age of 105. Her mother (Mary) was Wishram-Yakima, her father (George ktá) was

Yakima-Cowlitz. The father of Mrs. James and Mrs. Mesplie was Joe Northover. His mother was born in Kittitas County and was part Yakima; his father was William Northover, an Englishman. Mrs. James' first husband was Andrew Foster; she had two sons by him. Her second husband was Walter James (part Puyallup), and they had four sons and four daughters. She moved to Vashon Island in the early 1940s, and did not return to the Yakima area until about 1952. She died in 1974. Mrs. Mesplie's husband was August Mesplie (Wishram-French). She lived her entire life on the Yakima Reservation, and died there in 1992.

Mrs. James and Mrs. Mesplie had used Cowlitz only infrequently for a number of years before 1967, and were somewhat rusty in it at first, but remembered more and more as the summer progressed. Textual material was virtually impossible to obtain. Although their non-use of the Cowlitz language over many years undoubtedly resulted in an occasional erroneous form as shown by contradictory forms and some forms that disagree with older material (and no attempt has been made to identify, correct, or omit such forms), both women were clearly in command of the phonological, morphological, and syntactic structure and rules of the language. (Because of possible errors and contradictions in the data of the dictionary, linguistic theoreticians would be well advised to use this material with extreme caution.) A few very brief historical texts were recorded; otherwise the corpus consists entirely of words, phrases, and sentences. Because of this lack of texts, no attempt is made to include exemplifying sentences here. This constitutes the only known electronically recorded material in this language; very little other manuscript material is extant, and apart from five earlier word lists (and copies of them; the original word lists are Boas 1925, Curtis 1911, Gibbs n.d.b, Hale 1846, and Harrington 1942), only a few words have appeared in comparative articles and other manuscript or published materials. Thus we must all be extremely grateful to Mrs. James and Mrs. Mesplie for their cooperation in this project.

I have included in the dictionary vocabulary from all earlier sources that I have found. When my own data did not include these words, I have attempted to provide their probable phonemic form according to the transcription system I use; most of these guesses are based on known cognate forms in Upper Chehalis or from the manuscript materials of John P. Harrington, whose phonetic transcriptions were quite accurate. These sources of data (with the abbreviations used in citing their forms) are the following (full bibliographic citations may be found in the References at the end of this Introduction). **(a)** Horatio Hale (HH:1846) gives about 169 words of Cowlitz; his transcriptions are consistent and reasonably good, except that he does not write glottalization of consonants and does not distinguish front and back velars (these are both failings of all nineteenth century transcriptions of Cowlitz). **(b)** Albert Gallatin (AG:1848) lists 56 Cowlitz words for comparative purposes; they are copied from Hale, with some orthographic changes. **(c)** Robert G. Latham (RL:1862) lists these same 56 words, copied from Gallatin, and with the same changes. **(d)** George Gibbs (GGa:1853-60) has five words copied from a letter from Warbass (see Warbass 1858). **(e)** Gibbs (GGb:n.d.b) is a list of nearly 160 words, presumably collected by Gibbs himself; his transcriptions are consistent, but not as accurate as those of Hale. **(f)** Gibbs (GGc:1863) includes one Cowlitz word. **(g)** U. G. Warbass (UWa:1858) was an early settler at Toledo, who provided Gibbs with some information on Cowlitz in a letter in answer to a request from Gibbs; his transcriptions are poorer than those of Hale or Gibbs, and the letter includes 15 words in Cowlitz and a rough map of Cowlitz territory with several placenames on it. **(h)** Warbass also provided Gibbs with material which is contained in another manuscript by the latter (UWb:Gibbs n.d.a); it contains 23 words copied from Warbass. **(i)** F. L. O. Roehrig (FR:1870) put together a lengthy manuscript of comparative Salish; it includes between 110 and 115 words of Cowlitz taken from the manuscripts of Gibbs, and includes a few words from Warbass. **(j)** Edward Curtis (EC:1911) gives 188 words of Cowlitz and 29 placenames (some of which are Kiksht); these were actually written down by his assistant, W. E. Myers, and are reasonably accurate and well-transcribed. **(k)** The Franz Boas collection at the Library of the American Philosophical Society in Philadelphia includes a large manuscript of comparative Salishan vocabularies (FBa:Boas 1925). Mostly these data are not in Boas' handwriting, and were probably compiled by James A. Teit and Herman K. Haeberlin. The Cowlitz materials, consisting of roughly 640 words, were almost certainly collected by Teit sometime during the first decade of the twentieth century; the transcriptions are fairly good. **(l)** Boas himself collected a large body of Upper Chehalis material in 1927 (FBb); these incidentally include nearly 50 Cowlitz words from a Mrs. Youckton scattered through his notebooks, and the transcriptions are quite good. **(m)** The article by Boas and Haeberlin (BH:1927) includes 33 items taken from the comparative vocabularies (see **k** above). **(n)** Haeberlin also prepared an article on lexical suffixes which was not published until 1974 (HT); this includes 67 Cowlitz words, also taken from the comparative vocabularies. **(o)** Melville Jacobs' Sahaptin grammar (MJa:1931) includes six Cowlitz placenames in a specimen text at the end the volume; the text was dictated by Lewy Castama. **(p)** One of Jacobs' collections of Sahaptin folktales (MJb:1934) contains three Cowlitz words and a few personal names and place names from Mary Iley and her son Sam N. Iley, Jr., and several place names from Lewy Costima [Castama] (lc) and Jim Yoke (jy). Jacobs' transcriptions are quite accurate. **(q)** Thelma Adamson is reported to have collected a large amount of data on the Cowlitz language, but it has all disappeared. She did, however, publish a number of folktales in English (TAb:1934), and 68 Cowlitz words are scattered through them; her transcriptions leave much to be desired. Adamson's sources for these tales were Mary Iley (mi), Sophie Smith (ss), James Cheholts (jc), Lucy Youckton (ly), Frances Northover (fn), and Minnie Case (mc). **(r)** An extensive manuscript left by Adamson (TAa) pertaining to Upper Chehalis ethnography also includes a few Cowlitz place names obtained from George Sanders (gs), Peter Heck (ph), Marion Davis (md), and Pike Benn (pb) (the last three were

Upper Chehalis speakers, the first a Nisqually). This manuscript has been summarized and rearranged in Miller (1999), although most native words are omitted. **(s)** Verne F. Ray worked with Mrs. Emma Luscier at Bay Center between 1931 and 1936 collecting Lower Chinook ethnographic data. Mrs. Luscier's mother was Cowlitz, and Ray (VR:1938) includes three Cowlitz personal names. **(t)** John P. Harrington also collected data from Mrs. Luscier in 1942 (JH). He re-elicited much of the vocabulary in Curtis (1911), and his manuscripts include nearly 130 words from this source plus a number of placenames and personal names. He also collected about 35 words from Joe Peter (jp), a Cowlitz residing on the Yakima Reservation. Harrington's transcriptions are excellent, but significant discrepancies from other Cowlitz data in his transcriptions of Mr. Peter suggest that the latter had not used Cowlitz for some time, and was quite rusty. These materials also include a couple of Cowlitz words from Sarah Scarborough (ss), and a few place names obtained during a visit to Oakville from Minnie Case (mc) and Lizzie Johnson (lj). **(u)** In 1960 Silas Heck (SH) volunteered five Cowlitz words (which he had learned from his wife) while I was working with him on Upper Chehalis. In citing forms from these various sources, I have retained the transcriptions of the originals except in one respect: I have replaced Harrington's small, odd capital k with q, since this is now the usual symbol for this sound. I have replaced Adamson's small superscript right parenthesis (ʾ) with an apostrophe (') to indicate glottalization. My own transcriptions used in this dictionary are phonemic, not narrowly phonetic.

The system adopted here for entering items in the Cowlitz to English section of the dictionary may be illustrated by explaining several entries given under (1) /ʔáʔqiʔ, (2) /ʔácqʷ-, (3) /ʔə́x̣t-, (4) /c'ə́ka-, and (5) /ʔális-.

(1) An entry, such as /ʔáʔqiʔ, with no hyphen following may be used as is; it is a full word, and can be used in this unmodified form. It cannot be analyzed or broken down further, although it may be expanded as indicated by subentries. Entries with following hyphens may *not* be used in this hyphenated form, but must be expanded or modified in ways indicated by subentries. Subentries are given in the following order: inflected forms (that is, words with grammatical material added); derived forms (that is, words with affixes or reduplication added to create stems with somewhat different meanings); compounds (words made up of two or more roots); phrases (a short series of words, one of which is based on the root at the beginning of the entry). Words within each of these categories are more or less alphabetized. Subentries are numbered; a lead entry that is a full form is not numbered, but is considered to be the first item of the sequence.

(2) In a case like /ʔácqʷ-, the root (that is, the base of the word — as English *grow-* is the root of the word *growth* or *wid-* is the root of *width*) itself may be given a meaning, even though it may not be immediately apparent from the words derived from it; the root and its meaning are given first, then, on following lines, the words based on it. Prefixes and suffixes (such as *-n* or *-t-n*) are listed in the Grammatical Sketch, not in the body of the dictionary. In some cases, a root alone cannot be given a meaning (as in the case of /cáq-), and only the root occurs at the beginning of that entry; derived forms are then given on following lines.

(3) In a case like /ʔə́x̣t-, the root can be deduced only from derived forms; the simplest form which illustrates the basic meaning is then given immediately after this root and two question marks, and other inflected forms and derivatives follow. Additional information may be given following the meaning of a stem: principal parts, plurals, and possessed forms; a literal translation of a placename (set off by quotation marks); important grammatical information necessary for correct understanding or use of the form; identification as a loanword, with information about its source, when possible; cross-references (in parentheses).

(4) /c'ə́ka- illustrates an entry with "principal parts". First is given this root, then its approximate meaning 'win, defeat, use up, be gone'. Then in parentheses up to four forms may occur, depending on aspect and transitivity. If there are only two forms, the stem is either intransitive (no object) or transitive (must have an object), but not both; which it is will be clear from the endings of the forms. The two forms given differ according to aspect. Given first is perfective aspect, then imperfective aspect; since most words differ somewhat and in unpredictable ways in these two aspectual forms, it is necessary to give at least these two forms. If there are four forms, the first two are intransitive, the second two transitive, and each of these pairs represents perfective and imperfective aspect. There are several categories of transitive endings, and the correct category can be determined from the forms given. Any form missing from these principal parts is indicated by a dash in place of that form, which means it does not occur anywhere in the source material. If a transitive form has a meaning somewhat different from that of the intransitive form or from that of the stem by itself, that meaning is given immediately following the transitive forms. All forms given have third person subjects and/or objects, unless glossed otherwise. The four principal parts of /c'ə́ka- are: *c'ə́kɬ, sc'ə́kawn, c'ə́kn, sc'ə́ktn*. These may occur and be individually translated as: *ʔit c'ə́kɬ* 'it's gone, it's lost' (perfective intransitive), *sc'ə́kawn* 'it's getting lost, it's going away' (imperfective intransitive), *ʔit c'ə́kn* 'he used it up' (perfective transitive), *sc'ə́ktn* 'he's

using it up' (imperfective transitive). Perfective forms, which must be preceded by *ʔit* (or occasionally a similar particle), refer to a single event, usually in the past. Imperfective forms refer to an event that occurs over a period of time. A third major aspect, stative, is marked by prefixing *ʔac-* to perfective forms; these refer to states rather than events. The creation of additional forms with other persons as subject or object follows regularly from these principal parts according to the pronominal tables given in Appendix A, Inflectional and Derivational Suffixes. Sample paradigms can also be found there illustrating inflection for aspect, person (possessive, subjects, objects), and transitivity.

(5) An entry like /ʔális- does not have principal parts, but does have plural forms. For a form of this type, the collective, or plural, form ('chiefs') and/or the form with a third person possessor ('his chief') follow the plain singular entry. The forms following the main entry give derivatives of this root. Since the singular form may be a reduction of the full root indicated by various inflected or derived forms, the full root followed by a hyphen and a colon is given first. This is followed by a simple form with its meaning, or a specifically singular form with its meaning.

A slash (/) or a root sign (√) is used only before roots that can be further inflected or derived. A slash is used in the Cowlitz-English section of the dictionary, and root sign in the English-Cowlitz section, the latter for cross-references only; the import of the two symbols is equivalent. Such a symbol is not used before particles such as *ʔakʷu* or *tu*. It is omitted from words from earlier sources that were not verified in the 1967 and later elicitations because of uncertainties about the exact shape of these words, although it *is* used in hypothesized forms. A number of roots are given as unanalyzed forms which are probably ultimately analyzable as a string of smaller components. Synchronic evidence from available Cowlitz data is lacking for further breakdown of these forms.

Most grammatical information (usually abbreviated) is given in italics. Grammatical divisions within Cowlitz words are marked by hyphens (and are irrelevant for pronunciation). The location of a hyphen is sometimes arbitrary where a vowel could belong either to the root or a suffix.

If a given form or meaning does not occur in data I collected, the source is indicated by initials immediately adjacent to the stem or meaning to identify that source (see Abbreviations and Punctuation Conventions, p. xxii); the most usual of these is FB for Franz Boas, although (as indicated above) Boas himself was not usually the one who collected these forms. Sometimes my own elicitations of forms or meanings came either from Mrs. Mesplie or Mrs. James, but were either different from, or not confirmed, by the other; such forms or meanings are followed by ENM or LNJ. Occasionally their niece gave a different translation; that is indicated by her initials, KNM. If a gloss in an earlier source was not confirmed by Mrs. Mesplie or Mrs. James, I do not add it to theirs, but leave it with the form from the earlier source.

Cross-references are given when further information is given under a root that has a shape somewhat different from the form where the cross-reference is given, but usually not when they are identical. Compound words thus usually have a cross-reference to only half of the compound.

In the English-Cowlitz section of the dictionary, occasionally a form is given which does not actually occur in the source data, or which does not occur there in just the form cited; an asterisk precedes these forms to indicate that they are inferred rather than attested. These inferred forms are always based on earlier data. Such forms are included to provide the probable shape of particularly important words for anyone consulting this section of the dictionary alone. The actual attested transcriptions can be found in the Cowlitz-English section of the dictionary, and are given there as possible (*poss.*) or probable (*prob.*) transcriptions. These inferred shapes of words are based on similar Upper Chehalis words (see Kinkade

1991) or on probabilities from within Cowlitz itself. I am less sure of forms labelled *poss.* than on those labelled *prob.*

Cross-references are given when a piece of a word (a compound or a word with a prefix) is not initial, that is, is not at the beginning of the whole word. If the piece is initial, then what actually appears can be looked up (thus *ta7aɬ, tu7aɬ,* or *xaɬ* under the *7aɬ* entry can also be looked up under *ta, tu,* or *x*).

In the English to Cowlitz section of the dictionary, entries are essentially alphabetical. Sometimes one or more base forms will precede strictly alphabetical listings (for example 'night, darkness' precedes 'become night'). Only selected plurals are given here.

ALPHABETICAL ORDER

The alphabetical order used here for Cowlitz is: *7 a b c c' č č' d e ə g h i ǰ k k' kʷ ǩʷ l l' ɬ ƛ̓ m m' n n' o p p' q q' qʷ q̓ʷ s š t t' u w w' x xʷ x̣ x̣ʷ y y'.* Vowel length is largely ignored in alphabetization. Glottalized resonants are not always alphabetized separately from their unglottalized counterparts because of fluctuation in the occurrence of these sounds in the language. *b, d, g,* and *ǰ* occur in only three or four foreign words. Long vowels and sequences of vowel-glottal stop are usually in free variation, and are normally written as a long vowel. An epenthetic *ə* (not written) is regularly and predictably inserted before resonants (*l, m, n, w, y*) in consonant clusters, or after an initial resonant when followed by another consonant, and in a few other positions.

Since *s-* is a very common prefix in Cowlitz, many words begin with a cluster of *s* and another consonant. Except for a few words borrowed from English, such words are always alphabetized under the initial root consonant following the *s-,* even if the form is not known to occur without it. This *s-* normally becomes *š-* before *y.*

Since this dictionary is intended for the use of native people, linguists, and non-linguists alike, a guide to pronunciation is provided here to explain the phonological symbols (letters) used for those who are not familiar with Americanist transcription practices. International Phonetic Alphabet symbols are added in brackets.

b, d, g, h, k, m, n, p, s, t, w, y sound like English sounds those letters usually represent (y = IPA [j])

a - like the a of father ([a])

e - like the a of fat ([æ])

ə - varies a great deal depending on the consonants around it, but basically is like the u of but or the a of about ([ə]); when this sound is unstressed and completely predictable it is not normally written

i - like the a of late, or the i of machine ([e, i])

o - like the au of caught ([ɔ])

u - like the oa of coat, or the u of rule ([o, u])

long vowels (aˑ, eˑ, etc.) are identical to short vowels, but held about twice as long ([ː]); these long vowels are usually in free variation with a sequence of the vowel followed by ʔ

ʔ - represents the catch in your throat that you make when you say "Uh-uh" (meaning 'no') in English, although it is never written in English ([ʔ])

c - like the ts of hats ([t͡s]); in forms from BH, FB, JT, MJ, TA, and VR c = š

č - like the ch of church ([t͡ʃ])

l - like the l at the beginning of lean (not like the l at the end of call) ([l])

ł - sort of like an l, but is voiceless and very breathy ([ɬ])

q - like k, except that it is made by touching the back part of the tongue further back in the mouth ([q])

š - like the sh of shine ([ʃ])

x - the tongue should be in the same position as for k, but not quite touching the roof of the mouth, resulting in a light scraping noise ([x])

x̣ - the tongue should be in the same position as for q, but not quite touching the roof of the mouth, resulting in a scraping noise ([χ])

kʷ, qʷ, xʷ, x̣ʷ - like k, q, x, x̣, respectively, but with the lips slightly rounded; kʷ is like the q̲u̲ of q̲u̲ick ([kʷ, qʷ, xʷ, χʷ])

c', č', k', k̓ʷ, p', q', q̓ʷ, t' - these are like the same sounds without the ' beside them, but are made with a sharp popping sound; to get this popping sound, make a ʔ, hold it, and say the other sound (c, k, p, etc.) at the same time ([t͡s', t͡ʃ', k̓, k̓w, p̓, q̓, q̓w, t̓])

λ̓ - this has the same sort of sharp popping sound that the sounds immediately above have; to make it, begin with ʔ and make a t, keeping the tongue closed against the roof of the mouth; then, instead of letting the tip of the tongue come away from in back of the upper teeth, keep it there, but let the air out to one or both sides (just as in making l or ł) ([t͡ɬ'])

l', m', n', w', y' - like l, m, n, w, y interrupted by ʔ; at the end of a word the sound is chopped off abruptly; in the middle of a word, they may have a ʔ right in the middle of the sound, but mostly they just sound sort of "squeezed" or raspy ([l̓, m̓, n̓, w̓, y̓])

´ - this marks the part of the word that sounds loudest or most prominent (['])

A few other symbols will be found in forms cited from other sources:

α - the same as ə, or sometimes a

ç, ʃ = the same as š

E - the same as ə

ɩ - short i as in bi̲t ([ɩ or ɪ])

L - the same as either ł or λ̓

ʊ, ω - short u̲, like o̲o̲ in bo̲o̲k or u̲ in pu̲t ([ʊ, ᴜ, or ω])

ʸ - the sound is palatalized, that is, has a y-offglide ([ʲ])

ʒ - like z̲ in az̲ure or s̲ in plea̲s̲ure ([ʒ])

small raised letters (other than ʷ, ʸ, and ʰ) are short, murmured versions of those same letters when written normal size

ᵋ - the same as ʔ

` - like ´, but weaker, less prominent ([ `])
' - aspiration, a breathy release of a sound (['])

ABBREVIATIONS AND PUNCTUATION CONVENTIONS

Data Sources:

AG - Albert Gallatin 1848

BH - Franz Boas and Herman Haeberlin 1927

EC - Edward S. Curtis 1911

FBa - Franz Boas 1925

FBb - Franz Boas 1927

FR - F. L. O. Roehrig 1870

GGa - George Gibbs 1853-1860

GGb - George Gibbs n.d.b

GGc - George Gibbs 1863

HH - Horatio Hale 1846

HT - Herman Haeberlin 1974

JH - John P. Harrington 1942 (Emma Luscier, informant)

JHjp - John P. Harrington 1942 (Joe Peter, informant)

JHlj - John P. Harrington 1942 (Lizzie Johnson, informant)

JHmc - John P. Harrington 1942 (Minnie Case, informant)

JHgs - John P. Harrington 1942 (George Sanders, informant)

JHss - John P. Harrington 1942 (Sarah Scarborough, informant)

JT - James Teit 1907-1910

LY - Lillian Young (an Upper Chehalis speaker with some Cowlitz ancestry)

MJa - Melville Jacobs 1931

MJa-lc - Melville Jacobs 1931 (Lewy Costima [Castama], informant)

MJb - Melville Jacobs 1934

MJb-jy - Melville Jacobs 1934 (Jim Yoke, informant)

MJb-lc - Melville Jacobs 1934 (Lewy Costima [Castama], informant)

MJb-mi - Melville Jacobs 1934 (Mary Iley, informant)

MJb-si - Melville Jacobs 1934 (Sam N. Iley, Jr., informant)

RL - Robert G. Latham 1862

SH - Silas Heck

TAa - Thelma Adamson 1926-1927

TAa-gs - Thelma Adamson 1926-1927 (George Sanders, informant)

TAa-md - Thelma Adamson 1926-1927 (Marion Davis, informant)

TAa-pb - Thelma Adamson 1926-1927 (Pike Benn, informant)

TAa-ph - Thelma Adamson 1926-1927 (Peter Heck, informant)

TAb - Thelma Adamson 1934

TAb-fn - Thelma Adamson 1934 (Frances Northover, informant)

TAb-jc - Thelma Adamson 1934 (James Cheholts, informant)

TAb-ly - Thelma Adamson 1934 (Lucy Youckton, informant)

TAb-mc - Thelma Adamson 1934 (Minnie Case, informant)

TAb-mi - Thelma Adamson 1934 (Mary Iley, informant)

TAb-ss - Thelma Adamson 1934 (Sophie Smith, informant)

UWa - U. G. Warbass 1858

VR - Verne F. Ray 1938

Other abbreviations used in the grammatical sketch and dictionary (numbers indicate the section of the grammatical sketch where more information on this topic can be found)

1pl - first person plural

1sg - first person singular

2sg - second person singular

3sg - third person singular

appl - applicative 2.3.6

back - back, again 2.11.3

caus - causative 2.3.4

cj - conjunction 3.4.1

comp - complementizer 2.7.3

compar - comparative (see dictionary under *tk*)

def - definite –x̣

det - determiner, article 2.8

dev - developmental 2.11.1

dimin - 2.10

ENM - Emma Mesplie

epen - epenthetic 1.4.4, 1.4.5

evid - evidential (see dictionary under *ʔu*)

fdet - feminine determiner 2.8

fem - feminine 2.8

fut - future 2.6.2

hab - habitual 2.2.3

impl.tr. - implied transitive 2.3.7

imper - imperative 3.2.3

impf - imperfective aspect 2.2.1

inch - inchoative 2.11.2

inst - instrumental 2.11.5

intr - intransitive 2.3.1

LNJ - Lucy James

KNM - Kay Merritt

lnk - link 2.1.3

mdl - middle voice 2.5.1

n - noun

nom - nominalizer 2.0.1

obj - object 2.4.2
obl - oblique (preposition)
    (see dictionary under *ɬ*)
pass - passive 2.5.2
past - past tense 2.6.1
perf - perfective aspect 2.2.1
pl - plural 2.9
poss - possibly
posv - possessive 2.4.3
prob - probably
q - question marker 3.2.2
qi - qi 2.7
recip - reciprocal 2.4.6
refl - reflexive 2.4.5
rel - relational 2.3.5

repet - repetitive 2.1.1, 2.9.5
report - reportative (see
    dictionary under *(ʔ)akʷú*)
s - s-prefix of uncertain
    function
sg - singular
sp - species
st - stative aspect 2.2.2
subj - subject 2.4.1
t.o. - topical object 2.4.4
tr - transitive 2.3, 2.4.2
v - verb
voc - vocative
wi - wi 3.
ws - -ws on negative 3.3

Special symbols

* - unattested form inferred from other forms
- (hyphen) - bound form that cannot occur by itself; may occur
    with a root or with an affix
(?) - form or translation is dubious or uncertain
" " - literal translation, special explanation, special usage,
    explanation as given by a native speaker
( ) - some grammatical information; cross-references; loanword
    sources
[ ] - infixed material
√ - precedes the root (that is, base) of a word
/ - same as √, used in the Cowlitz-English part of the dictionary
= - precedes lexical suffixes (see Appendix A)
• - reduplication
+ - separates clitics from what precedes or follows

ADDITIONAL INSTRUCTIONS FOR NON-LINGUISTS

1. Ignore all non-alphabetic symbols except hyphens, accents
    and apostrophes.

2. Read small raised dots (ˑ), but not big ones (•).

3. The Cowlitz-English portion of the dictionary contains more information than the English-Cowlitz portion. If you look something up in the English-Cowlitz portion, follow up in the Cowlitz-English portion to learn more about this word.

4. The grammatical sketch is only a sketch, not a full grammar. Limited data preclude writing a full grammar.

5. Placenames and personal names are poorly attested, and early attempts at writing them down are not easily transposable into the transcription system used in this dictionary. For this reason, few are given in the body of the dictionary. Appendixes are provided that give all known placenames and personal names in their original transcriptions.

BIBLIOGRAPHY

Adamson, Thelma. 1926-27. [Unarranged Sources of Chehalis Ethnology.] (Manuscript in Box 77, Melville Jacobs Collection, University of Washington Libraries, Seattle, Washington.) [402 pp.] [TAa]

Adamson, Thelma, collector and ed. 1934. *Folk Tales of the Coast Salish. Memoirs of the American Folk-Lore Society* 27. New York. (Reprinted: Kraus Reprint, New York, 1969.) [TAb]

Boas, Franz. 1925. Comparative Salishan Vocabularies. (Manuscript No. [30(S.2)] in the American Philosophical Society Library, Philadelphia.) [FBa]

Boas, Franz. 1927. [Ch notebooks.] [Vol. X.581; ca. 40 items from Mrs. Youckton, 10 other items.] (or n.b.III?) [FBb]

Boas, Franz and Herman Haeberlin. 1927. Sound shifts in Salishan dialects. *International Journal of American Linguistics* 4(2-4):117-136. [BH]

Curtis, Edward S. 1911. *The North American Indian: Being a Series of Volumes Picturing and Describing the Indians of the United States, the Dominion of Canada and Alaska.*

Frederick Webb Hodge, ed. 20 vols. Norwood, Mass.: Plimpton Press. (Reprinted: Johnson Reprint, New York, 1970.) [Vol. 9, pp. 112-173, 182-194.] [EC]

Douglas, David. 1914. *Journal Kept by David Douglas During His Travels in North America, 1823-1827.* Published Under the Direction of the Royal Horticultural Society, London.

Gallatin, Albert. 1848. Hale's Indians of North-west America. *Transactions of the American Ethnological Society* 2:xxiii-clxxxviii, 1-130. New York. [P. 119.] [AG]

Gibbs, George. 1853-1860. Vocabularies, Washington Terry. 1 vol. (Manuscript No. 227 in National Anthropological Archives, Smithsonian Institution, Washington.) [copied from UWa] [230 pp. Cowlitz vocabulary of 5 terms on p. [224] in notebook, n.d.] [GGa]

Gibbs, George. 1855. Journal of the Expedition form (*sic*) the Conclusion of the Treaty of Nisqually. In James Doty, Records of the Proceedings of the Commission to hold Treaties with the Indian Tribes in Washington Territory and the Blackfoot Country. Ms.[GGd]

Gibbs, George. 1863. *A Dictionary of the Chinook Jargon, or Trade Language of Oregon.* New York. (*Shea's Library of American Linguistics* 12.) New York: Cramoisy Press. (Published also as: *Smithsonian Miscellaneous Collections* 7(10), Washington.) (Reprinted: AMS Press, Inc., New York, 1970.) [P. x.] [GGc]

Gibbs, George. n.d.a. Comparative vocabulary of Cowlitz and Chinook. The words in the Cowlitz language were collected by Dr. Warbass at Cowlitz Landing, Feb. 1858. Copied by George Gibbs. (Manuscript No. 724 in National Anthropological Archives, Smithsonian Institution, Washington.) [1 p., 23 words.] [UWb]

Gibbs, George. n.d.b. Comparative vocabulary of Cowlitz and Quileute (Kwillehyute). 19 pp., in printed schedule issued by Geog. and Geolog. Survey, Interior Department. (Manuscript No. 733 in National Anthropological Archives, Smithsonian Institution, Washington.) [158 Cz words.] [GGb]

Haeberlin, Herman. 1974. Distribution of the Salish substantival [lexical] suffixes. M. Terry Thompson, ed. *Anthropological Linguistics* 16(6):219-350. [HT]

Hale, Horatio. 1846. Synopsis and Vocabularies. Pp. 569-634 in Ethnography and Philology. Vol. 6 of *United States Exploring Expedition During the Years 1838, 1839, 1840, 1841, 1842*. Philadelphia: Lea and Blanchard. (Reprinted: Gregg Press, Ridgewood, N.J. 1968.) [Pp. 570-629.][HH]

Harrington, John P. 1942. [Lower Chehalis, Upper Chehalis, and Cowlitz Fieldnotes.] (Microfilm, reel Nos. 017-018, John Peabody Harrington Papers, Alaska/Northwest Coast, in National Anthropological Archives, Smithsonian Institution, Washington.)[JH]

Jacobs, Melville. 1931. A Sketch of Northern Sahaptin Grammar. *University of Washington Publications in Anthropology* 4(2):85-292. Seattle. [MJa]

Jacobs, Melville. 1934. *Northwest Sahaptin Texts*. 2 vols. *Columbia University Contributions to Anthropology* 19. New York. (Reprinted: AMS Press, New York, 1969.) [P. 172.] [MJb]

Kane, Paul. 1859. *Wanderings of an Artist Among the Indians of North America, from Canada to Vancouver's Island and Oregon....* London: Longmans, Brown, Green, Longmans, and Roberts. (Reprinted: C. E. Tuttle, Rutland, Vt., 1967.)

Kinkade, M. Dale. 1991. *Upper Chehalis Dictionary. University of Montana Occasional Papers in Linguistics* 7. Missoula.

Latham, Robert G. 1862. *Elements of Comparative Philology*. London: Walton and Maberly. [Pp. 399-400.] [RL]

Miller, Jay. 1999. Chehalis area traditions, a summary of Thelma Adamson's 1927 ethnographic notes. *Northwest Anthropological Research Notes* 33(1):1-72.

Notices & Voyages of the Famed Quebec Mission to the Pacific Northwest: Being the Correspondence, Notices, Etc., of Fathers Bolduc and Langlois. Containing Much Remarkable Information on the Areas and Inhabitants of the Columbia, Walamette, Cowlitz and Fraser Rivers, Nesqually Bay, Puget Sound, Whidby and Vancouver

Islands While on their Arduous Mission to the Engagés of the Hudson☐s Bay Company and the Pagan Natives, 1838 to 1847. Translated by Carl Landerholm. Portland: Oregon Historical Society, 1956.

Ray, Verne F. 1938. Lower Chinook Ethnographic Notes. *University of Washington Publications in Anthropology* 7(2):29-165. Seattle. [VR]

Reports of Explorations and Surveys, to Ascertain the Most Practicable and Economical Route For a Railroad From the Mississippi River to the Pacific Ocean, 1853-1854. Vol. 11, Part II. Washington, D. C. 1855-60. [PRR]

Roehrig, F. L. O. 1870. Three comparative vocabularies of the Salish languages. One dated Nov. 15, 1870, Ithaca, New York. 149 pp. total. / pt. 3. Synoptical vocabulary of the Selish languages. n.d. 16 pp., approximately 190 terms. (Manuscript No. 3072 in National Anthropological Archives, Smithsonian Institution, Washington.) [FR]

Ross, Alexander. 1855. *The Fur Hunters of the Far West.* 2 vols. London: Smith, Elder. (Reprinted: Donnelly and Sons, Chicago, 1924.)

Teit, James. 1907-10. Salish tribal names and distinctions. Manuscript, American Philosophical Society Library, Philadelphia, Pennsylvania. [125 pp., 5 slips, 3 maps, 2 notebooks.] [JT]

Tolmie, William F. 1963. *The Journals of William Fraser Tolmie, Physician and Fur Trader.* Vancouver, B. C.: Mitchell Press.

Warbass, U. G. 1857. George Gibbs Correspondence: Gibbs to Warbass. Semiahmoo Bay, Dec. 7, 1857. Inquiry concerning Klikitat and Cowlitz Indians. (Manuscript No. 726 in National Anthropological Archives, Smithsonian Institution, Washington.) [1 p.]

Warbass, U. G. 1858. George Gibbs correspondence: Warbass to Gibbs. Cowlitz Landing, Feb. 14, 1858. Klickitat and Cowlitz terminology; map of Cowlitz River with native place names. (Manuscript No. 726 in National Anthropological Archives, Smithsonian Institution, Washington.) [3 pp.][UWa]

Warner, Mikell de Lores Wormell, translator. 1972. *Catholic Church Records of the Pacific Northwest: Vancouver, Volumes I and II and Stellamaris Mission.* (Annotated by Harriet Duncan Munnick.) St. Paul, Oregon: French Prairie Press.

Cowlitz - English

ʔ

ʔáˑ yes; HH a, ᴜ.

/ʔáʔcti– remember. 1.
/ʔáʔcti–x, — caus.

/ʔáʔqiʔ maggots. 2.
ʔac/ʔáʔqi–t–m tit k̓ʷús the
meat is full of maggots pass.

ʔác=ayq inside (a container or
person) (see =ayaqi–
inside). 2. s–ác=iʔq–: 2a.
s–ác=iʔq–i its inside, its
bottom.

/ʔácqʷ– bake in ashes. 1.
/ʔácqʷ–n, s/ʔácqʷ–t–n tr.
2. /ʔácqʷ–il–n baking
potatoes dev.

ʔác=tq inside, in the house
(see =staqi– fire); FBa
aˊtstᴇk inside. 2. isaṃ
aˊts.tᴇk FBa go inside (see
/ʔís come).

/ʔacwánx doctor; FBa
atswaˊnux̣ shaman; JH
sẃáˑnᵘxˑ; JHjp swánx̣
medicine man. 1b.
s/wanə̌š–i his doctor.

ʔác=xan– track an animal. 1.
ʔác=xan–n, — tr. (see
=xan/=šn foot).

ʔac̓í interrogative (see ʔac–
stative aspect prefix, /ʔí
question).

ʔakʷu, kʷu interrogative
particle (enclitic). 2. ʔit̓í
akʷu what's the matter?,
what happened? (see /ʔí
question). 3. ɬ/ín–s kʷu it
doesn't matter. 4. /ʔíni kʷu
anything be done to it. 5. ʔit
/ʔin–áwmx kʷu What's the
matter with them? 6.
s/ʔíni–n–axʷ kʷu What are
you doing? 7.
s/ʔín–ẇən–cal–s kʷu What
is he doing to me? 8. /ʔít–m
kʷu fixed that way perf.
pass. 9. nks + /ʔít–aw–ctx
kʷu whatever is being done
with it impf. pass. 10. ʔit ʔítx
kʷu k… what did you do
with…? 11. /káʔ akʷu where
is it? 12. /kán–m kʷu to
where? 13. /kan–ím̓ kʷu
what way, which way. 14.
/kan–ém–m̓ kʷu Which
way is it?, How do you do it?
15. /tám akʷu what?, why?
16. tu /káˑ k akʷu Where
were you? 17. /wá akʷu who
is he?, someone. 18. /wá k
akʷu Who are you? 19. /wát
akʷu who he is.

(ʔ)akʷú reportative (?). 2. ɬit
/wí ʔakʷu ʔac/mán? She's
going to have a baby. (see
/maníʔ– son, daughter,
child). 3. ʔit /t̓úl–ɬ ʔakʷu
They said he came. 4. /míɬta
ʔakʷu t s/t̓úl–i He didn't
come.

/ʔálal– sneak up on. 1.

3

/ʔálal-n, s/ʔáll-t-n *tr.*

/ʔális-: 1a. /ʔáls chief, leader; HH álís chief; GGb álse chief; FR alse chief; EC al's chief; FBa aʹlls chief. 1b. /ʔális-umx *pl.* 1c. /ʔálilas-i his chief. 2. nx/ʔáls-tn̓ old people, grandparents *pl.* 3. /ƛ̓ʹ k̓ʷ t /ʔáls God.

/ʔálm̓aq- wait, rest, wait for. 1. /ʔálmq, —, /ʔálm̓q-n, — (also given as /ʔámlaq-). 2. s/ʔálmaq-i his waiting.

/ʔalq̓álm̓yusm January, "a month the people don't camp out" (*see* /q̓ə́l- camp).

/ʔalútq deep, long canoe; GGb ah-lóte-ké Chinook canoe; EC a–lótk small ocean canoe; FBa aloʹtɛks Chinook canoe (loanword; *see* Quileute ʔàˑʔlútqat 'sealing canoe').

/ʔáˑlwasi- balance, rock in one's arms. 1. /ʔáˑlwasi-x, — *caus.* 2. /ʔálwasi-n-aʔ balance it!

ʔaɬ to, in, into, on. 2. ʔáɬ/cani to him, to her, to it (*see* /cə́ni he, him). 2a. ʔac/x̣ʷúqʷ-aɬ/cani with him (*see* /x̣ʷúqʷa- together with). 2b. ʔac/x̣ʷúqʷ-aɬ/cəni-yawm x with them. 2c. x-ʔáɬ/cani to him, to her, to it (*see* x to). 3. ʔáɬ/ċiwq̓ left (*see* /ċiwq̓ left). 4. ʔáɬ/ənca to me (*see* /ʔə́nca I, me). 4a. ʔac/x̣ʷúqʷ-aɬ/ənca with me (*see* /x̣ʷúqʷa- together with). 4b. x-ʔáɬ/ənca to me (*see* x to). 5. ʔáɬ/inm to us (*see* /ʔiním we, us). 5a. ʔac/x̣ʷúqʷ-aɬ/inm with us (*see* /x̣ʷúqʷa- together with). 6. ʔáɬ/naw=axn to the right (*see* /náw-). 7. ʔáɬ/nawi to you (*see* /náwi you, *sg.*). 7a. ʔac/x̣ʷúqʷ-aɬ/nawi with you (*see* /x̣ʷúqʷa- together with). 7b. x-ʔáɬ/nawi to you (*see* x to). 8. ʔáɬ/təmx on the ground (*see* /tə́mx earth, land). 8a. x-ʔáɬ/tm̓x onto the ground (*see* x to). 9. ʔáɬ/x̣x be home, stay home (*see* /x̣áx house). 9a. ʔáɬ/x̣ax-umx they're home *pl.* 10. ta-ʔaɬ along, around. 11. tl ʔaɬ from, than, (off, out of). 12. tu ʔaɬ from, of. 13. x-aɬ, x-ʔaɬ to. 13a. ta-x-aɬ to.

ʔāʹmane FBa a wave (*prob.* /ʔámaniʔ).

ʔáml, ʔamlʔ unless, if, when.

ʔana, ana, na *interrogative particle.*

/ʔánaʔan? black-billed magpie *Pica pica*; FBa aʹn.an.

ʔanám̓ just. 2. ʔanám̓ u just, only (*see* /nám̓u- perhaps, maybe). 3. an-nám-ote-láht-lo GGb wood (*see* /x̣ʼə́x- tree, stick; *prob.* ʔanám̓ u tit /x̣ʼə́x·x̣ʼx just wood).

/ʔápls apple, apples (loanword; *see* English *apples*). 2. /ʔápls=anil-: 2a. /ʔápls=an̓ɬ apple orchard. 2b. /ʔápls=anil-i his orchard.

/ʔáps-: 1. s/ʔáps diarrhoea, excrement. 2. /ʔáps=ɬanil- "B.S." someone, talk nonsense to. 2a. /ʔáps=ɬanil-n, — *tr.*

/ʔáˑps- expect. 1. /ʔáˑps-mn, — *rel.*

ʔáqa now (loanword; *see* Kathlamet Chinook *aqa* 'then').

/ʔáqʷas-: 1a. /ʔáqʷs eel *Lampetra* sp(p).; EC aqs lamprey; JH ʼáˑqws̥. 1b. /ʔáqʷas-i his eel.

/ʔátaman- die, be dead. 1. /ʔátamn, s/ʔátman-n; GGb tat-áhm dead; FBa etaʹtamEn dead (*prob.* ʔit /ʔátamn) *intr.* 2. s/ʔátman-i his dying. 3. s/tmə́n-i his death.

/ʔátqʷil- row, paddle. 1. /ʔátqʷɬ, s/ʔátqʷil-n; FBa âʹkᵘteɬa paddle *intr.* 2. /ʔátqʷɬil-: 2a. /ʔátqʷɬil-i its fin ("paddler").

/ʔáwat-: 1. /ʔáwt behind, after. 2. ʔac/ʔáwat-lx it's

late *dev.* 3. /ʔáwt=ikn-: 3a. /ʔáwt=ičn, s/ʔáwt=ičn back, behind, back of. 3b. s/ʔáwt=kn-i his back. 4. /ʔáwt-ɬ=tumx behind, after. 5. /ʔáwt=psm back of the neck. 6. sāutaʹksx̣En FBa heel (*poss.* s/ʔawt-áqs=xn). 7. saʹᵘteka FBa back of the hand (*prob.* s/ʔáwt=aka). 8. /ʔáwt-ɬ/cani behind him, after him (*see* /cə́ni he, him). 9. /ʔáwt-ɬ/nawi behind you (*see* /nə́wi you, *sg.*). 10. /ʔáwt-ɬ/nca behind me, after me (*see* /ʔə́nca I, me).

ʔawəl or.

/ʔáwəl- ?? 1. /ʔáwəl=qs- sneeze. 1a. /ʔáwəl=qs, s/ʔáwəl=qs-t-n *intr.* 2. /ʔáw·awəl=qs keep sneezing *perf. intr.*

ʼάwìˑlk, ʼαwíˑʼlk JH Indian paint; EC awílk red paint (*prob.* /ʔawílk). 2. ow-well-kenkk UWa Paint-illahae (name of a prairie at Cowlitz Landing).

/ʔáxaq- snow(ing). 1. —, s/ʔáxaq-n *intr.*

/ʔáx̣ʷ- throw away (pl. objects). 1. /ʔáx̣ʷ-n, — *tr.* 2. s/ʔáx̣ʷ-mt-n̓ potlatch, giving, throwing away *impf. mdl.*

/ʔáx̣ʷa- pl. run, travel. 1.
/ʔáx̣ʷ-ɫ, s/ʔáx̣ʷa-w-n *intr.*
2. /ʔáˑx̣ʷ-kʷu- gallop. 2a.
—, s/ʔáˑx̣ʷ-kʷu-mit-n
mdl.

/ʔax̣ʷíl̓- ?? 1. s/ʔax̣ʷíl̓=qʷuʔ
tears (running down one's
face).

/ʔáx̣ʷyin-: 1a. /ʔáx̣ʷyn net;
FBa aˊxiem fishnet (long).
1b. /ʔáx̣ʷyin-i his net. 2.
/ʔáx̣ʷyn-m fish with a net
perf. mdl.

/ʔáy- change. 1. /ʔáy-ši-
change *appl.* 1a. /ʔáy-š-n,
s/ʔáy-ši-t-n *tr.* 2. /ʔáy̓-ši-
trade, exchange *appl.* 2a.
/ʔáy̓-š-n, s/ʔáy̓-ši-t-n or
s/ʔáy̓i-ši-t-n *tr.* 3. nks +
/ʔáy̓-ši-t-n trader. 4.
/ʔáy/nax̣=nut change one's
mind (*see* /nax̣-). 5.
/ʔáy-uk̓ʷ trade for
something. 5a. /ʔáy-uk̓ʷ, —
intr. 5b. —,
s/ʔáy-uk̓ʷ-staw-n *caus.* 6.
ʔnks + c/ʔáy̓-ši-t-n
/čóˑšm̓ he's always trading.

/ʔáy- have a good time, have
fun. 1. /ʔáy-lx, s/ʔáy-lt-n
dev.

/ʔáy- ?? 1. /ʔáy=aka-min-:
1a. /ʔáy=aka-mń thimble.
1b. /ʔáy=aka-min-i her
thimble.

/ʔáyax- follow, go with. 1.
/ʔáyaš-n, s/ʔáy̓x-ni-t-n
appl. tr.

/ʔayayáš dumb, stupid,
clumsy, stubborn (loanword;
see Sahaptin ʔayayaš
'stupid, clumsy, dumb').

ʔaiˊkamɛltɛn FBa fishhook
(*poss.* /ʔáyq-am̓ɫ-tń).

/ʔáyl- smooth, polish. 1. —,
s/ʔáyl-taw-n *caus.*

/ʔáyn- revenge. 1. /ʔáyn-x,
— *caus.*

/ʔayóʔ medicine. 1b. /ʔayóʔ-i
his medicine. 2. /sá/ʔayuʔ-
use for medicine or
seasoning. 2a. —,
/sá/ʔayuʔ-t-n *tr.* 3.
/sá/ʔayuʔ-či used it for
medicine.

/ʔáys again (usually
compounded with a
following stem).

/ʔáy̓s sick. 2. /ʔáy̓s-aw- get
sick *inch.* 2a. /ʔáy̓s-aw-m,
s/ʔáy̓s-u-mit-n; FBb
s'aˑˊismetɛn he is getting
well *mdl.* 3. s/ʔáy̓s-tn
disease. 4. /ʔáy̓s=akaʔ lame.

/ʔáytak-: 1. /ʔáytk lots of,
very, hard; HH aíitka many
(much); UWb iket many,
much; FBa aiˊ.tɛk much,
many. 2. /ʔáy̓tak-umx there
are lots of them. 3. tk /ʔáy̓tk
more. 4. aíítkt-x̣áx HH town,
village (*see* /x̣áx house;
prob. /ʔáy̓tk t /x̣áx).

/ʔéˑtil- bathe, swim. 1. /ʔéˑtl̓,
s/ʔéˑtil-n, /ʔéˑtl-n, —. 2.

s/púx̣ʷ-cši-s t s/ʔé·til-n
sweatbath (*see* /púx̣ʷ-).

/ʔə́ɬp̓- ?? 1. /ʔə́ɬp̓-l=k- lose
hold. 1a. /ʔə́ɬp̓-l=k-mn, —
rel.

/ʔə́mx̣kʷu cedar-root basket;
EC ŭ-mâḥ-ku
waterbasket; FBa aˊmoxko
woven basket (coiled); JH
ʼậmx̣kʋ, ʼɑ́mˣx̣kʋ
water-tight basket. 1b.
/ʔə́mx̣kʷu-yumx *pl*. 1c.
/ʔə́mx̣kʷu-ni her cedar
basket. 2. /ʔé·mx̣kʷu small
cedar-root basket, picking
basket. 3. /nak̓-áw/əmx̣kʷu
one basket. 4. /sá/ʔəmx̣kʷu
weave a cedar-root basket. 4a.
/sá/ʔəmx̣kʷu,
/sá/ʔəmx̣kʷuʔ-n *intr*.

/ʔə́nca I, me; HH ʋ́ntsa I;
AG,RL ʋntsa I; GGb úntsa I;
FR únt-sa, ún-tsa I; FBa
Eˊnntsa I. 2. s/əncá-yaɬ
my, mine. 3. ʔáɬ/ənca to me.
3a. x-ʔáɬ/ənca to me. 4.
/ʔáwt-ɬ/ənca behind me,
after me. 5. /ʔílp-ɬ/ənca in
front of me. 6. /p̓én/ə́nca
beside me. 7.
ʔac/x̣ʷúqʷ-aɬ/ənca with
me (*see* /x̣ʷúqʷa- together
with).

/ʔəsúl- lead, take to, take
with, take along. 1. /ʔə́sɬ,
s/ʔasúl-n *intr*.

/ʔə́w- howl. 1. /ʔə́w·ʔəw-
howl (loudly). 1a. —,
s/ʔə́w·ʔəw-mit-n *mdl*.

/ʔə́x̣ʷ- foreign, strange,
different, other. 1. /ʔə́x̣ʷ-ɬ,
— *intr*. 2. /ʔəx̣ʷ-t-ál=mx
strange people. 3.
s/ə́x̣ʷ-t-a=m̓x foreign
country. 4. /ʔə́x̣ʷ-ɬ t
s/ə́x̣-tm he looks serious. 5.
/tám ʔo ʔə́x̣ʷ-ɬ something
else. 6. /wá ʔo ʔə́x̣ʷ-ɬ
someone else.

/ʔə́x̣- see, look, look at. 1.
/ʔə́x̣-n, s/ʔə́x̣-t-n *tr*. 2.
ŭch-háh-met-lah GGb; FR
uch-háh-met-la *i.t.*?
imperative? 3. /ʔə́x̣-am̓ɬ
open one's eyes *i.t.* 4.
/ʔə́x̣·x̣- examine, read. 4a.
/ʔə́x̣·x̣-n, s/ʔə́x̣·x̣-t-n *tr*.
5. /ʔéx̣- read. 5a. /ʔéx̣-n, —
tr. 6. /ʔé·x̣-ni- see, look at,
watch, stare *appl*. 6a.
/ʔé·x̣-n, s/ʔé·x̣-ni-t-n *tr*.
6b. ʔac/ʔé·x̣-ni-tum kɬ
we're watching. 7.
s/ə́x̣-aml-i his seeing. 8.
s/ʔə́x̣-tu-s his seeing it. 9.
s/ə́x̣-tm appearance. 10.
/ʔáx̣-acx-tn̓ window,
mirror; FBa aˊxatstEn
mirror, looking-glass. 11.
/ʔáx̣-acx-tn-mn̓ drapes. 12.
/ʔáx̣-am̓ɬ-tn̓ eyeglasses, a
glass, telescope. 13.
/ʔáʔx̣-am̓ɬ-tn̓ book. 14.
/ʔáx̣-acx-tn=iĺs

eyeglasses. 15. /ʔax̣-ét/pipa read. 15a. /ʔax̣-ét/pipa, s/ʔax̣-ét/pipaʔ-n (*see* /pípa paper). 16. /x̣̌aq^w-s/éx̣-ni- take care of, watch for, guard, protect, pay attention, herd; be alarmed, be alerted, look out for, risk *appl.* 16a. /x̣̌aq^w-s/éx̣-n, s/x̣̌aq^w-s/éx̣-ni-t-n *tr.* 17. /x̣ə́p/ax̣-acx̣-tń window blinds. 18. ei.sExaˊmEɬ FBa handsome, beautiful (*see* /ʔíˑ good, nice; *prob.* /ʔíˑ s/ʔə́x̣-amɬ). 19. x̂ícsExaˊmEɬ FBa ugly (*see* /x̣ə́š bad; *prob.* /x̣ə́š s/ʔə́x̣-amɬ).

/ʔə́x̣t- ?? 1. ʔac/ʔə́x̣t=k^wlx Indian doctor; ECa t͡sŭħ-tqĭlħ medicine-man. 2. s/ə́xt=k^wlx spirit power; TAb-mi sɑˊx̣t'kwulc tamanoas; JHjp sɑ́x̣tkulᵃx̣ a supernatural spirit.

/ʔə́x̣^wa- fall, fall apart. 1. /ʔə́x̣^w-ɬ, s/ʔáx̣^wa-w-n *intr.* (*see* /ʔáx̣^w- throw away ?).

/ʔí question, interrogative. 2. ʔacíˊ interrogative (ʔac/ʔí). 3. ʔaks/ʔí which one? 4. ʔití why?; FBa iˈteˊ (ʔit /ʔí). 5. ʔití ak^wu what's the matter?, what happened?

/ʔí- bring, give to. 1. /ʔí-x, s/ʔí-staw-n *caus.*

/ʔíˑ, /ʔíy good, nice; HH íye, áie good; HH aie handsome; GGb,FR éh-yee; FBa 'ei good. 2. s/í-tan-i its goodness. 3. /ʔáy-lx get well *dev.* 4. /ʔéˑy̓ kind. 5. /ʔay=álnut in a good humor. 6. aiyalinóut HH friend (*prob.* ʔay=álnut). 7. /ʔay=ásqm good smell. 8. /ʔay=áyn? good music. 9. /ʔiy=áɬwn pretty. 10. ei.sExaˊmEɬ FBa handsome, beautiful (*see* /ʔə́x̣- see, look at; *prob.* ʔíˑ s/ʔə́x̣-amɬ). 11. tk /ʔíˑ better. 12. t̓im /ʔíˑ best.

ʔic perfective aspect; definite article (*feminine*).

/ʔícax̣^w- stand up, set up, stop. 1a. /ʔícax̣^w-m, s/ʔícx̣^w-mit-n *mdl.* 1b. /ʔícx̣^w-mi-x, s/ʔícx̣^w-m-staw-n *mdl. caus.* 2. it-so-hom-la UWb to stand (*prob.* /ʔícax̣^w-m-laʔ stand up!) 3. /ʔéˑcax̣^w-m stand *dimin.*

ʔic + l past, used to be (*feminine*) (*see* l past).

/ʔíka acre (loanword; *see* English *acre*).

/ʔikán everywhere, somewhere (*see* /káˑ where?). 2. ta /ʔikán everywhere. 3. tu /ʔikán from everywhere.

/ʔík^wa- go after. 1. /ʔík^w-n, s/ʔík^wa-t-n *tr.*

/ʔíkʷtaq- steal. 1. /ʔíkʷtq,
s/ʔíkʷtaq-n, /ʔíkʷtq-n, —.
2. /ʔékʷtq=lakaʔ thief. 3.
ʔak ʔit /ʔíkʷtq-ni-n-umx
ʔu they evidently stole it.

/ʔíkʷ- ?? 1. /ʔíkʷ=us-m wash
one's face *perf. mdl.*

/ʔikʷín few, a few (*see* /kʷí
how many?). 2. /ʔikʷéṅ few,
a few *dimin.*

/ʔílani- sing. 1a. /ʔíln,
s/ʔílaṅ-n; GGb síll; FR sill,
siḷl; FBa sī´len. 1b.
/ʔílani-x, — sing to *caus.* 2.
/ʔé·ḷn hum *dimin.* 3.
s/ʔé·ḷ·aḷ-n humming *impf.
intr.* 4. /ʔílṅ-ši- sing for
appl. 4a. /ʔílṅ-š-n,
s/ʔílṅ-ši-t-n *tr.* 5. sē´lEn
FBa song (*prob.* s/ʔílṅ).

/ʔilápaʔ you (pl.), you folks;
HH elápa ye; GGb el-láppa
ye; FR el-láp-pa ye; FBa
ela´pa you, ye.

/ʔiləp-: 1. /ʔílp first, in front.
2. /ʔílp-ɬ first, in front. 3a.
s/iləp ancestors, front. 3b.
s/iləp-i his ancestors, its
(front) end. 4. /ʔílp-ɬ=tumx
before. 5. /ʔílp-ɬ/ənca in
front of me (*see* /ʔənca I,
me). 6. či/ʔílp until, before.

ʔil-maí-tŭmḥ EC earth (*poss.*
/ʔilmx-áy=tmx and derived
from /ʔilmíx- Indian).

/ʔilmíx-: 1a. /ʔílmx Indian;
HH élamax Indian, people;
GGb éh-lumḥ an Indian; FR
eh-lumḥ Indians, people; EC
í-līmḥ. 1b. /ʔílmix-umx *pl.*
2. s/ilmé·x=tmx Indian
land. 3. s/ílmix=uliɬn
Indian food.

/ʔíɬani- eat. 1a. /ʔíɬn,
s/ʔíɬan-n; FBa ī´ɬEn *intr.*
(*see* /citén- food, meal). 1b.
/ʔíɬani-x, — feed *caus.* 1c.
/ʔíɬ-aʔ-n *pl.* 1d. éht-lin-la
GGb,FR (*prob.* /ʔíɬn-laʔ eat!).
2. s/ʔíɬén-i his eating. 3.
/ʔíɬn-ši-ctx feast. 4.
s/ʔíɬn-taw-ml-n feast. 5.
/ʔéʔɬn=alakaʔ camp robber
(gray jay *Perisoreus
canadensis*), "always
begging for something to
eat". 6. /ʔíɬ/ḱsḱs-tṅ
dandruff (*see* /ḱəsḱás-
hair). 7. /kʷəc-l/iɬṅ left
some food. 8. /nám/iɬn
finished eating. 9.
/pən/ʔíɬ-s/kʷinm
November (*see* /kʷiním-
chicken). 10.
/pən/ʔíɬ-s/qʷuʔqʷstm=iʔɬ
April (*see* /qʷóqʷstm- egg).
11. /sa-s/íʔɬan-i her
cooking.

/ʔíɬp- shoot an arrow, sting,
squirt. 1. /ʔíɬp-n,
s/ʔíɬp-t-n *tr.* 2.
/ʔíɬp-ta-ni- squirt *appl.* 2a.
/ʔíɬp-ta-ni-x, — *caus.* 3.
/ʔéʔɬp-tan-: 3a. /ʔéʔɬp-tṅ
arrow. 3b. /ʔéʔɬp-tin-umx

pl. 3c. /ʔéʔɬp-tan-i his arrow.

ʟɬta´ls TAb-mc "Little Rochester Prairie" (a prairie near Rochester in Upper Chehalis territory) (*prob.* /ʔiɬtáls*).

/ʔiX̣áp̓ useless, no-good.

/ʔímac-: 1a. /ʔémc grandchild; FBa ê´mts; FBb e·mts. 1b. nx/ʔímc-tn or nx/ʔémc-tn *pl.* 1c. /ʔimac-aw-i his grandchild. 1d. nx/ʔímc-tan-i his grandchildren.

/ʔímn- echo; hear noise; squeak. 1. /ʔímn-m̓, s/ʔímn-mt-n *mdl.* 2. s/ʔímn-mt-n a voice.

/ʔím̓ a grass for basket-making (from the mountains).

/ʔíni- do what. 1. /ʔín, s/ʔíni-n-n. 2. ɬ/ʔín kn I'll do whatever I want. 3. ɬ/ín-s kʷu it doesn't matter. 4. /ʔíni kʷu anything be done to it. 5. ʔit /ʔin-áwmx kʷu What's the matter with them? 6. s/ʔíni-n-axʷ kʷu What are you doing? 7. s/ʔín-ẃən-cal-s kʷu What is he doing to me?

/ʔiním we, us; HH eném we; GGb,FR eh-néhm we; FBa inē´m we. 2. s/iním-aɬ our, ours. 3. ʔáɬ/inm to us. 4./p̓én̓/inm beside us. 5. ʔac/x̣ʷúqʷa-ɬ/inm with us (*see* /x̣ʷúqʷa- together with).

/ʔínut- say what? 1. ʔit /ʔínut kʷu k What did you say?

lpɛ́ʔsa TAb-mi Thunder's slaves.

/ʔíqʷ- grunt. 1. /ʔíqʷ-m, s/ʔíqʷ-mt-n *mdl.*

/ʔís come. 1a. /ʔís, s/ʔís-n; FBb i·´s *intr.* 1b. ī´sa FBa come here!; GGb issa come!; FR ís-sa to come (*prob.* /ʔís-aʔ come!). 2. s/ís-i his coming. 3. /ʔís-m- come at. 3a. s/ʔís-m-cal-n it's coming at me. 4. isam̓ a´ts.tɛk FBa go inside (*see* /ʔáctq inside). 5. ʔit /cún kn ʔak/ʔís-tl-s I invited him.

/ʔíšt̓i clumsy, butterfingers.

ʔit perfective aspect; definite article (*non-feminine*).

/ʔít- do what, do with. 1. /ʔít-x, s/ʔít-aw-n (?) *caus.* (*tr.* of /ʔíni- ?). 2. /ʔít-m kʷu fixed that way *perf. pass.* 3. nks + /ʔít-aw-ctx kʷu whatever is being done with it *impf. pass.* 4. ʔit /ʔít-x kʷu k… what did you do with…? *caus.*

/ʔít- ?? 1. /ʔít/nak̓-u=šn whole (*see* /nák̓- one).

/ʔitám thing (*see* /tám what, thing). 2. /ʔitám̓-tan̓-: 2a. /ʔitám̓-tn̓ things. 2b. /ʔitám̓-tan-i his things. 3.

/míɬta t /ʔitám nothing. 4.
/t̓əm/xʷáʔkʷuʔ t /ʔitám
everything (*see* t̓əmx- all).
/ʔitámaʔ clothing. 1b.
/ʔitámaʔ-asi his clothing. 2.
/qə́x̣/itm-tn wealth, lots of
clothes.
ʔít + l past, used to be
(*non-feminine*) (*see* l past). 2.
ʔít + l /yás yesterday. 3.
ɬ-ítl-čak /yás yesterday.
/ʔiwát someone else (*see* /wá
who).
/ʔíwṅ- feel (by touching). 1.
/ʔíwṅ-x, — *caus.*
/ʔíy- (?) send. 1. /ʔíy-c, —
she sent me *perf. tr.*
/ʔiyə́q- clean (off), polish,
straighten out, brush off,
change. 1. /ʔayə́q-ɬ, —,
/ʔayə́q-n, s/ʔíyq-t-n. 2.
s/ʔíyq-tn a clearing. 3.
s/ʔáy̓q-amɬ-tṅ a brush.
/ʔiyə́q- launch. 1. /ʔayə́q-n,
s/ʔíyq-t-n *tr.*
ʔnks, ʔənks, nks habitually.
ʔu, u, ʔo, o evidently
(*enclitic*).
ʔú Oh!
/ʔuc- ?? 1. /ʔuc=ámac-: 1a.
/ʔuc=ámc trousers, pants,
overalls. 1b. /ʔuc=ámac-i
his trousers. 2. /táy/uc=amc
he doesn't have his pants on.
/ʔúc̓s one; HH,AG,RL ots; GGb
otes; FR otes, ó-tes; EC
ú-t͡sŭs; FBa ō´ts.s; JH
'u·'ts's (*see* /nák̓- one). 2.

/ʔó·c̓s alone. 3. /ʔó·c̓·uc̓s
single, bachelor. 4. ta/ʔúc̓s
another. 5. ʔaɬ ta/ʔúc̓s next.
6. tál/ʔuc̓s eleven (ENM); EC
tal-ó-t͡sŭs. 7. ō´ts panEks
kEɬt ō´ts.s FBa one hundred
and one (*prob.* /ʔúc̓s
/pánks-ɬ=tumx kl t
/ʔúc̓s). 8. ō´ts
panEksɬto´mEx FBa one
hundred (*prob.* /ʔúc̓s
/pánks-ɬ=tumx). 9.
/cəm=túmx kl t /ʔúc̓s
twenty-one; EC
t͡sŭm-tumħ-kĭl-t͡sŭs; FBa
tsEmtū´mEx kEɬ ō´ts.s. 10.
/pánačš kl t /ʔúc̓s eleven
(LNJ); HH panʊtç-kaltótsʊs;
GGb pah-natsh
kul-totes´ŭs; FR
pah-natsh kult-ótes-us,
pah-natsh kult ótes; FBa
pa´nets kEɬ ō´ts.s. 11.
autsis-kwil-lum GGb friend
(*see* /qʷələ́m- heart).
/ʔúlwasi- get even. 1.
/ʔúlwasi-x, — *caus.*
/ʔúlx̣- save, take care of. 1.
/ʔúlx̣, —, /ʔúlx̣-n, —. 2.
/ʔó·lx̣- raise an orphan. 2a.
/ʔó·lx̣-n, — *tr.* 3. s/úlx̣
slave. 4. .sō´laxEm FBa
orphan (*prob.* s/úlax̣-m).
/ʔúɬ- bare. 1. /ʔuɬ-áĺ=šn
barefoot (/ʔuɬ-áĺ-ɬ=šn ?).
2. /ʔúɬ=ay̓q empty. 2a.
/ʔúɬ=ay̓q, —,
/ʔúɬ=ay̓q-n, —.

/ʔúm- feed. 1. —, s/ʔúm-t-n
tr. 2. /ʔúm-laʔ feed it!

/ʔúmati- name. 1. /ʔúmt-n,
s/ʔúmati-t-n *tr.*

/ʔúpal- eat. 1. /ʔúpɬ,
s/ʔúpal-n *intr.* 2.
/ʔúpaɬ-aʔ eat it!

/ʔúpax̣- send to. 1. /ʔúpax̣-n,
— *tr.*

ʔus *see* wəs.

/ʔúšam- pity, be sorry for. 1.
/ʔúšam-n, — *tr.* (or -mn
rel.?). 2. ʔac/ʔúšm-s-m he
is pitied *pass.* 3. q̇aɬ
/úšm-ń̓ɬ poor. 4. q̇aɬ
/ó·šm-ń̓ɬ a little poor.

/ʔútaq-: 1a. /ʔútq paddle, oar.
1b. /ʔútaq-i his paddle. 2.
/ʔútq- paddle a canoe. 2a.
—, s/ʔútq-t-n *tr.* 3.

/ʔútq=wil- paddle a canoe.
3a. —, s/ʔútq=wil-n *intr.*

/ʔúx̌ʷa- teach. 1. /ʔúx̌ʷa-ni-
teach, advise *appl.* 1a.
/ʔúx̌ʷa-ni-x,
s/ʔúx̌ʷ-n-y-n *caus.* 2.
/ʔúx̌ʷ-n-tux̌ʷ- teach *appl.*
2a. ʔit /ʔúx̌ʷ-n-tux̌ʷ-c he
taught me *perf. tr.* 3.
/ʔúx̌ʷ-ši- blame *appl.* 3a.
/ʔúx̌ʷ-š-n, s/ʔúx̌ʷ-ši-t-n
tr. 4. nks + /ʔúx̌ʷ-ń̓-maɬ-n
teacher. 5.
s/ʔúx̌ʷ-n-kʷaw-n
interpreting, teaching *impf.
intr.*

/ʔúx̌ʷtqs dislike, disapprove.
2. O´x̣tιqs TAb-ss name of a
slave with a long nose (myth
character) (*poss.*
/ʔúx̌ʷt=qs).

b

bo´Ets FBa boots (loanword;
see English boots).

c

c indefinite article (*feminine*).
cac definite article (*feminine*).
2. cac-x̣-cá that one
(*feminine*).

tsa.kwa´mEn FBa Chinook
canoe.

/caɬxán-: 1a. /cáɬšn shoe,
shoes; HH tsʋ´txlçin shoes;
AG,RL tsʋtkhlshin shoes;
GGb chál-shin shoe; FR
chál-shin shoes; FBa
tca´ɬcEn shoes; FBa
tsa´lccEn moccasins. 1b.

/c⅃xán-i his shoe. 2.
/cá?⅃šn little shoe.
/cám– two (*see* /sáli? two).
1. /cám=aqʷ two days; FBa
tsa´mokxᵁ today. 2.
/cam=ə́šn two times,
twice, two at a time. 3.
/cám=l̓s two dollars. 4.
/cám=panxʷ two years
old. 5. /cám̓=xaẇ⅃ two
rows. 6. /cm=túmx
twenty; HH tçum-tómᴜx;
GGb tsum-tó-moh; FR
tsum-tó-mȯh,
tsum-tó-moh; EC
t͡sŭm-túmh̓; FBa
tsᴇmtū´mᴇx. 7.
/cm=túmx kl t /?úc̓s
twenty-one; EC
t͡sŭm-túmh̓-kĭl-tú-t͡sŭs;
FBa tsᴇmtū´mᴇx kᴇ⅃
ō´ts.s. 8. /cám/santi two
weeks (*see* /sánti Sunday,
week). 9. /cam-s/q̓íx̣
Tuesday (see /q̓íx̣– day).
/cam– ?? 1a. /cam=é·c̓a?
great-grandchild; FBa
tsᴇme´tsa
great-grandchild,
great-grandparent, ancestor.
1b. nx/cam=é·c̓a-tn *pl.*
/cámus eight; HH tçámos;
AG,RL tshamos; GGb,FR
tsam-mose; EC t͡sá-mos;
FBa tsā´mus (*see* /mús
four). 2. /cámus-l=šn
eight times. 3. /cámus=l̓s

eight dollars. 4.
/cámus-⅃=qʷ eight days.
5. /cámus-⅃=tumx eighty.
6. /pánačš kl t /cámus
eighteen (LNJ). 7.
/tál̓/camus eighteen (ENM).
8. /t̓əmx/cámus eightfold.
/cána– sew, mend, push
through. 1a. —,
s/cán-ml-n *impl.tr.* 1b. —,
s/cána-t-n *tr.* 2.
/can=ál̓wa-x sewed
together *caus.* 3.
/cána-m̓⅃-tṅ needle, pin.
4. cán.kə⅃tən HT cinch; FBa
tsa´n.kᴇ⅃tᴇn.
/cápx creek, little river, small
stream from a spring; FBa
tsê´.p.x creek; BH
tsā´p.x.
/cáq– ?? 1. /cáq-⅃=kʷu
thirsty.
/cáqa– bracken roots; EC
st͡sak; JH sts´q (*prob.*
s/cáq). 2. /cáqa=ṅ⅃
bracken fern *Pteridium
aquilinum*; JH stsá·q'´ṅ⅃.
/cáqʷ–: 1a. s/cáqʷ arrow. 1b.
s/caqʷ-íl-i his arrow.
/cáqʷa– paint. 1. /cáqʷ-⅃,
—, /cáqʷ-n, s/cáqʷa-t-n.
2. s/cáqʷ-ml-n he's
painting *impf. impl.tr.* 3.
/cáqʷa-m̓⅃-tṅ paint *n.* 4.
/cáqʷ=aẏs painted face. 5.
s/cáqʷ=us-m red face
powder.

/caqʷáʔɬ alder; EC t͡sa-qáȟl;
FBa tsakaʹɬ spruce ?*Picea
sitchensis* (Sitka spruce).

/caqʷə́l-: 1a. /cáqʷɬ potato
Sagittaria latifolia
(arrowhead); EC t͡saqȟl
arrowhead-roots; FBa
tsaʹqoɬ potato; JH
tsɑ̊ʹqwɬ potato. 1b.
/cáqʷaɬ-iɬ *pl.* 1c.
/caqʷə́l-i his potato.

/caqʷə́l-: 1a. /cáqʷɬ paddle,
oar; GGb sák-wtl paddle. 1b.
/cáqʷiɬ-umx *pl.* 1c.
s/caqʷə́l-i his paddle. 2a.
sāʹkoɬtɛn FBa paddle
(*prob.* /cáqʷɬ-tn). 2b.
/cáqʷɬ-tan-i his paddle,
his oar.

/catáwiʔ cedar *Thuja plicata*
(western redcedar); EC
t͡sa-tá-wi; FBa tsɛtáwạ; JH
tsɑ̊tâ·wɪʹ.

/cátaxʷ-: 1a. /cátxʷ creek,
water from a spring. 1b.
s/cátaxʷ-i its creek.

/cawaq-: 1. /cawaq-áwm̓x
twins *pl.*

tsauʹɬkaxa FBa a fly.

tsaʹwx̣ TAb-mi roe (deer).

/cá·ya- busy. 1. /cá·ya-ɬ,
s/cá·ya-w-n *intr.*

/cayá·-: 1. ʔnks + /cayá·-
imitate. 1a. —, ʔnks +
/cayá·-cši-t-n *refl.*

/cáyaʔ- bother, worry,
annoy, nervous. 1. /cáya-ɬ,

—, /cáyaʔ-n,
s/cáyaʔ-t-n.

/cé́ɬ lake; HH tselx; GGb
tséh-tl; EC tsĕ'ȟl; FBa,BH
tsê.ɬ. 2. sáʹts'ɑɬ TAb-mc
Black River (in Upper
Chehalis territory; *prob.*
/sá/cəɬɬ).

/cép- proud, stuck up. 1.
/cép-ɬ, — *intr.*

tsɛtseiʹkatɛn FBa elbow; EC
sa-t͡saí-ŭ-katn.

/cə́kʷa- lie down, go to bed.
1. /cə́kʷ-ɬ, s/cə́kʷa-w-n
intr. 2. /cə́kʷi-ɬ-aʔ lie
down!; UWb tso-quilt-ah
to sleep. 3. ʔac/cékʷ-ɬ
lying down. 4.
/cakʷ-éˑl=iɬ-tn̓,
/cakʷ-íl=iɬ-tn̓ cradle
basket, cradle; EC tsqi'l.

/cə́kʷluʔxʷ dish; FBa
tseʹokʷoleʹx plate. 1b.
/cə́kʷluʔxʷ-umx *pl.* 2.
/céʔkʷíxʷ small dish.

/cəɬə́qʷ- tear, rip. 1.
/caɬə́qʷ-ɬ, —,
/caɬə́qʷ-n, s/cə́ɬqʷ-t-n.
2. /cə́ɬ·caɬaqʷ- tear up. 2a.
/cə́ɬ·caɬaqʷ-n, — *tr.*

/cə́m- hug. 1. /cə́m-n,
s/cə́m-t-n *tr.*

/cə́ni he, him; HH tsuʹne
he; HH tsune, tçini this;
AG,RL tsuné he; GGb
tehts-ún-né he; FR
tehts-ún-ne teh'tsún-ne
he; FBa tsaʹneɬ he, she, it.

2. c /cə́ni she, her. 3.
s/caní-yaⱡ his, her, hers,
its. 4a. /cəni-yáwmx they,
them; HH tçiniáömux they;
GGb tsen-ni-ȧu̇m̓h they;
FR tsen-ni-ȧu̇m̓h,
tsen-niáü-m̓h they; FBa
tsɛnia´mux they. 4b.
ʔac/x̱ʷúqʷ-aⱡ/cəni-yawm
x with them (see /x̱ʷúqʷa-
together with). 4c.
s/cəni-yáwmix-aⱡ their,
theirs. 5a. ʔáⱡ/cani to him,
to her, to it. 5b.
ʔac/x̱ʷúqʷ-aⱡ/cani with
him (see /x̱ʷúqʷa- together
with). 5c. x-ʔáⱡ/cani to
him, to her, to it. 6.
/ʔáwt-ⱡ/cani behind him,
after him. 7. /ṗéń/cani
beside him. 8. /ták/cani
himself.

/cə́ni- greedy. 1.
ʔac/cə́ni-stumx he's
greedy.

/cənúp-: 1a. /cə́np bed; FBa
tsî´n.p. 1b. /cə́nap-umx
pl. 1c. /canúp-i his bed. 2.
/céńp little bed.

/cə́p-: 1. /cə́p=kʷu go after
water.

/cə́q- sit straight, set over a
fire, roast. 1. /cə́q-ⱡ, —,
/cə́q-n, —. 2. /caqáʔ-
roast on a stick. 2a.
/caqáʔ-n, — tr. 3.
/cə́q=stq- boil, can. 3a.
/cə́q=stq-m̓ⱡ, — impl.tr.

3b. /cə́q=stq-n,
s/cə́q=stq-t-n tr. 4a.
/cáq=stq-tń kettle,
bucket; HH tsákstuktin
kettle; GGb tsukst´k kettle;
FBa tsa´kstkɛn kettle. 4b.
/cáq=stq-tań-i his
bucket. 5. /cá̓ʔq=stq-tń
canoe bailer.

/cəqíẏ- kick. 1. /caqíẏn, —;
FBa tsa´ketse tr. 2. ʔit
/cə́qiẏ-c he kicked me
impf. tr. 3. tsa´ketsikɛn
FBa kick (poss. /cə́qiẏcikn).

/cəsúẇⱡ stiff.

/cəxáẏus-: 1a. s/cəxáʔis
partner. 1b. s/cəxáẏus-i his
partner.

/ciʔin- ?? (see /ʔíni- do
what ?). 1. /nám̓u-ⱡ
/ciʔín-stawt ⱡ t /x̱ə́š
perhaps we'll have bad
luck.

cic definite article (feminine;
diminutive). 2a. ci-cu that's
why (see cu because, so, so
that, for the reason that). 2b.
ʔací ci-cu /t̓ə́k̓ʷ-tuli Why
did he bite him?

/cíki- rub, scrape, crumple. 1.
/cík-ⱡ, —, /cík-n,
s/cíki-t-n.

/cíks bee, bees; FBa tsī´ks
wasp. 2. /cíks=lwltxʷ
beehive, hornet's nest.

/cílks- five (see /čílačš
five). 2. /cílks-ⱡ=panxʷ
five years old. 3.

/cílks-ɬ=qʷ five days. 4.
/cílks-ɬ=tumx fifty; EC
tsí-lĭksh̄l-tumħ. 5a.
/cílks-ɬ=ušn five times.
5b. /cílks-t-l=xan-s its
five times. 6.
/cilks-t-áĺ=xaẃɬ five
rows. 7. /cílks-t=ĺs five
dollars. 8.
/cilks-t-al-s/q̓íx̣ Friday
(*see* /q̓íx̣- day).

/cilxmtə́n-: 1. /cilxmtə́n-i
their children.

/ciɬ- ?? 1.
/ciɬ-á·l=axʷ=inp floor. 2a.
/ciɬ-á·ĺ=axʷ board,
boards. 2b. /ciɬ-á·ĺ=axʷ-i
his board.

/ciɬə́n-: 1a. /cíɬn food,
meal; FBa tsi´ɬEn salmon;
JH-jp tsítɬn any salmon;
JHjp tsíɬn (*see* /ʔíɬani-
eat). 1b. /ciɬə́n-i his food.

/cín- ?? 1. /cín=qs fall on
one's face.

/cípɬ- ?? 1. /cípɬ-tn
headband.

/cíqʷi- dig. 1a. /cíqʷ-am̓ɬ,
s/cíqʷ-ml-n *impl.tr.* 1b.
/cíqʷ-n, — *tr.* 2.
/cíqʷi-n-aʔ dig it! 3.
/céqʷ-š- dig *appl.* 3a.
/céqʷ-š-n, — *tr.* 4.
s/cíqʷ-ɬ hole. 5a.
s/cíqʷ=qʷĺ a well. 5b.
s/cíqʷ=qʷaĺ-i his well. 6.
tseqiapī´mEɬEn FBa hoe
(*poss.* /ciqʷ=yapí-m̓ɬ-n̓).

/cítpan-: 1a. s/cítpn fish
trap; TAb-fn tse´tpən. 1b.
s/cítpan-i his fish trap.

/cítxʷ stung by a bee.

/cíx̣i- show. 1. —,
s/cíx̣i-w-n, —,
s/cíx̣i-t-n. 2. ʔac/cé·x̣-ɬ
stick out. 3. /cíx̣-š- show
to *appl.* 3a. /cíx̣-š-n, — *tr.*
4. /cíx̣-tuxʷ- show to *appl.*
4a. /cíx̣-tuxʷt, s/cíx̣-txʷt-
tr. 5. ʔit txʷ/cíx̣-st-m it
came to the surface and
disappeared fast *caus. pass.*
6. tse´x̣ɬuk.ɬta´m FBa
sunrise (*see* /ɬukʷáɬ sun;
poss. /cíx̣/ɬukʷɬ-tm). 7.
s/put-s/cíx̣i-w-n tit
/ɬukʷáɬ sunrise.

tsei´.a FBa sister-in-law.

.tskwe´.kᵘ FBa copper (see?
/k̓ʷiq̓é- green).

c + l past (time) (*feminine*)
(*see* l past).

/cɬkə́n-: 1. /cɬkə́n-i its
skin.

/cɬqʷála- ?? 1a. /cɬqʷála-tn
brain; FBa tskwa´latEn. 1b.
/cɬqʷál-tn-i his brain.

/cɬt- ?? 1. /cɬt=álaxʷ cloud,
clouds, sky; HH txltálaxu
sky, heaven; AG
tkhltalakhu sky; RL
tkhltalakun sky; GGb
sl-táh-la-hwŏ sky; FR
st-tah-la-hŭ sky; EC
sh̄ltá-lahw sky; FBa
sElta´laux sky.

/cmús face; GGb
tsum-móse; FR
tsum-móse face, eye; EC
t͡sŭ-mús; FBa tsɛmuˊs; HT
cəmús (*see* /mús eye). 1b.
/cmús-i his face. 1c. HH
ntsʊmós *prob.* my face.

/cóˑ– plan, think, have an
idea. 1. /cóˑ-n think. 2.
/cóˑ-t think, plan. 3.
ʔac/cóˑ-tu-mx he blamed
me *caus.* 4. ʔac/cóˑ-n̓-x̣-n
/q̓íc̓x̣ it looks suspicious. 5.
/mí+ta t
s/cóˑ-t=ayn-min-i he
didn't pay attention.

/cóʔ– ?? 1. tk /cóʔ between.

cóʔa exhortative particle (?).

/cópsqʷli– ?? 1.
/cópsqʷli-m̓+-tan-i its
nest.

/cóˑtx̣kn important.

/csisín– ?? 1. /mí+ta
/csisín-i nothing's the
matter (*see* /ʔíni– do
what?).

cu because, so, so that, for the
reason that.

/cúl–: 1a. /cú+ leg, foot, lap;
HH tsótxl foot; HH tsoótxl
leg; AG,RL tsotkhl feet; GGb
tsóhtl; EC t͡suhl; FBa tsuˊ+
foot. 1b. /cu+-áwmx *pl.* 1c.
/cúl-i his leg, his foot. 1c.

/cu+-áwmiš-i his legs, his
feet *pl.* 2. /cóʔ+ lower leg
dimin.

/cúm– ?? 1a. /cúm=ay̓s
eyebrow; FBa tsuˊmas; HT
cúmas. 1b. /cúm=iʔs-i his
eyebrow.

/cúmaʔ wild crab apple, wild
crab apples *Malus fusca*
(Pacific crab apple); JH
tsʊˊˑmɑˈ. 1b. /cúmaʔ-i
his crabapple.

/cún tell. 1a. /cún,
s/cún-t-n *tr.* 2. /cún-c-
he told me. 2a. /cún-c,
s/cún-cal-n *tr.* 3. /cún̓-x̣
tell, answer. 4. /cú-t say. 4a.
/cú-t, s/cú-t-n *intr.* 5.
/cú-t-laʔ say! 6. nks +
/cú-ti-cal-n (?) she was
telling me.

/cúsaq nail. 1b.
/cúsaq-umx *pl.* 1c.
/cúsaq-i his nail.

cút– ?? 1. cút-kn evidently,
maybe (*see* kən– maybe).

/cútaqʷ–: 1a. s/cútqʷ bow.
1b. s/cútaqʷ-i his bow.

/cút̓x̣ say. 1a. /cút̓x̣, — *intr.*
2. /cóˑt̓x̣ want to *dimin.*

/cúy̓qs– stumble. 1.
/cúy̓qs-m, — *mdl.* 2.
s/cúy·cuyqs-mit-n he's
stumbling *impf. mdl.*

c'

/c'ácx̌ʷn weasel *Mustela*
spp.; EC át͡s-ḥum; JH
'â·'ts^αxom' (*prob.*
/ʔácx̌ʷm').

/c'ac'ə́p wren ?*Troglodytes
troglodytes* (winter wren);
TAb-ly ts'ats'ɛ´'αp. 1b.
/c'ac'ə́p-i his wren.

/c'aɬə́q- wreck, ruin. 1.
/c'aɬə́q-ɬ, —, /c'aɬə́q-n,
—. 2. /c'ɬq=ál'us fall
apart.

ts'a´max̌wʊl TAb-ly a little
black bird, about the size of
a lark, that lives near the
river (*prob.* /c'ámax̌ʷl).

/c'ám'- suckle. 1a. c'ám'-tn
breast, udder. 1b.
/c'əm-tə́n-i her breast.

/c'ápax̣-: 1a. /c'ápx̣ cedar
roots, cedar. 1b. s/c'ápax̣-i
her cedar roots.

/c'áqa- open sore, rotten. 1.
/c'áq-ɬ, s/c'áq-a-w-n
intr. 2. ʔac/c'áq-ɬ an open
sore. 3. s/c'áq a sore.

/c'as- wrinkled. 1.
ʔac/c'as=ús wrinkled face.

/c'áw- get out of. 1.
/c'áw-ɬ, — *intr.* 2.
/c'aw=úqs dish up, serve.

/c'áwɬ Chinook salmon
*Onchorhynchus
tshawytscha*; GGa tsow-olt;
GGb tsàủ wtl spring salmon;
UWa Tsow-olt; UWa

Tsow-olts trout; FR
tsàủ-wtl, tsa-u-wtl
salmon; FBa tsā´uɬ
Chinook or king salmon.

/c'ax̣- ?? 1. /c'ax̣-áy'=stq
charcoal; EC t͡sa-ḥaísk; FBa
tsexai´.stɛk.

/c'ax̣- ?? 1. /c'ax̣=íl's sand;
FBa tsaxhe´l.s. 2.
ʔac/c'ax̣=íl's-x-tan-i tit
/pípa sandpaper.

/c'áx̣č=n' fish spear; EC
t͡sáḥ-kǐn; FBa tsa´xkɛn
(*prob.* /c'áx̣k=n). 2.
sα´x̣kən TAb-ss Spear Boy
(*prob.* /c'áx̣k=n).

/c'ax̣íl- nail. 1a.
/c'ax̣íl=akaʔ fingernail;
FBa tsaxai´laka; FBa
tsaxilê´ka claw; HT
caxaílaka. 1b.
/c'ax̣íl=ka-l'-i his
fingernail. 1c.
/c'ax̣íl=ak-umiš-i his
fingernails. 2a. /c'ax̣íl=šn
toenail. 2b. s/c'ax̣íl=xan-i
his toenail. 2c.
/c'ax̣íl=šn-umiš-i his
toenails, his claws *pl.*

/c'ay- aim, try for, want. 1.
/c'ay-s/kʷaná-t-n he's
reaching for it *impf. tr.* (see
/kʷəná- get, take). 2.
/c'ay-s/tə́qʷči-ci-n he's
aiming at you *impf. tr.* (see

/təqʷə́či- shoot with a
gun).

/c'éˑt'- ?? 1.
?ac/c'éˑt'=xan-m he
balanced on his toes *perf.
mdl.*

/c'ə́ka- win, defeat, use up,
be gone. 1. /c'ə́k-ɬ,
s/c'ə́ka-w-n, /c'ə́k-n,
s/c'ə́k-t-n. 2.
/c'ə́ka-mal- win, earn. 2a.
/c'ə́ka-m'ɬ, s/c'ə́k-ml-n
impl.tr. 3. s/c'ə́ka-m'ɬ
game. 4. /c'ə́k-š- beat,
defeat *appl.* 4a. /c'ə́k-š-n,
— *tr.* 5. /c'ak-ál=nut give
up. 6. /c'ak-ál=nut-š-n
impatient, out of patience
appl. 7. /c'ə́k=ay'q be
empty, become empty. 7a.
/c'ə́k=ay'q,.— *intr.* 8.
/c'ə́k/lxʷkʷu? smother, be
out of breath. 8a.
/c'ə́k/lxʷkʷu?,
s/c'ə́k/lxʷkʷu-w-n,
/c'ə́k/lxʷkʷu-ən, — (*see*
/láxʷkʷu- breathe). 9.
/c'ə́k/tal'a spend all one's
money (*see* /tála money).

/c'ələ́m belted kingfisher
Ceryle alcyon; FBa
tse'lîˊm; JH sts'ɑlɑ̀m'.

/c'ələ́pa- spin, turn. 1. —,
s/c'ə́lpa-w-n, /c'alə́p-n,
—. 2. tsaˊ ltsalepEl FBa
whirlwind (*poss.*
/c'ə́l·c'əlp-ɬ). 3.
/c'ál'p-y=al's drunk. 4.

tsEɬpeˊs.ɬko FBa eddy; HT
cə́ɬpés.ɬko (*prob.*
/c'əlp-ís-ɬ=kʷu).

tsElėˊtcEn FBa swallow [bird]
(*prob.* /c'əl=íčn).

/c'əmə́k̓ʷ- blunt pointed,
come off. 1. /c'amə́k̓ʷ-ɬ,
— *intr.* 2. ?it
txʷ/c'amə́k̓ʷ-st-m part of
it came off *caus. pass.*

/c'əmə́xʷ- sharp pointed. 1.
/c'amə́xʷ-ɬ, —. 2.
?ac/c'amе́xʷ=qs pointed
nose. 3. ?ac/c'əm'xʷ-l'=s
tit /silháws pointed tipi.

/c'ə́p strong, stiff; HH tsʊp
strong; GGb tsúpp strong;
FR tsupp strong.

/c'ə́p'a- flood. 1. /c'ə́p'-ɬ,
s/c'ə́p'a-w-n *intr.* 2.
/c'ap'-úw-s its flooding.

/c'ə́q'- push in, press down.
1. /c'ə́q'-n, — *tr.* 2.
tsaˊ kaiᵘktEn FBa ramrod
(of a gun) (*poss.*
/c'ə́q'=iqʷ-tn *or*
/c'ə́q'=aykʷ-tn).

/c'əwə́k'- cut. 1.
/c'awə́k'-ɬ, —,
/c'awə́k'-n, s/c'ə́wk'-t-n
(*see* /c'uk̓ʷ- cut, chop). 2.
/c'ə́w·c'əwək'- cut up,
butcher, carve, operate on.
2a. /c'ə́w·c'awək'-n,
s/c'ə́w·c'əwk'-t-n *tr.* 3.
/c'áwk'-am'ɬ-tn' chisel;
FBa tsaˊ zhamEɬtEn chisel
(for cutting trees). 4.

/c'əwk'-ə́mn chips (from cutting wood). 5.
/c'uwk'=áka cut one's hand. 6.
/c'uwk'-áy=aqan-m cut one's hair *perf. mdl.*
/c'ə́xʷi– loose, loosen, unroll, unravel. 1. /c'ə́xʷ-ɬ, —, /c'ə́xʷ-n, s/c'ə́xʷ-t-n. 2. /c'ə́xʷi-n-aʔ unravel it! 3. /c'əxʷ=ál'wa– untangle. 3a. /c'əxʷ=ál'wa-x, s/c'əxʷ=ál'u-staw-n *caus.* 4. /c'ə́xʷ-l=k– unwrap. 4a. /c'ə́xʷ-l=k-n, s/c'ə́xʷ-l=k-t-n *tr.*
/c'əxʷúy'nwn'– ?? 1. /c'əxʷúy'nwn'=šn little toe; FBa tsoxonwai´cEn. 2. tsExwo´Enwaieka FBa finger (*poss.* /c'əxʷúynw-ay=aka).
/c'əx̣ám– ?? 1. /c'əx̣ám=us dirty face.
/c'ə́x̣ʷa– drip, leak. 1. /c'ə́x̣ʷ-m, s/c'ə́x̣ʷ-mt-n *mdl.* 2. s/c'ə́x̣ʷa-m-i its dripping.
/c'ə́x̣ʷi– wash. 1. /c'ə́x̣ʷ-ɬ, —, /c'ə́x̣ʷ-n, —. 2. /c'ə́x̣ʷi-n-aʔ wash it! 3. /c'ə́x̣ʷ-am'ɬ wash something. 3a. /c'ə́x̣ʷ-am'ɬ, s/c'ə́x̣ʷ-ml-n *impl.tr.* 4. /c'áx̣ʷ-am'ɬ-tn' soap. 5.

/c'ə́x̣ʷ=iqi-m'ɬ wash dishes.
/c'əyə́p'– pinch, squeeze. 1. /c'ayə́p'-n, s/c'íyp'-t-n *tr.*
tsei´uk FBa northern flicker *Colaptes auratus n.* (*prob.* /c'ə́yqʷ).
/c'əy'ə́qʷa– cave in. 1. /c'ay'ə́qʷ-ɬ, s/c'əy'qʷa-w-n *intr.*
/c'í– pink. 1. ʔaks/c'í pink, red.
/c'ík– squeak. 1. /c'ík-m, — *mdl.* 2a. /c'ík·c'ik wagon. 2b. /c'ík·c'ik-i his wagon. 2c. /c'ík·c'ik-umiš-i his wagons *pl.* 3a. /c'ék·c'ik little wagon. 3b. /c'ék·c'ik-i his little wagon.
/c'ík̓ʷ– ?? 1. /c'é·k̓ʷ-l-ši– make faces at *appl.* 1a. /c'é·k̓ʷ-l-š-n, s/c'é·k̓ʷ-l-ši-t-n *tr.* 2. /c'ík̓ʷ=us– frown, make faces. 2a. /c'ík̓ʷ=us-m, — *mdl.*
/c'ík̓ʷ– numb. 1. /c'ík̓ʷ-ɬ, — *intr.* 2. /c'ík̓ʷ=aka arm goes to sleep. 3. /c'ík̓ʷ=šn leg goes to sleep.
/c'ilíləɬ, TAb-mc tc'ili´ɩɬ Mount Adams.
/c'íp– ?? 1. /c'é·p-l=si– wink, squint. 1a. ʔit /c'é·p-l=si-c he winked at me *perf. tr.*

/c'ípxʷ– ?? 1. tse´pxolstEn FBa eyelash (*poss.* /c'ípxʷ=ls–tn). 2. tsepiakalsEmEn FBa eyelid; HT cepiakalsəmən (*prob.* /c'ipxʷ=yaq=al's–mn).

/c'íq– red, bay. 1. ?aks/c'íq red, bay; HH uktséaqu red; AG uktseakhu red; RL uktseakhu red; GGb uks–tsék red; FR uks–tsek red; EC aks–t͡síŭk red; FBa Ekstsê´.q red; FBa Exkstsê´q bay. 2. ts'í·q'q'ᵅs JH buzzard, turkey vulture *Cathartes aura* (*prob.* /c'íq=qs). 3. .xtseq awi´lEk FBa red paint (*poss.* ?aks/c'íq /?awílk).

/c'íq̓ʷ– press, mash. 1. /c'íq̓ʷ–ɬ, —, /c'íq̓ʷ–n, —.

/c'íq̓ʷa– step on. 1. /c'íq̓ʷ–n, — *tr.* 2. /c'é·q̓ʷa–mn' stairway. 3. /c'é·q̓ʷa–m'ɬ–tn' steps, stairs; stirrups. 4. kát/c'iq̓ʷi–m'ɬ–tn' stirrups.

/c'íwi– pray. 1. /c'é·w– pray. 1a. /c'é·w–m, s/c'é·w–mt–n *mdl.* 2. ?ac/c'íw–ši–tm prayer. 3. /c'é·wi–mn church (ENM). 4. /c'éwi–m'ɬ–tn' church (LNJ); FBa tsa´ᵘemaɬEn.

/c'íwq sturgeon *Acipenser* sp(p).

/c'íwq' left (side). 2. ?áɬ/c'iwq' left; FBa êɬtsê´uq left hand.

/c'íxʷ–: 1. s/c'íxʷ osprey, fish hawk *Pandion haliaetus*).

/c'íx̣– have a premonition. 1. /c'íx̣–ɬ, — *intr.*

ts'í·x̣p JH root *sp.*; EC t͡siħp an edible root (*prob.* /c'íx̣p).

/c'íyi– dark red. 1. ?aks/c'íyi dark red, cherry red.

/c'íykʷ– giggle, waste time, act silly. 1. /c'íykʷ–cx, s/c'íykʷ–cši–t–n *refl.* 2. s/c'íy·c'iykʷ–cši–t–n she's giggling *impf. refl.*

ts'kwai EG wood fern ?*Dryopteris* sp. (note Proto-Salish *c'əkʷí? wood fern.

ts'kwí·kw̩ JH blue elderberry *Sambucus cerulea*; JHjp tsk'w̩íkw̩ (*prob.* /c'kʷíkʷ).

/c'lə́m waterdogs (?) (*poss.* salamander sp.)

/c'mə́l'qn (an unidentified animal, perhaps mink *Mustela vison*); TAb-ly ts'mɑ´lqen mink.

/c'óps, /c'ó?ps seven; HH tsóps; AG,RL tsops; GGb,FR tsopes; EC t͡sops; FBa tsô´.ps. 2. /c'ó?ps–t–l=šn seven times. 3. /c'óps–ɬ=panxʷ seven years old. 4. /c'óps–ɬ=qʷ seven days. 5.

/c'óps-ł=tumx seventy. 6. /c'ó·ps-t=ls seven dollars. 7. /pánačš kl t /c'óps seventeen (LNJ). 8. /tál/c'ups seventeen (ENM). 9. /t'əmx/c'ó·ps sevenfold.

/**c'skíyaq**-: 1a. /c'skíyq ant, ants; FBa tsEskī´Ek. 1b. /c'skíyaq-i his ant. 2. /c'skíyq=lwltxʷ ant-hill.

/**c'uc'úq̇ʷ**-: 1a. /c'úc'q̇ʷ feather; HH tsótsqu feathers; GGb tsotes-ko. 1b. c'uc'úq̇ʷ-i its feather. 2. ?ac/c'úc'q̇ʷ having a feather.

/**c'uk̇ʷ**- cut, chop (see /c'əwə́k'- cut). 1. /c'uk̇ʷ-áy=kʷp cut wood, split wood, chop wood. 1a.

/c'uk̇ʷ-áy=kʷp, s/c'uk̇ʷ-áy=kʷp-n intr. 2. /c'uk̇ʷ-áy=qs-t-n topping a tree.

tso´lswaia FBa toad (prob. /c'úlstwaya Bufo boreas western toad).

/**c'úni**- soak. 1. —, s/c'úni-t-n tr.

/**c'úq̇ʷ**- set upright, straight up. 1. /c'úq̇ʷ-ł, —, /c'úq̇ʷ-n, —. 2. /c'úq̇ʷ-ši- set up for appl. 2a. —, s/c'úq̇ʷ-ši-t-n tr. 3a. ?ac/c'úq̇ʷ-ł a pole; GGb at-só-quutl tree. 3b. ?ac/c'úq̇ʷ-a?-ł posts pl. 4. /c'úq̇ʷ-ł noon; FBa tso´qEł. 5. /nám/c'uq̇ʷł afternoon.

č

(**tc** in older material = č)

tca´tst FBa hammer (for cutting trees); HT čáct.

/**čá·kat**-: 1. /čá·kt waist. 1b. /čá·kat-i his waist.

/**čanumíš** awkward.

/**čátqɬm'**-: 1. s/čátqɬm' cougar, lion; a mean animal; EC chát-h̄lĭm grizzly bear; TAb-jc ca´tqɬəm White Bear; JH tʃá·t.q'ɬɑm' grizzly.

.**stcai´tcil** FBa rosebush Rosa spp.

/**čáyni** Chinese; FBa tcai´ne (loanword; see Chinook Jargon chaynee 'Chinese', taken in turn from colloquial English [čayní], a back formation from English Chinese).

'**tcê´** FBa friend.

/**čé?xʷ**- sunburned. 1. —, s/čé?xʷ-mal-n impl.tr.

/čé·taq- argue. 1. /čé·taq-m, s/čé·tq-mit-n *mdl.*

tcɛlī´cɛn FBa hair seal, fur seal ?*Phoca vitulina* (harbor seal) (*here* c = [š]).

/čənóʔkʷšitm owl (hawk?); EC chĭ-núk-sĥitm; FBa tcinu´kc̦itɛm; JH tʃɪnu´kwʃɪtàm horned owl *Bubo virginianus* (great horned owl).

/čə́nq- stutter. 1. ʔnks + c/čə́n·čnq=ɬnal-n he stutters.

tcɛto'x̣we´ FBa fisher *Martes pennanti.*

/čə́txʷan'-: 1a. s/čə́txʷn' black bear *Ursus americanus*; GGb s'chet-hoot bear; EC stsít-ḥṇn; FBa stcî´tᵘx̣ʷɛn; JH stsít.xwɑn'. 1b. s/čə́txʷin'-umx *pl.* 1c. s/čə́txʷan'-i his bear. 2. s/čéʔtxʷan=iʔɬ bear cub.

/číə chickadee; TAb-ly Tci´ə a bird with red, white, yellow, and black spots all over the body, and with orange and red tail and wings (*prob.*

Colaptes auratus northern flicker: MDK).

/čílačš five; HH tc̦élatc̦; AG,RL tshelatsh; GGb chéh-latsh; FR chíh-latsh; EC t͡sí-lat͡s; FBa tcila´.ts·ˢ; HT čí·lac (*see* cílks- five). 2. /číl'-ɬ half dollar, fifty cents. 3. /pánačš kl t /čílačš fifteen (LNJ). 4. /tál'/čilačš fifteen (ENM). 5. /t'əmx/čílačš fivefold.

Tci·´ləkᵘ TAb-mi x̣ʷaní's dog.

/čílmi- ?? 1. /čílmi=kʷp carry wood. 2. /čílmi=kʷp-ši-c-aʔ bring me some wood! *appl.*

/číl'- ?? 1. /číl'=qʷuʔ tears coming out of the eyes.

/čín- ?? 1. /čín=ɬni-poison. 1a. —, s/čín=ɬni-t-n *tr.*

/čuɬ- ?? 1. tcɛlmî´nam FBa stepchild (see /mán? child). 2. tcuɬmánɛm FBa stepfather (see /mán father; *prob.* /čuɬ/mán-m). 3. tcuɬtánɛm FBa stepmother (*see* /tán mother; *prob.* /čuɬ/tán-m).

č'

tc'a´kum EG bracken rhizome *Pteridium aquilinum* (bracken fern) (*poss.* /č'ákʷm).

tc'a´latca EG brake fern upper part *Pteridium aquilinum* (bracken fern) (*poss.* /č'álača?).

/č'aláqʷ- hole. 1. ʔac/č'aláqʷ-ɬ cave, dugout, steep hole. 2. ʔac/č'aléqʷ-ɬ groove *dimin.*

/č'amúyq'aʔ snail, snails; JHss ts'ɑmu˙yq'ɑ', JH ts'ɑmmû˙yyɑq'ɑ (loanword; *see* Lower Chinook *c'əmó·ik̲xan* 'snail').

/č'áqʷ- ?? 1. s/č'áqʷ=psm nape of the neck.

/č'áš- dangerous. 1. q'aɬ /č'áš-nɬ dangerous.

/č'ayə́š grease, fat (on body). 1b. /č'ay'ə́š-i his fat.

/č'éʔ-: 1a. s/č'éʔ buttocks, rear part. 1b. s/č'éʔ-i his buttocks.

/č'ə́qʷ-: 1. s/č'ə́qʷ sucker.

/č'ə́qʷn-: 1. s/č'ə́qʷn hip joints.

/č'iátkʷu Stick Indians.

chĭlshh̓ EC corselet. (JH tʃˈîʃx 'Indian armor' *is unidentified for language, and may be Cowlitz.*)

/č'íl'k widow; FBa tȼe´lɛk, qe´l.k. 1b. /č'il'k-áwmx *pl.* 2. /č'íl'k-awilm widower.

/č'íɬ- scatter. 1. /č'íɬ-n, —. 2. /č'íɬ-l=s- mess up hair.

2a. /č'íɬ-l=s, —, /č'íɬ-l=s-n, —.

/č'in'úxʷ-: 1a. /č'é·n'xʷ pillow; FBa tȼê´nux̲. 1b. /č'é·n'ixʷ-umx *pl.* 1c. /č'in'úxʷ-i his pillow.

/č'ín'-: 1. s/č'ín' silver salmon or sockeye or humpback salmon; FBa .s'tȼe´n steelhead salmon.

/č'íp- ?? 1. /č'íp=qas-: 1a. /č'íp=qs beard; HH tȼiépakυs; GGb chéhpks; FBa tse´pɛks. 1b. /č'íp=qis-umx *pl.* 1c. s/č'íp=qas-i his beard. 2. /x̲ʷáq̓ʷ-s/č'p=qs-m shave. 3. qi s/x̲ʷáq̓ʷa-c /č'íp=qs he shaved me (?).

/č'ípt red elderberry *Sambucus racemosa*; EC t͡sipt black elderberries; JH stʃ'ı˙pt; JHjp tsípt.

/č'íq- whine, squeal. 1. /č'íq·č'q-m, s/č'íq·č'q-mit-n *mdl.* 2. s/č'éq·č'q-mit-n whining *dimin., impf. mdl.*

/č'íxʷip- iron, press. 1. /č'íxʷip-n, — *tr.* 2. /č'é·xʷip-m'ɬ-tn' an iron.

/č'íx̲i- fry. 1. —, s/č'íx̲i-t-n *tr.* 2. /č'éx̲-am'ɬ-tn' frying pan.

/č'iyúxʷiʔš Oregon grape *Mahonia* spp.; EC t͡si-yúhwis; JH tʃ'ıy'υ˙xwın's wild grapes; JH

tʃ'ɪyùxwɪ'ts' Oregon
grape.

Tc'qwɛ´ TAb-ly a bird (red
head, red breast, white
belly, rest black) (*prob.
?Sphyrapicus ruber* red-
breasted sapsucker.)

/č'šnóʔ-: 1a. s/č'šnóʔ
money. 1b. s/č'šnóʔ-i his
money.

/č'úš- ?? 1. /č'ó·š-m'
always. 2. /č'úš-aka
always.

/č'úyuk̓ʷ- crooked (e.g. a
limb). 1. /č'úyuk̓ʷ-ɬ, —
intr. 2. /č'úy·č'uyuk̓ʷ-ɬ
crooked, zigzag, wavy,
corrugated.

h

/háps hops *Humulus lupulus*
(loanword; *see* English
hops). 2. /pən/háps hop-
picking time.

/hə́ndəd hundred (loanword;
see English *hundred*). 2.
/káʔɬiʔ t /hə́ndəd three
hundred.

hùlhùl JHjp wood rat *Neotoma
cinerea* (bushy-tailed
woodrat) (loanword; *see*
Chinook Jargon *hóol-hool*
'mouse', taken in turn from
Lower Chinook -*kólxul*
'mouse').

k

/ká·, /kán- where?; FBa
ka´.; BH ka. 2. ʔi/kán
everywhere, somewhere. 3.
/kaʔ ak̓ʷu where is it? 4.
/ká ʔo somewhere else. 5.
/kán-m k̓ʷu to where? 6.
/kan-ím' k̓ʷu what way,
which way. 7. /kan-ém-m'
k̓ʷu Which way is it?, How
do you do it? 8. /pən/ká
when?; FBa pɛn.ka´. 9. ta
ʔi/kán everywhere. 10.

tɛkx'ka FBa which (*see* tk
more; *poss.* tk /ká·). 11. tu
ʔi/kán from everywhere. 12.
tu /ká· k ak̓ʷu Where were
you?

/káʔ- take away. 1. /káʔ-x-
aʔ take it away! *caus.*

/ká·ʔɬax̌ʷm little finger.

/káʔɬiʔ three; HH kátxle;
AG,RL katkhle; GGb káhtl;
FR kahtl, kaht'l; EC ká-ħli;
FBa,BH ka´ɬe (*see* /kán-

three). **2.** /ká?ɫi=numx three at a time. **3.** /tál'/ka?ɫi? thirteen (ENM). **4.** /pánačš kl t /ká?ɫi? thirteen (LNJ). **5.** /t'əmx/ká?ɫi? three at a time, triple. **6.** /ká?ɫi? t /hándəd three hundred.

/kác- down, put down, lay down. **1a.** /kác-ɫ, s/kácil-n *intr.* **1b.** /kác-x, — *caus.* **2.** /kác-ši- put down on *appl.* **2a.** —, s/kác-ši-t-n *tr.*

/kak- build. **1.** /kak=áltmt-n carpentering *impf. mdl.* **2.** /kak=áltxʷ-ši- build a house for *appl.* **2a.** /kak=áltxʷ-š-n, s/kak=áltxʷ-ši-t-n *tr.*

/kálmn-: **1.** s/kálmn otter *Lontra canadensis* (river otter); EC skál-umn; FBa sqa´lɛmɛn; JH ská·lⁿmɑn.

/kálax-: **1a.** /kálx hand, arm; HH kalex arm; GGb,FR káhleh arm; EC kalħ; FBa ka´lɛx arm; FBa ka´lɛx, ka´lex hand; FBb ka·lx̣; BH ka´lɛx. **1b.** /kálax-umx *pl.* **1c.** /kálaw-i his hand, arm. **2.** /ká·lax-um'x fingers *dimin. pl.* **3a.** /ká·l'x-mn glove. **3b.** /ká·l'x-min-i his glove.

/kál'kʷu- look for lice. **1.** /kál'kʷu-n, s/kál'kʷu-t-n *tr.*

/kál'wi- expect. **1.** ?ac/kál'wi-cx a guest *refl.*

kaɫ on, into.

/káɫ- give. **2.** /káɫ-t give to. **2a.** /káɫ-t, s/káɫ-t-n *tr.* **2b.** /káɫ-c he gave it to me *perf.* **3.** /káɫ-tu-mi- give away *rel.* **3a.** /káɫ-tu-mi-x, s/káɫ-t-m-staw-n *caus.* **4.** /káɫ-a?-tu-mi- distribute *pl. rel.* **4a.** /káɫ-a?-tu-mi-x, — *caus.* (or káɫ-a?-tmɫi-x ??). **5.** ?it /káɫ-c-n /?ánca he forgave me.

kamá'los EC to cover with a dish.

/kán-, /ká· where? (*see* /ká·*).

/kán- three (*see* /ká?ɫi? three). **2.** /kan-áw'=xaw'ɫ three rows. **3.** /kán'-aw=l's three dollars. **4.** /kán-u=šn three times. **5.** /kán-x=panxʷ three years old. **6.** /kán-x=qʷ three days. **7.** /kán-x=tumx thirty; HH kánix tómux; FR kah-nech-tóme, kah-nech-tó-me; EC ká-niħ-tumħ; FBa qa´ṇɛx tu´mɛx. **8.** /kan-al-s/q'íx̣ Wednesday (*see* /q'íx̣-day).

.ska´nn FBa short-tailed mouse ?*Clethrionomys* spp. (vole), or *Microtus* spp.

/kanílstx̣ʷ–: 1.
/kanílstx̣ʷ=ayaq-m kneel,
confess *perf. mdl.*

/kapú coat. 1b. /kapúh-i his
coat (loanword; *see*
Chinook Jargon *ca-pó*
'coat', taken in turn from
Canadian French *capot*). 2.
s/x̣asíl?/kapu raincoat
(*see* /x̣asíli?– rain).

/kás– ?? 1. kā´.s FBa train
(*prob.* /kás; loanword; *see*
English *cars*). 2. /kás-
l/xaw'ɬ railroad; (*see*
/xəwál– road).

/kási? star, stars; HH,AG,RL
kase; GGb kúss-sé; FR
kúss-seh; EC ká-si; FBa
qā´se; JH q'â·sɪ'. 1b.
/kási-n'i his star.

/kásuci– hide. 1. /kásc-n,
— *tr.* 2. /kásuci-cx hide
self. 2a. /kásuci-cx,
s/kásuc-cši-t-n *refl.*

kac TAb-ss something said by
bluejay (*here* c = š).

/katísa? strawberry *Fragaria*
spp.; EC ka-tí-sa; FBa,BH
katī´sa; JH kɑtí·sɑ',
ka·tí·sɑ'; JHjp kɑtísɑ'.

/kátyn be in charge, plan on.

/kátyn interpreter,
representative. 2.
katiya´pɛktɛn FBa
interpreter (*poss.*
/katy=aqp-tn). 3.
/kát/yay'=ɬuɬ interpret
(*see* /yáy– tell).

/kátyn fishnet. 1b. /kátyn-
tan-i his net.

/káw–: 1a. s/káw sister-in-
law; FBa .skā´ᵘ; BH .skā´u.
1b. s/káw-i his sister-in-
law.

/káw– ?? 1. /káw/yəq̓ʷ–
settle down. 1a. /káw/iq̓ʷ,
— *intr.* (*see* /yəq̓ʷ– move).
2. ?it /káw/yaq̓ʷ-umx they
settled down (to live) *pl.*

/káwanan– ?? 1.
s/káwanan-i t ɬukʷáɬ
July.

kaukou´lac FBa drum (*poss.*
kaw·káwlaš) (loanword;
see Sahaptin *kiwkíwlas*
'drum'). 2. kuku´ɛlic FBa
drum (*here* c = š).

/káwlic Cowlitz; FBb
Qauɛli´tsq; JH qɑwlíts
Cowlitz Prairie; JHjp
khawlɪts lower Cowlitz
River. 2. qɑ́wlítsq JH
Cowlitz tribe; JH
q'ɑwwɪlí·tsq' Cowlitz
River.

/ká·w'an lie down, be lying.
1. /ká·w'an, — *intr.*

/káw'l– pretend. 1. /káw'l-n,
— *tr.*

/kaw'ús–: 1a. /káw's
hazelnut, nut *Corylus
cornuta* (*see* /k'ap'úx̣ʷ
hazelnut). 1b. /káw'us-mx
pl. 1c. /kaw'ús-i its nut. 2.
kau´saɬ FBa hazel (*poss.*
/káw's=an'ɬ).

/kayíʔ–: 1a. /káyʔ grandmother; FBa ꞌkai. 1b. nx/káyʔ-tn *pl.* 1c. /kayíʔ-i his grandmother. 1d. nx/káyʔ-tan-i his grandmothers *pl.* 2. kə/káyʔ grandmother; FBa kukwaꞌi; FBb kakaꞌe.

kaiꞌlɛkcɛn FBa ankle; HT kaíləkšən.

/káywiɬi– forbid, don't want to tell, keep quiet. 1. /káywiɬi-x, s/káywəɬ-taw-n *caus.*

kêꞌtcits FBa mountain goat *Oreamnos americanus.*

kɛt kɛt kɛt TAb-ly what qaqɑꞌm says.

/kələx–: 1a. /kəlx reed mat, reeds; EC kíl-lŭħ mat. 1b. /kaləx-i his mat. 2. s/waɬ-áɬ/kalx tules *Scirpus acutus* (see /waɬ–).

/kə́m– cry. 1. —, s/kə́m-mt-n *mdl.*

/kə́m– bend over, stoop. 1. /kə́m'-ɬ, — *intr.* 2. /kə́m=ay'q fall out, tip over. 3. /kə́m'=nač-m bend over a little *mdl.*

/kə́n– ?? 1. /kan-ál'=xan-not know how, make mistakes. 1a. /kan-ál'=šn, s/kan-ál'=xan-n *intr.* 2. /kə́n'-mn- make a mistake. 2a. /kə́n'-mn, — *rel.*

kən– maybe. 1. kən ʔó maybe. 2. kən /q'íc'x̣ it seems that way. 3. cút-kn maybe.

.skɛnaꞌps FBa red-headed woodpecker ?*Picidae* spp., or ?*Dryocopus pileatus* (Pileated woodpecker).

/kə́nnam– dissatisfied. 1. /kə́nnam-n, — *tr.*

kîꞌs.x FBa serviceberry *Amelanchier* spp.; JH kɑsx wild currant (*prob.* /kə́sx). 2. kɑsá·x̣ɑn'ɬ JH wild currant plant or patch (*prob.* /kəsáx=n'ɬ).

/kə́w– pack. 1. /kə́w-n, — *tr.* 2. s/kə́w-cši-t-n he's packing it up *impf. refl.*

/kəwáɬ–: 1a. /kúwɬ wife, woman; HH kủwitxl woman; HH kủwitxl, kowitxl wife; AG kúwitxl woman; RL kawitkhl woman; GGb kó-wtl woman; EC kŭ-wȋħl woman; FBa qoꞌuɛɬ wife; FBa kauꞌɛɬ woman; FBb kaꞌwɬ woman; BH qoꞌuɛɬ, koꞌwɛɬ; TAb-mi koꞌwɬ woman; SH kə́wɬ woman. 1b. /kúwaɬ-mx or /kəwaɬ-mx *pl.* 1c. s/kawáɬ-ani his wife. 1d. /kúwaɬ-miš-i his wives *pl.* 1e. t´sun-kow-wtl GGb my wife, my woman; FR t'sun-kow-wtl my wife

(*prob.* c n-/kə́wɬ); 2a.
/kawá·ɬ=iʔɬ big girl; FBa
kauwāˊ.ɬəɬ girl; FBa
kauwaˊ.ɬEɬ young woman;
FBb kawa·ˊaɬiɬ young girl.
2b. /kawá·ɬ=iʔɬt-ili his
girl. 3a. /kéˑwʼɬ little girl;
GGb kow-ahtl girl, maid; EC
kĕ̆-wȋ̄hl girl; SH /kéˑwɬ
girl. 3b. /kéˑwʼaɬ-mx *pl.* 4.
/ləq-ál/kuwɬ buy a wife.
5. /ləq-ál/kwaʔɬ-uʔɬ buy
a woman, wedding.

/kíkʷəlikʷut skirt. 1b.
/kíkʷəlikʷut-i her skirt
(loanword; *see* Chinook
Jargon *keé-kwil-lie* 'low,
under, beneath', taken in
turn from Lower Chinook
kik"íli (?) 'below, under';
and Chinook Jargon *coat*
'dress, gown', taken in turn
from English *coat*).

kiˊmia FBa wooly dog *Canis*
familiaris.

kl with, and.

ksa again (*enclitic*).

k'

/k'á·c'- ?? 1.
ʔac/k'á·c'=kʷu a puddle.
/k'á·k'aʔ-: 1. s/k'á·k'aʔ
crow *Corvus*
brachyrhynchos (American
crow); EC s'ḳa; FBa 'kaˊka;
BH -s'k'āk'a; JH sk'â·k'α.
/k'ál- cramp, pain. 1.
/k'al=íqs=xn-t-m cramp
in a toe *pass.* 2.
/k'ál=lkstiʔ cramp, pain in
the side.
/k'ál- get in a fight. 1. /k'ál-
ɬ, — *intr.*
/k'al- ?? 1. /k'al=álus a
cross. 2. /k'al=álusi-t-m
he crossed himself *pass.* 3.
/k'al=áluʔs cross on a
rosary.

/k'ál'ax-: 1a. /k'ál'x branch,
limb; HH kálex leaf; FBa
kāˊlEx limb or branch. 1b.
/k'ál'ax-umx *pl.* 1c.
/k'al'áw-i its branch. 2a.
/k'ál'x-cx-tn' shirt; EC
kálh̄-t͡shkŭn; FBa
kaˊɬExstsxEn. 2b. /k'ál'x-
cx-tan-i his shirt. 3.
/k'ál'=xn'-tn' trousers,
pants; FBa kaˊlExEntEn. 4.
weiaxkaˊlExEkstEn FBa
shirt (of dressed skin); HT
weiax̱kálə̱x̱əkstən shirt
(*prob.* /wayə̱x/k'ál'x-cx-
tn'; *see* /wayə́x̱ tanned
deerskin).

/k'anáp' scissors; FBa,BH
qanaˊp.x. 1b. /k'ánap

umx *pl.* 1c. /k'anə́p'-i her
scissors.

/k'anə́p'- squeeze. 1.
/k'anə́p'-n, — *tr.*

/k'ápa- tame. 1. /k'áp-ɬ, —,
/k'áp-n, s/k'ápa-t-n. 2.
/k'áp-s/tiqiw train horses
(*see* s/tiqíw horse).

ḳá-p̣óħw EC hazelnut
Corylus cornuta; JH
k'á·p'ὑ·x̣w̥, k'α'p'ὑ·x̣
(*prob.* /k'ap'úx̣ʷ; *see*
/kaw'ús- hazelnut). 2.
q'α'p'ὑ·x̣wαn'ɬ JH hazel
bush (*prob.*
/k'ap'úx̣ʷ=n'ɬ).

/k'átap-: 1a. s/k'átp rib; FBa
.sqa´tEp. 1b. s/k'átap-
umx *pl.* 1c. s/k'átap-i his
rib.

/k'axʷóʔ grease, oil, lard,
tallow. 1b. /k'axóʔ-i its
grease, oil. 2. /k'axʷóʔ- oil.
2a. /k'axʷóʔ-n, — *tr.* 3.
/sá/k'axʷoʔ- grease. 3a.
/sá/k'axʷoʔ-n, — *tr.*

/k'áy-: 1. /k'áy·k'ay-
tickle. 1a. /k'áy·k'ay-ɬ,
—, /k'áy·k'ay-n,
s/k'áy·k'ay-t-n.

/k'ayáč- sleepy. 1. /k'ayáč-
ɬ, — *intr.*

/k'ayə́xʷ bitter.

/k'é·c little, a little bit, small;
FBa kê´Ets small, little. 2.
/k'é·c-i little. 3. kEtso´xe
FBa little finger.

/k'ə́c'- represent. 1. —,
sk'ə́c'-t-n *tr.*

/k'ə́c'a- be in, get in, ride in.
1a. /k'ə́c'-ɬ, s/k'ə́c'a-w-n
intr. 1b. /k'ə́c'-n, — put in
tr. 2. /k'ə́c'i-ɬ-aʔ get in! 3.
/k'ə́c'-acx be on, get on (a
horse) *refl.* 4. /k'ə́c'-š- put
into *appl.* 4a. /k'ə́c'-š-n,
— *tr.* 5. /k'c'·k'ə́c'- put in.
5a. /k'c'·k'ə́c'-n, — *tr.* 6.
/k'éc'·k'ac'- ride a horse.
6a. /k'éc'k'ac'-ɬ,
s/k'éc'·k'c'-w-n *intr.* 7.
ʔit /k'ə́c'-cx-as kn tit
s/tiqíw I rode a horse.

/k'ə́ɬa- drown, sink. 1.
/k'ə́ɬ, s/k'ə́ɬa-w-n,
/k'ə́ɬ-n, —.

/k'ə́ɬi- send, throw, throw
away, dump. 1. /k'ə́ɬ-n,
s/k'ə́ɬ-t-n *tr.* 2. /k'ə́ɬi-n-
aʔ dump it! 3. /k'ə́ɬ-š-
send to *appl.* 3a. /k'ə́ɬ-š-n,
— *tr.* 4. /k'ə́ɬ-tuxʷt throw
it at *appl.* 5. /k'ə́ɬ·k'ə́ɬ-
throw (them) in. 5a.
/k'ə́ɬ·k'ə́ɬ-n, — *tr.*

/k'ə́n- shiver, shake. 1. —,
s/k'ə́n-mt-n *mdl.*

/k'əsk'ə́s-: 1a. /k'ə́sk's
hair; HH kὑskυs; AG,RL
kυskυs; GGb,FR kús-kus;
EC kŭs-kŭs; FBa qî´ᶻqîᶻ;
FBb sk!Es. 1b. k'sk'ə́s-i his
hair; FBb sk!Esk!Eseᵋ her
hair. 2. /ʔíɬ/k'sk's-tn'
dandruff.

/k'əspə́n–: 1a. /k'ə́spn neck; HH kúspʊn; GGb kúss-pen; FR kuss-pen; EC ḵĕs-pŭn; FBa,BH kE´spen. 1b. /k'spə́n-i his neck.

/k'ə́t'– gnaw, nibble. 1a. —, s/k'ə́t'-mt-n *mdl.* 1b. /k'ə́t'-n, s/k'ə́t'-t-n *tr.*

sk'ɑwɑ̇w JHjp steelhead *Oncorhynchus mykiss (poss.* s/k'əwə́w).

/k'léh salalberry *Gaultheria shallon*; EC kŭ-lĕ; JH k'ɑl'lé. 2. /k'líh=an'ɬ salal bushes.

kʷ

/kʷac a little, somewhat. 2. kwātsä´ksnî´k FBa brown (*prob.* /kʷác ʔaks/nə́q; *see* /nə́q- black). 3. kwEtskwe´xta´n FBa dusk, evening (*prob.* /kʷac s/qʷíxʷ tan; see /qʷíx- night).

/kʷác– ?? 1. /kʷác=tum'x in two.

/kʷácili– name, call. 1. —, s/kʷácili-t-n *tr.* 2a. s/kʷácɬ a name; UWb s´qualts; FR stqualts; FBa sqwa´ts.ɬ. 2b. s/kʷácil-i his name.

/kʷá·hi– quiet. 1. ʔac/kʷá·hi-laʔ be quiet! 2. ʔac/kʷá·-l'aʔ hush!, be quiet!

/kʷal'úw– weave a mat or basket (other than cedar-root). 1. /kʷal'úw-n, — *tr.*

ḵʷaɬ so that, and (LNJ) (*see* ḵʷaɬ so that).

/kʷaɬá– parent's sibling. 1a. /kʷáɬa/mn uncle (father's brother, mother's brother); EC qá-h̄la-mĭn (*see* /mán father). 1b. /kʷáɬ/mn-aw-i his uncle. 2a. /kʷáɬ/tn aunt (father's sister, mother's sister); EC nĭ-qáh̄l (*see* /tán mother). 2b. /kʷáɬ/tan-aw-i her aunt. 3. kə/kʷáɬ/tn aunt. 4a. /kʷə́ɬ-uʔ aunt (father□s sister). 4b. nx/kʷaɬ-óʔ-tn *pl.* 4c. /kʷə́ɬ-á·w'-i his aunt, a man's aunt. 5. nx/kʷə́ɬ-uw'-tn aunts (mother's sisters) *pl.*

/kʷáqkʷaq duck (loanword; *see* English *quack quack*).

kwa´seɬ FBa yellow pine *Pinus ponderosa* (Ponderosa pine); HT kwáseɬ.

/kʷáta quarter, twenty-five cents (loanword; see Chinook Jargon *kwáta* 'quarter of a dollar', taken in turn from English *quarter*).

/kʷáta- swim, wade, ford. 1.
/kʷát-ɬ, s/kʷáta-w-n,
/kʷát-tas, —. 2.
/kʷát·kʷat-ɬ go wading
perf. intr.

sqa-túħqs EC nostril (may
begin with qʷ).

kwaxaʹlus FBa hayfork.

/kʷáxʷ- hammer on. 1.
/kʷáxʷ-n, — *tr.* 2.
/kʷaxʷ=ál'wa- nail
together. 2a.
/kʷaxʷ=ál'wa-x, — *caus.*
3. qi /kʷáxʷ-am'ɬ-tn' a
maul.

/kʷáxʷa- arrive, get there,
reach. 1. /kʷáxʷ-ɬ,
s/kʷáxʷa-w-n, —,
s/kʷáxʷ-tas-n.

kwaʹxoloks FBa long
leggings.

kwaiʹtɛnɛɬ FBa willow (red)
Cornus stolonifera (red-
osier dogwood).

/kʷə́c- ?? 1. /kʷə́c-l/iɬn'
left some food (see /ʔíɬani-
eat).

/kʷə́ɬ- ?? 1. /kʷaɬ=ál'wa-
share, divide, separate. 1a.
/kʷaɬ=ál'wa-x,
s/kʷaɬ=ál'u-staw-n *caus.*
2. /kʷaɬ=ál'was-i its
dividing. 3. /pút/kʷaɬ=lus
t s/qʷíx̣ midnight.

/kʷə́ɬə́q- split, crack. 1.
/kʷaɬə́q-ɬ, —, /kʷaɬə́q-
n, —. 2. ʔac/kʷaɬə́q-ɬ a
crack. 3. /kʷə́ɬ·kʷə́ɬqa-

split. 3a. —,
s/kʷə́ɬ·kʷɬqa-w-n, —,
s/kʷə́ɬ·kʷə́ɬq-t-n. 4.
/kʷɬqʷ-áy'=kʷp split
wood.

/kʷəná- carry, hold, get,
take, take away, grab. 1.
/kʷaná- take, grab, hang
on to, catch. 1a. —,
s/kʷaná-t-n. 1b. /kʷaná-c
he grabbed me. 2. s/kʷaná-
tawl-n touching *impf.*
recip. 3a. /kʷə́na, /kʷə́nna
carry, hold, get, take, take
away, grab, get married *tr.*
3b. s/kʷə́na-t-iɬt they are
getting it *impf. tr.* 3c.
/kʷə́na-laʔ grab it! 3d.
s/kʷə́na-ml-n taking *impf.*
impl.tr. 3e. ʔa-s-tu-
ɬ/kʷə́n-n-it what you'll be
getting. 4. /kʷə́na- catch,
get. 4a. /kʷə́na-xʷ,
s/kʷə́n-y-n *tr.* (*caus.?*). 5.
/kʷé·na hold, hold back,
hold still *tr.* 6. kʷə́na-n-
catch, get *appl.* 6a. /kʷə́na-
n-xʷ *caus.* 6b. /kʷə́n-n-
mx he caught me *perf.* 7.
/kʷə́n-s- grab away from.
7a. /kʷə́n-s-t, —. 7b.
kʷə́n-s-c, /kʷə́n-s-cal-n
he's grabbing it away from
me *appl.* 7c. /kʷə́n-s-t-aʔ
take it away! 8. /kʷə́n-ši-
get for *appl.* 8a. —,
s/kʷə́n-ši-t-n *tr.* 9.
/kʷən-táči-c he led me by

the hand; they shook hands.
10. /kʷaná·-mn' handle,
reins. 11. /kʷaná=tmix-
take land. 11a.
/kʷaná=tm'x,
s/kʷaná=tmiš-n *intr.* 12.
/kʷan-áw'- hang on. 12a.
/kʷan-áw'-am'ɬ, s/kʷən-
áw'-ml-n *impl.tr.* 12b.
/kʷan-áw-amiɬ-aʔ take
some!, get some! 13.
/kʷə́n-n-wali court. 14.
/c'ay-s/kʷaná-t-n he's
reaching for it.
/kʷə́nala ?? 1. /kʷə́na-la
/ɬáX̌p-m' upside down
(*poss.* "hold it upside
down"; *see* /kʷə́na-).
/kʷə́s- evening. 1. /kʷə́s·s-
w-n evening; HH
skwĭsawan darkness; HH
skwŭsawʊn evening; GGb
kwàis-soon; FR kwáis-
soon; EC qʉ́s-su-wʉn
darkness. 2. /kʷə́s-mn
supper. 3. kwî´sʊEnta´ne
FBa sunset (*prob.* /kʷə́s·s-
w-n tani).
/kʷə́šə́qa- pop. 1. /kʷašə́q-
ɬ, —, /kʷašə́q-n, —. 2.
s/kʷə́š·kʷšqa-w-n it's
popping *impf. intr.*
kʊ´təkʊtə TAb-mi big red-
headed woodpecker
Dryocopus pileatus
(pileated woodpecker).
kwExkwa´x.ɬ FBa limb,
branch.

/kʷəyóh- ?? 1.
s/kʷəyóh=ips squirrel-tail,
yarrow *Achillea millefolium*
(yarrow).
/kʷicám fir tree
?Pseudotsuga menziesii
(Douglas fir).
/kʷílt quilt (loanword; *see*
English *quilt*). 2. /sáʔ/kʷilt
make a quilt.
/kʷiním-: 1a. s/kʷínm
chicken *Gallus gallus*,
pheasant, turkey *Meleagris
gallopavo*; EC sqinm
pheasant; FBa .skwi´nEm
chicken; FBa .skwi̱´nEm
willow-grouse; JH
sk'wî·nǽm pheasant,
chicken; JHjp skwî·nɑm
pheasant. Probably
originally ruffed grouse
Bonasa umbellus. 1b.
s/kʷínim-umx *pl.* 1c.
s/kʷiním-i his chicken. 2.
s/kʷiné·m'=iɬ-umx baby
chickens *pl.* 3. /pən/ʔíɬ-
s/kʷinm November (*see*
/ʔíɬani- eat).
/kʷísk̯ʷs acorn; EC ḵwisqs
acorns; JH kwískw̩s. 2.
/kʷísk̯ʷs=n'ɬ oak tree
Quercus garryana (Garry
oak); EC qís-qĭ-sĭnh̄l; FBa
kwi´sksEnEɬ; HT
kwísksənəɬ; JH
kwí·skwɪsɑn'ɬ.
/kʷíti- distribute, give gifts.
1. /kʷíti-m'ɬ, — *impl.tr.* 2.

/pən-s/kʷíti-m'ɬ Saturday, time to get rations.

/kʷíwxʷ- polish. 1. —, s/kʷíwxʷ-t-n *tr.*

/kʷíyxʷ- ?? 1. tit qi /kʷíyxʷ-ctx axle.

kʷu, akʷu interrogative particle (*enclitic*). 2. ?it'í akʷu what's the matter?, what happened? (*see* /?í question). 3. ɬ/ín-s kʷu it doesn't matter. 4. /?íni kʷu anything be done to it. 5. ?it /?in-áwmx kʷu What's the matter with them? 6. s/?íni-n-axʷ kʷu What are you doing? 7. s/?ín-w'ən-cal-s kʷu What is he doing to me? 8. /?ít-m kʷu fixed that way *perf. pass.* 9. nks + /?ít-aw-ctx kʷu whatever is being done with it *impf. pass.* 10. ?it ?ítx kʷu k... what did you do with...? 11. /ká? akʷu where is it? 12. /kán-m kʷu to where? 13. /kan-ím' kʷu what way, which way? 14. /kan-ém-m' kʷu Which way is it?, How do you do it? 15. /k̓ʷi-n-áwmx kʷu how many?, several others. 16. /tám akʷu what?, why? 17. tu /ká· k akʷu Where were you? 18. /wá akʷu Who is he?, someone. 19. /wá k akʷu Who are you? 20. /wá t akʷu who he is.

/kʷúkʷ- cook. 1. /kʷúkʷ-m, — *mdl.* (loanword; *see* English *cook*).

kwokwê´nɛp FBa sister-in-law; BH skwokwe´nep brother-in-law.

skwo´kwols FBa top of head; HT skwókwols.

kwola´tux̣ FBa leaf.

kwolī´ca FBa,BH blackbird ?*Euphagus cyanocephalus* (Brewer's blackbird); ?*Agelaius phoeniceus* (red-winged blackbird) (*here* c = š).

/kʷumáy much, very, a lot.

/kʷumál-: 1a. /kʷúmɬ piece of wood; FBa kō´mɛɬ firewood. 1b. /kʷumál-i his wood. 2. /kʷó·m'ɬ little piece of wood (dimin).

/kʷúpa? grandfather; FBa,BH 'ku´pa; FBb kop!a. 1b. /kʷúpa-w'-i his grandfather. 1c. nx/kʷúpa-tan-i his grandfathers *pl.* 2. ka/kʷúpa? grandfather.

/kʷupám- ?? 1. /kʷupám=ap=šn palm of the hand; FBa,BH kopā´matscɛn instep.

/kʷústam- borrow, lend, rent. 1. /kʷústm, —, kʷústm-n, —. 2. /kʷústami- rent to. 2a. /kʷústami-x, — *caus.* 3.

/kʷústm-tuxʷt lend to *appl.*

/kʷušú pig, hog *Sus scrofa* (loanword; *see* Chinook Jargon *coʹ-sho* 'pig', taken in turn from French *cochon* 'pig'). 1a. /kʷušúh-i his pig. 2. ʔac/kʷušúh-icx greedy *refl.* 3.

/kʷušú=ɬc'iʔ pork.

/kʷúwa- ready. 1. /kʷúwa-cx, — *refl.* (= /kə́w- pack ?). 2. s/kʷúw-cš-i his being ready.

skuiʹ ux FBa whale (*prob.* s/kʷúyxʷ).

k̓ʷ

k̓ʷá but, it turned out to be.

/k̓ʷaléʔ red salmon *?Onchorhynchus tshawytscha* (fall run Chinook salmon); GGa Qul-a larger salmon, after harvest; UWa Qul-a large salmon which runs after harvest; FBa kwal'êʹ Chinook or king salmon.

/k̓ʷálan- hear about, find out. 1a. /k̓ʷál'an-m, — *mdl.* 1b. /k̓ʷáln-mn, — *rel.* (*see* /k̓ʷil=áyn- listen, hear about).

k̓ʷaɬ so that (*see* kʷaɬ so that).

/k̓ʷán- ?? 1a. s/k̓ʷán=ayuʔ rat *Neotoma cinerea* (Bushytail woodrat); FBa kwaʹnaiᵘ bush-tail rat. 1b. /k̓ʷán=ayu-mx *pl.*

/k̓ʷánan-: 1. s/k̓ʷánan sin.

/k̓ʷasə́n-: 1a. /k̓ʷásn belly, stomach; FBa kwaʹṣEn belly. 1b. /k̓ʷasə́n-i his belly, his stomach.

/k̓ʷat'án'-: 1a. s/k̓ʷat'án' mouse; FBa kʷotaʹn; JHjp skwɑts'áˑn' house mouse. 1b. s/k̓ʷat'an-áwmx *pl.* 1c. s/k̓ʷat'án'-i his mouse.

/k̓ʷáya- chew. 1. /k̓ʷáy-n, s/k̓ʷáya-t-n *tr.* 2. /k̓ʷáˑy-nibble (*dimin.*). 2a. —, s/k̓ʷáˑy-mt-n *mdl.*

/k̓ʷáy'us- separate, part hair. 1. /k̓ʷáy's-mn, — *rel.* 2. /k̓ʷáy's-ni-n-aʔ part it! *appl.* 3. /k̓ʷáy's part in hair. 4. /k̓ʷáyus-i its forks, its separating.

/k̓ʷél'u- peek at. 1. /k̓ʷél'u-xʷ, — *caus.* 2. s/k̓ʷél'-stu-mx (*sic*) he's peeking at me *impf. caus.*

/k̓ʷə́c- still, calm, not blowing. 1. ʔac-txʷ/k̓ʷə́c-t-m it's calm, not blowing *pass.*

k'wάl' JHjp coast huckleberry *Vaccinium* sp(p). (*prob.* /k̓ʷəl'*).

/k̓ʷə́na- count. 1a. /k̓ʷə́na-m'ɬ, s/k̓ʷə́n-ml-n *impl.tr.* 1b. /k̓ʷə́n-n, s/k̓ʷə́n-t-n *tr.* 2. /k̓ʷəná-m'ɬ vote *perf. impl.tr.* 3. /k̓ʷən=én'wa-predict. 3a. /k̓ʷən=én'wa-x, — *caus.* 4. /k̓ʷən=ínwas- think. 4a. /k̓ʷən=ínus-m, s/k̓ʷən=ínuwas-mit-n *mdl.* 4b. /k̓ʷən=ínwas-n, — *tr.*

/k̓ʷə́p very. 2. /k̓ʷə́p- right, correct, true, straight, even, very. 2a. /k̓ʷə́p-ɬ, —; FBa qô´p.ɬ straight *intr.* 2b. /k̓ʷə́p-n, — straighten *tr.* 3. /k̓ʷép-ɬ very, really. 4. /k̓ʷíp-ɬ just in time. 5. /k̓ʷap-ús tan better. 6. /k̓ʷə́p-st straighten it out *caus.* 7. /k̓ʷáp-am'ɬ-tn' court, courtroom. 8. /k̓ʷəp=ál'wa- stand up. 8a. /k̓ʷəp=ál'wa-x, — *caus.* 9. /k̓ʷəp=á·xn aim. 9a. /k̓ʷəp=á·xn, — *intr.* 9b. /k̓ʷəp=á·xn-mn, — *rel.* 10. /k̓ʷəp-l=ús-: 10a. s/k̓ʷə́p-l'=s forehead. 10b. s/k̓ʷp-l=ús-i his forehead. 11. s/k̓ʷə́p-aw-m'ɬ a choice. 12. qi ʔaɬc/k̓ʷəp=ičə́n-i its scales (fish). 13. kupā´ks

kwî´s FBa sorrel (*prob.* /k̓ʷə́p ʔaks/qʷə́s; *see* /qʷə́s- sorrel).

/k̓ʷí how many?, what time? 2. /k̓ʷí ʔo how many? 3. ʔi/k̓ʷé-n', ʔi/k̓ʷí-n few, a few. 4. /k̓ʷi-n-áwmx kʷu how many?, several others. 5. /k̓ʷí-n-l=šn how many times?

/k̓ʷík̓ʷ- stick into. 1. /k̓ʷík̓ʷ-n, — *tr.*

/k̓ʷil- ?? 1. /k̓ʷil=áyn-listen, hear, hear about, believe. 1a. /k̓ʷil=áyn, — *intr.* 1b. /k̓ʷil=áyn-mn, — *rel.* (*see* /k̓ʷáln- hear about).

/k̓ʷiq'é- green. 1. ʔaks/k̓ʷíq' green, gold; HH skwéqu yellow; GGb uks-kwék green, yellow; FR uks-kwe'h green, yellow; FR uks-kwék blue; EC aks-qíü'k yellow; FBa Eks'kwê´.q green; FBa Ekskwi´Eq yellow. 2. ʔaks/k̓ʷé·q'-m'ɬ yellow. 3. /k̓ʷéq'- pale, turn pale. 3a. /k̓ʷéq'-m'ɬ, s/k̓ʷéq'-mal-n *impl.tr.* 4. ʔaks/k̓ʷíq'=ps-m yellow tail (?). 5. /k̓ʷiq'é·-m=an'ɬ bark; greenish. 6. axsqwe´q awi´lEk FBa yellow paint (*prob.* ʔaks/k̓ʷíq' /ʔawílk).

/k̓ʷíx̱- buzz, jingle. 1. —,
s/k̓ʷíx̱-mt-n *mdl.*

/k̓ʷpyáluci- understand. 1.
/k̓ʷpyáluc-n,
s/k̓ʷpyáluci-t-n *tr.* 2.
/mí⁴ta t n-s/k̓ʷpyálcn-⁴ I
can't understand him.

k'o'ó·lɪ·tʃɪn JH berry basket;
EC ko-ó-lĭchn (*prob.*
/k̓ʷuʔúl=ičn).

/k̓ʷuk̓ʷ- stick in. 1.
/k̓ʷuk̓ʷ=ápsam- choke,
stick in the throat. 1a.

/k̓ʷuk̓ʷ=ápsm, —,
/k̓ʷuk̓ʷ=ápsam-n, —.

/k̓ʷús meat, flesh; HH kos;
AG,RL kos meat; GGb kóse
flesh; FBa 'qu´s. 1b. /k̓ʷús-i
its flesh, his meat. 2.
/k̓ʷús=⁴c'iʔ body, beef.

/k̓ʷuxʷá⁴ spruce *Picea* spp.; EC
ḳu-hwáh̄l; JH k'ʋxwá·⁴.

/k̓ʷúxʷniʔ small clam *sp.*
?*Protothaca staminea* (little-
neck clam).

l

l past (with indefinite and
definite articles t + l, c + l,
ʔit + l, ʔic + l).

/lakamín soup, gravy
(loanword; *see* Chinook
Jargon *lakamin* 'stew,
dumplings', taken in turn
from French *le commun* 'the
common pot').

/lakláš barn (loanword; *see*
Chinook Jargon *lekalash*
'garage', taken in turn from
French *le garage* 'garage').
1b. /lakláš-umx *pl.*

/lál, /láln stick game; TAb-jc
lal a game.

lala·´xʋm TAb-mi a place
where camas grows.

/lalupá ribbon, ribbons; FBa
le´lupa´ (loanword; *see*
Chinook Jargon *lalopa*
'ribbon', taken in turn from
French *la ruban* 'ribbon').
1b. /lalupáh-i her ribbon.

/lám whiskey; FBa la´m
(loanword; *see* Chinook
Jargon *lum* 'rum, whiskey',
taken in turn from English
rum, or possibly from
French *le rhum* 'rum'). 1b.
/lám-i his whiskey.

/lám-: 1. /lám·lam- blaze.
1a. —, s/lám·lm-w-n *intr.*
2. /lám=staq- blaze, fire is
too high. 2a. /lám=stq, —

intr. 3. s/lám·lm=staq-n
it's blazing *impf. intr.*

/**lapíp** pipe (loanword; *see*
Chinook Jargon *la-peep*
'pipe', taken in turn from
French *la pipe* 'pipe'). 1a.
/lapíp-i his pipe.

/**lapišmú** saddle blanket
(loanword; *see* Chinook
Jargon *le-pish-e-mo* 'saddle
blanket', taken in turn from
Ojibwa *appiššimo·n*
'something to lie or sit on',
with a French article
attached).

/**laplít** bridle, bit (loanword;
see Chinook Jargon
lableed' 'bridle', taken in
turn from French *le bride*
'bridle').

/**lapuén** pan (loanword; *see*
Chinook Jargon *la-po-êl'*
'frying pan', taken in turn
from French *la poele*
'frying pan').

la´p.hwaxEn FBa shield
(*poss.* /lápxʷ=ax̣n). 2.
la´phwaxEn FBa vest (*poss.*
/lápxʷ=ax̣n).

/**lapyó·š** hoe (loanword; *see*
Chinook Jargon *la-pe-osh'*
'hoe, mattock', taken in turn
from French *la pioche*
'pickaxe, mattock'). 2.
/lapyó·š- hoe. 2a.
/lapyó·š-n, — *tr.*

/**lasúp** soup, stew (loanword;
see Chinook Jargon *lasup*

'soup', taken in turn from
French *la soupe* 'soup').

/**lá·š-** clear forest. 1. —,
s/lá·š-mt-n *mdl.* (possibly
a loanword: *see* English
slash).

/**lašəmní** chimney
(loanword; *see* Chinook
Jargon *lashimney, la-shum-
ma-na* 'chimney', taken in
turn from French *la
cheminée* 'chimney').

/**latám** table (loanword; *see*
Chinook Jargon *latáhb, la-
tem* 'table', taken in turn
from French *la table*
'table'). 1b. /latám-umx
pl. 1c. /latám-i his table.

/**lawé·n** oats *Avena sativa*
(loanword; see Chinook
Jargon *la-wen'* 'oats', taken
in turn from French *l'avoine*
'oats').

/**lawə́p** (?) inside, middle,
bottom (?). 2. lúwp inside.

lawe´latə TAb-mc Mount St.
Helens; TAb-mi lawe´latɬa
(a Sahaptin name: lawilayt-
ɬá "the smoker").

/**law-** ?? 1. /law-úl=ikn-:
1a. /law-úl=ičn bottle,
bottles; FBb lawu·´likEn. 1b.
/law-úl=kn-i his bottle.

/**laxičn** cabbage *Brassica
oleracea capitata* (?).

/**láxʷ-** be full (stomach). 1.
/láxʷ-ɬ, — *intr.*

slaw-hatz UWb lightning.

/láx^wk^wu– breathe. 1.
/láx^wk^wu-n-m,
s/láx^wk^wu-mit-n *mdl.* 2.
/láx^wk^w-l-m-i his
breathing. 3.
s/láx^w·ləx^wk^wu-mit-n,
s/láx^w·ləx^wk^w-l-mit-n
he's breathing *impf. mdl.* 4.
/c'ək/lx^wk^wuʔ– smother,
be out of breath. 4a.
/c'ək/lx^wk^wuʔ,
s/c'ək/lx^wk^wu-w-n,
/c'ək/lx^wk^wu-ən, —. 5.
/táy/lax^wk^wuʔ he's out of
breath.

/lax̱– ?? 1. lax̱aíaka HH hand,
fingers; AG,RL lakhaiaka;
GGb sla-hái-yak-a hand,
finger; FBb lax̱a´yek!a
(*prob.* /lax̱-áy=aka). 2.
lax̱aíīsxin HH toes (KNM:
shoes?) (*prob.* /lax̱-áy-
s=xn).

/láx̱^wa– laugh. 1. /láx̱^w-ɬ,
s/láx̱^wa-w-n; FBa lau´xEɬ.
2. ʔac/lá?x̱^w he smiled. 3.
ʔac/lá?x̱^w-st-mx he
smiled at me *caus.* 4. q'aɬ
/lá?x̱^w-n'ɬ funny.

/léʔq soft, easy to tear. 2.
/lé·ʔq-ilix soften *dev.*

/lém' shallow.

/le·x̱iníʔ–: 1a. s/lé·x̱nʔ
earring. 1b. s/lé·x̱inʔ-umx
pl. 1c. s/ləx̱néʔ-i her
earring. 1d. s/lé·x̱inʔ-
umiš-i her earrings.

li–íls EC sea lion *Zalophus
californianus* (California
sea lion) (*prob.* /ləʔíls).

/lək' full. 1a. /lək', — *intr.*
1b. /lək'-n, — fill *tr.* 2.
/lék'– fill, load a gun. 2a.
/lék'-n, — *tr.* 3. /lk'·lək'–
fill. 3a. /lk'·lək'-n, — *tr.* 4.
/lək'-tač full. 5. .slî´k.ks
FBa flood tide.

/ləl– in a hurry. 1. /ləl-ɬ, —.

/ləláqa– shake. 1. /laláq-ɬ,
s/lə́lqa-w-n, /laláq-n,
—.

/lə́lqa– privilege. 1. s/lə́lqa-
w-n a privilege.

/ləmitén gloves (loanword;
see Chinook Jargon *lemitten*
'mitten', taken in turn from
French *la mitaine* 'mitten,
mitt').

/lə́p–: 1. /lə́p·ləp– boil. 1a.
—, s/lə́p·ləp-mit-n *mdl.*
1b. /lə́p·ləp-n, — *tr.*

/lə́pa– peel. 1. —, s/lə́pa-
w-n. 2. /lap=íl'si– peel. 2a.
/lap=íl's-n, s/lap=íl'si-
t-n *tr.*

/ləpáx̱^w– drill, drill a hole,
pierce, make a hole. 1.
/lapáx̱^w-ɬ, —, /lapáx̱^w-n,
—. 2. ʔac/lapáx̱^w-ɬ hollow.
3. /lápx̱^w-am'ɬ-tn' a drill.
4. /ləpx̱^w=án'i– pierce
one's ears. 4a. /ləpx̱^w=án'-
n, s/ləpx̱^w=án'i-t-n *tr.*

/ləq– buy. 1. /ləq-n, s/ləq-
t-n *tr.* 2. /ləq-š– buy for

appl. 2a. /ləq–š–n, — *tr.* 3. /ləq–ál/kuwɬ buy a wife (*see* /kəwáɬ– wife, woman). 4. /ləq–ál/kwaʔɬ–uʔɬ buy a woman, wedding (*see* /kəwáɬ– wife, woman).

/ləw– dig. 1a. /ləw–m, — *mdl.* 1b. /ləw–n, — *tr.* 2. /ləw'–ši– dig for *appl.* 2a. /ləw'–š–n, s/ləw'–ši–t–n *tr.* 3. lā´omEn FBa root digger (*prob.* /láw–mn).

/liǰúb devil (loanword; *see* Chinook Jargon *le-jaub* 'devil', taken in turn from French *le diable* 'devil').

/likát cards (loanword; *see* French *les cartes* 'cards').

/likáy spotted horse (black and white). (loanword; *see* Chinook Jargon *leky´e* 'piebald horse, spotted, speckled', taken in turn from French *le caille* 'piebald horse'). 1b. /likáy–i his spotted horse.

/likʷó·k rooster *Gallus gallus* (loanword; *see* Chinook Jargon *le-cock´* 'rooster', taken in turn from French *le coq* 'rooster').

/lílʔ far; GGb léhl far off; FBa le´l. 2. /lé·lʔ further away. 3. /lé·l–m' away. 4. /lé·l–l/xaw'ɬ out of the way, off the road (*see* /xəwál– road). 5. tk /lílʔ further. 6. tl

s/lé·l–a ɬ s/təq̓ʷ a foreign language. 7. tu /lílʔ foreign, from afar.

/limitú sheep *Ovis aries* (loanword; *see* Chinook Jargon *lamuto, le-mo-to* 'sheep', taken in turn from French *le mouton* 'sheep'). 2. /limitúh–al=aqn wool.

luˑ´niya TAb-mi Rainier, Oregon (loanword; *see* English *Rainier*).

/liplét priest (loanword; *see* Chinook Jargon *le-plét* 'priest', taken in turn from French *le prêtre* 'priest').

/lipuá peas *Pisum sativum* (loanword; see Chinook Jargon *le-pwau´, lepoah* 'peas', taken in turn from French *les pois* 'peas').

/lipúm apple *Malus sylvestris* (loanword; *see* Chinook Jargon *lapóme* 'apple', taken in turn from French *le pomme* 'apple').

/lisák sack, bag, pocket (loanword; *see* Chinook Jargon *le-sák* 'sack, bag', taken in turn from French *le sac* 'sack, bag'). 1b. /lisak–áwmx *pl.* 1c. /lisák–i his pocket.

/lísi– *pl.* travel, walk. 1. /lís–ɬ, s/lísi–w–n *intr.*

/lišál shawl; FBa le.cā´l (loanword; *see* Chinook Jargon *leshawl* 'shawl', taken in turn from French *le châle* 'shawl'). 1b. lišaláwmx *pl.* 2. ʔac/lišál have a shawl on.

/líxʷl– come down, get off, get out of. 1. /líxʷl–cx, s/líxʷl–cši–t–n *refl.*

/lkʷátat–: 1a. /lkʷátt mat. 1b. /lkʷátat–i his mat.

ɬ

slu EC arrow point; FBa .slōʹ arrowhead; FBa .sɬoʹ caps (for gun) (*prob.* s/lúw).

lui´pam TAb-mi [no translation given].

/luslús a striped bug. 2. luslu´spiap TAb-mi a dangerous being.

ɬ₁ in, on, with; oblique. 2. tu– ɬ from, of.

ɬ₂ and (links verbs and verb phrases).

/ɬaʔíɬn' blackberry ?*Rubus ursinus* (trailing wild blackberry); EC ẖlaé'ẖln; JH ɬɑ'íˑɬǽn', ɬáˑʹíˑɬɑn'.

/ɬáʔkʷ–: 1. /ɬáʔkʷ–m' upstream, upriver. 2. /ɬákʷ–u upriver, up above. 3. wileɬāʹkum FBa go downstream (*poss.* /wí–laʔ /ɬáʔkʷ–m' *imper.*; *see* /wí– go on).

/ɬáčicu– upstream. 1. ɬatcitsuwitila FBa go upstream (*prob.* /ɬáčicu /wí–ti–laʔ *imper.*; *see* /wí– go on). 2. tuɬaʹtcitso FBa west (*prob.* tu /ɬáčicu).

txlatçílis HH star (*prob.* /ɬač'=íls).

/ɬákʷ– other side. 1. ɬaʹko FBa west; JH ɬâˑku way down (*prob.* /ɬákʷ–u). 2. tʃt.ɬâˑku JH downriver people (*prob.* čt/ɬákʷ–u). 3. /ɬáʔkʷ–i=xaš–m' around the house. 4. /ɬákʷ–ay'=x̣x behind the house.

Klac–olks UWa, klac–olts UWa Cowlitz Landing (at Toledo).

Lāʹᵘkometsa FBa cape, cloak; HT λáˑᵘkomeca cape.

ɬáˑk'wɑ̀'ᵅmɑx wíˑɬ JH Chinook canoe.

ɬaɬiˑʹk'pc MJb-mi flying squirrel *Glaucomys sabrinus* (northern flying squirrel) (here c = š).

/ɬáX̣ʼp below, low, down. 2.
/ɬáX̣ʼp-m' downwards,
downstream. 3. /kʷə́na-la
/ɬáX̣ʼp-m' upside down
(*poss.* "hold it upside
down!"; *see* /kʷə́na-).

/ɬámtʼ- ?? 1. /ɬámtʼ=ayq-
trip someone. 1a.
/ɬámtʼ=ayq, —,
/ɬámtʼ=ayq-n or
/ɬámtʼ=iq-n,
s/ɬámtʼ=iq-t-n.

/ɬán- ?? 1. tɛkɛʼɬa´n FBa
day after tomorrow (*prob.*
tk /ɬán).

/ɬán-: 1. /ɬán=tmx wild
cranberry (?), kinnickinick
(?) (the Upper Chehalis
cognate means 'mint').

/ɬánaʔ- button. 1. /ɬán-n,
— *tr.* 2a. /ɬánaʔ-cx-tn' a
button. 2b. /ɬánaʔ-cx-tin-
umx *pl.* 2c. /ɬánaʔ-cx-
tan-i his button.

/ɬáq́ʷ there (/ɬáq́ʷ ?).

/ɬáq́ʷ-: 1. s/ɬáq́ʷ snow on
the ground; HH sxláqwʊ
snow; AG,RL skhlakhwʊ
snow; GGb slákʼw snow; FR
slak-w, slakw snow; EC
sH̄laʼk snow; FBa sɬā´qᵘ
snow; JH sɬá·kw̥ snow; JHjp
sɬɑ̇kʊ̥ snow.

/ɬáx̣- ?? 1. /ɬáx̣-lnmʼ-tn
plant *sp.* (has wide leaves;
used for seasoning). 2.
s/ɬáx̣-tnʼ woven tule mat,
rug (s/láx-tnʼ ?).

/ɬáx̣ʷ- vomit. 1. /ɬáx̣ʷ-m,
— *mdl.*

/ɬax̣ʷə́cʼ- squeeze out, pull
out. 1. txʷ/ɬax̣ʷə́cʼ-n, —
tr.

/ɬéʔspa-: 1. /ɬéʔspa-w-n
mist.

/ɬə́k- inside. 1. /ɬə́k-i its
insides (?). 2. /ɬə́k=staqi-
come inside, go in, enter. 2a.
/ɬə́k=stq, s/ɬə́k=staq-n
intr. 2b. /ɬə́k=staqi-x,
s/ɬə́k=stq-staw-n take
in, bring in *caus.*

/ɬə́k- ?? 1. /ɬak=ál'was-
come together, reach. 1a.
/ɬak=ál'us, s/ɬak=ál'us-
t-n *intr.* 1b.
s/ɬak=ál'was-i its coming
together; corner.

/ɬə́k- ?? 1. /ɬə́k=ayq- fall
over, fall down. 1a.
/ɬə́k=ayq, s/ɬə́k=iq-n
intr. 2. s/ɬə́k·ɬak=iq-n
bobbing up and down (on
land) *impf. intr.*

sɬɑ̇kʼtsʼɑm JH elk *Cervus
elaphus*; EC h̄lík-t͡sŭm cow
elk; FBa slɛ´k.tsɛm (*prob.*
s/ɬə́kcʼm).

/ɬə́kʼ sharp. 2. /ɬákʼ-ilix
sharpen *dev.* 3.
/ɬakʼ=áyaqs FBb Blue
Mountains.

/ɬə́kʼa- sore, hurt. 1. /ɬə́kʼ,
— *intr.* 2. /ɬákʼ-ilix sicken
dev. 3. ʔac/ɬə́kʼa-m-cx
he's sad *refl.* 4. ʔac/ɬə́kʼa-

mn be sorry, be too bad, feel bad, sad *rel.* 5. /ɬə́k'=lwltxʷ hospital. 6. /ták/ɬak'i- hurt, ache, sore, wound. 6a. /ták/ɬk', s/ták/ɬak'-n *intr.* 6b. /ták/ɬak'i-x, s/ták/ɬk'-staw-n *caus.* (*see* /ták-).

/ɬə́kʷ- peck, strike. 1. /ɬə́kʷ-c it pecked me *perf. tr.* 2. /ɬə́kʷ·ɬkʷ- pecking. 2a. —, s/ɬə́kʷ·ɬkʷ-mit-n *mdl.* 2b. —, s/ɬə́kʷ·ɬkʷ-t-n *tr.* 3. /ɬakʷ=ə́lqs, /ɬakʷ=ə́lqs-m woodpecker.

/ɬə́la- separate from something. 1. /ɬə́la-cx, — *refl.*

/ɬələ́p- chip, break off. 1. /ɬaləp-n, — *tr.* 2. /ɬə́l·ɬlp- chipping. 2a. —, s/ɬə́l·ɬlp-t-n *tr.*

/ɬə́mi- tie. 1. /ɬə́m-ɬ, —, /ɬə́m-n, s/ɬə́m-t-n. 2. /ɬə́mi-n-aʔ tie it! 3. /ɬam-ə́ni-t-m it was tied up, it was caught *pass.* 4. ʔac/ɬam=ál'wəs tied together. 5. tɬamɬeni´mEɬtEn FBa bridle (*poss.* /ɬam=ɬní-m'ɬ-tn').

/ɬə́p- shake off. 1. —, s/ɬə́p-cši-t-n *refl.*

/ɬə́pa- fire goes out, put out a fire, turn off a light, kill, be dead. 1. /ɬə́p-ɬ, s/ɬə́pa-w-n, /ɬə́p-n,

s/ɬə́p-t-n. 2. /ɬə́pi-n-aʔ put (the fire) out!

/ɬə́q- hit (with fist or rock). 1. /ɬə́q-n, — *tr.* 2. /ɬé?q·ɬq- play ball. 2a. /—, s/ɬé?q·ɬq-mal-n *impl.tr.* 3. ɬakalEne´x.p FBa war club (*poss.* /ɬaq-al=níxp). 4. leko´setsīkEn FBa strike (with the fist) (*prob.* /ɬəq=úsi-ci kn I hit you).

/ɬə́q'- wide. 1. /ɬə́q'-ɬ, — *intr.* 2. /ɬə́q'=ƛ̓k beaver, beavers *Castor canadensis;* GGb,FR klúk-ut-lŭk; EC ḥláktlk; FBa,BH ɬa´qtlEq; JH ɬɑ̇qtɬ'ɑk'; JHjp tɬ'ɑ̇ktɬ'ɑ̥k, tlɑ̇qtɬɑ̥q. 3. ɬɑ̇qtɬ'ɑq yá·nə́sɪ JH beaver teeth (*prob.* /ɬə́q'=ƛ̓k /yənís-i; *see* /yənís- tooth).

/ɬə́q̓ʷ- break (rope, string, etc.). 1. /ɬə́q̓ʷ-n, — *tr.*

/ɬə́t'-: 1. /ɬə́t'·ɬat'- bounce. 1a. /ɬə́t'·ɬat'-ɬ, s/ɬə́t'·ɬt'-w-n, /ɬə́t'·ɬt'-n, —.

/ɬəwála- leave behind. 1a. /ɬə́wɬ, s/ɬawál-n *tr.* 1b. /ɬawála-mx he left me *perf. caus.* 2. /ɬə́waɬ-aʔ leave him! 3. /ɬawál'=xn-desert, leave. 3a. /ɬawál'=xn-mn, — *rel.* 4. /ɬawaɬ=áyn leave word with *perf. intr.*

/ɬə́xʷa- run away, get away. 1. /ɬə́xʷ-m, s/ɬə́xʷ-mt-n *mdl.* 1b. /ɬə́xʷa-mn, — run away from *rel.*

/ɬə́x̣- ?? 1. /ɬə́x̣·ɬx̣-tn suet.

/ɬə́x̣a- burn, burn up. 1. /ɬə́x̣-ɬ, s/ɬə́x̣a-w-n, /ɬə́x̣-n, s/ɬə́x̣-t-n. 2. s/ɬə́x̣ a burn in a forest.

/ɬə́x̣ʷl'a- sun comes up. 1. —, s/ɬə́x̣ʷl'a-w-n *intr.*

/ɬə́x̣ʷa- kidnap. 1. /ɬə́x̣ʷa-mi-x he kidnapped her *rel. caus.* 2. /ɬə́x̣ʷm-st-m he was kidnapped *rel. caus. pass.*

sɬe'tsaˊu FBa table.

ɬi'tcaˊ FBa fish-net (gill-net) (*prob.* /ɬičáˑʔ).

/ɬilíq' slick.

/ɬíl'- along with, take part in. 1. /ɬíl'-s/tq̇ʷ- agree, answer. 1a. /ɬíl'-s/tq̇ʷ, —, /ɬíl'-s/tq̇ʷ-n, — *intr.* (*see* /təq̇ʷa- talk).

/ɬíɬ- ?? 1. /ɬíɬ=qs-m blow nose *mdl.*

/ɬíp-: 1. /ɬéʔp·ɬip- blink. 1a. /ɬéʔp·ɬip-ɬ, s/ɬéʔp·ɬp-w-n *intr.*

/ɬíqaq- jump. 1a. /ɬíqq, s/ɬíqaq-n; FBa xleˊqEɬ *intr.* 1b. /ɬíqq-mn, — jump over *rel.* 2. s/ɬíq·ɬiqaq-n he's jumping *imperf. intr.* 3. s/ɬéʔq·ɬiqaq-n it's bobbing up and down *imperf. intr.*

/ɬíq'i- slip, slide. 1. /ɬíq'-ɬ, s/ɬíq'i-w-n *intr.* 2. /ɬíq'=ayq slip.

/ɬíš- be cold. 1. /ɬíš-ɬ, —; FBa ɬiˊcEɬ cold (person) *intr.*

ɬit future (*non-continuative*; ɬ- *future*, ʔit *perfective aspect*).

ɬítlčak /yás yesterday (*see* /ʔít + I past).

/ɬíw come off. 1. /ɬíw- take off, uncover. 1a. /ɬíw-ɬ, — *intr.* 1b. /ɬíw-x, s/ɬíw-staw-n take off, take out *caus.* 2. /ɬiw=ál'wa- loosen, untangle, sort out. 2a. /ɬiw=ál'wa-x, s/ɬiw=álu-st-n *caus.*

ɬkaˊtsEmin e skowaˊkstEmiɬ FBa eggshell (*see* /qʷóqʷstm- egg).

ɬâˊmEn FBa spoon; HT ɬâmən (*prob.* /ɬómn).

/ɬukʷáɬ sun, moon, month; HH txlóqwatxl sun; HH txloqwatxl moon; AG tkhlokhwatkhl sun, moon; RL tkhlokhwaokin sun; RL tkhlokhwatkhl moon; GGb klo-quatl sun, moon; FR klo-kwatl sun, moon; EC ħlu-qáħl sun, moon; FBa tlo'kwaˊɬ sun, moon; FBa tlukwaˊɬ month; FBa ɬokwaˊɬ clock, watch. 2. tseˊxɬuk.ɬtaˊm FBa sunrise (*poss.* /cíx̣/ɬukʷɬ–tm; *see* /cíx̣i– show). 3. s/káwanan–i t /ɬukʷáɬ July.

/ɬúma– shrink, shrivel, cramp. 1. /ɬúm–ɬ, s/ɬúma–w–n *intr.* 2. /ɬúm·ɬum– wrinkle, pleat. 2a. /ɬúm·ɬum–ɬ, — *intr.* 3. ʔac/ɬúm·ɬama=k̓ɬ t /k̓ʷús–i his skin is wrinkled.

/ɬúmi– detour, climb through, squeeze through. 1. /ɬúmi–cx, — *refl.*

/ɬúni– push. 1. /ɬún–n, s/ɬúni–t–n *tr.*

/ɬúq̓ʷ– bald. 1. ʔac/ɬúq̓ʷ=ls baldheaded.

/ɬút̓am̓–: 1a. /ɬút̓m̓ grasshopper; FBa ɬūˊtεm. 1b. /ɬút̓am̓–i his grasshopper.

ƛ̓

ƛ̓a future (*see grammar* 2.6.2.2).

/ƛ̓áʔ–, /ƛ̓áˑl̓u– look for. 1a. /ƛ̓á–m̓ɬ, — *impl.tr.* 1b. /ƛ̓áʔ–n, s/ƛ̓áʔ–t–n *tr.* 2. /ƛ̓áˑl̓u– look for. 2a. /ƛ̓áˑl̓u–xʷ, s/ƛ̓áˑl̓–stawn *caus.* 3. /ƛ̓áˑl̓=us– look for. 3a. /ƛ̓áˑl̓=us–n, — *tr.* 4. /ƛ̓a/sámn fish, go fishing *perf. intr.* (*see* /sáman– fish). 4b. /ƛ̓a/sáman–i his fishing. 5. .sʟeswaˊl FBa scout.

/ƛ̓aʔáwi– pick berries. 1a. /ƛ̓aʔáw–m, s/ƛ̓aʔáw–mt–n *mdl.* 1b. /ƛ̓aʔáw–n, s/ƛ̓aʔáwi–t–n *tr.* 2. /ƛ̓aʔáw–mn picking basket.

/ƛ̓aláš–: 1a. s/ƛ̓aláš deer *Odocoileus* spp.; GGb slal–ash; EC stla–lásĥ; FBa tlalaˊc; JH stɬ̓aˑláˑʃ; JHjp tɬ̓ɑláˑʃ. 1b. s/ƛ̓aláš–in–umx *pl.* 1c. s/ƛ̓aláš–i his deer. 2. s/ƛ̓aláˑʔš=iʔɬ fawn. 3a. s/ƛ̓aláš–al=šn buckskin moccasins. 3b. s/ƛ̓aláš–al=šin–i his moccasins. 4. tlaˊleconiˊtsa FBa deer-skin robe; HT tláleconíca (*prob.* /ƛ̓álaš–n=ic̓a).

/ƛ̓álkʷ go upstream. 1. /ƛ̓álkʷ–m, — *mdl.*

/ƛ̓áln– ?? 1. /ƛ̓áln–al=ičn how many baskets?

/ƛ̓amə́mn chips (of wood or rock).

klá-mŭkȟl EC yew *Taxus brevifolia* (western yew); FBa tlaˊmEɬ.k.ɬ; HT tlámət.k.ɬ (*prob.* /X̌ámq'ɬ). 2. tɬ'áˑmáˑ'k'ɑn'ɬ JH yewwood (*prob.* /X̌ámaq=an'ɬ).

/X̌áp- ?? (*see* X̌əp deep ?) 1. /X̌áp-l=k- put hand into. 1a. /X̌áp-l=k-mn, — *rel.*

/X̌áq- hint. 1. /X̌áq-n, — *tr.* 2. s/X̌áq-cši-n he's hinting *impf. refl.*

/X̌áq- tease. 1. /X̌áq-n, s/X̌áq-t-n *tr.*

/X̌áq- long, tall. 1a. /X̌áq-ɬ, —; FBa Laˊ kEɬ. 1b. /X̌aq-a-ɬ-ti? or /X̌á?q-a?-ɬ-ti? *pl.* 2. /X̌áq · X̌aq-m' lengthwise. 3. /X̌á?q-ay=aqn have long hair. 4. /X̌áq=awaq-ti? big bird (long legs ?). 5. /X̌áq=axn longhouse (?). 6. L'aqaˊyɑqɬ TAb-mc Grand Mound Prairie (in Upper Chehalis territory) (*prob.* /X̌aq=áyqɬ). 7. /X̌aq=íl's-ti long berries (?). 8. /X̌áq=ɬanaws, /X̌áq=ɬanawxs long time. 9. /X̌áq=ɬan'ɬ, s/X̌áq=ɬnɬ long time, long time ago. 10. s/X̌áq=ɬaniɬat that long.

/X̌áˑq- attack. 1. /X̌áˑq-n, — *tr.* 2. ?it /X̌áˑq-tu-mulɬ they attacked us *perf. tr.*

/X̌aqám'- spring; HH txlakám; UWb klic.cul-sa (?). 1. /X̌aqám'-ilɬ spring. 2. s/X̌aqám-l-tn spring. 3. /pən/X̌aqám' spring, March; FBa pEntlakāˊm spring. 4. ?áqa tat s/wáks-n tit s/X̌aqám' February. 5. tu ?aɬ s/X̌aqám' east.

/X̌áq'- ?? 1. /X̌áq'-ɬ=kʷu thirsty; FBa .sLaˊk.ɬko; HT .sX̌ák.ɬko spring of water.

/X̌aqʷ- ?? 1. /X̌aqʷ-s/éx̣-ni- take care of, watch for, guard, protect, pay attention, herd; be alarmed, be alerted, look out for, risk *appl* 1a. /X̌aqʷ-s/éx̣-n, s/X̌aqʷ-s/éx̣-ni-t-n *tr.* (*see* /?áx̣- see, look). 1b. ?nks + ?ac/X̌aqʷ-s/éx̣-ni-cx k You want to look out for that.

/X̌aqʷú- jealous. 1. /X̌aqʷú-m, — *mdl.*

/X̌áq̓ʷ let's!, you'd better!, he'd better!, OK, agree, *exhortative.*

/X̌áq̓ʷ well, better, healed. 2. /X̌áˑq̓ʷ- be better, get better. 2a. /X̌áˑq̓ʷ-m, s/X̌áˑq̓ʷ-mit-n *mdl.* 3. X̌áq̓ʷ-aw-m, X̌aq̓ʷ-u-mit-n get well *inch. mdl.* 4. /X̌áq̓ʷ-n- heal *appl.* 4a. ?it /X̌áq̓ʷ-n-stu-mx he healed me *perf. caus.* 5.

ʔac/X̌aq̓ʷ=ínʼwa-x heʼs satisfied.

/X̌áq̓ʷtmʼx enough.

/X̌as- go to see, come to see. 1. /X̌as-wál-n, s/X̌as-wáli-t-n.

Lā́tɪ.ɬ FBa porcupine *Erithizon dorsatum.*

/X̌atə́x̣ stiff hide. 2. /X̌atə́x̣-ɬ hide gets hard before working on it *perf. intr.* 3. /X̌atə́x̣-lx hide gets hard while working on it *dev.*

.sˈLáˑxᵘs FBa forehead; HH txlóxos, txlaxóse.

/X̌áˑx̣an- hunt, go hunting. 1. X̌áˑx̣an-m, s/X̌áˑx̣n-mit-n; FBa tlā́xanɛm hunt *mdl.*

/X̌ax̣ánʼ- ?? 1a. /X̌ax̣ánʼ-tn gills. 1b. /X̌ax̣n-tə́n-i its gills.

tlax̣waiˈnut FBa aunt (*prob.* /X̌ax̣ʷ=ínut).

/X̌éʔq- ?? 1. s/X̌éʔq=kʷu a fish *sp. Acipenser transmontanus* (white sturgeon); GGb sléhkʼk-ko sturgeon; EC stlĕŭˈkˈku sturgeon; FBa .stlḗqko sturgeon; JH stɬˈíˑqˈkʊ, stɬˈéˑqʼ-kˈʊ white sturgeon; JH stɬˈíqˈkʊ sturgeon. 2. Lˈɛ́ʔqˈku TAb-mi a kind of spider that runs on top of the water.

/X̌éx̣ilʼqs- hail. 1. /X̌éx̣lʼqs-m, s/X̌éx̣ilʼqs-mit-n; HH txléxailaxs; GGb klúch-

héh-luks; FR kluch-héh-luks; FBa tlā́xel.ks *mdl.*

.stlɛˈaˈls FBa lead *n.*

/X̌əʔílkl-: 1. /X̌aʔílkɬ skin, hide; FBa .stlaiiˈlɛkɛɬ robe, blanket. 1b. s/X̌ə́lʼkəl-i its hide.

/X̌ə́la- quit, stop. 1. /X̌ə́la-cx, s/X̌ə́l-cši-t-n *refl.* 2. /X̌élʼ- quiet down, calm down, hold still. 2a. /X̌élʼ-cx, s/X̌élʼ-cši-t-n *refl.* 2b. /X̌élʼ-cxi-x, — *caus. refl.*

/X̌ə́lqʷ- spark, crackle. 1. —, s/X̌ə́lqʷ-mt-n *mdl.* 2. s/X̌ə́l·X̌ə́lqʷ-mit-n crackle *imperf. mdl.*

/X̌ə́ɬ bitter. 2. /X̌ə́ɬ·X̌ɬalʼ-ɬ bitter taste.

/X̌əmə́x̣- poke. 1a. /X̌amə́x̣-n, — *tr.* 1b. ʔit /X̌ə́mx̣-c he poked me *perf. tr.* 2. /X̌ə́m·X̌əmx̣- keep poking. 2a. s/X̌ə́m·X̌əmx̣-cal-n he keeps poking me *impf. tr.* 3. /X̌ámx̣-amɬ-tnʼ spear. 4. /X̌əmx̣=álʼus wrecked. 5. tlā́mhepɛɬɛxtɛn FBa skin dresser, skin softener.

.stlɛnawáˈlus FBa room.

/X̌ə́p deep; FBb SL!Ep. 2. s/X̌ə́p-tan-i its depth. 3a. /X̌ap-ál=ax̣n armpit. 3b. s/X̌ap-ál=x̣n-i his armpit. 4. .stlapaɬɛɬ FBa lips (*poss.* s/X̌apá=ɬnɬ). 5. X̌ap=éˈlʼs downhill, bottom of a hill; HH txlapélis valley. 6.

/ƛ̓ap=é·l'us-m' downhill, downstream. 7a.
/ƛ̓éʔp=awq bowl. 7b.
/ƛ̓éʔp=awaq-tiʔ *pl.* 8.
sʟ!po·mc FBb deep water (*prob.* s/ƛ̓p-úmš). (*See also* /ƛ̓púlmix- Cowlitz.)

/ƛ̓əqə́- go out. 1. /ƛ̓əq-ɬ, s/ƛ̓əqa-w-n or s/ƛ̓əqi-w-n *intr.* 2. /ƛ̓əqə́- put out, take out. 2a. /ƛ̓aqə́-x, s/ƛ̓áq-taw-n *caus.* 3. /ƛ̓aq=ucə́n- river mouth. 3a. /ƛ̓aq=ucə́n-i the river's mouth.

/ƛ̓ə́qx skin breaks out.

/ƛ̓ə́q'- claim. 1. /ƛ̓ə́q'-n, — *tr.*

/ƛ̓əsə́qʷ- powder, dust flying. 1. /ƛ̓asə́qʷ-ɬ, — *intr.*

k'ɬwe·´lk EG licorice fern *Polypodium* spp. (*poss.* /ƛ̓əwílqʷ; note Upper Chehalis *sƛ̓əwiləqʷ).

/ƛ̓ə́x-: 1a. /ƛ̓ə́x·ƛ̓x tree, limb, stick, pole; HH txlʊtxl wood; FBa tlî´xtlîx tree; FBb ʟ!î´x·ʟ!x· stick. 1b. /ƛ̓ə́x·ƛ̓ax-umx *pl.* 2a. /ƛ̓éʔx·ƛ̓x bush, small stick. 2b. /ƛ̓éʔx·ƛ̓ax-um'x *pl.* 3. LEXLExet FBa pipestem. 4. Le´x.ɬweɬtᵘx̣ FBa plank lodge (*prob.* /ƛ̓ə́x·ƛ̓x=lwltxʷ). 5. an-na´m-ote-láht-lo GGb wood (*prob.* /ʔanám' u tit

/ƛ̓ə́x·ƛ̓x; *see* /ʔanám' just).

/ƛ̓ə́x̣- ?? 1. ƛ̓ə́x̣-ɬ t s/múx̣ʷi-cal-s he can pay me.

/ƛ̓ə́x̣- fast, quick, soon. 1. /ƛ̓ə́x̣-ɬ, — *intr.* 2. /ƛ̓ə́x̣·ƛ̓ax̣- fast, hurry, soon, right away. 2a. /ƛ̓ə́x̣·ƛ̓ax̣-ɬ, /ƛ̓ə́x̣·ƛ̓ax̣-t-n *intr.*

/ƛ̓ə́x̣iʔ- emergency. 1. /ƛ̓ə́x̣iʔ-cx, — *refl.*

/ƛ̓ə́x̣ʷ stiff, firm, hard, tight, strong. 2. /ƛ̓áx̣ʷ-lx- stiff, in tight, harden *dev.* 2a. /ƛ̓áx̣ʷ-lx, s/ƛ̓ax̣ʷ-lt-n, /ƛ̓áx̣ʷ-ilix, —. 3. /ƛ̓ə́x̣ʷ=ip stiff (like leather). 4. /ƛ̓ə́x̣ʷ-l=s-tn bullhead: "hard head" *Cottidae* spp. (various sculpin).

/X̌íp- ?? 1. /X̌íp-ši- cover *appl.* 1a. /X̌íp-š-n, s/X̌íp-ši-t-n *tr.* 2. s/X̌íp-x-tan-i its cover. 3. ʔac/X̌íp-x tan it's covered.

/X̌íq- ?? 1. as'ʟi´qtʟiqtɬ FBa knife handle.

/X̌íqsn box. 1b. /X̌íqsin-umx *pl.* 1c. /X̌íqsən-i his box. 2. /X̌éqsn box *dimin.*

/X̌íq'a- stick, glue. 1. —, s/X̌íq'a-w-n, /X̌íq'-n, —. 2. /X̌iq'·X̌íq' sticky. 3. /X̌éq'a-m'ɬ-tn' glue. 4. /X̌iq'=álwas- stick

together. 4a. /ƛ'iq'=álus, —
intr. 4b. /ƛ'iq'=álwa-xʷ,
s/ƛ'iq'=ál'us-taw-n caus.
5. s/ƛ'íq'=nak-: 5a.
s/ƛ'íq'=nk diaper,
breechcloth; FBa
.stlē´kɛnɛk breech-clout.
5b. s/ƛ'íq'=nač-i his diaper.

/ƛ'iw'x̣ín'-: 1. s/ƛ'iw'x̣ín'
bald eagle ?*Haliaeetus
leucocephalus* or ?*Aquila
chrysaetos* (golden eagle);
EC stliŭ-ħén; FBa
.stlaxē´.n golden eagle,
bald-headed eagle; JH
stƛ'í·lᵅx̣ɑn' eagle.

/ƛ'íx cold, cool; HH txleq
cold; AG tkhlekh cold; RL
tkhlek cold; GGb kleh´h
cold; FR kleh'h cold; FBa
Lí´xɛɬ cold (person). 2.
s/ƛ'íš-il-i its getting cold,
its being a year dev. 3. s/ƛ'íx
year. 4. s/ƛ'íx-tn north. 5.
ne-kàus-tléh GGb year
(prob. /nak'-aw-s/ƛ'íx). 6.
/pən/ƛ'íx winter; GGb
pent-leh'h; UWb,FR pin-
klech; FBa pɛnLé.x; BH
pɛnLe´.x. 7.
/pən/ƛ'íx=uliɬn storage
place. 8. qi/ƛ'íš-ils winter.
9. qi s/ƛ'íš-lt-aw-am'ɬ a
fan.

/ƛ'íxʷ- stick under. 1.
/ƛ'íxʷ=stq- put into the
oven. 1a. /ƛ'íxʷ=stq-n, —
tr.

L!e·x̣ᵘ FBb house (prob. ƛ'íxʷ).

/ƛ'ó·x̣ʷ- ?? 1. ʔac/ƛ'ó·x̣ʷ=s
cross-eyed.

/ƛ'p-úl=mix-: 1. s/ƛ'p-
úl=mx Cowlitz; HH
txlpólamʊx name; FBb
sƛ'pálmxʷ; TAa-md stop o
muxʷ, stop'omuxᵘ; TAb
L'ɑpu·´l'əmʊx̣; JH
tƛ'pʊ·lmɪx Cowlitz tribe;
JH tƛ'pú·lmɑx Cowlitz
person (see /ƛ'əp- deep). 2.
s/ƛ'p-úl=mš Cowlitz; TAb-
mi L'epolms. 3.
s/ƛ'əp=úmš Cowlitz
territory; MJb ctl pő bc; TAa-
gs L' pomic Lower Cowlitz;
TAa-ph L'epomic, L' pomic;
TAb-ly asl' pomx Cowlitz
prairie. 4. /ƛ'p-úl=mix=q
Cowlitz language; FBb
SL!pɛlEmi´x̣q! 5.
tʃt'.tƛ'pʊ·lmɪx JH Cowlitz
people; JHmc,lj
tʃtɬpʊ·lɑməxᵛ (prob.
čt/ƛ'p-úl=mx).

stƛ'ʊ·'ɑlɑm' JH cockle
Clinocardium nuttalli
(prob. s/ƛ'úʔlm').

tlu´k.tɛn FBa woven bag.

/ƛ'úk̓ʷ above, high; FBa
Lo´ᵘqᵘ high. 2. /ƛ'úk̓ʷ-m'
up. 3. /ƛ'ó·k̓ʷ-m' up, going
up. 4. /ƛ'uk̓ʷ=íl's hill. 5.
/ƛ'uk̓ʷ=él's mountain. 6.
/ƛ'uk̓ʷ=é·lus-m' uphill. 7.
/ƛ'uk̓ʷ=é·l's-m' to the
mountains. 8. /ƛ'úk̓ʷ=ičn

top. 9. /ƛ́úk̓ʷ=lwltxʷ top of
a house. 10. /ƛ́úk̓ʷ-ɬ=tumx
top. 11. /ƛ́úk̓ʷ=stq fire on
top. 12. ntlu´kamatsa FBa
coat (poss. n/ƛ́úk̓ʷ-
ma=c'aʔ). 13. /ƛ́ùk̓ʷ t
/ʔáls God (see /ʔális-
chief, leader). 14. tu /ƛ́úk̓ʷ
ceiling, above. 15. Lūk
sau´tselEks FBa apron

(prob. /ƛ́úk̓ʷ /sál'cil'qs;
see /sál'cil'qas- dress).
/ƛ́úqʷi– dip. 1. /ƛ́úqʷ-n,
s/ƛ́úqʷi-t-n tr. 2. /ƛ́úqʷ-
am'ɬ-tn' dipnet; spoon,
canoe bailer. 3. qi s/ƛ́úqʷ-
am'ɬ dipnet.
/ƛ́xʷáy' dog salmon
Onchorhynchus keta; JHjp
tɬ'kwáy.

m

/máʔksns moccasin
(loanword: see English
moccasins). 1b. máʔksns-
umx pl. 2. /sáʔ/maksns
make moccasins.
/macál–: 1a. mî´tsiɬ FBa
thread (prob. /məcɬ). 1b.
/macál-i its line, string. 2.
matsa´litcEn FBa bowstring
(poss. /macál=ičn).
/macə́p a creek that flows
into the Cowlitz River at the
Toledo grange hall.
/máčn– testicles. 1.
atsEma´tcEn .stEke´u FBa
stallion (prob. ʔac/máčn
s/tiqíw).
/máč'iɬaʔ flea, fleas; FBa
mā´tseɬa. 1b.
/máč'iɬan'-i his flea.
/mák̓ʷ– put into one's
mouth. 1. /mák̓ʷ-n, — tr. 2.
/máʔk̓ʷ=iq eat berries from
the bush. 3. /mák̓ʷ=ɬanal-

kiss. 3a. /mák̓ʷ=ɬanal-n,
s/mák̓ʷ=ɬn-t-n tr.
/mak̓ʷə́t–: 1a. /mák̓ʷt dead;
dead person, corpse, ghost;
HH máqut dead; FBa
mā´qut corpse; JH
má·k'wɑ't' ghost. 1b.
/mak̓ʷə́t-i his corpse. 2.
mu-ku-tá-u-mŭħ EC
spirit (ghost). 3.
.sma´kotuɬEn FBa sister-
in-law (prob.
s/mák̓ʷt=uɬn').
/máli Virgin Mary
(loanword; see English
Mary).
/malyí marry (loanword; see
Chinook Jargon mal-i-éh
'marry', taken in turn from
French marier 'marry'). 2.
/malyíh-umx they marry.
/mál'wa– mix in. 1. —,
s/mál'wi-t-n tr. 2.

məl · /mál'wa– mix up. 2a.
/məl · mál'wa-x, — *caus.*

/**mán** father; FBa 'ma´. 1b.
/mán-aw-i his father; HH
tamánawe. 2. kə/má?
father! *voc.*; FBb kama´.ᵋ. 3.
kʷu/má? father! *voc.*; HH
komá; AG,RL koma; GGb
ko-máh my father; FR ko-
máh; EC kŭ-ni-má. 4.
kʷá+a/mn uncle (*see*
/kʷa+á– parent's sibling). 5.
tcu+ma´nEm FBa stepfather
(*prob.* /ču+/mán-m). 6. s-
nx/mán-tn relatives. 6b. s-
nx/mn-tán-i or s-nx/m-
tán-i his relatives.

/**mána–** ?? 1. ma´na+tse FBa
calf of the leg (*prob.*
/mána=+c'i?).

/**má·na–** spawn. 1. /má·na-
m, — *mdl.* 2. s/má·na-m-
i their spawning. 3.
s/má·na-m'-lu+
spawning.

manι´k'o+ TAb-mc a place
across the river from Gate
City (in Upper Chehalis
territory) (*prob.*
/manák'=uw'+).

/**maní?–**: 1a. son, daughter,
child; FBa Ema´n son,
daughter. 1b. numán HH
son; AG,RL numan son; GGb
n'mánn son; FR n'mánn
my son (*prob.* n/mán? my
son). 1c. HH tsunumán
daughter; AG,RL tsunumán

daughter; GGb ts'in na
mánn my daughter; FR
tsin-na-mánn my
daughter (*prob.* c n/mán?
my daughter). 1d.
nx/mán?-tn *pl.* 1e.
/maní?-i or /mané?-i his
son, his daughter. 1f.
nxə/m'-tán-i *pl.* 2a.
?ac/mán? have a baby. 2b.
+it /wí ?akʷu ?ac/mán?
She's going to have a baby.
(*see* /t'úla–). 3.
tcElmî´nam stepchild (*see*
/ču+–).

/**manít–** kill, butcher. 1.
/manít/umusməski
butcher (*see* /wəmúsmuski
cow).

manikalítxlin HH mosquito
(*poss.* /manik=alí+n).

/**mán'ac–**: 1a. /mán'c
fingerlings, small fish,
small trout. 1b. /mán'ac-
umx *pl.*

/**máq'–** old (objects). 1.
/máq'-+, —; HH maqtl old
(not new); GGb mak'tl,
mā-ktl old; FR maaktl.

/**máqʷm** prairie, valley; GGb
mók-um plain; FR mok-
um, mo-kum valley,
prairie; FBa mā´kom plain.

/**má·s–** cheap. 1. /má·s-+,
— *intr.*

/**masəntán–**: 1. /masántn
gall; FBa mêsî´ntEn. 1b.
/məsntán-i his gall. 2.

masɑ́ntən TAb-mi Urine Boy (*in myths*).

/mát- go after, go for, fetch. 1. /mát=ikʷp go after firewood. 2. /mat=ó·li˥n go for food.

/máta- sharpen, file. 1. /mát-n, s/máta-t-n *tr.* 2. /máta-m'˥-tn' grinding stone, sharpener. 3. /má?ta-m'˥-tn' a file *dimin.*

/mátaxʷ- ?? 1a. s/mátxʷ-tn son-in-law, father-in-law; FBa .smê´.tuxtEn father-in-law, mother-in-law, son-in-law, daughter-in-law; BH .smê´.tuxtEn father-in-law. 1b. s/mátxʷ-tan-i his son-in-law. 1c. nx/mátaxʷ-n-tan-i his sons-in-law *pl.*

/mátil- feed, give food to. 1. /mátil-n,— *tr.*

mā´tEna˥En FBa scalp (*prob.* /mátn=a˥n).

/máx̣ʷ- break to pieces. 1. /máx̣ʷ-n, — *tr.*

/may- ?? 1. ?ac/may=á·l's be surprised. 2. /may=á·l's- suspect, be surprised at. 2a. /may=á·l's-mn, s/may=á·l's-mit-n *rel.* 3. /may=á·l'us- stare, stare at, look at something strange. 3a. —, s/may=á·l's-mit-n *mdl.*

3b. /may=á·l'u-xʷ, s/may=á·l's-taw-n *caus.*

/má·y- stick out, come to the surface. 1. —, s/máy'·mi?=s-mit-n *mdl.* 2. ?ac/má·y=ičn stick out of the water. 3. ?ac/má·y=us-n stick out of the ground.

/máyan'-: 1a. s/máyn' skunk *Mephitis mephitis* (striped skunk); EC smá-in; FBa smai´En; JH smɑ' 'ɑyɑn'. 1b. s/máyan'-umx *pl.* 1c. s/máyan'-i his skunk. 2. s/má·y'an'-umx little skunks *dimin. pl.* 3. /máyn'=sqm skunk's smell.

/mayə́n new, fresh; HH maiien young (new); UWb,FR mi-en new; FBa maiyî´n new.

/mé?ščm' mink (muskrat ?) *Mustela vison* (mink); EC mě's-chǐm mink; FBa mî´stcEm mink; TAb-mi mɑ´stc'əm; JH mǽ·'stʃəm' mink.

/mé·l'- ?? 1. /mé·l'=m'x children.

/méX̌- sulk. 1. —, s/méX̌-t-n *intr.*

/mén'- ?? 1. ?ac-txʷ/mén'-st-m be still, calm. *caus. pass.*

/mə́ckʷ blackcaps *Rubus leucodermis*; EC mŭt͡sq

black raspberries; FBa
mî´ds.k raspberry; JH
mɑ́tskw̥ raspberry. 2.
/mə́ckʷ=an'ɬ blackcap
bushes.
/məkʷə́- poke. 1. /mə́kʷ-n,
— *tr.* 2. /makʷə́-min-: 2a.
/makʷə́-mn awl; FBa
mê'qo´mEn. 2b. /makʷə́-
min-umx *pl.* 2c. /makʷə́-
min-i his awl.
/məkʷúp-: 1a. /mə́kʷp fire;
HH móksip; AG,RL moksip;
GGb mook'w'p; EC m̥ukp;
FBa mô´q.p; HT mô̥q.p. 1b.
/mə́kʷap-umx *pl.* 1c.
/makʷúp-i his fire. 2.
/x̣aɬxʷm-s txʷt/mə́kʷp
firewood.
/mə́ḱʷ- pile, pile up. 1.
/mə́ḱʷ-ɬ, —, /mə́ḱʷ-n,
s/mə́ḱʷ-t-n. 2.
ʔac/mə́ḱʷ-ɬ a pile. 3.
ʔac/mə́ḱʷ·maḱʷ-ɬ little
piles, lumpy. 4. /mé·ḱʷ-
pile up. 4a. /mé·ḱʷ-n, —
tr. 5. ʔac/méḱʷ·maḱʷ-ɬ
lumpy. 6. /məḱʷ=úyq-
bake in ashes. 6a.
/məḱʷ=úyq, —,
/məḱʷ=úyq-n, —. 7.
/məḱʷ=úyaq-umx they
heap it up. 8.
/məḱʷ=úy=stq-ni-n-aʔ
bank the fire! *appl.*
/mə́lak-: 1.
ʔac/mə́l·malak-ɬ pleats.

/mələ́q́ʷ- wrap. 1. /malə́q́ʷ-
n, s/mə́lq́ʷ-t-n *tr.* 2.
/mélq́ʷ=ls have the head
covered, have something
wrapped around the head.
/mə́lqni- forget. 1. /mə́lqni-
x, s/mə́lqna-y-n *caus.*
/mə́lx̣ʷ- undress. 1. /mə́lx̣ʷ-
cx, — *refl.*
/mə́l'qsi- dive. 1.
/mə́l'qs-n, — *tr.* 2.
s/mə́l'qsi-cx diving *refl.*
/mə́ɬk- summer. 1.
/pən/mə́ɬk summer; HH
pʊnemʊ́txlqʊ; GGb pen-
ne-méhl-kie; UWb,FR pin-
milkh; FBa pEnÉmî´ltEk. 2.
/pən/yáq'-s/mə́ɬk fall,
autumn; HH pʊneáxsoman
autumn; UWb,FR pin-yalk-
so-milkh autumn (*see*
/yáq'a- tip, fall).
/mə́X̌a- try, test, taste, guess.
1. /mə́X̌-n, s/mə́X̌-t-n *tr.*
2. /mə́X̌a- take a chance. 2a.
/mə́X̌a-cx, s/mə́X̌-cši-
t-n *refl.* 3. /mə́X̌·məX̌-
act. 3a. —, s/mə́X̌·məX̌-
cši-t-n *refl.* 4.
/mə́X̌·məX̌- shoot at
targets. 4a. —,
s/mə́X̌·məX̌-cši-t-n *refl.*
5. /mé·X̌- shoot at targets.
5a. —, s/mé·X̌-t-n *tr.* 6.
/méX̌·məX̌- act. 6a. —,
s/méX̌·məX̌-cši-t-n *refl.*
7. /méX̌·məX̌-n a contest.

smuq' EG horsetail
Equisetum sp. (*poss.*
/sməq).

/məqsə́n–: 1. /mə́qsn nose;
HH mu̇kusun, máksun;
AG,RL mukusun; GGb,FR
muk-sn; EC mŭksn; FBa
mû́ksEn; HT mî́qsən, mě̇
qsĕn. 1a. /məqsə́n-i his
nose.

/məqʷál'č–: 1. s/məqʷál'č
chipmunk *Eutamius* spp. (=
/məx̣ʷ=á·l'as ?).

/məqʷayíʔ–: 1. /mə́qʷiʔ
cheek; FBa mêkwai´. 1b.
/məqʷyíʔ-i his cheek. 1c.
/mə́qʷay-umiš-i his
cheeks *pl.*

/mə́q̓ʷa– swallow. 1a.
/mə́q̓ʷ-m, — *mdl.* 1b.
/mə́q̓ʷ-n, — *tr.* 2.
/məq̓ʷá-min–: 2a.
/məq̓ʷá-mn throat; GGb
muk wah mil windpipe;
FBa mokwa´mEn. 2b.
/məq̓ʷá-min-i his throat.

/mə́q̓ʷskʷu– like, take a
liking to, wish for. 1.
/mə́q̓ʷskʷu-ən, — *tr.*

.smếc FBa grizzly bear
Ursus arctos (*prob.*
s/mə́š).

/məšín car, automobile,
machine (loanword; *see*
English *machine*).

/mətá·s leggings, Indian
stockings; FBa mita´s short
leggings (loanword; *see*

Chinook Jargon *mit-áss*
'leggings', taken in turn
from Ojibwa *mita·ss*
'leggings'). 1b. /mətá·s-i
his stockings.

/mət'ə́kʷ– mix, stir, shake
up. 1. /mat'ə́kʷ-ɬ, —, —,
s/mát'kʷ-t-n.

/mət'ús–: 1a. /mə́t's kidney;
FBa mî́tEs. 1b. /mat'ús-i
his kidney.

/mə́xkan'–: 1a. /mə́xčn'
head-louse; FBa mî́xtcEn
louse. 1b. /mə́xkan'-i his
head-louse.

/məx̣kán–: 1a. /mə́x̣kn
horn, antlers; FBa mî́x̣kEn
antler, spoon. 1b.
/məx̣kán-i its horns. 2.
tsma´x̣kEn FBa buck deer
(*poss.* ʔac/mə́x̣kn). 3.
/mə́x̣kan'-ɬ Lacamas
Creek.

/mə́x̣ʷ–: 1a. s/mə́x̣ʷ high
mountain, ridge; HH smox,
smaxo hill, mountain;
GGb,FR smo'h mountain;
UWa smuck mountain; FBa
.s.mo´x mountain. 1b.
s/məx̣ʷ-áwmx *pl.*

/məx̣ʷ– ?? 1. /məx̣ʷ=á·l'as
chipmunk ?, weasel ?, mink
?: "blinking eyes"
?*Eutamias* spp., or
?*Tamiasciurus douglasi*
(Chickaree); FBa
mox̣wa´lls squirrel; JHjp

mɑxwáˑlɑs timber squirrel.

/məyə́xʷ- bump, get bumped. 1. /mayə́xʷ-ɬ, — intr. 2. ʔit /mə́yxʷ-c he bumped me perf. tr. 3. ʔac/mayə́xʷ=qs have a hump on the nose.

/milúx̣ʷ- round, spherical. 1a. /milúx̣ʷ=akaʔ fist. 1b. /milúx̣ʷ=aka-n'-i his fist. 2. /milúx̣ʷ=akaʔ-ši- double one's fist at appl. 2a. /milúx̣ʷ=akaʔ-ši-c he doubled his fist at me perf. tr. 3a. /milúx̣ʷ=l's ball, round object. 3b. /milúx̣ʷ=l's-i his ball.

/míɬta no, not, never; HH mexlta no; GGb,FR méhlt no; FBa mīˊɬta no. 2. /méˑɬta no, not (emphatic).

/mín- be mean. 1. /mín-ɬ, — (loanword; see English mean).

/míq̓ʷi- make muddy, roil water. 1. /míq̓ʷ-ɬ, —, /míq̓ʷ-n, s/míq̓ʷi-t-n. 2. ʔac/míq̓ʷ-ɬ=kʷu muddy water.

/míwt a seal ?Phoca vitulina (harbor seal); EC mí-wṵt hair seal; JH míˑwʊt.

/móʔ- handful. 1. /nək'-u/móʔ a handful, cluster, bunch (see /nák'- one).

/móʔəm a grouse sp. ?Dendragapus obscurus (blue grouse); GGb móhm; EC mom; FBa môˊmx blue grouse; JH móˑm', móˑ'm'.

/móˑlukʷ- stubborn. 1. /móˑlukʷ-ɬ, — intr.

/móˑluqʷ- plug. 1. /móˑluqʷ-ɬ, — intr.

/móˑl'- keep warm. 1. /móˑl'-cx, — refl.

/múc- tangle. 1. /múc-ɬ, — intr.

/múc'- wring out, drain, seep. 1. /múc'-n, — tr.

/múlukʷ- crazy, dizzy, nod the head. 1. /múlukʷ-ɬ, s/múlkʷ-w-n intr. 2. txʷ/mulúkʷ=s-t-n he fainted. 3. ʔac/mulúkʷ=ls be dizzy, faint.

/múq̓ʷa- float, drift. 1. /múq̓ʷ-ɬ, s/múq̓ʷa-w-n intr. 2. s/múq̓ʷˑmuq̓ʷ-w-n waves. 3. tit ʔac/múq̓ʷ-aʔ-ɬ tit /ƛ̓ə́xˑƛ̓ax-umx driftwood.

/múq̓ʷi- pole a boat. 1. —, s/múq̓ʷi-t-n tr.

/mús four; HH,AG,RL mos; GGb mose; FR mose, mo-se; EC mus; FBa mūs. 2. /mus-al-s/q'íx̣ Thursday (see /q'íx̣- day). 3. /mus-ál'=xaw'ɬ four rows. 4. /mús=ls four dollars. 5. /mús-ɬ=panxʷ four years old. 6. /mús-ɬ=qʷ four days. 7. /mús-ɬ=tumx forty; EC mósh̄l-tumh̄; FBa mū´s.ɬ tū´mEX. 8. /mús-ɬ=ušn four times. 9. /pánačš kl t /mús fourteen (LNJ). 10. /tál'/mus fourteen (ENM). 11. /t'əmx/mús fourfold.

/mús eye; HH,AG,RL mos; GGb tsummose; UWb moos face; EC mus; FBa mu´s; FBb mo·s. 1b. /mus-áwmx pl. 1c. /mús-i his face. 1d. /mus-áwmiš-i his eyes. 2. c/mús face; GGb tsum-móse; FR tsum-móse face, eye; EC t͡sŭ-mús; FBa tsEmu´s; HT cəmús. 2b. c/mús-i his face. 2c. HH ntsʊmós (*prob.* n/cmús my face).

/mús- ?? 1. /mús-al=mx moth.

/músa- sleep, asleep. 1a. /mús-m, s/mús-mt-n *mdl.* 1b. /músa-mi-x, — put to sleep *mdl. caus.* 2. /mó·s- take a nap *dimin.* 2a. —, s/mó·s-mt-n *dimin. mdl.* 3. /mós-m=alaka sleepyhead.

/mút'i- suck, suck on. 1. /mút'-n, s/mút'i-t-n *tr.*

/múx̣ʷi- pay. 1. /múx̣ʷ-n, s/múx̣ʷi-t-n *tr.* 2. /múx̣ʷ·mux̣ʷi-c he paid me over and over *perf. tr.* 3. múx̣ʷ-ši- pay it for *appl.* 3a. —, s/múx̣ʷ-ši-t-n *tr.* 4. /?ays/múx̣ʷi-c he paid me again *perf. tr.*

/múx̣ʷi- punish. 1. /múx̣ʷi-x, s/múx̣ʷ-staw-n *caus.*

n

n and.

na, ?ana, ana *interrogative particle.* 2. ?a-ka-/ma? na tit /nawíɬ=m'x Is this man your father? 3. ?it /múx̣ʷi-t-m k na /yás Did he pay you yesterday? 4. s-yayús-t-alapt na Are you (*pl.*) working? 5. s-/yayús-t-ax̣ʷ ?u na Are you still working?

/ná?ɬ- rest, take a nap. 1. /ná?ɬ-cx, s/ná?ɬ-cši-t-n *refl.*

/nák'- one (bound form) (*see* /?úc's one). 1. /nák'-aw=l's one dollar. 2. /nák'-aw'=ɬ t /ɬukʷáɬ one month. 3a. /nák'-u=šn once, one time. 3b. /nák'·nak'-u=šn one at a time. 4. /?ít/nak'-u=šn whole. 5. /nák'-x=panxʷ

one year old; FBa
naˊkɛxpaˊnɛx year; HT
nákəx̣pánəx year. 6.
/nák'=x=qʷ (?) one day. 7.
/nak'-áw/əmx̣kʷu one
basket (see /ʔə́mx̣kʷu
cedar-root basket). 8.
/nak'-áw/santi one week
(see /sánti Sunday, week).
9. ne-kàùs-tléh GGb year
(prob. /nak'-aw-s/ƛ̓íx;
see /ƛ̓íx cold). 10. na-
koús-kéh GGb day (prob.
/nak'-áw-s/q'ix̣; see
/q'íx̣- day). 11. /nak'-
áw'=xaw'ł one row. 12.
.snakax hweˊmɛł FBa
fathom. 13. nàk'-u-
s/x̣ʷúqʷ together (see
/x̣ʷúqʷa- together with).
14. /nək'-u/móʔ a handful,
cluster, bunch (see /móʔ-
handful). 15. /nək'-u-
s/x̣ʷóqʷ bunch (see
/x̣ʷúqʷa- together with).
16. /nək̓ʷ/x̣ím handful (see
/x̣ím- grab, grab a
handful).

/náma- done, finish, stop,
end. 1. /nám-ł, s/náma-
w-n, /nám-n, s/náma-
t-n. 2a. ʔac/nám-l's ready.
2b. /nám-l's, s/nám-l's-
t-n intr. 3. /náˑm'=usi-
end, finish. 3a. /nám'=us,
—. 3b. /náˑm'=usi-x, —
caus. 3c. s/náˑm'=us-i its
end. 4. .snaˊmai.x FBa ebb

tide (poss. s/nám=iq). 5.
/nám/c'uq̓ʷ-ł afternoon
(see /c'úq̓ʷ- set upright,
straight up). 6. /nám/iłn
finished eating (see
/ʔíłani- eat). 7.
/nám/santi Monday (see
/sánti Sunday, week). 8.
/nám/t'ək-m dressed mdl.
(see /t'ə́k- wear, get
dressed). 9. s/put-
s/náma-t-n he just
finished it.

/nám'u perhaps, maybe,
might, wish (see /ʔanám'
just). 2. /nám'u-ł perhaps,
might, maybe. 3. /nám'u
qas wish, hope (see qas
want).

/nápis late, getting dark.

/napúl-: ?? 1. s/napúl=uł
load. 1a. s/napúl=ul-i his
load.

/natə́p a site on the Cowlitz
River (placename).

'naˊu FBa bluebird Sialia spp.
(prob. /náw). 1a. Nau TAb-jc
Bluejay's older sister.

/náw- ?? 1. /náw=ax̣n right
(side); FBa nauˊax̣ɛn
shoulder; HT naúax̣ən
shoulder. 2. ʔáł/naw=ax̣n
to the right; FBa
ałnaˊ ᵘax̣ɛn right hand; HT
ełnaˑúax̣ən right hand.

/náw- ?? 1a. /náw=łc'iʔ
body; HH náwitxltse; GGb
nah-wult-seh belly; FR

nah-wult-seh; FBa
nā´utse. 1b. /náw=ɬc'i-
n'i his body. 1c.
/nu=ɬc'íʔ-i body, trunk
(*prob.* his body).
/**náw-** ?? 1. nau´.ɬko FBa
river; HT naú.ɬko (*prob.*
/náw-ɬ=kʷu).
/**náwa-** old. 1. /náw-ɬ,
s/náwa-w-n *intr.* 2a.
ʔac/náw-ɬ old person; HH
tçunáwitxl old; FBa
tsɛnā´uɬ old, aged. 2b.
ʔac/náw-a-ɬ-tiʔ *pl.* 3.
/náw=aqʷ-m Big Prairie
(placename); UWa Now-ok
prairie, Hudson Bay farms
on Cowlitz River; TAb
na´waqυm Newaukum
River. 4. /naw=ín'wa-
respect, be proud of. 4a.
/naw=ín'wa-x, — *caus.* 5.
/ná·w'-ɬ=mx old woman;
FBa nā´uɬɛmɛx,
nāuɬta´mɛx old man, old
woman. 6. now-oo-tsou
UWa Monticello (now
Longview) (placename;
prob. /naw=úcn). 7.
naukīa´sˢ FBa day before
yesterday (*prob.* /naw-
ki/yás; *see* /yás yesterday).
8a. /náw/santi holiday (*see*
/sánti Sunday, week). 8b.
/náw'/san'ti-m'n flag. 9a.
/pən/náw/santi holiday
time, December. 9b.
/pən/náw'/san'ti-m'n

holiday, July, Christmas.
10a. /tals/náwaʔ
grandparent, old people. 10b.
nx-s/tas/náwa-tn *pl.* 10c.
/tals/náwa-tan-i his
grandparents. 11. tk
ʔac/náw-ɬ older.
/**nawíɬ=m'x** person, man;
HH nawétxlamax man; HH
nawítxlamυx Indian,
people; AG,RL
nawetkhlamakh man; SH
nawíɬəmx man.
/**náwqɬ** Bluejay's older
sister.
naw' or.
/**náxʷɬqʷul'as** thank you;
FBa nauxɬkola´te.
/**náxʷɬuʔ** true; GGb nŭhwhl
yes; FR núch-whl; FBa
nau´xɬo yes, true; FBa
no´xɬo now.
/**nax̣-** ?? 1. /ʔáy/nax̣=nut
change one's mind. 2.
/sá·/nax̣=nut plan, agree.
3. /sá·/nax̣=nut-ši- plan
appl. 3a. /sá·/nax̣=nut-
š-n, — *tr.*
/**néʔsk** younger brother; HH
nυsk brother; GGb nesk
brother; FR nesk younger
brother; EC nĕsk; FBb
nà·ɛsk, nàᵋsk, nɛ´ski. 1b.
nx/néʔsk-tn *pl.* 1c. /nsk-
éw'-i his younger brother.
1d. nx/néʔsk-tan-i his
younger brothers. 2.
neskɛnɛma´n FBa younger

brother (*prob.* /né?sk
n/mán?; *see* /mán? child).

/nə́ka- sink, weight down. 1.
/nək-ɬ, —, /nək-n,
s/nək-y-n. 2.
nê´.kam.ɬtɛn FBa sinker
(for line or net) (*prob.*
/nə́ka-m'ɬ-tn'). 3. qi
s/nə́ka-m'ɬ anchor.

/nək'ál'-: 1. /nək'ál'=us,
s/nək'ál'=us coyote *Canis
latrans*; EC sna-kŭ-lŭ;
FBa,BH snɛka´l; BH
sne'kî´l; TAb-jc snəkɑ´l?;
JH snɑk'ɑ́l fox.

nulk-tsulk UWa Newaukum
River (*prob.* nə́x̣ʷ/c'al'x̣).

/nə́ɬ- throw a person down.
1. /nə́ɬ-c he threw me
down *perf. tr.*

/nə́m- bury. 1. /nə́m-n,
s/nə́m-t-n *tr.*

/nə́q- black. 1. /né?q-
blacken, darken. 1a.
/né?q-m, s/né?q-mal-n
mdl. 2. ?aks/nə́q black; HH
ksnu̇qu; AG,RL ksnukhu;
GGb,FR uk-snúk; EC aks-
nŭk; FBa ɛks'nî´q. 3a.
?aks/naq=íl's black round
object. 3b. ?aks/naq=íl's-
ti? *pl.* 4. nîkana´mɛts FBa
Negro; HT nîkanámǝc
(*poss.* /nǝq=námc). 5.
tsnî´ks FBa pupil of eye
(*prob.* c/nǝ́q=s). 6.
kwātsä´ksnî´k FBa brown
(*prob.* /kʷác ?aks/nǝ́q; *see*

/kʷác a little, somewhat). 7.
?ac/né?q-m s/xam'álaxʷ
Negro.

/nǝqʷálm'- weasel *Mustela*
spp. 1. s/nǝqʷálm'.

/nǝwáp-: 1a. s/nǝ́wp
bottom, stump; FBa .sno´ᵘp
stump of a tree. 1b.
s/nawáp-i its bottom.

/nǝ́wi you (sg.); HH nu̇we
thou; AG,RL nuwé thou; GGb
nóo-weh thou; FR nóo-
weh, nū-weh thou; FBa
no´we thou. 2. s/nawí-yaɬ
your. 3. ?ac/x̣ʷúqʷ-
aɬ/nawi with you (*see*
/x̣ʷúqʷa- together with).
4a. ?áɬ/nawi to you. 4b. x̣-
?áɬ/nawi to you. 5. /?áwt-
ɬ/nawi behind you. 6.
p'én'/nawi beside you.

/nǝxánči a small chipmunk
sp. *Eutamias* spp.; TAb-mi,jc
Nǝx̣ɑ´ntci, TAb-mi X̣ɑ´ntci
animal similar to mouse,
but red in color; MJb-mi
Naha´ntci myth character.

/nǝ́x̣ʷ- ?? s/nǝ́x̣ʷ=x̣̌k=mx
become pregnant.

/nǝ́x̣ʷa- *pl.* talk, argue,
discuss. 1a. /nǝ́x̣ʷ-m,
s/nǝ́x̣ʷ-mt-n *mdl.* 1b.
/nǝ́x̣ʷ-n, — *tr.* 2. /?ilápa?
/nǝ́x̣ʷ-t-ila? You folks
discuss it! 3. /míɬta t qi
s/nǝ́x̣ʷa-mɬ they don't
talk to each other.

/níʔ-: 1. /níʔ-x̣ here. 2.
/néʔ-x̣ here.

.snicha´ FBa loon *Gavia* sp.

/níɬi- alive 1. /níɬ-ɬ,
s/níɬi-w-n *intr.* 2. /níɬ
alive; HH nétxl; GGb néh'tl;
FR neh'tl; FBa .sni´ɬtEn. 3a.
/níɬ-lx come back to life
dev. 3b. s/níɬi-l-i his
coming back to life. 4.
s/níɬ-n-t-n he's
becoming alive *impf. intr.* 5.
s/niɬ-tə́n-: 5a. s/níɬ-tn
soul, life; EC sni͡hltn human
spirit; FBa .s.nī´ɬtEn soul.
5b. s/niɬ-tə́n-i his life, his
soul.

/ninəmú LNJ, niminú turnip
Brassica compestris
(loanword; *see* Chinook
Jargon *lenawo* 'turnips',
taken in turn from Acadian
French *le navot* 'turnip').

/níq̓ʷɬ cottonwood *Populus
balsamifera* (black
cottonwood) and/or *Populus
tremuloides* (quaking
aspen); EC níŭ-qŭ͡hl; FBa
nê´ᵘkEɬ poplar (aspen); FBa
'ne´kuɬ poplar (balsam);
JH ní·q̓'w̥ɬ.

/níx here; FBa,BH nē´x. 2.
ʔaɬ/níx on this side. 3. tu
/níx from here.

nks, ʔnks habitually
(*proclitic*). 2. nks + t + l
ʔac/wé·x̣ xánʔ-x̣ He used
to live there. 3. ʔnks +
ʔac/ƛ̓aqʷ-s/éx̣-ni-cx k
You want to look out for
that.

nu-che-lip UWa Cowlitz
River below Cowlitz
Landing (*placename*).

/núkʷiɬ-: 1a. s/núkʷiɬ
nephew, niece (on man's
side). 1b. nx/núkʷiɬ-tn *pl.*
1c. s/núkʷiɬt-aw-i his
nephew.

.snū´nux̣ FBa dog salmon
Onchorhynchus keta; GGa
snoon-ocht large speckled
salmon; UWa snoon-ocht a
large speckled salmon with
stripes or belts around it
(*prob.* s/núnxʷ).

/nús- damp 1. /nús-ɬ, —
intr. 2. /nus-áy=tm'x
damp earth.

p

/palə́qʷ-: 1a. /plə́qʷ a
spring. 1b. /palə́qʷ-i his
spring.

/palúw'- leak. 1. /palúw'-ɬ,
— *intr.*

/paɬə́qʷ break open. 1a.
/paɬə́qʷ, — intr. (see
/pə́ɬqa- split ?).
/pá́ɬkʷu outside; FBa,b
pa´ɬko. 2. /pá?ɬkʷu-lm'
toward the outside, go
outside. 3. wilaxpa´ɬko FBa
go outside (prob. /wí-la?
/pá́ɬkʷu; see /wí- go on).
/paɬús tell a lie, bullheaded.
/pá́ɬx̣an-: 1a. s/pá́ɬx̣n
swamp, meadow, pasture;
GGb spáhl-hun island; FBa
spa´ɬxan valley. 1b.
s/pá́ɬx̣an-i his swamp. 2.
s/pá?ɬx̣n little swamp
dimin.
/pánaks(t)-: 1. /pánačš ten;
HH pánutç; AG,RL panutsh;
GGb,FR pah-natsh; EC pá-
nachs; FBa pa´netc; HT
páneč. 2a. /pánkst-l=šn
ten times. 2b.
/t'əmx/pánkst-l=šn one
hundred (times). 3.
/pánkst=l's ten dollars. 4.
/t'əmx/pánačš ten-fold. 5.
/pánačš kl t /?úc's LNJ
eleven; HH panutç-
kaltótsus; GGb pah-natsh
kul-totes´ŭs; FR pah-
natsh kult-ótes-us, pah-
natsh kult ótes; FBa
pa´nets kEɬ ō´ts.s. 6.
/pánačš kl t /sáli? twelve;
HH panutç-kaltsále; GGb
pah-natsh kult-sáh-leh;
FR pah-natsh kult-sah-

leh; FBa pa´nets kEɬ
sā´le. 7. /pánačš kl t
/ká?ɬi? thirteen. 8. /pánačš
kl t /mús fourteen. 9.
/pánačš kl t /čílačš
fifteen. 10. /pánačš kl t
/t'ax̣ə́m sixteen. 11.
/pánačš kl t /c'óps
seventeen. 12. /pánačš kl t
/cámus eighteen. 13.
/pánačš kl t /túwxʷ
nineteen. 14. pániks-txl-
tómux HH hundred; FR
páh-nak'sl-tome, páh-
naks'l-tó-me; EC pá-
nĭksħl-tumħ (prob.
/pánks-ɬ=tumx). 15. ō´ts
panEksɬto´mEx FBa one
hundred (prob. /?úc's
/pánks-ɬ=tumx). 16. ō´ts
panEks kEɬt ō´ts.s FBa one
hundred and one (prob.
/?úc's /pánks-ɬ=tumx kl
t /?úc's). 17. sa´les
paneksɬtū´mEx FBa two
hundred (poss. /sáli-s
/pánks-ɬ=tumx). 18.
pa´nets pa´neksɬtū´mEx
FBa one thousand (poss.
/pánačš /pánks-
ɬ=tumx).
/papáy- digit (?). 1a.
/papáy=aka? thumb, palm
(ENM); HH papaiaka nails;
GGb pa-pái-yak nail; FR
pa-pai-yak nails; EC pa-
paí-ya-ka fingernail. 1b.
/papáy=aka-n'-i his

thumb. 2a. /papáy=šn big toe, toenail, (sole of foot); HH papáiçin toes; GGb papái-shin toe; EC papaíŝhn toenail; FBa papai´cen toe; FBa pêpaicî´n toenail; HT papaíšən toe. 2b. /papáy=šn-i his big toe. 2c. /papá·y'=šn little toe, toes *dimin.*

/pástin-: 1a. /pástn White man (loanword; *see* Chinook Jargon *boston, pos-ton* 'white man, American', taken in turn from English *Boston*). 1b. /pástin-umx *pl.* 2. /pástin=u‡n', s/pástin=u‡n' American woman. 3. /pástin'=q, /pá?stin=q' English, talk English.

/patálan-: 1. s/patáln rock, rocks, stone; FBa spata´l.n; JH spα'tâ·lαn. 1b. s/patálan-i his rock. 2. s/patá·l'in-umx gravel, little rocks.

/pátaq-: 1a. /pátq tracks. 1b. /pátaq-i his tracks. 2. pa´t.kemen FBa footprint (*prob.* /pátq-mn). 3. /yə́q̓ʷ/pataq- step, take a step, walk. 3a. /yə́q̓ʷ/pataq-m, s/yə́q̓ʷ/patq-mit-n *mdl.*

patao´xemen FBa lobe of the ear (*poss.* /patáxʷ-mn).

/patáy's- visit. 1. /patáy's, s/patáy's-t-n *intr.* 2. /patáy's- visit. 2a. —, s/patáy's-mit-n *mdl.*

/pátk- reach for. 1. /pátk-mn, — *rel.*

patu´? TAb-mi Mt. Adams (Sahaptin name, *pátu* 'snowcap peak').

/paxʷán'x̣ when, at the same time.

/páy- foam, scum. 1. /páy-‡=kʷu foam, scum (on something being cooked).

pai´cîp FBa steamboat (*prob.* /páyəšəp) (loanword; *see* Chinook Jargon *piah-ship* 'steamer', taken in turn from English *fire* and *ship*).

/payúc·payuc cone (on a tree).

/pəcə́qʷ- dive. 1. /pacə́qʷ-m, s/pə́cqʷ-mt-n *mdl.* 2. s/pə́c·pcqʷ-mit-n he's diving *impf. mdl.*

/pə́ck‡ leaf, leaves, cabbage; GGb púts-ktl; FBa pî´tsek.‡.

spelewe´ FBa crane *Grus canadensis* (sandhill crane) (*prob.* s/pəlwé·?).

/pəl'ə́kʷa- have a hole, pierce, make a hole. 1. /pal'ə́kʷ-‡, —, /pal'ə́kʷ-n, —. 2. s/pə́l'·pəl'kʷa-mal-n making holes *impf.*

impl.tr. 3. ʔac/pal'ə́kʷ-ɬ hollow, hole. 4. /pál'kʷa-m'ɬ-tn' a drill. 5. s/pə́l'kʷ=iq-i its hole.

/pə́ɬ thick.

/pə́ɬqa- split. 1. —, s/pə́ɬqa-w-n *intr.* (= /paɬə́qʷ break open ?).

/pən- time. 1. /pən/ʔíɬ-s/kʷinm November (*see* /ʔíɬani- eat). 2. /pən/ʔíɬ-s/qʷuʔqʷstm=iʔɬ April (*see* /ʔíɬani- eat). 3. /pən/háps hop-picking time (*see* /háps hops). 4. /pən/ká when?; FBa pEn.ka´ (*see* /ká· where?). 5. /pən/ƛ̓aqám' Spring, March; FBa pEntlakā´m spring (*see* /ƛ̓aqám'- spring). 6. /pən/ƛ̓íx winter; GGb pent-leh'h; UWb,FR pin-klech; FBa,BH pEnLe´.x (*see* /ƛ̓íx cold). 7. /pən/ƛ̓íx=uliɬn storage place (*see* /ƛ̓íx cold). 8. /pən/mə́ɬk summer; HH punemútxlqu; GGb pen-ne-méhl-kie; UWb,FR pin-milkh; FBa pEnEmî´ltEk (*see* /mə́ɬk- summer). 9. /pən/náw/santi holiday time, December (*see* /náwa- old). 9a. /pən/náw'/san'ti-m'n holiday, July, Christmas (*see* /náwa- old). 10. /pən-s/kʷíti-m'ɬ Saturday, time to get rations (*see* /kʷíti-distribute). 11. /pən-s/q̓ʷáƛ̓-ši-tm-s t s/xís May (*see* /q̓ʷáƛ̓- pick). 12. /pən-s/tó·l'šn August (*see* /tó·l'xan- fruit, berries). 13. /pən/tíʔ-x this time (*see* /tíʔ- here, this). 14. /pən/típi-kʷn warrior (*see* /típi-). 15. pantolos HH winter; FBb pEntolo´s fall, autumn, late fall (*prob.* /pən/túlucn; *see* /túlucn ice). 16. /pən/xá·la-m'ɬ time to plant a garden (*see* /xála- plant). 17. /pən/xasílʔ-mn' raincoat (*see* /xasíliʔ- rain). 18. /pən/yáq'-s/mə́ɬk fall, autumn; HH puneáxsoman autumn; UWb,FR pin-yalk-so-milkh autumn (*see* /yáq'a- tip, fall). 19. /pən/yúpi-kʷn wartime (*see* /yúpi- war).

/pə́n- add to. 1. /pə́n-n, — *tr.* 2. /pén'-ši- add more to *appl.* 2a. —, s/pén'-ši-t-n *tr.*

/pə́n-: 1. s/pə́n wing, wings; GGb spínn; FBa .s'pî´n feather of an arrow. 1a. s/pə́n-i its wing; HH spúne wings.

/pə́na- land a canoe or boat. 1. /pə́n-ɬ, s/pə́na-w-n *intr.*

pu-natch GGa,UWa dog salmon *Onchorhynchus keta.*

/pə́nč–: 1. s/pə́nč squirrel ?*Sciurus griseus* (western gray squirrel), or ?*Tamiasciurus douglasi* (chickaree), or ?*Citellus lateralis* (golden-mantled squirrel).

/pə́n'– collapse, fall in. 1. /pə́n'-ɬ, — *intr.*

/pə́q uterus ??

/pə́qʷa– spill, pour out. 1. /pə́qʷ-ɬ, s/pə́qʷa-w-n, /pə́qʷ-n, s/pə́qʷ-t-n. 2. /pə́qʷ-ši– pour on, baptize *appl.* 2a. /pə́qʷ-š-n, s/pə́qʷ-ši-t-n *tr.* 3. /pə́qʷ/qal'– strain water out, drain. 3a. /pə́qʷ/qal'-n, — *tr.* (*see* /qalíʔ– water).

pə́s together with.

/pə́saʔ animal, dangerous being, malevolent Indian doctor woman; TAb-mi pɑ́ˑsa. 1b. /paséʔ-i his animal. 2. /péˑsaʔ bird, flying creature; GGb péh-sa bird. 3. /ps=áyq mosquito; UWb psi-ock; FBa pɛsaiˊɛk. 4. .spɛsaiˊɬtɛmɛx FBa ghost (*prob.* s/pəs-áy-ɬ=tmx).

/pəsén'–: 1. /péˑsn' younger sister; HH púsun sister; FBa pếˑᵣsɛn elder sister, younger sister; FBb pắˑsɛn younger sister. 1b. nx/pasén'-tn *pl.* 1c. /psn-áˑw'-i his younger sister. 1d. nx/pasén'-tan-i his younger sisters. 1e. GGb tsin-péss my sister; FR tsin-pess sister; EC nĭpě'sn (*prob.* c n/pə́sn' my younger sister.

/pəxʷ– lie. 1. /pəxʷ=áy's– tell a lie. 1a. /pəxʷ=áy's, — *intr.*

/pə́x̣ʷ– stain. 1. ʔac/pə́x̣ʷ a stain.

/pəx̣ʷ– ?? 1. /pəx̣ʷ-áy=aka index finger.

/pəyə́x̣ʷa– crumble. 1. /payə́x̣ʷ-ɬ, s/pə́yx̣ʷa-w-n, /payə́x̣ʷ-n, —.

/píʔx̣ʷ– crippled. 1. ʔac/píʔx̣ʷ=nk crippled in the legs.

pi´tspam TAb-mi [*no translation given; probably a Taitnapam Sahaptin name*].

/pícx̣ʷ, s/pícx̣ʷ a small gray bird (possibly thrush); TAb-mi Spi´tsx̣ᵘ snowbird.

/píɬi– scatter, spread out, distribute. 1. /píɬ-n, s/píɬi-t-n *tr.*

/pípa paper (loanword; *see* Chinook Jargon peh´-pa 'paper, letter, writing, book', taken in turn from English *paper*). 1b. pípa-ni

his paper. 2. /ʔax̣ét/pipa-
read. 2a. /ʔax̣ét/pipa,
s/ʔax̣ét/pipaʔ-n *intr.* (*see*
/ʔə́x̣- see). 3. /pó?t/pipa-
l'uʔɬ school (*see* /púti-
know).

/**píšpiš** cat *Felis domestica*;
FBa pi ́cpec; JH pí·ʃpɪʃ;
JHjp píṣpɪṣ (loanword; *see*
Chinook Jargon *pish-pish*
'cat'). 1b. /píšpiš-umx *pl.*
1c. /píšpiš-i his cat. 2a.
/pé?špiš kitten *dimin.* 2b.
/pé?špiš-umx *pl.* 2c.
/pé?špiš-i his kitten. 3.
/péšp=iɬ kitten.

/**plə́ms-** plum *Prunus* spp.
(loanword; see English
plums). 1. /plə́ms=an'ɬ
plum orchard.

/**púc̓ʷ-** get up late, be late
in the morning. 1.
/púc̓ʷ-ɬ, — *intr.*

spū ́kᴇls FBa top of the head
(*prob.* s/púkʷ=ls).

/**púla-** grow. 1. /púl-ɬ,
s/púla-w-n, /púl-n, —.
2. /púl-i its growing.

/**púqʷa-** moldy, mildew. 1.
/púqʷ-ɬ, s/púqʷa-w-n
intr.

/**púsa-** swell up. 1. /pús-ɬ,
s/púsa-w-n *intr.* 2.
ʔac/pús=ay's face is
swollen. 3. ʔac/pús·ps-m
mumps. 4. s/pó?s·ps-w-n
blistering *impf. intr.* 5a.

s/pús swelling. 5b. s/pús-i
its swelling.

/**pút-** just, only. 1. /pút-
akaʔ half done. 2.
/pút/kʷaɬ=lus t s/qʷíx̣
midnight (*see* /kʷə́ɬ-
divide). 3. s/put-s/cíx̣i-w-
n tit /ɬukʷáɬ sunrise (*see*
/cíx̣i- show). 4. s/put-
s/náma-t-n he just
finished it *impf. tr.* (*see*
/náma- done, finish). 5.
s/put-s/t'úla-w-anx I
just got home *impf. intr.*
(*see* /t'úla- arrive).

pū ́tᴇpt FBa ground squirrel
?*Spermophilus* sp(p). (*poss.*
/pútpt).

/**púti-** know. 1. /pút-n,
s/púti-t-n *tr.* 2. ʔac/pút-
al-i (?) her knowing. 3.
/pó?t-lk-mn lesson. 4.
/pó?t/pipa-l'uʔɬ school
(*see* /pípa paper). 5.
s/pót=alaka know how.

/**putis-** ?? 1. /putís-ɬ=kʷu
hornet.

/**pútmix-:** 1. /pútmx
downriver, down to the
river. 2. /pó?tmiš-m'
towards the river *mdl.* 3. tu
/pútmx up from the river.

/**púxʷ-** ?? 1. s/púxʷ-cši-s t
s/ʔé·til-n sweat bath *refl.*

/**púxʷ-** ?? 1. /púxʷ-ši- add
to (to increase value) *appl.*
1a. /púxʷ-š-n, s/púxʷ-
ši-t-n *tr.*

/púxʷ– smoke. 1. ʔac/pəxʷ–
   əm=ip tani already tanned.
   2. /pəxʷ–əm=ip– smoke a
   hide. 2a. /pəxʷ–əm=ip-n,
   — *tr.* 3. /púxʷ=isi-t-m
   smoked on the face *pass.*
/púxʷi– blow with the
   mouth. 1. —, s/púxʷi-t-n
   tr. 2. /púxʷ=iqi– blow a
   horn. 2a. /púxʷ=iq-n,
   s/púxʷ=iqi-t-n *tr.* 3.
   s/púxʷ·puxʷ=iʔqa–

mal-n he's blowing a horn
   impf. impl.tr.
poxe´ɬEn.ɬp FBa basket of
   cedar twigs.
/púy– bend. 1. /púy-n, — *tr.*
   2. ʔac/púy·puy-ɬ crooked
   (e.g. a stick).
/pyəx̣í, /pyax̣í bitterroots
   Lewisia rediviva (loanword;
   see Sahaptin *pyax̣í*
   'bitterroot'). 1b. /pyəx̣í-hi
   her bitterroots.

p'

p'a TAb-mi excrements; a
   yellow substance.
/p'ál– wake up. 1. /p'ál-ɬ,
   —, /p'ál-n, —. 2.
   ʔac/p'á·l-ɬ be awake.
/p'álan–: 1. p'áln' bark of a
   tree; HH palen bark; GGb,FR
   páh-len; FBa pā´l.n; JH
   p'â·lɑn' fir bark. 1b.
   /p'álan-i its bark.
/p'alé·č'–: 1. /p'alé·č'-m'
   inside out *mdl.* (*see*
   /p'ələk'– roll, turn over).
/p'áqʷ– fade. 1. —, s/p'áqʷ-
   mal-n *impl.tr.* 2. /p'áʔqʷ-
   m'ɬ gray. 3. ʔaks/p'áqʷ
   gray; FBa akspa´kᵘ. 4.
   ʔaks/p'áqʷ=l's gray rock.
   5. eks spa´konamts FBa
   roan (*prob.*
   ʔaks/p'áqʷ=namc). 6a.
   s/p'áqʷ=uyq ashes, dust;

EC spá-ko-yŭk ashes; FBa
   pa´qoiEk dust; FBa
   spa´koiEk ashes. 6b.
   s/p'áqʷ=uyq-i its ashes.
/p'asə́q̇ʷ– sprain. 1.
   /p'asə́q̇ʷ-n, — *tr.*
/p'ašə́xʷ– flat. 1.
   /p'ašə́xʷ-ɬ, — *intr.*
/p'át'a– splice, put end to
   end. 1. —, s/p'át'a-t-n *tr.*
/p'áx̣a– shine. 1. /p'áx̣-ɬ,
   s/p'áx̣a-w-n *intr.* 2. ʔaɬ
   c/p'áx̣ in the sun.
/p'ayə́ḱʷ blue jay *Cyanocitta
   stelleri* (steller's jay);
   mischievous; FBa paiû´qᵘ
   blue jay; JH p'ɑyu̇k' blue
   jay.
/p'é·l'– thin. 1. /p'é·l'-ɬ, —
   intr.
/p'én'– beside. 1. /p'é·n'-m
   aside, move aside *mdl.* 2.

/p'én=tmx beside, next to. 3. s/p'n-áy'=x̣ax-: 3a. s/p'n-áy'=x̣x neighbor. 3b. /p'n-áy'=x̣ax-i his neighbor. 4. /p'én/ən'ca beside me (*see* /ʔə́nca I, me). 5. /p'én-l/xawɫ by the road (*see* /xəwál- road). 6. /p'én'/cani beside him (*see* /cə́ni he, him). 7. /p'én'/inm beside us (*see* /ʔiním we, us). 8. /p'én'/nawi beside you (*see* /nə́wi you, *sg.*).

/p'étl-: 1. /p'étl-m' all over, completely.

/p'ə́č'm wildcat, bobcat *Lynx rufus*; EC pŭ-t͡sím; FBa pɛttcɛ´m lynx; JH p'ɑtʃ'ɑm'.

/p'ələ́k'- roll, roll over, turn over. 1. /p'alə́k'-n, s/p'ə́lk'-t-n *tr.* (*see* /p'alé·č'- inside-out). 2. /p'ə́lk'-cx, s/p'ə́lk'-cši-t-n *refl.* 3. /p'ə́lk'=iq-i-n-aʔ turn it inside-out! 4. /p'ə́l·p'əlk'-ši- swing around *appl.* 4a. —, s/p'ə́l·p'əlk'-ši-t-n *tr.*

/p'ələ́ƙʷ- dig up, root up. 1. /p'alə́ƙʷ-n, s/p'ə́lƙʷ-t-n *tr.* 2. ʔac/p'ə́lƙʷ=ip stump pulled over with roots sticking up. 3. /p'alə́ƙʷ=qas- pig *Sus scrofa*: 3a. /p'alə́ƙʷ=qs;

FBa pɛlu´xɛks. 3b. /p'alə́ƙʷ=qas-i his pig.

/p'ələ́qʷa- take out, pop out. 1. /p'alə́qʷ-ɫ, s/p'álaqʷa-w-n, /p'alə́qʷ-n, s/p'ə́lqʷ-t-n. 2. /p'ə́lqʷ-əc-t-m (?) bring it out *pass.*

/p'ə́ɫa- fall, fall off. 1a. /p'ə́ɫ or /p'ə́ɫ-ɫ, s/p'ə́ɫa-w-n *intr.* 1b. /p'ə́ɫ-n, — drop *tr.* 2. s/p'ə́ɫ=šq fog; EC spŭh̓ls͡hk cloud; FBa pî´ɫc.k (*see* /šə́q big white cloud).

/p'ə́n'c- ?? 1. ʔac/p'ə́n'c tani tit /qáwm' prepared camas.

/p'ə́xʷ-: 1a. s/p'ə́xʷ a boil. 1b. s/p'ə́xʷ-i his boil. 2. s/p'éʔxʷ pimple *dimin.*

/p'ə́x̣- smart, wise, know better. 1. /p'ə́x̣-ɫ, — *intr.* 2. ʔac/p'é·x̣-ɫ be smart *dimin.*

/p'ə́x̣- come to, revive. 1. /p'ə́x̣-ɫ, — *intr.*

/p'íʔi- tap on, touch. 1. /p'íʔ-n, s/p'íʔi-t-n *tr.* 2. /p'éʔ- tap on *dimin.* 2a. /p'éʔ-n, — *tr.*

/p'íc'- spray, sprinkle, squirt. 1. /p'íc'-ši- spray, sprinkle *appl.* 1a. /p'íc'-š-n, s/p'íc'-ši-t-n *tr.* 2. /p'íc'/qʷlmx- milk (a cow). 2a. /p'íc'/qʷlmx-n,

— *tr.* (*see* /qʷúlamx milk).
3. qi s/p'íc'-i t /qálʔ
faucet.

/p'íɬ- dig for, look for. 1.
/p'íɬ-n, — *tr.*

/p'íX̌i- flat. 1a. /p'íX̌-ɬ, —
intr. 1b. /p'íX̌-n, s/p'íX̌i-
t-n flatten *tr.* 2.
ʔac/p'íX̌·p'iX̌ flattened out.
3. ʔac/p'íX̌=ay's flat face. 4.
ʔac/p'íX̌=šn flat feet.

/p'íq'- scar. 1. /p'íq'-ɬ, —
intr. 2. ʔac/p'íq'=ay's scar
on the face.

/p'íq̓ʷluʔ rotten wood.

/p'itílstiʔ wheat. 1b.
/p'itíl'sti-n'i his wheat.

p̓itqʰl EC sea otter *Enhydra
lutris*; FBa pe᷄t.kuɬ otter;
JH p'ɪ̓·t'kw̥ɬ (*prob.*
/p'ítkʷɬ).

/p'íw' nighthawk *Chordeiles
minor* (common night-
hawk); FBa pē᷄uẋ
goatsucker.

/p'íẋ- roast underground. 1.
/p'íẋ-n, — *tr.*

/p'óʔ fart.

/p'óʔs- ?? 1. /p'óʔs=nk
mink (muskrat?) *prob.
Ondatra zibethicus*
(muskrat); FBa pô᷄sɛnɛk
muskrat.

/p'úc- float, float away. 1.
/p'úc-ɬ, — *intr.*
2.s/p'úc·p'c-w-n it's
floating *impf. intr.*

/p'úca- foam. 1. —,
s/p'úca-w-n (= /p'úc-
float ?). 2. s/p'úc·p'c-w-n
t /qálʔ rapids on a river
impf. intr.

/p'ús-: 1a. s/p'ús lungs; EC
spus; FBa .s'pu᷄s. 1b.
s/p'ús-i his lungs.

q

qa so that, instead, and.

q'ɑ̓'ɬ, q'ɑ̓''ɑɬ JH trout (*prob.*
/qáʔɬ).

qā᷄.tɛn FBa sweathouse; JH
sq'â·'ten' (*poss.* /qá·ʔ-
tn).

sqɑ̓tsɬ, sq'ɑtsɬ JH
arrowwood (*prob.* s/qácɬ).

/qalí- attack. 1. /qalí-n, —
tr. 2. /qalí-kʷani- fight. 2a.
/qalí-kʷn, s/qalí-kʷan-n,
/qalí-kʷani-x, —. 3.
/qalé·-kʷani- wrestle
dimin. 3a. —, s/qalé·-
kʷan-n *intr.* 4. /qalí-kʷa-
m'ɬ-tn' weapon. 5. /qalí-
kʷ=alakaʔ fighter.

/qalíʔ-: 1a. /qálʔ water,
river; HH,AG,RL kal water;
GGb kăh water; GGb káhl

river; FR kah water; FR kahl
river; EC kalˈl water; FBa
qaˊl water; BH qal. 1b.
/qalíʔ-i its water. 2.
kaˊn.ɬɬaɬ FBa saliva (*poss.*
/qálʔ=ɬnɬ). 3. /pə́qʷ/qalʼ-
strain water out, drain. 3a.
/pə́qʷ/qalʼ-n, — *tr.*
kaliˊtsɛnɛl FBa willow
(common) *Salix* sp(p).
(*prob.* /qalíc=nʼɬ).
qaˊls MJb-mi camas (or
another root?), *prob.*
Camassia sp(p).
qaɬ can, could (*irrealis*).
ska-móħl EC river canoe; JH
sqáˑmỏˑɬ; JHjp skɑmỏɬ
Chinook canoe (*prob.*
s/qamúɬ).
qaˊnɛks FBa paper.
/qanómʼ- quarrel. 1. ʔit
/qanómʼ-s kn I quarreled
with him *perf.* 2.
/qanómʼ=ɬn-cši-t-iɬt
they're quarreling *impf. refl.*
.nkêkaiˊaxa FBa shadow
(*prob.* n/qaqáy=ax̣n my
shadow).
qêˈqîˊm FBa red-headed
woodpecker; TAb-ly
qaqɑˊm woodpecker (red
head, tiny spot on wings)
(*prob.* /qaqə́m).
/qaqswéʔ hoof. 1b.
qaqswéʔ-i its hoof. 2.
kekauˊɛlscɛn FBa hoof
(*prob.* /qaqáwls=šn).

qas because, and. 2. qasi
because.
qas want, desiderative
(*enclitic*).
kaˊ.se FBa uncle (*prob.*
/qásiʔ).
/qašqáš strawberry roan
(loanword; *see* Sahaptin
qaˑšqáˑš 'strawberry roan').
1b. /qášqaš-i his
strawberry roan.
/qát- pet. 1. /qát-mn,
s/qát-mis-n *rel.* 2. /qáʔt-
like. 2a. qáʔt-mn, — *rel.* 3.
qʼaɬ /qát-nɬ nice, kind.
qaˊwinactpʼəˊn:
watciˑˊˑˑx̣utciˑˑx̣u
qaˊwinactpʼəˊn MJb-mi Are
you asleep yet? (*here* c =
[š]).
/qáwmʼ camas *Camassia*
sp(p).; JHjp qʼawm. 1b.
/qáwʼam-i her camas. 2.
ʔac/pʼə́nʼc tani tit
/qáwmʼ prepared camas
(*see* /pʼə́nʼc-).
/qáx̣- meet. 1. /qáx̣-t-
awlx-umx, s/qáx̣-t-
awll-iɬt *recip.* 2. ʔit /qáx̣-
tn-wʼlx-umx they met
each other *recip.* 3. ʔit
/qáx̣-tn-x kn we met each
other.
/qáx̣aʔ dog *Canis familiaris*;
HH kaxa; AG,RL kakha;
GGb,FR káh-ha; EC ká-ħa;
FBa qaˊxa; BH sqāˊxa; JH
qʼáˑx̣ɑʼ, qʼáˑx̣ɑ̇ʼ; JHjp

qὰx̣ɑ'. 1b. /qx̣ʔ-áwmx *pl.*
1c. /qax̣éʔ-i his dog. 1d.
/qx̣ʔ-áwmiš-i his dogs *pl.*
2a. /qά·ʔx̣aʔ little dog,
puppy *dimin.* 2b. /qx̣ʔ-
á·w'mx *pl.*

/qáy'x̣i- ?? 1. /qáy'x̣i=l's-
blind, dazzle. 1a.
/qáy'x̣i=l's-n, — *tr.*

/qémx̣- doubled up. 1.
/qémx̣-cx, — *refl.*

/qəlnús-: 1a. s/qə́lns cheek,
jaw, chin, chins; EC skalns
chin; FBa qa´lɛns; HT
qáləns chin. 1b. s/qəlnús-i
his chin, his jaw.

/qəɬə́x̣a- growl, be angry. 1.
/qaɬə́x̣-ɬ, s/qə́ɬx̣a-w-n
intr.

/qə́m'- smooth (water), still
air. 1. /qə́m'-ɬ, — *intr.*

/qənúx̣-: 1a. /qə́nx mouth;
HH kὺnix; AG,RL kunikh;
GGb,FR kún-neh; EC kŭn-
nĭ̈h mouth, lips; FBa
qê´nnɛx; FBb qɛnx̣,
qɛno´s; BH 'ka´dux̣ᵘ. 1b.
/qanús-i his mouth; FBb
qanu´se his mouth.

/qə́qa- choke, stick in throat.
1. /qə́q-ɬ, s/qə́qa-w-n
intr. 2. /qaq-ə́m choked
mdl.

kî´ṣiaka FBa drumstick
(*prob.* /qə́sy=akaʔ).

/qə́x̣- many, lots. 1. /qə́x̣-ɬ,
— *intr.* 2. /qə́x̣-wiwi,
/qéx̣-wiwi rich. 3.

/qə́x̣/itm-tn wealth, lots
of clothes (*see* ʔitámaʔ
clothing).

qi syntactic particle (*see
grammar* 2.7.3 and *appendix*
on *prefixes*).

/qílitn elk *Cervus elaphus*;
GGb,FR kȧi-let; EC ké-letn
bull elk; FBa kai´lētɛn,
kele´tɛn; JH q'ê·lɪ·tɑn,
q'î·lɪtɑn; JHjp qílɪtn. 2.
/qé·l'itn elk calf *dimin.* 3.
kala´tib FBa elk skin robe.

/qílk'- crawl. 1. —, s/qílk'-
mis-n crawl up to *rel.* 2.
s/qíl·qilk'-mit-n he's
crawling *impf. mdl.*

/qílq camas *Camassia* sp(p).;
EC ké-lŭk; FBa qe´lɛk
camas root; JH qí·lɑq,
q'é·l'ɑq', qî·lq.

/qín- want, like. 1. /qín-mn,
s/qín-mis-n *rel.* 2. /qín-s
want to (*followed by tr. or
intr. form*). 3. tom-tsi-en-
i-ken UWb to love, want; FR
tom-tsi-en-i-ken to love
(*poss.* /tám-či n/qín; *see*
/tám what?, thing).

/qinúy'- ?? 1. /qinúy'=ɬn'-
argue. 1a. —,
s/qinúy'=ɬn'-cši-t-n *refl.*

/qinúy'ɬn' wolf *Canis lupus*
(gray wolf); GGb keh-
noótl; EC ke-nún-h̄ln; FBa
kanū´ɬɛn; JH
sq'í'n'ὺ·yɬɑn'; JHjp
qɪnὺɪɬ.

ki´pixLE⁴ FBa hair seal, fur seal ?*Callorhinus ursinus* (northern fur seal), or ?*Phoca vitulina* (Harbor seal) (loanword; *see* Chinook -*gé·pixL* 'sea lion').

/qíq– hang up. 1. /qíq-n, — *tr.* 2. /qíq=⁴anal– choke, hang. 2a. /qíq=⁴n, —, /qíq=⁴anal-n, —.

/qíti– lift, pick up. 1. /qít-⁴, s/qíti-w-n, /qít-n, s/qíti-t-n.

/qíwal– smell. 1. —, s/qíwal-n *intr.* 2. /qiw=á⁴qs onion *Allium* sp(p).; EC ke-wá̄hlks; JH q'í·wá·⁴qs. 3. /qíw=nas smell through the nose. 3a. /qíw=nas, s/qíw=nas-n

intr. 4. /qíw=xan– track an animal, smell a track. 4a. —, s/qíw=xan-n *intr.* 4b. s/qíw=xn a track. 5. s/qiwá⁴=aln onion. 6. s/qíw⁴=kʷu ocean; HH skaíwitxlko sea; HH skéwitxlko river; AG,RL skewitkhlko river; GGb skéh-whlk sea; EC ské-wuh̄l-ku river; FBa ske´ᵘ⁴ko sea, salt, salty; HT skéʷ⁴ko sea.

qe´ EX FBa cold (weather).

/qíxʷ– fat. 1. /qíxʷ-⁴, — *intr.* 2. /qíxʷ-lx gain weight *dev.*

/qiy'áluqʷas–: 1a. /qiy'áluqʷs soup, broth. 1b. /qiy'áluqʷas-i his soup.

ql can, be able.

q'

/q'á?n berry sp., *poss.* ?*Crataegus douglasii* (black hawthorn); TAb-jc q'a?α´n berries similar to serviceberries, but grow in little bunches like crabapples; the bush is thorny.

/q'á?p short huckleberry, blueberry *Vaccinium* sp.; EC k̦ap blue huckleberries; JH q'α̇p shotberry; JHjp k'á·p

shotberry. 2. /q'á?p=an'⁴ huckleberry plant.

/q'ál'x̣i– get hurt, wound. 1a. /q'ál'x̣-m, s/q'ál'x̣-mt-n *mdl.* 1b. /q'ál'x̣-n, — *tr.* 2. ?ac/q'ál'x̣ crippled, limping; a wound. 3. ?ac/q'ál'·q'l'x̣ have a lot of wounds.

q'a⁴ (*see grammar* 2.7.1.)

/q'á⁴č'm' cougar (beaver?); FBa ka´⁴tcEm weasel (*prob.* weasel).

q'á·na·lʊ' JH a large trout *sp.*
(*prob.* /q'ánaluʔ).

/q'anápsu grass; GGb kún-
nup-so; UWb ka-nap-su
prairie.

/q'áp'a- heal up. 1. —,
s/q'áp'a-w-n *intr.*

/q'áxʷa- freeze, harden, set.
1a. /q'áxʷ-ɬ, s/q'áxʷa-
w-n *intr.* 1b. /q'áxʷ-aʔ-ɬ
pl. perf. intr. 2. s/q'áxʷ ice.
3. /q'áxʷ=akaʔ frostbitten
hands.

/q'áx̣a- paint, smear. 1.
/q'áx̣-ɬ, —, /q'áx̣-n, —.
2. /q'áx̣a-ctx tit /x̣áx̣
they're painting the house
impf. pass.

/q'áyc'- thread, twine. 1.
.sqai´.ts FBa thread of
Indian hemp Apocynum
cannabinum; HT .skaí.ic
thread (*prob.* s/q'áyc'). 2.
/q'áyc'-tan pack strap.

/q'ayúq̇ʷ swing, cradle. 1a.
/q'ayúq̇ʷ-i his swing. 2.
/q'ayó·q̇ʷ- sway, swing
back and forth. 2a.
/q'ayó·q̇ʷ-m,
s/q'ayó·q̇ʷ-mt-n *mdl.* 3.
kaia´kᵘomEn FBa swing,
hammock (*prob.*
/q'ayó·q̇ʷ-mn).

/q'áy'- ?? 1. /q'áy'=stq-tn'
kindling.

/q'ém'ɬ narrow. 2. /q'é·maɬ
slim.

/q'ét'a- fish, catch fish. 1.
/q'é·t'-m, s/q'é·t'-mit-n
mdl. 2. /q'ét'a-m'ɬ-tn'
bait, a hook. 3. /q'é·t'-mn'
implement for fishing.

/q'ə́kʷ- clot, clabber. 1.
/q'ə́kʷ-ɬ, — *intr.*

/q'əlá- camp. 1. /q'ə́l-m, —
mdl. 2. /q'al-ə́mn
campsite, camp, hotel. 3.
/q'al-ə́mn-tn
campground. 4. ʔal/q'ál-
m'-yus-m January: "a
month the people don't
camp out". 5. tit qi
s/q'alá-n-n /yəmyú the
whole camp (?).

/q'əláx̣an-: 1a. /q'əláx̣n
fence, corral. 1b. /q'láx̣an-i
his fence. 2. /sá·/q'lax̣n
build a fence.

/q'ələ́p'- coil up, bend. 1.
/q'alə́p'-ɬ, —, /q'alə́p'-
n, —. 2. ʔac/q'ə́lp'-cx be
coiled up *refl.*

/q'ə́lp'a- sway, swing. 1.
s/q'ə́l·q'lp'a-w-n he's
swaying back and forth
impf. intr.

/q'ə́ɬ sweet.

/q'ə́p soft (like cloth).

/q'əx̣áʔi- get muddy. 1. —,
s/q'əx̣áʔi-t-n *tr.* 2.
s/q'ə́x̣iʔ mud; FBa
.sqa'xe´i; BH sqa.xe´i.

/q'əx̣áp- tell a lie. 1. /q'ə́x̣p,
s/q'ax̣áp-n, /q'ax̣áp-n,
—. 2. ʔac/q'é·x̣p-stu-mx

he's unfaithful (to me?)
caus.

/q'íctm'x̌ fast, go on a fast.

/q'íc'x̌ thus, the same. 2. kən
q'íc'x̌ it seems that way. 3.
q'éc'i?x̌ that's the kind.

ka´ilet EG skunk cabbage
Lysichiton americanus
(*prob.* /q'ílt).

q'ím already.

/q'ímin-: 1a. /q'ímn
shoulder. 1b. /q'ímin-i his
shoulder. 1c. /q'ímin-
umiš-i his shoulders. 2.
/q'ím'=ax̌n upper arm,
shoulder blade (?)

/q'ít tomorrow (ENM); HH
qet; GGb kéht; FR keht; FBa
qe´.tɛt.

/q'itám without, not have
any, be gone.

/q'iwán'-: 1. s/q'iwán' plant
sp., prob. ?*Arctostaphylos
uva-ursi* (kinnikinnick); EC
ske-wán'ᵃ partridge-
berries; FBa skaᵘwa´n
bearberry berry and plant;
JH sq'í·wá·n' kinnickinick
berries, corn (*prob.*
kinnickinick).

/q'íwq- lock. 1. /q'íw'q-n,
— *tr.* 2. s/q'íwq a lock,
key.

/q'íw'- call, invite. 1. /q'íw'-
tas, s/q'íw'-tas-n *tr.*

/q'íx̌-: 1. s/q'íx̌ day,
daylight; HH sqaiex, sqex
day; AG,RL skhaiekh day;
EC at͡s-ḳéħħl day; FBa
.s'qe´x day. 1b. s/q'íx̌-i
his day. 2. /q'íx̌-m
daylight. 3. s/q'íx̌-ml-i its
burning. 4. s/q'íx̌·q'x̌-
w-n lightning, a light
flashes *impf. intr.* 5. s/q'íx̌-
tn day. 6. s/q'íx̌i-w-n it's
daytime, it's getting
daylight *impf. intr.*; HH
skexéwan light. 7. /q'éx̌-
light, shine, bright. 7a.
/q'éx̌-m'ɫ, s/q'éx̌-mal-n
impl.tr.; EC at͡s-kéa-ħa-
mȋhl light. 8. s/q'éx̌ light,
daylight. 9. /q'éx̌-am'ɫ-tn'
light, candle, torch. 10.
?aks/q'éx̌-m'ɫ silver. 11.
/q'ix̌-áy=tmix̌- get
daylight. 11a. —, s/q'ix̌-
áy=tmix̌-n *impf. intr.* 12.
/q'íx̌-ɫəqènqs (?) in the
morning. 13. .tsqê´.xɛltɛn
FBa light (*poss.* ?ac/q'íx̌-l-
tn). 14. /cam-s/q'íx̌
Tuesday. 15. /kan-al-
s/q'íx̌ Wednesday. 16.
/mus-al-s/q'íx̌ Thursday.
17. /cilks-t-al-s/q'íx̌
Friday. 18. ɫ tit s/q'íx̌
today; HH tetsxéx; GGb te-
téht atskéh. 19. ɫ tit
s/q'é?x̌ today. 20. na-
kóus-keh GGb day (*prob.*
/nak'-áw-s/q'ix̌ one day).
21. /taw'ət s/q'íx̌ Sunday,
big day.

/q'íx̌ʷus tomorrow (LNJ).

/q'íyax^wm worm.

/q'iyáx̣-: 1a. q'íyx̣ guts. 1b. /q'ayáx̣-i his guts. 2. /q'é·yx̣ navel, belly button *dimin.*

/q'iyúx^w-: 1a. s/q'iyúx^w bow; tanning frame; prop; temporary shelter. 1b. /q'iyúx^w-i his bow.

q^w

/q^wal- ?? 1. /q^wal=é·n'u?s- get hungry. 1a. —, s/q^wal=é·n'u?s-t-n *intr.*

qwɑ́lɑstì' JH smelt ?*Osmeridae* sp(p).; JHjp qwɑlístɪ' (*prob.* /q^wáləsti?).

/q^wálitn-: 1. s/q^wálitn a large clam sp.

.sqwa´lux̣ FBa bachelor.

/q^wá·l'ɬ a light.

/q^wamá·l'm slow.

/q^wán- fear, be afraid of. 1. /q^wán-tas, — *tr.* 2a. ?ac/q^wán-u? afraid; a coward. 2b. ?ac/q^wán-u?-i his fear. 3. /q^wané·- scare; insult. 3a. /q^wané·-n, — *tr.*

/q^wáq^w-: 1. s/q^wáq^w raven *Corvus corax* (common raven); FBa qwāqᵘ; TAb-mi qwaqᵂ; JH qwá·qw̥, q'wɑq'w̥.

/q^watíx̣a? body louse; EC qatíħa grayback louse; FBa kwote´xa louse; JH kwɑtí·xɑ'. 1b. /q^watix̣í?-i his louse.

/q^watúx̣^w-: 1a. /q^wátx̣^w trap for animals, traps. 1b. /q^watúx̣^w-i his trap.

qwáx HH salt.

/q^way'á-: 1. /q^wáy'=ɬ child, baby; HH kwaíítxl boy; HH tskwaíítxl, tçitskwaíitxl girl; GGb kwí-ihl boy; UWb quilt young; FBa kwai´eɬ young. 2a. s/q^way'á=iɬ baby; HH kwaiaíítxl infant, child; GGb skwi-ái-ihl infant, child; FR skwai-ai- ihl infant; EC sqai-yaí'ħl; FBa kwaiai´.ɬ infant; FBa skwo´iai.ɬ child; FBa .skwaiai´.ɬ doll; JH sqwɑ'yá·yɬ small baby. 2b. s/q^way'áy=iɬ-umx *pl.* 2c. s/q^way'á=iɬtil-i her baby. 3. ?it wi /q^wáy'=ɬ have a baby.

/q^wéx̣i?x^w (*see* /q^wíx̣- night) morning, early; HH kwéxaióxu morning; GGb kwéh-a-hài-hu morning; FR kwéh-a-hai-hu morning; FBb qwē´xeᵘx dawn; FBb kwa´xeux̣ morning. 2. /qʷéx̣iʔxʷ-mn breakfast.

qwûts FBa leg (*poss.* /qʷə́ts). 2. kwuˊtesumox FBa leg (*poss.* /qʷə́tis-umx legs).

/qʷə́cx̣aʔ-: 1. s/qʷə́cx̣aʔ meadowlark *Sturnella neglecta* (western meadowlark); FBa kʷûˊtsx̣a; TAb-mi qutsx̣aˊ lark. 2. s/qʷécx̣aʔ=iʔɬ little meadowlark.

/qʷələ́m-: 1a. s/qʷə́lm heart; HH skwálum; GGb,FR skwúl-lum; EC skó-lu̧m; FBa,BH .skwêˊlEm. 1b. s/qʷalə́m-i his heart. 2. autsis-kwil-lum GGb friend (*prob.* /ʔúc's s/qʷə́lm).

/qʷə́ɬx̣aʔ roe, salmon eggs.

/qʷə́na- sting. 1. /qʷə́n-c it stung me *perf. tr.* 2. /qʷə́n·qʷn nettles *Urtica dioica*; JH qwɑ̇n'qwɑ̇n'. 3. /qʷə́na-m'ɬ-tn' nettles.

kwêˊnnts FBa sea gull Larus spp. (*prob.* s/qʷə́ns).

/qʷə́q- become chapped. 1. /qʷə́q-ɬ, — *intr.*

/qʷə́s- sorrel. 1. ʔaks/qʷə́s sorrel; FBa aks kwîˊs chestnut. 2. kupāˊks kwîˊs FBa sorrel (*prob.* /k̓ʷə́p ʔaks/qʷə́s; *see* /k̓ʷə́p very). 3. /qʷas-áy'=qn-i its mane (sorrel mane ?).

sqwɑ̇y' JH canoe type (*poss.*

s/qʷə́y').

/qʷícqʷi- ?? 1. ʔit /sítm /qʷícqʷi-x s/ƛ̓á-m'ɬ t s/ə́x̣t=kʷlx looking for spirit power.

/qʷíla- bleed. 1. /qʷíl-ɬ, s/qʷíla-w'-n *intr.* 2a. s/qʷíɬ blood; HH skwaitxl; AG,RL skwaitkhl; GGb skwéhtl; FR skwéh-itl; EC sqeh̄l; FBa skwaiˊ.ɬ. 2b. s/qʷíl-i his blood.

/qʷílx̣ʷ in-law.

skwoiˊtlEm FBa war spear (*prob.* s/qʷíƛ̓-m).

/qʷíx̣-: 1. s/qʷíx̣ night; HH kwaíeq; AG,RL kwaiekh; GGb quéʼh; FBa kweˊxᵘ; FBa qweˊx dark. 2. s/qʷéx̣ night. 3a. /qʷíx̣-kʷu get dark on. 3b. ʔit /qʷíx̣-kʷu kn it got dark on me *perf. pass.* 4. s/qʷéx̣-kʷu become night. 5. /qʷíx̣-l-tn, s/qʷíx̣-l-tn night, darkness; HH sqwéxultun darkness. 6. kwEtskweˊxtaˊn FBa dusk, evening (*prob.* /kʷac s/qʷíx̣ tan; *see* /kʷac a little, somewhat). (See /qʷéx̣iʔxʷ morning, early.)

/qʷíym moss.

/qʷóʔ drink. 1. /qʷóʔ, s/qʷóʔ-n *intr.*; FBa tEˈkwoˊ (*prob.* t /qʷóʔ). 2. kwáll-la GGb drink (*prob.* /qʷóʔ-laʔ drink!). 3a.

/qʷóʔ-tn' cup; FBa
kâ´ɛtɛn. 3b. /qʷóʔ-tn-
umx *pl.* 3c. /qʷóʔ-tn-i his
cup.

/qʷóqʷstm-: 1a.
s/qʷóqʷstm=iʔɬ egg,
eggs; HH skwoxstumítxl;
GGb s'kaúks tmetl; FBa
skowa´kstɛmiɬ. 1b.
s/qʷóqʷstm=iɬt-il-i its
egg. 2. ɬka´tsɛmin e
skowa´kstɛmiɬ FBa
eggshell. 3. /pən/ʔíɬ-
s/qʷuʔqʷstm=iʔɬ April
(*see* /ʔíɬani- eat).

qo´kwɛn FBa lariat.

/qʷúlamx̣ milk; FBa
ku´lamux̣ breast (of
female); HT kúlamux̣ breast
of female. 1b. /qʷúlmš-i
his milk. 2. /p'íc'/qʷlmx-
milk (a cow). 2a.
/p'íc'/qʷlmx-n, — *tr.*

kumɬ EG crab apple (unripe)
Malus fusca (Pacific crab
apple) (*prob.* /qʷúmɬ; *see*
Lower Chehalis *sqʷúm'*,
Quinault *qʷəm'* ripe crab
apples). 1b. ku´mtlas EG
crab apple plant (-*as* is the
Sahaptin suffix for plant).

/qʷúpi- pad. 1a. /qʷúp-ɬ,
—, /qʷúp-n, —. 1b.
/qʷúpi-n-aʔ pad it! 2.
qo´pcɛn FBa stockings,
socks (*poss.* /qʷúp=šn).

/qʷút- blister. 1. /qʷút-ɬ, —

intr. 2a. ʔac/qʷút-ɬ a
blister. 2b. s/qʷút-i his
blister.

/qʷúx̣ʷ- white. 1.
ʔaks/qʷúx̣ʷ white; HH
ksqwóx; AG,RL kskhwokh;
GGb,FR uk-skóh; EC aks-
kóh; FBa ɛksqō´xᵘ. 2.
ʔac/qʷóx̣ʷ-m'ɬ whiten
impl.tr. 3. ʔaks/qʷúx̣ʷ-
ay=aqn white mane. 4.
ʔaks/qʷúx̣ʷ=iʔps white
tail. 5. ʔaks/qʷúx̣ʷ=ls have
gray hair. 6.
ʔaks/qʷúx̣ʷ=l's white
round object. 7.
ʔaks/qʷúx̣ʷ=l'wltxʷ white
house. 8. /qʷúx̣ʷ=ɬc'iʔ
swan, *prob. Cygnus
columbianus* (tundra swan);
EC skóhhl-t͡si; FBa
.sqo´x̣ɛltse; JH
q'ó·x̣ɬts'ɪ'. 9.
axskoxsī´ɬɛmux̣ FBa
white man (*prob.*
ʔaks/qʷúx̣ʷ /síɬmx; *see*
/síɬmix- man). 10.
.tsko´ke tse´ux̣we FBa
silver (*poss.* ʔaks/qʷúx̣ʷ
ʔac/yáyx̣ʷi; *see* /yáyx̣ʷi-
expensive, valuable).

qo´x̣.kox FBa mourning dove
Zenaida macroura (*poss.*
/qʷúx̣ʷqʷux̣ʷ/).

/qʷúx̣ʷa- bark. 1. /qʷúx̣ʷ-cx
or /qʷux̣ʷa-cx, s/qʷúx̣ʷ-
cši-tn *refl.*

/q̓ʷac'ə́ɬ–: 1. /sq̓ʷac'ə́ɬ chipmunk *Eutamias* sp(p).; FBa .skwê´ tsEɬ.

/q̓ʷál– ?? 1. s/q̓ʷál=ax̣n merganser, fish duck, *prob.* ?*Mergus merganser* (common merganser).

/q̓ʷalaní?–: 1a. /q̓ʷalán? ear; HH qoalán; AG,RL khoolan; GGb,FR kwal–lan; EC ḳwa–lá'n; FBa kwêla´n; HT kwêlán. 1b. /q̓ʷalan–áwmx *pl.* 1c. /q̓ʷəlní?–i his ear. 1d. /q̓ʷəln–áwmiš–i his ears.

/q̓ʷalí– smoke. 1. /q̓ʷalí–mɬ, s/q̓ʷalí–mal–n *impl.tr.* 2a. /q̓ʷalé–mɬ–tn' tobacco; HH kwalémᴜtxlin; GGb kwal–lab–´tl; FR kwal–láb–tl, kwal–lab–tl; EC qa–lĕ–mȋh̄ltn; FBa kwola´mEɬtEn; JH q'wá·læ̆·m'ᵅɬtɑn'. 2b. /q̓ʷalé–mɬ–tan–i his tobacco. 3a. /q̓ʷalé–m'ɬ–tn' pipe; EC qa–lă–mȋh̄ltn. 3b. /q̓ʷalé–m'ɬ–tan–i his pipe.

/q̓ʷalit'– ?? 1a. /q̓ʷalít'=k'n' skin. 1b. /q̓ʷəlt'=k'án'–i his skin.

/q̓ʷá·l's, /q̓ʷáls raccoon *Procyon lotor*; EC ḳwals; FBa kwā´l.s; JH k'wá·l's, k'wɑlá·s.

/q̓ʷál'x̣ʷ raspberry, (serviceberry, thimbleberry), *prob.* ?*Rubus parviflorus* (thimbleberry); EC ḳwá–lᴜh̓ red raspberries; JH q'wá·lox̣w̱, q'wá·lᵒx̣w. 2. /q̓ʷál'x̣ʷ=an'ɬ raspberry bush.

/q̓ʷáƛ̓– lay down. 1. /q̓ʷáƛ̓–n, — *tr.* 2. /q̓ʷáƛ̓–tx̣ʷ– lay down for *appl.* 2a. s/q̓ʷáƛ̓–tx̣ʷ–cal–n he's laying it down for me *impf. tr.*

/q̓ʷáƛ̓– pick. 1. /q̓ʷáƛ̓–ši– pick *appl.* 1a. s/q̓ʷaƛ̓–ə́š–i her picking, what she picked. 2. /pən–s/q̓ʷáƛ̓–ši–tm–s t s/x̣ís May.

/q̓ʷás–: 1. s/q̓ʷás crane, *prob. Ardea herodias* (great blue heron); FBa .s'kwa´ sˢ; TAb–fn sq'was.

/q̓ʷatə́x̣ʷ– fool. 1. nks + tx̣ʷ/q̓ʷatə́x̣ʷ–st–m get fooled *caus. pass.*

/q̓ʷátx̣ʷ bat, various *Chiroptera*.

/q̓ʷát'a– boil over, run over. 1. —, s/q̓ʷát'a–w–n *intr.*

/q̓ʷáx̣– get mad. 1. /q̓ʷáx̣=iq–ši– be mad at, threaten *appl.* 1a. /q̓ʷáx̣=iq–š–n, s/q̓ʷáx̣=iq–ši–t–n *tr.* 2. q'aɬ /q̓ʷáx̣–n=ɬna–t–i his getting mad.

/q̓ʷax̣ə́nw- ?? 1. /q̓ʷax̣ə́nw-ay=aka little finger; EC sqa-ħún-u-wai-ya-ka fingers.

/q̓ʷax̣ʷə́-: 1a. /q̓ʷax̣ʷə́-mn knife; HH kwaxómun; AG,RL kwakhomun; GGb kwo-hó-min; EC ḳwaħómn; FBa koˊxomEn. 1b. /q̓ʷax̣ʷə́-min-um'x pl. 1c. /q̓ʷax̣ʷə́-min-i his knife.

squai-i ihl GGb shovel-nosed canoe; FBa skwaiaiˊElut bark canoe; HT skwaiaíəlut bark canoe; JH sq'wȧy'áˑytɪtwɑt shovel-nose canoe (prob. s/q̓ʷay'áyt=ut; see Upper Chehalis qˊʷay'áit).

/q̓ʷáy's plant sp. (the membrane in the middle of its leaves was used on boils).

/q̓ʷél'xʷič white duck; TAb-jc kwɛˊlkwuc.

/q̓ʷə́la- ripe. 1. /q̓ʷə́l-t, s/q̓ʷə́la-w-n intr. 2. /q̓ʷalí- bake, cook. 2a. /q̓ʷalí-n, s/q̓ʷalí-t-n tr. 3. kwîˊl (saˊpEleˊl) FBa bread (prob. /q̓ʷə́l /saplə́l; see /saplə́l bread).

q̓ʷə́t so.

/q̓ʷə́té- mark, write, design, brand, vote. 1a. /q̓ʷə́té-m't, s/q̓ʷə́té-m'l-n impl.tr. 1b. /q̓ʷə́té-n, — tr. 2a. /q̓ʷə́t a brand, mark,

design. 2b. /q̓ʷə́t-i its marks, its design. 3a. Ɂac/q̓ʷə́t spots, design, something written. 3b. kt͡sqaħl EC it is marked. 4. Ɂac/q̓ʷéɁt spots. 5. /q̓ʷətéɁ-s- sign for appl. 5a. /q̓ʷətéɁ-s-c he signed for me perf. tr. 6. /q̓ʷəté-ši- write to appl. 6a. /q̓ʷəté-š-n, s/q̓ʷəté-ši-t-n tr. 7a. /q̓ʷəté-m't-tn' book, tablet, pencil, pen; FBa kwotaˊmEtten pencil. 7b. /q̓ʷəté-m't-tan'-i his book. 8. 'ɑtsq'wáˑtáˑ'p JH spotted butt (in reference to a placename). 9. Ɂac/q̓ʷət=éˑčn native speckled trout. 10. Ɂac/q̓ʷət=íl's spotted rock. 11. /q̓ʷət-ál=ičn design on a basket. 12. Ɂit /q̓ʷəté-n-n x-Ɂátt/ənca she wrote it to me (see Ɂə́nca I, me).

/q̓ʷə́mx-: 1. s/q̓ʷə́mx sweathouse.

/q̓ʷəyə́pa- wilt. 1. /q̓ʷayə́p-t, s/q̓ʷə́ypa-w-n intr.

/q̓ʷíc' dirty. 1. /q̓ʷíc', — intr. 2. /q̓ʷíc'=ay's dirty face. 3. /q̓ʷíc'=ps-m dirty neck. 4. /q̓ʷíc'=s dirty face.

/q̓ʷíc'i- smash, mash, grind, break in pieces. 1. /q̓ʷíc'-t, —, /q̓ʷíc'-n, s/q̓ʷíc'i-t-n. 2. /q̓ʷéˑc'-am't-tn' pestle;

FBa kwä´.tsamEɬtEn mortar.

/q̓ʷílɬ war paint.

/q̓ʷíɬ- ?? 1a. /q̓ʷíɬ=p root; EC qeħlp stump; FBa kwai´lp root of tree; HT qwaíɬp root of tree; JH q'wɪ·ɬp stump. 1b. /q̓ʷíɬ=ap-umx *pl.* 1c. /q̓ʷíɬ=ap-i its roots. 2. /q̓ʷéɬ=ap=lm'x wild celery ?*Apiaceae.*

/q̓ʷíɬi- itch. 1a. /q̓ʷíɬ-ɬ, s/q̓ʷíɬi-w-n *intr.* 1b. /q̓ʷíɬ-n, — scratch *tr.* 2. /q̓ʷíɬi- scratch oneself. 2a. /q̓ʷíɬi-cx, s/q̓ʷíɬ-cši-t-n *refl.*

sq'wê·wq' JH a gray-colored duck.

/q̓ʷíx̣- blue. 1. ?aks/q̓ʷíx̣ blue; HH ksqwex black; HH kuqwéx blue, green; GGb uks-kwé'h; FR uks-kwék; FR uks-kwe'h yellow; EC aks-qíüħ blue, green; FBa Eks'kwē´xᵘ. 2. /q̓ʷí?x̣=al's blue round object. 3. /q̓ʷé·x̣-a?=ičn blueback salmon ?*Oncorhynchus kisutch* (young Coho salmon).

/q̓ʷó·?ayq belch.

/q̓ʷó?c-: 1. ?aks/q̓ʷó?c a little while. 2. /q̓ʷó·c-an a little while, a little bit, soon, well.

/q̓ʷól'- happy. 1. /q̓ʷól'-ɬ, — *intr.* 2. /q̓ʷó·l'-ts-mi he made up with you. 3. ?ac/q̓ʷó·l-ts-wlx-umx they like each other *recip.*

/q̓ʷumə́t-: 1a. q̓ʷúmt head; HH qomut; AG,RL khomut; GGb,FR kóme-et; UWb,FR ko-mit forehead; EC ḳómut; FBa qo´m.t; FBb q!o·mEt, q!o·´m·t. 1b. /q̓ʷumə́t-i his head. 2. /q̓ʷumé·t-i his little head *dimin.*

/q̓ʷúx̣ʷ- smoke. 1. /q̓ʷúx̣ʷ-m, s/q̓ʷúx̣ʷ-mt-n *mdl.* 2. s/q̓ʷúx̣ʷ smoke; gunpowder; EC skoħ smoke; FBa .sqō´x gunpowder. 3. .s'qo´xom FBa smoke (*prob.* s/q̓ʷúx̣ʷ-m). 4. /q̓ʷúx̣ʷ=ayqs suck in smoke. 5. /q̓ʷúx̣ʷ=iqs-be bothered by smoke. 5a. —, s/q̓ʷúx̣ʷ=iqst-n *intr.* 5b. /q̓ʷúx̣ʷ=iqs-s-n, — smoke *tr.* 6. kwo´xElotsEn FBa soot (*poss.* /q̓ʷúx̣ʷ=lucn).

/q̓ʷúyuxʷ- crooked (e.g. a road). 1. /q̓ʷúyuxʷ-ɬ, — *intr.*

/q̓ʷúyx̣-: 1. s/q̓ʷúyx̣ arrow.

S

/sáʔa– do, make. 1. /sáʔ-ɬ,
/sáʔa-w-n, /sáʔ-n,
(s)/sá·-t-n. 2. /sá-m'ɬ,
(s)/sá-ml-n make *impl.tr.*
3. /sáʔ-ši- make for *appl.*
3a. /sáʔ-š-n, — *tr.* 4.
/saʔ=áḱʷt-il-iɬt they're
going to have a funeral
impf. intr. 5. /saʔ-ál-ɬ=šn
make moccasins *perf. intr.*
6. /saʔ=én'p make a bed
perf. intr. 7. /saʔ=én'p-ši-
make a bed for *appl.* 7a. —,
/saʔ=én'p-ši-t-n *tr.* 8.
/səʔ=ínp a bed or mat with
a blanket on top upon which
a bride is seated while
dowry gifts are piled around
her. 9. /saʔ-úɬ=x̣ax-n
build a house *impf. intr.* 10.
/saʔ-úɬ=x̣-ši- build a
house for *appl.* 10a. /saʔ-
úɬ=x̣-šn, — *tr.* 11.
/sá/ʔayuʔ- use for
medicine or seasoning. 11a.
—, /sá/ʔayuʔ-t-n *tr.* (*see*
/ʔayóʔ medicine). 12.
/sá/ʔayuʔ-či used it for
medicine *perf.* (*see* /ʔayóʔ
medicine). 13. /sáʔ/kʷilt
make a quilt *perf. intr.* (*see*
/kʷílt quilt). 14.
/sáʔ/maksns make
moccasins *perf. intr.* (*see*
/máʔksns moccasin). 15.
/sá/ʔəmx̣kʷu- make a
cedar-root basket. 15a.
/sá/ʔəmx̣kʷu,
/sá/ʔəmx̣kʷuʔ-n (*see*
/ʔəmx̣kʷu cedar-root
basket). 16. /sáʔ/stakn
make stockings (*see* /stákn
stockings). 17. /sáʔ/wəl-n
making a canoe *impf. intr.*
(*see* /wíl- canoe). 18.
/saʔ/x̣áw'il- make a road.
18a. —, /saʔ/x̣áw'il-n (*see*
/x̣əwál- road). 19.
sa´ts'ɑɬ TAb-mc Black
River (in Upper Chehalis
territory) (*prob.* /sá/cəl'ɬ;
see /cél'ɬ lake). 20.
/sá/k'axʷoʔ- grease. 20a.
/sá/k'axʷoʔ-n, — (*see*
/k'axʷóʔ grease). 21.
/sá·/nax̣=nut plan, agree
(*see* /nax̣-). 22.
/sá·/nax̣=nut-ši- plan
appl. 22a. /sá·/nax̣=nut-
š-n, — *tr.* (*see* /nax̣-). 23.
/sá·/q'lax̣n build a fence
perf. intr. (*see* /q'əláx̣an-
fence). 24. /sá/saplal-n
making bread *impf. intr.*
(*see* /saplǝl bread). 25.
/sa-s/íɬan-i her cooking
(*see* /ʔíɬani- eat). 26.
/sá/sult- salt. 26a.
/sá/sult-n, — *tr.* (*see*
/súlt- salt). 27. /ʔə́xʷ-ɬ qi
s/sáʔ-n-ml-i it's doing it
strangely.

/**sá?qʷs** mountain goat *Oreamnos americanus*.

/**sác–** ?? **1.** /sác=i?q-i its inside (e.g. a bucket), its bottom (*see* ?ác=ayq inside). **2.** /sác=inwas-i its stomach, its insides; FBa sê´tsɛmus stomach; FBa .sa´tcinos inside bark of a tree (*prob.* /sac=ínus).

satska´ustɛn FBa grave.

/**sác'u?** fish spear. **1b.** /sác'u?-ni his fish spear.

/**sákp–** ?? **1.** sɛksa´k.pɬɛɬ FBa feather bonnet.

/**sákʷa–** whisper. **1.** /sákʷ-n, /sákʷa-t-n *tr.*

sā´kotaxolwɛ´ɬtx̣ᵘ FBa bark lodge, tent; HT sá·kotaxolwəɬtx bark lodge; HT sá·kotaxolwə́ɬtxʷ tent.

/**sá·k̓ʷ,** nš/sá·k̓ʷ SH Mount St. Helens.

/**sáli?** two; HH,AG,RL sale; GGb sáh-leh; FR sah-leh; EC sál-li; FBa,BH sā´le (*see* /cám– two). **1b.** /sály-umx *pl.* **2.** /tál'/sali? (ENM) twelve; EC tál–sal. **3.** /t'əmx/sáli? both, double, together. **4.** /t'əmx/sáli-yumx each other, together *pl.* **5.** /pánačš kl t /sáli? twelve (LNJ); HH panutç-kaltsále; GGb pah-natsh kult-sáh-leh; FR pah-natsh kult-sah-leh; FBa

pa´nets kɛɬ sā´le. **6.** sa´les paneksɬtū´mɛx FBa two hundred (*poss.* /sáli-s /pánks-ɬ=tumx).

/**sálti** salty (loanword; *see* English *salty*).

/**sálwaxʷ** Chinook salmon; GGa sal-a-wah salmon used for salting; GGb sál-o-wéh'hu fall salmon; UWa Sal-a-wah middle-sized salmon with silver sides; FR sál-o-weh-hu fall salmon; FBa sa´luwox silver or coho salmon; JH sá·lwɑnuxw̥ silverside.

/**sál'–** ?? **1.** /sál'=ičn, /sál'=kn-n put a load on a horse *intr.*

/**sál'c–** ?? **1.** /sál'c=il'qas-: **1a.** /sál'c=il'qs dress; EC sa-wi-t͡sí-lŭks skirt; FBa sau´tselɛks Indian skirt or kilt. **1b.** /sál'c=l'qas-i her dress. **2.** LŪk sau´tselɛks FBa apron (*prob.* /ƛ́úk̓ʷ /sál'c=il'qs; *see* /ƛ́úk̓ʷ above, high). **3.** /táxʷ/sal'c=il'qs buy a dress.

/**sáman–:** **1a.** /sámn, /sémn fish (loanword; *see* English *salmon*). **1b.** /sáman-i his fish. **2.** /ƛ̓a/sáman fish, go fishing. **2a.** /ƛ̓a/sámn, — *intr.* **2b.** /ƛ̓a/sáman-i his fishing.

sā´mɛɬko FBa herring

Clupea harengus (Pacific herring) (*poss.* /sám-ɬ=kʷu).

/**sánti** Sunday, week (loanword; *see* Chinook Jargon *sun´-day* 'Sunday, week, flag', taken in turn from English *Sunday*). 2. /sán'ti-mn' flag. 3. /cám/santi two weeks. 4. /nak'-áw/santi one week. 5. /nám/santi Monday. 6. /náw/santi holiday. 7. /náw'/san'ti-m'n flag. 8. /pən/náw/santi holiday time, December. 9. /pən/náw'/san'ti-m'n holiday, July, Christmas.

/**sápan–**: 1a. /sápn daughter-in-law. 1b. /sápan-aw-i his daughter-in-law.

/**saplə́l** bread; FBa sa´pEle´l flour (loanword; *see* Chinook Jargon *sap´-o-lill* 'wheat, flour, bread'; further derivation is unclear). 1b. /saplə́l-i his bread. 2. kwî´l (sa´pEle´l) FBa bread (*see* /q̓ʷə́la-ripe). 3. /sá/saplal-n making bread *impf. intr.*

sa´**p.elEks** FBa old style apron; HT sáp.eleks apron (*prob.* /sáp'=il'qs).

/**saqáˑx̣–** make fun of, laugh at. 1. /saqáˑx̣-mi-tawɬ he made fun of us *perf. rel.* 2. /saqáˑx̣-tn– mock, make fun of. 2a. /saqáˑx̣-tn-mn, — *rel.*

/**sása** saucer (loanword; *see* English *saucer*). 1b. /sása-yum'x *pl.*

/**sáˑtə–** add to. 1. /sáˑtə-x, — *caus.*

/**sáwac'–**: 1a. /sáwc' bracelet. 1b. /sáwac'-i her bracelet. 1c. /sawác'-umiš-i her bracelets *pl.*

/**sawítak–**: 1a. /sawítk wild carrot ?*Apiaceae*. 1b. /sawítak-i her wild carrots.

/**sáw'la–** ask. 1. /sáw'li-x, s/sáw'la-y-n *caus.* 2. /sáw'la-ɬikʷn ask oneself. 3. /sáw'li-tmɬi- ask for. 3a. /sáw'li-tmɬi-x, — *appl.?* *caus.* 4. /sáw'li-tuxʷt ask him for it *appl. tr.*

sau´**xakEn** FBa handle of a root digger.

/**saxʷúcuɬn** iron; HH saxotsótxlin; UWb saw-holt-so-tle; FBa saho´tsuɬEn. 2. /saxʷó·ʔcuɬn wire *dimin.*

/**sáx̣–** scratch. 1. /sáx̣=kn scratched on the back.

/**sáx̣linm'** (?) sword fern.

/**séˑxʷ–** embarrass, bashful, confused, frown. 1. /séˑxʷ-ɬ, — *intr.* 2. ʔac/séˑxʷ-mi-cx he's embarrassed *rel. refl.* 3. ʔit /séˑxʷ-st-mx he embarrassed me *perf. caus.*

/sə́csuqʷ– weave a basket. 1. s/sə́csuqʷ-st-n *impf. caus.* 2. s/sə́csuqʷ-staw-n *impf. caus.*

/səc'ə́– stick in, stick on. 1. /sə́c'-n, /sə́c'-t-n *tr.* 2. /sə́c'-tuxʷt stick it on him *appl.* 3. /sə́c'·c'-w-n needles (?). 4a. /sac'ə́-mn fork. 4b. /sac'ə́-min-um'x *pl.* 4c. /sac'ə́-min-i his fork. 5. /sác'-m'ɬ-tan-i its needle. 6. /sac'=áx̣ʷc-tn' a pin. 7. /sac'=él'usi– point at. 7a. /sac'=él's-n, —, /sac'=él'us-n, /sac'=él'usi-t-n. 8. sa´tspakantEn FBa fork (table); HT sácpakantən fork (*poss.* /sác'=pakan-tn). 9. sê´.tsᴱˣ FBa tattoo marks. 10. sêtsa´lsEmetEn FBa first finger (*prob.* /səc'=áls-mit-n). 11. /səc'=ál'wa– pin together. 11a. /səc'=ál'wa-x, — *caus.*

/sə́k'– swim. 1. /sə́k'-m, — *mdl.* 2. sî´kEmla FBa swim (*prob.* /sə́k'-m-la? swim!). 3. /sə́k'·sk'-mit-n he's swimming *impf. mdl.* 4. sE´kEmɬax tEkExa´n FBa swim across (*prob.* /sə́k'-m xaɬ tk /xán?; *see* tk more, comparative).

/sə́k'– split, crack. 1. /sə́k'-i its splitting. 2a. /sə́k'-

áy'=tmx-tn' plow; FBa,BH sEkai´ tEmExEn. 2b. /sək'-áy'=tmx-tan-i his plow, his plowing.

/sə́ƙʷɬ some, other.

səlpê̝x̣.ks HT nostril.

Səmt'i´c TAb-mi a gray animal, similar to fox, *poss.* ?*Urocyon cinereoargenteus* (gray fox) (*here* c = [š]).

s/əncá-yaɬ my, mine (*see* /?ə́nca I, me).

sɑ̇nux̣ JHjp silverside, silver salmon *Oncorhynchus kisutch* (*prob.* /sə́nx̣ʷ) (loanword; *see* Sahaptin *sɨnx̣ʷ, sínux̣* 'coho or silver salmon').

/sə́pyuc–: 1. ?ac/sə́pyuc-n crumbs.

/sə́q̇ʷɬtn unidentified plant *sp.*

/sə́t'x̣ʷs unidentified root *sp.*

/səwə́– knock out, have wind knocked out, faint. 1a. txʷ/sə́w, — *intr.* 1b. txʷ/sawə́-x, txʷ/sə́w-staw-n *caus.* 2. ?ac-txʷ/séw he's knocked out.

/sə́xʷa– wet. 1. /sə́xʷ-ɬ, /sə́xʷa-w-n, /sə́xʷ-n, /sə́xʷ-t-n. 2. sůkwu HH rain; AG,RL sukwu; GGb súk-w (*prob.* /sə́xʷ). 3. /sə́xʷ·sxʷ dew (ENM). 4. /səxʷ-áy=tmx dew (LNJ). 5. /sə́xʷ-l'=s– wet one's head with. 5a. —,

/sə́xʷ-l'=s-mis-n *rel.*

/səxʷáy'- ?? 1. /səxʷáy'-min-i his penis (?).

/səx̣ə́p- scratch. 1. /sax̣ə́p-ɬ, —, —, /sə́x̣p-t-n.

/sík'lx- ?? 1a. /sík'lx=ayuʔ snake; HH sekalekaíu; GGb séh-kul-hái-yu; FBa sīkEɬxai´o. 1b. /sík'lx=ay-umx *pl.* 1c. /sík'lx=ayuʔ-ni his snake. (Stem includes -lx *dev.*?)

/sikʷámc- ?? 1. /sikʷámc=n'ɬ maple *Acer macrophyllum* (big-leaf maple); EC si-qám-t͡sĭnh̄l; FBa sEkwa´mtsEnEɬ maple (wide-leaved); FBb sikwa·´mtsEnɬ; JH sɪkwâ·m'tsɑn'ɬ, sɪkwá·m'ts. (Stem includes suffix =amc side?) (See sukwa´mtsEnEɬ common willow.)

/sík̓ʷ- rip off. 1. /sík̓ʷ-ɬ, —, /sík̓ʷ-n, —.

/síl cloth (loanword; *see* Chinook Jargon *sail* 'cloth, cotton', taken in turn from English *sail*). 1b. /síl-i her cloth. 2. ʔac/síl-x-tan-i t /wíɬ sailboat. 3. /síl-al=ikn-: 3a. /síl-al=ičn cloth bag. 3b. /síl=kn-i her bag. 4. /sil/háws tent (loanword; *see* Chinook Jargon *sēlhaus* 'tent', taken in turn from English *sail*

plus *house*).

silaxwa´ls FBa? pupil of the eye; HT silax̣wáls.

Sɪləma´tks TAb-ss a chief's name.

/silmátx give a dish of food.

/sílmix torch, fire drill.

selEmuxena FBa buffalo *?Bison bison.*

/síɬ bullet, bullets, shell, shells, gunpowder; HH sitxl arrow; GGb séhtl arrow; EC sih̄l arrow; FBa se´ɬ arrow, bullet. 1b. /síɬ-i his bullet.

/síɬ- ?? 1. /síɬ=mix-: 1a. /síɬ=mx man, male; HH sítxlamax man; GGb séht-lum-eh man; EC sí-h̄lĭmh̄ man; FBa si´ɬEmux, sī´lEmEx̣ man; FBb si·´tɬEmx· man; HT síɬəmux man. 1b. /síɬ=mix-umx *pl.* 2a. /sé·ɬ=m'x boy *dimin.* 2b. /sé·ɬ=mix-umx *pl.* 2c. /sé·ɬ=miš-i his boy. 2d. /sé·ɬ=mix-umiš-i his boys *pl.* 3. axskoxsī´ɬEmux̣ FBa white man (*prob.* ʔaks/qʷúx̣ʷ /síɬ=mx; *see* /qʷúx̣ʷ-white).

s/iním-aɬ our, ours (*see* /ʔiním we, us).

sê´çEk FBa clam.

/síq̓ʷ- turn off a road 1. /síq̓ʷ-lx, /síq̓ʷ-lt-n *dev.*

/síq̓ʷ-: 1. /síq̓ʷ-ɬ a good

class of people; people and an area in southern Cowlitz territory between Kelso and Toledo; TAb sɩˈˈ'q'w the Toutle River Cowlitz. 2. tk /síq̓ʷ a person from a good class of people.

/sítikan- go over a mountain pass, cross. 1. /sítikan-m, — *mdl.*

/sítm ?? 1. ?it /sítm /qʷícqʷi-x s/ƛ̓á-m'ɬ t /sə́x̣t=kʷlx looking for spirit power.

/síw too. 1. ?ac/síw a little bit more than. 2. /síw/i?s sick (*see* /?áy's sick).

/skáw ferryboat (loanword; *see* English *scow*).

sku´lhau´s FBa schoolhouse (*prob.* /skʷulháws) (loanword; *see* English *schoolhouse*).

/sópt stories of old times; FBa sâ´ɛpt myth; TAb sɔˈˈ'pt tales of the time when all the animals were people.

/spalyán Spaniard; cayuse (horse) (loanword; *see* Spanish *español* 'Spanish'). 2. spanyo´nolitsa FBa poncho; HT spanyónolica (*prob.* spanyún-ul=ic'a).

/spún spoon (loanword; *see* Chinook Jargon *spoon* 'spoon', taken in turn from English *spoon*). 1b. /spun-áwm'x *pl.*

/spún (name of a horse).

/stákn stockings (loanword; *see* Chinook Jargon *stocken*´ 'stocking', taken in turn from English *stocking*). 2. /sá?/stakn make stockings.

/súc'us-: 1a. /súc's cousin. 1b. nx/só·c's-tn *pl.* 1c. /súc'us-i his cousin. 1d. nx/súc's-tan-i his cousins *pl.*

sukwa´mtsɛnɛɬ FBa willow (common) (*see* /sikʷámc- maple).

/súk̓ʷi- skin, dress game. 1a. —, s/súk̓ʷ-mt-n *mdl.* 1b. /súk̓ʷ-n, /súk̓ʷi-t-n *tr.*

/súlt- salt (loanword; *see* Chinook Jargon *salt* 'salt', taken in turn from English *salt*). 1. /sá/sult- salt. 1a. /sá/sult-n, — *tr.* 2. /súlt-ɬ salt water. 3. /súlt-ɬ=kʷu beach.

/súmsə̀m inner side of a hide, the film on the inner side of a hide next to the flesh.

cu´ntc FBa large rush mat (*prob.* /súnč'). 2. su´natcɛɬwe´ltxᵘ FBa mat lodge; HT súnačəɬwéltx̣ʷ (*prob.* /súnač'=lwltxʷ).

/súp- ?? 1. /súp=aq- whistle. 1a. /súp=q, /súp=aq-n *intr.* 2. /súp=q-ši- whistle for

appl. **2a.** /súp=q-š-n, —
tr. **3.** /súp·sup=aq-n he's
whistling *impf. intr.*

/súps- ?? **1a.** /súps=n'k
tail; FBa su´psank; HT
súpsank. **1b.** /súps=n'č-i
its tail. **2.** /súps=n'k-tan-:
2a. /súps=n'k-tn crupper.
2b. /súps=n'k-tan-i his
crupper. **3.** /táy/sups=nk
bob tailed.

/súskp-: 1. /súskp=n'ɬ
hemlock, (cedar ENM)
?*Tsuga heterophylla*
(western hemlock); EC súskpŭnh̄l; FBa su´skepEnEɬ;
HT súskepǝnǝɬ; JH
sù·skɑpɑ̀n'ɬ. **2.**
sisku´pas EG hemlock
(includes the Sahaptin
suffix -*as* 'plant').

/súwl (?) a stick (?).

/súwn big rock; EC sú-wụn
rock. **1b.** /súwin-l-m'x *pl.*

š

(c in older material = š)

š ?? **1.** /k̓ʷə̀p š /ʔí· This is
very good.

/šáʔš liver; FBa cê´.c; BH
ce´.c. **1b.** /šáʔš-i his liver.

/šawíʔ-: 1a. /šáwʔ bone; HH
çáwʊ; GGb sháú; FR shàǔ,
shaǔ; EC s͡hôw; JH ʃá·w'.
1b. /šawéʔ-i his bone. **1c.**
/šaw'-áwmiš-i his bones.
2. cā´oks FBa iron
arrowhead; HT šá·oks,
šaúǝks arrowhead: "bone
point" (*prob.* /šawʔ=qs).

/šéʔ here. **2.** ta/šéʔ through
here. **3.** xʷ/šéʔ to here.

/šək̓ʷíy'-: 1. txʷ/šak̓ʷíy'-st-
be surprised, be startled
caus? **1a.** txʷ/šak̓ʷíy'-st-n,
— *tr.* **2.** /šə̀k̓ʷiy=axʷc
hiccough.

/šə́q big white cloud. **2.**
s/p'ə́ɬ/šq fog.

/šə́q- stain a cloth. **1.** /šə́q-
ɬ, — *intr.*

/šíp- (loanword; *see* English
sheep): **1.** /šíp=ɬc'iʔ
mutton.

/šíxn' there. **2.** /šíxn'-x̣
there, that.

/šúkʷa-: 1. sū´ga FBa sugar
(loanword; *see* Chinook
Jargon *shu´-kwa* 'sugar,
honey', taken in turn from
English *sugar*). **2.** /šó·kʷu-
mn sugar bowl.

/šúƛ̓- stick in, get stuck. **1.**
/šúƛ̓-ɬ, — *intr.*

/šúšukli God, angel, heaven
(loanword; *see* Chinook
Jargon *Sesu Kli* 'Jesus

Christ', taken in turn from French *Jésus Christ* 'Jesus Christ').

coˊ ᵘɬ FBa common marmot or groundhog; JHjp ʃúˈɬ mountain beaver (*prob.* /šúwɬ or /šə́wɬ *Aplodontia rufa* mountain beaver).

t

t indefinite article (*non-feminine*).

t'əaˊwən TAb-mc Oakville Reservation Prairie (in Upper Chehalis territory) (*prob.* /t?áwn).

ta- ?? preposition. 1. ta-?aɬ along, around. 2. ta/šé? through here. 3. ta-xaɬ to.

/tá-: 1. /tá-x̣ that; FBa taˊx.

/tá?- slope. 1. /tá?-ɬ, — *intr.*

/táčn- get attached to. 1. /táčn-mn, — *rel.*

/táčnmn baby getting hysterics.

tak with. 2. ták/cani himself (*see* /cə́ni- he, him).

/ták- ?? 1. /ták/ɬak'i- hurt, ache, sore, wound. 1a. /ták/ɬk', s/ták/ɬak'-n *intr.* 1b. /ták/ɬak'i-x, s/ták/ɬk'-staw-n *caus.* (*see* /ɬə́k'a- sore, hurt). 2. /ták-s/x̌ʷqʷ starve (*see* /x̌ʷə́qʷa- hungry, starve).

/ták- lean. 1. /ták-n, — *tr.* 2. /ták-cx, — *refl.* 3. ?ac/ták-cx-as kn I'm leaning against it *refl.*

takaɬ so that, in order to (?).

/tákʷl'kʷ- reach in, put a hand in. 1. /tákʷl'kʷ-mn, — *rel.*

takoˊmanwEld FBa east.

ta-kó-ni EC bowl.

/tál- (travel) by means of. 1. /tál'=uɬ go in a boat. 2. /tál-s/tiqiw, /tál-a-s/tiqiw by horse, horseback, on a horse (*see* /tiqíw- horse). 3. /tal-s/yə́p on foot, by walking (*see* /yə́pa- walk).

/tál- ?? 1. /tál=aqap- call, yell, shout, holler. 1a. /tál=aqp, s/tál=aqap-n, /tál=aqp-n, —. 2. /tál=aqp-ni-n-a? holler at him! 3. /tál·tal=aqap- call, shout, holler. 3a. /tál·tal=aqp, s/tál·tal=aqap-n, /tál·tal=aqap-n, —.

/tal- ?? 1. /tal=áyn- obey, listen to, send word to. 1a. /tal=áyn-mn, — *rel.*

/táˑl- *pass.* 1. /táˑl-y-m aqa /tál/?uc's eleven-thirty.

/tála money (loanword; *see* Chinook Jargon táh-la 'money, dollar', taken in turn from English *dollar*). 2. /c'ə́k/tal'a spend all one's money.

/talíči– help. 1. /talíč-n, s/talíči-t-n *tr.* 2. /talíč-l=k- help pack things out. 2a. s/talíč-l=k-cal-n he's helping me pack things out *impf. tr.* 3. /talíč-tn' helper.

/táln– *pass.* 1. /táln-mx he passed me *perf. caus.*

/táln'x–: 1. s/táln'x over, across.

/tals–: 1a. /tals/náwaʔ grandparent, old people (*see* /náwa- old). 1b. /tals/náwa-tan-i his grandparents.

/tált (?) back down.

/tál'– -teen. 1. /tál'/ʔuc's eleven; EC tal-ó-t͡sŭs (*see* /ʔúc's one). 2. /tál'/saliʔ twelve; EC tál-sal (*see* /sáliʔ two). 3. /tál'/kaʔɬiʔ thirteen (*see* /káʔɬiʔ three). 4. /tál'/mus fourteen (*see* /mús four). 5. /tál'/čilačš fifteen (*see* /čílačš five). 6. /tál'/t'x̣m sixteen (*see* /t'əx̣ə́m- six). 7. /tál'/c'ups seventeen (*see* /c'óps seven). 8. /tál'/camus eighteen (*see* /cámus eight). 9. /tál'/tuwx̌ʷ nineteen (*see*

/təwíx̌ʷ- nine).

/tál'– ?? 1. /tál'=ikn-: 1a. /tál'=ičn bag. 1b. /tál'=kn-i his bag.

/tál'–: 1. /tál'·tal-m' crosswise.

/tál'– ?? 1. s/tál'=iq=šn instep; end of toe; EC stá-liŭksh̑n toes.

/tá·l'a– let, allow. 1. /tá·l'-n, s/tá·l'a-t-n *tr.*

/tál'š–: 1. tál'š-l's- follow, chase *dev.?* 1a. /tál'š-l's, s/tál'š-l't-n *intr.* 1b. /tál'š-l's-x, — *caus.*

/tál'x̌ʷuc– young people. 1. /tál'x̌ʷuc-umx *pl.*

/táɬ– spread flat, lie flat. 1. /táɬ-ɬ, — *intr.* 2. ʔac/táʔɬ-cx kn I'm lying on my side *refl.* 3. ʔit tx̌ʷ/táɬ-st-m he flopped down flat *caus. pass.* 4. ta´ɬɪnk'ən TAb-mc Ford's Prairie (in Upper Chehalis territory) (*prob.* /tá·ɬ=n'k'n).

/tám what?, thing; FBa tā´.m what (*see* /ʔitám thing). 2. /tám akʷu what?, why? 3. /tám ʔo ʔə́x̌ʷ-ɬ something else. 4. tom-tsi-en-i-ken UWb to love, want; FR tom-tsi-en-i-ken to love (*poss.* /tám-či n/qín; *see* /qín- want, like).

/tám–: 1a. s/təm·tám beads, necklace; EC

stŭmtám dentalium shell;
FBa stɛmta´m money,
dentalia; JH stɑm'tá·m a
kind of necklace; JHjp
stɑtá·m bead. 1b.
s/təm·tám-i her beads. 2.
?ac/təm·tám'-i⁴x (?)
beaded (moccasins ?). 3.
/təm·tám'-i⁴-al=ikn–:
3a. /təm·tám'-i⁴-al=ičn
beaded bag, beaded
clothing. 3b. /təm·tám'-
i⁴-al=kn-i her beaded bag.
4. ?ac/c'úc'q̓ʷ ?a⁴ tit
?ac/təm·tám-i⁴šn feather
with a beaded headband.

/táma?as–: 1. /táma?as-i
his wealth, his clothes.

/tamán–: 1. /tamán-i its
pus.

tan now, already (enclitic). 2.
tani now (enclitic).

/tán mother; FBa 'ta´. 1b.
s/tán-aw-i his mother; HH
stánawe mother. 1c. /tán-
aw-⁴ their mothers. 2.
ka/tá? your mother; FBb
kata´ᵋ. 3. kn/tá? my
mother. 4. kʷu/tá? mother!
(voc.); HH kotá; AG,RL
kota; GGb ko-táh my
mother; FR ko-tah; EC ku-
tá. 5. tcu⁴ta´nɛm FBa
stepmother (prob.
/ču⁴/tán-m). 6. /kʷá⁴/tn
aunt (see /kʷa⁴á– parent's
sibling). 7. nx/tán·tan-i
his parents.

/tán–: 1. /tán·tan other,
something else.

/taníš–: 1. /taníš-i his
arteries.

/tan'ís–: 1a. /tán's
knee(cap); EC ta'ns; FBa
ta´nns knee. 1b. /tán'is-
umx pl. 1c. /tan'ís-i his
knee.

tapa´⁴ TAmc a creek
adjoining Dip Creek.

/taqə́m⁴ busy at (?).

tā´qɛs ti'tî´mɛ⁴ FBa ground,
surface of the earth (poss.
/táq-s tit /tə́mx; see
/tə́mx earth).

/táqtmix–: 1a. s/táqtmx
shade, shadow. 1b.
s/táqtmiš-i his shadow.

/taq'é·ma–: 1.
/taq'é·ma=c'a? underwear
(t' ?).

/taq'íx̣n' cedar roots (dried
and prepared) (t' ?). 2.
/taq'éx̣n cedar roots dimin.

/táqʷ– ?? 1. /táqʷ=n'⁴=kʷp
sparks from a fire, live
coals.

/tása– flop, flap. 1. —,
s/tása-t-n tr.

/tása– pound on. 1. /tás-n,
s/tása-t-n tr. 2. /tása-
m'⁴-n' drummer. 3. /tása-
m'⁴-tn' drum; whip, club.
4. ta´sɛnɛktɛn FBa whip; HT
tásənəktən (prob.
/tás=nk-tn).

tat definite article (*non-feminine*).

/taw- other side. 1. /taw-íɬ=kʷu across the river (?).

/taw-: 1. /taw=ó·yn' echo, noise, voice.

/tawáksi- stab. 1. /tawáks-n, s/tawáksi-t-n *tr.*

/tawasá-: 1a. /tawás=n'ɬ ash tree ?*Fraxinus latifolia* (Oregon ash); EC ta-wá-sĭnh̄l; FBa tauasē´ɬ; HT tauasé·ɬ. 1b. /tawəsá=n-i? his ash tree. 2. tawa´sɛnɛɬ FBa hayfork (*poss.* /tawás=n'ɬ). 3. tawa´shweyə TAb-mi roasting-stick (?).

/tawél'an'-: 1a. s/tawél'n' carrot, carrots *Daucus carota.* 1b. s/tawél'an'-i her carrots.

/taw-ílax- sit down *dev.* 1. /taw-ílx, —; UWb tow-wil-i-kow to sit. 2. /taw-ílax-a? sit down! 3. /taw-élx squat, sit *dimin.* 4. ?ac/taw-élx be sitting. 5. /taw-ílls-m be sat on *pass.* 6. /taw-éll-tan-: 6a. /taw-éll-tn' chair. 6b. /taw-éll-tan'-i his chair.

tu-íl-ŭ-pa-min EC breech-cloth.

/táwn- ?? 1. /táwn=ɬc'i? doe, female; FBa tau´ɛɬtse doe (of deer); HT taúəɬce doe. 2. tau´ɛɬtse stɛke´u FBa mare (*prob.* /táwn=ɬc'i? s/tiqíw; *see* /tiqíw- horse).

/taw'ət big, large; HH tuwʊtx great; AG,RL tuwʊtkh great; GGb,FR tów-ut great; EC ta-wút large; FBa tauwî´t large, big; FBb tawu´t big. 2. s/taw'ət-i its size, its bigness. 3. /taw'í·t very big (*emphatic*). 4. /taw'-ál=awɬ big kettle, big pan, big basket, big container. 5a. /taw'=íls big rock, big round object. 5b. /taw=íl's-ti? *pl.* 6. /taw'-íɬ=kʷu big body of water. 7. /táw'=kʷu?, s/táw'=kʷu-ən-mit-n flow (LNJ), high water *impf. mdl.* 8. s/táw'=stq-mit-n it's blazing higher *impf. mdl.* 9. /təw'-áy=tmx /təmx country, territory. 10. /siw /taw'ət-ɬ/ənca too big for me (*see* /?ənca I, me). 11. tawetxo´uɬ FBa road, trail (*prob.* /taw'ət /xəwɬ; *see* /xəwál- road).

/taxʷál'š- blend work in a basket. 1. /taxʷál'š-n, — *tr.*

/táxʷayway- sell. 1. /táxʷiwi, s/táxʷay-n *intr.* 2. /táxʷiway- sell to. 2a. /táxʷiway-əx, s/táxʷiwi-staw-n *caus.* 3. /táxʷiwi-c

sold to me *perf. tr.* 4.
s/táxʷiyu-stal-n selling
impf. caus. ? 5. /tá?xʷi-
mn' a store (ENM). 6.
/táxʷayu-mn' a store (LNJ).
7. /taxʷ-ál'=šn buy shoes.
8. /táxʷ/sal'c=il'qs buy a
dress (*see* sál'c=il'qas-
dress).
táxʷl' although.
/tᶻáx̱- ask for. 1. /tᶻáx̱-n, —
tr.
/táx̱ʷ- call for. 1. /táx̱ʷ-n,
— *tr.*
/táx̱ʷac- chest. 1a. /táx̱ʷc;
EC tᶻaẖwts; FBa ta´ᵘxts; HT
tá·uxc. 1b. /táx̱ʷac-i his
chest. 2. ntau´xtsEn FBa
breast (*prob.* n/táx̱ʷc-n).
/táx̱ʷu, s/táx̱ʷu only. 1. tu
s/táx̱ʷu only.
/táy- without, negative. 1.
/táy=nut refuse. 2.
/táy/sups=nk bobtailed
(*see* /súps=n'k tail). 3.
tai´.sxEnlêmEn FBa
spinster (*prob.* /táy-
s/x̱ən-lmn; *see* /x̱ə́n
husband). 4. /tay-s/x̱ʷáq̇ʷ
deerskin with hair still on it
(*see* /x̱ʷáq̇ʷa- scrape hair
off). 5. /táy/tmx have no
land (*see* /tə́mx earth,
land). 6. /táy/uc=amc He
doesn't have his pants on. 7.
/táy-s/put-n kn ?it
/?átamn I didn't know that
he died. 8. ?ac'í ana cu

/tay-s/tal=áyn-mn k
Why don't you care?
/táytnapam Taitnapam,
Upper Cowlitz; UWa Ti-tin-
a-pam Cowlitz River
above Cowlitz Landing. 1b.
/táytnapam-umx (a
Sahaptin name based on the
Tieton River).
Ta´ɪx· TAb-ss name of an
unidentified creek.
/təkál-: 1a. HH takális pipe;
HH tʊkálís stone; AG,RL
tʊkalis stone; GGb stuk-
úlse pipe; GGb stuk-álse
stone; FBa .staka´lls pipe
(*poss.* s/tək=áls). 1b.
s/təkál-i his Indian pipe.
/tə́ktkni hummingbird
?*Selasphorus rufus* (rufous
hummingbird); FBa,BH
tE´ktkanē.
tEko´leka FBa palm of the
hand; HT təkóleka.
/tə́k' (front or back) end (?).
/təkʷayí- braid. 1. —,
s/təkʷáy-n *intr.* 2.
/təkʷáyi-n-a? braid it! 3a.
s/tə́kʷi? a braid. 3b.
s/tkʷyí?-i her braid. 3c.
/tə́kʷay'-umiš-i her braids
pl.
tela´la FBa bye and bye, after
a while (*poss.* /təlá·la).
/tələ́pa- march. 1. /taləp-ɬ,
s/tə́lpa-w-n *intr.*
/tə́lkʷa- ring, make music. 1.
—, s/tə́lkʷa-w-n *intr.* 2.

s/tə́lkʷ-mt-n *impf. mdl.* 3. s/tə́lkʷ-min making music *impf. rel.* (?). 4. s/tə́l·tlkʷ-mit-n making music *impf. mdl.*

/təmán'a- ?? 1. /təmán'a=n'ɬ spruce (thistle ?) ?*Picea* sp(p).

/tə́mx earth, land, dirt, ground, country; HH tŭmʋx earth, land; AG,RL tʋmʋkh earth; GGb túm-'wh; FR túm'-wh; FBa ti'tî´mEɬ earth, country, land (*prob.* tit /tə́mx). 1b. /tamíwal-i his land; FBb tEme´wale ground, earth. 2a. ʔáɬ/tm'x on the ground. 2b. x-ʔáɬ/tm'x onto the ground. 3. /ɬán/tmx wild cranberry ?, kinnickinick ? 4. tā´qEs ti'tî´mEɬ FBa ground, surface of earth (*poss.* /táq-s tit /tə́mx). 5. /táy/tmx have no land.

/tə́m'š- cover. 1. /tə́m'š-n, — *tr.* 2. ta´miclEpstEn FBa crupper; HT támišləpstən (*poss.* /tám'š-l=ps-tn).

/tə́p- bump, run into. 1. /tə́p-n, s/tə́p-t-n *tr.* 2. /tap-álɬ bump feet together. 3. /tap=álwa-collide. 3a. /tap=álwa-x, — *caus.* 4. /tap=ál'us they collided, hit together. 5. ta´pxEnEmEn FBa spurs (*prob.* /táp=xn-mn). 6.

/tə́p=ls- bump one's head. 6a. —, s/tə́p=ls-t-n *tr.*

stEpu´xEks FBa nostril (*poss.* s/tapə́xʷ=qs).

/tə́q- close, shut. 1. /tə́q-ɬ, —, /tə́q-n, —. 2. ʔac/táq-ɬ it's invisible. 3. ʔac/tə́q-lix-kʷuʔ airtight *dev.* 4. /táʔq-am'ɬ-tn' gate. 5. /taq=álps-tan-: 5a. /taq=ál'ps-tn' door; FBa taka´l.pstEn door, doormat; HT takál.pstən. 5b. /taq=álps-tan-i its door. 6. /taq=án' deaf. 6a. /taq=án', s/taq=án-n *intr.* 7. /táq=l's-tan-i its lid. 8. /tə́q=nak-: 8a. s/tə́q=nk dam. 8b. s/tə́q=nak-umx *pl.* 8c. s/tə́q=nač-i his dam.

/tə́q'- ?? 1. /tə́q'=tum'x middle, close together, next to.

/təqʷə́či- shoot with a gun, explode, blow up. 1. /taqʷə́č-ɬ, s/tə́qʷča-w-n, /tə́qʷč-n or /taqʷə́č-n, s/tə́qʷči-t-n. 2a. /táqʷč-am'ɬ-tn' gun; dynamite; FBa ta´kucamEɬtEn gun. 2b. /táqʷč-m'ɬ-tan-i his gun. 3. /táʔqʷč-am'ɬ-tn' little gun *dimin.* 4. s/téqʷ·tqʷč-amal-n he's shooting (at) it *impf. impl.tr.* 5. s/tə́qʷ·tqʷč-am'ɬ the shooting. 6. s/tə́qʷ·tqʷči-

t–n he's shooting (at) it
impf. tr. **7.** /c'ay–s/təq̓ʷči–
ci–n he's aiming at you
impf. tr.

/tə́q̓ʷa– talk. **1.** /tə́q̓ʷ–ɬ,
s/tə́q̓ʷa–w–n; FBa t̪û´kEɬ
talk, speak *tr.* **2.** /taq̓ʷ–ə́xʷ,
s/tə́q̓ʷ–staw–n talk to
caus. **3.** ʔit /taq̓ʷ–ə́c he
quarreled with me. **4.** túk
weht la GGb to speak; FR
tuk–weht–la (*prob.*
/tə́q̓ʷi–ɬ–aʔ speak!). **5.**
/taq̓ʷí– scold, get after,
quarrel with. **5a.** /taq̓ʷí–n,
— *tr.* **6.** /tə́q̓ʷa– talk about.
6a. /tə́q̓ʷa–mn, — *rel.* **6b.**
s/tə́q̓ʷ–m–stawt we're
talking it over *impf. rel.* **7.**
s/tə́q̓ʷ·tq̓ʷ–n talking *impf.*
intr. **8.** s/tə́q̓ʷ word,
language, speech. **9.**
/tə́q̓ʷ=alakaʔ talkative,
talker. **10.** /ɬíl'–s/tq̓ʷ agree,
answer. **10a.** /ɬíl'–s/tq̓ʷ, —,
/ɬíl'–s/tq̓ʷ–n, —. **11.**
/x̌ál'–s/tq̓ʷ–m hush, be
quiet *mdl.* **12.** /x̌ám'–s/tq̓ʷ
finish talking. **13.** tl s/lé·la
ɬ s/tə́q̓ʷ a foreign
language.

/tə́w– pay. **1.** /tə́w–ɬ, — *intr.*
2. /tə́w–ši– pay to *appl.* **2a.**
—, s/tə́w–ši–t–n *tr.*

/təwíxʷ–: **1.** /túwxʷ nine; HH
tóoxu; AG,RL tookhu; GGb
to̓ oh; FR to̓–óh, to–óh; EC
tuħ; FBa t̪o´ᵘx̱. **2.**

/tawíxʷ=l's nine dollars. **3.**
/tawíxʷ–l'=šn nine times.
4. /tawíxʷ–ɬ=tumx ninety.
5. /tawíxʷ=qʷ nine days. **6.**
/túwxʷ–ɬ=panxʷ nine
years old. **7.** /tál'/tuwxʷ
nineteen (ENM). **8.**
/t'əmx/túwxʷ ninefold. **9.**
pánačš kl t túwxʷ nineteen
(LNJ).

/tə́wɬ bump. **1.** /tə́wɬ, —,
/tə́wɬ–n, —.

/təwúl– wool. **1.**
s/təwúl=ic'aʔ wool
blanket.

/tə́xʷis–: **1a.** /tə́xʷs enemy;
HH toxus friend; FBa 'tuxs.
1b. /tə́xʷis–i his enemy.

/tə́x̱– ?? **1.** /tə́x̱·tax̱–al=uɬ
platters.

/tə́x̱ʷ– pull. **1.** /tə́x̱ʷ–n, — *tr.*

/təx̱ʷ– half. **1.** /təx̱ʷ–ál=ičn
half a sack. **2.** /təx̱ʷ=ámc
half.

/tə́x̱ʷs– ?? **1.** /tə́x̱ʷs=kʷu
spit; FBa to´xsko spittle.

təx̱o´ma TAb-mc Mt. Rainier;
TAb-mi tax̱o´ma; TAb-jc
taqo´mən (*poss.*
/təx̱ʷúma).

/tíʔ–: **1.** /tíʔ–x̱, /tí–x̱ right
here, this one, just; FBa tê´x
this. **2.** /tíʔ–x̱–ɬ=panxʷ
this year. **3.** /pən/tíʔ–x̱ this
time.

/tíʔi– fly. **1.** —, s/tíʔi–w–n
intr. **2.** /téʔ– fly. **2a.** /téʔ–ɬ,
— *intr.*

/tíʔi- buzz. 1. —, s/tíʔi-w-n *intr.* 2. s/téʔ·ti-w-n it's buzzing around *impf. intr.*

/tíci- scatter. 1. /tíc-ɬ, —, /tíc-n, s/tíci-t-n.

te´mseka FBa hammer; FBa tēmsa´ka pestle; HT témseka hammer (*prob.* /tíms=akaʔ).

/tím'- across. 1. /tím'·tim-m' crosswise. 2. /tém'·tem-m' striped horizontally.

/tíntin- music, ring (loanword; *see* Chinook Jargon *tin´-tin* 'bell, music'; imitative). 1a. /tíntin-m, — *mdl.*

/tínix-: 1. /tínx muscle, sinew; FBa te´n.x; BH tī´nx. 1b. /tíniš-i his muscles.

.stī´p FBa cloud (*prob.* s/típ).

/típi- ?? 1. /pən/típi-kʷn warrior.

/tiqíw-: 1a. s/tiqíw horse *Equus caballus*; EC stiŭké-wu; FBa stêkē´u; JH stɪ·qé·ww. 1b. s/tiqiw-áwmx *pl.* 1c. s/tiqíw-i his horse. 2. s/tiqé·w'=iʔɬ colt; FBa,HT têkä´ uweɬ. 3. s/tiqíw=lwltuxʷ-: 3a. s/tiqíw=lwltxʷ barn. 3b. s/tiqíw=lwltuxʷ-i his barn. 4. /k'áp-s/tiqiw train horses. 5. /tál-s/tiqiw,

/tál-a-s/tiqiw by horse, horseback, on a horse. 6. atsɛma´tcɛn .stɛke´u FBa stallion (*prob.* ʔac/máčn s/tiqíw; *see* /mačn- testicles). 7. tau´ɛɬtse stɛke´u FBa mare (*prob.* /táwn=ɬc'iʔ s/tiqíw; *see* /táwn=ɬc'iʔ doe, female).

tit definite article (*non-feminine*). 2. titatí this one; GGb teht-a-téh this person or thing; FR teht-a-téh, teh-ta-téh this. 3. titató that one, way over there; GGb teh-ta-táh that person or thing; FR teht-a-táh, teh-ta-táh that. 4. titx̣tá that. 5. titx̣tí this one. 6. titx̣t'íst that.

/tíwat- cross, get across. 1. /tíwt, s/tíwat-n *intr.* 2. /tíw-x-t-n crossing a little creek *impf. appl.* (?). 3. te´utlatáluɬ FBa cross water. 4. tē´utɛmɛn FBa bridge, steps (*prob.* /tíwt-mn). 5. qi /téw't-tn' bridge.

/tixʷcál-: 1a. /tíxʷcɬ tongue; HH téxutsitxl; AG,RL tekhutsitkhl; GGb téh-hootsl; FR téh-hootsl, téh-hut-sl; EC ti'hwts̄hl; FBa te´uxtsɛl. 1b. /txʷcál-i his tongue.

tk more, *comparative degree.* 1. tk ʔac/náwɬ older (*see*

/náwa- old). 2. tk /ʔáy'tk more (see /ʔáy'tk lots of). 3. tk /ʔíˑ better (see /ʔíˑ good). 4. tk /cóʔ between (see /cóʔ-). 5. tEkx'kaˊ FBa which (poss. tk /káˑ; see /káˑ where?). 6. tk /lílʔ further (see /lílʔ far). 7. tEkE'ɬaˊn FBa day after tomorrow (prob. tk /ɬán; see ɬán-). 8. tk /síq̓ʷ a person from a good class of people (see /síq̓ʷ- a good class of people). 9. tk /xánʔ opposite, other side; FBa tEkExaˊn across, on the opposite side; BH tEkExaˊn across (see /xánʔ there). 10. sEˊkEmɬax tEkExaˊn FBa swim across (prob. /sə́k'-m xaɬ tk /xánʔ; see /sə́k'- swim).

t + l past (time) (non-feminine) (see l past). 2. t + l ʔaɬ from, out of, off, than.

/tóʔkʷ- hate, dislike. 1. /tóʔkʷ-mn, — rel.

/tólapi- begin. 1. /tólp, s/tólap-n intr. 2. /tóˑl'api- begin, start. 2a. /tóˑl'p, s/tóˑl'ap-n intr. 2b. /tóˑl'api-x, — caus.

/tóˑlu- find out about. 1. /tóˑlu-xʷ, — caus. 2. ʔac/tóˑl-ɬstmɬəx kn (?) I heard about it.

/tóˑl'u- mind, obey. 1. /tóˑl'u-x, s/tóˑl'-staw-n

caus.

/tóˑl'xan-: 1a. s/tóˑl'šn fruit, berries. 1b. s/tóˑl'xan-i her fruit. 2. /pən-s/tóˑl'šn August.

/tómʔɬ short; FBa tôˊmEɬ.

stâkt͡s EC mountain goat Oreamnos americanus; FBa .stûˊkts, .stauˊkts; FBa .staˊkᵒts sheep; JH stoq'ts' (prob. stóqʷc). 2. t̲akoˊne FBa ram (of mountain sheep).

tu from, of. 1. tuɬ from, of (see ɬ in, on, with). 2. tu ʔaɬ from, of. 3. tu /káˑ k akʷu Where were you? 4. tu /lílʔ foreign, from afar (see /lílʔ far). 5. tuɬaˊtcitso FBa west (prob. tu /ɬáčicu; see /ɬáčicu-). 6. tu s/táxʷu only. 7. tu s/t'íx now.

/túkʷa-l'ix- dream dev. 1. /túkʷa-l'ix or /túkʷa-l'x, s/túkʷa-llt-n intr. 2. s/túkʷ·tukʷa-llt-n he's dreaming impf. intr.

/túl- ?? 1. s/túl=nk basket hoops; start (the bottom of) a basket.

/túl- doctor sings; sing a lullaby. 1. /túl-m'ɬ, s/túl'-mal-n impl.tr. 2. s/tóˑl'-mal-n he's humming. 3. stú-lĭ-mĭ̄hl EC spirit creature (prob. s/túl-m'ɬ).

/**tuləm** digging stick; FBa
  tu'lî´m root- digger. 1b.
  tuləm-i her digging stick.
tul-ka´lɛx FBa south, down
  country.
/**túlkʷ** downward (?).
/**túlucn** ice, chunks of ice;
  HH tolótçun ice; GGb tó-
  lote-st ice; FR tóh-lote-st
  ice; EC tú-luṭsn ice; FBa
  tu´luṭstɛn frost, ice. 2.
  /túluc=u⁊=n glass. 3.
  pantolos HH winter; FBa
  pɛntolo´s fall, autumn, late
  fall (*prob.* /pən/túlucn).
tul.xa´u.ts FBa young man,
  youth; FBa to´lɛxau.ts boy;
  FBb sto·´lx·auts young
  man (*prob.* s/túlxawc).
/**túl'šl's** hint, guess. 1.
  /túl'šl's, s/túl'šl's-n *intr.*
  2. s/túl'šl's-mal-n he's
  hinting to me *impf. caus.*
/**tú⁊i**– stretch. 1. /tú⁊-n, —
  tr. 2. /tú⁊i- stretch self. 2a.

/tú⁊i-cx, s/tú⁊-cši-t-n
  refl. 3. /tú⁊·t⁊-ni-n-aʔ
  stretch it! *appl.* 4. qi t
  s/tú⁊·t⁊-w-n rubber.
.**stū´m.la** FBa north,
  upcountry.
/**tún**– release, let go. 1.
  /tún-n, — *tr.*
/**túpan'**–: 1a. /túpn' spider,
  spiders; EC ṭu'pn; JH
  tù·pɑn. 1b. /túpan'-i his
  spider. 2. /túpl' spider; FBa
  tū´pɛl.
.**stu´ps** FBa skin dresser, skin
  softener.
/**túqʷ**– thunder. 1. /túqʷ-m,
  s/túqʷ-mt-n *mdl.* 2.
  s/túqʷ thunder; HH stóqu
  thunder; HH stoqu
  lightning; GGb,FR stó-kw;
  UWb stook; EC stoq; FBa
  .s'to´k.
/**túxʷ**– hang. 1. /túxʷ-⁊, —
  intr.

t'

/**t'ačéʔ**–: 1a. s/t'ačéʔ island;
  HH statçié; UWb sta-cha.
  1b. s/t'ačéʔ-i his island.
t!ak!a·´ls FBb stone (*prob.*
  /t'ak'á=l's).
/**t'alá**– ?? 1. s/t'alá=šin-:
  1a. s/t'alá=šn foot, instep;
  HH staláçin foot; GGb stah-
  lásh-in foot; FR sta-lásh-

in foot; EC sta-lásŝhn foot;
  FBa tɛla´cxɛn sole of the
  foot. 1b. s/t'alá=šin-umx
  pl. 1c. s/t'alá=šin-i his
  foot. 2. staléka HH hand,
  fingers, nails (*prob.*
  s/t'al=ákaʔ). 3. tɛtala´ka
  FBa wrist.
/**t'ám**– mark. 1.

ʔac/t'ám·t'am-ɬ marks. 2.
/t'am=áka-mn bracelet
(ENM), ring (LNJ).

/t'aməx̌ʷ gooseberry *Ribes*
sp(p).; EC ṭa-múħw; JH
t'ɑ'ɑmὺxw. 2. tmuxwas
EG common gooseberry
(includes Sahaptin -*as*
'plant').

/t'amiɬə́n-: 1a. /t'amíɬn
rope; FBa tamê´ɬEn; FBa
tamī´ɬEna lariat. 1b.
/t'amíɬin-umx. 1c.
/t'amiɬə́n-i his rope. 2.
tami´ɬEn Eɬ tê hê´nns FBa
fishline (*prob.* /t'amíɬn ɬ t
/x̌ə́n's; *see* /x̌ən'ús-
fishhook).

/t'amín fur; FBa tê'mín hair
(of body and animals). 1b.
/t'amín-i its fur.

/t'amúl- ?? 1. /t'amúl=ikn-
: 1a. /t'amúl=ičn barrel. 1b.
/t'amúl=kn-i his barrel. 2.
/t'amó·l=ičn little barrel.

/t'aná- cross, go across, go
through, land (a canoe),
reach shore. 1. /t'án-ɬ,
s/t'ána-w-n *intr.* 2. /t'an-
ə́x, — get to the end,
continue *caus.* 3.
/t'an=ál'uʔs a cross,
crossed.

/t'anáp- dark, get dark. 1.
/t'anáp-m'ɬ, s/t'anáp-
mal-n *impl.tr.* 2. /t'anáp
/ɬukʷáɬ moon.

/t'anáw's- ?? 1.

/t'anáw's=n'k-tn' blanket
on top of a saddle.

/t'aními- measure. 1.
/t'ané·m-n, s/t'ané·mi-
t-n *tr.* 2. /t'aním'-ši-
signal *appl.* 2a. /t'aním'-š-
n, — *tr.* 3. s/t'aním'-ši-
ctx a signal *impf. pass.* 4.
tena´mectEn FBa picture
(*poss.* /t'aném-š-t-n). 5.
/t'aném=aka-ši- give
hand signals *appl.* 5a.
/t'aném=aka-š-n,
s/t'aném=aka-ši-t-n *tr.*
6. /t'anémi-m'ɬ-tn'
straight line, square.

/t'áp'- close, shut. 1.
ʔac/t'áp'=s he's blind. 2.
/t'áp'=s- blind. 2a.
/t'áp'=s-n, — *tr.* 3.
/t'á·p'=us- take a nap,
close one's eyes. 3a.
/t'á·p'=us-m, — *mdl.*

/t'áqaʔ salalberries
Gaultheria shallon.

/t'áqʷa- lick, lap. 1. /t'áqʷ-
n, s/t'áqʷa-t-n *tr.*

/t'awál's-: 1. s/t'awál's hay,
tall grass, straw.

stawúm EC cut, mow; JH
st'ɑwúm' cut grass (*prob.*
s/t'aw-ə́m').

ta-wí-t͡sʰl EC white fir; FBa
tau'i´tsEɬp white pine; HT
tau'ícəɬp white pine; JH
tɑ'wítsɬ white fir; JH
t'ɑ·wítsən'ɬ pine (*prob.*
/t'awíc'ɬ).

/t'ə́k- wear, get dressed. 1a.
/t'ə́k-m, s/t'ə́k-mt-n
mdl. 1b. /t'ə́k-n, — *tr.* 2.
ʔac/t'ə́k wear, have on. 3a.
s/t'ə́k jacket, jackets; FBa
.stî´qᵏ robe, blanket. 3b.
s/t'ə́č-i his jacket. 4.
s/t'ak-áwmix-: 4a.
s/t'ak-áwmx clothing *pl.*
4b. s/t'ak-áwmiš-i his
clothing. 5. /nám/t'ək-m
dressed *mdl.*

st'ɛ́ dkeɩq TAb-ss One-
Legged Man (myth
character; *prob.*
s/t'ə́k'=iq).

/t'ə́k̇ʷ- bite. 1. /t'ə́k̇ʷ-n,
s/t'ə́k̇ʷ-t-n *tr.* 2.
/t'ə́k̇ʷ·t'k̇ʷ-tm get all
bitten *perf. pass.* 3.
s/t'ə́k̇ʷ-ctx getting a
cramp *impf. pass.* 4.
/t'ak̇ʷ=á·n'i-cal-ctx I
have an earache *impf. pass.*
5. ʔac/t'ak̇ʷ=énusi-tm
have a stomachache *perf.
pass.* 6. /t'ak̇ʷ=énusi-cal-
ctx I have a stomachache
impf. pass.

/t'ə́k̇ʷ- a bow; HH stʊqu,
stǐqʊ; GGb stukw; FBa
.sta´kʷo (*prob.* s/t'ə́k̇ʷ). 2.
/t'ə́k̇ʷ=ɬn? bow; EC sta-
ḵwŭȟln.

/t'ələ́p- put around, put on,
hook on. 1. /t'alə́p-ɬ, —,
/t'alə́p-n, s/t'ə́lp-t-n. 2.

/t'ə́lp-ši- patch *appl.* 2a.
/t'ə́lp-š-n, — *tr.* 3.
/t'ə́l·t'lp-ši- patch *appl.*
3a. /t'ə́l·t'lp-š-n,
s/t'ə́l·t'lp-ši-t-n *tr.* 4.
/t'ə́l·lp-tuxʷt brush onto
appl. 5. ʔac/t'alə́p=nk a
mask. 6. /t'əlp=ál'wa-
splice, put together. 6a.
/t'əlp=ál'wa-x,
s/t'əlp=ál'u-staw-n *caus.*
7. ʔac/t'əlp=ál'us put
together side by side. 8.
ʔac/t'əlp-xʷ-tan-i his
shield.

/t'ə́lx̣- scream. 1. /t'ə́lx̣-cx,
— *refl.* 2. s/t'ə́l·t'lx̣-cši-
t-n he's screaming *impf.
refl.*

/t'əmx- all. 1. /t'əmx/sáliʔ
both, double, together (*see*
/sáliʔ two). 2. /t'əmx/sáli-
yumx each other, together
pl. (*see* /sáliʔ two). 3.
/t'əmx/káʔɬiʔ three at a
time, triple (*see* /kaʔɬiʔ
three). 4. /t'əmx/mús
fourfold (*see* /mús four). 5.
/t'əmx/čílačš fivefold (*see*
/čílačš five). 6.
/t'əmx/t'ax̣ə́m sixfold
(*see* /t'əx̣ə́m- six). 7.
/t'əmx/c'ó·ps sevenfold
(*see* /c'óps seven). 8.
/t'əmx/cámus eightfold
(*see* /cámus eight). 9.
/t'əmx/túwxʷ ninefold

(*see* /təwíxʷ- nine). 10. /t'əmx/pánačš tenfold (*see* /pánaks- ten). 11. /t'əmx/pánkst-l=šn one-hundred (*see* /pánaks- ten). 12. /t'əm/xʷáʔkʷuʔ all, every, whole (*see* /xʷáʔkʷuʔ all). 13. /t'əm/xə́mʔ both ends (*see* /xə́mʔ-).

/t'əp- ?? 1. /t'əp=qə́s-: 1a. /t'ə́p=qs snot. 1b. /t'p=qə́s-i his snot.

t'əpit'ə́pi TAb-mi (myth character).

/t'ə́qi- wind around, tie around, arrest, put in jail. 1. /t'ə́q-ɬ, —, /t'ə́q-n, —. 2. /t'éqi-mɬ-tn' jail. 3. qi /t'éʔqi-m'ɬ-tn' policeman. 4. /t'ə́q-am'ɬ-tn' something you tie around. 5. takaʹkEmEɬ.tEn FBa hobbles (*poss.* /t'aq=ák-am'ɬ-tn'). 6. s/t'éq=ls, s/t'éq=ls-mn' head-band (?). 7. /t'əq=iyúxʷ-: 7a. /t'ə́q=ixʷ belt, belts. 7b. /t'əq=iyúxʷ-i his belt. 8. t!ăqăyEqtinamaᵋ FBb tie your belt. 9. /t'ə́q-l=ikn- wrap up. 9a. /t'ə́q-l=kn, — *intr.* 10. ʔac/t'ə́q=lič-n a package. 11. taʹkshwaismEn FBa headband (*prob.* /t'ə́q-s/xʷay's-mn; *see*

/xʷay'ús- hat).

/t'ə́q's under, back under, bottom; FBa taʹq.s low. 2. ks/t'ə́q'-tm underneath. 3. /t'ə́q's-ɬ=kʷu under water. 4. /t'ə́q's-ɬ=tumx underneath.

/t'ə́q'x̣ʷ- slap, spank, paddle. 1. /t'ə́q'x̣ʷ-n, —. 2. ʔit /t'ə́q'x̣ʷ-cx he slapped himself *perf. refl.* 3. ʔit /t'ə́q'·t'q'x̣ʷ-cx he kept slapping himself *perf. refl.* 4. /t'ə́q'x̣ʷ=nk- spank. 4a. /t'ə́q'x̣ʷ=nk-n, s/t'ə́q'x̣ʷ=nk-t-n *tr.* 5. t'q'x̣ʷ=ási- slap. 5a. /t'q'x̣ʷ=ás-n, s/t'q'x̣ʷ=ási-t-n *tr.*

/t'ə́s- crack. 1. /t'ə́s-ɬ, — *intr.*

/t'ə́xʷ- brush off, shake out, thresh. 1. /t'ə́xʷ-n, s/t'ə́xʷ-t-n *tr.* 2. /t'ə́xʷ- inum thresh.

/t'əx̣ə́m-: 1. /t'ax̣ə́m six; HH táxam; AG,RL takham; GGb tuch-húm; GGc tukhʹum; FR túch-hum, tuch-húm; EC tá-h̆um; FBa ta'xîʹm. 2. /pánačš kl t /t'ax̣ə́m sixteen (LNJ). 3. /tál'/t'x̣m sixteen (ENM). 4. /t'əx̣ám-l=s six dollars. 5. /t'ə́x̣m-l=əšn six times. 6. /t'ə́x̣m-l=qʷ six days. 7. /t'ə́x̣m-ɬ=panxʷ six years old. 8. /t'ə́x̣m-ɬ=tumx sixty. 9.

/t'χm–ál'=xaw'ɬ six rows.
10. /t'əmx/t'axə́m sixfold.

/t'íc– splash. 1. s/t'íc·c–w–n
it's splashing *impf. intr.* 2.
/t'íc–ši– splash on *appl.* 2a.
—, s/t'íc–ši–t–n *tr.*

/t'ik'– ?? 1. /t'ik'=á·?ka?
revolver.

te´lɛka FBa elk calf (*prob.*
/t'ílq'ah). 2. tɛlɛ'ka´n FBa
fawn (of deer).

t'ím most, superlative degree.
1. t'im /?í· best (*see* /?í·
good). 2. t'im /χə́š worst
(*see* /χə́š bad).

/t'íqi– soak. 1. /t'íq–n,
s/t'íqi–t–n *tr.* 2. /t'éq–
am'ɬ–tn' something
soaked. 3. /t'é?q–am'ɬ–tn'
sinker *dimin.* 4. /t'é·q=s–
m (go) down, downwards.

/t'íχ while, now. 2. tu s/t'íχ
now. 3. tu s/t'íχu that's all.
4. /t'íχu only, only one,
only ones. 5. /t'íχ na c
?a/kúwɬ Is she your wife?

/t'k'n– ?? 1. /t'k'n=ámc
half-breed.

/t'ó?i– put away, put aside,
store, save. 1. /t'ó?–n,
s/t'ó?i–t–n *tr.*

/t'úla– arrive, come. 1a.
/t'úl–ɬ, s/t'úla–w–n *intr.*
1b. /t'úl–a?–ɬ *pl.* 1c. ?it
/t'úl–ɬ ?akʷu They said he

came. 1d. /míɬta ?akʷu t
s/t'úl–i He didn't come. 2.
/t'ul–ə́x, s/t'úl–taw–n
bring to, bring back *caus.* 3.
s/t'úl–m–cal–n it's
coming to me *impf. rel.* 4.
/t'úl–ms–m expect
company *perf. rel. pass.* (?).
5. ?ac/t'ó·l'–ms–m have
company, have guests *rel.
pass.* (?). 6. /t'úl–x– bring
to. 6a. ?it /t'úl–x–ci he
brought it to you *perf. tr.* 6b.
/t'úl–x–st–wal–iɬt they
are bringing it to each other
impf. caus. recip. 7. /t'ó·l–
x–ši– bring to *appl.* 7a. —,
s/t'ó·l–x–ši–t–n *tr.* 7b. n–
s/t'úl–x–ši–tm it was
brought for me *pass.* 8.
ti/t'úl– come again. 8a.
ti/t'úl–ɬ, — *intr.* 8b.
ti/t'ul–ə́x, — return *caus.*
9. s/put–s/t'úla–w–anx I
just got home *impf. intr.*

/t'úliq̇ʷ move over, move in.
1. /t'úliq̇ʷ, — *intr.*

/t'úqʷi– find, meet, catch at.
1. /t'úqʷ–n, s/t'úqʷi–t–n
tr.

/t'úq̇ʷ– describe. 1. /t'úq̇ʷ–
n, — *tr.* (q̇ʷ ?).

/t'úyxʷ– mix, stir. 1.
/t'úyxʷ–n, s/t'úyxʷ–t–n
tr. 2. t'úyxʷ–m'ɬ–tn' ladle.

W

wa ?? **1.** /ʔíɬn-laʔ ɬ tit /qiy'áluqʷs, k̓ʷaɬ ta /X̌áq̓ʷ-aw-m k wa /X̌əx̣-ɬ Eat the soup so you can get well fast! **2.** ʔí-x-c-aʔ tit /sac'ə́-mn, k̓ʷaɬ /c'aw=úqs kn wa Give me that fork so I can dish this up!

/wá(t) who, someone; HH wa who; GGb wáh who; FR wah who; FBa wa´ who. **2.** /wá ʔo someone else. **2a.** /wá ʔo /ʔə́xʷ-ɬ someone else. **3.** /wá ak̓ʷu who is he?, someone. **4.** /wá k ak̓ʷu Who are you? **5.** /wát ak̓ʷu who he is.

/wácxan– dance. **1.** /wácxan-m, s/wácxn-mit-n; GGb wáts-háh-num; FR wats-háh-num *mdl.* **2.** wa´tsxanɛmla FBa dance (*prob.* /wácxan-m-laʔ dance! *mdl.*).

/wáč clock, watch; FBa wa´tc (loanword; *see* English *watch*).

/wá·či– watch. **1.** —, s/wá·či-t-n *tr.* (possibly a loanword; *see* English *watch*).

watci·´··x̣utci··x̣u qa´winactp'ə´n MJb-mi Are you asleep yet? (*here* c = [š]).

/wakə́s– go. **1a.** /wáks, s/wáks-n; FBa wa´.ks *intr.* **1b.** /wák-aʔ-s *pl.* **1c.** FBb swa´ksanɛx I am going (*prob.* s/wáks-anx). **2.** s/wáks-in-anx I'm going *impf. intr.* **3.** ʔit /wákas-i-m-umx they kept on going. **4.** /wakə́s-i his going. **5.** /wáksa– go to. **5a.** /wáksa-mn, — *rel.* **6.** ʔit /cún kn ʔak/wáks-tl-s I told him to leave.

/wák'x– uncover. **1.** wák'š-n, —. **2.** ʔac/wák'x tani it's uncovered now.

/wálaʔ– be scary, horse shies. **1.** /wál-ɬ, —. (The initial w is lost after the prefix txʷ- in the following forms.) **2.** ʔac-txʷlá-x it's serious. **3.** txʷál?-st-m be surprised, be confused *caus. pass.* **4.** txʷálaʔ– stare, confuse, surprise. **4a.** txʷálaʔ-x, — *intr.* **5.** txʷláʔ-x-ši– stare at *appl.* **5a.** txʷláʔ-x-š-n, — *tr.*

/waləx soft.

/waɬ–: **1.** s/waɬ-áɬ/kalx tules *Scirpus acutus* (*see* /kələx– reed mat, reeds).

waɬa´lən TAb-jc,mc Scatter Creek (in Upper Chehalis territory; *prob.* /waɬá·ln).

/wánač– be lost, get lost. **1.**

/wánač-ɬ, — *intr.* 2.

/wán·wanač- get lost. 2a.

/wán·wanač-ɬ, — *intr.*

Wah-nookt UWa Klickitat Indians; MJb wânukt Taitnapam and Wanook: Silver Creek; TAb-pb wa nukt' a people; TAa-md Wawuk t, Wanukᵘt, Wanukut' people around Mossy Rock; TAa-ph wanukʷt', wan kᵘt, wanvkᵘt, wanakᵘt, wan&kᵘt¢ Upper Cowlitz, just east of the mountains; JH wáˑnʊkwt, wâˑnʊkt the Klickitats; JHmc wɑ̇nʊk't' the Upper Cowlitz (*poss.* wánəkʷt).

swaˊnxaxa FBa snipe *?Gallinago gallinago* (common snipe).

waˊpia FBa fishnet (bag net).

/**wáq'-** open. 1. /wáq'-n, — *tr.* 2. ʔac/wáq'-a-ɬ they are open *intr. pl.*

/**waq'íq'-**: 1a. š/waq'íq' frog; FBa .swakêˊkɬ. 1b. š/waq'íq'-umx *pl.* 1c. š/waq'íq'-i his frog. 2. š/wəq'éˑq'-umx little frogs *pl.* 3. s.wáq'iq'=čn a frog sp.; TAb-jc swaˊq'ex̣tcɪn a game animal.

/**wáq̇ʷan'ɬ** tanning.

/**wasáln** what is left ungathered after a basket is full.

wa'sêˊl FBa vein (*prob.* /wasəl').

/**wásqʷx̣ʷ** last year.

/**wáwaʔ-**: 1. s/wáwaʔ cougar, cougars *Felis concolor* (mountain lion); EC s'wáˊ-wa mountain lion; FBa .swa'waˊ.; TAb-mi swaˊwa; JH sw'âˑ'wɑ', sᵅw'áˑ'ᵅwɑ'; JHjp swɑ̇wɑ'.

/**wáx̣ʷ-** ?? 1. ʔac/wáx̣ʷ=ay's striped (?). 2. ʔac/wáx̣ʷ·wax̣ʷ-ɬ it's striped (vertically).

/**wáya-** leave. 1. /wáy-n, s/wáya-t-n *tr.* 2. /wáy-l'=k- let go. 2a. /wáy-l'=k-mn, — *rel.*

/**wayə́x̣** tanned deerskin; EC wai-yŭħ deerskin; FBa wei'eˊx deerskin, leather. 2. weiaxkaˊlɛxɛkstɛn FBa shirt (of dressed skin); HT weiax̣kálǝx̣ǝkstǝn shirt (*prob.* /wayǝx̣/k'ál'x-cx-tn'; *see* /k'ál'ax- branch).

/**wáylšip** mountain goat (loanword; *see* English *wild sheep*).

/**wéˑ-x̣-** live, stay, have. 1. /wéˑ-x̣, s/wéˑ-ni-x̣ *intr.* (*see* /wín- live, reside). 2. ʔac/wéˑ-x̣ o alive. 3. /níʔ-x̣ na t qi s/wéˑ-n-ilp-x̣ Do you folks live here? 4. wàˑˊnaxaˊlexʷ FBb goodbye (*prob.* /wéˑ-nax̣-alxʷ).

/wéta– store, put away. 1. —, s/wéˑta-w-n *intr.* 2. /wét-x, — *caus.*

/wəč'ál bracken roots, roots of *Pteridium aquilinum* (bracken fern).

/wə́l– herd, scare away. 1. —, s/wə́l-t-n *tr.* 2. s/wə́l-tn a herd.

/wələq'– smooth, level. 1. /waləq'-ɬ, —, —, s/wə́lq'-t-n.

wEl'kai´ FBa rattlesnake *Crotalus viridis.*

/wə́lk'– shine, polish. 1. —, s/wə́lk'-mt-n *mdl.*

/wəɬə́qa– bloom, open, spread out, stretch. 1. —, s/wə́ɬqa-w-n, /waɬə́q-n, s/wə́ɬq-t-n.

/wəmúsmuski, wəmúsəski (ENM) cow *Bos taurus;* FBa wemuˊsEmuske cattle, cow (loanword; *see* Chinook Jargon *moosˊ-moos* 'cow, cattle'; source unknown; possibly directly from Chinook rather than from Chinook Jargon; the initial *wə-* may represent a Chinook feminine gender prefix; the final *-ki* is unexplained). 1b. /wəmúsmuskiy-umx, /wəmúsəskiy-umx (ENM) *pl.* 1c. /wəmúsmuski-ni his cow. 2.

/wəmóʔsmuskiʔ=iʔɬ, /wəmóʔsəski=ʔɬ (ENM) calf. 3. /wəmúsmuski=ɬc'iʔ beef. 4. /manít/umusməski butcher a cow or steer.

/wənáy'x̣ mountain huckleberries, Yakima huckleberries *Vaccinium* sp.; JH wɑ́nnɑ́y'x̣, wáˑnáˑy'x̣; JHjp wɑnáyx̣. 2. /wənáy'x̣=an'ɬ huckleberry bush.

/wə́n'– fold. 1. /wə́n'-n, — *tr.* 2. /wə́n'·wan'– fold up. 2a. /wə́n'·wan'-ɬ, —, /wə́n'·wn'-n, s/wə́n'·wn'-t-n. 3. /wén'·wn'-ni-n-aʔ fold it up! 4. suwaˊnwEnuEn FBa pocketknife (*prob.* s/wə́n'·wən'-w-n). 5. /wan'=állwa– fold up. 5a. /wan'=állwa-x, — *perf. caus.*

wəpaˊls TAb-mi handle of a root digger.

wupkaiˊlExt FBa a quiver.

/wə́q'a– run. 1. /wə́q'-ɬ, s/wə́q'a-w-n; FBa waˊqEɬ *intr.* 2. /wə́q'-tas, — run after *tr.* 3. wa-kȧit-la GGb run (*prob.* /wə́q'i-ɬ-aʔ run!). 4. n-s/wə́q'·wəq' my running around.

wəs, ʔus be, focus or topic marker (*usually follows the negative* míɬta) (?).

/wə́tt-: 1. s/wə́tt lucky, smart, famous.

/wə́xa- pull, drag. 1. /wə́x-n, s/wə́x-t-n *tr.* 2. /wə́xa- paddle a canoe. 2a. /wə́xa-cx, s/wə́x-cši-t-n *refl.* 3. /wáxa-m'ɬ-tn' pulley. 4. /wə́x-iʔ- pull up. 4a. /wə́x-iʔ-n, — *tr.*

wi and, but.

/wi, /ʔu be, become, focus or topic marker. 2. /wi, s/win-n *intr.*

/wí- go on. 1. /wí-laʔ go on!; GGb will-la to go; UWb,FR we-la to walk; FR wil-la to go; FBa we´la go away! 2. la/wílatn you go on (analysis uncertain). 3. ta/wí-laʔ go away!, go back! 4. wileɬā´kum FBa go downstream (*prob.* /wí-laʔ /ɬáʔkʷ-m' *imper.*; *see* /ɬáʔkʷ- upstream). 5. wilaxpa´ɬko FBa go outside (*prob.* /wí-laʔ /páɬkʷu *imper.*; *see* /páɬkʷu outside).

/wíʔx̣, /wéʔx̣ do.

/wíl-: 1a. /wíɬ canoe, boat, car; HH wétxl canoe, boat; GGb weh´hl canoe; FBa wī´ɬ dug-out canoe; HT wí·ɬ dug-out canoe; JH wí·ɬ canoe; JHjp wíɬ. 1b. /wíl-i his canoe. 2. /sáʔ/wəl-n making a canoe *impf. intr.* 3.

ɬá·k'wɑ́'ᵅmɑx wí·ɬ JH Chinook canoe.

weɬ TAb-mi a boy's name (a bird?; *prob.* /wíɬ).

/wiɬ- ?? 1. /wiɬ-íɬ=kʷu riffle.

/wíɬax̣ʷu turtle *Chrysemys picta* (painted turtle); HH wetxláxo tortoise; FBa wi´ɬhaxo´.

/wín- ?? 1. /wín·wn- double up. 1a. —, s/wín·wn-t-n *tr.*

/wín- live, reside, stay, become. 1a. —, s/wín-n *intr.* 1b. /win-áwm'x they stayed, they became *perf. intr.* 2. s/wín·win-n he's acting like *impf. intr.* 3. /wín·win-x̣- stay, act like. 3a. /wín·wn-x̣, s/wín·win-n-x̣ *intr.*

wi-ni-ní-ḥu̱ks EC buzzard *Cathartes aura* (Turkey vulture).

/wiq'ə́s- ?? 1. /wiq'ə́s-tan-: 1a. /wiq'ə́s-tn axe; HH qu̇stn, wequ̇stin axe, hatchet; AG,RL khustn axe; GGb wuk-ús-tin; FBa we'ka´stEn. 1b. /wiq'ə́s-tan-i his axe. 1c. /wiq'ə́s-tin-umiš-i his axes *pl.*

/wítk- ?? 1. /wítk=n'ɬ willow ?*Cornus stolonifera* (red-osier dogwood); EC wít-kĭnh̄l; HT kwaítənəɬ red willow; JH wí·tsqɑn'ɬ.

/wítq'–: 1. s/wítq' robin *Turdus migratorius* (American robin); FBa .shwī´ s.k.k (*prob.* s/wísq'q').

wī´tuwit FBa snipe, *prob.* ?*Gallinago gallinago* (common snipe) (*poss.* /wítwit).

/wítx̱, /wétx̱ do. 1. /wítx̱,

s/wít-awn'-x̱ *intr.* 2. /mí+ta t ?a-ta-s/wítx̱ Never do that again!

/wít'aš grizzly bear *Ursus arctos*.

/wít'i– climb. 1. /wít'-+, s/wít'i-w-n *intr.* 2. /wé·t'a-tn' ladder, stairway.

wutse´s.ks FBa fish spear.

X

x to.

/xác–: 1. xác·xac– trot. 1a. —, s/xá?c·xc-w-n, /xác·xac-n, —.

/xáculx (?) supply gets short.

xa+, x?a+ to. 2. ta-xa+ to.

/xá+– club. 1. /xá+-n, — *tr.*

/xamyúp–: 1. s/xamyúp-i his side.

/xam'álaxʷ–: 1. s/xam'álaxʷ people; EC sha-má-lahw; FBa .sx̱amaˊlaux relative; FBa .sx̱amaˊlaux Indian; FBa .sx̱Emaˊlaux people. 2. s/xam'á·l'axʷ small people *dimin.* 3. ?ac/né?q-m s/xam'álaxʷ Negro (*see* /nə́q– black).

/xán? there, that one (remote); FBa xaˊn there. 2. /xán?-x̱ there. 3. ?a+ /xán? there. 4. tk /xán? opposite, other side; FBa

tEkExaˊn across, on opposite side; BH tEkExaˊn across. 5. sEˊkEm+ax tEkExaˊn FBa swim across (*prob.* /sə́k'-m xa+ tk /xán?; *see* /sə́k'– swim).

/xápan– yawn. 1. /xápn', — *intr.* 2. s/xáp·xapan-n he's yawning *impf. intr.*

/xasák̓ʷ wild. 2. /xasák̓ʷ-lx go wild *dev.*

/xašém' this way, this direction. 2. /xašém'-x̱ this way, this direction.

/xawáci+–: 1. s/xawáci+ nephew, niece (on woman's side).

/xay'álu– ?? 1. /xay'álu-min–: 1a. /xay'álu-mn saddle; FBa xaiaˊluEnEmEn; HT x̱aiáluənəmən. 1b. /xay'álu-min-i his saddle.

/xə́lk– drag, haul. 1. —, s/xə́lk-t-n *tr.* 2.

s/xə́l·xlk-cši-t-n he's dragging along *impf. refl.* 3. xalkáˊmɛɬtɛn FBa wagon (*prob.* /xalk-ám'ɬ-tn). 4. /xál'k-m'ɬ-tan-i its tugs.

/xə́mʔ- ?? 1. /t'əm/xə́mʔ both ends.

/xəmím' dove *Columba fasciata* (band-tailed pigeon); FBa xemīˊm.t pigeon. 2. /xəmím'-x mourning dove *Zenaida macroura.*

/xə́n husband; HH sxʊn; GGb sˊhúnn; FR s'hunn; FBa .sxîˊn. 1b. /xə́n-i her husband. 2. s/xaná-m marry (*from a Boas Upper Chehalis manuscript*). 3. taiˊ.sxɛnlêmɛn FBa spinster (*prob.* /táy-s/xən-lmn).

/xənáˑs- lie on one's back. 1. /xənáˑs-m', — *mdl.*

/xə́pa- cover. 1. —, s/xə́pa-w-n *intr.* 2a. s/xə́p blanket, bedding. 2b. s/xə́p-i his blankets. 3. ʔac/xə́p=ls be covered. 4. /xə́p/aẋ-acx-tn' window blinds (*see* /ʔə́ẋ- see).

/xəpayíʔ-: 1a. /xə́piʔ comb; FBa,BH xîˊpēi. 1b. /xpyíʔ-i his comb. 2. /xəpáyi-comb. 2a. /xəpáy-m, — *mdl.* 2b. /xəpáy-n, s/xəpáyi-t-n *tr.* 3.

/xəpáyi-mɬ-tn' a rake.

/xəwál-: 1a. /xə́wɬ, /xúwɬ road, row; EC ħŭwiħl road; FBa xêˊ.uɬ road, trail; HT x̣ê.uɬ road; JH x̣ɑ́wɬ road. 1b. /xúwiɬ-umx *pl.* 1c. /xawál-i his road. 2. /xéw'ɬ trail, path *dimin.* 3. /saʔ/xáw'il- make a road. 3a. —, /saʔ/xáw'il-n *intr.* 4. kás-l/xaw'ɬ railroad. 5. /léˑl-l/xaw'ɬ out of the way, off the road. 6. /p'én-l/xawɬ by the road. 7. tawetxoˊuɬ FBa road, trail (*prob.* /taw'ət/xə́wɬ; *see* /taw'ə́t big).

/xəwála- grow, raise. 1. /xə́wɬ, s/xawála-n *intr.* 2. /xə́waɬi-x, — *caus.*

/xə́y- back, backwards. 1. s/xə́y=nak-: 1a. s/xə́y=nk crab, crawfish; FBa .sxīˊ.nɛk crab; JH sxîˑnɪk' fresh-water crawfish. 1b. s/xə́y=nak-umx *pl.* 1c. s/xə́y=nač-i his crab. 2. s/xéy'=nak-umx little crabs. 3. /xə́y'=nak- step back, walk backwards. 3a. /xə́y'=nač-m', s/xə́y'=nk-mit-n *mdl.*

/xə́y'- mind, obey. 1a. /xə́y'-ɬ, — *intr.* 1b. /xə́y'-tas, — *tr.*

xʷ

/xʷáˑʔaʔs later on, after a
while; GGb hwáss bye and
bye.

/xʷáʔkʷuʔ all; HH xwako;
GGb hwáh-ko; FR hwáh-
ko, h'wáhko; FBa xwaˊko.
2. /t'əm/xʷáʔkʷuʔ all,
every, whole.

/xʷákʷa- sweep, clear off. 1.
/xʷákʷ-ɬ, s/xʷákʷa-w-n,
/xʷákʷ-n, s/-xʷákʷa-t-
n. 2. /xʷákʷ-ltam- sweep.
2a. /xʷákʷ-ltm, s/xʷákʷ-
ltam-n intr. 3. s/xʷákʷ-
lkʷ-cši-t-n the clouds are
travelling fast impf. refl. 4.
x̣waˊkwolᴇmtᴇn FBa
broom; HT xwákwoləmtən
(prob. /xʷákʷ-lm-tn).

/xʷál' dull, not sharp.

/xʷam'- ?? 1. /xʷam'=íčn
bent over, humpbacked.

hwanēˊkᵘ FBa humpback
salmon Onchorhynchus
gorbuscha (poss.
/xʷaníkʷ).

/xʷán' other side.

/xʷáw'kʷ- go across (=
/xʷúʔkʷ- over there ?). 1.
/xʷu·xʷáw'kʷ-m' go
across. 2. /xʷu·xʷáw'kʷ-
m'-x̣ over there, across.

.swai'aˊtok FBa chicken
hawk ?Accipiter sp(p). or
?Buteo jamaicensis (red-
tailed hawk) (poss.
s/xʷayát').

/xʷayə́q̓ʷ-: 1a. s/xʷayə́q̓ʷ
wrist. 1b. s/xʷayə́q̓ʷ-i his
wrist. 2. s/xʷiyq̓ʷ=ə́šan-:
2a. s/xʷiyq̓ʷ=ə́šn ankle; EC
sʰwi-ŭ-qŭsʰn ankle-joint.
2b. s/xʷiyq̓ʷ=ə́šan-i his
ankle.

/xʷáyp eagle; EC hwaips
golden eagle; TAb-jc
x̣waˊips mountain eagle;
JH sxwâyps bald eagle.

/xʷay'ús-: 1a. s/xʷáy's hat;
FBa .shwaiˊs. 1b.
s/xʷay'ús-i his hat. 2.
ʔac/x̣ə́q-s/xʷáy's
snowcap (see /x̣ə́q-). 3.
taˊkshwaismᴇn FBa
headband (prob. /t'ə́q-
s/xʷay's-mn; see /t'ə́q-
wind around, tie around). 4.
/x̣asílʔ-s/xʷay's rain hat.

/xʷc- ?? (possibly txʷ-
cúyn-). 1. /xʷc=úyn- be
barely audible, barely hear.
1a. —, /xʷc=úyn-mit-n
mdl. 2. /xʷc=úyn-mn', —
rel.

/xʷéˑk̓ʷ lightweight.

/xʷəl- ?? 1. /xʷəl-tm non-
Indian; GGb hwíl-tum a
white man; EC hwúl-i-tu̧m
people (white). 2a. /xʷəl-
tam-ul=ic'aʔ blanket. 2b.
/xʷəl-tam-ul=ic'a-yumx
pl. 2c. /xʷəl-tam-ul=ic'a-

ni his blanket.

/xʷə́lpa– turn. 1. —,
s/xʷə́lpa-w-n *intr.*

X̣wuˊlpios TAb-ss an old
man's name; MJb-si
hwilpiˊus old man giant
(myth character).

/xʷə́l'p– be last. 1. s/xʷə́l'p-
tn the last one.

/xʷə́na– tired, weak. 1.
/xʷə́n-ɬ, s/xʷə́na-w-n
intr. 2. /xʷə́na-mn,
s/xʷə́n-ms-n tire of *rel.*

X̣wαnαˊye TAb-mi Coyote's
daughter and name of a
river.

xontuˊlεms FBa rosebush
Rosa spp. (*poss.*
/xʷəntúlms).

/xʷə́plq, /xʷə́plq-tn
rainbow; EC hú-pĭ-lŭktn;
FBa hwoˊpεlkεn.

/xʷə́t'a– get up. 1a. /xʷə́t'-ɬ,
s/xʷə́t'a-w-n *intr.* 1b.
/xʷít'-iʔ-ɬ *pl.*

/xʷikʷi– wipe, wipe off. 1.
/xʷíkʷ-n, s/xʷíkʷi-t-n *tr.*
2. /xʷíkʷ=iq– dry (dishes).
2a. /xʷíkʷ=iq-n, — *tr.* 3.
/xʷíkʷ=qs– wipe one's
nose. 3a. /xʷíkʷ=qs-m, —
mdl.

/xʷík̓ʷ– wave, blow in the
wind. 1. /xʷík̓ʷ-ɬ, — *intr.*
2. s/xʷík̓ʷ·xʷk̓ʷ-w-n it's
waving *impf. intr.* 3.
/xʷí·xʷk̓ʷ– wave at. 3a.
/xʷí·xʷk̓ʷ-c he waved at

me *perf. tr.* 4. /xʷí·xʷk̓ʷ-
ši– wave at *appl.* 4a.
/xʷí·xʷk̓ʷ-š-n, — *tr.* 5.
/xʷík̓ʷ=ɬn' handkerchief,
scarf; FBa hwiˊkuɬεn
handkerchief.

/xʷíli– hang down, hang
over. 1. /xʷíl-ɬ, —, /xʷíl-
n, s/xʷíli-t-n. 2. qi s-
xʷíl-aʔ hanging racks.

/xʷim– ?? 1. /xʷim=ínut
lonesome. 2. /xʷim=ínut-
ši– be lonesome for *appl.*
2a. /xʷim=ínut-š-n, — *tr.*

/xʷíq̓ʷx̣– cut. 1. /xʷíq̓ʷx̣-n,
— *tr.*

/xʷísələs "Whistling Jack"
(marmot ?), *prob.*
?*Marmota caligata* (hoary
marmot); TAb-mi Hwιˊsələs
the Wolves.

/xʷít wheat (loanword; *see*
English wheat). 2.
/xʷé·t=lwltxʷ granary.

/xʷíy·xʷiy stingy, won't
share.

/xʷúʔkʷ– over there (=
/xʷáw'kʷ– go across ?). 1.
xʷu·/xʷúʔkʷ-m' over
there.

/xʷuʔú– cry. 1. /xʷuá-m,
s/xʷuʔú-mit-n; FBa
.s.xôˊm cry, weep *mdl.* 2.
xʷúʔ·xʷuʔ– howl. 2a. —,
s/xʷúʔ·xʷuʔ-mit-n *mdl.*
3. /xʷóˑʔ·xʷuʔ– howl. 3a.
—, s/xʷóˑʔ·xʷuʔ-mit-n
mdl.

/xʷúlup-: 1. ʔac/xʷúlup-ɬ
round, spherical, around.
/xʷúxʷa- wind blows. 1. —,
s/xʷúxʷa-w-n *intr.* 2.
s/xʷúxʷ wind; HH sxux,
sxox; GGb s'hoo'h; FR
s'hoo'h, s'hū'h; EC sḣoḣ;
FBa .s'xuˊx. 3. s/xʷóˑxʷ

breeze *dimin.* 4.
s/xʷúxʷkʷ-u-ən-stawt it
got windy on us, we're
having a windstorm. 5. tu
ʔaɬ t s/xʷúxʷ west.

hoˊxtɬ FBa dentalia
Dentalium pretiosum.

X̣

/x̣áḱʷa- gnaw, chew. 1. —,
s/x̣áḱʷa-t-n *tr.*
/x̣ála- plant, sow. 1. /x̣ál-n,
— *tr.* 2. s/x̣áˑl'a-m'ɬ
crops, garden. 2b. s/x̣áˑl'-
m'l-i his garden. 3. s/x̣ála-
m'ɬ-tn' seeds. 4.
/pən/x̣áˑla-m'ɬ time to
plant a garden.
/x̣aləw'-: 1. x̣aləw'·x̣aləw'
butterfly; FBa
x̣aleˊmxaiˊu. 2.
/x̣aláˑw'=iʔɬ little blue
butterfly.
/x̣ál'- ?? 1. /x̣ál'-s/tq̇ʷ-m
hush, be quiet (see /təq̇ʷa-
talk).
/x̣áˑl'- set a table. 1. /x̣áˑl'-
n, — *tr.* 2. /x̣ál'=txʷi-: 2a.
/x̣ál'=txʷ roof. 2b.
s/x̣ál'=txʷi-t-n he's
putting on the roof *impf. tr.*
/x̣ál'xʷil-: 1. s/x̣ál'xʷil-i
their stakes, their pot, what
they gamble.
/x̣áɬxʷa- play, laugh. 1.

/x̣áɬxʷ-m, s/x̣áɬxʷ-mt-n
mdl. 2. /x̣áɬxʷa-mi-x, —
play with, wrestle with
caus. 3. /x̣áɬxʷa- make
faces at, make fun of. 3a. —,
s/x̣áɬxʷ-m't-n *mdl.* 3b.
/x̣áɬxʷa-mn, — *rel.* 4.
s/x̣áɬxʷa-m'n toy, doll.
/x̣áɬxʷm ?? 1. /x̣áɬxʷm-s
txʷt/məkʷp firewood.
/x̣áƛ̓- ?? 1. s/x̣áƛ̓=tmx
brush, underbrush; EC
sḣátl-tŭmħl forest; JH
sx̣âɬtɑmɑx underbrush.
/x̣aƛ̓é- force. 1. /x̣aƛ̓é-n, —
tr.
x̣āˊtlolitsa FBa rabbit skin
robe; HT x̣áˑtlolica (*poss.*
/x̣áƛ̓-ul=ic'aʔ).
/x̣ám'- ?? 1. /x̣ám'-s/tq̇ʷ
finish talking (*see* /təq̇ʷa-
talk).
/x̣án- ?? 1. /x̣án=tmx
cranberry *Vaccinium
oxycoccos* (wild cranberry);
EC ħán-tŭm; JH x̣áˑntɑm,

x̣â·ntɑm.

/x̣anúmt- insult. 1.
/x̣anúmt-mn, — rel.

xaʼkaiˊ FBa bark basket
(poss. /x̣aqáy).

/x̣asíliʔ- rain. 1. /x̣asílʔ,
s/x̣asé·l-n intr. 2.
s/x̣asilíʔ-i its raining. 3.
s/x̣asílʔ-kʷù-stawt it's
raining on us, we got rained
on impf. non-control pass. 4.
s/x̣asílʔ (the) rain; EC s̓ha-
síl; FBa xasʼsél. 5.
/pən/x̣asílʔ-mnʼ raincoat
(ENM). 6. s/x̣asílʔ/kapu
raincoat (LNJ) (see /kapú
coat). 7. /x̣asílʔ-s/xʷayʼs
rain hat (see /xʷayʼús-
hat).

/x̣asíɬšn-: 1. s/x̣asíɬšn
driftwood, anything washed
up on a beach, brush; HH
x̣ásitxltҫin grass.

/x̣asó·l-: 1. s/x̣asó·l=ičn
openwork basket (also
given as səx̣ʷó·ʔcal=ičn);
EC ħa-só-lichn wallet
basket; FBb sx̣asɔ·ˊɛlikEn;
JH x̣ɑsó·lí·tʃɪn storage
basket.

/x̣átx̣at duck; HH xátxʊt;
GGb,FR haat-hat; FBa
xāˊtxEt; JH x̣áˑt.xɑt. 1b.
/x̣átx̣at-i his duck. 1c.
/x̣átx̣at-umiš-i his ducks
pl.

/x̣awə́lʔ fast. 2. /x̣aw-
íɬ=kʷu fast water.

/x̣áwqaɬ can't (loanword;
see Chinook Jargon howʹ-
kwutl 'cannot, stubborn'
taken in turn from Lower
Chinook x̣áoxaL 'cannot').

/x̣áwš cous, biscuitroot
?Lomatium cous (loanword;
see Sahaptin x̣áwš 'cous,
biscuitroot').

/x̣áx house; HH xax; AG,RL
khakh; GGb hách, hágh;
FR hagh; EC ħass̑h; FBb
x̣ax̣. 1b. /x̣áx-i his house.
2. /x̣áʔx little house dimin.
3. añtkt-x̣áx HH town,
village (prob. /ʔáyʼtk t
/x̣áx; see /ʔáyʼtk lots of).

ħá-ħe-wĩhl EC pine Pinus
sp(p).; JH x̣áˑɬɪˑwɪɬ pine
tree (prob. /x̣áxiwɬ).

/x̣áx̣- ?? 1. /x̣áx̣-l=us
Speckled Face (a kitten's
name).

xaiaˊm FBa fishhook (poss.
/x̣ayám).

/x̣ayímʼ a witch; unlucky.

/x̣ə́k̓ʷuwt hinge (?).

/x̣ə́lkʷ- rap. 1. —,
s/x̣ə́l·xlkʷ-mit-n mdl.

x̣əɬ so.

/x̣ə́ƛ̓- break in two. 1. /x̣ə́ƛ̓-
ɬ, —, /x̣ə́ƛ̓-n, s/x̣ə́ƛ̓-t-n.
2. s/x̣ə́ƛ̓·x̣ƛ̓-w-n it's
falling apart impf. intr. 3.
/x̣aƛ̓=áx̣an- break an arm.
3a. /x̣aƛ̓=áx̣n,
s/x̣aƛ̓=áx̣an-n intr. 4.
/x̣aƛ̓=éʔkʷn someone who

wants to argue, mean person; HH x̣atx̣lékwʊn warrior; GGb,FR haht-léh-kwun warrior; FBa x̣atʟā´kʷEn warrior. 5. /x̣ə́ƛ̓=qs break one's nose.

/x̣əƛ̓– ?? 1. /x̣aƛ̓=ált-mn, /x̣əƛ̓=ált-mn hard (work).

/x̣ə́m heavy. 2. /x̣ám-lx get heavy *dev.* 3. /x̣ə́m-tan-: 3a. /x̣ə́m-tn heavy, heaviness, weight. 3b. s/x̣ə́m-tan-i its weight.

xumxum EG horsetail roots (*Equisetum* sp.) (*prob.* /x̣ə́m'x̣əm').

/x̣ən'ús–: 1a. /x̣ə́n's fishhook; EC ħanˀns; FBa x̣ênns; HT x̣ênns. 1b. /x̣ə́n'is-umx *pl.* 1c. /x̣an'ús-i or /x̣an'ís-i his fishhook. 2. tami´ɬEn Eɬ tê hê´nns FBa fishline (*prob.* /t'amíɬn ɬ t /x̣ə́n's; *see* /t'amiɬə́n– rope).

/x̣ə́p– ?? 1. /x̣ə́p=ayq lazy.

/x̣ə́pa– dry. 1. /x̣ə́p-ɬ, s/x̣ə́pa-w-n, /x̣ə́p-n, —. 2. s/x̣ə́p-ɬ dried things. 3. /x̣ápa-m'ɬ-tn' drying rack. 4. .shapau´ɬiɬEn FBa dried salmon (*prob.* s/x̣ap=úliɬn). 5. /x̣ap=úl'mx-n spread to dry *perf. tr.* 6. /x̣ə́p-nx-tn drying rack. 7. tit qi /x̣ap-ánan-i /ká· t qi s/x̣ap-ə́t-s t s/ƛ̓aláš drying rack

where he dries the deer meat.

sx̣ɑp'ɑlɑm' JH small owl *sp.* (*prob.* s/x̣ə́p'lm').

/x̣ə́q– ?? 1. ?ac/x̣ə́q-s/xʷáy's snowcap (*see* /xʷay'ús– hat).

/x̣ə́q̓ʷ– squeeze. 1. /x̣ə́q̓ʷ-n, — *tr.* 2. /x̣ə́q̓ʷ-l=k-squeeze. 2a. —, s/x̣ə́q̓ʷ-l=k-mis-n *rel.*

/x̣ə́š bad. 1. /x̣ə́š, —; HH xuç bad, ugly; GGb,FR hush; FBa xêc *intr.* 2. /x̣aš-áwmx bad people *pl.* 3. /x̣aš-ə́x, — mistreat *caus.* 4. /x̣áš-lx- get bad, spoil *dev.* 4a. /x̣áš-lx, s/x̣áš-lt-n. 4b. /x̣áš-ili-x, — ruin, harm *caus.* 4c. ?ak-c/x̣áš-lx ?u It tastes spoiled. 4d. x̣ɑci·´lc FBb bad (*prob.* /x̣əš-ílš). 5. t'im /x̣ə́š worst. 6. /x̣ə́š-m' a fool. 7. s/x̣ə́š-tan-i his badness. 8. /x̣áš-lkʷukʷɬ thunderstorm. 9. /x̣aš=úl'mx coarse, bad food. 10a. s/x̣ə́š=tmx weeds. 10b. /x̣aš-áy=tmx trash, garbage, rough ground; sx̣ɑsâytɑm'ʃ JH underbrush. 11. /x̣š=ál'wn ugly. 12. xîcsExa´mEɬ FBa ugly (*prob.* /x̣ə́š s/?ə́x-am'ɬ; *see* /?ə́x– see).

/x̣əyə́k̓ʷ– curl. 1. /x̣ayə́k̓ʷ-ɬ, —, /x̣ayə́k̓ʷ-n, —. 2.

ʔac/x̣éyk̓ʷ-m’ɬ it’s
wrinkled (e.g. cloth) *impl.tr.*
3. /x̣əyk̓ʷ=óʔs hair is curly.

x̣íˑts’tɑmts JH dogwood
?Cornus nuttallii (Pacific
flowering dogwood) (*prob.*
/x̣íc’tmc).

/x̣ík’- ?? 1. /x̣ík’=lsi- peel.
1a. /x̣ík’=ls-n, s/x̣ík’=lsi-
t-n *tr.*

/x̣íli- attack. 1. /x̣íl-n,
s/x̣íli-t-n *tr.*

/x̣ím- grab, grab a handful. 1.
/x̣ím-n, — *tr.* 2.
/nək̓ʷ/x̣ím handful. 3.
s/x̣ím=usi-ctx he was
grabbed by the face *impf.*
pass.

/x̣íp’- forbid, stop. 1.
/x̣íp’-n, s/x̣íp’-t-n *tr.* 2.
ʔit /x̣íp’-tmɬi-x he
forbade it *perf. caus.*

/x̣íq’- whittle. 1. /x̣íq’-n, —
tr. 2. s/x̣íq’-ml’-n he’s
whittling *impf. impl.tr.*

/x̣ísi- bloom. 1. /x̣ís-ɬ,
s/x̣ísi-w-n *intr.* 2a. s/x̣ís
flower, flowers; FBa
.s’xeˊs. 2b. s/x̣ís-i her
flower. 3. /pən-s/q̓ʷáX̣-
ši-tm-s t s/x̣ís May.

/x̣íwq’-: 1. /x̣íw·x̣awq’- tell
on. 2. /x̣íw·x̣awq’-n, — *tr.*

/x̣íx̣aq’- race. 1. —,
s/x̣íx̣aq’-n *intr.*

/x̣íx̣i goose; EC sħe-ħé; FBa
xe'xeiˊ; JH sx̣ɑ̀yx̣ɑ̀yy. 2.
s/x̣ix̣í fish coming
upstream swinging its tail;
young person chasing
around.

/x̣íy- order, force to leave,
drive away 1. /x̣íy-n,
s/x̣íy-t-n *tr.*

/x̣íyap-: 1a. s/x̣íyəp fish
trap. 1b. s/x̣íy’ap-i his fish-
trap.

/x̣wíʔ- ?? 1. /x̣wíʔ=ičn
backbone.

x̣ʷ

ħŭ-t͡sé-a-má-ħŭn EC bat,
various *Chiroptera*; FBa
xatseˊmaxEn; JH
x̣wɑ̀tsǽˑ’mɑ̀x̣ɑ̀n’ (*prob.*
/x̣ʷacéʔm=ax̣n’).

/x̣ʷacíʔ- steep. 1. /x̣ʷacíʔ-ɬ,
— *intr.*

/x̣ʷál- gamble, play cards. 1.
—, s/x̣ʷál-mit-n *mdl.*

/x̣ʷál-: 1a. /x̣ʷáɬ, /x̣ʷáʔɬ
older sibling; FBa 'hwaˊɬ
elder brother. 1b. ne-whátl
my brother GGb; FR ne-
wharl my elder brother; EC
nŭ-ħwáȟl elder brother; EC
na-ħwáȟl elder sister
(*prob.* n/x̣ʷáɬ my elder
sibling. 1c. nx/x̣ʷáʔɬ-tn *pl.*

1d. /x̣ʷál-i his older sibling. 1e. nx/x̣ʷá?ɬ-tan-i his older siblings *pl.*

/x̣ʷalá? hot, warm. 1a. /x̣ʷalá?, —; HH xwála warm; GGb hwál-la hot; FR hwál-la warm; FBa x̣wola´ warm (person) *intr.* 1b. /x̣ʷalá?-n, — heat *tr.* 2. ?ac/x̣ʷála?-tn fever. 3. /x̣ʷalá?-lx- get warm *dev.* 3a. /x̣ʷalá?-lx, s/x̣ʷalá?-llt-n. 3b. /x̣ʷalá?-ili-x-a? heat it! 4. hwola´xtomᴇx FBa warm (weather). 5. /x̣ʷal=ílsi- heat rocks. 5a. —, s/x̣ʷal=ílsi-t-n *tr.* 6a. /x̣ʷal-íɬ=kʷu warm water. 6b. /x̣ʷal-íɬ=kʷu-m-i-ɬ-a? heat the water! *imper.*

/x̣ʷál'a- burn, catch fire. 1a. /x̣ʷál'-ɬ, s/x̣ʷá·l'a-w-n *intr.* 1b. /x̣ʷál'-n, — put in the fire *tr.* 2. /x̣ʷál'-š- put fire on *appl.* 2a. /x̣ʷál'-š-n, — *tr.* 3a. /x̣ʷál'=kʷp build a fire. 3b. /x̣ʷál'·x̣ʷl'=kʷp keep building fires. 3c. /x̣ʷál'=kʷp-mn' stove, heater.

/x̣ʷám- wear out. 1. /x̣ʷám-ɬ, —, /x̣ʷám-n, —.

/x̣ʷaní the transformer (myth character); TAb x̣wɑ´ni; JH x̣wɑní·x̣wɑnɪ.

/x̣ʷáqʷiy- *or* /x̣ʷáqʷay- miss, make a mistake. 1. /x̣ʷáqʷiy-n *or*

/x̣ʷáqʷay-n, — *tr.*

/x̣ʷáq̇ʷa- scrape hair off. 1. /x̣ʷáq̇ʷ-n, s/x̣ʷáq̇ʷa-t-n *tr.* 2a. s/x̣ʷáq̇ʷ-ml-n scraping a hide *impf. impl.tr.* 2b. /x̣ʷáq̇ʷa-m'ɬ-tn' scraper; FBa hwa´kwamᴇɬtᴇn skin-scraper, tanning- knife. 3. qi s/x̣ʷáq̇ʷa-c /č'íp=qs he shaved me (?). 4. /x̣ʷáq̇ʷ-s/č'p=qs-m shave *mdl.* (*see* /č'íp=qas- beard). 5. /tay-s/x̣ʷáq̇ʷ deerskin with hair still on it.

/x̣ʷatəqʷ- heat 1. /x̣ʷatəqʷ-n, — *tr.*

/x̣ʷáya- miss, be gone. 1. /x̣ʷáy'-ɬ, —, —, s/x̣ʷáy-taw-n. 2. /x̣ʷáya-cx disappear *refl.* 2a. /x̣ʷáya-cx, s/x̣ʷáy-cši-t-n. 3. /x̣ʷay=ó·ɬ=q- quiet, get quiet, shut up. 3a. /x̣ʷay=ó·ɬ=q, s/x̣ʷay=ó·ɬ=aq-n *intr.*

/x̣ʷáykas-: 1a. s/x̣ʷáyks rabbit *Lepus americanus* (Snowshoe hare); EC sḣhwaiks; FBa .shwai´.ks; TAb-mi sx̣wa´iks; JH sx̣wá·yɑqs small rabbit *sp.*; JHjp sx̣wáyks brush rabbit. 1b. s/x̣ʷáykis-umx *pl.* 1c. /x̣ʷáykas-i or s/x̣ʷayksən-i (LNJ) his rabbit. 2. /x̣ʷáy'kas=iɬ-um'x small rabbits.

/x̣ʷáy'–: 1. x̣ʷ · /x̣ʷáy' golden eagle *?Aquila chrysaetos.*

/x̣ʷay'əx̣ʷay'əx̣ʷ fly; HH xwaioxwaío; GGb hwió-hwio; FR hwáio-hwáio, hwái-o.-hwái-o.

/x̣ʷay'úp–: 1. /x̣ʷay'úp-i his side, his hip.

/x̣ʷél' young; HH xwéle small; HH xwelt young; GGb hwéll small; FR hwell small; EC ḥwel small.

/x̣ʷél'·l' become very sick. 2. s/x̣ʷél'-l't-n he's getting weak *impf. intr. dev.*

/x̣ʷəl– ?? 1. s/x̣ʷəl=ayq dust.

xolā´tEn FBa trout; JHjp x̣wɑlɑtn (*prob.* /x̣ʷəlátn).

/x̣ʷəl'a– sweat. 1. /x̣ʷəl'-ɬ, s/x̣ʷəl'a-w-n *intr.*

/x̣ʷənəx̣ʷ– ?? 1. s/x̣ʷənəx̣ʷ=qs nostril.

/x̣ʷəq'– ditch. 1. ʔac/x̣ʷəq'-ɬ big ditch. 2. ʔac/x̣ʷé·q'-ɬ a ditch *dimin.*

/x̣ʷəqʷa– hungry, starve. 1. /x̣ʷəqʷ-ɬ, s/x̣ʷəqʷa-w-n; FBa .tsho´k.ɬ hungry *intr.* 2. ʔac/x̣ʷəqʷ-tas kn I'm hungry for it *tr.* 3. /ták-s/x̣ʷq̇ʷ starve.

/x̣ʷəx̣ʷəl– (?) disappear, lose. 1. /x̣ʷəx̣ʷɬ, — *intr.* 2. /x̣ʷax̣ʷəl-st-i (?) their leaving it.

/x̣ʷíʔɬ–: 1. ʔac-x̣ʷí· /x̣ʷiʔɬ-kɬ Windy Point

(*placename*).

/x̣ʷilúq– ?? 1. /x̣ʷilúq=qs-snore. 1a. /x̣ʷilúq=qs-m, s/x̣ʷilúq=qs-mit-n *mdl.*

/x̣ʷóʔana– cough. 1. /x̣ʷóʔn, s/x̣ʷóʔan-n *intr.* 2. /x̣ʷóʔana-mn tuberculosis.

/x̣ʷúc'– bend. 1. /x̣ʷúc'-n, — *tr.* 2. s/x̣ʷúc'-i its corner.

/x̣ʷúlqʷ– purr. 1. —, s/x̣ʷúlqʷ-mt-n *mdl.*

.sxo´mEks FBa ridge of the nose; HT .sx̣óməks (*prob.* s/x̣ʷúm=qs).

/x̣ʷúqʷa– *or* /x̣ʷúqʷi– meet, gather, together with, pick up. 1. /x̣ʷúqʷ-ɬ, s/x̣ʷúqʷa-w-n, /x̣ʷúqʷ-n, s/x̣ʷúqʷi-t-n. 2. ʔac/x̣ʷúqʷ-aɬ/cani with him (*see* /cə́ni he, him). 3. ʔac/x̣ʷúqʷ-aɬ/cəni-yawmx with them (*see* /cə́ni he, him). 4. ʔac/x̣ʷúqʷ-aɬ/ənca with me (*see* /ʔə́nca I, me). 5. ʔac/x̣ʷúqʷ-aɬ/inm with us (*see* /ʔiním we, us). 6. ʔac/x̣ʷúqʷ-aɬ/nawi with you (*see* /nə́wi you, *sg.*). 7. ʔac/x̣ʷúqʷ-t-wlx-umx travelling companion. 8. /nàk̓ʷ-u-s/x̣ʷúqʷ together (*see* /nák'- one). 9. /nək̓ʷ-u-s/x̣ʷóqʷ a bunch (*see* /nák'- one). 10. s/x̣ʷuqʷ=álust-n coming

together *impf. intr.* 11.
/x̣ʷúqʷ·qʷ–i‡t club,
meeting.
/x̣ʷúx̣ʷ– lose. 1. /x̣ʷúx̣ʷ–‡,

—, /x̣ʷúx̣ʷ–n, s/x̣ʷúx̣ʷ–
t–n. 2. /x̣ʷux̣ʷí– owe, be in
debt. 2a. /x̣ʷux̣ʷí–n, — *tr.*

y

/yác'– take back. 1. /yác'–n,
s/yác'–staw–n *tr./caus.* 2.
s/yác'·yəc'–w–n
swinging, going back and
forth *impf. intr.* 3. /yác'–
‡=kʷu riffle, whirlpool. 4.
/yác'=s– turn around. 4a.
/yác'=s–n, — *tr.* 4b.
/yác'=us–m–la? turn
around! *mdl., imper.*
yáis ?? 1. yáis /mí‡ta t n–
s/láxʷkʷu–n–m I can't
breathe. 2. yais /x̣áwqa‡ t
n–s/láxʷkʷu–n–m I can't
breathe.
/yákm'x, /yá?km'x near,
close; HH iákamax near;
FBa ya´kɛmɛx near.
/yákp– catch up with. 1.
/yákp–n, s/yákp–taw–n
tr./caus. 2. GGb yáh–kahp
near; FR yah–kahp near
(*prob.* /yákp).
/yák̓ʷa– bony, thin, skinny. 1.
/yák̓ʷ–‡, s/yák̓ʷa–w–n
intr.
/yál– groan. 1. /yál–m,
s/yál–mt–n *mdl.*
/yal– around ?? 1.
/yal=á?ka–min–: 1a.
/yal=á?ka–mn ring; FBa

yele´ka´mɛn finger-ring.
1b. /yal=á?ka–min–i her
ring. 1c. /yal=á?ka–min–
umiš–i her rings.
/yaləm'– go around. 1.
/yaləm'–n, — *tr.*
/yaləqʷx̣ʷ–: 1. ?ac/yaləqʷx̣ʷ
temporary shelter.
/yálp wild celery ?*Apiaceae.*
/yálxʷtak–: 1a. s/yálxʷtk
brother-in-law; FBa
sia´luxtɛk. 1b. /yálxʷtač–i
his brother-in-law. 1c.
nx/yálxʷtk–tan–i his
brothers-in-law.
/yál'–: 1. ?ac/yál' like this.
/yál'i– go through (?) 1.
/yál', s/yáli–w–n *intr.*
/yáƛ̓a– go home. 1a. /yáƛ̓–‡,
s/yáƛ̓a–w–n *intr.* 1b.
/yaƛ̓–əx, — bring home
caus. 1c. /yáƛ̓–a?–‡ *perf.*
intr. pl. 2. FBa tɛtiat‡kɛn go
home, come home (*prob.* tit
/yáƛ̓–‡ kn I went home). 3.
/yáƛ̓=us–m turn around
mdl.
/yámac–: 1a. /yámc tree,
wood (Ponderosa pine);
prob. Pseudotsuga
menziesii (Douglas fir);

HH iámuts tree, pine; AG,RL iamuts tree; UWb yamps tree; EC yá-mĩts red fir; FBa yā´mɛts fir; FBb ya·ᵋmts fir; HT yá·məc fir; JH yá·m'ts fir. 1b. /yámac-umx *pl.* 2. /yá·m'ac-umx little trees *dimin. pl.*

/yamə́t'- hang over the edge. 1a. /yamə́t'-ɬ, — *intr.* 1b. /yamə́t'-n, — throw over *tr.*

/yamó?si- threaten, shake one's fist at. 1. /yamó?s-n, s/yamó?si-t-n *tr.*

/yá·n yarn (loanword; *see* English *yarn*).

/yanáq-: 1a. /yán'q necklace, halter; FBa ya´nɛk necklace, neckerchief. 1b. /yanáq-i her necklace.

/yáp'a- bend down. 1. —, s/yáp'a-t-n *tr.* 2. /yáp'-a?-ɬ bend down (e.g. limbs) *perf. intr. pl.*

/yáq'a- tip, tip over, fall, fell. 1. /yáq'-ɬ, s/yáq'a-w-n, /yáq'-n, s/yáq'a-t-n. 2. pən/yáq'-s/məɬk fall, autumn; HH puneáxsoman autumn; UWb, FR pin-yalk-so-milkh autumn (*see* /mə́ɬk-summer). 3. s/yáq' windfall, fallen tree, log. 4. /yáq'-ši- fall on *appl.* 4a. —, s/yáq'-ši-t-n *tr.* 5. ?aqa ta-s/yə́q'a-w-n

September.

/yáq'·iq'- rock back and forth. 1. /yáq'·iq'-n, s/yáq'·iq'-t-n *tr.* 2. s/yáq'·iq'-cši-t-n rocking oneself back and forth *impf. refl.* 3. /yéq'·iq'-taw-n rocking chair.

/yá·qʷɬ-: 1a. š/yá·qʷɬ hat (old kind). 1b. š/yá·qʷ-i his hat.

/yás yesterday; HH iás; GGb yáhs; FR yahs; FBa ya´s. 1. naukīa´sˢ FBa day before yesterday (*prob.* /naw-ki/yás; *see* /náwa- old).

/yasə́n hook, net (?) 1b. /yasə́n-i his hook.

/yasə́x̣an- *or* /yacə́x̣an- fringe. 1. /yasə́x̣an-i *or* /yacə́x̣an-i its fringe.

/yát- shake. 1. /yát=ips- run around swinging her tail (of women or fish). 1a. /yát=ips-m, — *mdl.* 2. /yát-l=us- shake one's head. 2a. /yát-l=us-m, — *mdl.*

/yáta- rattle. 1. —, s/yáta-w-n, /yát-n, s/yáta-t-n.

/yát'a- turn, stir, wind, twist, churn, wring out. 1. /yát'-ɬ, —, /yát'-n, s/yát'a-t-n. 2. /yát'-ši- turn around *appl.* 2a. —, s/yát'-ši-t-n *tr.*

/yáwa- skim off. 1. —,

s/yáwa-t-n *tr.*

/**yáwax̣an-** gamble at stick-game. 1a. /yáwax̣an-m, — *mdl.* 1b. /yáwax̣an-n, — *tr.*

/**yáxa-** pack, carry. 1. /yáš-n, s/yáxa-t-n *tr.* 2. /yáxa-ni- carry on the back *appl.* 2a. /yáxa-ni-x, — *caus.* 3. /yəx-ál'=kn-: 3a. /yəx-ál'=kn-i his pack (on the back), rolling its pack off (?). 4. /yəxá-n'-mn' pack (horse).

/**yax̣áw'at-:** 1a. /yax̣áw't fish trap, fish basket. 1b. /yax̣áw'at-i his fish trap.

/**yáx̣ʷa-** shake. 1. —, s/yáx̣ʷa-w-n *intr.* 2. /yáx̣ʷ=ipsi- wag its tail (at). 2a. —, s/yáx̣ʷ=ips-mit-n *mdl.* 2b. —, s/yáx̣ʷ=ipsi-t-n *tr.* 3. /yáx̣ʷ=nak- wiggle. 3a. /yáx̣ʷ=nač-m, s/yáx̣ʷ=nk-mit-n *mdl.*

/**yáy-** like, respect. 1. /yáy-n, — *tr.*

/**yáy-** tell, tell on. 1. /yáy-n, s/yáy-t-n *tr.* 2. ʔnks + t/yáy'·yay'-ši-c she's always telling me stories *appl.* 3. /yáy-ni-n-aʔ tell him! *appl.* 4. /yáy'=ɬwal-: 4a. /yáy'=ɬuɬ tell news, tell a story. 4b. s/yáy'=ɬuɬ story, news. 4c. s/yáy'=ɬwal-i his story. 5.

/kát/yay'=ɬuɬ interpret (*see* /kátyn interpreter). 6. /yáy'-ši- tell to *appl.* 6a. /yáy'-š-n, s/yáy'-ši-t-n *tr.* 7. /yáyay'-ši- tell to *appl.* 7a. —, s/yáyay'-ši-t-n *tr.* 7b. ɩt ya·´ix̣Entwalex̂ FBb he told him *perf. recip.* 8. /yáy'-tx̣ʷt tell him it *appl.*

/**yáy-** stingy. 1. —, s/yáy-n *intr.* 2. /yáy-ɬx stingy with food.

/**yayús** work. 1a. /yayús, s/yayúst-n *intr.*; FBb yayo´s do, work. 1b. —, s/yayús-mis-n work on *rel.* 2. ǰæ̌yayús-i SH work (*sic*; should be 'his work'). 3. /yayó·s-a-tn' tools. 4. /yayús=alakaʔ worker. 5. yei´usla FBa work (*prob.* /yayús-laʔ work!). 6. /yayús-ši- use, work for *appl.* 6a. /yayús-š-n, s/yayús-ši-t-n *tr.*

/**yáyx̣ʷi-:** 1. ʔac/yáyx̣ʷi expensive, valuable, high-priced. 2. .tstcē´euxwei FBa gold (*poss.* ʔac/yáyx̣ʷi). 3. .tsko´ke tse´uxwe FBa silver (*poss.* ʔac/qʷúx̣ʷ ʔac/yáyx̣ʷi; *see* /qʷúx̣ʷ- white).

/**yəcə́q-** tan a hide, work a hide. 1. /yacə́q-n, s/yə́cq-t-n *tr.* 2. s/yacə́q-ɬ tanned hide.

/yə́kʷa- move, change. **1.** —, s/yə́kʷa-t-n *tr.* **2.** yə́kʷa-move. **2a.** /yə́kʷa-cx, s/yə́kʷ-cši-t-n *refl.* **3.** yékʷ-cx-laʔ move over! *refl.* **4.** /yə́kʷ=iʔp-transplant, move a rooted plant to another hole. **4a.** /yə́kʷ=iʔp-n, — *tr.*

/yələ́k'- double up, twist, spin. **1.** /yalə́k'-ɬ, —, /yalə́k'-n, s/yə́lk'-t-n.

/yələ́kʷ- roll. **1.** —, s/yə́l'kʷa-w-n, /yalə́kʷ-n, s/yə́l'kʷ-t-n. **2.** s/yə́l'kʷa-w-n wheel, tire.

/yələ́p- doctor. **1.** —, s/yə́lpa-w-n *or* s/yalə́pa-w-n, /yalə́p-n, —. **2.** syél.pà·wə̀n JH singing for a patient (*prob.* s/yə́lpa-w-n).

/yəlqiní ʔ-: **1a.** s/yəlqínʔ slave; EC sil-kén; FBa sī.lqai´n; JH sy'ɪlq'ín'; JHjp sya·lk'ín'. **1b.** s/yəlqiníʔ-i his slave. **1c.** s/yəlqin-áwmiš-i his slaves.

/yəlúx̣ʷ- roll up (*see* /yúlux̣ʷ- coil, round). **1.** /yalúx̣ʷ-n, s/yə́l'x̣ʷ-t-n *tr.* **2.** /yəló·x̣ʷ-m' round. **3.** /yalúx̣ʷ=aka-n- double up one's fist. **3a.** /yalúx̣ʷ=aka-n-m, — *mdl.* **3b.** s/yalúx̣ʷ=aka-n-m-ši-taw-n he's doubling

up his fist (at him ?) *appl.*, *caus.*

/yəlwíči- go around. **1.** /yəlwíči-c he went around me *perf. tr.*

/yəmkə́s-: **1a.** /yə́mks tallow. **1b.** /yəmkə́s-i its tallow.

/yəmyú ?? **1.** tit qi s/q'alá-n-n /yəmyú the whole camp (?) (*see* /q'əlá- camp).

/yənís-: **1a.** /yə́ns tooth; HH, AG,RL yĕnis teeth; GGb yínnis; FR yín-nis teeth; EC yĭns teeth; FBa ye´nns; BH yĭnns; HT yénns. **1b.** /yə́nis-umx *pl.* **1c.** /yə́nis-i his tooth. **1d.** /yə́nis-umiš-i his teeth *pl.* **2.** ɬɑ́qtɬ'ɑq yá·nəsɪ JH beaver teeth (*prob.* /ɬə́q'=ƛ̓k /yənís-i; *see* /ɬə́q'- wide).

/yənkʷə́s-: **1a.** /yə́nkʷs pack strap, pack rope; FBa yĭ´nuks tumpline. **1b.** /yənkʷə́s-i her pack rope.

/yə́pa- walk. **1.** /yə́p-ɬ, s/yə́pa-w-n; FBa yĭ´pEɬ walk, leave *intr.* **2.** nkʷ/yə́p travelling companion. **3a.** s/yə́p trip, walk. **3b.** s/yə́p-i his trip. **4.** tal-s/yə́p on foot, by walking. **5.** /yáp·yap-ɬ go walking *perf. intr.*

/yə́q'- punch, pound. **1.**

/yəq'-n, s/yəq'-t-n *tr.* 2.
s/yáq'-am'ɬ-tn' a maul. 3.
s/yəq'·iq'-tawl-n they're
boxing *impf. recip.* 4.
/yaq'-ə́mn pound on it
perf. rel. 5. /yə́q'·iq'-t-m
it was pounded *pass.* 6.
/yə́q'=lusi-c he pounded
on my head *perf. tr.*
/yə́q̓ʷ- move 1. /yə́q̓ʷ-ɬ, —
intr. 2. s/yə́q̓ʷ·iq̓ʷ-iɬt ʔaɬ
tit /qál? They're moving
up and down river. 3.
/yə́q̓ʷ/pataq- step, take a
step, walk 3a.
/yə́q̓ʷ/pataq-m,
s/yə́q̓ʷ/patq-mit-n *mdl.*
(*see* /pátaq- tracks).
/yə́tawaʔ salmonberry *Rubus
spectabilis*; EC yǐ -to-wŭ;
JH yítta·wɑ', yíttɑwwɑ';
JHjp yítwɑ'; EG eʹtwan
salmonberries. 2. eʹtwanac
EG whole salmonberry plant
(includes Sahaptin -aaš
'plant').
yə́xa, yə́x- only, nothing but.
1. yəx/lasúp tan t ʔacwé·x
There's nothing but soup
left. 2. mí∤ta t ʔitám
yəx/saplə́l tan There's
nothing but bread left.
/yə́xʷa- melt, thaw, dissolve.
1. /yə́xʷ-ɬ, s/yə́xʷa-w-n
intr.
/yə́x̣- sort, make a choice. 1.
/yə́x̣-n, s/yə́x̣-t-n *tr.*
/yəx̣alíʔ-: 1a. yəx̣ál? back,

backbone; FBa yea'xaʹl
back. 1b. yəx̣líʔ-i his back.
/yə́x̣m'c lizard ?*Gerrhonotus
coeruleus* (northern
alligator lizard); FBa
yeʹxamts.
ye·ᵋ FBb Oh (*prob.* /yíʔ).
yitsaiʹ.ts FBa fire drill; FBa
iʹtsEaits matches (*poss.*
/yíc'a·yc').
yiʹtiit FBa small red hawk
(*poss.* /yə́tyət).
/yíy good (?).
/yó·luq̓ʷ- plug (?). 1.
yó·luq̓ʷ-ɬ, — *intr.*
/yó·xʷ- bully, brag. 1.
/yó·xʷ-cx, s/yó·xʷ-cši-
t-n *refl.*
/yúca- beat up, kill; put out a
fire. 1. /yúc-x, s/yúca-y-
n *caus.* 2. /yúca-mi-cx
kill oneself, commit suicide
perf. refl. 3. yoúts-hah GGb
to kill; FR yoúts-hah,
yoút's-hah (*prob.* /yúc-
x-a? kill it!).
/yul- ?? 1. /yul=ínut-ši-
worry about *appl.* 1a.
/yul=ínut-š-n, — *tr.* 2.
/yul=ínwati- worry, feel
bad, mistreat. 2a.
/yul=ínut, — *intr.* 2b.
/yul=ínwati-x,
s/yul=ínut-staw-n *caus.*
/yúlux̣ʷ- coil, round (*see*
/yəlúx̣ʷ- roll up). 1.
/yúlux̣ʷ-ɬ, — *intr.* 2.
/yúl·yulux̣ʷ-ɬ lumpy *perf.*

intr.

/**yúpi**– war. 1. /yúpi–kʷn, —
intr. 2. pən/yúpi–kʷn
wartime.

/**yúxʷctx** silver (?).

/**yúxʷi**– know. 1. /yúxʷ–n,
s/yúxʷi–t–n *tr.* 2. ʔit
/yó·xʷ–n he knew it *dimin.*
perf. tr.

English - Cowlitz

a

able be able, can: ql.
above above, ceiling: tu
  ƛúk̲ʷ. above, high: ƛúk̲ʷ.
ache ache, hurt, wound, sore:
  tákɬk' (√ták-, √ɬə́k'a-).
  earache: I have an earache:
  t'ak̲ʷá·n'icalctx (√t'ə́k̲ʷ-).
  stomachache: have a
  stomachache:
  ʔact'ak̲ʷénusitm
  (√t'ə́k̲ʷ-).
acorn: k̲ʷísk̲ʷs (√k̲ʷís-).
acre: ʔíka.
across across, get across: tíwt
  (√tíwat-). across, over:
  stáln'x (√táln'x-). across
  the river: tawíɬk̲ʷu (?)
  (√taw-). go across:
  x̲ʷux̲ʷáw'k'm'
  (√x̲ʷáw'k̲ʷ-). go across,
  cross, go through, land (a
  canoe),reach shore: t'ánɬ
  (√t'aná-).
act act like, stay: wínwnx̲
  (√wín-). act silly, giggle,
  waste time: c'íyk̲ʷcx
  (√c'íyk̲ʷ-). acting:
  sméx̲ʼməx̲ʼcšitn,
  smə́x̲ʼməx̲ʼcšitn (√mə́x̲ʼa-).
  acting like: swínwinn
  (√wín-).
add add to: pə́nn (√pə́n-);
  sá·təx (√sá·tə-). add to
  (to increase value): púx̲ʷšn
  (√púx̲ʷ-). adding more to:

spén'šitn (√pə́n-).
advise advise, teach:
  ʔúx̲ʷanix (√ʔúx̲ʷa-).
afar from afar, foreign: tu
  lílʔ.
afraid: ʔacq̲ʷánuʔ
  (√q̲ʷán-). be afraid of,
  fear: q̲ʷántas (√q̲ʷán-).
after: ʔáwt, ʔáwtɬtumx̲
  (√ʔáwat-). after a while,
  bye and bye: tela´la FBb.
  after a while, later on:
  x̲ʷá·ʔaʔs. go after: ʔík̲ʷn
  (√ʔík̲ʷa-).
afternoon: námc'uq̲ʷɬ
  (√náma-, √c'úq̲ʷ-).
again: ʔáys; ksa (*enclitic*).
agree agree, answer: ɬíl'stq̲ʷ
  (√ɬíl'-, √tə́q̲ʷa-). agree,
  plan: sá·nax̲nut (√sáʔa-,
  √nax̲-).
aim: k̲ʷəpá·x̲n (√k̲ʷə́p-).
  he's aiming at you:
  c'aystə́q̲ʷčicin (√c'ay-,
  √tə́q̲ʼə́či-).
airtight: ʔactə́qlixk̲ʷuʔ
  (√tə́q-).
alarm alarm, alert, risk, look
  out for; guard, protect,take
  care of, watch for, pay
  attention, herd: ƛaq̲ʷséx̲n
  (√ƛáq̲ʷ-, √ʔə́x̲-).
alder: caq̲ʷáʔɬ.
alert alert, alarm, risk, look
  out for; guard, protect,take

care of, watch for, pay
attention, herd: x̌aqʷséx̣n
(√x̌áqʷ-, √ʔə́x̣-).

alive: ʔacwé·x̣o (√wé·-x̣-);
níɬɬ (√níɬi-). come back
to life: níɬlx (√níɬi-). he's
becoming alive: sníɬntn
(√níɬi-).

all: xʷáʔkʷuʔ. all, every,
whole: t'əmxʷáʔkʷuʔ
(√t'əmx-, √xʷáʔkʷuʔ-).
all over, completely:
p'étlm' (√p'étl-). that's
all: tu st'íx̣u (√t'íx̣-).

allow allow, let: tá·l'n
(√tá·l'a-).

almost almost, soon, a little
while, a little bit, well:
q̇ʷó·can (√q̇ʷóʔc-).

alone: ʔó·c's (√ʔúc's-).

along along, around: taʔaɬ.

already: q'ím. already, now:
tan.

although: táxʷl'.

always: č'ó·šm', č'úšaka
(√č'úš-).

American woman:
pástinuɬn', spástinuɬn'
(√pástin-).

ancestor ancestor, great-
grandparent, great-
grandchild: camé·c'aʔ
(√cam-). ancestors, front:
siləp (√ʔiləp-).

anchor (n.): qi snəkam'ɬ
(√nəka-).

and: n, ɬ₂. and, because: qas.
and, but: wi. and, so that

LNJ: kʷaɬ. and, so that,
instead: qa. and, with: kl.

angel angel, God, heaven:
šúšukli.

angry angry, growl: qaɬə́x̣ɬ
(√qəɬə́x̣a-). be mad at,
threaten: q̇ʷáx̣iqšn
(√q̇ʷáx̣-). he's getting
mad: q'aɬ q̇ʷáx̣nɬnati
(√q̇ʷáx̣-).

animal animal, dangerous
being, malevolent Indian
doctor woman: pə́saʔ. a
gray animal, similar to a
fox: səmt'i´c TA. a mean
animal; lion, cougar:
sčátqɬm' (√čátqɬm'-).

ankle: sxʷiyq̇ʷə́šn
(√xʷayə́q̇ʷ-); kai´ lɛkcɛn
FBa.

annoy annoy, bother, worry,
nervous: cáyaɬ (√cáyaʔ-).

another: taʔúc's (√ʔúc's-).

answer answer, agree:
ɬíl'stq̇ʷ (√ɬíl'-, √təq̇ʷa-).
answer, tell: cún'x̣
(√cún-).

ant, ants: c'skíyq
(√c'skíyaq-). anthill:
c'skíyqlwltxʷ
(√c'skíyaq-).

antler antlers, horns: mə́x̣kn
(√mə́x̣kán-).

anything anything be done to
it: ʔini kʷu (√ʔini-).

appearance: sə́x̣tm
(√ʔə́x̣-).

apple: ʔápls, lipúm. apple

orchard: ʔáplsan'ɬ
(√ʔápls-).

April: pənʔíɬsqʷuʔqʷstmiʔɬ
(√pən-, √ʔíɬani-,
√qʷóqʷstm-).

apron: Lūk sauˊtselɛks FBa
(√x̌úkʷ-, √sál'c-). old
style apron: saˊp.elɛks
FBa.

argue: čéˑtaqm (√čéˑtaq-).
argue, discuss, talk (*pl.*):
nə́x̣ʷm (√nə́x̣ʷa-).
arguing: sqinúy'ɬn'cšitn
(√qinúy'ɬn'-). someone
who wants to argue, mean
person: x̣ax̌éʔkʷn
(√x̣ə́x̌-).

arm arm, hand: kálx (*pl.*
kálaxumx) (√kálax-).
upper arm, shoulder blade:
q'ím'ax̣n (?) (√q'ímin-).

armpit: x̌apálax̣n (√x̌ə́p-).

around around, along: taʔaɬ.
around, round, spherical:
ʔacxʷúlupɬ (√xʷúlup-).
around the house:
ɬáʔkʷix̣ašm' (√ɬákʷ-). go
around: yaləm'n
(√yaləm'-). he went
around me: yəlwíčic
(√yəlwíči-). turn around:
yáx̌usm (√yáx̌a-).

arrest arrest, put in jail, tie
around, wind around: t'ə́qn
(√t'ə́qi-).

arrive arrive, come: t'úlɬ
(√t'úla-). arrive, get there,
reach: kʷáxʷɬ (√kʷáxʷa-).

arrow: scáqʷ (√cáqʷ-);
ʔéʔɬptn' LNJ (√ʔíɬp-);
sq̇ʷúyx̣ ENM (√q̇ʷúyx̣-).
arrow, bullet: seˊɬ FBa
(√síɬ-). arrowhead: .slōˊ
FBa. iron arrowhead:
cāˊoks FBa (√šawíʔ-).

arrowwood: sqɑ́tsɬ JH
(*sqɑ́cɬ).

artery his arteries: taníši
(√taníš-).

articles: t, ʔit, tit, tat, c, ʔic,
cic, cac.

ash tree: tawásn'ɬ
(√tawasá-).

ashes ashes, dust: sp'áqʷuyq
(√p'áqʷ-). bake in ashes:
ʔácqʷn (√ʔácqʷ-).

aside aside, move aside:
p'éˑn'm (√p'én'-).

ask (*tr.*): sáw'lix
(√sáw'la-). ask for: táx̣n
(√táx̣-); sáw'litmɬix
(√sáw'la-). he asked him
for it: sáw'lituxʷt
(√sáw'la-).

asleep: ʔacmúsm
(√músami-). Are you
asleep yet?:
watciˑˊˑˑx̣utciˑˑx̣u
qaˊwinactp'ən MJb-mi.

attach get attached to:
táčnmn (√táčn-).

attack: x̌áˑqn (√x̌áˑq-);
qalín (√qalí-); x̣íln
(√x̣íli-).

attention pay attention:
cóˑtaynmn (√cóˑ-). pay

attention, watch for, guard, protect...: x̌aqʷséx̣n (√x̌áqʷ-, √ʔə́x̣-).

audible be barely audible, barely hear: xʷcúynmn' (√xʷc-).

August: pənstó·l'šn (√pən-, √tó·l'xan-).

aunt: kʷáɬtn, kəkʷáɬtn (pl. nxkʷə́ɬuw'tn mother's sisters) (√kʷaɬá-, √tán-); tlax̣wai´nut FBa. aunt (father's sister): kʷə́ɬuʔ (pl. nxkʷaɬóʔtn) (√kʷaɬá-). her aunt: kʷáɬtanawi (√kʷaɬá-, √tán-). his aunt: kʷəɬá·w'i (√kʷaɬá-).

automobile automobile, car, machine: məšín. car, boat, canoe: wíɬ (√wíl-).

autumn autumn, fall: pənyáq'sməɬk (√pən-, √yáq'a-, √mə́ɬk-).

awake: ʔacp'á·lɬ (√p'ál-).

away: lé·lm' (√lílʔ-). get away, run away: ɬə́xʷm (√ɬə́xʷa-).

awkward: čanumíš.

awl: makʷə́mn (pl. makʷə́minumx) (√mək̓ʷə́-).

axe: wiq'ə́stn (√wiq'ə́s-).

axle: tit qi kʷíyxʷctx (√kʷíyxʷ-).

b

baby: sqʷay'áiɬ (pl. sqʷay'áyiɬumx) (√q̓ʷáy'ɬ-). baby, child: q̓ʷáy'ɬ (√q̓ʷáy'ɬ-). baby basket, cradle basket: cakʷíliɬtn', cakʷé·liɬtn' (√cə́kʷa-). have a baby: ʔit wi q̓ʷáy'ɬ (√q̓ʷáy'ɬ-); ʔacmánʔ (√maníʔ-).

bachelor: .sqwa´lux̣ FBa. bachelor, single: ʔó·c'uc's (√ʔúc's-).

back back, back of, behind: ʔáwtičn, sʔáwtičn (√ʔáwat-). back, backbone: yəx̣álʔ (√yəx̣alíʔ-). back of the hand: sa´ᵘteka FBa (√ʔáwat-). back of the neck: ʔáwtpsm (√ʔáwat-).

back down: tált (?).

backbone: x̣wíʔičn ENM (√x̣wíʔ-). backbone, back: yəx̣álʔ (√yəx̣alíʔ-).

backwards walk backwards, step back: x̣ə́y'načm' (√x̣ə́y-).

bad: x̣ə́š. bad food, coarse: x̣ašúl'mx (√x̣ə́š-). bad people: x̣ašáwmx (√x̣ə́š-). feel bad, be too bad, be sorry, sad:

ʔacłə́k'amn (√łə́k'a-).
feel bad, worry, mistreat:
yulínut (√yul-).

bag: tál'ičn (√tál'-). bag,
sack, pocket: lisák (*pl.*
lisakáwmx). beaded bag,
beaded clothing:
təmtám'iłaličn (√tám-).
cloth bag: sílaličn (√síl-).
woven bag: tlu´k.tEn FBa.

bail canoe bailer:
X̌úqʷam'łtn' (√X̌úqʷi-);
cáʔqstqtn' (√cə́q-).

bait bait, a hook:
q'ét'am'łtn' (√q'ét'a-).

bake bake, cook: q̓ʷalín
(√q̓ʷə́la-). bake in ashes:
ʔácqʷn (√ʔácqʷ-);
mə́k̓ʷúyq (√mə́k̓ʷ-).
baking potatoes: ʔácqʷiln
(√ʔácqʷ-).

balance balance, rock in
arms: ʔá·lwasix
(√ʔá·lwasi-). balance on
one's toes: c'é·t'xanm
(√c'é·t'-).

bald bald, baldheaded:
ʔacłúq̓ʷls (√łúq̓ʷ-).

ball ball, round object:
milúx̣ʷl's (√milúx̣ʷ-).
playing ball: słéʔqłqmaln
(√łə́q-).

bank bank the fire!:
mə́k̓ʷúystqninaʔ
(√mə́k̓ʷ-).

baptize baptize, pour on:
pə́qʷšn (√pə́qʷa-).

barefoot: ʔułál'šn (√ʔúł-).

barely barely hear, be barely
audible: xʷcúynmn'
(√xʷc-).

bark (n.) bark, greenish:
k̓ʷiq'é·man'ł (√k̓ʷiq'é-).
bark of a tree: p'áln
(√p'álan-). bark lodge,
tent: sā´kotaxolwE´łtx̣ᵘ
FBa.

bark (v.): qʷúx̣ʷcx,
qʷúx̣ʷacx (√qʷúx̣ʷa-).

barn: stiqíwlwltxʷ
(√tiqíw-); laklás̆ (*pl.*
laklás̆umx).

barrel: t'amúličn
(√t'amúlikn-).

bashful bashful, confused,
frown, embarrass:
ʔacsé·xʷł (√sé·xʷ-).

basket baby basket, cradle
basket: cakʷíliłtn',
cakʷé·liłtn (√cə́kʷa-).
bark basket: xa'kai´ FBa.
basket of cedar twigs:
poxe´łEn.łp FBa. berry
basket: k'o'ó·lɪ·tʃɪn JH
(*k̓ʷuʔúličn). blend work in
a basket: taxʷál'šn
(√taxʷál'š-). cedar-root
basket: ʔə́mx̣kʷu. fish
basket, fish trap: yax̣áw't
(√yax̣áw'at-). one basket:
nak'áwəmx̣kʷu (√nák'-,
√ʔə́mx̣kʷu-). openwork
basket: sx̣asó·ličn,
səx̣ʷó·ʔcaličn ENM
(√x̣asó·l-). picking basket:
ʔé·mx̣kʷu (√ʔə́mx̣kʷu-);

X̣aʔáwmn (√X̣aʔáwi-).
start (the bottom of) a
basket, basket hoops:
stúlnk (√túl-). weave a
cedar-root basket:
sáʔəmx̣kʷu (√sáʔa-,
√ʔə́mx̣kʷu-). weaving a
basket: ssə́csuqʷstn
(√sə́csuqʷs-).

bat: q̇ʷátxʷ;
x̣wɑ̀ts'ǽˑ'mɑ̀x̣ɑ̀n' JH.

bathe bathe, swim: ʔéˑtl'
(√ʔéˑtil-).

bay bay, red: ʔaksc'íq
(√c'íq-).

beach: súltɬkʷu (√súlt-).

bead beads, necklace:
stəmtám (√tám-). beaded
(moccasins?):
ʔactəmtám'iɬx (?)
(√tám-). beaded bag,
beaded clothing:
təmtám'iɬaličn (√tám-).

bear: sčə́txʷn' (pl.
sčə́txʷin'umx)
(√čə́txʷan'-). bear cub:
sčéʔtxʷaniʔɬ
(√čə́txʷan'-). grizzly bear:
wít'aš; .smê´c FBa.

beard: č'ípqs (pl.
č'ípqisumx) (√č'ipqas-).

beat beat, defeat: c'ə́kšn
(√c'ə́ka-). beat up, kill, put
out a fire: yúcx (√yúca-).

beautiful beautiful,
handsome: ei.sᴇxa´mᴇɬ
FBa (√ʔíˑ-, √ʔə́x̣-).

beaver, beavers: ɬə́q'X̣k

(√ɬə́q'-). beaver, otter:
q'áɬč'm' (?).

be: wəs, ʔus. be, become:
wi, ʔu.

because: qasi, qas. because,
so, so that, for the reason
that: cu.

become become, be: wi, ʔu.
becoming, living, residing,
staying: swínn (√wín-).
they became, they stayed:
wináwm'x (√wín-).

bed: cónp (pl. cónapumx)
(√cənúp-). bed or mat
with a blanket on top upon
which a bride is seated and
dowry gifts are piled around
her: səʔínp (√sáʔa-).
bedding, blanket: sxə́p
(√xə́pa-). go to bed, lie
down: cə́kʷɬ (√cə́kʷa-).
make a bed: saʔén'p
(√sáʔa-). making a bed
for: saʔén'pšitn (√sáʔa-).

bee, bees: cíks. beehive,
hornet's nest: cíkslwltxʷ
(√cíks-).

beef: wəmúsmuskiɬc'iʔ
(√wəmúsmuski-). beef,
body: k̓ʷúsɬc'iʔ (√k̓ʷús-).

before: ʔílpɬtumx
(√ʔiləp-). before, until:
čiʔílp (√iləp-).

begin: tólp (√tólap-).
begin, start: tóˑl'p
(√tólap-).

behind: ʔáwt, ʔáwtičn,
sʔáwtičn, ʔáwtɬtumx

($\sqrt{}$ʔáwat-). behind the house: ⁴ákʷay'x̣x ($\sqrt{}$⁴ákʷ-).

belch: q̇ʷóˑʔayq.

believe believe, hear, hear about, listen: k̓ʷiláyn ($\sqrt{}$k̓ʷil-).

belly belly, stomach: k̓ʷásn ($\sqrt{}$k̓ʷasə́n-).

belly button belly button, navel: q'éˑyx̣ ($\sqrt{}$q'iyáx̣-).

below below, low, down: ⁴áx̓̌p.

belt, belts: t'əqixʷ ($\sqrt{}$t'əqi-).

bend: púyn ($\sqrt{}$púy-); x̣ʷúc'n ($\sqrt{}$x̣ʷúc'-). bend, coil up: q'aləp'⁴ ($\sqrt{}$q'ələp'-). bend down (e.g. limbs) (*pl.*): yáp'aʔ⁴ ($\sqrt{}$yáp'a-). bend over, stoop: kəm'⁴ ($\sqrt{}$kəm-). bend over a little: kəm'načm ($\sqrt{}$kəm-). bent over, humpbacked: ʔacx̣ʷam'íčn ($\sqrt{}$x̣ʷam'-).

berry berries, fruit: stóˑl'šn ($\sqrt{}$tóˑl'xan-). berry *sp.*: q'áʔn. blackberry: ⁴aʔí⁴n'. blackcap: məckʷ. blue elderberry: ts'kwíˑkw̥ JH (*c'kʷíkʷ). cranberry: x̣ántmx̣ ($\sqrt{}$x̣án-); ⁴ántmx̣ (?) ($\sqrt{}$⁴án-). gooseberry: t'aməx̣ʷ. Oregon grape: č'iyúx̣ʷiʔs. raspberry, serviceberry, thimbleberry LNJ: q̇ʷál'x̣ʷ. red elderberry: č'ípt.

salalberry: t'áqaʔ; k'léh. salmonberry: yə́tawaʔ. serviceberry: kîˑ́s.x̣ FBa (*kə́sx̣). short huckleberry, blueberry: q'áʔp; k'wɑ̀l' JH (*k̓ʷə́l'). strawberry: katísaʔ. Yakima huckleberry: wənáy'x̣.

beside: p'én'- (plus personal pronouns). beside, next to: p'éntmx ($\sqrt{}$p'én'-).

best: t'im ʔíˑ.

better: k̓ʷapús tan ($\sqrt{}$k̓ʷə́p-); tk ʔíˑ. better, well, healed: x̓̌áq̇ʷ. be better, get better: x̓̌áˑq̇ʷm ($\sqrt{}$x̓̌áq̇ʷ-). (you'd) better, OK (exhortative particle), let's!: x̓̌áq̇ʷ.

between: tk cóʔ.

big big, large: taw'ə́t.

bird bird, flying creature: péˑsaʔ ($\sqrt{}$pə́saʔ-). a bird (red head, red breast, white belly, rest black): Tc'qw'ɛ́ˑ TA. a little black bird, about the size of a lark, that lives near the river: ts'a´mᶏx̣wuɪ TA. a small gray bird, possibly thrush: spícx̣ʷ, pícx̣ʷ.

biscuitroot biscuitroot, cous: x̣áwš.

bit bit, bridle: laplít.

bite: t'ə́k̓ʷn ($\sqrt{}$t'ə́k̓ʷ-). get all bitten: t'ə́k̓ʷt'k̓ʷtm ($\sqrt{}$t'ə́k̓ʷ-).

bitter: x̓̌ə́⁴; k'ayə́x̣ʷ. bitter

taste: ƛ̓ə̓ɫƛ̓ɫal'ɫ (√ƛ̓ə̓ɫ-).

bitterroot: pyəx̣í, pyax̣í.

black: ʔaksnə̓q (√nə̓q-).
blacken, darken: né?qm
(√nə̓q-).

blackberry: ɫaʔíɫn'.

blackbird: kwolī´ca FBa.

blackcaps: mə̓ckʷ. blackcap
bushes: mə̓ckʷan'ɫ
(√mə̓ckʷ-).

blame: ʔúxʷšn (√ʔúxʷa-).
he blamed me: ʔaccó·tumx
(√có·-).

blanket: xʷə̓ltamulic'aʔ (*pl.*
xʷə̓ltamulic'ayumx)
(√xʷə̓l-). blanket, bedding:
sxə̓p (√xə̓pa-). blanket on
top of a saddle:
t'anáw'sn'ktn'
(√t'anáw's-). saddle
blanket: lapišmú. wool
blanket: stəwúlic'aʔ
(√təwúl-).

blaze blaze, fire is too high:
lámstq (√lám-). blazing:
slámlmwn, slámlmstaqn
(√lám-). it's blazing
higher: stáw'stqmitn
(√taw'ə̓t-).

bleed: qʷílɫ (√qʷíla-).

blend blend work in a basket:
taxʷal'šn (√taxʷál'š-).

blind blind (*tr.*): t'áp'sn
(√t'áp'-). blind, dazzle:
qáy'x̣il'sn (√qáy'x̣i-).
he's blind: ʔact'áp's
(√t'áp'-).

blinds window blinds:

xə̓pax̣acxtn' (√xə̓pa-,
√ʔə̓x̣-).

blink: ɫéʔpɫipɫ (√ɫíp-).

blister: qʷútɫ (√qʷút-). a
blister: ʔacqʷútɫ (√qʷút-).
blistering: spóʔspswn
(√púsa-).

blood: sqʷíɫ (√qʷíla-).

bloom: x̣ísɫ (√x̣ísi-).
blooming, opening,
spreading out, stretching:
swə̓ɫqawn (√wə̓ɫə̓qa-).

blow blowing (with mouth):
spúxʷitn (√púxʷi-). blow
a horn: púxʷiqn
(√púxʷi-). blow in the
wind, wave: xʷík̓ʷɫ
(√xʷík̓ʷ-). blow the nose:
ɫíɫqsm (√ɫíɫ-). blow up,
explode, shoot with a gun:
taqʷə̓čɫ (√təqʷə̓či-). wind
blowing: sxʷúxʷawn
(√xʷúxʷa-). not blowing,
still, calm: ʔactxʷk̓ʷə̓ctm
(√k̓ʷə̓c-).

blue: ʔaksq̓ʷíx̣ (√q̓ʷíx̣-).

blueback salmon:
q̓ʷé·x̣aʔičn (√q̓ʷíx̣-).

blueberry blueberry, short
huckleberry: q'áʔp. short
huckleberry plant:
q'áʔpan'ɫ (√q'áʔp-).

bluebird: 'na´u FBa.

blue jay blue jay;
mischievous: p'ayə̓k̓ʷ.
Bluejay's older sister:
náwqɫ.

blunt blunt-pointed, come

off: c'aмə́k̓ʷɬ
(√c'əмə́k̓ʷ-).

board, boards: ciɬá·l'axʷ
(√ciɬ-).

boat boat, canoe, car: wíɬ
(√wíl-). ferryboat: skáw.
go in a boat: tál'uɬ (√tál-).

bob bobbing up and down:
sɬé?qɬiqaqn (√ɬíqaq-);
sɬə́kɬakiqn (√ɬə́k-).

bobcat bobcat, wildcat:
p'ə́č'm.

bobtailed: táysupsnk
(√táy-, √súps-).

body: náwɬc'i? (√náw-).
body, beef ENM: k̓ʷúsɬc'i?
(√k̓ʷús-). body, trunk:
nuɬc'í?i (√náw-).

boil (n.): sp'ə́xʷ (√p'ə́xʷ-).

boil (v.): lə́pləpn (√lə́p-).
boil, can: cə́qstqn
(√cə́q-). boiling over,
running over: sq̓ʷát'awn
(√q̓ʷát'a-).

bone: šáw? (√šawí?-).

bonnet feather bonnet:
sEksa´k.pɬEɬ FBa
(√sákp-).

bony bony, skinny, thin:
yák̓ʷɬ (√yák̓ʷa-).

book: ?á?xam'ɬtn' (√?ə́x̣-).
book, tablet, pen, pencil:
q̓ʷaɬém'ɬtn' (√q̓ʷə́ɬé-).

boots: bo´Ets FBa.

borrow borrow, lend, rent:
k̓ʷústm.

both both, double, together:
t'əмxsáli? (√t'əмx-,

√sáli?-). both ends:
t'əмxə́m? (√t'əмx-,
√x̣ə́m?-).

bother bother, annoy, worry,
nervous: cáyaɬ (√cáya?-).
being bothered by smoke:
sq̓ʷúx̣ʷiqstn (√q̓ʷúx̣ʷ-).

bottle, bottles: lawúličn
(√lawúl-).

bottom bottom, middle,
inside: lawə́p (?). bottom,
stump: snə́wp (√nəwáp-).
bottom, under, back under:
t'ə́q's. bottom of a hill:
X̣apé·l's (√X̣ə́p-). its
bottom, its inside: sáci?qi
(√?ácayq-, √sác-).

bounce: ɬə́t'ɬat'ɬ (√ɬə́t'-).

bow: t'ə́k̓ʷɬn? ENM
(√t'ə́k̓ʷ-); scútqʷ
(√cútaqʷ-). bow, tanning
frame, prop, temporary
shelter: sq'iyúx̣ʷ
(√q'iyúx̣ʷ-). bowstring:
matsa´litcEn FBa
(√macál-).

bowl: X̣é?pawq (pl.
X̣é?pawqti?) (√X̣ə́p-);
ta-ko-ni EC.

box: X̣íqsn (pl. X̣íqsinumx),
X̣éqsn.

boxing: syə́q'iq'tawln
(√yə́q'-).

boy: sé·ɬm'x (pl.
sé·ɬmixumx) (√síɬmix-);
to´lExau.ts FBa.

bracelet: sáwc' (√sáwac'-).
bracelet ENM, ring LNJ:

t'amákamn (√t'ám-).

bracken: cáqan'ɫ (√cáqa-). bracken roots: wəč'ál; st̂sak EC (√cáqa-).

brag brag, bully: yóˑxʷcx (√yóˑxʷ-).

braid (n.): stəkʷiʔ (√təkʷayí-). braiding: stakʷáyn (√təkʷayí-).

brain: cɫqʷálatn (√cɫqʷála-).

branch branch, limb: k'ál'x (*pl.* k'ál'axumx) (√k'ál'ax-); kwɛxkwaˊx.ɫ FBa.

brand brand, mark, design, write, vote: q̇ʷaɫén (√q̇ʷəɫé-). a brand, mark, design: q̇ʷəɫ (√q̇ʷəɫé-).

bread: saplə́l; kwîˊl (saˊpɛleˊl) FBa (√q̇ʷə́la-). making bread: sásaplaln (√sáʔa-, √saplə́l-).

break break (rope, string): ɫə́q̇ʷn (√ɫə́q̇ʷ-). break in pieces, smash, grind, mash: q̇ʷíc'n (√q̇ʷíc'i-). break in two: xə́ƛ̓ɫ (√xə́ƛ̓-). break off, chip: ɫalə́pn (√ɫalə́p-). break one's arm: xaƛ̓áxn (√xə́ƛ̓-). break one's nose: xə́ƛ̓qs (√xə́ƛ̓-). break open: paɫə́q̇ʷ. break out (skin): ƛ̓ə́qx. break to pieces: mə́xʷn (√mə́xʷ-).

breakfast: q̇ʷéx̣iʔxʷmn (√q̇ʷéx̣iʔxʷ-).

breast: ntauˊxtsɛn FBa (√táx̣ʷac-). breast, udder: c'ám'tn (√c'ám'-).

breathe: láxʷkʷunm (√láxʷkʷu-). he's breathing: sláxʷləxʷkʷumitn, sláxʷləxʷkʷlmitn (√láxʷkʷu-). out of breath: táylaxʷkʷuʔ (√láxʷkʷu-); c'ə́klxʷkʷuʔ (√c'ə́ka-, √láxʷkʷu-).

breechcloth breechcloth, diaper: sƛ̓íq'nk (√ƛ̓íq'a-); tu-íl-ŭ-pa-min EC.

breeze: sxʷóˑxʷ (√xʷúxʷa-).

bridge: qi téw'ttn' (√tíwat-). bridge, steps: tēˊutɛmɛn FBa (√tíwat-).

bridle: tɫamɫeniˊmɛɫtɛn FBa (√ɫə́mi-). bridle, bit: laplít.

bright bright, shine, light: q'éxm'ɫ (√q'íx̣-).

bring bring, (give to): ʔíx (√ʔí-). bring back, bring to: t'ulə́x (√t'úla-). bring home: yaƛ̓ə́x (√yáƛ̓a-). bring in, take in: ɫə́kstaqix (√ɫə́k-). bring it out: p'əlqʷə́ctm (?) (√p'ələ́qʷ-). bring to: t'úlx- (√t'úla-); st'óˑlxšitn (√t'úla-).

broom: x̣waˊkwolɛmtɛn FBa (√xʷákʷa-).

broth broth, soup:

qiy'áluqʷs
(√qiy'áluqʷas-).
brother older brother: t
x̣ʷáɬ, t x̣ʷáʔɬ (*pl.*
nxx̣ʷáʔɬtn) (√x̣ʷál-).
younger brother: néʔsk (*pl.*
nxnéʔsktn).
brown: kwātsä´ksnî´k FBa
(√kʷac-, √náq-).
brush (n.) brush, driftwood:
sx̣así ɬšn (√x̣así ɬšn-).
brush, underbrush:
sx̣áx̌tmx (√x̣áx̌-).
brush (v.) brush off, clean
(off), change, polish,
straighten out: ʔayáqɬ
(√ʔiyáq-). brush off ENM,
shake out LNJ, thresh:
t'áx̣ʷn (√t'áx̣ʷ-). brush
onto: t'állptuxʷt
(√t'aláp-). a brush:
sʔáy'qam'ɬtn' (√ʔiyáq-).
bucket bucket, kettle:
cáqstqtn' (√cáq-).
buffalo: selEmuxena FBa.
bug a striped bug: luslús.
build build a fence:
sá·q'lax̣n (√sáʔa-,
√q'aláx̣an-). build a fire:
x̣ʷál'kʷp (√x̣ʷál'a-). build
a house: kakáltxʷ (√kak-);
saʔúɬx̣axn (√sáʔa-). build
a house for: kakáltxʷšn
(√kak-); saʔúɬx̣šn
(√sáʔa-). keep building
fires: x̣ʷál'x̣ʷl'kʷp
(√x̣ʷál'a-).
bullet bullet, bullets, shell,

shells, gunpowder: síɬ.
bullhead: x̌'áx̣ʷlstn
(√x̌'áx̣ʷ-).
bullheaded bullheaded, tell a
lie: paɬús.
bully bully, brag: yó·x̣ʷcx
(√yó·x̣ʷ-).
bump: mayáx̣ʷɬ
(√mayáx̣ʷ-); táwɬ. bump,
run into: tápn (√táp-).
bump feet together: tapálɬ
(√táp-). bumping head:
stáplstn (√táp-).
bunch: nák̓ʷusx̣ʷóqʷ
(√nák'-, √x̣ʷúqʷa-).
bunch, cluster, handful:
nák̓ʷumóʔ (√nák'-,
√móʔ-).
burn burn, burn up: ɬáx̣ɬ
(√ɬáx̣a-). burn, catch fire:
x̣ʷál'ɬ (√x̣ʷál'a-). a burn
(in a forest): sɬáx̣
(√ɬáx̣a-). its burning:
sq'íx̣mli (√q'íx̣-).
bury: námn (√nám-).
bush bush, small stick:
x̌'éʔxx̌'x (*pl.* x̌'éʔxx̌'axum'x)
(√x̌'áx̣-).
busy: cá·yaɬ (√cá·ya-).
busy at: taqámɬ (?).
but but, and: wi. but, it
turned out to be: k̓ʷá.
butcher butcher a cow *or*
steer: manítumusmáski
(√manít-,
√wamúsmuski-). butcher,
cut up, carve, operate on:
c'áwc'awák'n

(√c'əwə́k'–).
butterfingers butterfingers, clumsy: ʔíšt'i.
butterfly: x̣aləw'x̣aləw' (√x̣aləw'–). little blue butterfly: x̣alá·w'iʔɬ (√x̣aləw'–).
buttocks buttocks, rear part: sč'éʔ (√č'éʔ–).
button button (*tr.*): ɬánn (√ɬánaʔ–). a button: ɬánaʔcxtn' (*pl.* ɬánaʔcxtinumx) (√ɬánaʔ–).
buy: ləqn (√ləq–). buy a dress: táx̣ʷsal'cil'qs

(√táx̣ʷayway–, √sál'c–).
buy a wife: laqálkuwɬ (√ləq–, √kəwáɬ–). buy a woman, wedding: ləqálkwaʔɬuʔɬ (√ləq–, √kəwáɬ–). buy for: ləqšn (√ləq–). buy shoes: tax̣ʷál'šn (√táx̣ʷayway–).
buzzard: wi-ni-ní-ḥuks EC; ts'í·q'q'ᵅs JH.
buzzing: stíʔiwn (√tíʔi–). buzzing, jingling: sk̓ʷíx̣mtn (√k̓ʷíx̣–). it's buzzing around: stéʔtiwn (√tíʔi–).
bye bye and bye, after a while: tela´la FBa.

c

cabbage: laxičn (?); pə́ckɬ.
calf: wəmóʔsmuskiʔiʔɬ, wəmóʔsəskiʔɬ ENM (√wəmúsmuski–). elk calf: qé·l'itn (√qílitn–); te´lEka FBa.
calf of the leg: ma´naɬtse FBa (√mána–).
call call, invite: q'íw'tas (√q'íw'–). call, shout, holler: táltalaqp (√tál–). call, yell, shout, holler: tálaqp (√tál–). call for: táx̣ʷn (√táx̣ʷ–). calling, naming: sk̓ʷácilitn (√k̓ʷácili–).
calm calm, be still: ʔactx̣ʷmén'stm (√mén'–).

calm, still, not blowing: ʔactx̣ʷk̓ʷəctm (√k̓ʷəc–). calm down, quiet down, hold still: ƛ̓él'cx (√ƛ̓əla–).
camas: qáwm'; qílq. prepared camas: ʔacp'ən'c tani tit qáwm' (√p'ən'c–).
camp: q'əlm (√q'əl–). campground: q'aləmntn (√q'əl–). campsite, camp, hotel: q'alə́mn (√q'əl–).
camp robber (gray jay): ʔéʔɬnalakaʔ (√ʔíɬani–).
can can, be able: ql. can, could: qaɬ. can't: x̣áwqaɬ (√x̣áw–, √qaɬ–).
can (*v.*) can, boil: cə́qstqn (√cə́q–).

candle candle, light, torch: q'éx̱am'ɬtn' (√q'íx̱-).

canoe canoe, boat, car: wíɬ (√wíl-). bark canoe: skwaiaiˊElu‡ FBa. canoe type: sqwǻy' JH (*sqʷǽy'). Chinook canoe: tsa.kwaˊmEn FBa; ɬáˑk'wǻ'ᵅmɑx wíˑ‡ JH deep, long canoe, Chinook canoe: ʔalútq. river canoe: sqáˑmùˑ‡ JH (*sqamú‡). making a canoe: sáʔwəln (√sáʔa-, √wíl-).

canoe bailer: x̌úqʷam'ɬtn' (√x̌úqʷi-); cáʔqstqtn' (√cə́q-).

cape cape, cloak: Lāˊᵘkometsa FBa.

caps caps (for gun): .sɬoˊ FBa.

car car, automobile, machine: məšín. car, boat, canoe: wíɬ (√wíl-).

cards: likát.

care take care of, guard, protect...: x̌ʼaqʷséx̱n (√x̌ʼáqʷ-, √ʔə́x̱-). take care of, save: ʔúlx̱n (√ʔúlx̱-).

carpentering: kakáltmtn (√kak-).

carrot, carrots: stawél'n' (√tawél'an'-). wild carrot: sawítk (√sawítak-).

carry carry, hold, get, take, take away, grab, get married: kʷə́na, kʷə́nna (√kʷəná-). carry, pack: yášn (√yáxa-). carry on back: yáxanix (√yáxa-). carry wood: čílmikʷp (√čílmi-).

carve carve, cut up, butcher, operate on: c'ə́wc'awək'n (√c'əwə́k'-).

cat: píšpiš (*pl.* píšpišumx). kitten: pé?špiš (*pl.* pé?špišumx), péšpi‡ (√píšpiš-).

catch catch, get: kʷə́naxʷ, kʷə́nanxʷ (√kʷəná-). catch, take, grab, hang on to: skʷanátn (√kʷəná-). catch at, find, meet: t'úqʷn (√t'úqʷi-). catch fire, burn: x̌ʷál'‡ (√x̌ʷál'a-). catch fish, fish: q'ét'm (√q'ét'a-). catch up with: yákpn (√yákp-). it was caught, it was tied up: ɬamə́nitm (√ɬə́mi-).

cave cave, dugout, steep hole: ʔacč'aléqʷ‡ (√č'aléqʷ-).

cave in: c'ay'ə́qʷ‡ (√c'əy'ə́qʷa-).

cayuse cayuse (horse), Spaniard: spalyán.

cedar, cedars: catáwi?. cedar roots, cedar: c'ápx̱ (√c'ápax̱-). cedar roots (dried and prepared): taq'íx̱n',taq'éx̱n.

ceiling ceiling, above: tu x̌úk̓ʷ.

celery wild celery: yálp;

q̓ʷét̓aplm'x (√q̓ʷít̓ap-).

chair: tawélltn'
(√tawílax-). rocking chair:
yéq'iq'tawn (√yáq'iq'-).

chance take a chance:
mə́x̌acx (√mə́x̌a-).

change: ʔáyšn (√ʔáy-).
change, clean, polish,
straighten out, brush off:
ʔayə́qt̓ (√ʔiyə́q-). change
one's mind: ʔáynax̣nut
(√ʔáy-, √nax̣-). changing;
moving: syə́kʷatn
(√yə́kʷa-).

chap become chapped:
qʷə́qt̓ (√qʷə́q-).

charcoal: c'ax̣áy'stq
(√c'ax̣-).

charge be in charge, plan on:
kátyn.

chase chase, follow: tál'šl's
(√tál'š-). young person
chasing around; fish coming
upstream swinging its tail:
sx̣ix̣í (√x̣í-).

cheap: ʔacmá·st̓ (√má·s-).

cheek: mə́qʷiʔ
(√məqʷayíʔ-). cheek, jaw,
chin: sqə́lns (√qəlnús-).

chest: táx̣ʷc (√táx̣ʷac-).

chew: k̓ʷáyn (√k̓ʷáya-).
chewing, gnawing:
sx̣ák̓ʷatn (√x̣ák̓ʷa-).

chickadee: číə.

chicken chicken, pheasant,
turkey: skʷínm (*pl.*
skʷínimumx) (√kʷiním-).
baby chickens:

skʷiné·m'it̓umx
(√kʷiním-). rooster:
likʷó·k.

chicken hawk: .swai'a´tok
FBa.

chief chief, leader: ʔáls (*pl.*
ʔálisumx) (√ʔális-).

child child, baby: qʷáy'+.
child, son, daughter: mánʔ
(*pl.* nxmánʔtn) (√maníʔ-).
children: mé·l'm'x
(√mé·l'-); nxmánʔtn
(√manʔí-). his child, his
son, his daughter:
manéʔi, maníʔi (√manʔí-).
their children: cilxmtə́ni
(√cilxmtə́n-). stepchild:
tcElmî´ nam FBa (√ču+-,
√manʔí-).

chimney: lašəmní.

chin chin, chins, jaw, cheek:
sqə́lns (√qəlnús-).

Chinese: čáyni.

Chinook salmon ENM:
sálwax̌ʷ; c'áw+.

chip chip, break off: +alə́pn
(√+ələ́p-). chipping:
st̓ə́l+lptn (√+ələ́p-). chips
(from cutting wood):
c'əwk'ə́mn (√c'əwə́k'-).
chips of wood *or* rock:
x̌amə́mn.

chipmunk: sməqʷál'č LNJ
(√məqʷál'č-); məx̣ʷá·l'as
ENM (√məx̣ʷ-); sq̓ʷac'ə́+
(√q̓ʷac'ə́+-). a small
chipmunk: nəx̌ánči.

chisel: c'áwk'am'+tn'

(√c'əwə́k'-).

choice a choice:
sk̓ʷə́pawm'ɬ (√k̓ʷə́p-).
make a choice, sort: yə́x̣n
(√yə́x̣-).

choke choke, hang: qíqɬn
(√qíq-). choke, stick in the
throat: k̓ʷuk̓ʷápsm
(√k̓ʷuk̓ʷ-); qə́qɬ
(√qə́qa-). choked: qaqə́m
(√qə́qa-).

chop chop wood, cut wood,
split wood: c'uk̓ʷáyk̓ʷp
(√c'uk̓ʷ-).

Christmas Christmas,
holiday, July:
pənnáw'san'tim'n
(√pən-, √náwa-,
√sánti-).

church: c'éˑwimn ENM,
c'éwim'ɬtn' LNJ (√c'íwi-).

churn churn, turn, twist,
wring out, wind, stir: yát'n
(√yát'a-).

cinch: tsaˊn.kEɬtEn FBa
(√cána-).

clabber clabber, clot: q'ə́k̓ʷɬ
(√q'ə́k̓ʷ-).

claim: ƛ̓ə́q'n (√ƛ̓ə́q'-).

clam: sêˊçEk FBa. large clam
sp.: sqʷálitn (√qʷálitn-).
small clam *sp.*: k̓ʷúxʷni?.

class a good class of people, a
people and an area on the
Cowlitz River between
Kelso and Toledo: síq̓ʷɬ
(√síq̓ʷ-). a person from a
good class of people: tk

síq̓ʷ.

clean clean (off), polish,
brush off, change,
straighten out: ?ayə́qɬ
(√?iyə́q-).

clear clear off, sweep:
xʷák̓ʷɬ (√xʷák̓ʷa-). a
clearing: s?íyqtn
(√?iyə́q-). he's clearing
forest: sláˑšmtn (√láˑš-).

climb: wít'ɬ (√wít'i-). climb
through, squeeze through,
detour: ɬúmicx (√ɬúmi-).

cloak cloak, cape:
Lāˊᵘkometsa FBa.

clock clock, watch: wáč.

close close, near: yákm'x,
yá?km'x. close together,
next to, middle: tə́q'tum'x
(√tə́q'-).

close (*v.*) close, shut: tə́qɬ
(√tə́q-). close one's eyes:
t'áˑp'usm (√t'áp'-).

clot clot, clabber: q'ə́k̓ʷɬ
(√q'ə́k̓ʷ-).

cloth: síl. cloth bag: sílaličn
(√síl-).

clothing: st'akáwmx
(√t'ə́k-); ?itáma?. beaded
clothing, beaded bag:
təmtám'iɬaličn (√tám-).
his clothes, his wealth:
táma?asi (√táma?as-).
lots of clothes, wealth:
qə́x̣itmtn (√qə́x̣-,
√?itáma?-).

cloud: .stīˊp FBa. cloud,
clouds, sky: cɬtálaxʷ

(√cɬt–). big white cloud: šə́q. the clouds are travelling fast: sxʷákʷlkʷcšitn (√xʷákʷa–).

club club (*tr*.): xáɬn (√xáɬ–). club, whip, drum: tásam'ɬtn' (√tása–). war club: ɬakalɛneˊx.p FBa (√ɬə́q–).

club club, meeting: x̌ʷúqʷqʷiɬt (√x̌ʷúqʷa–).

clumsy clumsy, butterfingers: ʔíšt'i. clumsy, stupid, dumb, stubborn: ʔayayáš.

cluster cluster, bunch, handful: nək̓ʷumóʔ (√nák'–, √móʔ–).

coals coals (live), sparks from a fire: táqʷn'ɬkʷp (√táqʷn'ɬ–).

coarse coarse, bad food: x̌ašúl'mx (√x̌ə́š–).

coat kapú; ntluˊkamatsa FBa (√ƛ̓úk̓ʷ–). raincoat: sx̌asílʔkapu (√x̌asílʔ–, √kapú–); pənx̌asílʔmn' (√x̌asílʔ–).

cockle: stɬ'ʋˑ'αlαm' JH (*sƛ̓úʔlm').

coil coil, round: ʔacyúlux̣ʷɬ (√yúlux̣ʷ–). coil up, bend: q'alə́p'ɬ (√q'ələ́p'–). be coiled up: ʔacq'ə́lp'cx (√q'ələ́p'–).

cold cold, cool: ƛ̓íx. cold (weather): qeˊɛx FBa. be cold: ɬíšɬ (√ɬíš–).

collapse collapse, fall in: pə́n'ɬ (√pə́n'–).

collide: tapálwax (√tə́p–). they collided, hit together: tapál'us (√tə́p–).

colors black: ʔaksnə́q (√nə́q–). blue: ʔaksq̓ʷíx̣ (√q̓ʷíx̣–). brown: kwātsäˊksnîˊk FBa (√kʷac–, √nə́q–). gray: ʔaksp'áqʷ, p'áʔqʷm'ɬ (√p'áqʷ–). green, gold: ʔaksk̓ʷíq' (√k̓ʷiq'é–). pink, red: ʔaksc'í (√c'í–). red, bay: ʔaksc'íq (√c'íq–). dark red, cherry red: ʔaksc'íyi (√c'íyi–). roan: eks spaˊkonamts FBa (√p'áqʷ–). silver: ʔaksq'éx̣m'ɬ (√q'íx̣–). sorrel: ʔaksqʷə́s (√qʷə́s–). white: ʔaksqʷúx̣ʷ (√qʷúx̣ʷ–). yellow: ʔaksk̓ʷé·q'm'ɬ (√k̓ʷiq'é–).

colt: stiqéˑw'iʔɬ (√tiqíw–).

comb comb (*intr*.): xəpáym (√xəpayíʔ–). a comb: xə́piʔ (√xəpayíʔ–).

come: ʔís. come, arrive: t'úl'ɬ (√t'úla–). come again: tit'úlɬ (√t'úla–). come down, get off, get out of: líxʷlcx (√líxʷl–). come inside, go in, enter: ɬə́kstq (√ɬə́k–). come off: ɬíw. come off, blunt pointed: c'amə́k̓ʷɬ (√c'əmə́k̓ʷ–).

come to, revive: p'ə́x̣ɫ
(√p'ə́x̣-). come to see, go
to see: X̌aswáln
(√X̌aswáli-). come
together, reach: ɫakál'us
(√ɫək-). coming to the
surface, sticking out:
smáy'mi?smitn (√má·y-).
coming together:
sx̣ʷuqʷálustn
(√x̣ʷúqʷa-). he's coming
at me: s?ísmcaln (√?ís-).
his coming: sísi (√?ís-).
sun comes up: sɫə́x̣ʷl'awn
(√ɫə́x̣ʷl'a-).

commit commit suicide, kill
oneself: yúcamicx
(√yúca-).

companion travelling
companion:
?acx̣ʷúqʷtwlxumx
(√x̣ʷúqʷa-); nkʷyə́p
(√yə́pa-).

company expect company:
t'úlmsm (√t'úla-). have
company, have guests:
?act'ó·l'msm (√t'úla-).

comparative *comparative
degree*, more: tk.

completely completely, all
over: p'étlm' (√p'étl-).

cone (on a tree):
payúcpayuc.

confess confess, kneel:
kanílstx̣ʷayaqm
(√kanílstx̣ʷ-).

confuse confuse, surprise,
stare: tx̣ʷála?x (√wála?-).

confused, frown, bashful,
embarrass: ?acsé·x̣ʷɫ
(√sé·x̣ʷ-). be confused, be
surprised: ?actx̣ʷál?stm
(√wála?-).

conjunctions and: n, ɫ₂. and,
but: wi. because: qasi.
because, and: qas. because,
so, so that, for the reason
that: cu. if, unless, when:
?aml, ?aml?. or: ?awəl;
naw'. so that ENM: k̓ʷaɫ. so
that, and LNJ: kʷaɫ. so that,
in order to: takaɫ. so that,
instead, and: qa. with, and:
kl.

contest (n.): méX̌məX̌n
(√mə́X̌a-).

continue continue, get to the
end (*tr.*): t'anə́x (√t'aná-).

cook: kʷúkʷm (√kʷúkʷ-).
cook, bake: q̓ʷalín
(√q̓ʷə́la-). bake in ashes:
?ácqʷn (√?ácqʷ-);
məkʷúyq (√mə́kʷ-). boil:
cə́qstqn (√cə́q-). frying:
sč'íxitn (√č'íxi-). roast on
a stick: caqá?n (√cə́q-).
roast underground: p'íx̣n
(√p'íx̣-). half done:
pútaka? (√pút-). her
cooking: sasíɫani (√sáʔa-,
√?íɫani-).

cool cool, cold: X̌íx.

copper: .tskwe´.kᵘ FBa.

corner corner, its coming
together: sɫakál'wasi
(√ɫək-). its corner:

sx̣ʷúc'i (√x̣ʷúc'-).

corpse corpse, ghost, dead, dead person: mák̓ʷt (√mak̓ʷət-).

corral corral, fence: q'əláx̣n (√q'əláx̣an-).

correct correct, right, true, very, straight, even: k̓ʷə́pɬ (√k̓ʷə́p-).

corrugated corrugated, crooked, zigzag, wavy: č'úyč'uyuk̓ʷɬ (√č'úyuk̓ʷ-).

corselet: čhǐlshh̓ EC.

cottonwood: níq̓ʷɬ.

cougar, cougars: swáwaʔ (√wáwaʔ-). cougar LNJ, beaver: q'áɬč'm' (?). cougar, lion; a mean animal: sčátqɬm' (√čátqɬm'-).

cough: x̣ʷóʔn (√x̣ʷóʔan-).

could could, can: qaɬ.

count: k̓ʷə́nn (√k̓ʷə́na-).

country country, earth, dirt, land, ground: tə́mx. country, territory: təw'áytmx tə́mx (√taw'ə́t-). foreign country: sə́x̣ʷtam'x (√ʔə́x̣ʷ-).

court (*n.*) court, courtroom: k̓ʷápam'ɬtn' (√k̓ʷə́p-). court (*v.*): kʷə́nnwali (√kʷəná-).

cousin: súc's (*pl.* nxsóˑc'stn) (√súc'us-).

cover: λ̓ípšn (√λ̓íp-);

tə́m'šn (√tə́m'š-). cover with a dish: kamáˑlos EC. covering (*intr.*): sx̣ə́pawn (√x̣ə́pa-). be covered: ʔacx̣ə́pls (√x̣ə́pa-). have the head covered, have something wrapped around the head: mélq̓ʷls (√mələ́q̓ʷ-). its cover: sλ̓ípxtani (√λ̓íp-).

cow: wəmúsmuski, wəmúsəski ENM (*pl.* wəmúsmuskiyumx, wəmúsəskiyumx. beef: wəmúsuskiɬc'iʔ (√wəmúsmuski-). calf: wəmóʔsmuskiʔiʔɬ, wəmóʔsəskiʔɬ ENM (√wəmúsmuski-).

coward: ʔacqʷánuʔ (√qʷán-).

Cowlitz: káwlic. Cowlitz language: λ̓púlmixq (√λ̓púlmix-). Cowlitz person, Cowlitz tribe: sλ̓púlmx (√λ̓púlmix-). Upper Cowlitz: táytnapam (*pl.* táytnapamumx).

coyote: nək'ál'us, snək'ál'us (√nək'ál'-).

crab crab, crawfish: sx̣íynk (*pl.* sx̣ə́ynakumx) (√x̣ə́y-).

crab apple, crab apples: cúmaʔ. unripe (?) crab apple: *q̓ʷúmɬ (kumɬ).

crack crack, split: kʷaɬə́qɬ

(√kʷəɬə́q–). a crack:
ʔact'ə́sɬ (√t'ə́s–);
ʔackʷaɬə́qɬ (√kʷəɬə́q–).

crackling: sX̌ə́lX̌əlqʷmitn
(√X̌ə́lqʷ–). crackling,
spark: sX̌ə́lqʷmitn
(√X̌ə́lqʷ–).

cradle cradle, cradle basket,
baby basket: cakʷíliɬtn',
cakʷé·liɬtn' (√cə́kʷa–).
cradle, swing: q'ayúq̓ʷ.

cramp cramp, pain in the
side: ʔack'állksti?
(√k'ál–). cramp LNJ,
shrink, shrivel: ɬúmɬ
(√ɬúma–). cramp in a toe:
k'alíqsxntm (√k'ál–).
getting a cramp: st'ə́k̓ʷctx
(√t'ə́k̓ʷ–).

cranberry: x̌ántmx
(√x̌án–); ɬántmx (?)
(√ɬán–).

crane: sq̓ʷás (√q̓ʷás–);
spElEwe´ FBa.

crawfish crawfish, crab:
sxíynk (*pl.* sxə́ynakumx)
(√xə́y–).

crawl crawling up to:
sqílk'misn (√qílk'–). he's
crawling: sqílqilk'mitn
(√qílk'–).

crazy crazy, dizzy, nodd the
head: múlukʷɬ
(√múlukʷ–).

creek creek, little river, small
stream from a spring: cápx.
creek, water from a spring:
cátxʷ (√cátaxʷ–).

crippled crippled, limping, a
wound: ʔacq'ál'x̣
(√q'ál'x̣i–). crippled in the
legs: ʔacpí?x̣ʷnk
(√pí?x̣ʷ–).

crooked crooked (e.g. a
limb): ʔacč'úyuk̓ʷɬ
(√č'úyuk̓ʷ–). crooked (e.g.
a road): ʔacq̓ʷúyuxʷɬ
(√q̓ʷúyuxʷ–). crooked
(e.g. a stick): ʔacpúypuyɬ
(√púy–). crooked, zigzag,
wavy, corrugated:
č'úyč'uyuk̓ʷɬ
(√č'úyuk̓ʷ–).

crops crops, garden:
sx̣á·l'am'ɬ (√x̣ála–).

cross (*n.*): k'alálus (√k'al–).
cross on a rosary: k'alálu?s
(√k'al–). a cross, crossed:
t'anál'u?s (√t'aná–). he
crossed himself: ?it
k'alálusitm (√k'al–).

cross (*v.*) cross, get across:
tíwt (√tíwat–). cross, go
across, go through, land (a
canoe), reach shore: t'ánɬ
(√t'aná–). cross, go over a
mountain pass: sítikanm
(√sítikan–). cross water:
te´utlataluɬ FBa
(√tíwat–). crossing a little
creek: tíwxtn (√tíwat–).

cross-eyed: ʔacX̌ó·x̣ʷs
(√X̌ó·x̣ʷ–).

crosswise: tál'talm'
(√tál'–); tím'timm'
(√tím'–).

crow: sk'á·k'a?
(√k'á·k'a?–).

crumble: payə́xʷɬ
(√payə́xʷ–).

crumbs: ?acsə́pyucn
(√sə́pyuc–).

crumple crumple, rub,
scrape: cíkɬ (√cíki–).

crupper: súpsn'ktn
(√súpsn'k–);
ta´miclEpstEn FBa
(√tə́m'š–).

cry: xʷuám (√xʷu?ú–).
crying: skə́mmtn
(√kə́m–).

cup: qʷó?tn' (*pl.*
qʷó?tnumx) (√qʷó?–).

curl: x̣ayə́k̓ʷɬ (√x̣əyə́k̓ʷ–).
curly hair: ?acx̣əyk̓ʷó?s
(√x̣əyə́k̓ʷ–).

cut: c'awə́k'ɬ (√c'əwə́k'–);
xʷíq̓ʷx̣n (√xʷíq̓ʷx̣–). cut
grass: st'ɑwúm' JH
(*st'awə́m'). cut hair:
c'uwk'áyaqanm
(√c'əwə́k'–). cut one's
hand: c'uwk'áka
(√c'əwə́k'–). cut up,
butcher, carve, operate on:
c'ə́wc'awək'n
(√c'əwə́k'–). cut wood,
split wood, chop wood:
c'uk̓ʷáyk̓ʷp (√c'uk̓ʷ–).

d

dam (*n.*): stə́qnk (*pl.*
stə́qnakumx) (√tə́q–).

damp: núsɬ (√nús–). damp
earth: nusáytm'x (√nús–).

dance: wácxanm
(√wácxan–).

dandruff: ?íɬk'sk'stn'
(√?íɬani–,√k'əsk'ə́s–).

dangerous: q'aɬ č'ášnɬ
(√č'áš–). a dangerous
being: luslu´spiap TA
(√luslús–). dangerous
being, animal, malevolent
Indian doctor woman:
pə́sa?.

dark dark, get dark:
t'anápm'ɬ (√t'anáp–).
darken, blacken: né?qm

(√nə́q–). darkness, night:
qʷíx̣ltn, sqʷíx̣ltn
(√qʷíx̣–). get dark on:
qʷíx̣kʷu (√qʷíx̣–). getting
dark, late: nápis.

daughter daughter, son:
mán? (*pl.* nxmán?tn)
(√maní?–).

day day, daylight: sq'íx̣,
sq'íx̣tn (√q'íx̣–). daylight:
q'íx̣m (√q'íx̣–). daylight,
light: sq'éx̣ (√q'íx̣–).
getting daylight:
sq'ix̣áytmix̣n (√q'íx̣–).
it's daytime, it's getting
daylight: sq'íx̣iwn
(√q'íx̣–).

days of the week Monday:

námsanti (√náma-,
√sánti-). Tuesday:
camsq'íx̱ (√cám-,
√q'íx̱-). Wednesday:
kanalsq'íx̱ (√kán-,
√q'íx̱-). Thursday:
musalsq'íx̱ (√mús-,
√q'íx̱-). Friday:
cilkstalsq'íx̱ (√cílks-,
√q'íx̱-). Saturday:
pənskʷítim'ɬ (√pən-,
√kʷíti-). Sunday: taw'ə́t
sq'íx̱ (√q'íx̱-).

dazzle dazzle, blind:
qáy'x̱il'sn (√qáy'x̱i-).

dead dead, dead person,
corpse, ghost: mák̓ʷt
(√mak̓ʷə́t-). be dead, die:
ʔátamn (√ʔátaman-). be
dead, fire goes out: ɬə́pɬ
(√ɬə́pa-).

deaf: ʔactaqán' (√tə́q-).

death his death: stmə́ni
(√ʔátaman-).

debt be in debt, owe:
x̱ʷux̱ʷín (√x̱ʷúx̱ʷ-).

December: pənnáwsanti
(√pən-, √náwa-,
√sánti-).

deep: ƛ̓ə́p. its depth:
sƛ̓ə́ptani (√ƛ̓ə́p-).

deer: sƛ̓aláš (*pl.*
sƛ̓alášinumx) (√ƛ̓aláš-).
buck deer: tsma´xkEn FBa
(√məx̱kán-). fawn:
sƛ̓alá·ʔši?ɬ (√ƛ̓aláš-). roe
(deer?): tsa´wx̱ TA.

deerskin deerskin (tanned):

wayə́x̱. deerskin robe:
tɬa´leconi´tsa FBa
(√ƛ̓aláš-). deerskin with
hair still on it: taysx̱ʷáq̓ʷ
(√táy-, √x̱ʷáq̓ʷa-).

defeat defeat, beat: c'ə́kšn
(√c'ə́ka-). defeat, win, use
up, be gone: c'ə́kɬ
(√c'ə́ka-).

deictics

articles

	non-feminine	feminine
indefinite	t	c
definite	tit	cic
	ʔit	ʔic
	tat	cac

demonstratives

	non-feminine	feminine
this	titatí	titx̱tí
that (near)	——	titx̱t'íst
that (remote)	titató	titx̱tá	cacx̱cá
this one	tí?x̱, tíx̱	
that, that one	xán?	
that	táx̱	

adverbials

here	šé?	ní?x̱, níx̱
there	ɬáq̓ʷ	xán?x̱, šíxn'
that, there	šíxn'x̱	
there	ʔaɬ xán?	
to here	x̱ʷšé?	
through here	tašé?	
this way	xašém', xašém'x̱	
over there	x̱ʷux̱ʷú?kʷm'	

dentalia: ho´xtɬ FBa.

describe: t'úq̓ʷn (√t'úq̓ʷ-).

desert desert, leave:
ɬawál'xnmn (√ɬəwála-).

desiderative desiderative

particle, want: qas
(*enclitic*).

design design, mark, a brand:
q̓ʷə┼ (√q̓ʷə┼é-). design,
mark, write, brand, vote:
q̓ʷa┼én (√q̓ʷə┼é-). design,
spots, something written:
ʔacq̓ʷə┼ (√q̓ʷə┼é-). design
on a basket: q̓ʷa┼álič̓n
(√q̓ʷə┼é-).

detour detour, climb through,
squeeze through: ┼úmicx
(√┼úmi-).

devil: lijúb.

dew: səxʷáytmx LNJ;
sə́xʷsxʷ ENM (√sə́xʷa-).

diaper diaper, breechcloth:
sƛ̓íq'nk (√ƛ̓íq'a-).

diarrhoea diarrhoea,
excrement: sʔáps
(√ʔáps-).

die die, dead: ʔátamn
(√ʔátaman-). his death:
stmə́ni (√ʔátaman-).

different different, foreign,
strange, other: ʔə́xʷ┼
(√ʔə́xʷ-).

dig dig (a hole): lə́wm
(√lə́w-). dig for: lə́w'šn
(√lə́w-). dig for, look for:
p'í┼n (√p'í┼-). dig roots:
cíqʷn, cíqʷšn (√cíqʷi-).
dig up, root up: p'alə́k̓ʷn
(√p'ələ́k̓ʷ-).

digging stick: tulə́m. root
digger: lā´omEn FBa
(√lə́w-). handle of a root
digger: sau´xakEn FBa.

dip: ƛ̓úqʷn (√ƛ̓úqʷi-).

dipnet: qi sƛ̓úqʷam'┼,
ƛ̓úqʷam'┼tn' (√ƛ̓úqʷi-).

dirt dirt, earth, land, ground,
country: tə́mx.

dirty: ʔacq̓ʷíc' (√q̓ʷíc'-).
dirty face: c'əx̣ámus
(√c'əx̣ám-);
q̓ʷíc's,q̓ʷíc'ay's (√q̓ʷíc'-).
dirty neck: q̓ʷíc'psm
(√q̓ʷíc'-).

disappear: xʷáyacx
(√xʷáya-). disappear, lose:
xʷə́xʷ┼ (√xʷəxʷə́l-).

disapprove disapprove,
dislike: ʔúxʷtqs.

discuss discuss, talk (*pl.*),
argue: nə́xʷm (√nə́xʷa-).

disease: sʔáy'stn (√ʔáy's-).

dish: cə́kʷluʔxʷ (*pl.*
cə́kʷluʔxʷumx).

dish up dish up, serve:
c'awúqs (√c'áw-).

dislike dislike, disapprove:
ʔúxʷtqs. dislike, hate:
tóʔkʷmn (√tóʔkʷ-).

dissatisfied: ʔackə́nnamn
(√kə́nnam-).

dissolve dissolve, melt, thaw:
yə́xʷ┼ (√yə́xʷa-).

distribute: ká┼aʔtumix
(√ká┼-). distribute, give
gifts: kʷítim'┼ (√kʷíti-).
distribute, scatter, spread
out: pí┼n (√pí┼i-).

ditch (n.): ʔacxʷé·q'┼
(√xʷə́q'-). big ditch:
ʔacxʷə́q'┼ (√xʷə́q'-).

dive: mə́l'qsn (√mə́l'qsi-);
pacə́qʷm (√pəcə́qʷ-).

he's diving: spə́cpcqʷmitn
(√pəcə́qʷ-).

divide divide, share, separate:
kʷaⱡál'wax (√kʷəⱡ-).

dizzy dizzy, crazy, nod the
head: múlukʷⱡ
(√múlukʷ-).

do: sáʔn (√sáʔa-); wíʔx̣,
wéʔx̣, wítx̣, wétx̣
(√wiʔx̣-). do with, do what:
ʔítx (√ʔít-). anything be
done to it: ʔíni kʷu
(√ʔíni_). I'll do whatever I
want: ⱡiʔín kn (√ʔíni-).
what are you doing?:
sʔíninax̣ kʷu (√ʔíni-).
what did you do with...?: ʔit
ʔítx kʷu k... (√ʔít-). what
he is doing to me:
sʔínw'əncals kʷu (√ʔíni-).
whatever is being done with
it: nks + ʔítawctx kʷu
(√ʔít-).

doctor (*n.*) a doctor:
ʔacwánx. Indian doctor:
ʔacʔə́x̣tkʷlx (√ʔə́x̣t-).
malevolent Indian doctor
woman, dangerous being,
animal: pə́saʔ.

doctor (*v.*) doctor (*tr.*):
yalə́pn (√yələ́p-).

doe doe, female: táwnⱡc'iʔ
(√táwn-).

dog: qáx̣aʔ (*pl.* qx̣ʔáwmx).
little dog, puppy: qáˑʔx̣aʔ
(*pl.* qx̣áˑw'mx)
(√qáx̣aʔ-). wooly dog:
kiˑ´mia FBa.

dog salmon: ƛ'x̣ʷáy';

.snūˑ´nux̣ FBa; pu-natch
GGa,UWa.

dogwood: x̣íˑts'tɑmts JH
(*x̣íc'tmc).

doll doll, toy: sx̣áⱡx̣ʷam'n
(√x̣áⱡx̣ʷa-).

dollar one dollar: nák'awls
(√nák'-). half dollar, fifty
cents: číl'ⱡ (√čílačš-).

done: ʔacnámⱡ (√náma-).
half done: pútakaʔ
(√pút-).

door: taqál'pstn' (√tə́q-).

double double, both,
together: t'əmx̣sáliʔ
(√t'əmx̣-,√sáliʔ-). double
up one's fist: yalúx̣ʷakanm
(√yəlúx̣ʷ-). doubled up,
twist, spin: yalə́k'n
(√yələ́k'-). doubling up:
swínwntn (√wín-). be
doubled up: ʔacqémx̣cx
(√qémx̣-). he doubled his
fist at me: milúx̣ʷakaʔšic
(√milúx̣ʷ-).

dove dove, pigeon: x̣əmím'.
mourning-dove: x̣əmím'x
(√x̣əmím'-); qoˑ´x.kox
FBa.

down down, downwards:
t'éˑqsm (√t'íqi-). down,
low, below: ⱡáX̣p. down,
put down, lay down: kácⱡ
(√kác-). down country,
south: tul-kaˑ´lEx FBa.
come down, get off, get out
of: líx̣ʷlcx (√líx̣ʷl-). fall
down, fall over: ⱡə́kayq
(√ⱡə́k-). lie down, be

lying: ká·w'an. lie down,
go to bed: cə́kʷɬ
(√cə́kʷa-). putting down
on: skácšitn (√kác-).
upside down: kʷə́nala
ɬáƛ'pm' (√kʷə́nala-,
√ɬáƛ'p-).

downhill downhill, bottom of
a hill: ƛ'apé·l's (√ƛ'ə́p-).
downhill, downstream:
ƛ'apé·l'usm' (√ƛ'ə́p-).

downriver downriver, down
to the river: pútmx
(√pútmix-).

downstream: ɬáƛ'pm LNJ
(√ɬáƛ'p-); ƛ'əpé·l'usm'
ENM (√ƛ'ə́p-). downstream,
downhill: ƛ'apé·l'usm'
(√ƛ'ə́p-). downwards,
downstream: ɬáƛ'pm
(√ɬáƛ'p-). go downstream:
wileɬā´kum FBa (√wí-,
√ɬá?kʷ-).

downward: túlkʷ (?)

downwards downwards,
down: t'é·qsm (√t'íqi-).
downwards, downstream:
ɬáƛ'pm (√ɬáƛ'p-).

drag drag, pull: wə́xn
(√wə́xa-). dragging,
hauling: sxə́lktn (√xə́lk-).
he's dragging along:
sxə́lxlkcšitn (√xə́lk-).

drain drain, seep, wring out:
múc'n (√múc'-). drain,
strain water out: pə́qʷqal'n
(√pə́qʷa-, √qalí?-).

drapes drapes, (window
shades): ?áxacxtnmn'
(√?ə́x-).

dream: túkʷal'ix, túkʷal'x
(√túkʷa-). he's dreaming:
stúkʷtukʷalltn (√túkʷa-).

dress (n.): sál'cil'qs
(√sál'c-). buy a dress:
táxʷsal'cil'qs
(√táxʷayway-, √sál'c-).

dress (v.) dress, get dressed,
wear: t'ə́km (√t'ə́k-).
dress game, skin: súk̓ʷn
(√súk̓ʷi-). dressed:
námt'əkm (√náma-,
√t'ə́k-). skin dresser, skin
softener: .stu´ps FBa;
tla´mhepEɬExtEn FBa
(√ƛ'əmə́x-).

dried salmon:
.shapau´ɬiɬEn FBa
(√xə́pa-).

drift drift, float: múq̇ʷɬ
(√múq̇ʷa-).

driftwood: tit ?acmúq̇ʷa?ɬ
tit ƛ'ə́xƛ'axumx
(√múq̇ʷa-, √ƛ'ə́x-).
driftwood, brush: sxasíɬšn
(√xasíɬšn-).

drill drill, drill a hole, make a
hole, pierce: lapə́xʷɬ
(√ləpə́xʷa-). a drill:
lápxʷam'ɬtn' LNJ
(√ləpə́xʷa-);
pál'k̓ʷam'ɬtn' ENM
(√pəl'ə́k̓ʷ-). fire drill:
yitsai´.ts FBa. fire drill,
torch: sílmix.

drink: qʷó?.

drip drip, leak: c'ə́x̣ʷm
(√c'ə́x̣ʷa-).

drive drive away, force to leave, order: x̣íyn (√x̣íy–).

drop: p'ə́ɬn (√p'ə́ɬa–).

drown drown, sink: k'ə́ɬ (√k'ə́ɬa–).

drum: kaukou´lac FBa; kuku´Elic FBa. drum, club, whip: tásam'ɬtn' (√tása–).

drummer: tásam'ɬn' (√tása–).

drumstick: kî´ṣiaka FBa.

drunk: c'ál'pyal's (√c'ələp–).

dry: x̣ə́pɬ (√x̣ə́pa–). dry (dishes): x̌ʷík̓ʷiqn (√x̌ʷík̓ʷi–). dried salmon: .shapau´ɬiɬEn FBa (√x̣ə́pa–). dried things: sx̣ə́pɬ (√x̣ə́pa–). drying rack: x̣ápam'ɬtn', x̣ə́pnxtn (√x̣ə́pa–). spread to dry: x̣apúl'mxn (√x̣ə́pa–).

duck: x̣átx̣t (√x̣átx̣at–);

kʷáqkʷaq. duck *sp.* (gray-colored): sq'wê·wq' JH. fish duck, merganser: sq̓ʷálax̣n (√q̓ʷál–). a white duck: q̓ʷél'x̣ʷič.

dugout dugout, cave, steep hole: ʔacč'aləqʷɬ (√č'aləqʷ–).

dull dull, not sharp: x̌ʷál'.

dumb dumb, stupid, clumsy, stubborn: ʔayayáš.

dump dump, throw, throw away, send: k̓ʷə́ɬn (√k̓ʷə́ɬ–).

dusk dusk, evening: kwEtskwe´xta´n FBa (√kʷac–, √q̓ʷíx̣–).

dust (n.): sx̣ʷə́layq (√x̣ʷə́l–). dust, ashes: sp'áqʷuyq (√p'áqʷ–). dust flying, powder: x̌'asə́qʷɬ (√x̌'əsə́qʷ–).

dynamite dynamite; gun táqʷčam'ɬtn' (√təqʷə́či–).

e

each each other, together: t'əmxsáliyumx (√t'əmx–, √sáliʔ–).

eagle: x̣ʷáyp. bald eagle: sx̌'iw'x̣ín' (√x̌'iw'x̣ín'–). golden eagle: x̣ʷx̣ʷáy' (√x̣ʷáy'–).

ear: q̓ʷalánʔ (*pl.* q̓ʷalanáwmx)

(√q̓ʷalaníʔ–). lobe of the ear: patao´xEmEn FBa.

earache I have an earache: t'ak̓ʷá·n'icalctx (√t'ə́k̓ʷ–).

early early, morning: q̓ʷéx̣iʔx̣ʷ.

earn earn, win: c'ə́kam'ɬ (√c'ə́ka–).

earring: slé·x̣nʔ (*pl.*

slé·x̣in'umx) (√lé·x̣-).

earth: il-maí-tŭmħ EC.
earth, dirt, land, ground,
country: tə́mx.

east: tu ʔaⱡ sX̣aqám'
(√X̣aqám'-);
tako´manwEld FBa.

easy easy to tear, soft: lé́ʔq.

eat: ʔíⱡn (√ʔíⱡani-); ʔúpⱡ
(√ʔúpal-). eat berries from
the bush: má́ʔkʷiq
(√mákʷ-). finished eating:
námiⱡn (√náma-,
√ʔíⱡani-).

ebb tide: .sna´mai.x FBa
(√náma-).

echo echo, hear noise,
squeak: ʔímnm' (√ʔímn-).
echo, noise, voice:
tawó·yn' (√taw-).

eddy: tsEⱡpe´s.ⱡko FBa
(√c'ə́lə́p-).

eel: ʔáqʷs (√ʔáqʷas-).

egg, eggs: sqʷóqʷstmiʔⱡ
(√qʷóqʷstm-). eggshell:
ⱡka´tsEmin e
skowa´kstEmiⱡ FBa.
salmon eggs, roe: qʷə́ⱡx̣aʔ.

eight: cámus. eighteen:
pánačš kl t cámus;
tál'camus. eighty:
cámusⱡtumx (√cámus-).

elbow: tsEtsei´katEn FBa;
sa-t͡saí-ŭ-katn EC.

elderberry blue elderberry:
ts'kwí·kw̥ JH (*c'kʷík̇ʷ).
red elderberry: č'ípt.

eleven: pánačš kl t ʔúc's;

tál̇ʔuc's.

elk: qílitn. cow elk:
sⱡɑ́k'ts'ɑm JH. elk calf:
qé·l'itn (√qílitn-). elk
skin robe: kala´tib FBa
(√qílitn-).

else someone else: wáʔo,
wáʔo ʔə́xʷⱡ (√wá-);
ʔiwát. something else:
támʔo ʔə́xʷⱡ (√tám-);
tántan (√tán-).
somewhere else: káʔo
(√ká·-).

embarrass embarrass,
confused, frown, bashful:
sé·xʷⱡ (√sé·xʷ-). he
embarrassed me: ʔit
sé·xʷstmx (√sé·xʷ-).
he's embarrassed:
ʔacsé·xʷmicx (√sé·xʷ-).

emergency: ʔacX̣ə́x̣iʔcx
(√X̣ə́x̣iʔ-).

empty: ʔúⱡay'q (√ʔúⱡ-). be
empty, become empty:
c'ə́kay'q (√c'ə́ka-).

end end, finish: ná·m'usix
(√náma-). end, finish,
stop: námn (√náma-).
end of toe; instep: stál'iqšn
(√tál'-). both ends:
t'ə́mxə́mʔ (√t'ə́mx-,
√x̣ə́mʔ-). get to the end,
continue (tr.): t'aná́x
(√t'aná-). its end:
sná·m'usi (√náma-); tək'
(?). its front end: silə́pi
(√ʔilə́p-).

enemy: tə́xʷs (√tə́xʷis-).

English English language, talk English: pástin'q,páʔstinq' (√pástin-).

enough: x̌áq̓ʷtm'x.

enter enter, come inside, go in: ɬə́kstq (√ɬə́k-).

even even, get even: ʔúlwasix (√ʔúlwasi-). even, very, right, straight, correct, true: k̓ʷə́pɬ (√k̓ʷə́p-).

evening: kʷə́sswn (√kʷə́s-). evening, dusk: kwɛtskwe´xta´n FBa (√kʷac-, √qʷíx̣-).

every every, all, whole: t'əmx̌ʷáʔkʷuʔ (√t'əmx-, √x̌ʷáʔkʷuʔ-).

everything: t'əmx̌ʷáʔkʷu t ʔitám (√t'əmx-, √x̌ʷáʔkʷuʔ-).

everywhere: ta ʔikán. everywhere, somewhere: ʔikán. from everywhere: tu ʔikán.

evidently: ʔo, o, ʔu, u (*enclitic*). evidently, maybe:

examine examine, read: ʔə́x̣x̣n (√ʔə́x̣-).

exchange exchange, trade: ʔáy'šn (√ʔáy-).

excrement excrement, diarrhoea: sʔáps (√ʔáps-); p'a TA.

expect: ʔá·psmn (√ʔá·ps-). expect company: t'úlmsm (√t'úla-).

expensive expensive, valuable, high-priced: ʔacyáyx̣ʷi (√yáyx̣ʷi-).

explode explode, shoot with a gun, blow up: taqʷə́čɬ (√təqʷə́či-).

eye: mús (*pl.* musáwmx). pupil of the eye: tsnî´ks FBa (√nə́q-); silaxwa´ls FBa.

eyebrow: cúmay's.

eyeglasses: ʔáx̣acxtnil's, ʔáx̣am'ɬtn' (√ʔə́x̣-).

eyelash: tse´pxolstɛn FBa (√c'ípxʷ-).

eyelid: tsepiakalsɛmɛn FBa (√c'ípxʷ-).

f

face: cmús. dirty face: c'əx̣ámus (√c'əx̣ám-). make faces, frown: c'ík̓ʷusm (√c'ík̓ʷ-). make faces at: c'é·k̓ʷlšn (√c'ík̓ʷ-). make faces at, make fun of: x̣áɬx̣ʷamn

(√x̣áɬx̣ʷa-).

fading: sp'áq̓ʷmaln (√p'áq̓ʷ-).

faint faint, be dizzy: ʔacmúlukʷls (√múlukʷ-). faint, have wind knocked out: txʷsə́w (√səwə́-). he

fainted: txʷmulúkʷstn
(√múlukʷ-).

fall (*n*.) fall, autumn:
pənyáq'sməɬk (√pən-,
√yáq'a-, √məɬk-).

fall (*v*.) fall, fall off: p'əɬ,
p'əɬɬ. fall, tip, tip over:
yáq'ɬ (√yáq'a-). fall apart:
c'ɬqál'us (√c'aɬəq-). fall
apart, fall (*pl*.): ʔə́xʷɬ
(√ʔə́xʷa-). fall in, collapse:
pə́n'ɬ (√pə́n'-). fall on
one's face: cínqs (√cín-).
fall out, tip over: kə́may'q
(√kə́m-). fall over, fall
down: ɬə́kayq (√ɬə́k-).
fallen tree, windfall, log:
syáq' (√yáq'a-). falling
on: syáq'šitn (√yáq'a-).
it's falling apart: sx̣əƛ̓x̣ƛ̓wn
(√x̣ə́ƛ̓-).

famous famous, lucky, smart:
swə́tt (√wə́tt-).

fan (*n*.): qi sƛ̓íšltawam'ɬ
(√ƛ̓íx-).

far: lílʔ. further: tk lílʔ
(√tk-, √lílʔ-). further
away: lé·lʔ (√lílʔ-).

fart: p'óʔ.

fast: x̣awə́lʔ. fast, quick,
soon: ƛ̓ə́x̣ɬ (√ƛ̓ə́x̣-). fast,
soon, hurry, right away:
ƛ̓ə́x̣ƛ̓ax̣ɬ (√ƛ̓ə́x̣-). fast
water: x̣awíɬkʷu
(√x̣awə́lʔ-).

fast (*v*.) fast, go on a fast:
q'íctm'x.

fat: qíxʷɬ (√qíxʷ-). grease,

fat (on the body): č'ayə́š.

father: mán. father! (address
form): kəmáʔ, kʷumáʔ
(√mán-). his father:
mánawi (√mán-).
stepfather: tcuɬmánɛm FBa
(√čuɬ-, √mán-).

fathom: .snakax hweˊmɛɬ
FBa (√nák'-).

faucet: qi sp'íc'i t qálʔ
(√p'íc'-).

fawn: sƛ̓alá·ʔšiʔɬ
(√ƛ̓aláš-); tɛlɛ'ka´n FBa.

fear fear, be afraid of:
qʷántas (√qʷán-).

feast (*n*.): sʔíɬntawmln,
ʔíɬnšictx (√ʔíɬani-).

feather: c'úc'q̓ʷ
(√c'uc'úq̓ʷ-). feather
bonnet: sɛksa´k.pɬɛɬ FBa
(√sákp-).

February: ʔáqa tat swáksn
tic ƛ̓aqám' (√wakə́s-,
√ƛ̓aqám'-).

feed: ʔíɬanix (√ʔíɬani-).
feed, give food to: mátiln
(√mátil-). he's feeding
him: sʔúmtn (√ʔúm-).

feel feel (by touching):
ʔíwn'x (√ʔíwn'-). feel bad,
be sorry, sad, be too bad:
ʔacɬə́k'amn (√ɬə́k'a-).
feel bad, worry, mistreat:
yulínut (√yul-).

fell (a tree): yáq'n
(√yáq'a-).

female female, doe:
táwnɬc'iʔ (√táwn-).

fence fence, corral: q'əláx̣n
(√q'əláx̣an-). build a
fence: sá·q'lax̣n (√sáʔa-,
√q'əláx̣an-).

fern bracken fern: cáqan'ɬ
(√cáqa-). bracken fern,
upper part: *č'álača?
(tc'a´latca). bracken roots:
wəč'ál; st̂sak EC (√cáqa-).
licorice fern: *ƛ̓əwílqʷ
(k'ɬwe·´lk). rhizome of
bracken fern: *č'ákʷm
(tc'a´kum). sword fern:
sáx̣linm' (?) wood fern:
*c'əkʷíʔ (ts'kwai).

ferryboat: skáw.

fever: ʔacx̣ʷaláʔtn
(√x̣ʷaláʔ-).

few: ʔiǩʷín, ʔiǩʷén'.

fifteen: pánačš kl t čílačš;
tál'čilačš.

fifty: cílksɬtumx (√cílks-).

fight: qalíkʷn (√qalí-).
fighter: qalíkʷalaka?
(√qalí-). get in a fight:
k'álɬ (√k'ál-).

file file, sharpen: mátn
(√máta-). a file:
máʔtam'ɬtn' (√máta-).

fill fill (a container): lək'n,
lk'lək'n (√lək'-). fill, load
a gun: lék'n (√lək'-). full
(stomach): ʔacláx̣ʷɬ
(√láx̣ʷ-).

fin its fin: ʔátqʷɬili
(√ʔátqʷil-).

find find, meet, catch at:
t'úqʷn (√t'úqʷi-). find

out, hear about: ǩʷál'anm
(√ǩʷálan-). find out about:
tó·luxʷ (√tó·lu-).

finger: tsEx̣wo´Enwaieka
FBa (√c'əx̣ʷúy'nwn'-).
fingers: ká·laxum'x
(√kálax-). fingers, hand:
laxaíaka HH. fingers, hand,
nails: staléka HH (√t'alá-).
first finger: sêtsa´IsEmetEn
FBa (√sə́c'-). index finger:
pəx̣ʷáyaka ENM (√pəx̣ʷ-).
little finger: q̓ʷax̣ə́nwayaka
(√q̓ʷax̣ə́nw-); ká·ʔɬax̣ʷm;
kEtso´xe FBa.

fingerling fingerlings, small
fish, small trout: mán'c
(√mán'ac-).

fingernail: c'ax̣ílaka?
(√c'ax̣íl-).

finish finish, end: ná·m'usix
(√náma-). finish, end,
stop: námn (√náma-).
finish talking: x̣ám'stq̓ʷ
(√x̣ám'-, √təq̓ʷa-).
finished eating: námiɬn
(√náma-, √ʔíɬani-). he
just finished it:
sputsnámatn (√pút-,
√náma-).

fir: kʷicám; yámc (?). white
fir: ta-wí-tsh̄l EC.

fire: mə́kʷp (*pl.*
mə́kʷapumx). build a fire:
x̣ʷál'kʷp (√x̣ʷál'a-). catch
fire, burn: x̣ʷál'ɬ
(√x̣ʷál'a-). fire goes out:
ɬə́pɬ (√ɬə́pa-). fire is too

high, blaze: lámstq
(√lám-). fire on top:
x̣úk̓ʷstq (√x̣úk̓ʷ-). keep
building fires: x̣ʷál'x̣ʷl'k̓ʷp
(√x̣ʷál'a-). put fire on:
x̣ʷál'šn (√x̣ʷál'a-). put in
the fire: x̣ʷál'n (√x̣ʷál'a-).
put out a fire, beat up, kill:
yúcx (√yúca-). put out a
fire, put out a light, kill:
ɬə́pn (√ɬə́pa-).

fire drill: yitsai´.ts FBa. fire
drill, torch: sílmix.

firewood: x̣áɬx̣ʷms
tx̣ʷtmə́k̓ʷp (√x̣áɬx̣ʷm-,
√mə́k̓ʷúp-).

firm firm, hard, stiff, strong,
tight: ƛ̓ə́x̣ʷ.

first first, in front: ʔílp, ʔílpɬ
(√ʔílə́p-).

fish (*n.*): sámn, sémn
(√sáman-). fish *sp.*:
sƛ̓éʔqk̓ʷu (√ƛ̓éʔq-) (*see*
sturgeon). small fish, small
trout, fingerlings: mán'c
(√mán'ac-).

fish (*v.*) fish, catch fish:
q'é·t'm (√q'ét'a-). fish,
go fishing: ƛ̓asámn
(√ƛ̓áʔ-, √sáman-). fish
with a net: ʔáx̣ʷynm
(√ʔáx̣ʷyin-).

fisher: tcEto'x̣we´ FBa.

fish hawk fish hawk, osprey:
sc'íx̣ʷ (√c'íx̣ʷ-).

fishhook: x̣ə́n's (*pl.*
x̣ə́n'isumx) (√x̣ən'ús-);
ai´kamEltEn FBa; xaia´m

FBa.

fishline: tami´ɬEn Eɬ tê
hê´nns FBa (√t'amiɬə́n-,
√x̣ən'ús-).

fishnet: ʔáx̣ʷyn
(√ʔáx̣ʷyin-); kátyn;
yasə́n; li'tca´ FBa; wa´pia
FBa.

fish trap: scítpn (√cítpan-);
sx̣íyəp (√x̣íyap-). fish
trap, fish basket: yax̣áw't
(√yax̣áw'at-).

fist: milúx̣ʷakaʔ
(√milúx̣ʷ-). double up
one's fist: yalúx̣ʷakanm
(√yəlúx̣ʷ-). he doubled up
his fist at me:
milúx̣ʷakaʔšic
(√milúx̣ʷ-).

five: čílačš.

fix fixed that way: ʔítm k̓ʷu
(√ʔít-).

flag: sán'timn';
náw'san'tim'n (√náwa-,
√sánti-).

flap flapping, flopping:
stásatn (√tása-).

flash a light flashing,
lightning: sq'íx̣q'x̣wn
(√q'íx̣-).

flat: p'íƛ̓ɬ (√p'íƛ̓i-);
p'asə́x̣ʷɬ (√p'asə́x̣ʷ-).
flatten: p'íƛ̓n (√p'íƛ̓i-).
flattened out: ʔacp'íƛ̓p'iƛ̓
(√p'íƛ̓i-). flat face:
ʔacp'íƛ̓ay's (√p'íƛ̓i-). flat
feet: ʔacp'íƛ̓šn (√p'íƛ̓i-).
he flopped down flat: ʔit

txʷtáɬstm (√táɬ-). spread
flat, lie flat: táɬɬ (√táɬ-).

flea, fleas: máč'iɬaʔ.

flesh flesh, meat: k̓ʷús.

flicker (*n*.): tseiˊuk FBa.

float float, drift: múq̓ʷɬ
(√múq̓ʷa-). float, float
away: p'úcɬ (√p'úc-). it's
floating: sp'úcp'cwn
(√p'úc-).

flood: c'ə́p'ɬ (√c'ə́p'a-).
flood tide: .slîˊ k.ks FBa
(√lə́k'-). high water, flow
LNJ: táw'k̓ʷuʔ (√táw'-).

floor: ciɬáˑlaxʷinp (√ciɬ-).

flop flopping, flapping:
stásatn (√tása-). he
flopped down flat: ʔit
txʷtáɬstm (√táɬ-).

flow flow LNJ, high water:
táw'k̓ʷuʔ (√táw'-).

flower, flowers: sx̣ís
(√x̣ísi-).

fly (*n*.): x̣ʷay'ə́x̣ʷay'ə́x̣ʷ;
tsauˊɬkaxa FBa.

fly (*v*.): téʔɬ (√tíʔi-). it's
flying: stíʔiwn (√tíʔi-).

flying squirrel: ɬaɬiˑˊk'pc
MJb-mi.

foam foam, scum (on
something being cooked):
páyɬk̓ʷu (√páy-).
foaming: sp'úcawn
(√p'úca-).

fog: sp'ə́ɬšq (√p'ə́ɬa-,
√šə́q-).

fold: wə́n'n, wan'állwax
(√wə́n'-). fold up:

wə́n'wn'n (√wə́n'-).

follow follow, chase: tál'šl's
(√tál'š-). follow, go with:
ʔáyašn (√ʔáyax-).

food food, meal: cíɬn
(√ciɬə́n-). bad food,
coarse: x̣ašúl'mx (√x̣ə́š-).
give a dish of food:
silmátx. Indian food:
sílmixuliɬn (√ʔilmíx-).
left some food: k̓ʷə́cliɬn'
(√k̓ʷə́c-, √ʔíɬani-).

fool (*n*.): x̣ə́šm' (√x̣ə́š-). get
fooled: nks +
txʷq̓ʷatə́x̣ʷstm
(√q̓ʷatə́x̣ʷ-).

foot foot, leg, lap: cúɬ (*pl*.
cuɬáwmx) (√cúl-). foot,
instep: st'alášn (*pl*.
st'alášinumx) (√t'alá-).
on foot, by walking:
talsyə́p (√tál-, √yə́pa-).

footprint: paˊt.kEmEn FBa
(√pátaq-).

forbid forbid, don't want to
tell, keep quiet: káywiɬix
(√káywiɬi-). forbid, stop:
x̣íp'n (√x̣íp'-).

force: x̣aƛ̓én (√x̣aƛ̓é-).
force to leave, drive away,
order: x̣íyn (√x̣íy-).

ford ford, wade, swim: k̓ʷátɬ
(√k̓ʷáta-).

forehead: sk̓ʷə́pl's
(√k̓ʷə́p-); s'Laˊx̣ᵘs FBa.

foreign foreign, strange,
different, other: ʔə́x̣ʷɬ
(√ʔə́x̣ʷ-). foreign, from

afar: tu líl?. foreign
country: sə́xʷtam'x
(√ʔə́xʷ-). foreign language:
tl slé·la ɬ stə́q̓ʷ (√líl?-,
√tə́q̓ʷa-).

forget: mə́lqnix
(√mə́lqni-).

fork hayfork: kwaxa´lus
FBa; tawa´sɛnɛɬ FBa
(√tawasá-). table fork:
sac'ə́mn (*pl.*
sac'ə́minum'x);
sa´tspakantɛn FBa
(√sə́c'-). its forks, its
separating: k̓ʷáyusi
(√k̓ʷáy'us-).

forty: mə́sɬtumx (√mə́s-).

four: mús.

fourteen: pánačš kl t mús;
tál'mus.

frame frame for tanning,
bow, prop, temporary
shelter: sq'iyúxʷ
(√q'iyúxʷ-).

freeze freeze, harden, set:
q'áxʷɬ (√q'áxʷa-).

fresh fresh, new: mayə́n.

Friday: cilkstalsq'íx̣
(√cílks-, √q'íx̣-).

friend: autsis-kwil-lum GGb
(√ʔúc's, √qʷələ́m-);
aiyalinóot HH (√ʔí·-).

fringe its fringe: yacə́x̣ani *or*
yasə́x̣ani (√yasə́x̣an-).

frog: šwaq'íq' (*pl.*
šwaq'íq'umx)

(√waq'íq'-). frog *sp.*:
swáq'iq'čn (√waq'íq'-).

from from, of: tu; tu ʔaɬ;
tuɬ. from, off, out of, than:
tl ʔaɬ.

front front, ancestors: silə́p
(√ʔilə́p-). in front, first:
ʔílp, ʔílpɬ (√ʔilə́p-).

frostbite frostbitten hands:
q'áxʷakaʔ (√q'áxʷa-).

frown frown, bashful,
embarrass, confused:
sé·xʷɬ (√sé·xʷ-). frown,
make faces: c'ík̓ʷusm
(√c'ík̓ʷ-).

fruit fruit, berries: stó·l'šn
(√tó·l'xan-).

fry frying (*tr.*): sč'íx̣itn
(√č'íx̣i-). frying pan:
č'éx̣am'ɬtn' (√č'íx̣i-).

full: lə́k', lə́k'tač. full
(stomach): ʔacláxʷɬ
(√láxʷ-).

fun have fun, have a good
time: ʔáylx (√ʔáy-). make
fun of, make faces at:
x̣áɬxʷamn (√x̣áɬxʷa-).
make fun of, mock:
saqá·x̣tnmn (√saqá·x̣-).

funeral they're going to have
a funeral: saʔák̓ʷtiliɬt
(√sáʔa-).

funny: q'aɬ láʔx̣ʷn'ɬ
(√láxʷa-).

fur: t'amín.

future: ɬ-; ɬit; ƛ̓a.

g

gain gain weight: qíxʷlx
(√qíxʷ–).

gall: masə́ntn
(√masəntə́n–).

gallop it's galloping:
s?á·x̣ʷk̓ʷumitn (√?áx̣ʷa–).

gamble gambling, playing
cards: sx̣ʷálmitn (√x̣ʷál–).
gamble at stick-game:
yáwax̣anm (√yáwax̣an–).
what they gamble, their
stakes, their pot: sx̣ʷál'x̣ʷili
(√x̣ál'x̣ʷil–).

game: sc'ə́kam'ɫ (√c'ə́ka–).
playing ball: sɫé?qɫqmaln
(√ɫə́q–). playing cards:
sx̣ʷálmitn (√x̣ʷál–). stick-
game: lál, láln.

garbage garbage, trash, rough
ground: x̣ašáytmx
(√x̣ə́š–).

garden garden, crops:
sx̣á·l'am'ɫ (√x̣ála–). time
to plant a garden:
pənx̣á·lam'ɫ (√pən–,
√x̣ála–).

gate: tá?qam'ɫtn' (√tə́q–).

gather gather, together with,
meet: x̣ʷúqʷɫ (√x̣ʷúqʷa–).

get get, carry, hold, take, take
away, grab, get married:
kʷə́na, kʷə́nna (√kʷəná–).
get, catch: kʷə́nax̣ʷ,
kʷə́nanx̣ʷ (√kʷəná–). get
after, scold, quarrel with:
taq̓ʷín (√tə́q̓ʷa–). get

away, run away: ɫə́x̣ʷm
(√ɫə́x̣ʷa–). get even:
?úlwasix (√?úlwasi–). get
in, be in, ride in: k'ə́c'ɫ
(√k'ə́c'a–). get on a horse,
be on a horse: k'ə́c'acx
(√k'ə́c'a–). get out of (a
canoe, train, car): c'áwɫ
(√c'áw–). get out of, get
off, come down: líxʷlcx
(√líxʷl–). get there, reach,
arrive: kʷáx̣ʷɫ (√kʷáx̣ʷa–).
get to the end, continue (*tr.*):
t'anə́x (√t'aná–). get up:
x̣ʷə́t'ɫ (√x̣ʷə́t'a–). get up
late, be late in the morning:
púck̓ʷɫ (√púck̓ʷ–). getting
it for him: sk̓ʷə́nšitn
(√k̓ʷəná–).

ghost: .spɛsai´ɫtɛmɛx FBa
(√pə́sa?–). ghost, corpse,
dead person, dead: mák̓ʷt
(√mak̓ʷə́t–).

giggle giggle, waste time, act
silly: c'íykʷcx (√c'íykʷ–).

gills gills of a fish: ƛ'ax̣án'tn
(√ƛ'ax̣án'–).

girl big girl: kawá·?ɫi?ɫ
(√kəwáɫ–). little girl:
ké·w'ɫ (*pl.* ké·w'aɫmx)
(√kəwáɫ–).

give to: káɫt (√káɫ–). give a
dish of food: silmátx. give
away: káɫtumix (√káɫ–).
give food to, feed: mátiln
(√mátil–). give gifts,

distribute: kʷítim'ɬ
(√kʷíti-). give hand
signals: t'anémakašn
(√t'aními-). give to, bring:
ʔíx (√ʔí-). give up:
c'akálnut (√c'əka-).
giving, potlatch, throwing
away: sʔáx̣ʷmtn'
(√ʔáx̣ʷ-).

glass glass, a glass: túlucuɬn
(√túlucn-). eyeglasses:
ʔáx̣acxtnil's (√ʔə́x̣-).
eyeglasses, telescope, a
glass: ʔáx̣am'ɬtn' (√ʔə́x̣-).

glove: káˑl'xmn (√kálax-);
ləmitén.

glue glue, stick: x̣̌íq'n
(√x̣̌íq'a-). glue (n.):
x̣̌éq'am'ɬtn' (√x̣̌íq'a-).

gnaw gnaw, nibble: k'ə́t'n
(√k'ə́t'-). gnawing,
chewing: sx̣ák̓ʷatn
(√x̣ák̓ʷa-).

go: wáks (√wakə́s-). go
across: xʷuxʷáw'kʷm'
(√xʷáw'kʷ-). go after:
ʔíkʷn (√ʔíkʷa-). go after
firewood: mátikʷp
(√mát-). go after water:
cə́pkʷu (√cə́p-). go
around: yalə́m'n
(√yalə́m'-). go around: he
went around me: yəlwíčic
(√yəlwíči-). go away!, go
back!: tawílaʔ (√wí-). go
for food: matóˑliɬn
(√mát-). go home: yáx̣̌ɬ
(√yáx̣̌a-). go in, come

inside, enter: ɬə́kstq
(√ɬə́k-). go in a boat:
tál'uɬ (√tál-). go inside:
isam̓ aˊts.tɛk FBa (√ʔís-).
go on!: wílaʔ (√wí-). go
out: x̣̌ə́qɬ (√x̣̌ə́qə́-). go
outside, toward the outside:
páʔɬkʷulm' (√páɬkʷu-).
go over a mountain pass,
cross: sítikanm
(√sítikan-). go through:
yál' (√yál'i-). go through,
go across, cross, land (a
canoe),reach shore: t'ánɬ
(√t'aná-). go to: wáksamn
(√wakə́s-). go to bed, lie
down: cə́kʷɬ (√cə́kʷa-).
go to see, come to see:
x̣̌aswáln (√x̣̌aswáli-). go
walking: yápyapɬ
(√yə́pa-). go with, follow:
ʔáyašn (√ʔáyax-). going
back and forth, swinging:
syác'yəc'wn (√yác'-).
going up, up: x̣̌óˑk̓ʷm'
(√x̣̌úk̓ʷ-). they kept on
going: ʔit wákasimumx
(√wakə́s-).

goat mountain goat: sáʔqʷs;
wáylšìp; kêˊtcitc FBa;
stóq'ts' JH.

God: x̣̌ùk̓ʷ t ʔáls. God,
angel, heaven: šúšukli.

gold: .tstcēˊeuxweⁱ FBa
(√yáyx̣ʷi-). gold, green:
ʔakskʷíq' (√kʷiq'é-).

gone gone, use up, defeat,
win: c'ə́kɬ (√c'ə́ka-). be

gone, miss: x̣ʷáy'ɬ
(√x̣ʷáya–). be gone,
without, not have any:
q'itám.

good good, nice: ʔíˑ, ʔíy.
good (at): yíy (?). good
music: ʔayáynʔ (√ʔíˑ–).
good smell: ʔayásqm
(√ʔíˑ–). have a good time,
have fun: ʔáylx (√ʔáy–). in
a good humor: ʔayálnut
(√ʔíˑ–). no-good, useless:
ʔiX̌áp'.

goodbye: wàˑ´nax̣álexʷ FBb
(√wéˑ–x̣–).

goose: x̣ix̣í (√x̣í–).

gooseberry: t'amə́x̣ʷ.

grab grab, catch, take, hang
on to: skʷanátn
(√kʷəná–). grab, grab a
handful: x̣ímn (√x̣ím–).
grab, take, hold, carry, get,
take away, get married:
kʷə́na, kʷə́nna (√kʷəná–).
grab away from: kʷə́nst
(√kʷəná–).

granary: x̣ʷéˑtlwltxʷ
(√x̣ʷít–).

grandchild: ʔém'c (*pl.*
nx̣ʔém'ctn, nx̣ʔímctn)
(√ʔímac–). great-
grandchild, great-
grandparent, ancestor:
caméˑc'aʔ (√cam–).

grandfather: kʷúpaʔ,
kakʷúpaʔ.

grandmother: káyʔ (*pl.*
nxkáyʔtn) (√kayíʔ–).

grandparent grandparents,
old people: nx̣ʔálstn'
(√ʔális–); talsnáwaʔ
(√tals–, √náwa–). great-
grandparent, great-
grandchild, ancestor:
caméˑc'aʔ (√cam–).

grass: q'anápsu. a mountain
grass for baskets: ʔím'. tall
grass, hay, straw: st'awál's
(√t'awál's–).

grasshopper: ɬút'm'
(√ɬút'am'–).

grave: satska´ustEn FBa.

gravel gravel, little rocks:
spatáˑl'inumx
(√patálan–).

gravy gravy, soup: lakamín.

gray: ʔaksp'áqʷ, p'áʔqʷm'ɬ
(√p'áqʷ–). gray hair:
ʔaksqʷúx̣ʷls (√qʷúx̣ʷ–).
gray rock: ʔaksp'áqʷl's
(√p'áqʷ–).

grease (*n.*) grease, fat (on
body): č'ayə́š. grease, lard,
tallow, oil: k'axʷóʔ.

grease (*v.*) grease (*tr.*):
sák'axʷoʔn (√sáʔa–,
√k'axʷóʔ–).

greedy: ʔaccónistumx
(√cáni–); ʔackʷušúhicx
(√kʷušú–).

green green, gold: ʔaksk̓ʷíq'
(√k̓ʷiq'é–). greenish; bark:
k̓ʷiq'é·man'ɬ (√k̓ʷiq'é–).

grind grind, mash, break in
pieces, smash: q̓ʷíc'n
(√q̓ʷíc'i–). grinding stone,

sharpener: mátam'ɬtn'
(√máta-).

groan: yálm (√yál-).

groove: ʔacč'aléqʷɬ
(√č'aláqʷ-).

ground ground, earth, dirt,
land, country: támx.
ground, surface of earth:
tā´qɛs ti'tî´mɛɬ FBa. on
the ground: ʔáɬtm'x
(√ʔaɬ-, √támx-). onto the
ground: xʔáɬtm'x (√x-,
√ʔaɬ-, √támx-).

groundhog groundhog *or*
common marmot: co´ᵘɬ
FBa.

ground squirrel: pū´tɛpt
FBa.

grouse *sp.*: mó?əm.

grow: púlɬ (√púla-). grow,
raise: xáwɬ (√xəwáli-).

growl growl, be angry:
qaɬáxɬ (√qəɬáxa-).

grunt: ʔíqʷm (√ʔíqʷ-).

guard guard, protect, look
out for, herd...: λ̓aqʷséx̣n
(√λ̓áqʷ-, √ʔáx̣-).

guess guess, hint: túl'šl's.
guess, try, test, taste: máλ̓n
(√máλ̓a-).

guest: ʔackál'wicx
(√kál'wi-). have guests,
have company:
ʔact'ó·l'msm (√t'úla-).

gun gun; dynamite:
táqʷčam'ɬtn' (√təqʷáči-).
revolver: t'ik'á·ʔkaʔ.

gunpowder gunpowder,
bullet, shell: síɬ.
gunpowder, smoke: sq̓ʷúx̣ʷ
(√q̓ʷúx̣ʷ-).

guts: q'íyx̣ (√q'iyáx̣-).

h

habitually (proclitic): nks,
ʔnks.

hail: λ̓éx̣l'qsm
(√λ̓éx̣il'qs-).

hair: k'ásk's (√k'əsk'ás-).
gray hair: ʔaksqʷúx̣ʷls
(√qʷúx̣ʷ-). hair is curly:
ʔacx̣əyk̓ʷó?s (√x̣əyák̓ʷ-).
have long hair: λ̓á?qayaqn
(√λ̓áq-).

half: təx̣ʷámc (√təx̣ʷ-).
half a sack: təx̣ʷáličn
(√təx̣ʷ-). half-breed:
t'k'námc (√t'k'n-). half

dollar, fifty cents: číl'ɬ
(√čílačš-). half done:
pútaka? (√pút-).

halter halter, necklace: yán'q
(√yanáq-).

hammer (*n.*): te´mseka FBa.
hammer for cutting trees:
tca´tst FBa. hammer on:
kʷáx̣ʷn (√kʷáx̣ʷ-).

hammock hammock, swing:
kaia´kᵘomɛn FBa
(√q'ayúq̓ʷ-).

hand hand, arm: kálx (*pl.*
kálaxumx) (√kálax-).

hand, fingers: laxaíaka HH.
hand, fingers, nails: staléka
HH ($\sqrt{}$t'alá-). back of the
hand: sa´ᵘteka FBa
($\sqrt{}$ʔáwat-).

handful: nək̓ʷx̣ím ($\sqrt{}$nák'-,
$\sqrt{}$x̣ím-). handful, cluster,
bunch: nək̓ʷumóʔ
($\sqrt{}$nák'-, $\sqrt{}$móʔ-). grab a
handful, grab: x̣ímn
($\sqrt{}$x̣ím-).

handkerchief handkerchief,
scarf: xʷík̓ʷɬn' ($\sqrt{}$xʷík̓ʷ-).

handle handle, reins:
kʷaná·mn' ($\sqrt{}$kʷəná-).
handle of a root digger:
sau´xakEn FBa; wəpa´ls
TA. knife handle:
as'Li´qtLiqtɬ FBa.

handsome handsome,
beautiful: ei.sExa´mEɬ FBa
($\sqrt{}$ʔí·-, $\sqrt{}$ʔə́x̣-).

hang: ʔactúxʷɬ ($\sqrt{}$túxʷ-).
hang, choke: qíqɬn
($\sqrt{}$qíq-). hang down, hang
over: xʷílɬ ($\sqrt{}$xʷíl-). hang
on: kʷanáw'am'ɬ
($\sqrt{}$kʷəná-). hang on to,
take, grab, catch: skʷanátn
($\sqrt{}$kʷəná-). hang over the
edge: yamə́t'ɬ ($\sqrt{}$yamə́t'-).
hang up: qíqn ($\sqrt{}$qíq-).
hanging racks: qi sxʷílaʔ
($\sqrt{}$xʷíl-).

happen what happened?: ʔit'í
akʷu ($\sqrt{}$ʔí-).

happy: ʔacq̓ʷól'ɬ ($\sqrt{}$q̓ʷól'-).

hard hard (of work):
x̣ax̌áltmn, x̣əx̌áltmn.
hard, lots of, very: ʔáy'tk
($\sqrt{}$ʔáy'tak-). hard, stiff,
tight, firm, strong: x̌ə́x̣ʷ.
harden, set, freeze: q'áxʷɬ
($\sqrt{}$q'áxʷa-). harden, stiff,
in tight: x̌áx̣ʷlx ($\sqrt{}$x̌ə́x̣ʷ-).

harm harm, ruin: x̣ášilix
($\sqrt{}$x̣ə́š-).

hat: sxʷáy's ($\sqrt{}$xʷay'ús-);
šyá·qʷɬ ($\sqrt{}$yá·qʷɬ-). rain
hat: x̣asílʔsxʷay's
($\sqrt{}$x̣asíliʔ-, $\sqrt{}$xʷay'ús-).

hate hate, dislike: tóʔkʷmn
($\sqrt{}$tóʔkʷ-).

haul hauling, dragging:
sx̣ə́lktn ($\sqrt{}$x̣ə́lk-).

have have, live, stay: wé·x̣
($\sqrt{}$wé·-x̣-). have on, wear:
ʔact'ə́k ($\sqrt{}$t'ə́k-). not have
any, without, be gone:
q'itám.

hawk chicken hawk:
.swai'a´tok FBa. small red
hawk: yi´tiit FBa.

hay hay, tall grass, straw:
st'awál's ($\sqrt{}$t'awál's-).

hayfork: kwaxa´lus FBa;
tawa´sEnEɬ FBa
($\sqrt{}$tawasá-).

hazelnut hazelnut, nut:
káw's (*pl.* káw'usmx)
($\sqrt{}$kaw'ús-); ḳá-p̓óḣw EC.
hazel bush:
q'α'p'ú·x̣wαn'ɬ JH.

he he, him, it: cə́ni. his, her,
hers, its: scaníyaɬ ($\sqrt{}$cə́ni-).

head: q̓ʷúmt ($\sqrt{}$q̓ʷumə́t-).

top of head: skwoˊkwols
FBa; spūˊkEls FBa.

headband: cípɬtn (√cípɬ-);
st'éqls,st'éqlsmn' (?)
(√t'əqi-); taˊkshwaismEn
FBa (√t'əqi-, √xʷay'ús-).

heal healed, well, better:
ƛ'áq̇ʷ. healing up:
sq'áp'awn (√q'áp'a-).

heap they heap it up:
mək̇ʷúyaqumx (√mə́k̇ʷ-).

hear hear, hear about, listen,
believe: k̇ʷiláyn (√k̇ʷil-).
hear about, find out:
k̇ʷál'anm (√k̇ʷálan-). hear
noise, echo, squeak:
ʔímnm' (√ʔímn-). barely
hear, be barely audible:
xʷcúynmn' (√xʷc-). I
heard about it:
ʔactóˑlɬstmɬəx kn (?)
(√tóˑlu-).

heart: sqʷə́lm (√qʷələ́m-).

heat heat (tr.): xʷalá?n
(√xʷalá?-); xʷatə́qʷn
(√xʷatə́qʷ-). heating
rocks: sx̣ʷalílsitn
(√xʷalá?-).

heater heater, stove:
x̣ʷál'k̇ʷpmn' (√x̣ʷál'a-).

heaven heaven, God, angel:
šúšukli.

heavy: x̣ə́m. heavy,
heaviness, weight: x̣ə́mtn
(√x̣ə́m-). get heavy:
x̣ámlx (√x̣ə́m-).

heel: sāutaˊksx̣En FBa
(√ʔáwat-).

help: talíčn (√talíči-). he's
helping me pack things out:
stalíčlkcaln (√talíči-).

helper: talíčtn' (√talíči-).

hemlock: súskpn'ɬ
(√súskp-).

her she, her: c cə́ni. her,
hers, his, its: scaníyaɬ
(√cə́ni-).

herd (n.): swə́ltn (√wə́l-).

herd (v.) herd, guard, protect,
take care of...: ƛ'aqʷséx̣n
(√ƛ'áq̇ʷ-, √ʔə́x̣-). herding,
scaring away: swə́ltn
(√wə́l-).

here: níʔx̣, néʔx̣ (√níʔ-);
níx̣; šéʔ. right here, this
one: tíʔx̣, tíx̣ (√tíʔ-). to
here: xʷšéʔ (√šéʔ-).

herring: sāˊmEɬko FBa.

hiccough: šə́k̇ʷiyax̣ʷc
(√šə́k̇ʷíy'-).

hide (n.) hide, skin: ƛ'aʔílkɬ
(√ƛ'əʔílkl-). deerskin with
hair still on it: taysx̣ʷáq̇ʷ
(√táy-, √x̣ʷáq̇ʷa-). inner
side of a hide, the film on
the inner side of a hide next
to the flesh: súmsəm'. stiff
hide: ƛ'atə́x̣. tanned
deerskin: wayə́x̣. tanned
hide: syacə́qɬ (√yəcə́q-).

hide (v.): káscn (√kásuci-).
hide self: kásucicx
(√kásuci-).

high high, above: ƛ'úk̇ʷ. high
water, flow LNJ: táw'k̇ʷuʔ
(√táw'-).

high-priced high-priced,
expensive, valuable:
ʔacyáyx̣ʷi (√yáyx̣ʷi-).
hill: x̌uk̓ʷíl's (√x̌úk̓ʷ-).
bottom of a hill, downhill:
x̌apé·l's (√x̌əp-).
him him, he, she, her, it:
cə́ni.
hinge: x̣ə́k̓ʷuwt (?).
hint: x̌áqn (√x̌áq-). hint,
guess: túl'šl's.
hip his hip, his side: x̣ʷay'úpi
(√x̣ʷay'úp-). hip joints:
sč'ə́qʷn (√č'ə́qʷn-).
his his, her, hers, its:
scaníyaɬ (√cə́ni-).
hit hit (with fist *or* rock):
ɬə́qn (√ɬə́q-). hit together,
they collided: tapál'us
(√tə́p-).
hobbles: taka´ kɛmɛɬ.tɛn
FBa (√t'ə́qi-).
hoe (*n.*): lapyó·š;
tseqiapī´ mɛɬɛn FBa
(√cíqʷi-). hoe (*tr.*):
lapyó·šn (√lapyó·š-).
hog hog, pig: k̓ʷušú.
hold hold, carry, take, take
away, get, grab, get
married: k̓ʷə́na, k̓ʷə́nna
(√k̓ʷəná-). hold, hold
back, hold still: k̓ʷé·na
(√k̓ʷəná-). hold still, quiet
down, calm down: x̌él'cx
(√x̌əla-). lose hold:
ʔə́ɬp'lkmn (√ʔə́ɬp'-).
hole: scíqʷɬ (√cíqʷi-). hole,
drill, drill a hole, make a

hole, pierce: lapə́x̣ʷɬ
(√ləpə́x̣ʷa-). hole, hollow:
ʔacpal'ə́k̓ʷɬ (√pəl'ə́k̓ʷ-).
its hole: spə́l'k̓ʷiqi
(√pəl'ə́k̓ʷ-). make a hole,
have a hole, pierce:
pal'ə́k̓ʷɬ (√pəl'ə́k̓ʷ-).
making holes:
spə́l'pəl'k̓ʷamaln
(√pəl'ə́k̓ʷ-). steep hole,
cave, dugout: ʔacč'aləqʷɬ
(√č'aləqʷ-).
holiday: náwsanti
(√náwa-, √sánti-).
holiday, Christmas, July:
pənnáw'san'tim'n
(√pən-, √náwa-,
√sánti-). holiday time,
December: pənnáwsanti
(√pən-, √náwa-,
√sánti-).
holler holler, shout, call:
táltalaqp (√tál-). holler,
yell, shout, call: tálaqp
(√tál-).
hollow: ʔaclapə́x̣ʷɬ
(√ləpə́x̣ʷa-). hollow, hole:
ʔacpal'ə́k̓ʷɬ (√pəl'ə́k̓ʷ-).
home home, at home, stay
home: ʔáɬx̣x (√ʔaɬ-,
√x̣áx-). bring home:
yax̌ə́x (√yáx̌a-). go home:
yáx̌ɬ (√yáx̌a-). I just got
home: sputst'úlawanx
(√pút-, √t'úla-).
hoof: qaqswéʔ;
kekau´ ɛlscɛn FBa.
hook hook LNJ, net ENM:

yasə́n. a hook, bait:
q'ét'am'ɬtn' (√q'ét'a-).
fishhook: x̣ə́n's (*pl.*
x̣ə́n'isumx) (√x̣ə́n'ús-);
aiˊkamEltEn FBa; xaiaˊm
FBa. hook on, put on, put
around: t'alə́pn
(√t'ələ́p-).

hoop hoops on the edge of a
basket; start (the bottom of)
a basket LNJ: stúlnk
(√túl-).

hope hope, wish: nám'uqas
(√nám'u-).

hops: háps. hop-picking
time: pənháps (√pən-,
√háps-).

horn horns, antlers: mə́x̣kn
(√məx̣kán-).

hornet: putísɬkʷu
(√putís-). hornet's nest,
beehive: cíkslwltxʷ
(√cíks-).

horse: stiqíw (*pl.*
stiqiwáwmx) (√tiqíw-).
cayuse; Spaniard: spalyán.
colt: stiqéˑw'iʔɬ
(√tiqíw-). mare:
tauˊEɬtse stEkeˊu FBa
(√táwn-, √tiqíw-). roan:
eks spaˊkonamts FBa
(√p'áqʷ-). sorrel:
ʔaksqʷə́s (√qʷə́s-).
spotted horse (black and
white): likáy. stallion:
atsEmaˊtcEn .stEkeˊu FBa
(√máčn-, √tiqíw-).
strawberry roan: qašqášˊ.

train horses: k'ápstiqiw
(√k'ápa-, √tiqíw-).

horseback horseback, by
horse, on a horse:
tálstiqiw,tálastiqiw
(√tál-, √tiqíw-).

horsetail: *smə́q (smuq').
horsetail roots: *x̣ə́m'x̣əm'
(xumxum).

hospital: ɬə́k'lwltxʷ
(√ɬə́k'a-).

hot hot, warm: x̣ʷaláʔ.

hotel hotel, campsite, camp:
q'alə́mn (√q'ə́l-).

house: x̣áx̣; L!eˑx̣ᵘ FBb. in
the house: ʔáctq.
longhouse: ƛ'áqax̣n (tit
x̣áx̣) (√ƛ'áq-). plank lodge:
Leˊx̣.ɬweɬtᵘx̣ FBa
(√ƛ'ə́x̣-). top of a house:
ƛ'úkʷlwltxʷ (√ƛ'úkʷ-).

how how many?: k̓ʷíʔo
(√k̓ʷí-). how many?,
several others: k̓ʷináwmx
kʷu (√k̓ʷí-). how many?,
what time?: k̓ʷí. how many
baskets: ƛ'álnaličn
(√ƛ'áln-). how many
times?: k̓ʷínlšn (√k̓ʷi-).
How do you do it?, Which
way is it?: kanémm' kʷu
(√káˑ-).

howling: sxʷúʔxʷuʔmitn,
sxʷóˑʔxʷuʔmitn
(√xʷuʔú-). howling
loudly: sʔə́wʔəwmitn
(√ʔə́w-).

huckleberry mountain

huckleberry (tall bush), Yakima huckleberry: wənáy'x̣. mountain huckleberry bush: wənáy'x̣an'ɬ (√wənáy'x̣-). short huckleberry, blueberry: q'áʔp; k'wɑ̓l' JH (*k̓wə́l'). short huckleberry plant: q'áʔpan'ɬ (√q'áʔp-).

hug: cə́mn (√cə́m-).

hum: ʔé·l'n (√ʔílani-). humming: sʔé·l'al'n (√ʔílani-); stó·l'maln (√túl-).

hummingbird: tə́ktkni.

humor in a good humor: ʔayálnut (√ʔíˑ-).

hump hump on the nose: ʔacmayə́x̣ʷqs (√məyə́x̣ʷ-). humpbacked, bent over: ʔacx̣ʷam'íčn (√x̣ʷam'-).

humpback salmon: hwanē´ kᵘ FBa.

hundred one hundred: ʔúc's hə́ndəd; t'əmx̣pánkstlšn

(√t'əmx-, √pánaks-); ō´ts panɛksɬto´mɛx FBa.

hungry hungry, starve: ʔacx̣ʷə́qʷɬ (√x̣ʷə́qʷa-). getting hungry: sqʷalé·n'uʔstn (√qʷal-). I'm hungry for it: ʔacx̣ʷə́qʷtas kn (√x̣ʷə́qʷa-).

hunt hunt (game), go hunting: ƛ̓á·x̣anm (√ƛ̓á·x̣an-).

hurry hurry, fast, soon, right away: ƛ̓ə́x̣ƛ̓ax̣ɬ (√ƛ̓ə́x̣-). in a hurry: ʔaclə́lɬ (√lə́l-).

hurt hurt, ache, sore, wound: tákɬk' (√ták-, √ɬə́k'a-). hurt, sore: ɬə́k' (√ɬə́k'a-). get hurt, wound: q'ál'x̣m (√q'ál'x̣i-).

husband: x̣ə́n.

hush hush, be quiet: x̣ál'stq̓ʷm (√x̣ál'-, √tə́q̓ʷa-). hush!, be quiet!: ʔackʷá·l'aʔ (√kʷá·hi-).

hysterics baby getting hysterics ENM: táčnmn.

i

I I, me: ʔə́nca. my: səncáyaɬ (√ʔə́nca-).

ice ice (in solid areas): sq'áx̣ʷ (√q'áx̣ʷa-). ice, chunks of ice: túlucn.

if if, unless, when: ʔáml, ʔaml?.

imitate: ʔnks + cayá·cšitn (√cayá·-).

impatient impatient, out of patience: c'akálnutšn (√c'ə́ka-).

important: ʔaccó·tx̣kn (√có·tx̣kn-).

in in, on, with; oblique: ɬ. in, to, into, on: ʔaɬ. be in, get in, ride in: k'ə́c'ɬ (√k'əc'a-). go in, come inside, enter, bring in, take in: ɬə́kstq (√ɬə́k-). in order to, so that: takaɬ. put in: k'c'k'əc'n (√k'əc'a-). put into: k'ə́c'šn (√k'ə́c'a-).

Indian: ʔílmx (*pl.* ʔílmixumx) (√ʔilmíx-). Indian food: sílmixuliɬn (√ʔilmíx-). Indian land: silmé·xtm'x (√ʔilmíx-). non-Indian: xʷə́ltm (√xʷə́l-). Stick Indians: č'iátkʷu.

in-law: qʷílx̣ʷ. brother-in-law: syálxʷtk (√yálxʷtak-); skwokwe´nep BH. daughter-in-law: sápn (√sápan-). father-in-law, son-in-law: smátxʷtn (√mátaxʷ-). sister-in-law: skáw; tsei´.a FBa; kwokwê´nEp FBa; .sma´kotuɬEn FBa (√mak̉ʷə́t-).

inside inside, middle, bottom: lawə́p (?), lúwp. inside a container *or* person: ʔácayq. inside a house: ʔáctq. go inside: isaṃ a´ts.tEk FBa (√ʔís-). its insides: ɬə́ki (?) (√ɬə́k-). its insides (e.g a bucket),

bottom: sáci?qi (√ʔácayq-, sác-). its insides, its stomach: sácinwasi (√sác-).

inside out: p'alé·č'm' (√p'alé·č'-).

instead instead, so that, and: qa.

instep: stál'iqšn ENM (√tál'-); kopā´matscEn FBa. instep, foot: st'alášn (*pl.* st'alášinumx) (√t'alá-).

insult: x̣anúmtmn (√x̣anúmt-). insult, scare: qʷané·n (√qʷán-).

interpret: kátyay'ɬuɬ (√kátyn-, √yáy-). interpreting, teaching: s?úxʷnkʷawn (√ʔúxʷa-).

interpreter: katiya´pEktEn FBa (√kátyn-). interpreter, representative: kátyn.

interrogative interrogative, question: ʔac'í; akʷu; ʔana,ana, na; ʔí.

into into, on: kaɬ. into, to, in, on: ʔaɬ.

invisible: ʔactáqɬ (√táq-).

invite invite, call: q'íw'tas (√q'íw'-).

iron (*n.*): saxʷúcuɬn.

iron (*v.*) iron, press: č'íxʷipn (√č'íxʷip-). an iron: č'é·xʷipm'ɬtn' (√č'íxʷip-).

island: st'ačé? (√t'ačé?-).

it it, he, him, she, her: cə́ni.

its, his, her, hers: scaníyaⱡ
(√cə́ni–).

itch: q̓ʷíⱡⱡ (√q̓ʷíⱡi–).

j

jacket, jackets: st'ə́k
(√t'ə́k–).
jail: t'éqimⱡtn' (√t'ə́qi–).
put in jail, arrest, tie around,
wind around: t'ə́qn
(√t'ə́qi–).
January: ʔalq'álm'yusm
(√q'əl–).
jaw jaw, chin, cheek: sqə́lns
(√qəlnús–).
jay blue jay; mischievous:
p'ayə́k̓ʷ. gray jay, camp
robber: ʔéʔⱡnalakaʔ
(√ʔíⱡani–).
jealous: ʔacX̌aq̓ʷúm

(√X̌aq̓ʷú–).
jingle jingling, buzzing:
sk̓ʷíx̣mtn (√k̓ʷíx̣–).
joint hip joints: sč'ə́qʷn
(√č'ə́qʷn–).
July: pənnáw'san'tim'n
(√pən–, √náwa–,
√sánti–); skáwanani t
ⱡuk̓ʷáⱡ (√káwanan–,
√ⱡuk̓ʷáⱡ–).
jump: ⱡíqq (√ⱡíqaq–). jump
over: ⱡíqqmn (√ⱡíqaq–).
just: ʔanám'u, ʔanám';
pút–. just, right here, this
one: tíʔx̣, tíx̣ (√tíʔ–).

k

kettle kettle, bucket:
cáqstqtn' (√cə́q–).
key key, lock: sq'íwq
(√q'íwq–).
kick: caqíy'n (√cəqíy'–).
kidnap he was kidnapped:
ⱡə́x̣ʷmstm (√ⱡə́x̣ʷm–).
kidney: mə́t's (√mət'ús–).
kill kill, beat up, put out a
fire: yúcx (√yúca–). kill,
butcher: manítumusməski
(√manít–,
√wəmúsmuski–). kill, put

out a fire, turn off a light:
ⱡə́pn (√ⱡə́pa–). kill
oneself, commit suicide:
yúcamicx (√yúca–).
kind: ʔé·y' (√ʔí·–). kind,
nice: q'aⱡ qátnⱡ (√qát–).
kind that's the kind: q'éc'iʔx̣
(√q'íc'x̣–).
kindling: q'áy'stqtn'
(√q'áy'–).
kingfisher: c'ə́lə́m.
kinnickinick: ⱡántmx LNJ
(?) (√ⱡán–).

kiss: mákᵂɬanaln
(√mákᵂ-).

kitten: pé?špiš (*pl.*
pé?špišumx), péšpiɬ
(√píšpiš-).

Klickitat Indians: Wah-
nookt UWa.

knee knee, kneecap: tán's
(*pl.* tán'isumx)
(√tan'ís-).

kneel kneel, confess:
kanílstx̣ᵂayaqm
(√kanílstx̣ᵂ-).

knife: q̓ᵂax̣ᵂə́mn (*pl.*
q̓ᵂax̣ᵂə́minum'x)
(√q̓ᵂax̣ᵂə́min-). knife
handle: as'Li´qtLiqtɬ FBa.

pocketknife:
suwa´nwEnuEn FBa
(√wə́n'-).

knock out: txᵂsawə́x
(√sawə́-). have wind
knocked out, faint: txᵂsə́w
(√sawə́-).

know: yúxᵂn (√yúxᵂi-);
pútn (√púti-). know
better, smart, wise:
?acp'ə́x̣ɬ (√p'ə́x̣-). know
how: spótalaka (√púti-).
he knew it: ?it yó·xᵂn
(√yúxᵂi-). not know how,
make mistakes: kanál'šn
(√kə́n-).

l

ladder ladder, stairway:
swé·t'atn' (√wít'i-).

ladle: t'úyxᵂm'ɬtn'
(√t'úyxᵂ-).

lake: cél'ɬ.

lame: ?áy'saka? (√?áy's-).

land (*n.*) land, earth, dirt,
ground, country: tə́mx.
have no land: táytmx
(√táy-, √tə́mx-). Indian
land: silmé·xtm'x
(√?ilmíx-).

land (*v.*) land (a canoe),
cross, go across, go
through,reach shore: t'ánɬ
(√t'aná-). land a canoe or
boat: pə́nɬ (√pə́na-).

language language, speech,
word: stə́q̓ᵂ (√tə́q̓ᵂa-).
foreign language: tl slé·la ɬ
stə́q̓ᵂ (√líl?-,√tə́q̓ᵂa-).

lap (*n.*) lap, leg, foot: cúɬ
(√cúl-).

lap (*v.*) lap, lick: t'áq̓ᵂn
(√t'áq̓ᵂa-).

lard lard, grease, oil, tallow:
k'axᵂó?.

large large, big: taw'ə́t.

lariat: qo´kwEn FBa.

last the last one: sxᵂə́l'ptn
(√xᵂə́l'p-). last year:
wásqᵂx̣ᵂ.

late: ?ac?áwatlx (√?áwat-).
late ENM, getting dark LNJ:

nápis. later on, after a
while: xʷá·ʔaʔs. be late in
the morning, get up late:
púckʷɬ (√púcḱʷ-).

laugh: láxʷɬ (√láxʷa-).
laugh, play: x̣áɬxʷm
(√x̣áɬxʷa-).

launch launch a canoe:
ʔayə́qn (√ʔiyə́q-).

lay down: q̇ʷáƛ̓n (√q̇ʷáƛ̓-).
lay down, put down: kácx
(√kác-). he's laying it
down for me: sq̇ʷáƛ̓txʷcaln
(√q̇ʷáƛ̓-).

lazy: ʔacx̣ə́payq (√x̣ə́p-).

lead (*n.*): .stlE'a´ls FBa.

lead (*v.*) lead, take to, take
with, take along: ʔə́sɬ
(√ʔəsúl-). lead by the
hand, shake hands:
kʷəntáčic (√kʷəná-).

leader leader, chief: ʔáls (*pl.*
ʔálisumx) (√ʔális-).

leaf leaf, leaves, cabbage:
pə́ckɬ; kwola´tux̣ FBa.

leak: palúw'ɬ (√palúw'-).
leak, drip: c'ə́x̣ʷm
(√c'ə́x̣ʷa-).

lean lean (*intr.*): tákcx
(√ták-). lean (*tr.*): tákn
(√ták-).

leave leave (*tr.*): wáyn
(√wáy-). leave, desert:
ɬawál'xnmn (√ɬəwála-).
leave behind (*tr.*): ɬə́wɬ
(√ɬəwála-). leave word
with: ɬawaɬáyn
(√ɬəwála-). left some

food: kʷə́cliɬn' (√kʷə́c-,
√ʔíɬani-). their leaving it:
x̣ʷax̣ʷə́lsti (√x̣ʷax̣ʷə́l-).
what is left ungathered after
a basket is full: wasáln.

left (side): c'íwq', ʔáɬc'iwq'.

leg: qwûts FBa;
kwu´tesumox FBa. leg,
foot, lap: cúɬ (*pl.*
cuɬáwmx) (√cúl-). calf of
the leg: ma´naɬtse FBa
(√mána-). lower leg: có?ɬ
(√cúl-).

leggings leggings (long):
kwa´xoloks FBa. leggings,
Indian stockings: mətá·s.

lend lend, borrow, rent:
kʷústm (√kʷústam-).
lend to: kʷústmtuxʷt
(√kʷústam-).

lesson: pó?tlkmn (√púti-).

let let, allow: tá·l'n
(√tá·l'a-). let go:
wáyl'kmn (√wáy-). let go,
release: túnn (√tún-).
let's!, OK, you'd better
(exhortative particle): ƛ̓áq̇ʷ.

level level, smooth:
ʔacwaləq'ɬ (√wələ́q'-).

lick lick, lap: t'áqʷn
(√t'áqʷa-).

lid its lid: táql'stani
(√tə́q-).

lie lie down, be lying:
ká·w'an. lie down, go to
bed: cə́kʷɬ (√cə́kʷa-). lie
flat, spread flat: táɬɬ
(√táɬ-). lie on one's back:

xəná·sm' (√xəná·s-). lie
on one's side: ʔactáʔɬcx
(√táɬ-).

lie, tell a lie: q'əx̣p
(√q'əx̣áp-); pəx̣ʷáy's
(√pə́x̣ʷ-). tell a lie,
bullheaded: paɬús.

life life, soul: sníɬtn
(√níɬi-). come back to life:
níɬlx (√níɬi-).

lift lift, pick up: qítn
(√qíti-).

light: qʷá·l'ɬ; .tsqê´.x̣EltEn
FBa (√q'íx̣-). light, candle,
torch: q'éx̣am'ɬtn'
(√q'íx̣-). light, daylight:
sq'éx̣ (√q'íx̣-). light,
shine, bright: q'éx̣m'ɬ
(√q'íx̣-). a light flashes,
lightning: sq'íx̣q'x̣wn
(√q'íx̣-).

lightning: slaw-hatz UWb.
lightning, a light flashes:
sq'íx̣q'x̣wn (√q'íx̣-).

lightweight: x̣ʷé·k̓ʷ.

like: qáʔtmn (√qát-). like,
respect: yáyn (√yáy-).
like, take a liking to, wish
for: mə́q̓ʷskʷuən
(√mə́q̓ʷskʷu-). like, want:
qínmn (√qín-). they like
each other:
ʔacq̓ʷó·lcwlxumx
(√q̓ʷól'-).

like this: ʔacyál' (√yál'-).

limb limb, branch: k'ál'x (pl.
k'ál'axumx) (√k'ál'ax-);
kwExkwa´x.ɬ FBa. limb,

tree, stick, pole: x̓ə́x̣x̓x (pl.
x̓ə́x̣x̓axumx) (√x̓ə́x̣-).

limp limping, crippled, a
wound: ʔacq'ál'x̣
(√q'ál'x̣i-).

line fishline: tami´ɬEn Eɬ tê
hê´nns FBa (√t'amiɬə́n-,
√x̣ən'ús-). its line, string:
macáli (√macál-). straight
line, square: t'anémim'ɬtn'
(√t'aními-).

lion lion, cougar; a mean
animal: sčátq̓m'
(√čátq̓m'-).

lips: .stlapaɬEɬ FBa (√x̓ə́p-).

listen listen, hear, hear about,
believe: k̓ʷiláyn (√k̓ʷil-).
listen to, send word to,
obey: taláynmn (√tal-).

little: k'é·ci (√k'é·c-). little,
a little bit, small: k'é·c. a
little, somewhat: kʷac. a
little while, a little bit,
almost, soon, well: q̓ʷó·can
(√q̓ʷóʔc-).

live live, have, stay: wé·x̣
(√wé·-x̣-). living,
residing, staying, becoming:
swínn (√wín-).

liver: šáʔš.

lizard: yə́x̣m'c.

load a load: snapúluɬ
(√napúl-). load a gun, fill:
lék'n (√lə́k'-). put a load
on a horse: sál'ičn
(√sál'ikn-).

lobe of the ear:
patao´x̣EmEn FBa.

lock: q'íwqn ($\sqrt{}$q'íwq-). a
lock, key: sq'íwq
($\sqrt{}$q'íwq-).

lodge bark lodge, tent:
sā´kotaxolwE´ɬtx̣ᵘ FBa.
mat lodge:
su´natcEɬwe´ltxᵘ FBa.
plank lodge: Le´x.ɬweɬtᵘx̣
FBa ($\sqrt{}$ƛ'ə́x-).

log log, fallen tree, windfall:
syáq' ($\sqrt{}$yáq'a-).

lonesome: ʔacxʷimínut
($\sqrt{}$xʷim-). be lonesome for:
xʷimínutšn ($\sqrt{}$xʷim-).

long long, tall: ƛ'áqɬ
($\sqrt{}$ƛ'áq-). long time:
ƛ'áqɬanaws, ƛ'áqɬanawxs
($\sqrt{}$ƛ'áq-). long time, long
time ago:
ƛ'áqɬan'ɬ,sƛ'áqɬnɬ
($\sqrt{}$ƛ'áq-). have long hair:
ƛ'áʔqayaqn ($\sqrt{}$ƛ'áq-).
lengthwise: ƛ'áqƛ'aqm'
($\sqrt{}$ƛ'áq-). that long:
ƛ'áqɬaniɬaɬ ($\sqrt{}$ƛ'áq-).

longhouse: ƛ'áqax̣n (?)
($\sqrt{}$ƛ'áq-).

look look, look at, see: ʔə́x̣n
($\sqrt{}$ʔə́x̣-). look at, see,
watch, stare: ʔé·x̣n
($\sqrt{}$ʔə́x̣-). look at something
strange, stare, stare at:
mayá·l'uxʷ ($\sqrt{}$may-). look
for: ƛ'á·ʔn, ƛ'á·l'ux,
ƛ'á·l'usn ($\sqrt{}$ƛ'áʔ-). look for,
dig for: p'íɬn ($\sqrt{}$p'íɬ-).
look for lice: kál'kʷun
($\sqrt{}$kál'kʷu-). look out for,

alarm, alert, risk...:
ƛ'aqʷséx̣n ($\sqrt{}$ƛ'áqʷ-,
$\sqrt{}$ʔə́x̣-). he looks serious:
ʔə́xʷɬ t sə́x̣tm ($\sqrt{}$ʔə́xʷ-,
$\sqrt{}$ʔə́x̣-).

loon: .snicha´ FBa.

loose loose, untied:
ʔacc'ə́xʷɬ ($\sqrt{}$c'ə́xʷi-).
loosen, unroll, unravel:
c'ə́xʷn ($\sqrt{}$c'ə́xʷi-). loosen,
untangle, sort out:
ɬiwál'wax ($\sqrt{}$ɬíw-).

lose: x̣ʷúx̣ʷɬ ($\sqrt{}$x̣ʷúx̣ʷ-).
lose, disappear: x̣ʷə́xʷɬ
($\sqrt{}$x̣ʷə́xʷə́l-). lose hold:
ʔə́ɬp'lkmn ($\sqrt{}$ʔə́ɬp'-). be
lost, get lost: wánačɬ
($\sqrt{}$wánač-). get lost:
wánwanačɬ ($\sqrt{}$wánač-).

lots lots, many: qə́x̣ɬ
($\sqrt{}$qə́x̣-). lots of, very,
hard: ʔáy'tk ($\sqrt{}$ʔáy'tak-).
lots of clothes, wealth:
qə́x̣itmtn ($\sqrt{}$qə́x̣-,
$\sqrt{}$ʔitámaʔ-). a lot, much,
very: kʷumáy.

louse body louse: qʷatíx̣aʔ.
head louse: mə́xčn'
($\sqrt{}$mə́xkan'-). look for
lice: kál'kʷun ($\sqrt{}$kál'kʷu-).

love love, want: tom-tsi-
en-i-ken UWb ($\sqrt{}$tám).

low low, down, below: ɬáƛ'p.

lucky lucky, smart, famous:
swə́tt ($\sqrt{}$wə́tt-).

lumpy: yúlyulux̣ʷɬ
($\sqrt{}$yúluxʷ-). lumpy, little
piles: ʔacmə́k'ʷmaǩʷɬ

($\sqrt{}$mə́k̓ʷ-).

lungs: sp'ús ($\sqrt{}$p'ús-).

m

machine machine, car,
automobile: məšín.
mad be mad at, threaten:
q̓ʷáx̣iqšn ($\sqrt{}$q̓ʷáx̣-). he's
getting mad: q'aɬ
q̓ʷáx̣nɬnati ($\sqrt{}$q̓ʷáx̣-).
maggots: ʔáʔqiʔ.
magpie: ʔánaʔanʔ.
make: sám'ɬ ($\sqrt{}$sáʔa-).
make, do: sáʔn ($\sqrt{}$sáʔa-).
make a bed: saʔén'p
($\sqrt{}$sáʔa-). make a bed for:
saʔén'pšitn ($\sqrt{}$sáʔa-).
make a cedar-root basket:
sáʔəmx̣k̓ʷu ($\sqrt{}$sáʔa-,
$\sqrt{}$ʔə́mx̣k̓ʷu-). make a
choice, sort: yə́x̣n ($\sqrt{}$yə́x̣-).
make a mistake, miss:
x̣ʷáqʷiyn, x̣ʷáqʷayn
($\sqrt{}$x̣ʷáqʷiy-). make a quilt:
sáʔk̓ʷilt ($\sqrt{}$sáʔa-, $\sqrt{}$k̓ʷílt-).
make faces, frown:
c'ík̓ʷusm ($\sqrt{}$c'ík̓ʷ-). make
faces at: c'é·k̓ʷlšn
($\sqrt{}$c'ík̓ʷ-). make faces at,
make fun of: x̣áɬx̣ʷamn
($\sqrt{}$x̣áɬx̣ʷa-). make for:
sáʔšn ($\sqrt{}$sáʔa-). make fun
of, mock: saqá·x̣tnmn
($\sqrt{}$saqá·x̣-). make
moccasins: saʔálɬšn
($\sqrt{}$sáʔa-); sáʔmaksns
($\sqrt{}$sáʔa-, $\sqrt{}$máʔksns-).

make stockings: sáʔstakn
($\sqrt{}$sáʔa-, $\sqrt{}$stákn-). making
a canoe: sáʔwəln ($\sqrt{}$sáʔa-,
$\sqrt{}$wíl-). making a road:
saʔxáw'iln ($\sqrt{}$sáʔa-,
$\sqrt{}$xəwál-). making bread:
sásaplaln ($\sqrt{}$sáʔa-,
$\sqrt{}$saplə́l-). making music:
stə́lkʷawn, stə́lkʷmitn,
stə́ltlkʷmitn ($\sqrt{}$tə́lkʷ-). he
made up with you:
q̓ʷó·l'cmi ($\sqrt{}$q̓ʷól'-).
male male, man: síɬmx (*pl.*
síɬmixumx) ($\sqrt{}$síɬmix-).
man man, male: síɬmx (*pl.*
síɬmixumx) ($\sqrt{}$síɬmix-).
man, person: nawíɬm'x.
young man, youth:
tul.xa´u.ts FBa.
mane its mane: qʷasáy'qni
($\sqrt{}$qʷə́s-).
many many, lots: qə́x̣ɬ
($\sqrt{}$qə́x̣-). how many?: k̓ʷíʔ,
k̓ʷíʔo. how many?, several
others: k̓ʷináwmx kʷu
($\sqrt{}$k̓ʷí-).
maple: sikʷámcn'ɬ
($\sqrt{}$sikʷámc-).
March: pənƛ̓aqám'
($\sqrt{}$pən-, $\sqrt{}$ƛ̓aqám'-).
march (*v.*): talə́pɬ
($\sqrt{}$talə́pa-).
mare: tau´Eɬtse stɛke´u

FBa (√táwn-, √tiqíw-).

mark mark, a brand, design: q̓ʷə́ɬ (√q̓ʷəɬé-). mark, write, design, brand, vote: q̓ʷaɬén (√q̓ʷəɬé-). marks: ʔact'ámt'amɬ (√t'ám-).

marmot marmot, "Whistling Jack": xʷísələs. common marmot or groundhog: co´uɬ FBa.

marry: sxanám (√xə́n-); malyí. get married, take, take away, get, hold, carry,grab: kʷə́nna, kʷə́na (√kʷəná-). they marry: malyíhumx (√malyí-).

Mary Virgin Mary: máli.

mash mash, press: c'íq̓ʷɬ (√c'íq̓ʷ-). mash, smash, break in pieces, grind: q̓ʷíc'n (√q̓ʷíc'i-).

mask (*n.*): ʔact'alə́pnk (√t'ələ́p-).

mat: lkʷátt. large rush mat: cu´ntc FBa. mat lodge: su´natcEɬwe´ltxᵘ FBa. reed mat, reeds: kə́lx (√kələ́x-). woven tule mat, rug: sɬáxtn' (√ɬáx-).

matter it doesn't matter: ɬínskʷu (√ʔíni-). nothing's the matter: míɬta csisíni (√csisín-). what's the matter?: ʔit'í akʷu (√ʔí-).

maul (*n.*): syáq'am'ɬtn' (√yə́q'-); qi kʷáxʷam'ɬtn' (√kʷáxʷ-).

May: pənsq̓ʷáƛ̓šitm scxís (√pən-,√q̓ʷáƛ̓-, √xísi-).

maybe: kən̓ʔó (√kən-). maybe, evidently: cútkn (√cút-, √kən-). maybe, perhaps, might: nám'uɬ (√nám'u-).

me me, I: ʔə́nca.

meadow meadow, swamp, pasture: spáɬxn (√páɬxan-).

meadowlark: sqʷə́cxaʔ (√qʷə́cxaʔ-).

meal meal, food: cíɬn (√ciɬə́n-).

mean be mean: mínɬ ENM (√mín-). mean person, someone who wants to argue: xaƛ̓éʔkʷn (√xə́ƛ̓-).

means by means of: tál-. go in a boat: tál'uɬ (√tál-). horseback, by horse, on a horse: tálstiqiw,tálastiqiw (√tál-, √tiqíw-). on foot, by walking: talsyə́p (√tál-, √yə́pa-).

measure: t'ané·mn (√t'aními-).

meat meat, flesh: kʷús.

medicine: ʔayóʔ. used it for medicine: sáʔayuʔči (√sáʔa-,√ʔayóʔ-). using it for medicine or seasoning: sáʔayuʔtn (√sáʔa-, √ʔayóʔ-).

meet: qáx̣tawlxumx (√qáx̣-). meet, find, catch at: t'úqʷn (√t'úqʷi-).

meet, gather, together with: x̌ʷúqʷɬ (√x̌ʷúqʷa-).
meeting, club: x̌ʷúqʷqʷiɬt (√x̌ʷúqʷa-). we met each other: ʔit qáx̣tnx kn (√qáx̣-).

melt melt, thaw, dissolve: yə́xʷɬ (√yə́xʷa-).

mend mending, sewing, pushing through: scánatn (√cána-).

merganser merganser, fish duck: sq̓ʷálax̣n (√q̓ʷál-).

mess mess up hair: č'íɬls (√č'íɬ-).

middle middle, inside, bottom: lawə́p (?). middle, next to, close together: tə́q'tum'x (√tə́q'-).

midnight: pútkʷaɬlus t sqʷíx̣ (√pút-, √kʷə́ɬ-, √qʷíx̣-).

might might, maybe, perhaps: nám'uɬ (√nám'u-).

mildew mildew, mold: púqʷɬ (√púqʷa-).

milk (*n.*): qʷúlamx. milk (a cow): p'íc'qʷlmxn (√p'íc'-, √qʷúlamx-).

mind mind, obey: tó·l'ux (√tó·l'u-); x̣ə́y'ɬ (√x̣ə́y'-). change one's mind: ʔáynax̣nut (√ʔáy-, √nax̣-).

mink: p'óʔsnk ENM (?) (√p'óʔs-); méʔščm' LNJ; c'mə́l'qn (?); məx̣ʷá·l'as (?) (√məx̣ʷ-).

mirror mirror, window: ʔáx̣acxtn' (√ʔə́x̣-).

mischievous mischievous; blue jay: p'ayə́k̓ʷ.

miss miss, be gone: x̣ʷáy'ɬ (√x̣ʷáya-). miss, make a mistake: x̣ʷáqʷiyn, x̣ʷáqʷayn (√x̣ʷáqʷiy-).

mist: ɬéʔspawn (√ɬéʔspa-).

mistake make a mistake: kə́n'mn (√kə́n-). make a mistake, miss: x̣ʷáqʷiyn, x̣ʷáqʷayn (√x̣ʷáqʷiy-). make mistakes, not know how: kanál'šn (√kə́n-).

mistreat: x̣ašə́x (√x̣ə́š-). mistreat, worry, feel bad: yulínut (√yul-).

mix mix, stir: t'úyxʷn (√t'úyxʷ-). mix, stir, shake up: mat'ə́kʷɬ (√mət'ə́kʷ-). mix up: məlmál'wax (√mál'wa-). mixing in: smál'witn (√mál'wa-).

moccasins: máʔksns (*pl.* máʔksnsumx). buckskin moccasins: sX̌alášalšn (√X̌aláš-). make moccasins: saʔálɬšn (√sáʔa-); sáʔmaksns (√sáʔa-, √máʔksns-).

mock mock, make fun of: saqá·x̣tnmn (√saqá·x̣-).

moldy moldy, mildew: púqʷɬ (√púqʷa-).

Monday: námsanti (√náma-, √sánti-).

money: tála; sč'šnóʔ
(√č'šnóʔ-).

month month, moon, sun:
ɫukʷáɫ.

months January:
ʔalq'álm'yusm (√q'əl-).
February: ʔáqa tat swáksn
tic X̌aqám' (√wakə́s-,
√X̌aqám'-). March:
pənX̌aqám' (√pən-,
√X̌aqám'-). April:
pənʔíɫsqʷuʔqʷstmiʔɫ
(√pən-,√ʔíɫani-,
√qʷóqʷstmiʔɫ-). May:
pənsq̓ʷáX̌šitm scx̣ís
(√pən-,√q̓ʷáX̌-, √x̣ísi-).
July: skáwanani t ɫukʷáɫ
(√káwanan-,√ɫukʷáɫ-);
pənnáw'san'tim'n
(√pən-, √náwa-,
√sánti-). August:
pənstó·l'šn (√pən-,
√tó·l'xan-). September:
ʔáqa tasyə́q'awn
(√yáq'a-). October:
paxʷán'x̣ ʔáqa t qi sq̓ʷə́li
t wənáy'x̣ (√paxʷán'x̣-,
√q̓ʷə́la-,√wə́nay'x̣-).
November: pənʔíɫskʷinm
(√pən-,√ʔíɫani-,
√kʷiním-). December:
pənnáwsanti (√pən-,
√náwa-,√sánti-).

moon: ɫukʷáɫ; t'anáp
ɫukʷáɫ.

more: tk ʔáy'tk
(√ʔáy'tak-). more,
comparative degree: tk. a

little bit more than: ʔacsíw
(√síw-).

morning morning, early:
qʷéx̣iʔxʷ. in the morning:
q'íx̣ɫəqə̀nqs (√q'íx̣-).

mosquito, mosquitoes:
psáyq (√pə́saʔ-);
manikalítxlin HH.

moss: qʷíym.

most most, superlative
degree: t'ím.

moth: músalmx (√mús-).

mother: tán. mother (*voc.*):
kʷutáʔ (√tán-). his
mother: stánawi (√tán-).
my mother: kntáʔ (√tán-).
stepmother: tcuɫtánEm FBa
(√čuɫ-,√tán-).

mountain: X̌uk̓ʷél's
(√X̌úk̓ʷ-). high mountain,
ridge: smə́x̣ʷ (*pl.*
smax̣ʷáwmx) (√mə́x̣ʷ-).
to the mountains:
X̌uk̓ʷé·l'sm' (√X̌úk̓ʷ-).
mountain beaver: ʃú'ɫ JH
(*šúwɫ).

mountain goat: sáʔqʷs;
wáylšip; kê´tcits FBa;
stóq'ts' JH.

mourning dove: xəmím'x
(√xəmím'-); qo´x.kox
FBa.

mouse: sk̓ʷat'án' (*pl.*
sk̓ʷat'anáwmx)
(√k̓ʷat'án'-). short-tailed
mouse: .ska´nn FBa.

mouth: qə́nx (√qənúx-).
mouth of a river:

ƛ̓aqʷucə́ni (√ƛ̓əqə́-). put
into the mouth: mákʷn
(√mákʷ-).
move: yə́kʷacx (√yə́kʷa-).
move (away): yə́q̓ʷɬ
(√yə́q̓ʷ-). move a rooted
plant to another hole,
transplant: yə́kʷi?pn
(√yə́kʷa-). move aside,
aside: p'é·n'm (√p'én'-).
move over!: yékʷcxla?
(√yə́kʷa-). move over,
move in: t'úliq̓ʷ. moving,
changing: syə́kʷatn
(√yə́kʷa-). they're moving
up and down river:
syə́q̓ʷiq̓ʷiɬt ?aɬ tit qál?
(√yə́q̓ʷ-).
much much, very, a lot:
kʷumáy.
mud: sq'ə́x̣i? (√q'ə́x̣á?i-).

muddy water: ?acmíq̓ʷɬkʷu
(√míq̓ʷi-). getting muddy:
sq'əx̣á?itn (√q'əx̣á?i-).
make muddy, roil water:
míq̓ʷɬ (√míq̓ʷi-).
mumps: ?acpúspsm
(√púsa-).
muscle muscle, sinew: tínx
(√tínix-).
music music, ring: tíntinm
(√tín-). good music:
?ayáyn? (√?í·-). making
music: stə́lkʷmln,
stə́ltlkʷmitn (√tə́lkʷ-).
making music, ringing:
stə́lkʷawn,stə́lkʷmitn
(√tə́lkʷ-).
muskrat: mé?ščm' ENM (?);
p'ó?snk LNJ (√p'ó?s-).
mutton: šípɬc'i? (√šíp-).
my: səncáyaɬ (√?ə́nca).

n

nail (*n.*): cúsaq (*pl.*
cúsaqumx). nail together:
kʷax̣ʷál'wax (√kʷáx̣ʷ-).
nails nails, fingers, hand:
staléka HH (√t'alá-).
name (*v.*): ?úmtn
(√?úmati-). a name:
skʷácɬ (√kʷácili-).
naming, calling: skʷácilitn
(√kʷácili-).
nap take a nap, close eyes:
t'á?·p'usm (√t'áp'-). take
a nap, rest: ná?ɬcx

(√ná?ɬ-). taking a nap:
smó·smtn (√músami-).
nape of the neck:
sč'áqʷpsm (√č'áqʷ-).
back of the neck (lower
than above): ?áwtpsm
(√?áwat-).
narrow: q'ém'ɬ.
navel navel, belly button:
q'é·yx̣ (√q'iyáx̣-).
near near, close: yákm'x,
yá?km'x.
neck: k'ə́spn (√k'əspə́n-).

back of the neck: ʔáwtpsm
(√ʔáwat-). nape of the
neck: sč'áqʷpsm
(√č'áqʷ-).

necklace necklace, beads:
stəmtám (√tám-).
necklace; halter: yán'q
(√yanáq-).

needle needle, pin:
cánam'ɬtn' (√cána-).
needles: səc'c'wn (?)
(√səc'-). its needle:
sác'm'ɬtani (√səc'-).

Negro: ʔacnéʔqm
sxam'álaxʷ (√nəq-,
√xam'álaxʷ-);
nîkana´mEts FBa (√nəq-).

neighbor: sp'náy'x̣x
(√p'én'-).

nephew nephew, niece (on
man's side): snúkʷiɬ (pl.
nxnúkʷiɬtn) (√núkʷiɬ-).
nephew, niece (on woman's
side): sxawáciɬ
(√xawáciɬ-).

nervous nervous, bother,
worry, annoy: cáyaɬ
(√cáyaʔ-).

nest its nest:
cópsqʷlim'ɬtani
(√cópsqʷli-).

net net ENM, hook LNJ:
yasə́n. a big net: ʔáx̣ʷyn
(√ʔáx̣ʷyin-). dipnet: qi
sx̣̌úqʷam'ɬ, x̣̌úqʷam'ɬtn'
(√x̣̌úqʷi-). fishnet: kátyn.
fishnet (bag net): wa´pia
FBa. fishnet (gill): ɬi'tca´

FBa.

nettles: qʷə́nqʷn,
qʷə́nam'ɬtn' (√qʷə́na-).

never never, no, not: míɬta.

new new, fresh: mayə́n.

news news, story: syáy'ɬuɬ
(√yáy-).

next: ʔaɬ taʔúc's (√ʔúc's-).
next to, beside: p'éntmx
(√p'én'-). next to, close
together, middle:
təq'tum'x (√təq'-).

nibble nibble, gnaw: k'ə́t'n
(√k'ə́t'-). nibbling:
sk̓ʷá·ymtn (√k̓ʷáya-).

nice nice, good: ʔí·, ʔíy. nice,
kind: q'aɬ qátnɬ (√qát-).

niece niece, nephew (on
man's side): snúkʷiɬ (pl.
nxnúkʷiɬtn) (√núkʷiɬ-).
niece, nephew (on woman's
side): sxawáciɬ
(√xawáciɬ-).

night: sqʷíx̣, sqʷéx̣
(√qʷíx̣-). night, darkness:
sqʷíx̣ltn, qʷíx̣ltn
(√qʷíx̣-). become night:
sqʷéx̣kʷu (√qʷíx̣-).
midnight: pútkʷaɬlus t
sqʷíx̣ (√pút-, √kʷə́ɬ-,
√qʷíx̣-).

nighthawk: p'íw'.

nine: túwxʷ (√təwíxʷ-).
nineteen: pánačš kl t
túwxʷ; tál'tuwxʷ
(√təwíxʷ-). ninety:
tawíxʷɬtumx (√təwíxʷ-).

no no, not, never: míɬta. no-good, useless: ʔiX̌áp'.

nod nod the head, dizzy, crazy: múlukʷɬ (√múlukʷ-).

noise noise, voice, echo: tawóˑyn' (√taw-). hear noise, echo, squeak: ʔímnm' (√ʔímn-).

noon: c'úq̇ʷɬ (√c'úq̇ʷ-). afternoon: námc'uq̇ʷɬ (√náma-, √c'úq̇ʷ-).

north: sX̌íxtn (√X̌íx-). north, upcountry: .stū´m.la FBa.

nose: məqsn (√məqsə́n-). ridge of the nose: .sxo´mEks FBa.

nostril: sx̣ʷənə́x̣ʷqs (√x̣ʷənə́x̣ʷ-); stEpu´xEks FBa; ṣqa-túħks EC; səlpê̱x̣ˑks HT

not not, no, never: míɬta.

nothing: míɬta t ʔitám. nothing's the matter: míɬta csisíni (√csisín-).

November: pənʔíɬskʷinm (√pən-, √ʔíɬani-, √kʷiním-).

now: ʔáqa; tu st'íx̣ (√t'íx̣-). now, already: tan, tani. now, while: t'íx̣.

numb: c'ík̇ʷɬ (√c'ík̇ʷ-).

numbers one: ʔúc's. two: sáliʔ. three: káʔɬiʔ. four: mús. five: čílačš. six: t'ax̣ə́m (√t'əx̣ə́m-). seven: c'óps. eight: cámus. nine: túwxʷ

ten: pánačš (√pánaks-). eleven: pánačš kl t ʔúc's; tálʔuc's. twelve: pánačš kl t sáliʔ; tál'sali?. thirteen: pánačš kl t káʔɬiʔ; tál'kaʔɬiʔ. fourteen: pánačš kl t mús; tál'mus. fifteen: pánačš kl t čílačš; tál'čilačš. sixteen: pánačš kl t t'ax̣ə́m; tál't'x̣m (√t'əx̣ə́m-). seventeen: pánačš kl t c'óps; tálc'ops. eighteen: pánačš kl t cámus; tál'camus. nineteen: pánačš kl t túwxʷ; tál'tuwxʷ (√təwíxʷ-). twenty: cmtúmx (√cám-). twenty-one: cmtúmx kl t ʔúc's (√cám-). thirty: kánxtumx (√kán-). forty: músɬtumx (√mús-). fifty: cílksɬtumx (√cílks-). sixty: t'ax̣mɬtumx (√t'əx̣ə́m-). seventy: c'ópsɬtumx (√c'óps-). eighty: cámusɬtumx (√cámus-). ninety: tawíxʷɬtumx (√təwíxʷ-). one hundred: ʔúc's hándəd; t'əmxpánkstlšn (√t'əmx-, √pánaks-); ō´ts panEksɬto´mEx FBa.

nut nut, hazelnut: káw's (*pl.* káw'usmx) (√kaw'ús-).

o

oak tree: kʷískʷsn'ɬ
(√kʷís-).

oar oar, paddle: cáqʷɬ,
sā´koɬtEn FBa
(√caqʷəl-); ʔútq
(√ʔútaq-).

oats: lawé·n.

obey obey, listen to, send
word to: taláynmn
(√tal-). obey, mind: xə́y'ɬ
(√xə́y'-); tó·l'ux
(√tó·l'u-).

ocean: sqíwɬkʷu (√qíwa-).

October: paxʷán'x̱ ʔáqa t
qi sq̓ʷəli t wənáy'x̱
(√paxʷán'x̱-, √q̓ʷəla-,
√wənay'x̱-).

of of, from: tu; tu ʔaɬ; tuɬ.

off off, from, out of, than: tl
ʔaɬ. get off, get out of,
come down: líxʷlcx
(√líxʷl-). off the road, out
of the way: lé·llxaw'ɬ
(√líl?-, √xəwál-). take
off, take out, uncover: ɬíwx
(√ɬíw-).

oh!: ʔú; ye·ʔ FBb.

oil (*v.*): k'axʷóʔn
(√k'axʷóʔ-). oil, grease,
lard, tallow: k'axʷóʔ.

OK OK, let's!, you'd better
(*exhortative particle*):
ƛ̓áq̓ʷ.

old: ʔacnáwɬ (√náwa-). old
(object): máq'ɬ (√máq'-).
old people, grandparents:

nx̱ʔálstn' (√ʔális-);
talsnáwaʔ (√tals-,
√náwa-). old person:
ʔacnáwɬ (*pl.* ʔacnáwaɬtiʔ)
(√náwa-). old woman:
ná·w'ɬmx (√náwa-).
older: tk ʔacnáwɬ (√tk-,
√náwa-).

on on, in, with; oblique: ɬ.
on, into: kaɬ. on, to, in,
into: ʔaɬ. be on, get on (a
horse): k'ə́c'acx
(√k'ə́c'a-).

once once, one time:
nák̓ʷušn (√nák'-).

one: ʔúc's. one hundred:
ʔúc's hə́ndəd;
t'əmxpánkstlšn
(√t'əmx-, √pánaks-);
ō´ts panEksɬto´mEx FBa.
twenty-one: cmtúmx kl t
ʔúc's (√cám-).

onion: qiwáɬqs, sqiwáɬaln
(√qíwa-).

only: táx̱ʷu, stáx̱ʷu, tu
stáx̱ʷu; yə́xa. only, just:
ʔanám'u (√ʔanám'-);
pút-. only, only one, only
ones: t'íx̱u (√t'íx̱-).

open: wáq'n (√wáq'-).
open one's eyes: ʔə́x̱am'ɬ
(√ʔə́x̱-). opening,
spreading out, blooming,
stretching: swə́ɬqawn
(√wə́ɬəqa-).

operate operate on, cut up,

butcher, carve:
c'əwc'awək'n
(√c'əwə́k'-).

opposite opposite, other side:
tk xán? (√tk-,√xán?-).

or: ?awəl; naw'.

orchard apple orchard:
?áplsan'ł (√?ápls-). plum
orchard: plə́msan'ł
(√plə́ms-).

order order, drive away,
force to leave: x̣íyn
(√x̣íy-).

Oregon grape: č'iyúxʷi?s.

orphan: .sō´laxEm FBa
(√?úlx̣-). raise an orphan:
?ó·l'x̣n (√?úlx̣-).

osprey, fish hawk: sc'íxʷ
(√c'íxʷ-).

other other, foreign, strange,
different: ?ə́xʷł (√?ə́xʷ-).
other, some: sə́k̓ʷł. other,
something else: tántan
(√tán-). other side: xʷán'.
other side, opposite: tk
xán? (√tk-,√xán?-). each
other, together:
t'əmxsáliyumx (√t'əmx-,
√sáli?-). several others,
how many?: k̓ʷináwmx
k̓ʷu (√k̓ʷí-).

otter: skálmn (√kálmn-);
pe´t.kuł FBa (*p'ítkʷł).
sea otter: pitqh̄l EC
(*p'ítkʷł).

our, ours: siními̇ł
(√?iním-).

out bring it out: p'əlqʷə́ctm
(?) (√p'ələ́qʷ-). get out of
(canoe, etc.): c'áwł
(√c'áw-). get out of, get
off, come down: líxʷlcx
(√líxʷl-). go out: ƛ'ə́qł
(√ƛ'əqə́-). out of, from,
off, than: tl ?ał. out of
breath: táylaxʷk̓ʷu?
(√láxʷk̓ʷun-);
c'ə́klxʷk̓ʷu? (√c'ə́ka-,
√láxʷk̓ʷun-). out of the
way, off the road:
lé·llxaw'ł (√líl?-,
√xəwál-). put out, take
out: ƛ'aqə́x (√ƛ'əqə́-). put
out a fire, fire goes out, turn
off a light, kill, be dead:
łə́pł (√łə́pa-). squeeze
out, pull out: txʷłax̣ʷə́c'n
(√łax̣ʷə́c'-). take out, pop
out: p'alə́qʷn (√p'ələ́qʷ-).

outside: pátk̓ʷu. toward the
outside, go outside:
pá?łk̓ʷulm' (√pátk̓ʷu-).

oven put into the oven:
ƛ'íxʷstqn (√ƛ'íxʷ-).

over over, across: stáln'x
(√táln'x-).

overalls overalls, trousers,
pants: ?ucámc
(√?ucámac-).

owe owe, be in debt:
x̣ʷuxʷín (√x̣ʷúx̣ʷ-).

owl: čənó?k̓ʷšitm;
sx̣ɑ́p'ɑlɑm' JH
(*sx̣ə́p'lm').

p

pack: kə́wn (√kə́w–). pack
(horse): yəxán'mn'
(√yáxa–). pack, carry:
yášn (√yáxa–). he's
packing it up: skə́wcšitn
(√kə́w–). his pack (on
back), rolling its pack off
(?): yəxál'kni (√yáxa–).
package: ʔact'ə́qličn
(√t'ə́qi–).
pack strap ENM: q'áyc'tan
(√q'áyc'–). pack strap,
pack rope: yə́nkʷs
(√yənkʷə́s–).
pad: qʷúpɬ (√qʷúpi–).
paddle (*n.*) paddle, oar: ʔútq
(√ʔútaq–); cáqʷɬ,
sā´koɬtEn FBa (√caqʷə́l–).
paddle a canoe: wə́xacx
(√wə́xa–); ʔátqʷɬ
(√ʔátqʷil–). paddling a
canoe: sʔútqtn, sʔútqwiln
(√ʔútaq–).
paddle (*v.*) paddle, spank,
slap: t'ə́q'x̣ʷn (√t'ə́q'x̣ʷ–).
pain pain or cramp in one's
side: ʔack'allksti?
(√k'ál–).
paint (*v.*): cáqʷɬ (√cáqʷa–).
paint (n.): cáqʷam'ɬtn'
(√cáqʷa–). paint, smear:
q'áx̣ɬ (√q'áx̣a–). red
paint: .xtseq awi´lEk FBa
(√c'íq–); 'ὰwì·lk JH
(*ʔawílk). war paint: q̇ʷílɬ.
yellow paint: axsqwe´q

awi´lEk FBa (√k̇ʷiq'é–,
*ʔawílk).
pale pale, turn pale:
k̇ʷéq'm'ɬ (√k̇ʷiq'é–).
palm palm of the hand:
kʷupámapšn ENM;
tEko´leka FBa. palm of the
hand ENM, thumb:
papáyaka? (√pap–).
pan: lapuén.
pants pants, trousers:
k'ál'xn'tn' (√k'ál'ax–).
pants, trousers, overalls:
ʔucámc (√ʔucámac–). he
doesn't have his pants on:
táyucamc (√ʔucámac–).
paper: pípa; qa´nEks FBa.
parents his parents:
nxtántani (√tán–).
part part hair, separate:
k̇ʷáy'smn (√k̇ʷáy'us–).
part in hair: k̇ʷáy's
(√k̇ʷáy'us–).
particles akʷu *interrogative.*
ʔana, ana, na
interrogative. ʔanám' just.
ʔanám'u just, only. ʔáqa
now. ʔáys again (*proclitic*).
ʔu, u, ʔo, o evidently
(*enclitic*). ʔú Oh! cicu that's
why (√cic–). có?a
exhortative (?). cu because,
so, so that, for the reason
that. cútkn evidently,
maybe (√cút–, √kən–).
kən?ó maybe (√kən–).

kənq'íc'x̣ it seems that way
(√kən-, √q'íc'x̣-). ksa
again (*enclitic*). k̓ʷac a
little, somewhat. k̓ʷá but, it
turned out to be. l *past*. ʔicl
past (ʔic + l). ʔitl *past* (ʔit
+ l). cl *past* (c + l). tl *past*
(t + l). ɬit *future* (ɬ- + ʔit).
x̣̓a *future*. x̣̓áq̓ʷ *exhortative*:
OK, better!, let's! nám'uɬ
perhaps, maybe, might
(√nám'u-). nám'uqas
wish, hope (√nám'u-).
nks, ʔnks habitually
(*proclitic*). qaɬ modal: can,
could. qas *desiderative*:
want (*enclitic*). qi syntactic
particle (*see grammar* 2.7.3
and appendix on prefixes).
ql *modal*: can, be able
(past?). q'aɬ ?*modal* (*see
grammar* 2.7.1). q'íc'x̣ thus,
the same. q'ím already.
q̓ʷəɬ so. š ?? ta ?? tan,
tani now, already. táx̣ʷl'
although. táx̣ʷu, stáx̣ʷu, tu
stáx̣ʷu only. tela´ la FBa
bye and bye, after a while.
tk *comparative degree*:
more. t'im *superlative
degree*: most. t'íx̣ while,
now. t'íx̣u only, only one,
only ones. tu st'íx̣ now. tu
st'íx̣u that's all. wa ?? wi
?? x̣áwq'aɬ can't. x̣əɬ so.
yáis ?? yəx̣a only.
partner: scəx̣áʔis
(√cəx̣áy'us-).

pass: tá·lym (√tá·ly-). he
passed me: tálnmx
(√táln-).
past: l, t + l, ʔít + l (*non-
feminine*), c + l, ʔíc + l
(*feminine*).
pasture pasture, swamp,
meadow: spáɬx̣n
(√páɬxan-).
patch: t'əlpšn, t'əlt'lpšn
(√t'ələp-).
path path, trail: x̣éw'ɬ
(√x̣əwál-).
patience out of patience,
impatient: c'akálnutšn
(√c'əka-).
pay: múx̣ʷn (√múx̣ʷi-);
təwɬ (√təw-). pay
attention: có·taynmn
(√có·-). pay attention,
watch for, guard...:
x̣̓aqʷséx̣n (√x̣̓áqʷ-,
√ʔə́x̣-). paying it for:
smúx̣ʷšitn (√múx̣ʷi-).
paying to: stəwšitn
(√təw-). he paid me again:
ʔaysmúx̣ʷic (√ʔáys-,
√múx̣ʷi-). he paid me over
and over: múx̣ʷmux̣ʷic
(√múx̣ʷi-).
peas: lipuá.
peck pecking: sɬə́k̓ʷɬk̓ʷmitn
(√ɬə́k̓ʷ-). it pecked me: ʔit
ɬə́k̓ʷc (√ɬə́k̓ʷ-).
peek at: k̓ʷél'ux̣ʷ
(√k̓ʷél'u-).
peel: lapíl'sn (√ləpa-);
x̣ík'lsn (√x̣ík'-). it's

peeling: sləpawn
(√ləʔpa-).

pencil pencil, pen, book,
tablet: q̇ʷałém'łtn'
(√q̇ʷəłé-).

penis his penis: səxʷáy'mini
(?) (√səxʷáy'-).

people: sxam'álaxʷ
(√xam'álaxʷ-). a good
class of people; people and
an area in southern Cowlitz
territory between Kelso and
Toledo: síq̇ʷł (√síq̇ʷ-).
bad people: x̣ašáwmx
(√x̣ə́š-). old people,
grandparents: nxʔálstn'
(√ʔális-); talsnáwaʔ
(√tals-, √náwa-). young
people: tál'xʷucumx
(√tál'xʷuc-).

perfective aspect, definite
article (*non-feminine*): ʔit

perhaps perhaps, maybe,
might: nám'uł
(√nám'u-).

person person, man:
nawíłm'x. a person from a
good class of people: tk
síq̇ʷ. non-Indian: xʷə́ltm
(√xʷə́l-). old person:
ʔacnáwł (*pl.* ʔacnáwałtiʔ)
(√náwa-).

pestle: q̇ʷé·c'am'łtn'
(√q̇ʷíc'i-); tēmsa´ka FBa.

pet: qátmn (√qát-).

pheasant pheasant, chicken,
turkey: skʷínm (*pl.*
skʷínimumx) (√kʷiním-).

pick pick berries: x̌aʔáwm
(√x̌aʔáwi-). her picking,
what she picked: sq̇ʷax̌ə́ši
(√q̇ʷáx̌-).

pick up: xʷúqʷn
(√xʷúqʷa-). pick up, lift:
qítn (√qíti-).

picture: tena´mectEn FBa
(√t'aními-).

pierce pierce, drill, drill a
hole, make a hole: lapə́xʷł
(√ləpə́xʷa-). pierce, have
a hole, make a hole:
pal'ə́kʷł (√pəl'ə́kʷ-).
pierce one's ears:
ləpxʷán'n (√ləpə́xʷa-).

pig: kʷušú; p'alə́kʷqs
(√p'ələ́kʷ-). pork:
kʷušúłc'iʔ (√kʷušú-).

pigeon pigeon, dove:
xəmím'. mourning dove:
xəmím'x (√xəmím'-).

pile pile, pile up: mə́kʷł,
mə́kʷn, mé·kʷn
(√mə́kʷ-). a pile:
ʔacmə́kʷł (√mə́kʷ-). little
piles, lumpy:
ʔacmə́kʷmakʷł
(√mə́kʷ-).

pillow: č'é·n'xʷ (*pl.*
č'é·n'ixʷumx)
(√č'in'úxʷ-).

pimple: sp'éʔxʷ (√p'ə́xʷ-).

pin (*n.*): sac'áxʷctn'
(√sə́c'-). pin, needle:
cánam'łtn' (√cána-). pin
together: səc'ál'wax
(√sə́c'-).

pinch pinch, squeeze: c'ayə́p'n (√c'əyə́p'–).

pine: yámc (*pl.* yámacumx) (√yámac–); ħá–ħe–wĩ̀hl EC (*x̣áx̣iw⅃). white pine: tau'i´tsE⅃p FBa. yellow pine: kwa´se⅃ FBa.

pink pink, red: ʔaksc'í (√c'í–).

pipe: q̓ʷalém'⅃tn' (√q̓ʷalí–); lapíp. pipestem: LEXLExet FBa (√ƛ'ə́x–). his Indian pipe: stəkáli (√təkál–).

pity pity, be sorry for: ʔúšamn (√ʔúšam–).

plan: sá·nax̣nut, sá·nax̣nutšn (√sáʔa–, √nax̣–). plan, think: có·t (√có·–). plan on, be in charge: kátyn.

plant *sp.*: ⅃áx̣lnm'tn.

plant *sp.*: sq'iwán? (√q'iwán'–).

plant *sp.*: q̓ʷáy's.

plant *sp.*: sə́q̓ʷ⅃tn.

plant (*v.*) plant, sow: x̣áln (√x̣ála–). time to plant a garden: pənx̣á·lam'⅃ (√pən–, √x̣ála–).

platters: tə́x̣tax̣alu⅃ (√tə́x̣–).

play play, laugh: x̣á⅃x̣ʷm (√x̣á⅃x̣ʷa–). play with, wrestle with: x̣á⅃x̣ʷamix (√x̣á⅃x̣ʷa–). playing ball: sté̓ʔq⅃qmaln (√⅃əq–). playing cards, gambling:

pleats: ʔacmə́lmalak⅃ (√mə́lak–). pleated, wrinkled: ʔac⅃úm⅃um⅃ (√⅃úma–).

plow (*n.*): sək'áy'tmxtn' (√sə́k'–).

plug: mó·luqʷ⅃ (√mó·luqʷ–); ʔacyó·luq̓ʷ⅃ (?) (√yó·luq̓ʷ–).

plum plum orchard: plə́msan'⅃ (√plə́ms–).

pocket pocket, sack, bag: lisák (*pl.* lisakáwmx).

point point at: sac'él'usn (√sə́c'–). pointed: ʔacc'ə́m'x̣ʷl's (√c'əmə́x̣ʷ–). blunt-pointed, come off: c'amə́k̓ʷ⅃ (√c'əmə́k̓ʷ–). sharp-pointed: ʔacc'amə́x̣ʷ⅃ (√c'əmə́x̣ʷ–).

poisoning: sčín⅃nitn (√čín⅃ni–).

poke: mə́kʷn (√məkʷə́–); ƛ'amə́x̣n (√ƛ'əmə́x̣–).

pole (*n.*): ʔacc'úq̓ʷ⅃ (√c'úq̓ʷ–). pole, tree, limb, stick: ƛ'ə́xƛ'x (*pl.* ƛ'ə́xƛ'axumx) (√ƛ'ə́x–). poling a boat: smúq̓ʷitn (√múq̓ʷi–).

policeman: qi t'éʔqim'⅃tn' (√t'ə́qi–).

polish polish, clean (off), change, straighten out, brush off: ʔayə́q⅃ (√ʔiyə́q–).

getting smooth and
polished: ʔáyltawn
(√ʔáyl–). polishing:
skʷíwxʷtn (√kʷíwxʷ–).
polishing, shining:
swəlk'mtn (√wəlk'–).

poncho: spanyoˊnolitsa FBa
(√spalyán–).

poor: q'aɬ úšmn'ɬ
(√ʔúšam–).

pop: kʷašəqɬ (√kʷəšə́q–).
pop out, take out: p'aléqʷn
(√p'əléqʷ–). popping:
skʷə́škʷšqawn
(√kʷəšə́q–).

porcupine: Lāˊtɪ.ɬ FBa.

pork: kʷušúɬc'iʔ
(√kʷušú–).

posts: ʔacc'úq̇ʷaʔɬ
(√c'úq̇ʷ–).

pot their pot, their stakes,
what they gamble:
sx̣ál'xʷili (√x̣ál'xʷil–).

potato: cáqʷɬ (√caqʷə́l–).
baking potatoes: ʔácqʷiln
(√ʔácqʷ–).

potlatch potlatch, giving,
throwing away: sʔáx̣ʷmtn'
(√ʔáx̣ʷ–).

pound pound, punch: yə́q'n
(√yə́q'–). pound on: tásn
(√tása–); yaq'ə́mn
(√yə́q'–). he pounded on
my head: yə́q'lusic
(√yə́q'–). it was pounded:
yə́q'iq'tm (√yə́q'–).

pour pour on, baptize:
pə́qʷšn (√pə́qʷa–). pour

out, spill: pə́qʷɬ
(√pə́qʷa–).

powder powder, dust flying:
ʔacƛasə́qʷɬ (√ƛəsə́qʷ–).
gunpowder, shell, bullet:
síɬ. gunpowder, smoke:
sq̇ʷúx̣ʷ (√q̇ʷúx̣ʷ–). red
face powder: scáqʷusm
(√cáqʷa–).

power spirit power: sə́x̣tkʷlx
(√ʔə́x̣t–).

prairie prairie, valley:
máqʷm.

pray: c'éˑwm (√c'íwi–).
prayer: ʔacc'íwšitm
(√c'íwi–).

predict: k̓ʷənén'wax
(√k̓ʷə́na–).

pregnant become pregnant:
snə́x̣ʷƛ̓kmx (√nə́x̣ʷ–).

premonition have a
premonition: ʔacc'íx̣ɬ
(√c'íx̣–).

prepare prepared camas:
ʔacp'ə́n'c tani tit qáwm'
(√p'ə́n'c–).

prepositions ʔaɬ to, in, into,
on. kaɬ on, into. kl with,
and. ɬl in, on, with;
oblique. taʔaɬ along,
around. tak with. taxaɬ to.
tl ʔaɬ from, off, out of,
than. tu from, of. tu ʔaɬ
from, of. tuɬ from, of. x to.
xaɬ, xʔaɬ to.

press press, iron: č'íxʷipn
(√č'íxʷip–). press, mash:
c'íq̇ʷɬ (√c'íq̇ʷ–). press

down, push in: c'ə́q'n
(√c'ə́q'-).
pretend: káw'ln (√káw'l-).
pretty: ʔiyál'wn (√ʔíˑ-).
priest: liplét.
privilege: slə́lqawn
(√lə́lqa-).
pronouns, personal ʔə́nca I,
me. nə́wi you (*sg.*). cə́ni he,
him, she, her, it. ʔiním we,
us. ʔilápaʔ you (*pl.*), you
folks. cəniyáwmx they,
them (√cə́ni-).
pronouns, possessive
səncáyaɬ my, mine
(√ʔə́nca-). snawíyaɬ your,
yours (√nə́wi-). scaníyaɬ
his, her, hers, its (√cə́ni-).
siním aɬ our, ours
(√ʔiním-).
scəniyáwmixaɬ their,
theirs (√cə́ni-).
prop prop, tanning frame,
temporary shelter, bow:
sq'iyúxʷ (√q'iyúxʷ-).
protect protect, guard, take
care of, watch for...:
x̌aqʷséx̣n (√x̌áqʷ-,
√ʔə́x̣-).
proud proud, stuck-up:
ʔaccépɬ (√cép-). be proud
of, respect: ʔacnawín'wax
(√náwa-).
puddle: ʔack'áˑc'kʷu
(√k'áˑc'-).
pull: tə́x̣ʷn (√tə́x̣ʷ-). pull,
drag: wə́xn (√wə́xa-). pull
out, squeeze out:

txʷɬax̣ʷə́c'n (√ɬax̣ʷə́c'-).
pull up: wə́xiʔn (√wə́xa-).
stump pulled over with
roots sticking up:
ʔacp'ə́lk̓ʷip (√p'ələ́k̓ʷ-).
pulley: wáxam'ɬtn'
(√wə́xa-).
punch punch, pound: yə́q'n
(√yə́q'-).
punish: múx̣ʷix (√múx̣ʷi-).
pupil pupil of the eye:
tsnî́ˑks FBa (√nə́q-);
silaxwaˊls FBa.
puppy puppy, little dog:
qáˑʔx̣aʔ (*pl.* qx̣ʔáˑw'mx)
(√qáx̣aʔ-).
purr it is purring:
sx̣ʷúlqʷmtn (√x̣ʷúlqʷ-).
pus its pus: tamáni
(√tamán-).
push: ɬúnn (√ɬúni-). push
in, press down: c'ə́q'n
(√c'ə́q'-). pushing
through, sewing, mending:
scánatn (√cána-).
put put a load on a horse:
sál'ičn (√sál'ikn-). put
away, put aside, store, save:
t'óʔn (√t'óʔi-). put away,
store: wétx (√wéta-). put
down, lay down: kácx
(√kác-). put fire on:
x̣ʷál'šn (√x̣ʷál'a-). put
hand in, reach in:
tákʷl'kʷmn (√tákʷl'kʷ-).
put hand into: x̌áplkmn
(√x̌áp-). put in: k'ə́c'n,
k'c'k'ə́c'n (√k'ə́c'a-). put

in, be in, get in: k'ə́c'ɬ
(√k'ə́c'a-). put in jail,
arrest, tie around, wind
around: t'ə́qn (√t'ə́qi-).
put in the fire: x̣ʷál'n
(√x̣ʷál'a-). put into:
k'ə́c'šn (√k'ə́c'a-). put
into the mouth: mákʷn
(√mákʷ-). put into the
oven: ƛ̓íxʷstqn (√ƛ̓íxʷ-).
put on, put around, hook on:
t'aləpn (√t'ələp-). put
out, take out: ƛ̓aqə́x

(√ƛ̓əqá-). put out a fire,
beat up, kill: yúcx
(√yúca-). put out a fire,
turn off a light, kill: ɬə́pn
(√ɬə́pa-). put together,
splice: t'əlpál'wax
(√t'ələp-). put together
side by side: ʔact'əlpál'us
(√t'ələp-). putting down
on: skácšitn (√kác-).
putting end to end, splicing:
sp'át'atn (√p'át'a-).

q

quarrel quarrel with, scold,
get after: taq̓ʷín
(√təq̓ʷa-). he quarrelled
with me: ʔit taq̓ʷə́c
(√təq̓ʷa-). I quarrelled
with him: ʔit qanóm's kn
(√qanóm'-). they're
quarrelling:
qanóm'ɬncšitiɬt
(√qanóm'-).
quarter quarter, twenty-five
cents: kʷáta.
question question,
interrogative: ʔac'í; akʷu;
ʔana,ana, na; ʔí.
quick quick, fast, soon: ƛ̓ə́x̣ɬ
(√ƛ̓ə́x̣-).
quiet quiet, get quiet, shut up:

ʔacx̣ʷayó·ɬq (√x̣ʷáya-).
quiet down, calm down,
hold still: ƛ̓él'cx (√ƛ̓əla-).
be quiet!: ʔackʷá·hilaʔ
(√kʷá·hi-). be quiet, hush:
x̣ál'stq̓ʷm (√x̣ál'-,
√təq̓ʷa-). be quiet!, hush!:
ʔackʷá·l'aʔ (√kʷá·hi-).
keep quiet, don't want to
tell, forbid: káywiɬix
(√káywiɬi-).
quilt: kʷílt. make a quilt:
sáʔkʷilt (√sáʔa-, √kʷílt-).
quit quit, stop: ƛ̓əlacx
(√ƛ̓əla-).
quiver (*n.*): wupkai´lɛxt
FBa.

r

rabbit: sx̣ʷáyks (*pl.* sx̣ʷáykisumx) (√x̣ʷáykas–). rabbit skin robe: xā´tlolitsa FBa.

raccoon: q̓ʷá·ls, q̓ʷáls.

racing: sx̣íx̣aq'n (√x̣íx̣aq'–).

rack drying rack: x̣ápam'ɬtn', x̣əpnxtn (√x̣əpa–). hanging racks: qi sx̣ʷíla? (√x̣ʷíl–).

railroad: káslxaw'ɬ (√kás–, √x̣əwál–).

rain: x̣asíl? (√x̣asíli?–); sùkwʊ HH (√səx̣ʷa–). rain (*n.*): sx̣asíl? (√x̣asíli?–).

rainbow: x̣ʷəplq, x̣ʷəplqtn.

raincoat: pənx̣asíl?mn', sx̣asíl?kapu LNJ (√x̣asíli?–, √kapú–).

rain hat: x̣asíl?sx̣ʷay's (√x̣asíli?–, √x̣ʷay'ús–).

raise raise, grow: x̣əwɬ (√x̣əwáli–). raise an orphan: ?ó·l'x̣n (√?úlx̣–).

rake (*n.*): x̣apáyimɬtn' (√x̣əpayí?–).

ram (of mountain sheep): t̲ako´ne FBa.

ramrod (of a gun): tsa´kaiᵘktɛn FBa (√c'əq'–).

rapids on a river: sp'úcp'cwn t qál? (√p'úca–).

rapping: sx̣əlx̣lkʷmitn

(√x̣əlkʷ–).

raspberry: q̓ʷál'x̣ʷ. raspberry bush: q̓ʷál'x̣ʷan'ɬ (√q̓ʷál'x̣ʷ–).

rat: skʷánayu? (*pl.* k̓ʷánayumx) (√k̓ʷán–). wood rat: hùlhùl JHjp.

rations Saturday, time to get rations: pənskʷítim'ɬ (√pən–, √kʷíti–).

rattle: yátn (√yáta–).

rattlesnake: wɛl'kai´ FBa.

raven: sqʷáqʷ (√qʷáqʷ–).

reach reach, get there, arrive: kʷáxʷɬ (√kʷáxʷa–). reach for: pátkmn (√pátk–). reach in, put a hand in: tákʷl'kʷmn (√tákʷl'kʷ–). reach shore, land (a canoe), cross, go across, go through: t'ánɬ (√t'aná–). reaching, come together: ɬakál'us (√ɬək–). he' reaching for it: c'ayskʷanátn (√c'ay–, √kʷəná–).

read: ?əx̣x̣n, ?éx̣n, ?ax̣étpipa (√?əx̣–, √pípa–).

ready: kʷúwacx (√kʷúwa–); náml's (√náma–).

really really, very: k̓ʷépɬ (√k̓ʷəp–).

rear rear part, buttocks: sč'é? (√č'é?–).

reason for the reason that, so

that, so, because: cu.

red red, bay: ʔaksc'íq
(√c'íq–). pink, red: ʔaksc'í
(√c'í–). dark red, cherry
red: ʔaksc'íyi (√c'íyi–).
red paint: .xtseq awi´lɛk
FBa (√c'íq–,*ʔawílk). red
salmon: ƙʷaléʔ.

reed reeds, reed mat: kə́lx
(√kələ́x–).

refuse: táynutšn (√táy–).

reins reins, handle:
kʷaná·mn' (√kʷəná–).

relatives: snxmántn
(√mán–).

release release, let go: túnn
(√tún–).

remember: ʔáʔctix
(√ʔáʔcti–).

rent rent, borrow, lend:
kʷústm (√kʷústam–). rent
to: kʷústamix
(√kʷústam–).

represent representative,
interpreter: kátyn.
representing: sk'ə́c'tn
(√k'ə́c'–).

reside residing, living,
staying, becoming: swínn
(√wín–).

respect respect, be proud of:
ʔacnawín'wax (√náwa–).
respect, like: yáyn
(√yáy–).

rest rest, take a nap: náʔɬcx
(√náʔɬ–). rest, wait: ʔálmq
(√ʔálm'aq–).

return: tit'uləx (√t'úla–).

revenge: ʔáynx (√ʔáyn–).

revive revive, come to: p'ə́xɬ
(√p'ə́x–).

revolver: t'ik'á·ʔkaʔ
(√t'ik'–).

rib: sk'átp (*pl.* sk'átapumx)
(√k'átap–).

ribbon, ribbons: lalupá.

rich: qə́x̣wiwi, qéx̣wiwi
(√qə́x̣–).

ride ride a horse: k'ə́c'k'ac'ɬ
(√k'ə́c'a–). ride in, be in,
get in: k'ə́c'ɬ (√k'ə́c'a–).

ridge ridge, high mountain:
smə́x̣ʷ (*pl.* smə́x̣ʷáwmx)
(√m'ə́x̣ʷ–). ridge of the
nose: .sxo´mɛks FBa.

riffle: wiɬíɬkʷu (√wiɬ–).
riffle, whirlpool: yác'ɬkʷu
(√yác'–).

right right, very, correct, true,
straight, even: ƙʷə́pɬ
(√ƙʷə́p–). right away, fast,
hurry, soon: ƛ'ə́xƛ'axɬ
(√ƛ'ə́x–).

right (side): náwax̣n
(√náw–). to the right:
ʔáɬnawax̣n (√náw–).

ring (*n.*): yaláʔkamn
(√yal–). ring LNJ, bracelet
ENM: t'amákamn
(√t'ám–).

ring (sound) ring, music:
tíntinm (√tín–). ringing,
making music:
stə́lkʷwn, stə́lkʷmtn
(√tə́lkʷ–).

rip rip, tear: caɬə́qʷɬ

(√cə⁴əqʷ-). rip off: síḱʷ⁴
(√síḱʷ-).

ripe: q̇ʷə́l⁴ (√q̇ʷə́la-).

risk risk, look out for, alarm,
alert...: X̌aqʷsé x̣n
(√X̌áqʷ-, √ʔə́x̣-).

river: nau´.⁴ko FBa. river,
water: qál? (√qalí?-).
mouth of a river:
X̌aqʷucə́ni (√X̌əqə́-).

road road, row: xə́w⁴, xúw⁴
(*pl.* xə́wi⁴umx)
(√xəwál-). making a
road: saʔxáw'iln (√sá?a-,
√xəwál-).

roan: eks spa´konamts FBa
(√p'áqʷ-). strawberry
roan: qašqáš.

roast roast, set over a fire, sit
straight: cə́q⁴ (√cə́q-).
roast on a stick: caqá?n
(√cə́q-). roast
underground: p'íx̣n
(√p'íx̣-). roasting stick:
tawa´shweyə TA.

robe deerskin robe:
tla´leconi´tsa FBa
(√X̌aláš-). elk skin robe:
kala´tib FBa. rabbit skin
robe: xā´tlolitsa FBa.

robin: swítq' (√wítq'-).

rock (*n.*) rock, rocks, stone:
spatáln (√patálan-);
t!ak!aˑ´ls FBb. big rock:
súwn (*pl.* súwinlm'x).
little rocks, gravel:
spatáˑl'inumx
(√patálan-).

rock (*v.*) rock back and forth:
yáq'iq'n (√yáq'iq'-). rock
in one' arms, balance:
?áˑlwasix (√?áˑlwasi-).
rocking chair: yéq'iq'tawn
(√yáq'iq'-). rocking self
back and forth:
syáq'iq'cšitn (√yáq'iq'-).

roe roe, salmon eggs:
qʷə́⁴xa?.

roil roil water, make muddy:
míq̇ʷ⁴ (√míq̇ʷi-).

roll (*tr.*): yalə́kʷn
(√yələ́kʷ-). roll, roll over,
turn over: p'alə́k'n
(√p'ələ́k'-). roll up:
yalúx̣ʷn (√yəlúx̣ʷ-).
rolling: syə́l'kʷawn
(√yələ́kʷ-). rolling its pack
off (?), his pack (on back):
yəxál'kni (√yáxa-).

roof: x̣ál'txʷ (√x̣ál'-). he's
putting on the roof:
sx̣ál'txʷitn (√x̣ál'-).

room: .stlEnawa´lus FBa.

rooster: likʷóˑk.

root: q̇ʷí⁴p (*pl.* q̇ʷí⁴apumx)
(√q̇ʷí⁴ap-). root *sp.*: qaˑ´ls
MJb-mi. root *sp.*: sət'x̣ʷs.
root *sp.*: ts'íˑx̣p JH
(*c'íx̣p). bracken roots:
wə̌č'ál; st͡sak EC
(√cáqa-). cedar roots
(dried and prepared):
taq'íx̣n', taq'éx̣n. cedar
roots, cedar: c'ápx̣
(√c'ápax̣-).

root digger: lā´omEn FBa

(√ləw–). handle of a root digger: sau´xakɛn FBa; wəpa´ls TA.

root up root up, dig up: p'alək̓ʷn (√p'ələ́k̓ʷ–).

rope: t'amíɬn (*pl.* t'amíɬinumx) (√t'amiɬə́n–).

rosebush: .stcai´tcil FBa; xontu´lɛms FBa.

rotten rotten, open sore: c'áqɬ (√c'áqa–). rotten wood: p'íq̓ʷluʔ.

rough rough ground, trash, garbage: x̣ašáytmx (√x̣ə́š–).

round: yəló·x̣ʷm' (√yəlúx̣ʷ–). round, coil: yúlux̣ʷɬ (√yúlux̣ʷ–). round, spherical, around: ʔacx̣ʷúlupɬ (√x̣ʷúlup–). round object, ball: milúx̣ʷl's (√milúx̣ʷ–).

row (*n.*) row, road: xə́wɬ, xúwɬ (*pl.* xúwiɬumx) (√xəwál–).

row (*v.*) row, paddle: ʔátqʷɬ (√ʔátqʷil–).

rub rub, scrape, crumple: cíkɬ (√cíki–).

rubber: qi t stúɬtɬwn (√túɬi–).

rug rug, woven tule mat: sɬáx̣tn' (√ɬáx̣–).

ruin ruin, harm: x̣ášilix (√x̣ə́š–). ruin, wreck: c'aɬə́qɬ (√c'aɬə́q–).

run run (*sg.*): wə́q'ɬ (√wə́q'a–). run (*pl.*), travel: ʔáx̣ʷɬ (√ʔáx̣ʷa–). run after: wə́q'tas (√wə́q'a–). run around swinging her tail (of women or fish): yátipsm (√yát–). run away, get away: ɬə́x̣ʷm (√ɬə́x̣ʷa–). run away from: ɬə́x̣ʷamn (√ɬə́x̣ʷa–). run into, bump: tə́pn (√tə́p–). running over, boiling over: sq̓ʷát'awn (√q̓ʷát'a–). it's galloping: sʔá·x̣ʷk̓ʷumitn (√ʔáx̣ʷa–).

S

sack sack, bag, pocket: lisák (*pl.* lisakáwmx).

sad: ʔacɬə́k'amcx (√ɬə́k'a–). sad, feel bad, sorry, be too bad: ʔacɬə́k'amn (√ɬə́k'a–).

saddle: xay'álumn (√xay'álu–). saddle blanket: lapišmú.

sailboat: ʔacsílxtani t wíɬ (√síl–).

salalberry: k'léh; t'áqaʔ. salal bushes: k'líhan'ɬ (√k'léh–).

saliva: ka´n‑ɫɫaɫ FBa
(√qalíʔ‑ ?).

salmon blueback salmon:
q̓ʷé·x̣aʔičn (√q̓ʷíx̣‑).
Chinook salmon: c’áwɫ.
Chinook salmon ENM:
sálwax̌ʷ. dog salmon:
ƛ̓x̌ʷáy’; .snū´nux̣ FBa;
pu‑natch GGa,UWa. dried
salmon: .shapau´ɫiɫEn FBa
(√x̣ə́pa‑). humpback
salmon: hwanē´kᵘ FBa. red
salmon: k̓ʷaléʔ. silver
salmon, silverside: sɑ́nux̣
JH (*sə́nx̌ʷ). silver salmon,
sockeye, humpback: sč’ín’
(√č’ín’‑).

salmonberry: yə́tawaʔ.

salmon eggs salmon eggs,
roe: q̓ʷə́ɫx̣aʔ.

salt: qwáx̌ HH. salt (*tr.*):
sásultn (√sáʔa‑, √súlt‑).
salt water: súltɫ (√súlt‑).
salty: sálti.

same at the same time, when:
pax̌ʷán’x̣. the same, thus:
q’íc’x̣.

sand: c’ax̣íl’s (√c’ax̣‑).

satisfied: ʔacƛ̓aq̓ʷín’wax
(√ƛ̓áq̓ʷ‑).

Saturday: pənskʷítim’ɫ
(√pən‑, √kʷíti‑).

saucer: sása (*pl.*
sásayum’x).

save save, store, put away,
put aside: t’óʔn (√t’óʔi‑).
save, take care of: ʔúlx̣n
(√ʔúlx̣‑).

say: cút (√cún‑); cút’x̣.
what did you say?: ʔit ʔínut
kʷu k (√ʔínut‑).

scales (of fish) its scales
(fish): qi ʔaɫck̓ʷəpičə́ni
(√k̓ʷə́p‑).

scalp: mā´tEnaɫEn FBa.

scar: ʔacp’íq’ɫ (√p’íq’‑).
scar on the face:
ʔacp’íq’ay’s (√p’íq’‑).

scare scare, insult: qʷané·n
(√qʷán‑). scaring away,
herding: swə́ltn (√wə́l‑).

scarf scarf, handkerchief:
x̌ʷík̓ʷɫn’ (√x̌ʷík̓ʷ‑).

scary scary, shy (of a horse):
wálɫ (√wálaʔ‑).

scatter: tícɫ (√tíci‑); č’íɫn
(√č’íɫ‑). scatter, spread
out, distribute: píɫn
(√píɫi‑).

school: póʔtpipal’uʔɫ
(√púti‑, √pípa‑).
schoolhouse: sku´lhau´s
FBa.

scissors: k’anáp’ (*pl.*
k’ánap’umx).

scold scold, get after, quarrel
with: taq̓ʷín (√tə́q̓ʷa‑).

scout: .sleswa´l FBa.

scrape scrape, rub, crumple:
cíkɫ (√cíki‑). scrape hair
off: x̌ʷáq̓ʷn (√x̌ʷáq̓ʷa‑).
scraper: x̌ʷáq̓ʷam’ɫtn’
(√x̌ʷáq̓ʷa‑). scraping a
hide: sx̌ʷáq̓ʷmln
(√x̌ʷáq̓ʷa‑).

scratch: sax̣ə́pɫ (√sə́x̣əp‑);

q̓ʷíɬn (√q̓ʷíɬi-). scratch
oneself: q̓ʷíɬicx (√q̓ʷíɬi-).
scratched on the back:
sáx̣kn (√sáx̣-).

scream: t'ə́lx̣cx (√t'ə́lx̣-).
he's screaming:
st'ə́lt'lx̣cšitn (√t'ə́lx̣-).

scum scum, foam (on
something being cooked):
páyɬkʷu (√páy-).

sea gull: kwê´nnts FBa.

seal: míwt. hair seal, fur seal:
tcɛlī´cɛn FBa; ki´pixLEɬ
FBa.

sea lion: li-íls EC.

sea otter: p̓itqh̄l EC.

season using it for medicine
or seasoning: sáʔayuʔtn
(√sáʔa-, √ʔayóʔ-).

see see, look, look at: ʔə́x̣n
(√ʔə́x̣-). see, look at,
watch, stare: ʔé·x̣n
(√ʔə́x̣-). come to see, go to
see: ƛ̓aswáln (√ƛ̓aswáli-).
his seeing: sə́x̣amli
(√ʔə́x̣-).

seeds: sx̣álam'ɬtn'
(√x̣ála-).

seem it seems that way:
kənq'íc'x̣ (√kən-,
√q'íc'x̣-).

seep seep up, drain, wring
out: múc'n (√múc'-).

sell: táx̣ʷiwi
(√táx̣ʷayway-). sell to:
táx̣ʷiwayəx
(√táx̣ʷayway-). selling:
stáx̣ʷiyustaln

(√táx̣ʷayway-).

send send, throw, throw
away, dump: k'ə́ɬn
(√k'ə́ɬ-). send to: ʔúpax̣n
(√ʔúpax̣-); k'ə́ɬšn
(√k'ə́ɬ-). send word to,
listen to, obey: taláynmn
(√tal-). she sent me: ʔíyc
(√ʔíy-).

separate separate, divide,
share: kʷaɬál'wax
(√kʷə́ɬ-). separate, part
hair: k̓ʷáy'smn
(√k̓ʷáy'us-). separate from
something: ɬə́lcx (√ɬə́la-).

September: ʔáqa
tasyə́q'awn (√yáq'a-).

serious: ʔactx̣ʷláx
(√wálaʔ-). he looks
serious: ʔə́x̣ʷɬ t sə́x̣tm
(√ʔə́x̣ʷ-, √ʔə́x̣-).

serve serve, dish up:
c'awúqs (√c'áw-).

serviceberry: kî´s.x FBa;
q̓ʷál'x̣ʷ (?). serviceberry
bush: kɑsá·x̣ɑn'ɬ JH.

set set, harden, freeze: q'áx̣ʷɬ
(√q'áx̣ʷa-). set a table:
x̣á·l'n (√x̣ál'-). set over a
fire, sit straight, roast: cə́qɬ
(√cə́q-). set up: ʔícx̣ʷmix
(√ʔícax̣ʷmi-). set upright,
straight up: c'úq̓ʷɬ
(√c'úq̓ʷ-). setting up for:
sc'úq̓ʷšitn (√c'úq̓ʷ-).

settle down: káwiq̓ʷ
(√káw-, √yə́q̓ʷ-).

seven: c'óps. seventeen:

pánačš kl t c'óps;
tálc'ops. seventy:
c'óps⁴tumx (√c'óps-).

several several others, how
many?: k̓ináwmx k̓ʷu
(√k̓ʷí-).

sew sewed together:
canál'wax (√cána-).
sewing, mending, pushing
through: scánatn
(√cána-).

shade shade, shadow:
stáqtmx (√táqtmix-).
shadow: .nkêkai´axa FBa.

shake: laləq⁴ (√lələqa-).
shake hands, lead by the
hand: k̓ʷəntáčic
(√k̓ʷəná-). shake one's fist
at, threaten: yamóʔsn
(√yamóʔsi-). shake one's
head: yátlusm (√yát-).
shake out, brush off, thresh:
t'əx̌ʷn (√t'əx̌ʷ-). shake
up, mix, stir: mat'ək̓ʷ⁴
(√mət'ək̓ʷ-). shaking:
syáx̌ʷawn (√yáx̌ʷa-).
shaking, shivering:
sk'ənmtn (√k'ən-).
shaking off: s⁴əpcšitn
(√⁴əp-).

shallow: lém'.

share share, divide, separate:
k̓ʷa⁴ál'wax (√k̓ʷə⁴-).
won't share, stingy:
x̌ʷíyx̌ʷiy.

sharp: ⁴ək'. sharp-pointed:
c'aməx̌ʷ⁴ (√c'əməx̌ʷ-).

sharpen: ⁴ák'ilix (√⁴ək'-).

sharpen, file: mátn
(√máta-). sharpener,
grinding-stone:
mátam'⁴tn' (√máta-).

shave: x̌ʷáq̓ʷsč'pqsm
(√x̌ʷáq̓ʷa-, √č'ípqas-).

shawl: lišál (*pl.* lišaláwmx).
have a shawl on: ʔaclišál
(√lišál-).

she she, he, him, her, it: cə́ni.

sheep: limitú; .sta´k'ºts.
mutton: síp⁴c'iʔ (√šíp-).
wool: limitúhalaqn
(√limitú-).

shell shell, shells, bullet,
bullets, gunpowder: sí⁴.

shelter temporary shelter:
ʔacyaláq̓ʷx̌ʷ
(√yaláq̓ʷx̌ʷ-); sq'iyúx̌ʷ
(√q'iyúx̌ʷ-).

shield: la´p.hwaxɛn FBa his
shield: ʔact'əlpx̌ʷtani
(√t'ələp-).

shine: p'áx̌⁴ (√p'áx̌a-).
shine, bright, light:
q'éx̌m'⁴ (√q'íx̌-). shining,
polishing: swəlk'mtn
(√wəlk'-).

shirt: k'ál'xcxtn'
(√k'ál'ax-). shirt of
dressed skin:
weiaxka´lɛxɛkstɛn FBa
(√wayəx̌-, √k'ál'ax-).

shiver shivering, shaking:
sk'ənmtn (√k'ən-).

shoe, shoes: cá⁴šn
(√ca⁴xán-).

shoot shoot an arrow, sting,

squirt: ʔíɬpn (√ʔíɬp-).
shoot with a gun, explode,
blow up: taqʷə́čɬ
(√təqʷə́či-). shooting at
targets: smé·ƛ̓tn,
smə́ƛ̓məƛ̓cšitn (√mə́ƛ̓a-).
he's shooting (at) it:
stéqʷtqʷčamaln,
stə́qʷtqʷčitn (√təqʷə́či-).
short: tóm'ɬ. supply gets
short: xáculx (?).
shoulder: q'ímn
(√q'ímin-). shoulder
blade, upper arm: q'ím'axn
(?) (√q'ímin-).
shout shout, holler, call:
táltalaqp (√tál-). shout,
yell, holler, call: tálaqp
(√tál-).
show: cíx̣tuxʷt, cíx̣šn
(√cíx̣i-). showing it:
scíx̣itn (√cíx̣i-).
shrink shrink, shrivel, cramp:
ɬúmɬ (√ɬúma-).
shrivel shrivel, shrink, cramp:
ɬúmɬ (√ɬúma-).
shut shut, close: tə́qɬ
(√tə́q-). shut up, get quiet,
quiet: ʔacx̣ʷayó·ɬq
(√x̣ʷáya-).
shy shy (a horse), scary: wálɬ
(√wála?-).
sibling older sibling: x̣ʷáɬ,
x̣ʷá?ɬ (pl. nxx̣ʷá?ɬtn)
(√x̣ʷál-).
sick: ʔáy's; síwi?s (√síw-,
√ʔáy's-). sicken: ɬák'ilix
(√ɬə́k'a-). become very

sick: x̣ʷél'l'. get sick:
ʔáy'sawm.
side his side: sxamyúpi
(√xamyúp-). his side, his
hip: x̣ʷay'úpi
(√x̣ʷay'úp-). on this side:
ʔaɬníx (√níx-). other side:
x̣ʷán'.
sign he signed for me:
q̓ʷaɬé?sc (√q̓ʷəɬé-).
signal (v.): t'aním'šn
(√t'aními-). a signal:
st'aním'šictx (√t'aními-).
give hand signals:
t'anémakašn (√t'aními-).
silly act silly, giggle, waste
time: c'íykʷcx (√c'íykʷ-).
silver: ʔaksq'éx̣m'ɬ
(√q'íx̣-); yúx̣ʷctx (?);
.tsko´ke tse´ux̣we FBa
(√q'úx̣ʷ-, √yáyx̣ʷi-).
silver salmon, silverside:
sɑ́nux̣ JH (*sə́nx̣ʷ). silver
salmon, sockeye,
humpback: sč'ín'
(√č'ín'-).
sin: sk̓ʷánan (√k̓ʷánan-).
sinew sinew, muscle: tínx
(√tínix-).
sing: ʔíln (√ʔílani-). sing
for: ʔíln'šn (√ʔílani-). sing
to: ʔílanix (√ʔílani-).
doctor sings, sing a lullaby:
stúlm'ɬ (√túl-). singing
for a patient: syél.pà·wə̀n
JH (*syə́lpawn).
single single, bachelor:
ʔó·c'uc's (√ʔúc's-).

sink: nə́k⁴ (√nə́ka–). sink,
drown: k'ə́⁴ (√k'ə́⁴a–).
sinker: t'é?qam'⁴tn' ENM
(√t'íqi–); nê´.kam.⁴tɛn
FBa (√nə́ka–).

sister older sister: c x̣ʷá⁴, c
x̣ʷá?⁴ (*pl.* nxx̣ʷá?⁴tn)
(√x̣ʷál–). younger sister:
pé·sn' (*pl.* nxpasén'tn)
(√pəsén'–).

sit sit, squat: tawélx
(√tawílax–). sit down:
tawílx (√tawílax–). sit
straight, set over a fire,
roast: cə́q⁴ (√cə́q–). be sat
on: tawíllsm (√tawílax–).
be sitting: ?actawélx
(√tawílax–).

six: t'ax̣ə́m (√t'əx̣ə́m–).
sixteen: pánačš kl t
t'ax̣ə́m; tál't'x̣m
(√t'əx̣ə́m–). sixty:
t'əx̣m⁴tumx (√t'əx̣ə́m–).

size its size, its bigness:
staw'ə́ti (√taw'ə́t–).

skim skimming off: syáwatn
(√yáwa–).

skin (*n.*): q̓ʷalít'k'n'
(√q̓ʷalit'–). skin, hide:
ƛ̓a?ílk⁴ (√ƛ̓ə?ílkl–). skin
dresser, skin softener:
tla´mhepɛ⁴ɛxtɛn FBa
(√ƛ̓əmə́x̣–); .stu´ps FBa.
deerskin (tanned): wayə́x̣.
deerskin with hair still on it:
taysx̣ʷáq̓ʷ (√táy–,
√x̣ʷáq̓ʷa–). its skin:
c⁴kə́ni (√c⁴kə́n–).

skin (*v.*) skin, dress game:
súk̓ʷn (√súk̓ʷi–).

skinny skinny, thin, bony:
yák̓ʷ⁴ (√yák̓ʷa–).

skirt: kík̓ʷəlik̓ʷut.

skunk: smáyn' (*pl.*
smáyan'umx)
(√máyan–). little skunks:
smá·y'an'umx
(√máyan–). skunk smell:
máyn'sqm (√máyan–).

skunk cabbage: *q̓ílt
(ka´ilet).

sky sky, cloud, clouds:
c⁴tálaxʷ.

slap: t'q'x̣ʷásn (√t'ə́q'x̣ʷ–).
slap, spank, paddle:
t'ə́q'x̣ʷn (√t'ə́q'x̣ʷ–). he
kept slapping himself: ?it
t'ə́q't'q'x̣ʷcx (√t'ə́q'x̣ʷ–).

slave: syəlqín? (√yəlqiní?–);
súlx̣ (√?úlx̣–). Thunder's
slaves: lpɛ´?sa TA.

sleep sleep, asleep: músm
(√músami–). sleepy:
k'ayáč⁴ (√k'ayáč–).
sleepyhead: mósmalaka
(√músami–). arm went to
sleep: c'ík̓ʷaka (√c'ík̓ʷ–).
leg went to sleep: c'ík̓ʷšn
(√c'ík̓ʷ–). Are you asleep
yet?: watci·´·´·x̣ᵘtci·´·x̣ᵘ
qa´winactp'ə´n MJb-mi.

slick: ⁴ilíq'.

slim: q'é·ma⁴ (√q'ém'⁴–).

slip: ⁴íq'ayq (√⁴íq'i–). slip,
slide: ⁴íq'⁴ (√⁴íq'i–).

slope: ʔactáʔɬ (√táʔ–).

slowly: qʷamá·l'm.

small small, little, a little bit: k'é·c.

smart: ʔacp'é·x̣ɬ (√p'ə́x̣–). smart, famous, lucky: swə́tt (√wə́tt–). smart, wise, know better: ʔacp'ə́x̣ɬ (√p'ə́x̣–).

smash smash, break to pieces, grind, mash: q̓ʷíc'n (√q̓ʷíc'i–).

smear smear, paint: q'áx̣ɬ (√q'áx̣a–).

smell smell through the nose: qíwnas (√qíwa–). smelling: sqíwaln (√qíwa–). smelling a track, tracking an animal: sqíwxann (√qíwa–). a good smell: ʔayásqm (√ʔí·–).

smelt: qwɑ́lɑstì' JH (*qʷáləstiʔ).

smile: ʔacláʔx̣ʷ (√láx̣ʷa–).

smoke: q̓ʷúx̣ʷm (√q̓ʷúx̣ʷ–). smoke (*n.*), gunpowder: sq̓ʷúx̣ʷ (√q̓ʷúx̣ʷ–). smoke a hide: pəx̣ʷə́mipn (√púx̣ʷi–). smoked on the face: púx̣ʷisitm (√púx̣ʷi–). being bothered by smoke: sq̓ʷúx̣ʷiqstn (√q̓ʷúx̣ʷ–). suck in smoke: q̓ʷúx̣ʷayqs (√q̓ʷúx̣ʷ–).

smoke tobacco: q̓ʷalímɬ (√q̓ʷalí–).

smooth smooth, level: ʔacwaláq'ɬ (√waláq'–).

smooth (water), still air: ʔacqə́m'ɬ (√qə́m'–).

getting smooth and polished: sʔáyltawn (√ʔáyl–).

smother smother, be out of breath: c'ə́klx̣ʷk̓ʷuʔ (√c'ə́ka–, √láx̣ʷk̓ʷu–).

snail, snails: č'amúyq'aʔ.

snake: sík'lxayuʔ (*pl.* sík'lxayumx). rattlesnake: wɛl'kai´ FBa.

sneak sneak up on: ʔálaln (√ʔálal–).

sneeze: ʔáwəlqs.

snipe: swa´nxaxa FBa; wî´tuwit FBa.

snore: x̣ʷilúqqsm (√x̣ʷilúq–).

snot: t'ə́pqs (√t'əpqə́s–).

snow (*n.*): sɬáq̓ʷ (√ɬáq̓ʷ–). it's snowing: sʔáxaqn (√ʔáxaq–). snowcap: ʔacx̣ə́qsx̣ʷáy's (√x̣ə́q–, √x̣ʷay'ús–).

snowbird: Spi´tsx̣ᵘ TA (√pícx̣ʷ–).

so: q̓ʷə́ɬ; x̣ə́ɬ. so, so that, for the reason that, because: cu. so that ENM: k̓ʷaɬ. so that, and LNJ: k̓ʷaɬ. so that, in order to: takaɬ. so that, instead, and: qa.

soak: t'íqn (√t'íqi–). soaking it: sc'únitn (√c'úni–). something soaked: t'éqam'ɬtn'

(√t'íqi-).

soap: c'áx̣ʷam'ⱡtn' (√c'áx̣ʷa-).

soft soft (like cloth): q'ə́p. soft, easy to tear: lé?q. soft (more than lé?q): walə́x̣. soften: léˑ?qilix (√lé?q-).

sole sole of the foot, big toe LNJ, toenail: papáyšn (?) (√pap-).

some some, other: sə́k̉ʷⱡ. someone, who: wá. someone, who is he?: wá ak̉ʷu. someone else: wá?o, wá?o ?ə́x̣ʷⱡ (√wá-); ?iwát. something else: tám?o ?ə́x̣ʷⱡ (√tám-); tántan (√tán-). somewhat, a little: k̉ʷac. somewhere, everywhere: ?ikán. somewhere else: ká?o (√káˑ-).

son son, daughter: mán? (pl. nx̣mán?tn) (√maní?-).

song: sēˊlEn FBa (√?ílani-).

soon soon, almost, a little while, a little bit, well: q̉ʷóˑcan (√q̉ʷó?c-). soon, fast, hurry, right away: ƛ̉ə́x̣ƛ̉ax̣ⱡ (√ƛ̉ə́x̣-). soon, fast, quick: ƛ̉ə́x̣ⱡ (√ƛ̉ə́x̣-).

soot: kwoˊxElotsEn FBa (√q̉ʷúx̣ʷ-).

sore sore, hurt: ⱡə́k' (√ⱡə́k'a-). sore, hurt, ache, wound: tákⱡk' (√ták-, √ⱡə́k'a-). a sore: sc'áq (√c'áqa-). open sore:

?acc'áqⱡ (√c'áqa-). open sore, rotten: c'áqⱡ (√c'áqa-).

sorrel: ?aksqʷə́s (√qʷə́s-); kupāˊks kwîˊs FBa (√k̉ʷə́p-, √qʷə́s-).

sorry sorry, sad, feel bad, be too bad: ?acⱡə́k'amn (√ⱡə́k'a-). be sorry for, pity: ?úšamn (√?úšam-).

sort sort, make a choice: yə́x̣n (√yə́x̣-). sort out, loosen, untangle: ⱡiwál'wax (√ⱡíw-).

soul soul, life: sníⱡtn (√níⱡi-).

soup soup, broth: qiy'áluqʷs (√qiy'áluqʷas-). soup, gravy: lakamín. soup, stew: lasúp.

south south, down country: tul-kaˊlEx FBa.

sow sow, plant: x̣áln (√x̣ála-).

Spaniard Spaniard; cayuse (horse): spalyán.

spank: t'ə́q'x̣ʷnkn (√t'ə́q'x̣ʷ-). spank, slap, paddle: t'ə́q'x̣ʷn (√t'ə́q'x̣ʷ-).

spark spark, crackling: sƛ̉ə́lqʷmtn (√ƛ̉ə́lqʷ-). sparks from a fire, live coals: táqʷn'ⱡkʷp (√táqʷn'ⱡ-).

spawn: máˑnam (√máˑna-).

spear: ƛ̉ámx̣amⱡtn'

(√ƛ'əmə̀x̣-). fish spear:
sác'uʔ; c'áx̣čn';
wutseˊs.ks FBa. Spear
Boy: sɑˊx̣kən TA. war
spear: skwoiˊtlEm FBa.

speech speech, language,
word: stə̀q̓ʷ (√tə̀q̓ʷa-).

spend spend all one's money:
c'ə́ktal'a (√c'ə́ka-,
√tála-).

spherical spherical, round,
around: ʔacx̣ʷúlupɬ
(√x̣ʷúlup-).

spider, spiders: túpn', túpl'
(√túpan'-). a kind of
spider that runs on top of
the water: L'ɛˊʔq'ku TA
(√ƛ'éʔq-).

spill spill, pour out: pə́q̓ʷɬ
(√pə́q̓ʷa-).

spin spin, turn: c'alə́pn
(√c'ələ̀p-). spin, twist,
double up: yalə́k'n
(√yələ́k'-).

spinster: taiˊ.sxEnlêmEn FBa
(√táy-, √x̣ə̀n-).

spirit (ghost): mu-ku-tá-u-
mŭh EC (√mak̓ʷə́t-). spirit
creature: stú-lĭ-mĭ̄hl EC.

spirit power: sə́x̣tkʷlx
(√ʔə́x̣t-).

spit: tə́x̣ʷskʷu (√tə́x̣ʷs-).

splash splashing on: st'ícšitn
(√t'íc-). it's splashing:
st'íccwn (√t'íc-).

splice splice, put together:
t'əlpál'wax (√t'ələ̀p-).
splicing, putting end to end:

sp'át'atn (√p'át'a-).

split split, crack: kʷatə́qɬ
(√kʷətə́q-). split wood:
c'uk̓ʷáyk̓ʷp (√c'uk̓ʷ-);
kʷɬq̓ʷáy'k̓ʷp (√kʷətə́q-).
splitting: spə́ɬqawn
(√pə́ɬqa-);
skʷə́ɬkʷɬqawn
(√kʷətə́q-). its splitting:
sə́k'i (√sə̀k'-).

spoil spoil, get bad: x̣ášlx
(√x̣ə̀š-).

spoon: ƛ̓úqʷam'ɬtn' LNJ
(√ƛ̓úqʷi-); ɬâˊmEn FBa;
spún (*pl.* spunáwm'x).

spots: ʔacq̓ʷéʔɬ (√q̓ʷəɬé-).
spots, design, something
written: ʔacq̓ʷə́ɬ
(√q̓ʷəɬé-). spotted horse:
likáy. spotted rock:
ʔacq̓ʷaɬíl's (√q̓ʷəɬé-).

sprain: p'asə́q̓ʷn
(√p'asə́q̓ʷ-).

spray spray, sprinkle: p'íc'šn
(√p'íc'-).

spread spread flat, lie flat:
táɬɬ (√táɬ-). spread out,
scatter, distribute: píɬn
(√píɬi-). spread to dry:
x̣apúl'mxn (√x̣əpa-).
spreading out, opening,
blooming, stretching:
swə́ɬqawn (√wəɬə́qa-).

spring (of water): plə́q̓ʷ
(√palə́q̓ʷ-). water coming
from a spring, creek: cápx;
cátxʷ (√cátaxʷ-).

spring, springtime:

sx̣aqámltn,x̣ʼaqámʼil⁺,
pənx̣ʼaqámʼ (√x̣ʼaqámʼ-,
√pən-).

sprinkle sprinkle, spray:
pʼícʼšn (√pʼícʼ-).

spruce: kʼʷuxʷá⁺; tsakaʹ⁺
FBa (√caqʷáʔ⁺-). spruce,
(thistle?) LNJ: təmánʼanʼ⁺
(√təmánʼa-).

spurs: taʹpxᴇnᴇmᴇn FBa.

square square, straight line:
tʼanémimʼ⁺tnʼ
(√tʼaními-).

squat squat, sit: tawélx
(√tawílax-).

squeak: cʼíkm (√cʼík-).
squeak, hear noise, echo:
ʔímnmʼ (√ʔímn-).

squeal squeal, whine:
čʼíqčʼqm (√čʼíq-).

squeeze: x̣ə́q̇ʷn (√x̣ə́q̇ʷ-);
kʼanə́pʼn (√kʼanə́pʼ-).
squeeze, pinch: cʼayə́pʼn
(√cʼəyə́pʼ-). squeeze out,
pull out: txʷ⁺ax̣ʷə́cʼn
(√⁺ax̣ʷə́cʼ-). squeeze
through, climb through,
detour: ⁺úmicx (√⁺úmi-).
squeezing: sx̣ə́q̇ʷlkmisn
(√x̣ə́q̇ʷ-).

squint squint, wink: he
winked at me: ʔit cʼéʹplsic
(√cʼíp-).

squirrel: spə́nč (√pə́nč-).
flying squirrel: ⁺a⁺iʹkʼpc
MJb-mi. ground squirrel:
pūʹtᴇpt FBa.

squirrel-tail squirrel-tail,

yarrow: skʷəyóhips.

squirt: ʔí⁺ptanix (√ʔí⁺p-).
squirt, sting, shoot an
arrow: ʔí⁺pn (√ʔí⁺p-).

stab: tawáksn (√tawáksi-).

stain (*n*.): ʔacpə́x̣ʷ
(√pə́x̣ʷ-). stain a cloth:
šə́q⁺ (√šə́q-).

stairs stairs, steps, stirrups:
cʼéʹq̇ʷamʼ⁺tnʼ (√cʼíq̇ʷa-).
stairway: cʼéʹq̇ʷamnʼ
(√cʼíq̇ʷa-). stairway,
ladder: wéʹtʼatnʼ
(√wítʼi-).

stakes their stakes, their pot,
what they gamble:
sx̣álʼxʷili (√x̣álʼxʷil-).

stallion: atsᴇmaʹtcᴇn
.stᴇkeʹu FBa (√máčn-,
√tiqíw-).

stand: ʔéʹcaxʷm
(√ʔícaxʷmi-). stand up:
ʔícaxʷm (√ʔícaxʷmi-).
stand up (*tr*.): kʼʷəpálʼwax
(√kʼʷə́p-).

star, stars: kási?; txlatçílis
HH.

stare stare, see, look at,
watch: ʔéʹx̣n (√ʔə́x̣-).
stare, stare at, look at
something strange:
mayáʹlʼux (√may-). stare,
surprise, confuse: txʷálaʔx
(√wálaʔ-). stare at:
ʔactxʷláʔxšn (√wálaʔ-).

start start, begin: tóʹlʼp
(√tólap-). start (the
bottom of) a basket, basket

hoops: stúlnk (√túl-).

startle startled, surprised: txʷšak̓ʷíy'stn (√šək̓ʷíy'-).

starve: táksx̣ʷqʷ (√ták-, √x̣ʷəqʷa-). starve, hungry: x̣ʷəqʷɬ (√x̣ʷəqʷa-).

stay stay, act like: wínwnx̣ (√wín-). stay, live, have: wéˑx̣ (√wéˑ-x̣-). stay home, be home: ʔáɬxx (√ʔaɬ-, √x̣áx-). staying, living, residing, becoming: swínn (√wín-). they stayed, they became: wináwm'x̣ (√wín-).

steal: ʔík̓ʷtq (√ʔík̓ʷtaq-).

steamboat: paiˊcîp FBa.

steelhead: sk'αwἀw JH.

steep: ʔacx̣ʷací?ɬ (√x̣ʷací?-).

step (v.) step, take a step, walk: yə́q̓ʷpataqm (√yə́q̓ʷ-, √pátaq-). step on: c'íq̓ʷn (√c'íq̓ʷa-).

step-relative stepchild: tcɛlmîˊnam FBa (√ču̓ɬ-, √maní?-). stepfather: tcuɬmánɛm FBa (√ču̓ɬ-, √mán-). stepmother: tcuɬtánɛm FBa (√ču̓ɬ-, √tán-).

steps steps, bridge: tēˊutɛmɛn FBa (√tíwat-). steps, stairs, stirrups: c'éˑq̓ʷam'ɬtn' (√c'íq̓ʷa-).

stew stew, soup: lasúp.

stick (n.): súwl (?). stick, tree, pole, limb: λ̓əx̣λ̓x (pl. λ̓əx̣λ̓axumx) (√λ̓əx̣-).

stick game: lál, láln.

digging stick: tuləm.

roasting stick: tawaˊshweyə TA. small stick, bush: λ̓é?x̣λ̓x (pl. λ̓é?x̣λ̓axum'x) (√λ̓əx̣-).

stick (v.) stick, glue: λ̓íq'n (√λ̓íq'a-). stick in, get stuck: šúλ̓ɬ (√šúλ̓-). stick in, stick on: sə́c'n (√sə́c'-). stick in the throat, choke: k̓ʷuk̓ʷápsm (√k̓ʷuk̓ʷ-); qə́qɬ (√qə́qa-). stick into: k̓ʷík̓ʷn (√k̓ʷík̓ʷ-). stick it on him: sə́c'tuxʷt (√sə́c'-). stick out: ʔaccéˑx̣ɬ (√cíx̣i-). stick out of the ground: ʔacmáˑyusn (√máˑy-). stick out of the water: ʔacmáˑyičn (√máˑy-). stick together: λ̓iq'álus (√λ̓íq'a-). sticking out, coming to the surface: smáy'mi?smitn (√máˑy-).

Stick Indians: č'iátk̓ʷu.

sticky: λ̓iq'λ̓íq' (√λ̓íq'a-).

stiff stiff (leather) ENM: ʔaccəsúw'ɬ (√cəsúw'ɬ-). stiff (like leather): λ̓ə́x̣ʷip (√λ̓ə́x̣ʷ-). stiff, harden, in tight: λ̓áx̣ʷlx (√λ̓ə́x̣ʷ-). stiff, strong: c'ə́p. stiff, strong, hard, firm, tight: λ̓ə́x̣ʷ.

still still, calm:
ʔactxʷmén'stm
(√m'én'–). still air, smooth
(water): qə́m'ɬ (√qə́m'–).
be still, calm, not blowing:
ʔactxʷk̓ʷə́ctm (√k̓ʷə́c–).
hold still, quiet down, calm
down: ƛ̓él'cx (√ƛ̓ə́la–).

sting sting (bee): cítxʷ. sting
(nettles): it stung me:
qʷə́nc (√qʷə́na–). sting,
squirt, shoot an arrow:
ʔíɬpn (√ʔíɬp–).

stingy: syáyn (√yáy–).
stingy, won't share:
xʷíyxʷiy. stingy with food:
ʔacyáyɬx (√yáy–).

stir stir, mix: t'úyxʷn
(√t'úyxʷ–). stir, mix, shake
up: mat'ə́kʷɬ
(√mət'ə́kʷ–). stir, twist,
wind, turn, churn, wring
out: yát'n (√yát'a–).

stirrups: c'éˑq̓ʷam'ɬtn'
LNJ, kátc'iq̓ʷim'ɬtn' ENM
(√c'íq̓ʷa–).

stockings: stákn. stockings,
socks: qoˑ́pcEn FBa
(√qʷúpi–). Indian
stockings, leggings:
mətáˑs. make stockings:
sáʔstakn (√sáʔa–,
√stákn–).

stomach stomach, belly:
k̓ʷásn (√k̓ʷasə́n–). have a
stomachache:
ʔact'ak̓ʷénusitm
(√t'ə́k̓ʷ–). its stomach, its

insides: sácinwasi
(√sác–).

stone stone, rock, rocks:
spatáln (√patálan–);
t!ak!aˑ´ls FBb.

stoop stoop, bend over:
kə́m'ɬ (√kə́m–).

stop: ʔícxʷmix
(√ʔícaxʷmi–). stop, end,
finish: námn (√náma–).
stop, forbid: x̣íp'n
(√x̣íp'–). stop, quit:
ƛ̓ə́lacx (√ƛ̓ə́la–).

store (*n.*): táxʷayumn' LNJ,
táʔxʷimn' ENM
(√táxʷayway–).

store (*v.*) store, put away:
wétx (√wéta–). store, put
away, put aside, save: t'óʔn
(√t'óʔi–). storage place:
pənƛ̓íxuliɬn,qi
pənƛ̓íxuliɬn' (√pən–,
√ƛ̓íx–).

storm thunderstorm:
x̣ášlk̓ʷukʷɬ (√x̣ə́š–).

story story, news: syáy'ɬuɬ
(√yáy–). stories of old
times: sópt.

stove stove, heater:
x̣ʷál'k̓ʷpmn' (√x̣ʷál'a–).

straight straight, very, right,
correct, true, even: k̓ʷə́pɬ
(√k̓ʷə́p–). straight line,
square: t'anémim'ɬtn'
(√t'aními–). straight up,
set upright: c'úq̓ʷɬ
(√c'úq̓ʷ–). straighten:
k̓ʷə́pn (√k̓ʷə́p–).

straighten it out: k̓ʷə́pst
(√k̓ʷə́p-). straighten out,
change, clean (off),
polish,brush off: ʔayə́qɬ
(√ʔiyə́q-).

strain strain water out, drain:
pə́qʷqal'n (√pə́qʷa-,
√qalíʔ-).

strange strange, foreign,
different, other: ʔə́xʷɬ
(√ʔə́xʷ-). strange people:
ʔəxʷtálmx (√ʔə́xʷ-).

straw straw, hay, tall grass:
st'awál's (√t'awál's-).

strawberry: katísaʔ.

stretch stretch (*tr.*): túɬn
(√túɬi-). stretch oneself:
túɬicx (√túɬi-).
stretching, spreading out,
blooming, opening:
swə́ɬqawn (√wə́ɬəqa-).

strike strike, peck: it pecked
me: ɬə́k̓ʷc (√ɬə́k̓ʷ-).

string its string, line: macáli
(√macál-).

stripe striped horizontally:
tém'temm' (√tím'-).
striped vertically:
ʔacwáx̣ʷwax̣ʷɬ (√wáx̣ʷ-).

strong strong, hard, stiff,
firm, tight: λ̓ə́x̣ʷ. strong,
stiff: c'ə́p.

stubborn: ʔacmó·luk̓ʷɬ
(√mó·luk̓ʷ-). stubborn,
stupid, clumsy, dumb:
ʔayayáš.

stuck-up stuck-up, proud:
ʔaccépɬ (√cép-).

stumble: cúy'qsm
(√cúy'qs-).

stump stump, bottom: snə́wp
(√nəwáp-). stump pulled
over with roots sticking up:
ʔacp'ə́lk̓ʷip (√p'ələ́k̓ʷ-).

stupid stupid, dumb,
stubborn, clumsy: ʔayayáš.

sturgeon: c'íwq; sλ̓éʔqkʷu
(√λ̓éʔq-).

stutter: ʔnks +
čə́nčnqɬnaln (√čə́nq-).

suck suck, suck on: mút'n
(√mút'i-). suck in smoke:
q̓ʷúx̣ʷayqs (√q̓ʷúx̣ʷ-).

sucker (fish): sč'ə́qʷ
(√č'ə́qʷ-).

suet: ɬə́x̣ɬx̣tn (√ɬə́x̣-).

sugar: sū´ga FBa
(√šúk̓ʷa-). sugar bowl:
šó·k̓ʷumn (√šúk̓ʷa-).

suicide commit suicide, kill
oneself: yúcamicx
(√yúca-).

sulking: sméλ̓tn (√méλ̓-).

summer: pənmə́ɬk (√pən-,
√mə́ɬk-).

sun sun, moon, month:
ɬukʷáɬ. sunrise:
sɬə́x̣ʷl'awn tit ɬukʷáɬ
(√ɬə́x̣ʷl'a-); sputscíx̣iwn
tit ɬukʷáɬ (√pút-,
√cíx̣i-); tse´x̣ɬuk.ɬta´m
FBa (√cíx̣i-). sunset:
sx̣ə́pawn tit ɬukʷáɬ
(√x̣ə́pa-); kwî´ suɛnta´ne
FBa (√kʷə́s-).

sunburned: sčéʔxʷmaln

(√čéʔxʷ–).
Sunday: taw'ə́t sq'íx̣ (√q'íx̣–).
superlative *superlative degree*, most: t'ím.
supper: kʷə́smn (√kʷə́s–).
surface surface of earth, ground: tā´qᴇs ti'tî´mᴇɬ FBa. coming to surface, sticking out: smáy'miʔsmitn (√má·y–). it came to the surface and disappeared fast: ʔit txʷcíx̣stm (√cíx̣i–).
surprise surprise, confuse, stare: txʷálaʔx (√wálaʔ–). be surprised: ʔacmayá·l's (√may–). be surprised, be confused: ʔactxʷálʔstm (√wálaʔ–). be surprised, be startled: txʷšak̓ʷíy'stn (√šək̓ʷíy'–). be surprised at, suspect: mayá·l'smn (√may–).
suspect suspect, be surprised at: mayá·l'smn (√may–).
suspicious it looks suspicious: ʔaccó·n'x̣n q'íc'x̣ (√có·–).
swallow (*v.*): mə́q̓ʷm (√mə́q̓ʷa–).
swallow (bird): tsᴇle´tcᴇn FBa.
swamp swamp, meadow, pasture: spáɬx̣n (√páɬx̣an–).
swan: qʷúx̣ʷɬc'iʔ (√qʷúx̣ʷ–).
sway sway, swing back and forth: q'ayó·q̓ʷm (√q'ayúq̓ʷ–). swaying back and forth: sq'ə́lq'lp'awn (√q'ə́lp'a–).
sweat: x̣ʷə́l'ɬ (√x̣ʷə́l'a–). sweat bath: spúxʷcšis t sʔé·tiln (√púxʷ–, √ʔé·til–). sweathouse: sq̓ʷə́mx (√q̓ʷə́mx–); qā´.tᴇn FBa (*qá·ʔtn).
sweep: xʷákʷltm (√xʷákʷa–). sweep, clear off: xʷákʷɬ (√xʷákʷa–).
sweet: q'ə́ɬ.
swell swell up: púsɬ (√púsa–). a swelling: spús (√púsa–). face is swollen: ʔacpúsay's (√púsa–).
swim swim, bathe: ʔé·tl' (√ʔé·til–). swim, wade, ford: kʷátɬ (√kʷáta–). fish swims: sə́k'm (√sə́k'–).
swing (*n.*) swing, cradle: q'ayúq̓ʷ. swing, hammock: kaiạ´kᵘomᴇn FBa (√q'ayúq̓ʷ–).
swing (*v.*) swing back and forth, sway: q'ayó·q̓ʷm (√q'ayúq̓ʷ–). swinging, going back and forth: syác'yəc'wn (√yác'–). swinging around: sp'ə́lp'əlk'šitn (√p'ələ́k'–). fish coming

table 203 **tan**

upstream swinging its tail; young person chasing around: sx̣ix̣í (√x̣í-). run

around swinging her tail (of women *or* fish): yátipsm (√yát-).

t

table: latám (*pl.* latámumx); sɬe'tsa´u FBa.
tablet tablet, book, pencil, pen: q̇ʷaɬém'ɬtn' (√q̇ʷəɬé-).
tail: súpsn'k (√súps-). bobtailed: táysupsnk (√táy-, √súps-).
take take, carry, take away, hold, get, grab, get married: kʷə́na, kʷə́nna (√kʷəná-). take, grab, hang on to, catch: skʷanátn (√kʷəná-). take a chance: məx̌ʼacx (√məx̌ʼa-). take back: yác'n (√yác'-). take care of, guard, protect, watch for...: x̌ʼaqʷséx̣n (√x̌ʼáqʷ-, √əx̣-). take care of, save: ʔúlx̣n (√ʔúlx̣-). take in, bring in: ɬəkstaqn (√ɬək-). take it away!: káʔxaʔ (√káʔ-); kʷə́nstaʔ (√kʷəná-). take land: kʷanátm'x (√kʷəná-). take off, take out, uncover: ɬíwx (√ɬíw-). take out, pop out: p'aləq̇ʷn (√p'ə
ləq̇ʷ-). take out, put out: x̌ʼaqəx̣ (√x̌ʼəqə́-). take with, take along, take to,

lead: ʔə́sɬ (√ʔəsúl-).
talk: təq̇ʷɬ (√təq̇ʷa-). talk (*pl.*), discuss, argue: nəx̣ʷm (√nəx̣ʷa-). talk about: təq̇ʷamn (√təq̇ʷa-). talk English: pástin'q, páʔstinq' (√pástin-). talk nonsense to, "BS" someone: ʔápsɬaniln (√ʔáps-). talk to: taq̇ʷəx̣ʷ (√təq̇ʷa-). talkative, talker: təq̇ʷalakaʔ (√təq̇ʷa-). talking: stəq̇ʷtq̇ʷn (√təq̇ʷa-). finish talking: x̣ám'stq̇ʷ (√x̣ám'-, √təq̇ʷa-). we're talking it over: stəq̇ʷmstawt (√təq̇ʷa-).
tall tall, long: x̌ʼáqɬ (√x̌ʼáq-).
tallow: yəmks (√yəmkə́s-). tallow, grease, lard, oil: k'axʷóʔ.
tamanous spirit power: səx̣tkʷlx (√ʔə́x̣t-).
tame: k'ápɬ (√k'ápa-).
tan tan a hide, work a hide: yacəqn (√yəcəq-). tanned deerskin: wayə́x̣. tanned hide: syacəqɬ (√yəcəq-). tanning: wáq̇ʷan'ɬ. tanning frame, bow, prop, temporary shelter: sq'iyúxʷ

(√q'iyúxʷ-). already
tanned: ʔacpəxʷəmip tani
(√púxʷi-).

tangle: múc⁴ (√múc-).

tap tap on: p'éʔn (√p'íʔi-).
tap on, touch: p'íʔn
(√p'íʔi-).

target shooting at targets:
smé·ƛ̓tn,məƛ̓məƛ̓cšitn
(√məƛ̓a-).

taste taste, try, test, guess:
məƛ̓n (√məƛ̓a-).

tattoo marks: sê´.ts'ᴱˣ FBa
(√səc'-).

teach teach, advise, interpret:
ʔúxʷanix (√ʔúxʷa-).
teacher: nks +
ʔúxʷn'mal'n (√ʔúxʷa-).
teaching, interpreting:
sʔúxʷnkʷawn (√ʔúxʷa-).

tear tear, rip: ca⁴əqʷ⁴
(√cə⁴əqʷ-). tear up:
cə⁴ca⁴aqʷn (√cə⁴əqʷ-).

tears tears (running down
face): sʔaxʷíl'qʷuʔ
(√ʔaxʷíl'-). tears coming
out of the eyes: číl'qʷuʔ
(√číl'-).

tease: ƛ̓áqn (√ƛ̓áq-).

telescope telescope,
eyeglasses, a glass:
ʔáxam'⁴tn' (√ʔəx-).

tell tell (*tr.*): cún. tell,
answer: cún'x (√cún-).
tell, tell on: yáyn (√yáy-).
tell him it: yáy'txʷt
(√yáy-). tell news, tell a
story: yáy'⁴u⁴ (√yáy-). tell

on: x̌íwx̌awq'n (√x̌íwq'-).
tell to: yáy'šn (√yáy-).
telling to: syáyay'šitn
(√yáy-). don't want to tell,
keep quiet, forbid:
káywi⁴ix (√káywi⁴i-).
she's always telling me
stories: ʔnks +
tyáy'yay'šic (√yáy-).

ten: pánačš (√pánaks-).

tent: silháws (√síl-). tent,
bark lodge:
sā´kotaxolwᴇ´⁴txᵘ FBa.

territory territory, country:
təw'áytmx təmx
(√taw'ət-).

test test, try, taste, guess:
məƛ̓n (√məƛ̓a-).

than than, from, off, out of: tl
ʔa⁴.

thank thank you:
náxʷ⁴qʷul'as.

that: titxt'íst, titxtá, titató
(√tit-); táx̣ (√tá-). that,
there: šíxn'x̣ (√šíxn'-).
that one: cacx̣cá (*feminine*)
(√cac-). that one (remote),
there: x̌ánʔ. that one, way
over there: titató (√tit-).
that's all: tu st'íx̣u
(√t'íx̣-). that's the kind:
q'éc'iʔx̣ (√q'íc'x̣-). that's
why: cicu (√cic-).

thaw thaw, melt, dissolve:
yəx̣ʷ⁴ (√yəx̣ʷa-).

their, theirs: scəniyáwmixa⁴
(√cəni-).

them them, they: cəniyáwmx

(√cə́ni-).

there: ɬáq̇ʷ; ʔaɬ xánʔ, xánʔx̣ (√xánʔ-); šíxn'. there, that: šíxn'x̣ (√šíxn'-). there, that one (remote): xánʔ. over there: x̣ʷux̣ʷúʔkʷm' (√x̣ʷúʔkʷ-). that one, way over there: titató (√tit-).

they they, them: cəniyáwmx (√cə́ni-). their, theirs: scəniyáwmixaɬ (√cə́ni-).

thick: pə́ɬ.

thief: ʔékʷtqlakaʔ (√ʔíkʷtaq-).

thimble: ʔáyakamn' (√ʔáy-).

thimbleberry: q̇ʷál'x̣ʷ (?).

thin: p'é·l'ɬ. thin, bony, skinny: yák̇ʷɬ (√yák̇ʷa-).

thing: ʔitám. thing, what?: tám. things: ʔitám'tn' (√ʔitám-).

think: k̇ʷənínusm (√k̇ʷə́na-); ʔaccó·n (√có·-). think, plan: có·t (√có·-).

thirsty: ʔacX̣áq'ɬkʷu (√X̣áq'-); cáqɬkʷu (√cáq-).

thirteen: pánačš kl t káʔɬiʔ; tál'kaʔɬiʔ.

thirty: kánxtumx (√kán-).

this this one: titatí, titx̣tí (√tit-). this one, right here, just: tíʔx̣, tíx̣ (√tíʔ-). this time: pəntíʔx̣ (√pən-, √tíʔ-). this way, this direction: xašém', xašém'x̣. this year: tíʔx̣ɬpanxʷ (√tíʔ-). on this side: ʔaɬníx̣ (√níx̣-).

thistle: təmán'an'ɬ (?) (√təmán'a-).

thread: mî´tsiɬ FBa (√macál-); .sqai´.ts FBa.

threaten threaten, be mad at: q̇ʷáx̣iqšn (√q̇ʷáx̣-). threaten, shake fist at: yamóʔsn (√yamóʔsi-).

three: káʔɬiʔ.

thresh: t'ə́x̣ʷinum (√t'ə́x̣ʷ-). thresh, shake out, brush off: t'ə́x̣ʷn (√t'ə́x̣ʷ-).

throat: məq̇ʷámn (√mə́q̇ʷa-).

through go through: yál' (?) (√yál'i-). go through, go across, cross, land (a canoe), reach shore: t'ánɬ (√t'aná-). squeeze through, climb through, detour: ɬúmicx (√ɬúmi-). through here: tašéʔ (√šéʔ-).

throw throw, throw away, send, dump: k'ə́ɬn (√k'ə́ɬ-). throw away (pl. obj.): ʔáx̣ʷn (√ʔáx̣ʷ-). throw it at: k'ə́ɬtuxʷt (√k'ə́ɬ-). throw over: yamə́t'n (√yamə́t'-). throw (them) in: k'ə́ɬk'ə́ɬn (√k'ə́ɬ-). throwing away, giving, potlatch: sʔáx̣ʷmtn'

(√ʔáx̣ʷ–). he threw me
down: nə̓c (√nə̓–).

thrush: pícx̣ʷ, spícx̣ʷ (?).

thumb thumb LNJ, palm ENM:
papáyakaʔ (√pap–).

thunder (*n*.): stúqʷ
(√túqʷ–). thunder (*v*.):
túqʷm (√túqʷ–).
thunderstorm: x̣ášlkʷukʷɬ
(√x̣ə̓š–). Thunder's slaves:
lpɛ´ʔsa TA.

Thursday: musalsq'íx̣
(√mús–, √q'íx̣–).

thus thus, the same: q'íc'x̣.

tickle: k'áyk'ayɬ (√k'áy–).

tide ebb tide: .sna´mai.x FBa
(√náma–). flood tide:
.slî´k.ks FBa (√lə́k'–).

tie: ɬə́mɬ (√ɬə́mi–). tie
around, wind around, arrest,
put in jail: t'ə́qn (√t'ə́qi–).
it was tied up, it was
caught: ɬamə́nitm
(√ɬə́mi–). something you
tie around: t'ə́qam'ɬtn'
(√t'ə́qi–).

tight tight, stiff, firm, hard,
strong: x̌'ə̣x̣ʷ. in tight, stiff,
harden: x̌'áx̣ʷlx (√x̌'ə̣x̣ʷ–).

time at the same time, when:
paxʷán'x̣. have a good
time, have fun: ʔáylx
(√ʔáy–). just in time: k̓ʷípɬ
(√k̓ʷə́p–). long time:
x̌'áqɬanaws, x̌'áqɬanawxs
(√x̌'áq–). long time, long
time ago: x̌'áqɬan'ɬ,
sx̌'áqɬnɬ (√x̌'áq–). this

time: pəntíʔx̣ (√pən–,
√tíʔ–). what time?, how
many?: k̓ʷí.

tip tip, tip over, fall: yáq'ɬ
(√yáq'a–). tip over, fall
out: kə́may'q (√kə́m–).

tire (*n*.) tire, wheel:
syə́l'kʷawn (√yələ́kʷ–).

tire (*v*.) tire of: x̣ʷə́namn
(√x̣ʷə́na–). tired, weak:
ʔacx̣ʷə́nɬ (√x̣ʷə́na–).

to: x; xaɬ, x̣ʔaɬ; taxaɬ. to,
in, into, on: ʔaɬ.

toad: tso´lswaia FBa.

tobacco: q̓ʷalémɬtn'
(√q̓ʷalí–).

today: ɬ tit sq'íx̣, ɬ tit
sq'éʔx̣ (√q'íx̣–);
tsa´mokxʷ FBa (√cám–).

toe, toes: laxaíîsx̣in HH. big
toe, toenail: papáyšn
(√pap–). end of toe; instep:
stál'iqšn (√tál'–). little
toe: c'əx̣ʷúy'nwn'šn
(√c'əx̣ʷúy'nwn'–);
papá·y'šn (√pap–).

toenail: c'ax̣ílšn (√c'ax̣íl–).
toenail, big toe: papáyšn
(√pap–).

together: t'əmx̣sáliʔ,
t'əmx̣sáliyumx (√t'əmx̣–,
√sáliʔ–); nàk̓ʷusx̣ʷúqʷ
(√nák'–, √x̣ʷúqʷa–).
together with: pə́s. together
with, gather, meet: x̣ʷúqʷɬ
(√x̣ʷúqʷa–). come
together, reach: ɬakál'us
(√ɬə́k–). coming together:

sx̌ʷuqʷálustn
(√x̌ʷúqʷa-). put together,
splice: t'əlpál'wax
(√t'ələp-). put together
side by side: ʔact'əlpál'us
(√t'ələp-).

tomorrow: q'ít; q'íx̌ʷus LNJ.
day after tomorrow:
tɛkɛ'ɬa´n FBa (√tk-,
√ɬán-).

tongue: tíx̌ʷcɬ (√tix̌ʷcəl-).

too: síw.

tools: yayó·satn'
(√yayús-).

tooth: yə́ns (*pl.* yə́nisumx)
(√yənís-).

top: x̌úk̓ʷičn, x̌úk̓ʷɬtumx,
x̌úk̓ʷm' (√x̌úk̓ʷ-). top a
tree: c'uk̓ʷáyqstn
(√c'uk̓ʷ-). top of a house:
x̌úk̓ʷlwltxʷ (√x̌úk̓ʷ-). top
of the head: skwo´kwols
FBa; spū´kɛls FBa.

torch torch, fire-drill: sílmix.
torch, light, candle:
q'éx̌am'ɬtn' (√q'íx̌-).

touch touch, tap on: p'íʔn
(√p'íʔi-). touching:
skʷanátawln (√kʷəná-).

town town, village: aíɨtkt-
x̌áx HH (√ʔáy'tak-,
√x̌áx-).

toy toy, doll: sx̌áɬx̌ʷam'n
(√x̌áɬx̌ʷa-).

track track (*tr.*): ʔácxann
(√ʔácxən-). a track (*n.*):
sqíwxn (√qíwa-). tracks:
pátq (√pátaq-). tracking

an animal, smelling a track:
sqíwxann (√qíwa-).

trade trade, exchange: ʔáy'šn
(√ʔáy-). trader: nks +
ʔáy'šitn (√ʔáy-). trade for:
ʔáyuk̓ʷ (√ʔáy-).

trail trail, path: xéw'ɬ
(√xəwál-).

train train horses: k'ápstiqiw
(√k'ápa-, √tiqíw-).

transformer: x̌ʷaní. x̌ʷani's
dog: Tci·´ləkᵘ TA.

transplant transplant, move a
rooted plant to another hole:
yə́k̓ʷiʔpn (√yə́k̓ʷa-).

trap trap, traps (for animals):
qʷátx̌ʷ (√qʷatúx̌ʷ-). fish
trap: scítpn (√cítpan-);
sx̌íyəp (√x̌íyap-). fish
trap, fish basket: yax̌áw't
(√yax̌áw'at-).

trash trash, garbage, rough
ground: x̌ašáytmx
(√x̌ə́š-).

travel travel, *pl.* run: ʔáx̌ʷɬ
(√ʔáx̌ʷa-). travel, *pl.* walk:
lísɬ (√lísi-). travelling
companion:
ʔacx̌ʷúqʷtwlxumx
(√x̌ʷúqʷa-); nkʷyə́p
(√yə́pa-). the clouds are
travelling fast:
sx̌ʷák̓ʷlkʷcšitn
(√x̌ʷák̓ʷa-).

tree tree, stick, limb, pole:
x̌'ə́xx̌'x (*pl.* x̌'ə́xx̌'axumx)
(√x̌'ə́x-). tree, wood, pine:
yámc (*pl.* yámacumx)

(√yámac-). fallen tree, log, windfall: syáq' (√yáq'a-).

trip (*n.*) trip, walk: syə́p (√yə́pa-).

trip (*v.*): ɬámt'ayq (√ɬámt'-).

triple triple, three at a time: t'əmxká?ɬi? (√t'əmx-, √ká?ɬi?-).

trot trotting: sxá?cxcwn (√xác-).

trousers trousers, pants: k'ál'xn'tn' (√k'ál'ax-). trousers, pants, overalls: ?ucámc (√?ucámac-).

trout: x̣waláɬtn JH (*x̣ʷəlátn). large trout *sp.*: q'á·na·lu' JH (*q'ánalu?). native speckled trout: ?acq̇ʷaɬé·čn (√q̇ʷəɬé-); q'ɑ̇''ɑ̇ɬ JH (*qá?ɬ). small trout, small fish, fingerlings: mán'c (√mán'ac-).

true: náxʷɬu?. true, right, correct, straight, even, very: k̓ʷə́pɬ (√k̓ʷə́p-).

trunk trunk, body: nuɬc'í?i (√náw-).

try try, test, taste, guess: mə́x̣n (√mə́x̣a-).

tuberculosis: x̣ʷó?anamn (√x̣ʷó?an-).

Tuesday: camsq'íx̣ (√cám-, √q'íx̣-).

tugs his tugs: x̣ál'km'ɬtani (√x̣ə́lk-).

tules: swaɬáɬkalx (√wáɬ-,

√kələ́x-).

turkey turkey, chicken, pheasant: skʷínm (*pl.* skʷínimumx) (√kʷiním-).

turn turn, spin: c'alə́pn (√c'ələ́p-). turn, wind, twist, stir, churn, wring out: yát'n (√yát'a-). turn around: yác'sn (√yác'-); yáƛ̓usm (√yáƛ̓a-); syát'šitn (√yát'a-). turn around!: yác'usmla? (√yác'-). turn it inside out!: p'ə́lk'iqina? (√p'ələ́k'-). turn off a light, put out a fire, kill: ɬə́pn (√ɬə́pa-). turn off a road: síq̇ʷlx (√síq̇ʷ-). turn over, roll, roll over: p'alə́k'n (√p'ələ́k'-). turning: sxʷə́lpawn (√xʷə́lpa-). it turned out to be, but: k̓ʷá.

turnip: ninəmú LNJ, niminú (?).

turtle: wíɬax̣ʷu.

twelve: pánačš kl t sáli?; tál'sali?.

twenty: cmtúmx (√cám-). twenty-one: cmtúmx kl t ?úc's (√cám-).

twice twice, two times, two at a time: camə́šn (√cám-).

twins: cawaqáwm'x (√cawaq-).

twist twist, spin, double up: yalə́k'n (√yələ́k'-). twist, turn, wind, stir, churn,

wring out: yát'n (√yát'a–).
two: sáli?. in two:

k▾áctum'x (√k▾ác–).

u

udder udder, breast: c'ám'tn
(√c'ám'–).
ugly: x̱šál'wn (√x̱ə́š–);
x̱îcsExa´mE⁴ FBa (√x̱ə́š–,
√?ə́x̱–).
uncle: k▾á⁴amn (√k▾a⁴á–,
√mán–); ka´.se FBa. his
uncle: k▾á⁴mnawi
(√k▾a⁴á–, √mán–).
uncover: wák'šn
(√wák'x–). uncover, take
off, take out: ⁴íwx (√⁴íw–).
it's uncovered now:
?acwák'x tani (√wák'x–).
under under, back under,
bottom: t'ə́q's. underneath:
t'ə́q's⁴tumx, kst'ə́q'tm
(√t'ə́q's–). under water:
t'ə́q's⁴k▾u (√t'ə́q's–).
underbrush underbrush,
brush: sx̱áX̌tmx (√x̱áX̌–);
sx̱ɑsâ·ytɑm'ʃ JH (√x̱ə́š–).
understand: ƙ▾pyálucn
(√ƙ▾pyáluci–).
underwear: taq'é·mac'a
(√taq'é·ma–).
undress: mə́lx̱▾cx
(√mə́lx̱▾–).
unfaithful: ?acq'é·x̱pstumx
(√q'ə́x̱áp–).
ungathered what is left
ungathered after a basket is

full: wasáln.
unless unless, if, when: ?áml,
?aml?.
unlucky unlucky LNJ, a
witch: x̱ayém'.
unravel unravel, loosen,
unroll: c'ə́x▾n (√c'ə́x▾i–).
unroll unroll, unravel, loosen:
c'ə́x▾n (√c'ə́x▾i–).
untangle: c'əx▾ál'wax
(√c'ə́x▾i–). untangle,
loosen, sort out: ⁴iwál'wax
(√⁴íw–).
until until, before: či?ílp
(√?ilə́p–).
unwrap: c'ə́x▾lkn
(√c'ə́x▾i–).
up up, going up: X̌ó·ƙ▾m'
(√X̌úƙ▾–). up above,
upriver: ⁴ák▾u (√⁴á?k▾–).
upcountry, north: .stū´m.la
FBa.
uphill: X̌uƙ▾é·lusm'
(√X̌úƙ▾–).
upright set upright, straight
up: c'úq̇▾⁴ (√c'úq̇▾–).
upside down: k▾ə́nala
⁴áX̌pm' (√k▾ə́nala–,
√⁴áX̌p–).
upstream upstream, upriver:
⁴á?k▾m' (√⁴á?k▾–). go
upstream: X̌álk▾m

(√x̌álkʷ–); łatcitsuwitila
FBa. upriver, up above:
łákʷu (√łáʔkʷ–).

us us, we: ʔiním.

use use, work for: yayússn
(√yayús–). use up, be
gone, defeat, win: c'əkł
(√c'əka–). used it for
medicine: sáʔayuʔči
(√sáʔa–,√ʔayóʔ–). using

for medicine or seasoning:
sáʔayuʔtn (√sáʔa–,
√ʔayóʔ–).

used to used to be, past: ʔít +
l (*non-feminine*); ʔíc + l
(*feminine*).

useless useless, no-good:
ʔix̌áp'.

uterus: pə́q (?).

V

valley valley, prairie:
máqʷm.

valuable valuable, expensive,
high-priced: ʔacyáyx̣ʷi
(√yáyx̣ʷi–).

vein: wa'sê´l FBa.

very: kʷə́p. very, hard, lots
of: ʔáy'tk (√ʔáy'tak–).
very, much, a lot: kʷumáy.
very, really: k̓ʷépł
(√k̓ʷə́p–). very, right,
correct, true, straight, even:
k̓ʷə́pł (√k̓ʷə́p–).

vest: la´phwaxEn FBa.

village village, town: aȋtkt-
xáx HH (√ʔáy'tak–,
√x̣áx–).

Virgin Mary: máli.

visit: patáy's.

voice: sʔímnmtn (√ʔímn–).
voice, noise, echo:
tawó·yn' (√taw–).

vomit: łáx̣ʷm (√łáx̣ʷ–).

vote: k̓ʷənám'ł (√k̓ʷəna–).
vote, mark, write, design,
brand: q̓ʷałén (√q̓ʷəłé–).

W

wade wade, ford, swim:
kʷátł (√kʷáta–). go
wading: kʷátkʷatł
(√kʷáta–).

wag wagging its tail (at):
syáx̣ʷipsmitn (√yáx̣ʷa–).

wagon: c'íkc'ik (√c'ík–);

xalka´mEłtEn FBa
(√xə́lk–).

waist: čá·kt (√čá·kat–).

wait wait, wait for: ʔálmq
(√ʔálm'aq–).

wake up: p'álł (√p'ál–).

walk: yə́pł (√yə́pa–). walk,

step, take a step:
yə́q̓ʷpataqm (√yə́q̓ʷ-,
√pátaq-). walk (*pl.*),
travel: lísɬ (√lísi-). walk,
trip (*n.*): syə́p (√yə́pa-).
walk backwards, step back:
xə́y'načm' (√xə́y-). by
walking, on foot: talsyə́p
(√tál-,√yə́pa-). go
walking: yápyapɬ
(√yə́pa-).

want want, desiderative
particle: qas (*enclitic*).
want, like: qínmn (√qín-).
want, love: tom-tsi-en-i-
ken UWb (√tám). want to:
ʔaccó·t'x̣ (√cút'x̣-).

war: yúpikʷn (√yúpi-). war
club: ɬakalɛne´x.p FBa
(√ɬə́q-). war paint: q̓ʷílɬ.
wartime: pənyúpikʷn
(√pən-, √yúpi-).

warm warm, hot: x̣ʷalá?.
warm (weather):
hwola´xtomɛx FBa
(√x̣ʷalá?-). warm water:
x̣ʷalíɬkʷu (√x̣ʷalá?-). get
warm: x̣ʷalá?lx
(√x̣ʷalá?-). keep warm:
mó·l'cx (√mó·l'-).

warrior: pəntípikʷn ENM
(√pən-, √típi-).

wash: c'ə́x̣ʷɬ (√c'ə́x̣ʷa-).
wash dishes: c'ə́x̣ʷiqim'ɬ
(√c'ə́x̣ʷa-). wash one's
face: ʔíkʷusm (√ʔíkʷ-).

waste waste time, act silly,
giggle: c'íykʷcx

(√c'íykʷ-).

watch (*n.*) watch, clock: wáč.

watch (*v.*) watch, look at, see,
stare: ʔé·x̣n (√ʔə́x̣-).
watch for, guard, take care
of, protect...: ƛ̓aqʷséx̣n
(√ƛ̓áqʷ-, √ʔə́x̣-). he's
watching him: swá·čitn
(√wá·či-).

water water, river: qál?
(√qalí?-). go after water:
cə́pkʷu (√cə́p-). high
water, flow LNJ: táw'kʷu?
(√táw'-). salt water: súltɬ
(√súlt-).

waterdogs: c'lə́m.

wave (*v.*) wave, blow in the
wind: x̣ʷíḱʷɬ (√x̣ʷíḱʷ-).
wave at: x̣ʷíx̣ʷḱʷšn
(√x̣ʷíḱʷ-). he waved at me:
ʔit x̣ʷíx̣ʷḱʷc (√x̣ʷíḱʷ-).
it's waving: sx̣ʷíḱʷx̣ʷḱʷwn
(√x̣ʷíḱʷ-).

waves: smúq̓ʷmuq̓ʷwn
(√múq̓ʷa-); ā´mane FBa.

wavy wavy, crooked, zigzag,
corrugated: č'úyč'uyuḱʷɬ
(√č'úyuḱʷ-).

we we, us: ʔiním.

weak weak, tired: ʔacx̣ʷə́nɬ
(√x̣ʷə́na-). he's getting
weak: sx̣ʷél'l'tn
(√x̣ʷél'l'-).

wealth wealth, lots of clothes:
qə́x̣itmtn (√qə́x̣-,
√ʔitáma?-). his wealth, his
clothes: táma?asi
(√táma?as-).

weapon: qalíkʷam'ɬtn' (√qalí-).

wear wear, get dressed: t'ə́km (√t'ə́k-). wear, have on: ʔact'ə́k (√t'ə́k-). wear out: x̣ʷámɬ (√x̣ʷám-).

weasel: c'ácx̣ʷn ENM; snəqʷálm' LNJ (√nəqʷálm'-); məx̣ʷá·l'as (?) (√məx̣ʷ-).

weave weave a cedar-root basket: sáʔəmx̣kʷu (√sáʔa-, √ʔə́mx̣kʷu-). weave a mat or basket (other than cedar-root): kʷal'úwn (√kʷal'úw-). weaving a basket: ssə́csuqʷstn (√sə́csuqʷs-).

wedding wedding, buy a woman: ləqálkwaʔɬuʔɬ (√lə́q-, √kəwáɬ-).

Wednesday: kanalsq'íx̣ (√kán-, √q'íx̣-).

weeds: sx̣ə́štmx (√x̣ə́š-).

week week, Sunday: sánti.

weight weight, heaviness, heavy: x̣ə́mtn (√x̣ə́m-). weight down, sink: nə́kn (√nə́ka-). gain weight: qíx̣ʷlx (√qíx̣ʷ-).

well (n.): scíqʷqʷl' (√cíqʷi-).

well well, a little while, a little bit, almost, soon: q̓ʷó·can (√q̓ʷóʔc-). well, better, healed: ƛ̓áq̓ʷ. get

well: ƛ̓áq̓ʷawm (√ƛ̓áq̓ʷ-); ʔáylx (√ʔí·-).

west: tu ʔaɬ t sx̣ʷúx̣ʷ (√x̣ʷúx̣ʷa-); ɬa´ko FBa; tuɬa´tcitso FBa.

wet: sə́x̣ʷɬ (√sə́x̣ʷa-). wetting one's head with: sə́x̣ʷl'smisn (√sə́x̣ʷa-).

whale: skui´ux FBa.

what what?, thing: tám. what?, why?: tám akʷu. what are you doing?: sʔíninax̣ʷ kʷu (√ʔíni-). what did you do with...?: ʔit ʔítx kʷu k... (√ʔít-). what did you say?: ʔit ʔínut kʷu k (√ʔínut-). what he is doing to me: sʔínw'əncals kʷu (√ʔíni-). what time?, how many?: k̓ʷí. what way?, which way?: kaním' kʷu (√ká·-). what's the matter?, what happened?: ʔit'í akʷu (√ʔí-). whatever is being done with it: nks + ʔítawctx kʷu (√ʔít-). do what, do with: ʔítx (√ʔít-). I'll do whatever I want: ɬiʔín kn (√ʔíni-).

wheat: p'itílstiʔ; x̣ʷít.

wheel wheel, tire: syə́l'kʷawn (√yələ́kʷ-).

when when?: pənká (√pən-, √ká·-). when, at the same time: pax̣ʷán'x̣. when, if, unless: ʔáml, ʔamlʔ.

where: ká·. to where?:

kánm kʷu (√káˑ-). where
is it?: ká? akʷu (√káˑ-).
which: tɛkxˈka FBa (√tk-,
√káˑ-). which one?: ?aksí
(√?í-). which way?, what
way?: kaním' kʷu
(√káˑ-). which way is it?,
how do you do it?:
kanémm' kʷu (√káˑ-).
while while, now: t'íx̣. after a
while, bye and bye: tela´la
FBa. after a while, later on:
xʷáˑ?a?s. a little while:
?aksq̓ʷó?c (√q̓ʷó?c-). a
little while, a little bit,
almost, soon, well:
q̓ʷóˑcan (√q̓ʷó?c-).
whine whine, squeal:
č'íqč'qm (√č'íq-).
whining: sč'éqč'qmitn
(√č'íq-).
whip (*n*.): ta´sɛnɛktɛn FBa
(√tása-). whip, club,
drum: tásam'ɬtn'
(√tása-).
whirlpool whirlpool, riffle:
yác'ɬkʷu (√yác'-).
whirlwind: tsa´ltsalepɛl FBa
(√c'ələ́p-).
whiskey: lám.
whisper: sákʷn (√sákʷa-).
whistle: súpq (√súpaq-).
whistle for: súpqšn
(√súpaq-). he's whistling:
súpsupaqn (√súpaq-).
white: ?aksqʷúx̣ʷ
(√qʷúx̣ʷ-). whiten:
?acqʷóx̣ʷm'ɬ (√qʷúx̣ʷ-).

White man: pástn (*pl.*
pástinumx) (√pástin-);
akskoxsī´ɬɛmux̣ FBa
(√qʷúx̣ʷ-, √síɬmix-).
non-Indian: xʷə́ltm
(√xʷə́l-).
whittle: x̣íq'n (√x̣íq'-).
who who?, someone: wá.
who he is: wát akʷu
(√wá-). who is he?,
someone: wá akʷu.
whole: yəmyú (?). whole,
all, every: t'əmxʷá?kʷu?
(√t'əmx-, √xʷá?kʷu?-);
?ítnak̓ʷušn (√?ít-,
√nák'-).
why: ?it'í (√?í-). why?,
what?: tám akʷu. that's
why: cicu (√cic-).
wide: ɬə́q'ɬ (√ɬə́q'-).
widow: č'íl'k (*pl.*
č'il'káwmx). widower:
č'íl'kawilm (√č'íl'k-).
wife wife, woman: kə́wɬ (*pl.*
kúwaɬmx *or* kə́waɬmx)
(√kəwáɬ-). buy a wife:
ləqálkuwɬ (√lə́q-,
√kəwáɬ-).
wiggle: yáx̣ʷnačm
(√yáx̣ʷa-).
wild: xasə́k̓ʷ. go wild:
xasák̓ʷlx (√xasə́k̓ʷ-).
wildcat wildcat, bobcat:
p'ə́č'm.
willow: wítkn'ɬ (√wítk-);
kali´tsɛnɛl FBa;
sukwa´mtsɛnɛɬ FBa. red
willow: kwai´tɛnɛɬ FBa.

wilt: q̓ʷayə́pɫ (√q̓ʷəyə́pa–).

win win, defeat, use up, be gone: c'ə́kɫ (√c'ə́ka–). win, earn: c'ə́kam'ɫ (√c'ə́ka–).

wind (*n.*): sxʷúxʷ (√xʷúxʷa–). breeze: sxʷó·xʷ (√xʷúxʷa–). wind blowing: sxʷúxʷawn (√xʷúxʷa–). have wind knocked out, faint: txʷsə́w (√səwə́–).

wind (*v.*) wind, turn, twist, stir, churn, wring out: yát'n (√yát'a–). wind around, tie around, arrest, put in jail: t'ə́qn (√t'ə́qi–).

windfall windfall, log, fallen tree: syáq' (√yáq'a–).

window window, mirror: ʔáx̣acxtn' (√ʔə́x̣–). window blinds: x̣ə́pax̣acxtn' (√x̣ə́pa–, √ʔə́x̣–).

wing, wings: spə́n (√pə́n–).

wink he winked at me: ʔit c'é·plsic (√c'íp–).

winter: pənƛ̓íx (√pən–, √ƛ̓íx–); qi ƛ̓íšils (√ƛ̓íx–); pantolos HH (√pən–, √túlucn–).

wipe wipe, wipe off: xʷíkʷn (√xʷíkʷi–). wipe one's nose: xʷíkʷqsm (√xʷíkʷi–).

wire: sax̣ʷó·ʔcuɫn (√sax̣ʷúcuɫn–).

wise wise, smart, know better: ʔacp'ə́x̣ɫ (√p'ə́x̣–).

wish wish, hope: nám'uqas (√nám'u–). wish for, take a liking to, like: mə́q̓ʷskʷuən (√mə́q̓ʷskʷu–).

witch witch; unlucky LNJ: x̣ayím'.

with: tak. with, and: kl. with, in, on; oblique: ɫ. go with, follow: ʔáyašn (√ʔáyax–). together with: pə́s.

without without, not have any, be gone: q'itám.

wolf: qinúy'ɫn'.

woman woman, wife: kúwɫ (*pl.* kúwaɫmx *or* kə́waɫmx) (√kəwáɫ–). buy a woman, wedding: ləqálkwaʔɫuʔɫ (√lə́q–, √kəwáɫ–). old woman: ná·w'ɫmx (√náwa–).

won't won't share, stingy: xʷíyxʷiy.

wood: an-nám-ote-láht-lo GGb (√ʔanám'–, √ƛ̓ə́x–). wood, tree, pine: yámc (*pl.* yámacumx) (√yámac–). piece of wood: kʷúmɫ (√kʷumə́l–).

woodpecker: ɫak̓ʷə́lqsm LNJ, ɫak̓ʷə́lqs ENM (√ɫə́k̓ʷ–). red-headed woodpecker: s.kᴇna´ps FBa; qê'qî´m FBa. big red-headed woodpecker: kʊ´təkʊtə TA.

wool: limitúhalaqn
(√limitú–).
word word, language, speech:
stə́q̇ʷ (√tə́q̇ʷa–).
work: yayús. work a hide,
tan a hide: yacə́qn
(√yəcə́q–). work for, use:
yayússn (√yayús–).
worker: yayúsalakaʔ
(√yayús–). working on:
syayúsmisn (√yayús–).
worm: q'íyaxʷm.
worry worry, bother, annoy,
nervous: cáyaɬ (√cáyaʔ–).
worry, feel bad, mistreat:
ʔacyulínut (√yul–).
worst: t'im x̣ə́š.
wound wound, get hurt:
q'ál'x̣m (√q'ál'x̣i–).
wound, hurt, ache, sore:
tákɬk' (√ták–, √ɬə́k'a–). a
wound: ʔacq'ál'x̣
(√q'ál'x̣i–). have a lot of
wounds: ʔacq'ál'q'l'x̣
(√q'ál'x̣i–).
wrap: malə́q̇ʷn
(√malə́q̇ʷ–). wrap up:
t'ə́qlkn (√t'ə́qi–). have
something wrapped around
one's head, have one's head
covered: mélq̇ʷls

(√malə́q̇ʷ–).
wreck wreck, ruin: c'aɬə́qɬ
(√c'aɬə́q–). wrecked:
ƛ'əmx̣ál'us (√ƛ'əmə́x̣–).
wren: c'ac'ə́p.
wrestle wrestle with, play
with: x̣áɬxʷamix
(√x̣áɬxʷa–). wrestling:
sqalé·kʷann (√qalí–).
wring wring out, drain, seep:
múc'n (√múc'–). wring
out, turn, twist, wind, stir,
churn: yát'n (√yát'a–).
wrinkle wrinkled (e.g. a
cloth): ʔacx̣éykʷm'ɬ
(√x̣əyə́k̇ʷ–). wrinkled,
pleated: ʔacɬúmɬumɬ
(√ɬúma–). wrinkled face:
ʔacc'asús (√c'as–). his
skin is wrinkled:
ʔacɬúmɬamak' ɬ t k̇ʷúsi
(√ɬúma–, √k̇ʷús–).
wrist: sxʷayə́q̇ʷ
(√xʷayə́q̇ʷ–); tɛtala´ka
FBa (√t'alá–).
write write, mark, design,
brand, vote: q̇ʷaɬén
(√q̇ʷəɬé–). write to:
q̇ʷaɬéšn (√q̇ʷəɬé–).
something written, design,
spots: ʔacq̇ʷə́ɬ (√q̇ʷəɬé–).

y

yarn: yá·n.

yarrow yarrow, squirrel-tail: skʷəyóhips.

yawn: xápn' (√xápan-). he's yawning: sxápxapann (√xápan-).

year: sƛ̓íx (√ƛ̓íx-). last year: wásqʷxʷ. this year: tíʔx̣ɬpanxʷ (√tíʔ-).

yell yell, shout, holler, call: tálaqp (√tál-).

yellow: ʔaksk̓ʷé·q'm'ɬ (√k̓ʷiq'é-). yellow paint: axsqwe´q awi´lɛk FBa (√k̓ʷiq'é-, *ʔawílk).

yes: ʔá·.

yesterday: yás, ʔítl yás, ɬítlčak yás. day before yesterday: naukīa´s'ˢ FBa (√náwa-, √yás-).

yew: tla´mɛɬ.k.ɬ FBa.

you (*sg.*): nə́wi. you (*pl.*), you folks: ʔilápaʔ. your, yours (*sg.*): snawíyaɬ (√nə́wi-).

young: x̣ʷél'. young man, youth: tul.xa´u.ts FBa. young people: tál'xʷucumx (√tál'xʷuc-).

youth youth, young man: tul.xa´u.ts FBa.

z

zigzag zigzag, crooked, wavy, corrugated: č'úyč'uyuk̓ʷɬ (√č'úyuk̓ʷ-).

217

This sketch[1] should provide some idea of Cowlitz grammar. Given the limited amount of data about the language available, a full grammar is not possible. Many of the concepts that exist in the language are minimally attested, but this sketch is possible in part because of the similarity of Cowlitz to Upper Chehalis, about which much more is known,[2] and it is possible to extrapolate morpheme functions from the latter to Cowlitz. Forms themselves are not so extrapolated in the text of this sketch in order not to mislead readers into thinking that forms provided here are actually attested in Cowlitz data when that is

---

[1] I thank Henry Davis and Lisa Matthewson for reading a preliminary version of this sketch and making comments and suggestions, which proved to be very useful in completing the sketch. Errors, infelicities, awkward passages, and omissions remain my responsibility.

[2] Upper Chehalis was spoken directly north of Cowlitz, in the drainage of the Chehalis River from about Satsop upstream. The two languages were very similar, but not quite mutually intelligible.

not the case, hence the blanks in paradigms marked by ??; however, I have provided my best guess as to what these missing forms might be in footnotes. Morphemes discussed in this sketch are also listed in the appendixes on affixes or in the body of the dictionary. Abbreviations and special symbols used in this sketch are listed on pages xxii and xxiv.

1. Sound system (Phonology). The Cowlitz in this sketch and dictionary is written using a standard Americanist system. A pronunciation guide is given in the Introduction beginning on page xx.

1.1. Consonants. There are 36 consonants, articulated at bilabial, dental, lateral, palato-alveolar, velar, uvular, and glottal positions; velar and uvular stops and fricatives occur both plain and labialized. *c, c', ƛ, č,* and *č'* are affricates. Note that *ʔ* patterns with resonants in Cowlitz, as it does elsewhere in Salish.

(1) Cowlitz consonants

stops, voiceless	p	t	c		č	k	kʷ	q	qʷ	
stops, ejective	p'	t'	c'	ƛ'	č'	k'	k̓ʷ	q'	q̓ʷ	
fricatives (voiceless)			s	ɬ	š	x	xʷ	x̣	x̣ʷ	h
resonants, plain	m	n		l	y		w			ʔ
resonants, glottalized	m'	n'		l'	y'		w'			

Non-ejective voiceless stops are aspirated in word-final position, or when they occur before another stop. Resonants are often syllabic, or may occur with an excrescent *ə* preceding them (see **1.2.1**). On the unexpected (for Salish) presence of both a č–series and a k–series of obstruents, see **1.4.1** below.

1.2. Vowels. There are four basic vowels, but each can occur short or long. The long manifestation of *ə* is a short *e*.

(2) Cowlitz vowels

i   u

ə   e,eˑ   oˑ

a   aˑ

1.2.1. Schwa. The mid-central vowel [ə] (schwa) appears under three conditions, the third of which is not well understood. The occurrence of schwa and its alternations with other vowels is quite complex, and will not be gone into in great detail here. Much of what happens to schwa in Cowlitz is like what happens to it in neighboring Upper Chehalis, and that has been described in detail in Kinkade 1998.

(a) The most important condition for the appearance of schwa has to do with stress. Stress is not predictable in Cowlitz, and hence must be written. The Cowlitz word appears to have slots between consonants where it can occur; if there is not already a vowel (*i, a, u,* or a long vowel) in the position where stress is assigned, then [ə] is inserted (epenthesized) as a vocalic carrier of this stress. If stress is not assigned to an eligible slot, then *a* is inserted if the slot precedes the syllable where *ə́* is inserted. Such a vowel appears in *ʔit sə́k'-m* 'he swam', and between the first two consonants of *sə́k'·sk'-mit-n* 'he's swimming' but not between the second *s-k'* sequence. An example of an inserted *a* before stressed *ə́* is seen in *ʔit t'alə́p-n* 'he attached it'.

(b) A schwa, or a schwa-like vowel (that is, a central vowel with front or back coloring, depending on surrounding consonants) is regularly inserted before a resonant in any consonant cluster. These vowels are excrescent, and are completely predictable. Speakers do not hear them. They may be extremely short, or the resonant may just be syllabic with no vowel at all. Thus a word like *s-x̣ə́q̓ʷlk-mis-n* 'he is squeezing it' is phonetically [sx̣ə́q̓ʷəlkᵊmisən] or [...misṇ]. No schwa is inserted between obstruent clusters, and homorganic obstruents in clusters are rearticulated.

(c) The third kind of schwa may simply be a reduced variety of a true vowel when it is unstressed, or it may be an excrescent vowel inserted under unclear circumstances (that is, in consonant clusters not involving resonants), as in *yác'·yəc'-w-n* 'it's going back and forth'. Note that an epenthetic schwa (type a) appears as [a] when stress is elsewhere in the word, but syllable structure requires that a vowel be present. Thus *s-*

t'ə́lp-t-n 'he is attaching it' has an epenthetic schwa because stress is assigned between the *t'* and the *l*, but *ʔit t'alə́p-n* 'he attached it' has *a* in this same position because stress has been assigned to a position between the *l* and the *p*. The reasons for such stress shifts are not understood.

1.2.2. Vowel length. Only stressed vowels can be lengthened. Vowel length is actually a process of lengthening (adding a mora) and lowering vowels. Since /a/ is already low, it only lengthens, but /i/ and /u/ become both long and low. [ə] is essentially nothing; lengthening makes it a true vowel, and adds features that make it low and front, but short, since zero (no mora) plus length (one mora) can only result in a short vowel. However, there is considerable inconsistency in the Cowlitz data regarding /e, eˑ/, so long /i/ sometimes appears as a short /e/, and long [ə] sometimes appears as long /eˑ/. Vowel length may also appear as /ʔ/ or glottalization of a resonant, or one of these in addition to vowel lengthening. The /ʔ/ is actually the source of the lengthening. Vowel lengthening occurs under at least seven circumstances, classifiable into four categories:

(a) Compensatory lengthening
<u>Consonant loss</u>. In a few cases vowel length compensates for a lost consonant. One clear case is káˑ 'where'; the full form of this root is seen in ʔikán 'everywhere, somewhere'.

<u>Phonological</u>. Sometimes the sequence *iy* is heard as *iˑ*. Thus *ʔíy* 'good, nice' is usually heard as *ʔíˑ*, but note that when the basic vowel is lengthened, as in *ʔéˑy'* 'kind', the *y* must remain.

(b) Morphological
<u>Diminutive formation</u>. This is an active process, and many examples can be found in the dictionary, such as *ʔéˑl'n* 'hum' from *ʔíln* 'sing' and *yáˑm'ac-umx* 'little trees' from *yámac-umx* 'trees' (see **2.10**).

(c) Lexical
<u>Lexical</u>. In many cases, the only form of a root or stem recorded had a long vowel. It is likely that many of these had a

form with a short vowel that was not elicited, but many have, in fact, lost the short form in the modern language. Examples are the roots *ʔéˑtil–* 'bathe, swim', *cáˑya–* 'busy', and *máˑs–* 'cheap'.

Derivational. A few stems have a long vowel that is clearly derived from a root or stem with a short vowel, but the function of the lengthening is not to create a diminutive or emphatic form. An example is the stem *ʔéˑx̱-ni–* 'look at, watch, stare' derived from *ʔə́x̱–* 'see'.

Borrowed. A few words were borrowed with long vowels. In these cases the length may reflect word stress in the original language. Examples are *lapyóˑš* 'hoe', *lawéˑn* 'oats', *likʷóˑk* 'rooster', *mətáˑs* 'leggings', and *yáˑn* 'yarn' (the first three of these are from French, the fourth from Ojibwa, and the last from English; all except *yáˑn* probably came into Cowlitz via Chinook Jargon).

(d) Pragmatic
Emphatic. Only a few instances occur using vowel length for emphasis. Examples are *méˑɬta* 'no!' from *mi̱ɬta* 'no, not', or *s-x̱aséˑl-n* 'it's raining (hard)' from *x̱asílʔ* 'it rained'.

1.3. Stress. As just noted, stress location is not predictable in Cowlitz. Most suffixes have both stressed and unstressed variants. When a suffix is not stressed, one or all of its vowels may sometimes be deleted. This is an area requiring further study.

1.4. Morphophonemics. In addition to variations among vowels discussed in section **1.2**, there are alternations among certain consonants and vowels.

1.4.1. k vs. č. The consonant pairs k/č, k'/č', and x/š contrast in Cowlitz, as in *ʔit kén'-mn* 'he made a mistake' vs. *ʔnks c-čán·čnq=ɬnal-n* 'he stutters', or in *s-xawáciɬ* 'nephew, niece' vs. *šáwʔ* 'bone'. Nevertheless, there are circumstances under which they may alternate in the same morpheme, depending on surrounding sounds. Usually the palato-alveolar member of the pair (*č, č', š*) appears before or after a front vowel (*i*). Thus the reflexive ending is *–cx* in perfective aspect forms but *–cši–* in imperfective aspect forms, and *tál'=ičn* 'bag' is *tál'=kn–i* when a third person possessive suffix is added. (For further details of this alternation see Kinkade 1973.)

1.4.2. *w* vs. *u*; *y* vs. *i*. The glides *w* and *y* may become homorganic vowels when they occur between consonants. Examples of *w* to *u* can be seen in the plural suffix *–áwmx* when the stress occurs earlier in the word and the vowel of the suffix is lost, as in *cúsaq–umx*, from *cúsaq* 'nail'; note *cuɬ-áwmx* 'feet', from *cúɬ* 'foot', where the *w* appears. For *y* see *s–yáq'·iq'–cši–t–n* 'rocking oneself back and forth', where the reduplicated part of the word has *i*. This change does not always occur; note *wə́n'·wn'–n* 'he folded it up', where instead an excrescent [ə] occurs between the second *w* and the second *n'* (and another before the final *n*). The circumstances under which *w* becomes *u* and *y* becomes *i*, rather than inserting an excrescent [ə], are unknown.

1.4.3. *l* vs. *ɬ*. There are clear instances where *l* is voiced within a word but devoiced to *ɬ* word-finally, as in *s–t'anáp–mal–n* 'it's getting dark' vs. *ʔit t'anáp–m'ɬ* 'it got dark'. The rules for this alternation are more complicated than this, however, and are not completely understood.

1.4.4. Vowel deletion and retention. The patterns of retention and deletion of unstressed vowels in Cowlitz are complex, and not fully understood. (a) On the one hand, unstressed vowels are generally retained in open syllables and deleted in closed syllables (as in Upper Chehalis to the north; Kinkade 1998:199-200). For this purpose, a final resonant (especially *n* following another consonant) is syllabic, and does not trigger vowel deletion. In addition, certain suffixes, notably imperfective subject suffixes, count as syllabic (whether they actually are or not) for purposes of deletion and retention (see **2.4.1**). (b) On the other hand, some suffixes have variants with and without vowels: imperfective relational *–mis–/–ms–* (**2.3.5**), imperfective middle *–mit–/–mt–* (**2.5.1**), and to some extent imperfective implied transitive *–mal–/–ml–* (**2.3.7**). In these cases the form without a vowel usually follows a short stem (CVC), but the form with a vowel follows any longer stem, including reduplicated CVC stems. In these short stems *ə́* plus a resonant (especially *ə́l*) counts as the vowel. (c) A further complication is presented by noun plurals (**2.9.2**) and perfective third person plural forms with *-umx*, which require an *-i-* to be inserted before the final consonant of a stem longer than CVC, although this *-i-* does not always replace a vowel that is already there.

1.4.5. Epenthetic consonants. Two consonants occasionally appear epenthesized: *n* may appear between vowels (see example 170), and *t* may appear after an *s* (see example 168) or following the imperfective reflexive suffix *-cši-* (**2.4.5**).

2.0. Word structure (Morphology). Cowlitz words, especially verbs, are often complex. They require aspectual, transitivity, and person marking, although since some of these categories are null, some verbs can be used relatively unmarked. In addition to these three basic categories, any of several other inflectional categories may be applied, and several derivational affixes and processes are available for further development of word stems (see especially **2.1** and **2.11.5 - 2.11.8**). Nouns are optionally marked for plural or diminutive. It should be noted that the categories 'verb' and 'noun' are not as obvious as we believe them to be in English; verbal forms can easily be used as arguments, and nouns can easily be turned into predicates, with the addition of appropriate affixes.

2.0.1. Parts of speech. Cowlitz words can be classed as verbs, nouns, adjectives, or particles. Particles include articles, adverbs, prepositions, and conjunctions. Verbs, nouns, and adjectives can be identified by the different plurals they take. Verb use reduplication to indicate plural activity (repetitive) (**2.1.1**, **2.9.5**); nouns rarely do. Verbs take full sets of person marking in two different aspects. Nouns have articles (determiners) preceding them, and can take possessive inflection. They have distinctive plural suffixes (**2.9**). Adjectives also have distinctive plural marking (**2.9.3**). There is considerable shifting between parts of speech: verbs can be nominalized (usually with an *s-* prefix), and can then have possessive inflection. When nominalized, they can serve as arguments: subjects, objects, objects of prepositions, etc. Stative verbs are often used as adjectives. Nouns can serve as the main predicate of a clause, and can then be considered verbs. They can also be used as modifiers, that is, adjectives. Adjectives can be nominalized by the addition of a preceding article. Adjectives can also be marked for comparative and superlative (see **2.12**).

2.1. Word building. In addition to the grammatical categories given above, a number of other processes and affixes are used to create words in Cowlitz. Some of these are common, others occur only infrequently in available data. Nearly all are probably productive, given the appropriate circumstances, except perhaps *-c* (**2.11.8**).

2.1.1. Reduplication. Several sorts of reduplication occur in Cowlitz, but only one is productive with grammatical significance. $C_1C_2 \cdot C_1(V)C_2$ reduplication for 'repetitive' is discussed in **2.9.5**. This pattern also occurs in words of various origin, including onomatopoeia. Reduplication is marked with a bullet (•).

(3) ʔó·c'·uc's 'single, bachelor', from ʔóc's 'one' (the
　　　　second ʔ has merged with the preceding c')
　　ƛ̓áq·ƛ̓aq-m 'lengthwise', from ƛ̓áq- 'long'
　　wítwit 'snipe'
　　x̣átx̣at 'duck'
　　kʷís·kʷs 'acorn'

It has been found used for plural of a noun in only one form.

(4) tə́x̣·tax̣-al=uɬ 'platters' (singular not recorded)

$C_1C_2 \cdot C_1(V)C_2$ reduplications are rare, especially in texts; only eight instances can be found, and no semantic pattern can be identified.

(5) ƛ̓iq'·ƛ̓íq' 'sticky'

məl·mál'-wax 'he mixed them up'[3]
stəm·tám 'beads, necklace'
x̣ʷu·x̣ʷáw'kʷ-m' 'go across' (with *u* from *w*)
lk'·lə́k'-n 'he filled them'

-C₂ reduplication is equally rare, and, again, no semantic pattern emerges. (The reduplicated consonant is rearticulated, with no intervening vowel.)

(6) s-ʔə́x̣·x̣-t-n 'he's examining it', from *s-ʔə́x̣-t-n* 'he sees it'
k ʷə́s·s-w-n 'evening'
ʔit ɬíq·q̣ 'he jumped'
sx̣ʷél'·l'-t-n 'he's getting weak'
s-t'íc·c-w-n 'it's splashing'

C₁(V)- reduplication is found in only four forms.

(7) ʔac-x̣ʷí·x̣ʷiʔɬkɬ 'Windy Point' (unanalyzable place name; once in texts)
x̣ʷ·x̣ʷáy' 'golden eagle'
ʔit x̣ʷí·x̣ʷk̓ʷ-c 'he waved at me'
x̣ʷu·x̣ʷúʔkʷm' 'over here'

Among the few reduplications that do not fit any of these patterns are:

(8) sk'á·k'aʔ 'crow'
payúcpayuc 'cone (on a tree)'
x̣íx̣i 'goose'
x̣ʷay'əx̣ʷay'əx̣ʷ 'fly' (once in texts)

2.1.2. Compounding. The compounding of two roots to create a new stem occurs frequently in the available data. A compound is distinguished by having two roots, but only one primary stress. Compounds are most frequently simply juxtaposed, but a linking element may occur between the two parts; this can be

---

[3] Third person forms do not distinguish gender in Cowlitz. For simplicity, third person forms will henceforth be indicated solely by 'he', but can be read as having 'she' or 'it' as subjects (or as the analogous object forms of these English pronouns where relevant). Similarly, third person possessives can be 'his', 'her', 'its', or 'their'.

-*ál*-, -*al*-, -*l*-, -*áɬ*-, -*ɬ*-, or -*a*-. All further derivation and inflection follows the last root of the compound.

(9) ləq-ál-kuwɬ 'buy a wife' (ləq- 'buy', kəwáɬ- 'wife')
    p'én-l̩-xawɬ 'by the road' (p'én'- 'beside', xəwál-
       'road')
    swaɬ-áɬ-kalx 'tules' (waɬ- '?', kə́lx 'reeds')
    p'én-nawi 'beside you' (p'én'- 'beside', nə́wi 'you,
       sg.')
    ʔíɬ-k'sk's-tn' 'dandruff' (ʔíɬani- 'eat', k'ə́sk's 'hair')
    x̣asíl?-sx̣ʷay's 'rainhat' (x̣asíli?- 'rain', xʷay'ús- 'hat')

Loan words freely enter into compounds.

(10) manít-umusməski 'butcher' (manít- 'kill, butcher',
       wəmúsmuski 'cow')
    ƛ'a-sámn 'fish, go fishing' (ƛ'aʔ- 'look for', sáman-
       'fish')

Up to three roots have been found in a compound.

(11) pən-ʔíɬ-skʷinm 'November' (pən- 'time', ʔíɬani-
       'eat', kʷiním- 'chicken, pheasant')

This last is an example of the creation of a word in Cowlitz when the older word had been forgotten.

Even prepositions can be compounded to a limited extent, as can prepositions with independent pronouns and a few other words.

(12) x-aɬ, x-ʔaɬ 'to' (x 'to', ʔaɬ 'to, in, into, on')
    ta-x-aɬ 'to' (ta *preposition*, x 'to', ʔaɬ 'to, in, into, on')
    ʔáɬ-inm 'to us' (ʔaɬ 'to, in, into, on', ʔiním 'we, us')
    ʔáɬ-c'iwq' 'left (side)' (ʔaɬ 'to, in, into, on', c'íwq'
       'left')
    x-ʔáɬ-tm'x 'onto the ground' (x 'to', ʔaɬ 'to, in, into,
       on', tə́mx 'earth, land')

Note that it is a preposition that receives word stress in the last three examples.

2.1.3. Lexical suffixes. The most frequently used word building devices in Cowlitz are lexical suffixes. These are suffixes with semantic content like nouns, but which are usually completely or partially different from the independent noun with the same meaning. A few lexical suffixes and their source nouns are identical, suggesting that compounding was historically the origin of this large class of suffixes. Lexical suffixes are preceded by a small equals sign here and in the dictionary. Some suffixes and nouns with the same meaning are:

(13) =akaʔ / kálx 'hand, arm'
   =xan, =ayaq / cúɬ 'foot, leg'
   =axʷ, =txʷ, =lwltxʷ, =x̣ax / x̣áx 'house'
   =aniʔ / q̓ʷalán' 'ear'
   =aqʷ / máqʷm 'prairie'
   =kʷu, =iqi– / qálʔ 'water'

Lexical suffixes designate familiar objects such as body parts, people, geographical objects, and common cultural items. A few examples follow.

(14) s-x̣ʷal=ílsi-tn 'heat rocks' (x̣ʷaláʔ 'hot, warm', =il'usi– 'rock, mountain')
   ʔac-má·y=ičn 'stick out of the water' (má·y– 'stick out', =ikə́n 'back')
   x̓áʔq-ay=aqn 'have long hair' (x̓áq– 'long, tall', =aqan 'hair')
   ʔáwt=psm 'back of the neck' (ʔáwat– 'behind, after', =apsam 'neck')
   x̓úk̓ʷ=lwltxʷ 'top of a house' (x̓úk̓ʷ 'above, high', =lwltxʷ 'house')
   x̓úk̓ʷ=stq 'fire on top' (x̓úk̓ʷ 'above, high', =staqi– 'fire')
   taq=án' 'deaf' (tə́q– 'close, shut', =ániʔ 'ear')
   s-tə́q=nk 'dam' (tə́q– 'close, shut', =nak 'hind part, rear end')

Lexical suffixes are often preceded by an extender (stressed or unstressed) which has no discernable meaning. There are several of these extenders; –al– and –ay– are the most common; also found are –l–, –uɬ–, –ul–, –iɬ–, and –ɬ–. There are upwards of 100 of these suffixes. A complete list, with roots in which they have been found, is given in Appendix B.

2.2. Aspect. Every verbal construction must be marked for aspect, a category that indicates the internal structure of the activity expressed by the verb. There are two basic aspect categories, for which every verb is inflected, and four secondary ones, which are supplemental to the first two.

2.2.1. Perfective vs. imperfective. Perfective aspect, which views the activity of the verb as a discrete whole, is usually translated into English by using past tense. Perfective forms are usually preceded by a member of the article system, most often ʔit. Subject enclitics follow the verb itself. Since the third person subject enclitic is zero, no overt subject appears in some of the following examples. (Clitic status is indicated by a small plus (+)). Thus we find:

(15) ʔit cə́kʷ-ɬ + kn 'I lay down., I went to bed'. (kn 'I')
     ʔit ɬíqq '(S)he jumped'.
     ʔit ʔíkʷtq '(S)he stole'.

Imperfective views the activity of the verb over a period of time, and is usually translated into English as a progressive (-*ing*) form. Imperfective forms nearly always occur with an intial *s-*, and require a suffixed subject, which is always overt in this aspect. Thus the imperfective equivalents of the three perfective forms given just above are:

(16) s̲-cə́kʷa-w-anš 'I'm going to bed'. (-anš 'I')
     s̲-ɬíqaq-n '(S)he's jumping'. (-n 'he, she, it')
     s̲-ʔíkʷtaq-n '(S)he's stealing'. (-n 'he, she, it')

Perfective forms are usually the shortest in a set, whereas the imperfective forms usually appear with a vowel preceding the last consonant of the stem; this vowel should be considered as part of the stem. It is not deleted, due to complex vowel deletion rules that retain vowels in open syllables; the final *n* is syllabic here (see **1.4.4**), hence allowing these words to end in open syllables. Perfective forms usually end in a consonant that is not syllabic, and which close the finally syllable; in these cases the final stem vowel is deleted.

2.2.2. Stative ʔac-. Stative aspect shows that the verb indicates a (resulting) state or condition. Stative aspect forms use perfective inflection, but replace an initial *ʔit* (or the like) with the prefix *ʔac-*. A stative form can be the main or entire predicate of a sentence.

(17) ʔac-cékʷ-ɬ '(S)he's lying down'.
      ʔac-ƛ́áq-ɬ 'It's long.', 'It's tall.'
      ʔac-táʔɬ-cx + kn 'I'm lying on my side.'

English adjectives are often expressed in Cowlitz by verbs in the stative aspect, showing that adjectives are a subclass of verbs in Cowlitz. Such deverbal adjectives take the usual adjective plural *-aʔ-* (see **2.9.3**) and can be made comparative (**2.12.1**).

2.2.3. Habitual *nks* +. The proclitic *nks* + (or *ʔnks* +) is used to specify that something happens regularly. It precedes the past marker using *l* (that is *l, t + l, ʔit + l, c + l*, and *ʔic + l;* see **2.6.1**). Examples of its use are:

(18) nks + t + l ʔac-wéˑx xánʔ-x̣ 'He used to live there.'
      ʔnks + ʔac-ƛ́aqʷ-s-éx̣-ni-cx k 'You want to look out for that.'

2.2.4. Mutative *tx̌ʷ-*. To indicate that there is a change of state, a prefix (here labelled 'mutative') *tx̌ʷ-* is used between other aspect markers and the verb root:

(19) ʔit tx̌ʷ-c'amə́k̓ʷ-stm 'Part of it came off.'
      ʔac-tx̌ʷ-k̓ʷə́c-tm 'It's calm.'

2.3. Transitivity. In addition to aspect, every verbal construction must be indicated as either transitive or intransitive, although intransitive is usually indicated by the absence of an overt marker.

2.3.1. Intransitive. Intransitivity is basically unmarked. However, two suffixes appear to indicate 'intransitive' specifically, possibly by historical accident (Kinkade 1995). These suffixes are *-w-* 'imperfective' and *-ɬ* 'perfective'. These suffixes are restricted to short roots, namely CVC(V)- and CVRC(V)- (where R is a resonant), but since these are the most common root shapes, they turn up quite frequently. It is typical that the imperfective forms have a vowel in the stem of the word that is not found in the perfective forms. This difference is due to complex syllabification requirements (see **1.4.4** above).

(20) s-yáx̌a-w-n 'He's going home.' / ʔit yáx̌-ɬ 'He went home.'

s-qʷíla-w'-n 'He's bleeding.' / ʔit qʷíl-ɬ 'He bled.'

s-níɬi-w-n 'He's living.' / ʔac-níɬ-ɬ 'He's alive.'

Roots of the shape CəRC(V)- regularly shift the stress in perfective forms from the first vowel to a *ə* inserted after the second consonant, and change the first vowel to *a*.

(21) s-tə́lpa-w-n 'He's marching.' / ʔit talə́p-ɬ 'He marched.'

s-c'ə́y'qʷa-w-n 'It's caving in.' / ʔit c'ay'ə́qʷ-ɬ 'It caved in.'

This change is possible, but not common, in imperfectives as well:

(22) s-yə́lpa-w-n *or* s-yalə́pa-w-n 'He is doctoring.'

It is also found in perfective transitives of CəCC(V)- roots. Other intransitives are formed by the use of middles, passives, implied transitives, reflexives, and reciprocals, all discussed below. Paradigms are given in **2.4.1**.

2.3.2. Simple transitive. The basic, and most common, way of creating transitive forms was probably originally accomplished in Proto-Salish by adding *-nt-* to an uninflected root or stem. Cowlitz has modified the use of this suffix in several ways, and uses only either *-n* or *-t-*. *-n* appears only on perfective forms with a zero third person object (the *-n* in these cases could alternatively be interpreted as being the marker of perfective third person object). The *-t-* has fused with an initial *s* of several object suffixes as *c*, but in other cases appears as *-t-*. A paradigm with third person singular subjects is given in **2.4.2** (**32**).

A second set of object suffixes occurs; these suffixes lack both *-n* and *-t-* transitivizers, and the first and second singular and plural object suffixes begin with *m* rather than *c*. These (and their cognates elsewhere in Salish) have come to be called 'causative objects' (not to be confused with the causative suffix itself). They occur following the causative suffixes, the *−tas−* transitive, and one applicative suffix. They can also occur with none of these being present. A paradigm can be found in 2.4.2 (33).

A very few verbs combine features of both these transitive paradigms, and may have features different from either. One such verb is *ɬəwála−* 'leave behind'. A partial paradigm is given in 2.4.2 (34). Although the data for this paradigm are defective, it can be seen that the first person singular object forms follow the causative object paradigm, and the third person singular, the reciprocal, and the passive forms have no transitive marking suffix at all.

2.3.3. Causative. Cowlitz has two suffixes that create causative verbs; either can replace other transitive suffixes. Both require causative object suffixes. One suffix is basically *−staw−*, the other *−taw−*; no difference is discernable between them. A causative paradigm is given in 2.4.2 (35).

A number of verbs have *−y−* rather than *−staw−* in imperfective third person singular forms. Its distinctive function and origin are unknown. An example can be seen in the paradigm for 'ask' in (33). Other examples are *s−ʔúxʷn−y−n* 'he's teaching him', *s−kʷə́n−y−n* 'he's catching him', and *s−mə́lqna−y−n* 'he's forgetting it'.

2.3.4. Relational. It is possible to create derived forms by means of a suffix called 'relational'. This suffix creates transitives especially from intransitive roots and from stems that include lexical suffixes. If there is a simple transitive or causative of the root, then the relational provides a meaning semantically related to the basic meaning of the root. A specific meaning for this suffix is difficult to pin down. Examples of derivations created by the relational suffix are:

- Intransitive *s−tə́qʷa−w−n* 'he is talking' has the causative (transitive) *s−tə́qʷ−staw−n* 'he is talking to him'; the relational suffix creates *ʔit tə́qʷa−mn* 'he talked about it'.

- From intransitive *s–xʷə́na–w–n* 'he is tired', the relational will derive *s–xʷə́n–ms–n* 'he is tiring of it'.

- The middle voice form *s–x̣ə́ɬxʷ–mt–n* 'he is playing, laughing' has the causative *ʔit x̣ə́ɬxʷa–mi–x* 'he played with him'; the relational suffix creates *ʔit x̣ə́ɬxʷa–mn* 'he is making fun of him'.

- The root *kʷə́p* 'very, right, straight' can be expanded with the lexical suffix *=ax̣n* 'upper arm' to mean 'aim'; the relational suffix added to this creates *ʔit kʷəp=áˑx̣n–mn* 'he aimed at it'.

A partial paradigm illustrating the relational suffix is given in 2.4.2 (36) (not all forms were elicited). The relational suffix appears as *–mi–* before first and second person singular and first person plural object suffixes; it is *–m–* before the transitive *–n* suffix. Note that *–mis–* occurs only in third person imperfective forms with a zero third person object, before the reciprocal suffix, and in perfective (here stative) passive forms before passive *–m*. The origin and relationship between the *s*-forms and transitive suffixes is unclear. For the alternation betwen *–mis–* and *–ms–* in third person imperfective forms see 1.4.4.

The relational suffix precedes simple transitive, causative, passive suffixes, and all object and subject suffixes.

2.3.5. Other transitive. An infrequent transitivizing suffix is *–tas–*. Its function is unknown. It is probably a second relationala suffix. It is followed by causative object suffixes. A paradigm is given in 2.4.2 (37). This suffix has been found with only eight roots.

2.3.6. Applicative. Cowlitz has five verbal suffixes that allow a speaker to change an indirect (or other non-direct) object to a direct object. All applicatives immediately precede transitive and object suffixes. Four precede *–t–* objects, and one precedes the *–y–* type of causative object suffixes. Only a few instances of the last three occur in available Cowlitz data.

(a) –ši–. Constructions with this suffix often include 'for' in their translation ('make a bed for', 'pay it for', 'sing for') or indicate that there is a benefit for the object ('show to', 'send to', 'baptize', 'wave at'). However, this suffix cannot be considered a simple benefactive in light of other translations ('make faces at', 'double one's fist at', 'threaten', 'worry about'). It is not tied to a particular set of thematic roles, but rather can promote all kinds of indirect objects to direct object status. The simple transitive form *sáʔ-n* means 'he made it', and the item made is the direct object. Adding an applicative suffix creates *sáʔ-š̠-n* 'he made it for him', where the person for whom the object is made is direct object. The item made could still be indicated, but it would have to be expressed by a following prepositional phrase (e.g. *ʔit sáʔ-š̠-n ɬ tit X̌íqsn* 'he made the box for him'). A paradigm showing the variants of *-š̠i-* is given in 2.4.2 (38). This is the most frequently used applicative.

(b) –tuxʷt. Few examples of *-tuxʷt* were recorded, so its precise function cannot be determined. Comparative evidence (with Upper Chehalis, although its role there is not entirely clear either) suggests that it is used when an oblique object is raised to direct object status, and the original (unexpressed) direct object is possessed by someone (presumably the "it" in the examples given here is what is possessed). A partial paradigm is given in 2.4.2 (39). A complete paradigm was not obtained, and it occurs in the available data on only eight roots. Other examples of its use are

(23)   ʔit k'ə́ɬ-<u>tuxʷt</u> 'he threw it at him'
        ʔit sáw'li-<u>tuxʷt</u> 'he asked him for it'
        ʔit sə́c'-<u>tuxʷt</u> 'he stuck it on him'.

(c) –ni-₁. Two applicatives with the form *-ni-* occur, one taking *-t-* objects, the other taking *-y-* type causative objects. Neither occurs frequently, and only a few instances of either can be found. The one with *-t-* objects occurs in such constructions as *s-ʔáy'x-<u>ni</u>-t-n* 'he's following him, he's going with him', and *s-ʔé·x-<u>ni</u>-t-n* 'he's looking at it, he's watching it'. It has been found with no more than eight roots.

(d) –ni-₂. A second *-ni-* occurs, but this one requires *-y-* type causative objects. Examples of its use are

(24) s-ʔúxʷ-<u>n</u>-y-n 'he's teaching him'
      ʔit kʷə́n-<u>n</u>-mx 'he caught me'
      ʔit yaxa-<u>ni</u>-x 'he carried it on his back.'

(e) –s(t)–. The least common applicative is *–s(t)–*; it has been found with no more than three roots. Examples of its occurrence are

(25) s-kʷə́n-<u>s</u>-cal-n
      IMPERF-take-APPL-1SG.OBJ-3SG.SUBJ
      He's grabbing it away from me.

(26) ʔit   q̓ʷałéʔ-<u>s</u>-c
      PERF mark,write-APPL-1SG.OBJ
      he signed for me

2.3.7. Implied transitive. One suffix pair allows a speaker to change an intransitive verbal construction into one in which transitivity is strongly implied but not indicated by any transitive inflection. This is done by using a variant of the suffix *–amal–*. These constructions are felt to be transitive in some way by speakers, and they are usually translated with a non-specific object like 'something' (that is, 'I am counting something'). A paradigm is given in 2.4.2 (40).

A specific object can still be mentioned, but it must be in a prepositional phrase. The change of the *l* to *ł* is accounted for above in 1.4.3. A variant of *–ml–* occurs in *s-púxʷ·puxʷ=iʔqa-mal-n* 'he's blowing (a horn)' (see 1.4.4).

2.4. Person. Cowlitz marks first, second, and third persons, singular and plural, as pronominal categories. Third person plural is somewhat optional, but is used frequently. Third person singular is zero as subject of perfective forms and as object in many cases (transitive or causative markers might also be considered as indicating third person object when no other object is specified). Few forms with second person plural marking were obtained. Third person plural perfective subjects and third person plural objects add the noun plural *–i-awmx* to third person singular forms.

Perfective subject markers are enclitic, and first and second person singular possessive markers are proclitic; the clitic vs. suffix status of other possessive markers is unclear.

(27) **Pronominal affixes**

	POSSESSIVE	SUBJECT		OBJECT	
		Imperfective	Perfective	Imperfective	Perfective
1 sg	n +	−anx	+ kn	−cal−, −mal−	−c, −mx
2 sg	ʔa +	−axʷ	+ k	−ci−, ?	−ci, −mi
3 sg	−i, −s	−n	∅	−t−, −y−, −∅−	−n, −x, −xʷ, −∅
1 pl	−kɬ	−stawt⁴	+ kɬ	−taw−, ?	−tawɬ, −mulɬ
2 pl	−ilp	−alapt	+ kp	?, ?	−tawɬ, ?
3 pl	−ɬ	−iɬt	−i−umx	3 sg. endings + −áwmx	

The second forms of object suffixes (those beginning with m for first and second persons, and the −*y*−, −*x*−, and −*x*ʷ− for third person) are causatives, and occur following causative markers and after certain other transitive and applicative markers. Independent pronominal words also exist, but they are not used for inflection. They are essentially verbs, and can also be used as nouns (see **4.1**).

2.4.1. Subjects. The two sets of subjects are instrumental in distinguishing aspect. The suffixes are used for imperfective aspect, and the enclitics *kn*, *k*, *kɬ*, and *kp* are used for perfective aspect. Stems with the imperfective set of suffixes are treated as if they ended in an open syllable (whether this is actually the case or not — as it clearly is with −*n*, which is syllabic in this position). The perfective clitics have no bearing on this issue. A paradigm of a bare intransitive verb (with no further derivation) follows.

(28) root *ʔílan'*- 'sing' + simple pronouns

IMPERFECTIVE		PERFECTIVE	
sʔílan'anx	I am singing	ʔit ʔíln kn	I sang
sʔílan'axʷ	you (sg.) are singing	ʔit ʔíln k	you (sg.) sang

---

⁴ The origin of −*stawt* in Cowlitz and Upper Chehalis has long been mysterious. It consists of −*staw*− 'causative' and the old Salish first person plural subject suffix −*t*. Why this combination came to be the imperfective first person plural subject suffix is unknown.

s?ílan'n	he/she is singing	?it ?íln	he/she sang
s?ílan'stawt	we are singing	?it ?íln k⁴	we sang
s?ílan'alapt	you (pl.) are singing	?it ?íln kp	you (pl.) sang
s?ílan'i⁴t	they are singing	?it ?ílinumx	they sang

Two paradigms of intransitive verbs requiring the *-w-* / *-⁴* suffixes (see **2.3.1**) follow.

(29) root *qʷíla-* 'bleed' + *-w'-* / *-⁴* + pronouns

	IMPERFECTIVE		PERFECTIVE
sqʷílaw'anx	I am bleeding	?it qʷíl⁴ kn	I bled
sqʷílaw'axʷ	you (sg.) are bleeding	?it qʷíl⁴ k	you (sg.) bled
sqʷílaw'n	he/she is bleeding	?it qʷíl⁴	he/she bled
sqʷílaw'stawt	we are bleeding	?it qʷíl⁴ k⁴	we bled
sqʷílaw'alapt	you (pl.) are bleeding	?it qʷíl⁴ kp	you (pl.) bled
sqʷílaw'i⁴t	they are bleeding	?it qʷíli⁴umx	they bled

(30) root *qə́⁴x̣a-* 'get angry' + *-w-* / *-⁴* + pronouns

	IMPERFECTIVE		STATIVE
sqə́⁴x̣awanx	I am getting angry	?acqa⁴ə́x̣⁴ kn	I am angry
sqə́⁴x̣awaxʷ	you (sg.) are getting angry	?acqa⁴ə́x̣⁴ k	you (sg.) are angry
sqə́⁴x̣awn	he/she is getting angry	?acqa⁴ə́x̣⁴	he/she is angry
sqə́⁴x̣awstawt	we are getting angry	?acqa⁴ə́x̣⁴ k⁴	we are angry
sqə́⁴x̣awalapt	you (pl.) are getting angry	?acqa⁴ə́x̣⁴ kp	you (pl.) are angry
sqə́⁴x̣awi⁴t	they are getting angry	?acqa⁴ə́x̣i⁴umx	they are angry

(31) <u>Middle</u> voice (see **2.5.1**) — root *X̣á·x̣an-* 'hunt' + *-mit-* / *-m*

	IMPERFECTIVE		PERFECTIVE
sX̣á·x̣nmitanx	I am hunting	?it X̣á·x̣anm kn	I hunted
sX̣á·x̣nmitaxʷ	you (sg.) are hunting	?it X̣á·x̣anm k	you (sg.) hunted
sX̣á·x̣nmitn	he/she is hunting	?it X̣á·x̣anm	he/she hunted
sX̣á·x̣nmitstawt	we are hunting	?it X̣á·x̣anm k⁴	we hunted
sX̣á·x̣nmitalapt	you (pl.) are hunting	?it X̣á·x̣anm kp	you (pl.) hunted
sX̣á·x̣nmiti⁴t	they are hunting	?it X̣á·x̣animumx	they hunted

2.4.2. Objects. The third person singular object suffixes listed in **2.4** are actually transitive and causative markers, and third person object is actually zero. They serve very nicely to fill out object paradigms, and can be seen to serve dual roles. Causative *-x* is a delabialized form of *-xʷ* (which occurs rarely), which in turn is a devoiced from of the w at the end of *-staw-*. The *c* of several object suffixes is historically **-t-s*, but this sequence has been merged into a single sound. The −*t*− here is an old transitive suffix, and shows up without an *s* in several endings of the set. Transitive paradigms follow.

(32) <u>Simple transitive</u> (see **2.3.2**) — root *tal'íči*- 'help' + object suffixes + subjects

IMPERFECTIVE		PERFECTIVE	
stal'íčicaln	he is helping me	ʔit tal'íčic	he helped me
stal'íčicin	he is helping you (sg.)	ʔit tal'íčici	he helped you (sg.)
stal'íčitn	he is helping him/her/it	ʔit tal'íčn	he helped him/her/it
stal'íčituln	he is helping the other one	ʔit tal'íčtwali	he helped the other one
stal'íčitawn	he is helping us	ʔit tal'íčitaw+	he helped us
??[5]	he is helping you (pl.)	ʔit tal'íčitaw+	he helped you (pl.)
stal'íčtwaln	they are helping each other	ʔit tal'íčitawəlx	they helped each other
stal'íčicšitn	he is helping himself	ʔit tal'íčicx	he helped himself
stal'íčictx	he is being helped	ʔit tal'íčitm	he was helped

(33) <u>Causative paradigm</u> (see **2.3.2**) — root *sáw'la*- 'ask' + *m*- object suffixes

IMPERFECTIVE		PERFECTIVE	
sáw'lamaln	he is asking me	ʔit sáw'lamx	he asked me
sáw'lamin	he is asking you (sg.)	ʔit sáw'lami	he asked you (sg.)
sáw'layn	he is asking him/her	ʔit sáw'lix	he asked him/her
sáw'lawaln	he is asking the other one	ʔit sáw'lawali	he asked the other one
??	he is asking us	ʔit sáw'lamul+	he asked us
??	they are asking each other	ʔit sáw'lawəlx	they asked each other
??	he is asking himself	ʔit sáw'licx	he asked himself
??[6]	he is being asked	ʔit sáw'laym	he was asked

(34) Mixed features (see **2.3.2**) — root *+awála*- 'leave'

IMPERFECTIVE		PERFECTIVE	
s+awálamaln	he is leaving me	ʔit +awálamx	he left me
s+awáln	he is leaving him/her	ʔit +áw+	he left him/her
??	he is leaving us	ʔit +awálamul+	he left us
??	they are leaving each other	ʔit +aw'ál'wəlx	they left each other
??[7]	he is being left	ʔit +awálm	he was left

---

[5] The missing form here may be something like *stalíčitawn*.
[6] The missing forms here may be something like *sáw'lamawn, sáw'lawaln, sáw'licšitn*, and *sáw'lamctx* (or *sáw'lictx*).
[7] The missing forms here may be something like *s+awálamawn, s+awá-lwaln*, and *s+awálmctx*.

(35) Causative with *-staw-* (see **2.3.3**) — root *múx̣ʷ-* 'punish' + *-staw-*

IMPERFECTIVE		PERFECTIVE	
smúx̣ʷstumaln	he is punishing me	ʔit múx̣ʷstmx[8]	he punished me
smúx̣ʷstumin	he is punishing you (sg.)	ʔit múx̣ʷstumi	he punished you (sg.)
smúx̣ʷstawn	he is punishing him/her	ʔit múx̣ʷix̣	he punished him/her
??	he is punishing the other one	ʔit múx̣ʷstwali	he punished the other one
??	he is punishing us	ʔit múx̣ʷstumuɬ	he punished us
??[9]	he is being punished	ʔit múx̣ʷstm	he was punished

(36) Relational (see **2.3.4**) — root *qín-* 'want' + *-mis- / -mi-*

IMPERFECTIVE		STATIVE	
sqínmicaln	he is wanting me	ʔacqínmic	he wants me
sqínmicin	he is wanting you (sg.)	ʔacqínmici	he wants you (sg.)
sqínmisn	he is wanting him/her	ʔacqínmn	he wants him/her
??	he is wanting us	ʔacqínmitawɬ	he wants us
??	he is wanting them	ʔacqínminumx	he wants them
??	they are wanting each other	ʔacqínmistawlx	they want each other
??[10]	he is being wanted	ʔacqínmism	he is wanted

(37) *-tas-* paradigm (see **2.3.5**) — root *q'íw'-* 'call' + *-tas-*

IMPERFECTIVE		PERFECTIVE	
sq'íw'tsmaln	he is calling me	ʔit q'íw'tsmx	he called me
sq'íw'tsmin	he is calling you (sg.)	ʔit q'íw'tsmi	he called you (sg.)
sq'íw'tasn	he is calling him/her	ʔit q'íw'tas	he called him/her
sq'íw'tswaln	he is calling the other one	ʔit q'íw'tswali	he called the other one
??	he is calling us	ʔit q'íw'tsmuɬ	he called us
??	they are calling each other	ʔit q'íw'tswəlx	they called each other
??[11]	he is being called	ʔit q'íw'tasm	he was called

The *ts* sequence in these forms does not merge to [c], but is pronounced with a slight release of the *t*.

---

[8] There is some variation between *-stumx* and *-stmx* for perfective first person singular.

[9] The missing forms here may be something like *smúx̣ʷstwaln*, *smúx̣ʷ-stumawn*, and *smúx̣ʷstuctx*.

[10] The missing forms here may be something like *sqínmsawn*, *sqínmisn*, *sqínmswaln*, and *sqínmictx*.

[11] The missing forms here may be something like *sq́íwtsmawn*, *sq́íwts-waln*, and *sq́íwtasctx*.

(38) Applicative *–ši–* (see **2.3.6.a**) — root *ʔúxʷ–* 'blame' + *–ši–*

IMPERFECTIVE		PERFECTIVE	
sʔúxʷšicaln	he is blaming me	ʔit ʔúxʷšic	he blamed me
sʔúxʷšicin	he is blaming you (sg.)	ʔit ʔúxʷšici	he blamed you (sg)
sʔúxʷšitn	he is blaming him/her	ʔit ʔúxʷšn	he blamed him/her
sʔúxʷšituln	he is blaming the other one	ʔit ʔúxʷštwali	he blamed the other one
sʔúxʷšitawn	he is blaming us	ʔit ʔúxʷšitawɬ	he blamed us
sʔúxʷšitawaln	they are blaming each other	ʔit ʔúxʷšitawəlx	they blamed each other
sʔúxʷšicšitn	he is blaming himself	ʔit ʔúxʷšicx	he blamed himself
sʔúxʷšictx	he is being blamed	ʔit ʔúxʷšitm	he was blamed

(39) Applicative *–tuxʷt* (see **2.3.6.b**) — root *cíx̣–* 'show' + *–tuxʷt*

IMPERFECTIVE		PERFECTIVE	
scíx̣tx̣ʷcaln	he is showing it to me	ʔit cíx̣tuxʷc	he showed it to me
scíx̣tx̣ʷcin	he is showing it to you (sg.)	ʔit cíx̣tx̣ʷci	he showed it to you (sg)
scíx̣tx̣ʷtn	he is showing it to him	ʔit cíx̣tuxʷt	he showed it to him

(40) Implied transitive (see **2.3.7**) — root *kʷə́n–* 'count' + *–mal– / –m'ɬ*

IMPERFECTIVE		PERFECTIVE	
skʷə́nmlanx	I am counting	ʔit kʷə́nam'ɬ kn	I counted
skʷə́nmlaxʷ	you (sg.) are counting	ʔit kʷə́nam'ɬ k	you (sg.) counted
skʷə́nmln	he/she is counting	ʔit kʷə́nam'ɬ	he/she counted
skʷə́nmlstawt	we are counting	ʔit kʷə́nam'ɬ kɬ	we counted
skʷə́nmlalapt	you (pl.) are counting	ʔit kʷə́nam'ɬ kp	you (pl.) counted
skʷə́nmliɬt	they are counting	ʔit kʷə́nam'iɬumx	they counted

2.4.3. Possessives. Possessive markers are mixed as to where they are attached to a noun (or nominalized verb); first and second person singular are indicated by proclitics (separated by +), and may sometimes move to a preceding element in a phrase. Other persons are indicated by suffixes (some may be enclitics, but existing data provide no way to tell).

(41) root **stiqíw** 'horse'

n + stiqíw	my horse
ʔa + stiqíw	your (sg.) horse
stiqíw–i	his horse
stiqíw–kɬ	our horse
stiqíw–ilp	your (pl.) horse

stiqíw-ɫ̣   their horse

The third person singular possessive occurs in two forms, discussed in 2.4.3.1 and 2.4.3.2. Kin terms have additional complications when possessed (2.4.3.3).

2.4.3.1. *–i.* The most common third person possessive suffix encountered is a suffixed *–i.* If the root or stem to which it is attached ends in a consonant cluster, a vowel appears between the last two consonants. Since this vowel is not predictable, it is best considered as part of the stem, and is retained when the suffix *–i* creates an open syllable that allows its retention (see 1.4.4). This stem vowel is *a* about 46% of the time, but any vowel can appear, either stressed or unstressed.

(42) ciɫá·l'axʷ–i 'his board', *from* ciɫá·l'ax 'board'
       cúl–i 'his leg, his foot', *from* cúɫ 'leg, foot'
       sč'éʔ–i 'his buttocks', *from* sč'éʔ 'buttocks'
       lám–i 'his whiskey', *from* lám 'whiskey'
       mətá·s–i 'his stockings', *from* mətá·s 'leggings, Indian stockings'
       sqʷíl–i 'his blood', *from* sqʷíɫ 'blood'
       súps=n'č–i 'its tail', *from* súps=n'k 'tail'

(43) with stem vowel *a*
       məx̣kán–i 'its horns, its antlers', *from* mə́x̣kn 'horn, antlers'
       s–č'íp=qas–i 'his beard', *from* č'íp=qs 'beard'
       p'n–áy'=x̣ax–i 'his neighbor', *from* s–p'n–áy'=x̣x 'neighbor'
       ɫán–aʔcx–tan–i 'his button', *from* ɫán–aʔcx–tn' 'button'

(44) with stem vowel *i*
       qalíʔ–i 'its water', *from* qálʔ 'water, river'
       yənís–i 'his tooth', *from* yə́ns 'tooth'
       təx̣ʷis–i 'his enemy', *from* tə́x̣ʷs 'enemy'
       s–lé·x̣in'–umiš–i 'her earrings', *from* s–lé·x̣in'–umx 'earrings'

(45) with stem vowel *u*
       cənúp–i 'his bed', *from* cə́np 'bed'

sxʷay'ús-i̱ 'his hat', *from* sxʷáy's 'hat'
súc'us-i̱ 'his cousin', *from* súc's 'cousin'
stiqíw=lwltuxʷ-i̱ 'his barn', *from* stiqíw=lwltxʷ 'barn'

(46) with stem vowel *ə*
ciɫə́n-i̱ 'his food', *from* cíɫn 'food'
məqsə́n-i̱ 'his nose', *from* mə́qsn 'nose'
sqʷalə́m-i̱ 'his heart', *from* sqʷə́lm 'heart'
wakə́s-i̱ 'his going', *from* ʔit wáks 'he went'

If the unpossessed word ends in a vowel or vowel + *ʔ*, then -*ni*
is suffixed.

(47) ʔə́mx̣kʷu-ni 'her cedar-root basket', *from* ʔə́mx̣kʷu
'cedar-root basket'
máč'iɫa-n'i 'his flea', *from* máč'iɫaʔ 'flea'
milúxʷ=aka-n'i 'his fist', *from* milúxʷ=akaʔ 'fist'
pípa-ni 'his paper', *from* pípa 'paper'
sác'u-n'i 'his fish spear', *from* sác'uʔ 'fish spear'

In a very few vowel-final borrowed words, -*hi* is suffixed.

(48) kapú-hi 'his coat', *from* kapú 'coat'
kʷušú-hi 'his pig', *from* kʷušú 'pig'
lalupá-hi 'her ribbon', *from* lalupá 'ribbon'
pyəx̣í-hi 'her bitterroots', *from* pyəx̣í 'bitterroots'

Words ending in the lexical suffix =*iʔɫ* add -*ili*. The -*t*- that
appears is historically part of the lexical suffix.

(49) sqʷay'á=iɫt-ili 'her baby', *from* sqʷay'á=iɫ 'baby'
sqʷóqʷstm=iʔɫt-ili 'its egg', *from* sqʷóqʷstm=iʔɫ
'egg'

Other instances of apparent -*ili* are actually just -*i* with a
preceding lateral appearing in its voiced form.

(50) sníɫil-i̱ 'his coming back to life', *from* ʔacníɫɫ 'he's
alive'

In a small number of words a vowel is deleted.

(51) s-x̣'ap-ál=x̣n-i̱ 'his armpit', *from* x̣'ap-ál=ax̣n 'armpit'
qʷúl=mš-i̱ 'his milk', *from* qʷúl=amx 'milk'
t'am=úlkn-i̱ 'his barrel', *from* t'am=úličn 'barrel'

For some words, the possessive formation is best considered irregular.

(52) ʔitámaʔasi 'his clothing', *from* ʔitámaʔ 'clothing'
 paləqʷ-i 'his spring', *from* pləqʷ 'a spring'
 paséʔ-i 'animals', *from* pə́saʔ 'animal'
 qax̣éʔ-i 'dogs', *from* qáx̣aʔ 'dog'
 qʷatix̣íʔ-i 'his louse', *from* qʷatíx̣aʔ 'louse'
 tamí-wali 'his land', *from* tə́mx 'land, earth'

2.4.3.2. -s. The third person possessive suffix is *-s* everywhere else in Salish, and *-s* is to be found in Cowlitz as well, but only under very restricted circumstances. Most textual examples have it after a transitive verb (with or without a transitive suffix (*-n-* or *-t-*) present). Other examples in texts are unclear.

(53) tat pástn   táktə mí⁺ta t   ql
  DET white.man doctor not   DET can
   s-tal'íč-t-wal-s.
   NOM-help-TR-T.O.-3POSV
  The white doctor couldn't help him.

(54) ʔa⁺ tám tat s-pút-n-s   cə́ni.
  to   what DET NOM-know-TR-3POSV he/she
  She knew that.

(55) taw'é·t   t   t'amúličn t   qi t + l
  bi··g   DET barrel   DET QI DET + PAST
   s-k'ə́c'-s   tit cream
   NOM-put.in-3POSV   DET cream
  a bi··g barrel to put the cream in

2.4.3.3. -aw-. Several kinterms add an extender *-aw-* before the third person possessive *-i*. Some of these are:

(56) mán-aw-i 'his father', *from* mán 'father'
 ʔímac-aw-i 'his grandchild', *from* ʔém'c 'grandchild'
 kʷúp-aw'-i 'his grandfather', *from* kʷúpaʔ 'grandfather'
 nsk-éw'-i 'his younger brother', *from* néʔsk 'younger
  brother'
 snúkʷi⁺t-aw-i 'his nephew', *from* snúkʷi⁺ 'nephew,
  niece'

See **4.4** for a complete list of kin terms. Several of the possessed forms are irregular.

Two non-kin words were given with this suffix before –*i*.

(57) kál-<u>aw</u>–i 'his hand, his arm', *from* kálx 'hand, arm'
k'al'-<u>áw</u>–i 'its branch', *from* k'ál'x 'branch, limb'

2.4.3.4. Possessives of independent pronouns. Independent pronominal words are made possessive ('my', 'mine', 'your', 'yours', etc.) with a nominalizing *s-*, often a stress shift, and a suffixed *–(y)a*ɬ. For the full set of these see **4.1** (213).

2.4.4. Topical object. In addition to indicating regular third person object, Cowlitz has a suffix *–wal–* or *–ul–* / *–wali* or *–uli* called 'topical object'. This suffix indicates that the topic of discourse is a direct object rather than a subject. Verbs with this suffix are included in paradigms above. Examples of its use are:

(58) ʔit   caqíy'–n   tit   qáx̣aʔ, wi   ʔit
      PERF   kick-TR   DET   dog   WI   PERF
      t'ə́k̉ʷ–t–uli   ʔu
      bite-TR-T.O.   EVID
He kicked the dog, but it bit him anyway.

(59) ʔit   tálaqap–n,   wi   ʔit   ʔə́x̣–t–uli
      PERF   call-TR   WI   PERF   see-TR-T.O.
      He$_1$ called him$_2$, and he$_2$ looked at him$_1$.

Topical object suffixes are used commonly in narratives, conversation, and other kinds of discourse where it is important to keep track of the topic of a section of discourse. The subject of a sentence is most commonly also the topic, but sometimes a new subject will be introduced while keeping the old topic the same; in such a case, the topic may be the direct object of the verb, and is indicated as such in Cowlitz by use of a topical object suffix.

2.4.5. Reflexive. A reflexive suffix is used when the subject and object of a sentence refer to the same person or thing. These are indicated in English with *-self* suffixed to a possessive or object pronoun (*myself, yourself, herself, himself, themselves,* etc.). In Cowlitz, reflexives are created by suffixing *-cši-* / *-cx* to the end of a transitive verb in place of object and subject suffixes. Although the transitive (or causative) marking is still present (at least historically), these verbs are intransitive. Examples are:

(60) ʔac-q'ə́lp'-<u>cx</u> 'it's coiled up'
s-tú<del></del>-<u>cši</u>-t-n 'he's stretching (himself)'
ʔit tú<del></del>i-<u>cx</u> 'he stretched (himself)'.

Cowlitz often uses reflexives where one is not required in English, as in:

(61) ʔac-sé·x^w-mi-<u>cx</u> 'he's embarrassed'
qanóm'<del></del>n-<u>cši</u>-t-i<del></del>t 'they're quarreling'.

2.4.6. Reciprocal. A reciprocal suffix is used when the subject and object affect each other, as in ʔit qáx̣-tn-<u>w'lx</u>-umx 'they met each other', ʔac-q̓^wó·l-ts-<u>wlx</u>-umx 'they like each other', s-yə́q'·iq'-t-<u>awl</u>-n 'they're boxing', t'úlx-st-<u>wal</u>-i<del></del>t 'they're bringing it to each other'. Few examples occur in available data, and the shape of this suffix shows irregularities: *-wal-* and *-awl-* are found on imperfective forms, and *-wlx-*, *-w'lx*, *-awlx* are found on perfective forms. Like reflexives, reciprocals are intransitive, even though they are built on transitive stems.

2.5. Voice. The grammatical category that specifices the relation of the verbal action to the subject of the verb is voice; it is usually expressed as active or passive (as in English), or these plus middle voice. Cowlitz is a language of the latter type, expressing all three voices. The basic category is active voice, which is unmarked, and indicates that the agent of the verb is its subject.

2.5.1. Middle. Middle voice indicates that the action of the verb reflects back on the subject in some way. This is expressed in Cowlitz as *-mit-* or *-mt-* in the imperfective aspect (see **1.4.4** for the choice between these two), and as *-m* in the perfective aspect. A paradigm of a verb inflected for the middle voice was given in **2.4.1** (31).

Other examples of the use of middle voice are:

(62) s–ʔíqʷ–<u>mt</u>–n 'he's grunting' / ʔit ʔíqʷ–m 'he grunted'
s–yáx̣ʷ=nk–<u>mit</u>–n 'he's wiggling' / ʔit yáx̣ʷ=nač–m
'he wiggled'
s–təlkʷ–<u>mt</u>–n 'it's ringing', s–təl·tlkʷ–mit–n 'he's
making music'.

Middle voice endings are always used on intransitive forms after the inchoative suffix, as in *s–ʔáy's–u–<u>mit</u>–n* 'he's getting well', *ʔit ʔáy's–aw–<u>m</u>* 'he got well' (see **2.11.2**).

2.5.2. Passive. Passive inflection shifts relationships such that the subject undergoes the action of the verb. In such constructions, the former direct object becomes the subject of the verb, and the original subject is expressed (if at all) as the object of a preposition. Cowlitz has three passive constructions.

2.5.2.1. Main clause passive. The usual Cowlitz passive is formed by suffixing *–ctx* on imperfective forms or *–m* on perfective forms. These suffixes (at least the perfective passive) follow the imperfective form of a transitive or transitivizing suffix (*–t–*, *–st–*, *–y–*, *–tas–*, *–mis–*). Examples follow, with the transitive suffix underlined. Few examples of imperfective passive passives were recorded, but the forms correspond to those in Upper Chehalis in both use and shape.

(63) ʔít–aw–<u>ctx</u> kʷu 'whatever is being done with it'
ʔac–ʔáʔqi–<u>t</u>–m tit k̓ʷús 'the meat is full of maggots'
ɬə́x̣ʷm–<u>st</u>–m 'he was kidnapped'
ʔit sáw'la–<u>y</u>–m 'he was asked'
ʔac–q'íw'–<u>tas</u>–m 'he was called'
ʔac–qín–<u>mis</u>–m 'he is wanted'

In sentences like those in (64), the experiencer is expressed in English by a subject pronoun, but must be expressed in Cowlitz by an object pronominal preceding the imperfective passive suffix. Such forms are rare, however. In the examples in (64), *–cal–* is the first person singular object suffix.

(64) t'ak̓ʷ=á·n'i–<u>cal</u>–<u>ctx</u> 'I have an earache'
t'ak̓ʷ=énusi–<u>cal</u>–<u>ctx</u> 'I have a stomachache'

Note that passives are often translated into English as active forms.

2.5.2.2. Subordinate clause passive *–(i)t.* Another passive, which is very infrequent in available data, is a suffix *–(i)t* used in subordinate clauses, as in:

(65) ʔac–qín–mn + k   na   t   qi
     ST-want-REL + 2SG.SUBJ   Q   DET   COMP
       s–ləp·ləp–mi–t̲   tit   qál?
       NOM-boil-MDL-PASS   DET   water
     Do you want that water to boil?

(66) ...ʔał pástn   ʔał   t   qi   s–ʔúmati–t̲.
     ...in   white.man   in   DET   COMP   NOM-name-PASS
     ...as it's called in English.

(67) ʔaqa   ł   t   nák'–aw'=ł   łukʷáł.
     then   OBL   DET   one-LNK=??   moon
       s–təw–ši–t–i̲t̲–umx   cəniáwmx.
       s-pay-APPL-TR-PASS-PL   they/them
     In one month then they got paid.

In the first example, 'dry' is *x̌əp–*; there is a stress shift rightwards, and the second *x̌əp–* is followed by *–t* 'subordinate passive', followed in turn by *–s*, one of the variants of 'third person possessive'. The passive verbs in these three sentences are preceded by *qi* 'complementizer' and a nominalizing *s–* (as are most attested instances of this suffix).

     Cognates of this subordinate passive *–t* have been attested in Upper Chehalis and most Central Salish languages to the north.

2.5.2.3. Non-control passive *–kʷu.* An infrequent passive in Cowlitz can best be labelled 'non-control passive'. This is indicated with a suffix *–kʷu.* A following subject suffix or clitic indicates the patient or recipient of the action of the verb. These constructions are translated with active English sentences or "get-passive" forms. In these constructions the equivalent of the English object is expressed with a subject clitic or suffix.

(68) ʔit   qʷíx̲–k̲ʷu̲ + kn
     PERF   dark-pass + 1SG.SUBJ
     it got dark on me

(69) s-x̣asíl?-k̲ʷu̲–stawt
IMPERF-rain-PASS-1PL.SUBJ
it's raining on us, we are getting rained on

Further details of the use of this suffix in Cowlitz are unknown, although it is cognate with *tači* in Upper Chehalis which is used similarly (cognates are unknown elsewhere in Salish).

2.6. Tense. Past or future time may be specified for a verb or noun, and appears to be optional. Usually, however, perfective aspect is translated as past time, and other past time marking is unnecessary. Imperfective aspect indicates action over a period of time, and can be translated as either present or past, depending on context or the use of tense particles.

2.6.1. Past. Past time is indicated by a clitic /*l* placed between an article and the verb. It is usually encliticized to the article, so one hears *t + l, c + l, ?it + l, ?ic + l*, etc.

(70) mí⁴ta   t + l̲   s-wáks-k⁴
not   DET + PAST   NOM-go-1PL.POSV
We didn't go.

(71) nks + t̲ +̲ l̲   t   s-múx̣ʷ-ši-t-anx
HAB + DET + PAST   DET   IMPERF-pay-APPL-TR-1SG.SUBJ
t   mé·lmx
DET   children
I was paying it for children.

(72) ?átman-n   tit   nawí⁴mx   tit̲ +̲ l̲
die-3SG.SUBJ   DET   man   DET + PAST
?áy's-ms-t-ul-n
get.well-REL-TR-T.O.-3SG.SUBJ
The man who was getting well died.

What looks like an additional article or determiner often occurs after the /*l* (as in the second example just above), but its purpose is unknown.

2.6.1.1. *ta*. There may be a second past marker *ta*; the actual meaning of this particle is not clear, although it occurs very frequently. It may be the same as Upper Chehalis *ta* 'past'. Another *ta*, meaning 'back, again', also occurs; this one is cognate with Upper Chehalis *t'a*, but the two appear to have merged in Cowlitz.

2.6.2. Future. Future time may be indicated in two ways — by using one or the other of the particles ƛ̓a or ɫit. ɫit may be composed of ɫ and a perfective marker or article ʔit (the examples with verbs are all in perfective aspect).

2.6.2.1. ɫit. The particle ɫit occurs before perfective verb forms and before nouns. Neither the usual perfective marker ʔit nor an article occurs when ɫit does, suggesting that ɫit is composed of ɫ and ʔit.

(73) ʔi(t)   cút   <u>ɫ–i(t)</u>   táxʷiwi–c   ɫ   tax̣ʷáˑmc.
     PERF   say   FUT-PERF   sell-1SG.OBJ   OBL   half
     He said he'll sell me half.

(74) <u>ɫ–it</u>   yáy–š–n + kn   ʔac'í   t + l
     FUT-DET   tell-APPL-TR + 1SG.SUBJ   ST-Q   DET + PAST
     s–wáks–kɫ ...
     NOM-go-1PL.POSV
     I'm going to tell them how we went,

(75) qaɫ   <u>ɫ–i(t)</u>   tóˑl'–st–m   ɫ   ʔit
     can   FUT-DET   find.out-CAUS-PASS   OBL   DET
     sxam'álaxʷ   tit   kí   ʔac–k̓ʷəl=áˑy'n.
     people   DET   ??   ST-hear.about=hearing
     People might find out about him, hear about him.

(76) ɫ   yát=ips–il–m   wə   q'íc'x̣   ɫ   tit
     CJ   shake=tail-??-PASS   ??   thus   OBL   DET
     kʷúwaɫ–mx.   (t)   <u>ɫ–it</u>   sámn.
     woman-PL   ??   FUT-DET   salmon
     That's how the women shook their tails. The salmon. (??)

There may, in fact, be a particle ɫ used for future actions, or actions to be realized after the time of a preceding clause. This may be the role of the ɫ in the following examples; see also (92).

(77) ʔac–máɬqni–x + kn   tan   ʔac'í   t
     ST-forget-CAUS + 1SG.SUBJ   now   ST-Q   DET

n + qi   ɬ   s-yáy-ən   titx̣t'íst
1SG.POSV + QI ??   NOM-tell-TR   that
tit   x̣ə́wɬ
DET   road

I forget now how I should tell (about how) that road

(78) ʔáml qi ɬ   tóˑlp ʔaqa ...
      if   QI ?? begin then ...
      If I begin ...

This position between *qi* and the verb is a common position for tense markers to occur.

2.6.2.2. *X̌a.* The particle *X̌a* precedes a verb to indicate future time. Its usage, which is infrequent, is not fully understood. In all of the few available examples, it occurs before a nominalized and possessed verb.

(79) k'ə́c'-n ʔaɬ t   lúwp ʔaɬ t'amúličn
      put.in-TR in DET inside in   barrel
         ɬ   X̌a s-iɬə́n-i   pən√X̌íx.
         CJ FUT NOM-eat-3POSV time√winter
      it was put inside a barrel for them to eat in the winter.

(80) ʔac-qìns tóˑlu-xʷ   ʔac'í X̌a
      ST-want   find.out-CAUS ST-Q   FUT
         n + s-wáks.
         1SG.POSV + NOM-go
      They want to find out how I'll go.

2.7. Mode. The category of mode, used to indicate the attitude of the speaker to what is being said, is not widely developed or used in Cowlitz, and is not well understood.

2.7.1. *q'aɬ.* A particle *q'aɬ* historically indicated 'irrealis' (as it still does in Upper Chehalis). It has been found on only five roots, and the result is an adjective, where the irrealis meaning is no longer clearly present.

(81) q'aɬ láʔx̣ʷ-n'ɬ 'funny'
      q'aɬ ʔušm-n'ɬ 'poor'
      q'aɬ q̓ʷáx̣-nɬ-nat-i 'his getting mad'

All these forms have an unidentified suffix *-nɬ*, *-n'ɬ*.

2.7.2. **ʔak +**. A proclitic ʔak + occurs in several places and appears to be modal. It is usually translated 'might, should, could, evidently'.

(82) ʔit   cún + kn   <u>ʔak</u> + wáks–tl–s
     PERF   tell + 1SG.SUBJ   might + go-??-3POSV
     I told him to leave.

(83) <u>ʔak</u> + ʔit   ʔíkʷtq–n–i–n–umx   ʔu
     might + PERF   steal-TR-PL-??-PL   EVID
     They evidently stole it.

It is not clear whether or not ʔaks- 'indefinite, which, what' is the same prefix, with s- 'nominalizer'. It occurs preceding the interrogative predicate ʔí and q̓ʷóʔc- 'a little while'.

(84) <u>ʔaks</u> + ʔí   xánʔ–x̣
     ?? + Q   there-DEF
     What kind is it?

(85) ʔit   t'úl–ɬ   wi <u>ʔaks</u> + q̓ʷóʔc   t   s–wé·nax̣
     DET   arrive-INTR   WI ?? + little.while DET   NOM-stay
      He came but he didn't stay long.

2.7.3. **Complementizer (?)**. The particles *qi* and *ql* are used to create subjunctive clauses, and clauses that can be translated as infinitives and participles. They are usually followed by a verb nominalized with s- 'nominalizer'. First (and presumably second) person singular possessive clitics precede *qi* and *ql*. *t* + *l* 'past' (and possibly other tense markers), or a *t*- that is not understood follow them. Some uses of these two particles are given in (a) through (g).

(a) *qi*: subjunctive, subordinate (derives adjuncts from predicates; 'for the purpose X, in order to'; usually occurs with *tit* and *ʔac-*, and often with *-tani-*, *-min-* 'instrumentals', or possessive affixes; takes non-imperfective endings).

(86) taw'ət <u>qi</u>   q'alə–mn
     big   QI   camp-INST
     big camp (i.e. 'big [place] for camping')

(87) tit <u>qi</u>   x̣apá–n–ani   ká·   t   qi
     DET QI   dry-3OBJ-3POSV? where DET QI

s–x̣apə́–t–s   t   sƛ̓aláš
NOM-dry-TR-3POSV   DET   deer
drying rack where he dries the deer meat

(b) *qi s-*: subjunctive, subordinate (less restricted than *qi-* alone; occurs with various affixes on the verb, although rarely with *-n* 3rd person imperfective).

(88) mítta   n + qi   s–ʔə́x̣–i–n–umx
     not   1SG.POSV + QI   NOM-see-PL-TR-PL
     I can't see them.

(89) ʔac–qín–mn + k + na   t   qi
     ST-want-REL + 2SG.SUBJ + Q   DET   QI
       s–lə́p·ləp–mit   tit   qálʔ
       IMPERF-boil-MDL   DET   water
     Do you want that water to boil?

(90) ʔáy'tk   t   qi   s–x̣ʷə́l'–i
     lots   DET   QI   NOM-sweat-3POSV
     He sweats a lot.

(c) *qi ɬ*: subjunctive plus *ɬ* (indicates future possibility).

(91) mítta   t   n + qi   ɬ   s–wéˑ–x̣,
     not   DET   1SG.POSV + QI   FUT   NOM-do-DEF,
       ʔus   nə́wi + kn
       if   you,sg. + 1SG.SUBJ
     I wouldn't do that if I were you.

(92) qi   ɬ   tit   ƛ̓áq̓ʷ–aw–m + kn + na,
     QI   FUT   DET   well-INCH-MDL + 1SG.SUBJ + Q,
       n + qi   ɬ   ʔúpɬ
       1SG.POSV + qi   FUT   eat(tr.)
     Will I get well if I eat it?

(d) *qi t + l s-*: past subjunctive (same as *qi s-* with *t + l* 'past' included).

(93) níʔ–x̣   t   qi t + l   s–wéˑ–x̣–kɬ
     here-DEF   DET   QI   DET + PAST   NOM-live-DEF-1PL.POSV
     We used to live there.

(e) *qi t s-*: subjunctive, subordinate (same as *qi s-*, but always has imperfective endings; always preceded by an article).

(94) tit   q̲i   t   s–yác'·yəc'–w–n
DET QI DET IMPERF-swinging-IMPERF-3SG.SUBJ
taq=ál'ps–tn'
close=door-INST
swinging door

(95) tk   ʔáy'tk   t   q̲i   t   s–kʷə́n–y–n
COMPAR lots.of DET QI DET IMPERF-get-TR-3SG.SUBJ
tl   ʔáɬ–ənca
from   to-I
He gets more than I do.

(f) *qi* preceded by *ta* (of unknown function) is often used in expressions best translated as 'how to'.

(96) ʔac–qíns   pút–n   ʔac'í   ta q̲i   t + l
ST-want   know-TR   ST-Q   ?? QI DET + PAST
s...məḱʷ=uyq.   ɬ   t   qáwəm'.
s...bake.in.ashes OBL DET camas
They want to know how we baked camas in a steam pit.

(97) ʔac–qíns   pút–n + akʷu   ʔac'í   ta   q̲i
ST-want   know-TR + report ST-Q   ??   QI
t + l   st... wáks t + l   λ̓a–sámn.
DET + PAST ... go   DET + PAST look.for-salmon
They want to know how to look for salmon.

(g) *ql s–*: subjunctive (often translated 'can, be able, should'; commonly occurs with *míɬta* 'negative', with the meaning 'can't'; it often has possessive affixes).

(98) míɬta   t   n + q̲l   s–ʔéˑtl'
not   DET   1SG.POSV + can NOM-swim
I can't swim.

(99) s–ʔáy's–u–mit–anx   q̲l
IMPERF-sick-INTR-MDL-1SG.SUBJ can
s–láx̣ʷ–m + kn
s-laugh-MDL + 1SG.SUBJ
I feel like throwing up.

2.8. Gender and deixis. Feminine and non-feminine genders are specified in Cowlitz by means of articles and demonstratives. Feminine gender is applied to animate females and sometimes to diminutives. Otherwise, non-feminine gender is used. There are eight articles, four in each gender:

(100)

	NON-FEMININE	FEMININE
INDEFINITE	t	c
DEFINITE	tit	cic
	ʔit	ʔic
	tat	cac

The definite articles indicate proximity in time and space, with *tit* and *cic* being closest, and *tat* and *cac* most distant; *tat* and *cac* can sometimes be translated 'that'. *ʔit* is used mostly as the marker of a perfective verb, but can also be used with nouns. Gender is also distinguished in demonstratives:

(101)

	NON-FEMININE		FEMININE	
'this'	titatí	titx̣tí		
'that (near)'	—	titx̣t'íst		
'that (remote)'	titató	titx̣tá	cacx̣cá	

Other feminine forms were not recorded, although some probably existed. The difference between the two sets of demonstratives listed under 'non-feminine' is unknown; those in the first set were not found to occur in available textual material.[12]

When one of these demonstratives occurs before a noun or a nominalized verb, one of the articles (usually *tit*) occurs between the demonstrative and the noun.

(102)   titx̣tí tit təmx 'this land'
       titx̣t'íst tit ɬəq'x̌k 'that beaver'

titx̣t'íst	tit	n + s-yáyay'-ši-ci
that	DET	1SG.POSS + NOM-tell-APPL-2SG.OBJ

       what I told you

2.9. Plurality. Third person plural subjects and objects are often indicated on verbs (see **2.4.1** and **2.4.2** for some verbs inflected

---

[12] This distinction also occurs in Upper Chehalis, but is also obscure there.

with third person plural subjects and objects), but are not always mandatory if this plurality is clear from the context in which the verb is used. Much the same is true for noun plurals. The same plural suffix is used for perfective verb subjects and objects as is used for nouns (2.9.2). A different plural affix (2.9.1) is used with verbs (and their derivatives) when the activity expressed is of a multiple nature, and under other unclear circumstances. Adjectives have a special plural suffix (2.9.3). Kin terms have a plural formation peculiar to them (2.9.4). A distinctive type of verb plurality is repetitive activity; this is indicated in Cowlitz by $\cdot C_1(V)C_2$ reduplication (2.9.5).

2.9.1. -a(ʔ). Only a small number of examples of multiple activity plurals were recorded. In these cases, -aʔ is suffixed to C_2 of the verb root; if the root has a third consonant, this affix goes between C_1 and C_3. The emphasis in these forms is presumably on the multiple arrivals, freezings, bending, or eating as multiple individual events (that is, they arrived individually rather than together).

(103) ʔit t'úl-<u>aʔ</u>-ɬ 'they arrived' (*see* ʔit túl-ɬ 'he arrived')
       ʔit q'áxʷ-<u>aʔ</u>-ɬ 'they froze' (*see* ʔit q'áxʷ-ɬ 'it froze')
       ʔit yáp'-<u>aʔ</u>-ɬ 'they bent down (e.g. limbs)' (*see* s-yáp'a-t-n 'it's bending down')
       ʔit ʔíɬ[<u>aʔ</u>]n 'they ate' (*see* ʔit ʔíɬn 'he ate')

One instance of -iʔ occurred (this may have to do with the ə́ in the root):

(104) ʔit xʷít'-<u>iʔ</u>-ɬ 'they got up' (*see* ʔit xʷə́t'-ɬ 'he got up')

Deverbal nouns may also use this affix:

(105) ʔac-c'úq̓ʷ-<u>aʔ</u>-ɬ 'posts' (*see* ʔit c'úq̓ʷ-ɬ 'he set it upright')
       qi s-xʷíl-<u>aʔ</u> 'hanging racks' (see ʔit xʷíl-ɬ 'it hung down')

2.9.2. -i-awmix and variants. The most common noun plural marker is the complex suffix -i-awmix. This suffix has several shapes, depending on stress valence and the ending of the noun to which it is attached. The -i- portion of the suffix is infixed before the final consonant of the root or stem when it ends in a consonant cluster, although no examples of this were found when the stressed variant of the suffix occurred. This suffix is also used to indicate perfective third person plural subjects (and objects, although examples of objects are rare). An *i* appears between *m* and *x* before *-i* '3rd person possessive' and elsewhere if the *x* begins an open syllable (see 'his teeth' in (107)).

(a) *-áwmx*. A few roots and stems are unpredictably weak, and lose primary stress to this plural suffix. Except for 'dog', they retain their vowels when pluralized. Several loan words are in this category. Some examples are:

(106)   cuɬ-<u>áwmx</u> 'feet, legs', *from* cúɬ 'foot, leg'
        sk̓ʷat'an-<u>áwmx</u> 'mice', *from* sk̓ʷat'án' 'mouse'
        lisak-<u>áwmx</u> 'sacks, bags', from lisák 'sack, bag'
        stiqiw-<u>áwmx</u> 'horses', *from* stiqíw 'horse'
        qx̣ʔ-<u>áwmx</u> 'dogs', from qáx̣aʔ 'dog'

All other variants of this plural suffix leave stress on the root or stem, the vowel of the suffix is deleted, and the *-w-* is vocalized to *u*.

(b) *-i-umx*. The commonest variant inserts *-i-* between the two final consonants of the stem, and suffixes *-umx*. Note that *-umx* appears as *-umiš-* before third person possessive *-i*.

(107)   ʔális-<u>umx</u> 'chiefs, leaders', *from* ʔáls 'chief, leader'
        cáqʷiɬ-<u>umx</u> 'paddles, oars', *from* cáqʷɬ 'paddle, oar'
        sčə́txʷin'-<u>umx</u> 'black bears', *from* sčə́txʷn' 'black
          bear'
        ɬán-aʔcx-tin-<u>umx</u> 'buttons', *from* ɬán-aʔcx-tn' 'a
          button'
        pástin-<u>umx</u> 'White men', *from* pástn 'White man'
        yə́nis-<u>umx</u> 'teeth', *from* yə́ns 'tooth'
        yə́nis-<u>umiš</u>-i 'his teeth', *from* yanís-i 'his tooth'

A number of noun plurals look as if an *-a-* is inserted, rather than *-i-*, but these are best considered retentions of an underlying root vowel that is deleted in the singular forms.

(108)   kálax-<u>umx</u> 'hands, arms', *from* kálx 'hand, arm'

ƛ́əxƛ́ax-<u>umx</u> 'trees, limbs, sticks', *from* ƛ́əxƛ́x 'tree, limb, stick'

smáyan'-<u>umx</u> 'skunks', *from* smáyn 'skunk'

sxə́ynak-<u>umx</u> 'crabs, crawfish', *from* sxə́ynk 'crab, crawfish'

yámac-<u>umx</u> 'trees', <u>from</u> yámc 'tree, wood'

In two cases -*a*- replaces an underlying -*u*-.

(109) cə́nap-<u>umx</u> 'beds', *from* cə́np 'bed' (*see* canúp-i 'his bed')

mə́kʷap-<u>umx</u> 'fire', from mə́kʷp 'fire' (*see* makʷúp-i 'his fire')

(c) -*umx*. If the singular noun has a vowel (stressed or unstressed) before the final consonant of the root or stem, a simple -*umx* is added to indicate plurality.

(110) cúsaq-<u>umx</u> 'nails', *from* cúsaq 'nail'

šwaq'íq'-<u>umx</u> 'frogs', *from* šwaq'íq' 'frog'

latám-<u>umx</u> 'tables', *from* latám 'table'

píšpiš-<u>umx</u> 'cats', *from* píšpiš 'cat'

táytnapam-<u>umx</u> 'Taitnapam Indians', *from* táytnapam 'Taitnapam Indian'

This is also the plural of at least one loanword without a vowel between final consonants.

(111) má?ksns-<u>umx</u> 'moccasins', *from* má?ksns 'moccasin'

(d) -*yumx*. Words that end in a vowel in the singular add -*yumx* in the plural.

(112) ?ə́mx̣kʷu-<u>yumx</u> 'cedar-root baskets', *from* ?ə́mx̣kʷu 'cedar-root basket'

sása-<u>yum'x</u> 'saucers', *from* sása 'saucer'

wəmúsmuski-<u>yumx</u>, wəmúsəski<u>yumx</u> 'cattle', *from* wəmúsmuski, wəmúsəski 'cow'

One word ending in *a?* loses the glottal stop and adds -*yumx*.

(113) xʷə́ltam=ulic'a-<u>yumx</u> 'blankets', *from* xʷə́ltam=ulic'a? 'blanket'

Two words which end in *yuʔ* in the singular drop the glottal stop and add just *-mx*, making them look like *-yumx* endings.

(114) kʷánayu-<u>mx</u> 'rats', *from* sk̓ʷánayuʔ 'rat'
       sík'-lx=ayu-<u>mx</u> 'snakes', *from* sík'-lx=ayuʔ 'snake'

(e) Irregular. A few nouns have irregular plurals, but still involve at least *-mx*.

(115) káw'us-<u>mx</u> 'hazelnuts, nuts', *from* káw's 'hazelnut, nut'
       kúwaɬ-<u>mx</u> *or* kəwaɬmx 'wives, women', *from* kúwɬ 'wife, woman'
       sX̌aláš-<u>inumx</u> 'deer (pl.)', *from* sX̌aláš 'deer'
       súwin-<u>lm'x</u> 'big rocks', *from* súwn 'big rock'

2.9.3. Adjective plural. Five adjective plurals were recorded with *-tiʔ.* This follows all other suffixes.

(116) X̌áʔq-aʔ-ɬ-<u>tiʔ</u> 'long or tall objects'
       X̌éʔp=awaq-<u>tiʔ</u> 'bowls, deep round objects'
       ʔaks-naq=íl's-<u>tiʔ</u> 'black round objects'

(These are translated into English as nouns, but are actually adjectives in Cowlitz.) Note that the verbal *-aʔ* plural may co-occur with *-tiʔ*, as in 'long or tall objects'.

2.9.4. Plurals of kin terms. Cowlitz kin terms require a special plural consisting of a prefix *nx-* and a suffix *-tn*. It is apparently used on all kin terms, and only on kin terms. See **4.4** for a complete list of kin terms.

(117) nx-ʔém'c-<u>tn</u>   'grandchildren',   *from*   ʔém'c 'grandchild'
       nx-káyʔ-<u>tn</u> 'grandmothers', *from* káyʔ 'grandmother'
       nx-néʔsk-<u>tn</u> 'younger brothers', *from* néʔsk 'younger brother'
       nx-x̣ʷáʔɬ-<u>tn</u> 'older brothers, older sisters', *from* x̣ʷáʔɬ, x̣ʷáʔɬ 'older brother, older sister'
       nx-só·c's-<u>tn</u> 'cousins', *from* súc's 'cousin'

2.9.5. Repetitive reduplication. As noted in **2.1.1**, $C_{1V}C_2 \cdot C_1(\acute{V})C_2$ is the only reduplication pattern used productively in Cowlitz. It indicates repetitive activity or a repetitive pattern. There are four subvarieties.

(a) The root vowel is repeated.

(118) s-cúy·<u>cuyq</u>s-mit-n 'he's stumbling', *from* ʔit
      cúyqs-m 'he stumbled'
      ʔit k'áy·<u>k'ay</u>-n 'he tickled him'
      ʔac-ɫúm·<u>ɫum</u>-ɫ 'it's wrinkled, it's pleated', *from* ʔit
      ɫúm-ɫ 'it shriveled'
      s-máƛ·<u>məƛ</u>'-cši-t-n 'he's shooting at targets', *from*
      ʔit máƛa-cx 'he took a chance'
      ʔit múx̣ʷ·<u>mux̣ʷ</u>i-c 'he paid me over and over', *from*
      ʔit múx̣ʷ-n 'he paid him'
      n + s-wə́q'·<u>wəq</u>'-n 'my running around', *from* ʔit
      wə́q'ɫ 'he ran'
      tém'·<u>tem</u>-m' 'striped horizontally'
      s-xáp·<u>xapa</u>-n-n 'he's yawning', *from* ʔit xáp-n' 'he
      yawned'

(b) The root vowel is changed to *a*.

(119) ʔit ɫə́t'·<u>ɫat</u>'-ɫ 'it bounced' (but s-ɫə́t'·ɫt'-w-n 'it's
      bouncing')
      ʔac-ɫúm·<u>ɫamak</u>' ɫ t k̓ʷús-i 'his skin is wrinkled'
      ʔac-mék̓ʷ·<u>mak̓ʷ</u>-ɫ 'it's lumpy', *from* ʔit mə́k̓ʷ-n 'he
      piled it up'
      ʔit wə́n'·<u>wan</u>'-n 'he folded it up', *from* ʔit wə́n'-n
      'he folded it'
      ʔit x̣íw·<u>xawq</u>'-n 'he told on him'

(c) The root vowel is changed to *ə*; only two examples have been found.

(120) s-yác'·<u>yəc</u>'-w-n 'it's going back and forth', *from* ʔit
      yác'-n 'he took it back'
      s-láx̣ʷ·<u>ləx̣ʷ</u>k̓ʷu-mit-n 'he's breathing', *from* ʔit
      láx̣ʷk̓ʷu-n-m 'he breathed'

(d) The root vowel is deleted.

(121) s-č'éq·<u>č'q</u>-mit-n 'he's whining'

s–pó?s·<u>ps</u>–w–n 'it's blistering', ?ac–pús·<u>ps</u>–m 'mumps', *from* ?it pús–ɬ 'it swelled up'

?ac–q'ál'·<u>q'l'</u><u>x</u> 'he has a lot of wounds', *from* ?ac–q'ál'x 'crippled; a wound'

qi t s–túɬ·<u>tɬ</u>–w–n 'rubber', *from* ?it túɬ–n 'he stretched it'

s–xa?c·<u>xc</u>–w–n 'it's trotting'

s–yə́q'·<u>iq'</u>–tawl–n 'they're boxing', from ?it yə́q'–n 'he punched him'

There is no difference between pattern (a) and pattern (d) if the root vowel is *ə* and C$_2$ is a resonant (especially *l*).

2.10. Diminutive. Diminutives are formed on nouns, verbs, and adjectives. When applied to nouns and adjectives, the new form indicates a small or secondary exemplar of the non-diminutive thing. When applied to verbs, it indicates diminished or slow action, or gives a secondary meaning to the non-diminutive verb (such as 'watch' or 'read' from 'see'; 'hum' from 'sing'; 'nap' from 'sleep').

Cowlitz diminutives are formed by lengthening the stressed vowel of the word, by adding a glottal stop after it, or both. *é·* from *é* is sometimes shortened, and *é* from *ə́* is sometimes lengthened, confusing the source of *é* and *é·* (see **1.2.2**). The glottal stop merges with an adjacent resonant as a glottalized resonant.

(122)   papá·<u>y</u>'=šn 'little toe', *from* papáy=šn 'big toe'
        tá<u>?q</u>ʷč–am'ɬ–tn' 'little gun', *from* táqʷč–am'ɬ–tn' 'gun'
        sx̌álá·<u>?š</u>=i?ɬ 'fawn', *from* sx̌aláš 'deer'

(123)   q'é·<u>y</u>x 'navel, belly-button', *from* q'íyx 'guts'
        pé<u>?š</u>pis 'kitten', *from* píšpiš 'cat'
        qé·<u>l'</u>itn 'elk calf', *from* qílitn 'elk'
        s–č'é<u>q</u>·č'q–mit–n 'he's whining', *from* s–č'íq·č'q–mit–n 'he's whining, he's squealing'

(124)   sqʷé<u>c</u>xa?=i?ɬ 'little meadowlark', *from* sqʷə́cxa? 'meadowlark'

ƛ̓éʔxƛ̓x 'bush, small stick', *from* ƛ̓əxƛ̓x 'tree, limb, stick'

ʔac-x̌ʷé·q'ɬ 'a small ditch', *from* ʔac-x̣ʷə́q'ɬ 'a big ditch'

(125) s-x̌ʷó·x̌ʷ 'breeze', *from* s-x̌ʷúx̌ʷ 'wind'

có̱ʔɬ 'lower leg', *from* cúɬ 'leg, foot'

sax̌ʷó·ʔcuɬn 'wire', *from* sax̌ʷúcuɬn 'iron'

2.11. Miscellaneous affixes and clitics. Affixes which occur less frequently, or have specialized meanings, are given here.

2.11.1. *-i/x* developmental. The suffix *-i/x* and its variants express notions like 'get or become some quality', and can generally be translated into English with 'get X' or 'go X'. Emphasis is on the process of change, not on its beginning or end. Most of the roots that take this suffix are expressed in English as adjectives. The actual shape of the suffix is quite irregular, particularly in the imperfective aspect.

(126) ʔáy-lx 'he got well', s-ʔáy-lt-n 'he's getting well', *from* ʔí·, ʔíy 'good, nice'

qíx̌ʷ-lx 'gain weight', *from* qíx̌ʷ 'fat'

ʔac-təq-lix-kʷu 'air tight', *from* təq- 'close, shut'

xasák̓ʷ-lx 'go wild', *from* xasə́k̓ʷ 'wild'

Stems with *-i/x* transitivize with causative suffixes.

(127) lé·ʔq-ili-x 'soften', *from* lé·ʔq 'soft, easy to tear'

ɬák'-ili-x 'sharpen', *from* ɬə́k' 'sharp'

ɬák'-ili-x 'sicken', *from* ɬə́k' 'sore, hurt'

x̌ʷaláʔ-ili-x-aʔ 'heat it!', *from* x̌ʷaláʔ 'hot, warm'

Some roots do not occur without this suffix.

(128) ʔit taw-ílx 'he sat down', ʔac-taw-élx 'be sitting'

ʔit túkʷa-l'x 'he dreamed', s-túkʷa-llt-n 'he's dreaming'

This suffix appears to be a conflation of two original suffixes. The main source is *-wíl'x* 'developmental', found in several Interior Salish languages. The other is *-i/x* 'autonomous', common in Interior Salish, but appearing to a much more limited extent in most Central Salish languages.

The 'developmental' suffixes have much the same meaning as this Cowlitz suffix. The suffixes labelled 'autonomous' are described as referring to acts controlled by a specific agent. This seems to be a much more limited function of the use of *-ilx* in Cowlitz.

2.11.2. *-aw-* **inchoative.** The label "inchoative" is usually applied to a morpheme marking the beginning of action. It is not clear that that is the specific function of Cowlitz *-aw-*, which I label "inchoative". With only two examples of its use, an exact explanation of its function is impossible, as is an explanation of how it differs from *-ilx* 'developmental' (2.11.1). The inchoative suffix in Cowlitz is *-aw-*, and is always followed by a middle suffix. No transitive inchoative forms appear in the data, but in neighboring Upper Chehalis inchoatives are transitivized using a suffix from the causative object paradigm. Inchoatives of only two roots were found.

(129) s-ʔáy's-<u>u</u>-mit-n;   ʔit ʔáy's-<u>aw</u>-m
       IMPERF-sick-INCH-MDL-3SG.SUBJ; PERF sick-INCH-MDL
       he's getting sick; he got sick

(130) ƛ̓áq̓ʷ-<u>aw</u>-m
       well,better-INCH-MDL
       he got well

2.11.3. *ta-* **'back, again'.** Only four examples of this prefix were found.

(131) <u>ta</u>-wí-laʔ
       back-go.on-imper
       go away!, go back!

(132) mí⁺ta   t   ʔa + <u>ta</u>-s-wítx̣
       not   DET   2SG.POSV + back-IMPERF-do
       never do that again!

(133) <u>ta</u>-s-wáks-n
       back-IMPERF-go-3SG.SUBJ

       <u>ta</u>-s-ƛ̓əq-aw-n
       back-IMPERF-go.out-IMPERF-3SG.SUBJ
       he's going back out

2.11.4. Locative prefixes. Locative prefixes appear to be rare in Cowlitz. Only one example was found with a verb root.

(134) nitl–i⁴n   t'ix̣   s–wáks–n
going.along-eat   while   IMPERF-go-3SG.SUBJ
he ate while he was going along

Elsewhere in Salish, locative prefixes are commonly found with placenames, but only one of the few known Cowlitz placenames appears to have a locative prefix, and that is *nx*- on the name for Lacamas Prairie, *nɪxk'wâ·naxt'an*.[13]

2.11.5. Instrumental. Two instrumental suffixes, *–min–* and *–tan–* (and their variants), are used commonly to derive new words, often acculturation items. No apparent difference between the two is obvious, and sometimes one speaker used one, and the second the other for the same concept.

(135) Ɂáx̣–acx–tn' 'window, mirror', *from* Ɂə́x̣– 'see', –acx
      'reflexive'
      ɁéɁ⁴p–tan–i 'his arrow', *from* Ɂí⁴p– 'shoot an arrow'
      c'é·q̓ʷa–m'⁴–tn' 'steps, stairs', *from* c'íq̓ʷa– 'step on'
      s–yáq'–am'⁴–tn' 'a maul', *from* yə́q'– 'punch, pound'

(136) c'əwk'ə́–mn 'chips (from cutting wood)', *from*
      c'əwə́k'– 'cut'
      c'é·q̓ʷa–mn 'stairway', *from* c'íq̓ʷa– 'step on'
      ká·l'x–min–i 'his glove', *from* kálax– 'hand, arm'
      sac'ə́–mn 'fork', *from* səc'ə́– 'stick in'

The two instrumental suffixes can also occur together.

(137) Ɂáx̣–acx–tn–mn' 'drapes', *from* Ɂə́x̣– 'see', –acx
      'reflexive'
      q'alə́–mn–tn 'campground', *from* q'əlá– 'camp'

2.11.6. čt– 'person from'. Only one example of this prefix was found, but it would presumably be usable with any village or people name.

(138) čt–ƛ̓púlmx 'Cowlitz people', *from* sƛ̓púlmx 'Cowlitz'

---

[13] This is John P. Harrington's transcription, and probably represents either nxq̓ʷánxtn or nx̣k̓ʷánxtn.

2.11.7. *nkʷ-* **'companion'.** Only one example of this prefix was found, but it would presumably be usable with other roots, as appropriate.

(139) nkʷ-yə́p-i 'his companion, someone walking with him', *from* yə́pa- 'walk'

2.11.8. *c-*. This is a rare formative, and its meaning is unknown.

(140) c-íɬn 'food, meal', *from* ʔíɬani- 'eat'
       c-mús 'face', *from* mús 'eye'

2.12. Comparison of adjectives. Cowlitz, along with Upper Chehalis, is somewhat unusual in Salish in having a formal means of creating comparatives and superlatives of adjectives. Special comparative and superlative particles are placed before the adjective. *tk* 'comparative' may precede the stative prefix *ʔac-*; *t'im* 'superlative' may do so too, but only the two examples given below occur in the available data.

2.12.1. *tk* **'more', comparative degree.**

(141) tk ʔíˑ 'better', *from* ʔíˑ 'good'
       tk ʔáy'tk 'more', *from* ʔáy'tk 'lots of'
       tk lílʔ 'further', *from* lílʔ 'far'
       tk ʔac-náwɬ 'older', *from* náwa- 'old'

Some unexpected combinations also result from the use of *tk*, but a comparative notion is still apparent.

(142) tk cóʔ 'between', *from* cóʔ- '??'
       tk káˑ 'which', *from* káˑ 'where?'
       tk ɬán 'day after tomorrow', *from* ɬán- '??'
       tk xánʔ 'opposite, other side', *from* xánʔ 'there'

2.12.2. *t'ím* **'most', superlative degree.** Superlatives are formed by preposing the particle *t'im* before an adjective.

(143) t'im ʔíˑ 'best, *from* ʔíˑ 'good'
       t'im x̣ə́š 'worst', *from* x̣ə́š bad'

3. Sentence and clause structure (Syntax). Little of a systematic nature can be said about Cowlitz syntax, and only a few topics will be discussed here. Although a few pages of text are available, this material is of limited use. The speakers had not had occasion to speak Cowlitz for several years, and frequently reverted to English when they tried. Sentences frequently appear to be fragmentary, and heavily influenced by English. This makes it difficult to make syntactic generalizations based on this material. Sentences are indicative **3.2.1**, interrogative **3.2.2**, or imperative **3.2.3.** Clauses are main and subordinate. Subordinate clauses have special marking for passive (**2.5.2.2**).

Verb phrases consist of a verb, a subject suffix or clitic, and optionally a tense marker, a mode marker, and one or more adverbs or other particles. Noun phrases consist minimally of an article (**2.8**) and a noun or nominalized verb or adjective. Prepositional phrases begin with a preposition, which is followed by a noun phrase. Phrases and clauses may be conjoined by a variety of conjunctions. Particles, prepositions, and conjunctions are listed under those headings in the English-Cowlitz section of the dictionary.

A few clause-level particles can be identified in the textual material, and at least two occur fairly often: *wi* and *ta*. *wi* may serve in part as a focus marker, but beyond this the function and meaning of these two particles is not understood, and they will not be dealt with further in this sketch.

3.1. Word order. It is not possible at this time to make more than a few remarks about Cowlitz word order. Basic word order in a sentence is verb-subject or verb-object; more detail is given below under sentence types (**3.2**). Special attention needs to be given to adjective-noun order and the use of articles with such noun phrases.

3.1.1. Adjective-noun order. Most adjectives precede the noun they modify. An article usually precedes the adjective or the noun or both, but examples also exist with no article. Some 85 adjective-noun sequences are to be found in existing texts, including sequences of a quantifier (a numeral, ʔáy'tk 'lots', xʷáʔkʷuʔ 'all', or kʷumáy 'a lot, much'; about 61% of the examples involve a quantifier). Of these 36.5% are in the order modifier + article + noun.

(144) ʔac-qíns   nám-n + kn   sáli   t
 ST-want   finish-TR + 1SG.SUBJ two   DET
  ʔə́mx̣kʷu–yumx   ɬ   tit   pən√ƛ̓íx.
  basket-PL   OBL   DET   time√cold
 I want to finish two baskets this winter.

(145) t + l   ʔáy'tk   ká́ɬ-tu-mix + kn
 DET + PAST   lots   give-CAUS-3PL + 1SG.SUBJ
  xʷáʔkʷuʔ   ʔit   n + cíɬn,
  all   DET   1SG.SUBJ + food
 I gave away all of my food.

(146) ʔáqa   n   t'óqʷi-stawt   t   xéˑw'ɬ   ʔaɬ ...
 then   and find-1PL.SUBJ   DET trail   at   ...
  p'éntmx   kaɬ   taw'ə́t   tə...   máqʷm
  beside   on   big   DET   prairie
 And then we find a trail at ... beside a big prairie.

Note that this is the same order required when a demonstrative precedes a noun (see **2.8**).

Another 11.7% have the order article-modifier-noun.

(147) ʔaqa   ɬ   t   nák'-aw'=ɬ   ɬukʷáɬ.
 then   OBL   DET one-LNK=??   moon
  s-təw-ši-tit‑umx   cəniáwmx.
  s-pay-APPL-??-PL   they/them
 In one month then they got paid. (?)

(148) k̓ʷə́p-ɬ   x̣aƛ̓áltmn t + l   s-ʔís-kɬ
 very-PERF hard   DET + past NOM-come-1PL.POSV
  t + l   ʔaɬ   tit   taw'ə́t   s-wít'.
  DET + past   on   DET   big   NOM-climb
 It was very hard for us to come on the big climb.

Another 18.8% have an article before both the modifier and the noun.

(149) t + l   t   sáli   t   s-q'íx̣   t + l
 DET + PAST DET two   DET NOM-day   DET + PAST
  s-wán·wanač-ɬ-kɬ.
  NOM-get.lost-PERF-1PL.POSV
 We were lost for two days.

(150) wáks-n   ʔaks-yayús   tan   xán'   ɬ   <u>tit</u>
     go-3SUBJ   ??-work   now   there   in   DET

     <u>qi</u>   <u>taw'ət</u>   <u>tit</u>   <u>xáx̌</u>,
     QI   big   DET   house

     I'll work there in the big house,

14% lack any article at all.

(151) qi   kʷəna + kɬ   ʔiǩʷín   <u>čílačš</u>   <u>ʔáwl</u>   <u>mús</u>
     QI   get + 1PL.SUBJ   a.few   five   or   four

     <u>mán'ac–umx</u>
     little.fish-PL

     we get only five or four trout

(152) míɬta   wə   s-caní-yaɬ.   <u>səx̌ʷ–ta–ɬ</u>   <u>kə́wɬ</u>.
     not   wi   s-he-POSV   foreign-??-PERF   wife

     She wasn't his. She was a foreign woman.

There are few examples with two modifiers, and no particular patterns are evident in regard to article location.

(153) s-t'úqʷ-n + kn   <u>ʔáy'tk</u>   <u>q̇ʷə́l–ɬ</u>   <u>t</u>
     s-find-TR + 1sg.SUBJ   lots   ripe-PERF   DET

     <u>wənáy'x</u>,   <u>k'éˑciʔ</u>.
     huckleberries   small

     I found lots of ripe huckleberries, little ones.

Of the half dozen examples of sentences with a modifier following the noun only one had a quantifier (and the syntax of that sentence is not entirely clear). In none of these cases is there an article before this post-nominal modifier.

(154) kl   t   ʔíˑ   t'əq'ixʷ-tm   <u>x̌ʷáˑˑʔkʷuʔ</u>
     and   DET   good   belt-??   all

     <u>t</u>   <u>ʔitám</u>   <u>ʔíˑ</u>
     DET   thing   good

     and a good belt — all the good things.

(155) qaɬ   púl–ɬ   ta   <u>k'əsk's</u>   <u>ƛ̓áq–ɬ</u>.
     can   grow-PERF   ??   hair   long-PERF

     (You) can grow long hair.

3.1.1.1. Order of possessed noun and its modified noun. The order of a possessed noun (with –*i* suffixed) and the noun it modifies is the reverse of English constructions with a possessive *'s*, but follows the usual Cowlitz pattern of having the modifier precede the modified.

(156) ...ʔawəl   t   qi   s–xʷə́na–w–n<u>t</u>
  ...or DET QI   IMPERF-tired-IMPERF-3SUBJ
  <u>cúl–i</u>   t   nawíɬmx.
  DET foot-3POSV DET person/man
  ...or where a person's foot is tired.

(157) míɬta t n + s–pút–n   <u>t</u>
  not DET 1SG.POSV + NOM-know-TR DET
  <u>s–kʷácil–i</u>   t <u>sə́q̓ʷɬ</u>. tit ʔayó·ʔ
  NOM-name-3POSV DET other   DET medicine
  I don't know the name of that other. Medicine.

The reverse order occurred five times, but always in precisely the same construction when asking about the children of some nephews and nieces.

(158) Well, uh, k̓ʷí   <u>c</u>   Frances <u>t</u>
  Well, uh, how.many FDET Frances DET
  <u>nx–əm'tə́n–i</u>.
  PL-child-3POSV
  Well, how many children does Frances have?

3.2. Sentence types. Because so much information can be included in a verb by means of various kinds of prefixes and suffixes, it is not uncommon that a single word constitutes a sentence.

(159) s–kʷə́n–s–cal–n
  IMPERF-take-APPL-1SG.OBJ-3SG.SUBJ
  He's grabbing it away from me.

(160) s–ɬéʔq·ɬiqaq–n
  IMPERF-jump•REPET-3SG.SUBJ
  It's bobbing up and down.

(161) ʔac–má·y=us–n
  ST-stick.out=face-3SG.SUBJ
  It's sticking out of the ground.

(162)   ʔnks + ʔáy'i–š–t–wal–ɨɬt
        HAB + change-APPL-TR-RECIP-3PL.SUBJ
        They keep trading with each other.

3.2.1. Indicative. The most frequent type of sentence is indicative. It ordinarily begins with the verb, which is followed by the subject or object and/or a prepositional phrase. There is usually no more than one third person noun argument present — the subject if the verb is intransitive (163), the object if it is transitive (164). Oblique arguments and prepositional phrases usually follow the single noun argument (165). An argument can be focussed by placing it before the verb with the particle *wi* between them (166).

(163)   s–púsa–w–n   t   mus–áwmiš–i.
        IMPERF-swell.up-IMPERF-3SUBJ   DET   eye-PL-3POSV
        His eyes swelled up.

(164)   ʔnks + t   x̣ə́p–n   tit   k̓ʷús
        HAB + DET   dry-TR   DET   meat
        They would dry the meat,

(165)   ʔac–qíns   nám–n + kn   sáli   t
        ST-want   finish-TR + 1SG.SUBJ two   DET
            ʔə́mx̣k̓ʷu–yumx   ɬ   tit   pən√x̓íx.
            basket-PL   OBL   DET   time√cold
        I want to finish two baskets this winter.

(166)   t   sxam'álaxʷ   wi   əˑ... ʔaqi   yáwax̣an–m
        DET people   wi   uh   then   play.stick.game-MDL
        people play stick game,

A nominalized verb can also be used as an argument (167).

(167)   nks + x̓ə́l–cši–t–n   t
        HAB + stop-REFL-EPEN-3SUBJ   DET
            s–x̓aʔáw–n.
            NOM-pick.berries-3SUBJ
        they stopped picking berries.

Subordinate clauses are often introduced by a nominalized and possessed verb, and have the same word order as main clauses.

3.2.2. Interrogative. A yes-no question is formed by placing *na* (or *ana*) after the verb and its pronominal subject.

(168) s-yayús-t-axʷ   ʔu   na
     IMPERF-work-EPEN-2SG.SUBJ   EVID   Q
     Are you still working?

(169) t'íx̣   na   c   ʔa + kúwɬ
     now   Q   FDET   2SG.POSV + wife
     Is she your wife?

(170) níʔ-x̣   na   t   qi s-wéˑ-n-ilp-x̣
     here-DEF   Q   DET   QI NOM-live-EPEN-2PL.POSV-DEF
     Do you folks live here?

A verb meaning 'question' is used to ask 'why', and for other general interrogative purposes. The initial glottal stop is merged with the final consonant of a preceding stative or perfective marker.

(171) ʔac-'í   cicu   t'ə́kʷ-t-uli
     ST-Q   that's.why   bite-TR-T.O.
     Why did he bite him?

(172) ʔit-'í   akʷu
     PERF-Q   Q
     What's the matter?, What happened?

The root *ʔíni-* expresses the notion 'do what?'

(173) ʔit   ʔin-áwmx   kʷu
     PERF   do.what-3PL   Q
     What's the matter with them?

(174) s-ʔíni-n-axʷ   kʷu
     IMPERF-do.what-TR-2SG.SUBJ Q
     What are you doing?

(175) s-ʔín-w'ən-cal-s   kʷu
     NOM-do.what-??-1SG.OBJ-3POSV   Q
     What is he doing to me?

A general interrogative particle *kʷu, akʷu* is frequently used, and follows the verb and its pronominal subject, as in the last four examples above. It can also be used after other interrogative words. Interrogative words such as 'what', 'where', 'who', and 'when' appear clause initially, and may be followed by subject clitics.

(176)　ká?　　akʷu
　　　　where　Q
　　　　Where is it?

(177)　kan-ém-m'　　kʷu
　　　　where-??-MDL　Q
　　　　Which way is it?, How do you do it?

(178)　tu　　ká· + k　　　　akʷu
　　　　from　where + 2SG.SUBJ　Q
　　　　Where were you?

(179)　wá　akʷu
　　　　who Q
　　　　Who is he?

(180)　wá + k　　　　akʷu
　　　　who + 2SG.SUBJ　Q
　　　　Who are you?

3.2.3. Imperative. Several variants of an imperative suffix are used to create commands. After intransitives not ending in ɬ, the suffix is *-la?*.

(181)　yác'=us-m-la?
　　　　take.back=face-MDL-IMPER
　　　　turn around!

(182)　?ac-kʷá·-l'a?
　　　　ST-quiet-IMPER
　　　　hush!, be quiet!

(183)　yékʷ-cx-la?
　　　　move-REFL-IMPER
　　　　move over!

The variant *-i-a?* is used when the imperative word ends in ɬ (which may be *-ɬ* 'intransitive' or part of *-mɬ* 'implied transitive'.

(184) cə́kʷ-i-ɬ-aʔ
      lie.down-IMPER-INTR-IMPER
      lie down!

(185) k'ə́c'-i-ɬ-aʔ
      get.in-IMPER-INTR-IMPER
      get in!

(186) xʷal-íɬ=kʷu-m-i-ɬ-aʔ
      hot-link=water-IMPL.TR-IMPER
      heat the water!

Note, however, *ʔúpal-aʔ* 'eat it!' and *ɬə́waɬ-aʔ* 'leave him!', where the vowel preceding the final lateral is the root vowel, not part of the imperative suffix. *ʔís-aʔ* 'come!' and *tawílax-aʔ* 'sit down!' also add only *-aʔ*.

Transitives ending in *-n* also add the discontinuous *-i-aʔ*.

(187) cíqʷ-i-n-aʔ
      dig-IMPER-TR-IMPER
      dig it!

(188) c'ə́xʷ-i-n-aʔ
      wash-IMPER-TR-IMPER
      wash it!

(189) p'ə́lk'=iq-i-n-aʔ
      turn.over=inside-IMPER-TR-IMPER
      turn it inside-out!

Other transitives add *-aʔ* alone.

(190) ká?-x-aʔ
      take.away-caus-IMPER
      take it away!

(191) xʷalá?-ili-x-aʔ
      hot-DEVL-caus-IMPER
      heat it!

(192) čílmi=kʷp-ši-c-aʔ
      carry=wood-APPL-1SG.OBJ-IMPER
      bring me some wood!

(193) ʔíx-c-<u>aʔ</u>
     give-1SG.OBJ-IMPER
     give it to me!'

Only one example of a plural imperative has been found, and the suffix for this is *-ilaʔ*.

(194) ʔilápaʔ néx̌ʷ-t-<u>ilaʔ</u>
     you.PL *pl.*talk-TR-PL.IMPER
     You folks discuss it!

One prohibitive was found.

(195) míɫta   t   ʔa + ta-s-wítx̣
     not   DET   2SG.POSV + back-NOM-do
     Never do that again!

Here the negative begins the sentence, and is followed by a nominalized verb beginning with a second person singular possessive proclitic.

3.3. Negative clauses. A negative clause begins with the all-purpose negative predicate *míɫta*. Before verbs it is followed by a subordinate clause consisting minimally of the verb, which is nominalized with *s-*. The subject of this subordinate, nominalized verb is indicated with a possessive clitic/affix.

(196) míɫta   t   <u>n</u> + s-pút-n
     not   DET   1SG.POSV + NOM-know-TR
     I don't know.

(197) míɫta   t   q<u>l</u>   s-tal'íč-t-wal-<u>s</u>
     not   DET   can   NOM-help-TR-T.O.-3POSV
     He couldn't help him.

(198) míɫta   t + l   s-wáks-<u>kɫ</u>
     not   DET + PAST   NOM-go-1PL.POSV
     We didn't go.

(199) míɫta   x̣̌a   <u>n</u> + s-tó·lp
     not   FUT   1SG.POSV + NOM-begin
     I won't begin

No special syntax is required before a noun.

(200) mí‡ta   tit   q'anápsu. kl   tit   sáx̣linm'.
       not   DET   grass   and   DET   sword.fern
       Not grass or sword fern.

Before adverbs, adjectives, personal names, and emphatic pronouns *mí‡ta-ws* is used. It is not clear whether the *-ws* of this form is a suffix, an enclitic, or a particle.

(201) mí‡ta-<u>ws</u>   ʔáy'tk   t + l
       not-ws   lots   DET + PAST
            n + s-x̣̓aʔáw-m   wásqʷxʷ.
            1SG.POSV + NOM-pick.berries-MDL   last.year
       I didn't pick many berries last year.

(202) mí‡ta-<u>ws</u>   q̓ʷə́l-‡
       not-ws   ripe-PERF
       They're not ripe.

(203) mí‡ta-<u>ws</u>   s-caní-ya‡.
       not-ws   NOM-he-POSV
       It wasn't his.

3.4. Phrase and clause conjoining. Cowlitz has a variety of conjunctions, expressing equivalents to English 'and', 'and then', 'or', 'because', 'so that', 'if, unless, when', etc. One, possibly two, conjunctions are loanwords (*ʔaqa* 'and then' from Chinook Jargon, and possibly *n* 'and', which may be from a reduced form of English *and*). Both are used widely, and probably have replaced native conjunctions to some extent, although these sometimes occur along with a native conjunction. Different conjunctions are used to link verb phrases than are used for other conjoining.

3.4.1. Verb conjoining. The particle *‡₂* links two (or more) verb phrases that belong to the same speech situation, each of which has its own person inflection. If the second verb is subordinate, first and second person possessive clitics precede this conjunction.

(204) s-ʔasúl-n   John t   n + ʔitám'-tn'
       s-take.along-3SUBJ John DET   1SG.POSV + things-INST
            ‡·· cúq̓ʷ-n;   ‡   kʷə́n-ši-c-‡   t
            CJ set.up-TR CJ   get-APPL-1SG.OBJ-??   DET

kʷúmɬ ʔaqa n ɬ ta-ʔís-n.
wood then and CJ back-come-3SUBJ

I'll take John along to set my things up; and he'll get me (wood?), and then he'll come back.

(205) yát'-n + k ʔílp ɬ c'áxʷ-m
twist-TR + 2SG.SUBJ first CJ drip-MDL

tit qaléʔ-i.
DET water-3POSV

You twist it to let the water drip out first.

The two verbs may, but need not, have the same tense markers.

(206) k'ác'-n ʔaɬ t lúwp ʔaɬ t'amúličn
put.in-TR in DET inside in barrel

ɬ ƛ'a + s-iɬán-i pən√ƛíx.
CJ FUT + NOM-eat-3POSV time√winter

It was put inside a barrel for them to eat in the winter.

(207) ɬ-it wáks + kn ʔaml ʔa + ɬ wáks
FUT-DET go + 1SG.SUBJ when 2SG.POSV + CJ go

náwi
you,sg

I'll go when you do.

It frequently follows *kl* 'and' or *ʔaqa* 'and then' (or other conjunctions).

(208) ʔac-qìns pút-i-n-umx ... kl ɬ
ST-want know-PL-TR-3PL ... and CJ

yáy'-ši-n-umx + kn ...
tell-APPL-TR-3PL + 1SG.SUBJ ...

They want to know ... and I told them ...

(209) ʔac-ə... qín-mi-c-tn ʔaqa ɬ
ST-uh want-rel-1SG.OBJ-?? then CJ

yáy-n ʔánca
tell-TR I

They (want) me to tell (it).

It is homophonous with the preposition *ɬ₁* 'in, on', which is also used as a marker of oblique arguments, and is always accompanied by an article of some sort.

3.4.2. *kl*. The most common expression of 'and' is *kl*. This links nouns, noun phrases, and clauses (including some where *ł* might be expected).

(210) ʔúc's   t   wəmúsəski   taw'ə́t   k̲l̲   t
      one   DET   cow   big   and   DET
         k'éˑc'   t   wəmósəski?-ł̲
         little   DET   cow-3PL.POSV
      one big cow and a little cow

(211) wi   ł–it   yáy–š–n + kn   ʔac'í
      ??   FUT-DET   tell-APPL-TR + 1SG.SUBJ   ST-Q
      t + l   s–wáks–kł ...   k̲l̲   c
      DET + PAST   NOM-go-1PL.POSV   and   FDET
      n + x̣ʷáł   k̲l̲   ...   ʔic + l
      1SG.POSV + older.sister   and   ...   FDET + PAST
      yúyx̣ənət   k̲l̲   Susy,
      [name]   and   Susy
      and I'm going to tell them how we went, with my older
          sister ... and yúyx̣ənət, and Susy,

(212) wáks + kn   ʔə́nca   wi   k̲l̲   t
      go + 1SG.SUBJ   I   wi   and   DET
      x̣ə́pa–m'ł + kn   ł   t   ʔik̲ʷéˑn
      dry-IMPL.TR + 1SG.SUBJ   OBL   DET   few
      I'm going to dry a few.

kl is also used to link 'ten' with a following lower number to create the teens (see **4.3**).

(213) ʔaqs   nks + t   ʔə́s–ł̲   pánačš   k̲l̲
      then   HAB + DET   took.along-PERF   ten   and
         t   čílačš.
         DET   five
      Then he took along fifteen.

3.4.3. *n*. *n* also appears in the texts in a few cases where *ł* might be expected.

(214) qa   ta   ʔáys   x̣̌aʔáw–m + kł   ʔaqa
      so.that ??   again   pick.berries-MDL + 1PL.SUBJ   then

<u>n</u>   ta–yáx̌'–u–stawt
and   back-go.home-IMPF-1PL.SUBJ

so that we picked berries again and then went back home

4. Lexicon. Some words can be grouped together in lexical sets. Some of these entail special syntax or inflection.

4.1. Predicative personal pronouns (emphatic). Independent personal pronouns exist which are not part of the pronominal inflection system. They are used for emphasis, and are often predicative.

(215) PERSONAL PRONOUNS

ʔə́nca	I, me
nə́wi	you (sg.)
cə́ni	he, him, she, her, it
ʔiním	we, us
ʔilápaʔ	you (pl.), you folks
cəniyáwmx	they, them

(216) POSSESSIVE PRONOUNS

səncáyał	my, mine
snawíyał	your, yours
scaníyał	his, her, hers, its
sinímał	our, ours
ʔilápaʔ	your (pl.), you folks'
scəniyáwmixał	their, theirs

4.2. Demonstratives. There are numerous demonstratives. They are arranged in sets here to show their interrelationships (repeated from **2.8** above).

(217)   <u>articles</u>:

	NON-FEMININE	FEMININE
INDEFINITE	t	c
DEFINITE	tit	cic
	ʔit	ʔic
	tat	cac

(218)   <u>demonstratives</u>:

		NON-FEMININE		FEMININE
INDEFINITE		titatí	titx̣tí	
'this'		—	titx̣t'íst	
'that (near)'		ʔit		
'that (remote)'		titató	titx̣tá	cacx̣cá

tíʔx̣, tíx̣	this one
xánʔ	that, that one
táx̣	that

(219)   <u>adverbials</u>:[14]

here	šéʔ	níʔx̣, níx̣
there	ɬáq̓ʷ	xánʔx̣, šíxn'

šíxn'x̣	that, there
ʔaɬ xánʔ	there
xʷšéʔ	to here
tašéʔ	through here
xašém', xašém'x̣	this way
xʷuxʷúʔkʷm'	over there

4.2.1.   −x̣. Several demonstratives were recorded with the suffix −x̣. This means 'definite', and can probably occur with others than those given above.

4.3.   Numerals. There are two equally acceptable ways of forming the teens; one speaker used one pattern, the other speaker used the other when forms were elicited, but both used only the first type given here in textual material.

one - ʔúc's	eleven - pánačš kl t ʔúc's; tálʔuc's
two - sáliʔ	twelve - pánačš kl t sáliʔ; tál'sali?
three - káʔɬiʔ	thirteen - pánačš kl t káʔɬiʔ; tál'kaʔɬi?
four - mús	fourteen - pánačš kl t mús; tál'mus
five - čílačš	fifteen - pánačš kl t čílačš; tál'čilačš
six - t'ax̣ə́m	sixteen - pánačš kl t t'ax̣ə́m; tál't'x̣m
seven - c'óps	seventeen - pánačš kl t c'óps; tálc'ops

---

[14] It has not been possible to determine what difference in meaning or use there might be between the different forms of 'here' and 'there'.

eight - cámus

nine - túwxʷ

ten - pánačš

eighteen - pánačš kl t cámus; tál'camus

nineteen - pánačš kl t túwxʷ; tál'tuwxʷ

twenty - cəm'túmx

thirty - kánxtumx

forty - músɬtumx

fifty - cílksɬtumx

sixty - t'əx̣mɬtumx

seventy - c'ópsɬtumx

eighty - cámusɬtumx

ninety - tawíxʷɬtumx

one-hundred - ʔúc's həndəd; t'əmxpánkstlšn; ō´ts
   panEksɬto´mEx FBa

twenty-one - cəm'túmx kl t ʔúc's

4.4. Kin terms.

Words for relatives constitute a special class that uses a unique plural formation, a prefixed *nx-* and a suffixed *-tn*. Kin terms also usually have a suffix *-aw-* preceding the third person possessive *-i*. (Blanks indicate lack of a relevant form in available data.)

English	Cowlitz	PLURAL	POSSESSED	POSV.PL
grandparent	talsnáwaʔ	nxstasnáwatn		talsnáwatani
grandfather	kʷúpaʔ		kʷúpaw'i	nxkʷúpatani
grandmother	káyʔ	nxkáyʔtn	kayíʔi	nxkáyʔtani
father	mán		mánawi	
mother	tán		stánawi	nx–tán–tan–i 'his parents'
aunt	kʷə́ɬuʔ	nxkʷaɬóʔtn	kʷəɬá·w'i	
aunt (mother's sister)	kʷáɬtn	nxkʷə́ɬuw'tn	kʷáɬtanawi	
uncle	kʷáɬamn		kʷáɬmnawi	
older sibling	x̣ʷáɬ, x̣ʷáʔɬ	nxx̣ʷáʔɬtn	x̣ʷáli	nxx̣ʷáʔɬtani
younger brother	néʔsk	nxnéʔsktn	nskéw'i	nxnéʔsktani
younger sister	pé·sn'	nxpasén'tn	psná·w'i	nxpasén'tani
son, daughter, child	mánʔ	nxmánʔtn	maníʔi, nxəm'téni	manéʔi
grandchild	ʔém'c	nxʔímctn, nxʔém'ctn	ʔímacawi	nxʔímctani

great-grandchild	camé·c'aʔ	nxcamé·c'atn		
cousin	súc's	nxsó·c'stn	súc'usi	nxsúc'stani
nephew, niece (on man's side)	snúkʷi⁴	nxnúkʷi⁴tn	snúkʷi⁴tawi	
nephew, niece (on woman's side)	sxáwaci⁴			
husband	xə́n		xə́ni	
wife	kə́w⁴	kəwá⁴mx, kuwá⁴mx	skawá⁴ani	kúwa⁴miši
son-in-law, father-in-law	smátxʷtn		smátaxʷtani	nxmátaxʷntani
daughter-in-law	sápn		sápanawi	
brother-in-law	syálxʷtk		syálxʷtači	nxyálxʷtktani
widow	č'íl'k	č'il'káwmx		
widower	č'íl'kawilm			

4.5. Colors. Basic color terms constitute a special class marked by the prefix *ʔaks-*.[15]

ʔaksqʷúx̣ʷ	'white'
ʔaksnə́q	'black'
ʔaksc'íq	'red'
ʔaksḱʷíq'	'green, gold'
ʔaksq̇ʷíx	'blue'
ʔaksp'áqʷ	'gray'
ʔaksc'í	'pink, red'
ʔaksqʷə́s	'sorrel'

---

[15] It is usual in other Tsamosan and in several Central Salish languages for color terms to have special affixation (although only the Upper Chehalis prefix is cognate with this Cowlitz morpheme).

References

Kinkade, M. Dale. 1971. Third person possessives in Cowlitz. Paper presented at the 6th International Conference on Salish Languages. Victoria, B.C.

Kinkade, M. Dale. 1973. The alveopalatal shift in Cowlitz Salish. *International Journal of American Linguistics* 39(4):224-231.

Kinkade, M. Dale. 1995. Speculations on the origins of an empty morpheme in Upper Chehalis. Paper presented at the 30th International Conference on Salish and Neighbouring Languages. Victoria, B.C.

Kinkade, M. Dale. 1998. How much does a schwa weigh? Pp. 197-216 in *Salish Languages and Linguistics: Theoretical and Descriptive Perspectives*, Ewa Czaykowska-Higgins and M. Dale Kinkade, eds. (Trends in Linguistics, Studies and Monographs 107.) Berlin: Mouton de Gruyter.

Appendix A. Affixes

The following is a complete list of Cowlitz affixes. The list is divided into several parts: (a) lexical suffixes, (b) prefixes, (c) grammatical suffixes, (d) unclear endings. Further comments are included preceding each section.

Lexical Suffixes

Lexical suffixes are word endings peculiar to Salishan and a few other languages which have specific, concrete meanings (unlike grammatical or derivational endings) such as 'head', 'hand', 'house', or 'water'. Ordinarily, these lexical suffixes are totally unlike the independent words for these same meanings. This list includes all lexical suffixes, and some suffixes of uncertain status which seem best termed lexical also. The latter are those which often occur with only one root, but to which no meaning can be assigned. Clear suffixes are given first in their underlying shape (starred) with approximate translations; then all actually occurring surface forms of the suffix are listed (under "variants"). After "in" are listed all combinations of roots with that lexical suffix that have been found to occur, in the form given in the dictionary (many other combinations are probably acceptable). Probable lexical suffixes are given first in their surface form, and without meanings; then follow actually occurring combinations of roots with the suffix. Some of these suffixes here considered probable may actually be misrecorded or misanalyzed, although this cannot be determined from the data available. Inferred forms of root-and-suffix combinations drawn from earlier data are starred.

Under each main suffix heading are given the various expanded suffixes using stem extenders (-al-, -ay-, etc.; no separate gloss can be given for these extenders). The following stem extenders have been found: –al–, –aw–, –ay–, –iɬ–, –ɬ–, –t–, –ul–, –uɬ–, –x̱–. Of these, –aw–, –x̱–, and –t– occur only with numerals (the first two only with nák'– one and kán– three), and they are not cited in this section.

*=áka? hand, arm, finger
  variants: =áka, =aka?,
    =aka, =á?ka, =á·?ka?,
    =ak–, =ka–
  in: *s/?áwt=aka back of
    the hand
  /?áy=aka–mn' thimble
  /?áy's=aka? lame
  /c'ax̱íl=aka? fingernail
  /c'uwk'=áka cut one's
    hand
  /c'ík̓ʷ=aka arm goes to
    sleep
  /milúx̱ʷ=aka? fist
  */qə́sy=aka? drumstick
  /q'áx̱ʷ=aka? frostbitten
    hands
  */tíms=aka? hammer
  *s/t'al=áka? hand,
    fingers, nails
  tɛtala´ka wrist
  /t'am=áka–mn bracelet
    (ENM), ring (LNJ)
  /t'aném=aka–ši– give
    hand signals
  */t'aq=ák–am'ɬ–tn'
    hobbles
  /t'ik'=á·?ka? revolver
  /yal=á?ka–mn ring
  /yalúx̱ʷ=aka–n– double

up one's fist
*–al=áka? by means of the
  hand, using the hand
  variants: –l=k–, –l'=k–
  in: /?ə́ɬp'–l=k– lose hold
  /c'ə́x̱ʷ–l=k– unwrap
  /ƛ̓áp–l=k– put one's
    hand into
  /talíč–l=k– help pack
    things out
  tɛko´leka palm of the
    hand
  /wáy–l'=k– let go
  /x̱ə́q̓ʷ–l=k– squeeze
*–áy=aka? finger
  variants: –áy=aka?,
    –áy=aka, –ay=aka
  in: */c'ə́x̱ʷúynw–ay=aka
    finger
  */lax̱–áy=aka hand,
    finger
  /pap–áy=aka? thumb,
    palm
  /pəx̱ʷ–áy=aka index
    finger
  /q̓ʷax̱ə́nw–ay=aka little
    finger
*=ak̓ʷə́t dead person
  variants: =ak̓ʷə́t–, =ák̓ʷt
  in: /mák̓ʷt dead; dead

person, corpse, ghost

/saʔ=áƙʷt-il-iɬt they're
going to have a funeral

*=**alakaʔ** *nomen actoris*,
person who character-
istically does something

variants: =alakaʔ, =alaka,
=lakaʔ

in: /ʔékʷtq=lakaʔ thief
(/ʔíkʷtaq-)

/ʔéʔɬn=alakaʔ camp
robber (gray jay)

/mós-m=alaka
sleepyhead

s/pót=alaka know how

/qalí-kʷ=alakaʔ fighter

/təq̓ʷ=alakaʔ talkative,
talker

/yayús=alakaʔ worker

=**álaxʷ**

in: /cɬt=álaxʷ cloud, sky

=**álps** door

variants: =álps, =ál'ps

in: /taq=ál'ps-tn' door

=**ált**

in: /kak=ált-mt-n
carpentering

/xaƛ̓=ált-mn,
/xəƛ̓=ált-mn hard
(work)

*=**álwasi-** middle, together,
two parts

variants: =ál'was-,
=álwa-, =ál'wa-,
=állwa-, =álusi-,
=álus, =ál'us, =áluʔs,

=ál'uʔs, =lus

in: /can=ál'wa-x sewed
together

/c'ɬq=ál'us fall apart

/c'əxʷ=ál'wa- untangle

/k'al=álus a cross

/k'al=áluʔs cross on a
rosary

/k'al=álusi-t-m he
crossed himself

kwaxaʹlus hayfork

/kʷaxʷ=ál'wa- nail
together

/kʷaɬ=ál'wa- share,
divide, separate

/pút/kʷaɬ=lus t s/qʷíx̣
midnight

/ƙʷəp=ál'wa- stand up

/ɬak=ál'was- come
together, reach

s/ɬak=ál'was-i its
coming together; corner

ʔac/ɬam=ál'wəs tied
together

/ɬiw=ál'wa- loosen,
untangle, sort out

/ƛ̓əmx̣=ál'us wrecked

.stlɛnawaʹlus room (?)

/ƛ̓iq'=álwas- stick
together

/pút/kʷaɬ=lus t s/qʷíx̣
midnight

/sac'=él'usi- point at

/səc'=ál'wa- pin
together

/tap=álwa- collide

/t'an=ál'uʔs a cross,
  crossed
/t'əlp=ál'wa- splice, put
  together
ʔac/t'əlp=ál'us put
  together side by side
/wan'=állwa- fold up
s/x̣ʷuqʷ=álust-n
  coming together
*=ál'as eyes
  variants: =áˑl'as, =áˑl'u-,
    =áˑl's, =al's, =ls
  in: */c'ípxʷ=ls-tn eyelash
    */c'ipxʷ=yaq=al's-mn
      eyelid
    ʔac/may=áˑl's be
      surprised
    /may=áˑl's- suspect, be
      surprised at
    /may=áˑl'us- stare, stare
      at, look at something
      strange
    /məx̣ʷ=áˑl'as chipmunk
      ?, weasel ?, mink ?:
      "blinking eyes"
    /q̇ʷíʔx̣=al's blue round
      object
    *silaxwaˊls pupil of the
      eye
  *-ay=al's
  variants: -y=al's
  in: /c'ál'p-y=al's drunk
*=ál'wn appearance
  variants: =ál'wn
  in: /ʔiy=ál'wn pretty
    (/ʔíˑ-)

/x̣š=ál'wn ugly
=aɬn
  in: */mátn=aɬn scalp
=áɬqs
  in: /qiw=áɬqs onion
*=ámac- side
  variants: =ámac-, =ámc,
    =amc
  in: /ʔuc=ámac- trousers,
    pants, overalls
    /táy/uc=amc he doesn't
      have his pants on
    */nəq=námc Negro
    *ʔaks/p'áqʷ=namc roan
    /sikʷ=ámc=n'ɬ maple
    /təx̣ʷ=ámc half
    /t'k'n=ámc half-breed
*=áni?- ear
  variants: =án'i-, =áˑn'i-,
    =níʔ-, =néʔ-, =ánʔ,
    =án'-, =án-, =an-,
    =nʔ, =n'-
  in: s/k̓ʷat'án' mouse
    s/léˑx̣nʔ earring
    /ləpxʷ=án'i- pierce
      one's ears
    /q̇ʷalánʔ ear
    /taq=án' deaf
    /t'ak̓ʷ=áˑn'i-cal-ctx I
      have an earache
*=an'il- tree, plant, orchard
  variants: =anil-, =an'ɬ,
    =n'ɬ, =n-
  in: /ʔápls=an'ɬ apple
    orchard
    /cáqa=n'ɬ bracken fern

*/káw's=an'ɬ hazel

*/kəsáx=n'ɬ wild
  currant plant or patch

*k'ap'úx̣ʷ=n'ɬ hazel
  bush

/k'líh=an'ɬ salal bushes

kwaiˊ tɛnɛɬ red-osier
  dogwood

/kʷískʷs=n'ɬ oak tree

/kʷiq'éˑ-m=an'ɬ bark;
  greenish

*/ƛ́ámaq=an'ɬ
  yewwood

/məckʷ=an'ɬ blackcap
  bushes

/pləms=an'ɬ plum
  orchard

/qalíc=n'ɬ willow

/q'áʔp=an'ɬ huckleberry
  plant

/q̇ʷál'x̣ʷ=an'ɬ raspberry
  bush

/sikʷ=ámc=n'ɬ maple

/súskp=n'ɬ hemlock

/táqʷ=n'ɬ=kʷp sparks
  from a fire, live coals

/tawás=n'ɬ ash tree

*/tawás=n'ɬ hayfork

/təmán'a=n'ɬ spruce

t'ɑˑwíˑtsən'ɬ pine

/wənáy'x̣=an'ɬ
  huckleberry bush

/wítk=n'ɬ willow

*=áp bottom, base
  variants: =áp, =ap, =p
  in: /kʷupám=ap=šn palm

of the hand

/q̇ʷéɬ=ap=lm'x wild
  celery

/q̇ʷíɬ=p root

*=ápsam neck
  variants: =ápsam,
    =ápsm, =psm
  in: /ʔáwt=psm back of the
    neck
  s/č'áqʷ=psm nape of the
    neck
  /k̇ʷuk̇ʷ=ápsam- choke,
    stick in the throat
  /q̇ʷíc'=ps-m dirty neck

*=aq voice
  variants: =aq, =q, =q'
  in: */káwlic=q Cowlitz
    River
  /ƛ́p-úl=mix=q Cowlitz
    language
  /pástin'=q,
    /páʔstin=q' English,
    talk English
  /súp=aq- whistle

*-úɬ=aq
  variants: -óˑɬ=aq-,
    -óˑɬ=q
  in: /x̣ʷay=óˑɬ=q- quiet,
    get quiet, shut up

*=aqan hair
  *-al=aqan
  variants: -al=aqn
  in: /limitúh-al=aqn wool
  *-áy=aqan-
  variants: -áy=aqan-,
    -ay=aqn, -áy'=qn-

in: /c'uwk'-áy=aqan-m
cut one's hair
/X̌áʔq-ay=aqn have long
hair
/qʷas-áy'=qn-i its mane
(sorrel mane ?)
ʔaks/qʷúx̣ʷ-ay=aqn
white mane
*=aqap voice, sound
variants: =aqap-, =aqp
in: */katy=aqp-tn
interpreter
/tál=aqap- call, yell,
shout, holler
/tál·tal=aqap- call,
shout, holler
*=áqʷ- prairie
variants: =áqʷ-, =aqʷ-
in: /máqʷm prairie, valley
/náw=aqʷ-m Big Prairie
*=aqʷ day
variants: =aqʷ, =qʷ
in: /cám=aqʷ two days
/kán-x=qʷ three days
/nák'=x=qʷ (?) one day
/tawíxʷ=qʷ nine days
*-al=aqʷ
variants: -l=qʷ
in: t'áx̣m-l=qʷ six days
*-ɬ=aqʷ
variants: -ɬ=qʷ
in: /cámus-ɬ=qʷ eight
days
/cílks-ɬ=qʷ five days
/c'óps-ɬ=qʷ seven days
/mús-ɬ=qʷ four days

*=ási- ??
variants: =ási-, =ás-
in: /t'q'x̣ʷ=ási- slap
*=ásqm smell
variants: =ásqm, =sqm
in: /ʔay=ásqm good smell
(/ʔír-)
/máyn'=sqm skunk's
smell
*=awaq- legs
variants: =awaq, =awq
in: /X̌áq=awaq-tiʔ big
bird (long legs ?)
/X̌éʔp=awq bowl (?)
*=axʷ house
*-ál=axʷ board
variants: -á·l=axʷ,
-á·l'=axʷ
in: /ciɬ-á·l=axʷ=inp floor
/ciɬ-á·l'=axʷ board,
boards
*=áx̣an- upper arm,
shoulder, edge
variants: =áx̣an-, =áx̣n,
=á·x̣n, =ax̣n
in: ʔáɬ/naw=ax̣n to the
right
/k̓ʷəp=á·x̣n aim
*/lápxʷ=ax̣n shield; vest
/náw=ax̣n right (side)
*n/qaqáy=ax̣n shadow
/q'ím'=ax̣n upper arm,
shoulder blade (?)
s/q̓ʷál=ax̣n merganser,
fish duck
/x̣aX̌=áx̣an- break an

arm
   */x̣ʷacéʔm=ax̣n' bat
*-ál=ax̣n
   variants: –ál=ax̣n,
      –ál=x̣n–
   in: /x̌ʾap-ál=ax̣n armpit
=ax̣n
   in: /x̌ʾáq=ax̣n longhouse
      (?)
*=áx̣ʷac– chest
   variants: =áx̣ʷac–, =áx̣ʷc,
      =ax̣ʷc
   in: /sac'=áx̣ʷc-tn' a pin
      /šə́k̓ʷiy=ax̣ʷc hiccough
      /táx̣ʷc chest
*=ayaq leg, foot
   variants: =ayaq–, =ayq,
      =íq–, =ciq–
   in: /kanílstx̣ʷ=ayaq-m
      kneel, confess
      /ɬámt'=ayq– trip
      someone
      /ɬə́k=ayaq– fall over, fall
      down
      s/ɬə́k·ɬak=iq-n
      bobbing up and down
      (on land)
      /ɬíq'=ayq slip
      s/tál'=iq=šn instep; end
      of toe
      *s/t'ə́k'=iq One-Legged
      Man (*myth character*)
*=ayaqi– inside
   variants: =ayq, =ay'q,
      =yaq–, =iqi–, =iq,
      =iʔq–

in: /ʔác=ayq inside (a
   container or person)
   /ʔúɬ=ay'q empty
   /c'ə́k=ay'q be empty,
   become empty
   */c'ipx̣ʷ=yaq=al's-mn
   eyelid
   /kə́m=ay'q fall out, tip
   over
   s/pə́l'k̓ʷ=iq-i its hole
   /p'ə́lk'=iq-i-n-aʔ turn it
   inside-out!
   /q̓ʷáx̣=iq-ši– be mad at,
   threaten
   /sác=iʔq-i its inside (e.g.
   a bucket), its bottom
   s/tál'=iq=šn instep;
   end of toe
   /x̣ə́p=ayq lazy
=áyaqs
   in: /ɬak'=áyaqs Blue
      Mountains
*=ayn hearing (?) (*see* =úyn)
   variants: =ayn
   in: /ʔay=áynʔ good music
      (/ʔíˑ–)
      /míɬta t s/cóˑ-t=ayn-
      min-i he didn't pay
      attention /k̓ʷil=áyn-
      listen, hear, hear about,
      believe
      /ɬawaɬ=áyn leave word
      with
      /tal=áyn– obey, listen to,
      send word to
*=áyq ??

variants: =áyq, =ayq

in: /ps=áyq mosquito

s/x̣ʷə́l=ayq dust

=áyqs

in: /c'uk̓ʷ-áy=qs-t-n

topping a tree

*=ayqs ??

variants: =ayqs, =iqs-

in: /q̓ʷúx̣ʷ=ayqs suck in

smoke

/q̓ʷúx̣ʷ=iqs- be

bothered by smoke

*=ayuʔ animal

variants: =ayuʔ, =ayu

in: s/k̓ʷán=ayuʔ bushytail

woodrat

/sík'lx=ayuʔ snake

*=áy's face

variants: =áy's, =ay's,

=iʔs-

in: /cáq̇ʷ=ay's painted

face

/cúm=ay's eyebrow

s/máy'·miʔs-mit-n

stick out, come to the

surface /pəx̣ʷ=áy's-

tell a lie

ʔac/pús=ay's face is

swollen

ʔac/p'íX̣=ay's flat face

ʔac/p'íq'=ay's scar on

the face

/q̓ʷíc'=ay's dirty face

ʔac/wáx̣ʷ=ay's striped

(?)

*=ə́xan- time, times

variants: =ə́šn, =ušn

in: /ʔít/nak'-u=šn whole

/cam=ə́šn two times,

two at a time

/kán-u=šn three times

/nák'-u=šn once, one

time

/nák'·nak'-u=šn one at

a time

/ʔít/nak'-u=šn whole

*-l=ə́xan- times

variants: -l=xan-,

-l=ə́šn, -l=šn, -l'=šn

in: /cámus-l=šn eight

times

/cílks-t-l=xan-s its five

times

/c'óʔps-t-l=šn seven

times

/k̓ʷí-n-l=šn how many

times?

/pánkst-l=šn ten times

/t'əmx/pánkst-l=šn

one hundred (times)

/tawíx̣ʷ-l'=šn nine times

/t'ə́x̣m-l=ə́šn six times

*-ɬ=ə́xan times

variants: -ɬ=ušn

in: /cílks-ɬ=ušn five times

/mús-ɬ=ušn four times

*=iʔɬti- child, offspring,

young of

variants: =iʔɬt-, =iɬti-,

=iʔɬ, =iɬ, =ɬ

in:/pən/ʔíɬ-s/q̇ʷuʔq̇ʷstm

=iʔɬ April

/cakʷ-íl=iɬ-tn' cradle
    basket, cradle
s/čéʔtxʷan=iʔɬ bear cub
/kawá·ɬ=iʔɬ big girl
s/kʷiné·m'=iɬ-umx
    baby chickens
s/ƛ'alá·ʔš=iʔɬ fawn
/péšp=iɬ kitten
/qʷáy'=ɬ child, baby
s/qʷay'á=iɬ baby
s/qʷécxaʔ=iʔɬ little
    meadowlark
s/qʷóqʷstm=iʔɬ egg
s/tiqé·w'=iʔɬ colt
/wəmóʔsmuskiʔ=iʔɬ
    calf
/xalá·w'=iʔɬ little blue
    butterfly
/x̣ʷáy'kas=iɬ-um'x
    small rabbits

*=íc'aʔ blanket
variants: =ic'aʔ, =é·c'aʔ,
    =nic'a, =c'aʔ
in: /cam=é·c'aʔ great-
    grandchild
    Lā´ᵘkometsa cape, cloak
    */ƛ'álaš-n=ic'a deer-skin
    robe
    *n/ƛ'úk'ʷ-ma=c'aʔ coat
    /taq'é·ma=c'aʔ
    underwear

*-ul=ic'aʔ
variants: -úl=ic'aʔ,
    -ul=ic'aʔ, -ul=ic'a
in: *spanyún-ul=ic'a
    poncho

s/təwúl=ic'aʔ wool
    blanket
/xʷəl-tam-ul=ic'aʔ
    blanket
*/x̣áƛ'-ul=ic'aʔ rabbit
    skin robe

*=ikə́n- back, basket,
    container
variants: =kn, =ičə́n-,
    =íčn, =ičn, =é·čn, =čn
in: /ʔáwt=ikn- back,
    behind, back of
    /c'əl=íčn swallow [bird]
    qi ʔaɬc/k'ʷəp=ičə́n-i its
    scales (fish)
    */k'ʷuʔúl=ičn berry
    basket
    /law-úl=ikn- bottle
    /ƛ'úk'ʷ=ičn top
    */macál=ičn bowstring
    ʔac/má·y=ičn stick out
    of the water
    ʔac/q̓ʷaɬ=é·čn native
    speckled trout
    /q̓ʷé·x̣-aʔ=ičn blueback
    salmon
    /sál'=ičn, /sál'=kn-n
    put a load on a horse
    /sáx̣=kn scratched on
    the back
    /tál'=ičn bag
    /t'amúl=ičn barrel
    /t'amó·l=ičn little barrel
    s.wáq'iq'=čn a frog sp.
    /xʷam'=íčn bent over,
    humpbacked

s/x̣asó·l=ičn openwork
  basket
/x̣wíʔ=ičn backbone
*-ál=ikə́n- bag, container
variants: -al=kn-,
  -ál'=kn-, -l=kn, =kn,
  -ál=ičn, -al=ičn,
  -l=ičn
in: /ƛ́áln-al=ičn how
  many baskets?
  /q̇ʷaɬ-ál=ičn design on
  a basket
  /síl-al=ičn cloth bag
  /təm·tám'-iɬ-al=ičn
  beaded bag, beaded
  clothing
  /təx̣ʷ-ál=ičn half a sack
  /t'ə́q-l=ikn- wrap up
  ʔac/t'ə́q=lič-n a
  package
  /yəx-ál'=kn- pack (on
  the back)
*=ikʷúp fire, firewood
variants: =kʷúp, =ikʷp,
  =kʷp
in: /čílmi=kʷp carry wood
  /mát=ikʷp go after
  firewood
  /mə́kʷp fire
  /táqʷ=n'ɬ=kʷp sparks
  from a fire, live coals
  /x̣ʷál'=kʷp build a fire
  /x̣ʷál'·x̣ʷl'=kʷp keep
  building fires
  /x̣ʷál'=kʷp-mn' stove,
  heater

*-áy=kʷp
variants: -áy=kʷp,
  -áy'=kʷp
in: /c'uk̓ʷ-áy=kʷp cut
  wood, split wood,chop
  wood
  /kʷɬqʷ-áy'=kʷp split
  wood
*=il'qas- dress
variants: =il'qs, =ilqs,
  =l'qas-
in: /sál'c=il'qs dress
  */sáp'=il'qs old style
  apron
  /táxʷ/sal'c=il'qs buy a
  dress
*=íl'si- peel, covering
variants: =íl'si-, =íl's,
  =lsi-, =ls-
in: /lap=íl'si- peel
  ʔaks/naq=íl's black
  round object
  /x̣ík'=lsi- peel
*=íl'usi- rock, mountain,
  terminus
variants: =ílsi-, =íl's,
  =íls, =él's, =é·l's,
  =é·lus-, =él'us-,
  =é·l'us-, =él'usi-, =l's
in: /c'ax̣=íl's sand
  */ɬač'=íls star
  /ƛ́aq=íl's-ti long berries
  (?)
  /ƛ́ap=é·l's downhill,
  bottom of a hill,valley
  /ƛ́ap=é·l'us-m'

downhill, downstream
/ƛ̓ukʷ=íl's hill
/ƛ̓ukʷ=él's mountain
/ƛ̓ukʷ=éˑlus-m' uphill
/ƛ̓ukʷ=éˑl's-m' to the
mountains
ʔaks/p'áqʷ=l's gray
rock
ʔaks/qʷúx̣ʷ=l's white
round object
ʔac/q̓ʷaɬ=íl's spotted
rock
*/səc'=áls-mit-n first
finger
/sac'=él'usi- point at
/taw'=íls big rock, big
round object
*s/tək=áls stone (or
stone pipe)
*/t'ak'á=l's stone
/x̣ʷal=ílsi- heat rocks

*=ínp floor, bed
variants: =ínp, =inp,
=én'p
in: /ciɬ-áˑl=axʷ=inp floor
/saʔ=én'p make a bed
/səʔ=ínp a bed or mat
with a blanket on top
upon which a bride is
seated while dowry gifts
are piled around her

*=ínwasi- stomach, belly
variants: =ínwas-,
=inwas-, =ínuwas-,
=ínus-, =énusi-,
=éˑnusi-, =éˑn'uʔs-,

=ín'wa-, =én'wa-
in: /k̓ʷən=én'wa- predict
/k̓ʷən=ínwas- think
ʔac/ƛ̓aq̓ʷ=ín'wa-x he's
satisfied
/naw=ín'wa- respect, be
proud of
/qʷal=éˑn'uʔs- get
hungry
/sác=inwas-i its
stomach, its insides
*/sac=ínus inside bark
of a tree
/t'ak̓ʷ=énusi-cal-ctx I
have a stomachache

*=ínwati- mind
variants: =ínwati-, =ínut,
=nut
in: /ʔáy/nax̣=nut change
one's mind
*/ƛ̓ax̣ʷ=ínut aunt
/sáˑ/nax̣=nut plan,
agree
/sáˑ/nax̣=nut-ši- plan
/táy=nut refuse
/x̣ʷim=ínut lonesome
/yul=ínut-ši- worry
about
/yul=ínwati- worry, feel
bad, mistreat

*-al=ínut
variants: -ál=nut
in: /ʔay=álnut in a good
humor (ʔíˑ-)
*/ʔay=álnut friend (ʔíˑ-)
/c'ak-ál=nut give up

/c'ak-ál=nut-š-n
  impatient
*=ip base, bottom
  variants: =ip, =i?p
  in: ?ac/p'əlk̓ʷ=ip stump
    pulled over with roots
    sticking up
  /yə́kʷ=i?p- transplant,
    move a rooted plant to
    another hole
=ip skin, hide
  in: tla´mhepEɬExtEn FBa
    skin dresser, skin
    softener
  /ƛ̓ə́x̣ʷ=ip stiff (like
    leather) /pəxʷ-
    ə́m=ip- smoke a hide
*=ipsi- tail
  variants: =ipsi-, =ips,
    =i?ps, =ps
  in: s/kʷəyóh=ips squirrel-
    tail, yarrow
  ?aks/k̓ʷíq'=ps-m
    yellow tail (?)
  ?aks/qʷúx̣ʷ=i?ps white
    tail
  /xʷáyp(s) eagle
  /yát=ips- run around
    swinging her tail (of
    women or fish)
  /yáx̣ʷ=ipsi- wag its tail
    (at)
  *-al=ips
  variants: -l=ps
  in: */tám'š-l=ps-tn
    crupper

=iq
  in: /má?kʷ=iq eat berries
    from the bush
*=iqi- horn
  variants: =iqi-, =iq,
    =i?q-
  in: /púxʷ=iqi- blow a horn
*=iqi- water
  variants: =iqi-, =iq
  in: /c'ə́x̣ʷ=iqi-m'ɬ wash
    dishes
  *s/nám=iq ebb tide
  /xʷíkʷ=iq- dry (dishes)
=iqs
  in: /k'al=íqs=xn-t-m
    cramp in a toe
*=iyúx̣ʷ waist
  variants: =iyúx̣ʷ, =ix̣ʷ
  in: /t'əq=iyúx̣ʷ- belt
*=k'án'- skin
  variants: =k'án'-, =k'n',
    =k', =kə́n- (?)
  in: /cɬkə́n-i its skin
  ?ac/ɬúm·ɬama=k' ɬ t
    /k̓ʷús-i his skin is
    wrinkled /q̓ʷalít'=k'n'
    skin
*=kʷlx spirit power
  variants: =kʷlx
  in: ?ac/?ə́xt=kʷlx Indian
    doctor
  /sə́xt=kʷlx looking for
    spirit power
*=kʷu water
  variants: =kʷu, =kʷu?
  in: /?ə́mx̣kʷu cedar-root

basket
/cə́p=kʷu go after water
ʔac/k'á·c'=kʷu a puddle
s/ƛ́éʔq=kʷu a fish sp.
s/qíwɬ=kʷu ocean
/táw'=kʷuʔ flow (LNJ),
  high water
/təx̣ʷs=kʷu spit

*-íɬ=kʷu
variants: -íɬ=kʷu, -ɬ=kʷu
in: /cáq-ɬ=kʷu thirsty
  */c'əlp-ís-ɬ=kʷu eddy
  /ƛ́áq'-ɬ=kʷu thirsty
  ʔac/míq̇ʷ-ɬ=kʷu muddy
    water
  */náw-ɬ=kʷu river
  /páy-ɬ=kʷu foam, scum
  /putís-ɬ=kʷu hornet
  */sám-ɬ=kʷu herring
  /súlt-ɬ=kʷu beach
  /taw-íɬ=kʷu across the
    river
  /taw'-íɬ=kʷu big body
    of water
  /t'əq's-ɬ=kʷu under
    water
  /wiɬ-íɬ=kʷu riffle
  /x̣aw-íɬ=kʷu fast water
  /x̣ʷal-íɬ=kʷu warm
    water
  /yác'-ɬ=kʷu riffle,
    whirlpool
*=lkstiʔ insides
variants: =lkstiʔ
in: /k'ál=lkstiʔ cramp, pain
  in the side

*=lm'x ??
variants: =lm'x
in: /q̇ʷéɬ=ap=lm'x wild
  celery
=lucn
in: */q̇ʷúx̣ʷ=lucn soot
*=lwltxʷ house
variants: =lwltxʷ,
  =l'wltxʷ, =lwltuxʷ-
in: /cíks=lwltxʷ beehive,
  hornet's nest
  /c'skíyq=lwltxʷ ant-hill
  /ɬə́k'=lwltxʷ hospital
  */ƛ́ə́x·ƛ́x=lwltxʷ plank
    lodge
  /ƛ́úkʷ=lwltxʷ top of a
    house
  ʔaks/qʷúx̣ʷ=l'wltxʷ
    white house
  *sā´kotaxolwᴇ´ɬtxᵘ
    bark lodge, tent
  /súnač'=lwltxʷ mat
    lodge
  s/tiqíw=lwltxʷ barn
  /x̣ʷé·t=lwltxʷ granary
*=l's dollar
variants: =l's, =ls
in: /cám=l's two dollars
  /cámus=l's eight dollars
  /cílks-t=l's five dollars
  /c'ó·ps-t=ls seven
    dollars
  /kán'-aw=l's three
    dollars
  /mús=ls four dollars
  /nák'-aw=l's one dollar

/pánkst=l's ten dollars
/tawíxʷ=l's nine dollars
/t'əx̣ám-l=s six dollars

=ɬ
  in: /nák'-aw'=ɬ t /ɬukʷáɬ
    one month

*=ɬanal- mouth
  variants: =ɬanal-,
    =ɬanil-, =ɬnal-,
    =ɬna-, =ɬní-, =ɬni-,
    =ɬn, =ɬn'
  in: /ʔáps=ɬanil- talk
    nonsense to
    ʔnks +
    c/čə́n·čnq=ɬnal-n he
    stutters
    /čín=ɬni- poison
    */ɬam=ɬní-m'ɬ-tn'
    bridle
    *s/ƛ̓apá=ɬnɬ lips
    /mákʷ=ɬanal- kiss
    */qálʔ=ɬnɬ saliva
    /qanóm'=ɬn-cši-t-iɬt
    they're quarreling
    /qinúy'=ɬn'- argue
    /qíq=ɬanal- choke, hang
    /q̓ʷáx̣-n=ɬna-t-i his
    getting mad

*=ɬan'ɬ time
  variants: =ɬan'ɬ, =ɬnɬ,
    =ɬanaws, =ɬanawxs,
    =ɬaniɬat
  in: /ƛ̓áq=ɬanaws long
    time
    /ƛ̓áq=ɬan'ɬ, s/ƛ̓áq=ɬnɬ
    long time, long time ago

*=ɬc'íʔ body, meat
  variants: =ɬc'íʔ, =ɬc'iʔ
  in: /kʷušú=ɬc'iʔ pork
    /kʷús=ɬc'iʔ body, beef
    */mána=ɬc'iʔ calf of the
    leg
    /náw=ɬc'iʔ body
    /qʷúx̣ʷ=ɬc'iʔ swan
    /šíp=ɬc'iʔ mutton
    /táwn=ɬc'iʔ doe, female
    /wəmúsmuski=ɬc'iʔ
    beef

*=ɬn' implement
  variants: =ɬn'
  in: /t'ə́k̓ʷ=ɬnʔ bow
    /xʷík̓ʷ=ɬn' handkerchief,
    scarf

*=ɬwal- story
  variants: =ɬwal-, =ɬuɬ
  in: /kát/yay'=ɬuɬ interpret
    /yáy'=ɬwal- tell news,
    tell a story
    s/yáy'=ɬuɬ story, news

*=ƛ̓k belly
  variants: =ƛ̓k
  in: /ɬə́q'=ƛ̓k beaver
    s/nə́xʷ=ƛ̓k=mx become
    pregnant

*=míx person, people
  variants: =míx, =mix,
    =mx, =m'x, =miš-
  in: /ʔílmx Indian
    /mé·l'=m'x children
    /nawíɬ=m'x person, man
    s/nə́xʷ=ƛ̓k=mx become
    pregnant

/síɬ=mx man, male
/sé·ɬ=m'x boy
*-ál=mix people
variants: -ál=mx,
  -al=mx, -l=m'x,
  -a=m'x
in: /ʔəxʷ-t-ál=mx strange
  people
/mús-al=mx moth
*-ɬ=mix
variants: -ɬ=mx
in: /ná·w'-ɬ=mx old
  woman
*-úl=mix
variants: -úl=mix,
  -úl=mx, -ú=mx,
  -úl=mš, -ú=mš
in: s/ƛ̓p-úl=mx Cowlitz
  s/ƛ̓p-úl=mš Cowlitz
  s/ƛ̓əp=úmš Cowlitz
  territory
/ƛ̓p-úl=mix=q Cowlitz
  language
čt/ƛ̓p-úl=mx Cowlitz
  people
*=nak- hind part, rear end
variants: =nak-, =nk,
  =n'k, =nač-, =n'č-
in: /kəm'=nač-m bend
  over a little
  s/ƛ̓íq'=nk diaper,
  breechcloth
  ʔac/píʔxʷ=nk crippled in
  the legs
/p'óʔs=nk mink
  (muskrat?)

/súps=n'k tail
/súps=n'k-tn crupper
*/tás=nk-tn whip
s/təq=nk dam
s/túl=nk basket hoops;
  start (the bottom of) a
  basket
/t'anáw's=n'k-tn'
  blanket on top of a
  saddle
ʔac/t'aláp=nk a mask
/t'əq'xʷ=nk- spank
s/xəy=nk crab, crawfish
/xəy'=nak- step back,
  walk backwards
/yáxʷ=nak- wiggle
=nas
in: /qíw=nas smell
  through the nose
=níx̣p
  -al=níx̣p
in: */ɬaq-al=níx̣p war
  club
*=numx at a time
variants: =numx
in: /káʔɬi=numx three at a
  time
*=n' implement, place
variants: =n', =n
in: /c'áx̣č=n' fish spear
  /tása-m'ɬ-n' drummer
  /túluc=uɬ=n glass
*=pakan ??
variants: =pakan
in: */sác'=pakan-tn fork
*=panxʷ years

variants: =panxʷ

in: /cám=panxʷ two years
  old
  /kán-x=panxʷ three
  years old
  /nák'-x=panxʷ one year
  old

*-ɬ=panxʷ

variants: -ɬ=panxʷ

in: /cílks-ɬ=panxʷ five
  years old
  /c'óps-ɬ=panxʷ seven
  years old
  /mús-ɬ=panxʷ four
  years old
  /túwxʷ-ɬ=panxʷ nine
  years old
  /tíʔ-x̣-ɬ=panxʷ this
  year
  /t'ə́x̣m-ɬ=panxʷ six
  years old

*=qə́s- nose, front end

variants: =qə́s-, =qas-,
  =qs

in: /ʔúxʷt=qs dislike,
  disapprove
  /cín=qs fall on one's
  face
  ʔac/c'améxʷ=qs pointed
  nose
  */c'íq=qs buzzard,
  turkey vulture
  /č'íp=qs beard
  sqa-túħqs nostril
  /x̣ʷáq̇ʷ-s/č'p=qs-m
  shave

/ɬíɬ=qs-m blow nose
/mə́qsn nose
  ʔac/mayə́xʷ=qs have
  a hump on the nose
/p'aləḱʷ=qs pig
səlpê x̣.ks nostril
*/šawʔ=qs arrowhead:
  "bone point"
*s/tapə́x̣ʷ=qs nostril
/t'ə́p=qs snot
wi-ni-ní-ħu̥ks buzzard
wutse´s.ks fish spear
/x̣ʷíkʷ=qs- wipe one's
  nose
/x̣ə́λ̓=qs break one's
  nose
s/x̣ʷənə́x̣ʷ=qs nostril
/x̣ʷilúq=qs- snore
*s/x̣ʷúm=qs ridge of the
  nose

*-al=qs

variants: -ə́l=qs, -l=qs

in: /ʔáwəl=qs- sneeze
  Klac-olks Cowlitz (?)
  /ɬaḱʷ=ə́lqs woodpecker

=qʷl̓

in: s/cíqʷ=qʷl̓ a well

*=qʷuʔ tears

variants: =qʷuʔ

in: s/ʔax̣ʷíl̓=qʷuʔ tears
  (running down one's
  face)
  /číl̓=qʷuʔ tears coming
  out of the eyes

*=staqi- fire

variants: =staqi-, =staq-,

=stq

in: ʔác=tq inside, in the
   house
/cə́q=stq- boil, can
/cáq=stq-tn' kettle,
   bucket
/cáʔq=stq-tn' canoe
   bailer
/lám=staq- blaze, fire is
   too high
/ɬə́k=staqi- come
   inside, go in, enter
/ƛ̓íxʷ=stq- put into the
   oven
/ƛ̓úk̓ʷ=stq fire on top
/mək̓ʷ=úy=stq-ni-n-
   aʔ bank the fire!
/q̓áy̓=stq-tn' kindling
s/táw̓=stq-mit-n it's
   blazing higher

*-áy=stq

variants: -áy̓=stq
in: /c̓ax̣-áy̓=stq charcoal

*=šq cloud

variants: =šq
in: /p̓ə́ɬ=šq fog

*=tamix earth, land

variants: =tam'x, =tmix,
   =tmx, =tm'x,=tmiš-
in: s/ə́xʷ-t-a=m'x foreign
   country
s/ilmé·x=tm'x Indian
   land
/kʷaná=tmix- take land
/ɬán=tmx wild
   cranberry (?),

kinnickinick (?)
s/x̣áƛ̓=tmx brush,
   underbrush
/x̣án=tmx cranberry
s/x̣ə́š=tmx weeds

*-ay=tamix

variants: -áy=tmix-,
   -áy=tmx, -áy̓=tmx-,
   -áy=tm'x
in: */ʔilmx-áy=tmx earth
/nus-áy=tm'x damp
   earth
/q̓ix-áy=tmix- get
   daylight
/sək̓-áy̓=tmx-tn' plow
/səxʷ-áy=tmx dew
/təw̓-áy=tmx /tə́mx
   country, territory
/x̣aš-áy=tmx trash,
   garbage, rough ground

*-áy-ɬ=tamix

variants: -áy-ɬ=tmx
in: *s/pəs-áy-ɬ=tmx
   ghost

*=túmx ten, decade

variants: =túmx, =tumx
in: /cm=túmx twenty
/kán-x=tumx thirty

*-ɬ=tumx

variants: -ɬ=tumx
in: /cámus-ɬ=tumx
   eighty
/cílks-ɬ=tumx fifty
/c̓óps-ɬ=tumx seventy
/mús-ɬ=tumx forty
/pánks-ɬ=tumx

hundred
/tawíxʷ-ɬ=tumx ninety
/t'ə̣xm-ɬ=tumx sixty
*=tumx next to, adjacent
variants: =tum'x, =tmx
in: /kʷác=tum'x in two
/p'én=tmx beside, next
to
/tə́q'=tum'x middle,
close together, next to
*-ɬ=tumx
variants: -ɬ=tumx
in: /ʔáwt-ɬ=tumx behind,
after
/ʔílp-ɬ=tumx before
/ƛ́úk̓ʷ-ɬ=tumx top
/t'ə́q's-ɬ=tumx
underneath
*=txʷi- house
variants: =txʷi-, =txʷ
in: /x̣ál'=txʷ roof
*-al=txʷi-
variants: -ál=txʷ-
in: /kak=áltxʷ-ši- build a
house for
*=ucə́n- river mouth
variants: =ucə́n-, =úcn
in: /ƛ́aq=ucə́n- river
mouth
*/naw=úcn Monticello
(now Longview)
*=úliɬn food
variants: =uliɬn, =uliɬn',
=ó·liɬn, =alíɬn, =áɬaln
in: s/ílmix=uliɬn Indian
food

/pən/ƛ́íx=uliɬn storage
place
*/manik=alíɬn mosquito
/mat=ó·liɬn go for food
s/qiwáɬ=aln onion
*s/x̣ap=úliɬn dried
salmon
*=úl'mx berries
variants: =úl'mx
in: /x̣ap=úl'mx-n spread
to dry
/x̣aš=úl'mx coarse, bad
food
*=uɬn' woman
variants: =uɬn'
in: *s/mák̓ʷt=uɬn' sister-
in-law
/pástin=uɬn',
s/pástin=uɬn'
American woman
=úqs
in: /c'aw=úqs dish up,
serve
*=úsi- face
variants: =úsi-, =usi-,
=ús, =us, =óʔs, =si-,
=s
in: /ʔík̓ʷ=us-m wash one's
face
s/cáqʷ=us-m red face
powder
/cmús face
ʔac/c'as=ús wrinkled
face
/c'əx̣ám=us dirty face
/c'ík̓ʷ=us- frown, make

faces

*/ɬəq=úsi-ci kn I hit
   you

.sʻLaˊxᵘs forehead

ʔac/ƛ̓óˑx̣ʷ=s cross-eyed

ʔac/máˑy=us-n stick
   out of the ground

txʷ/mulúkʷ=s-t-n he
   fainted

/náˑm'=usi- end, finish

/nək'ál'=us,
   s/nək'ál'=us coyote

c/nəq=s pupil of the eye

/púxʷ=isi-t-m smoked
   on the face

/q̓ʷíc'=s dirty face

/t'áp'=s- blind

/t'áˑp'=us- take a nap,
   close one's eyes

/t'éˑq=s-m (go) down,
   downwards

/x̣əyk̓ʷ=óʔs hair is curly

s/x̣ím=usi-ctx he was
   grabbed by the face

/yác'=s- turn around

/yáƛ=us-m turn around

*-al=usi-

variants: -l=usi-, -l=ús-,
   -l=us-, -l'=us-,
   -l'=u-, -l=si-, -l=s,
   -l'=s, -íl=s, -il'=s

in: /ʔáx̣-acx-tn=il's
   eyeglasses

ʔac/c'əm'x̣ʷ-l'=s tit
   /silháws pointed tipi

/c'éˑp-l=si- wink,
squint

/č'íɬ-l=s- mess up hair

skwoˊkwols top of the
   head

s/k̓ʷə́p-l'=s forehead

ʔac/ɬúq̓ʷ=ls baldheaded

/ƛ̓áˑl'=us- look for

/ƛ̓əx̣ʷ-l=s-tn bullhead:
   "hard head"

/mélq̓ʷ=ls have the head
   covered, have
   something wrapped
   around the head

/milúx̣ʷ=l's ball, round
   object

ʔac/mulúkʷ=ls be dizzy,
   faint

*s/púkʷ=ls top of the
   head

/qáy'x̣i=l's- blind,
   dazzle

ʔaks/qʷúx̣ʷ=ls have
   gray hair

/sə́x̣ʷ-l'=s- wet one's
   head with

/tə́p=ls- bump one's
   head

/táq=l's-tan-i its lid

s/t'éq=ls, s/t'éq=ls-
   mn' head-band (?)

ʔac/x̣ə́p=ls be covered

/x̣áx̣-l=us Speckled
   Face (a kitten's name)

/yát-l=us- shake one's
   head

/yə́q'=lusi-c he pounded

on my head
=úy–
  in: /məkʷ=úy=stq-ni-n-
    aʔ bank the fire!
*=úyn noise, voice (see
  =ayn)
  variants: =úyn, =óˑyn',
    =áyn, =áynʔ
  in: /taw=óˑyn' echo, noise,
    voice
    /xʷc=úyn– be barely
    audible, barely hear
*=úyaq– ashes
  variants: =úyaq–, =úyq,
    =uyq
  in: /məḱʷ=úyq– bake in
    ashes
    /məḱʷ=úyaq-umx they
    heap it up
    s/p'áqʷ=uyq ashes, dust
*=wil– canoe, container
  variants: =wil–, =wəl–,
    =ul–, =uɬ, =úɬ, =úw'ɬ
  in: /ʔútq=wil– paddle a
    canoe
    */manək'=uw'ɬ a place
    across the river from
    Gate City
    s/napúl=uɬ load
    *s/qamúɬ river canoe
    *s/q̓ʷay'áyɬ=uɬ shovel-
    nose canoe
    /tál'=uɬ go in a boat
    /túluc=uɬ-n glass
*–ál=awil–
  variants: –ál=awɬ, –al=uɬ

in: /taw'-ál=awɬ big
  kettle, big pan, big
  basket, big container
  /təx̣·tax̣-al=uɬ platters
  teˊutlatalúɬ cross water
*=xán foot, leg
  variants: =xán–, =xan,
    =xn, =šn, =šin,
    =əšan– , =əšn
  in: ʔác=xan– track an
    animal
    *s/ʔawt-áqs=xn heel
    /cáɬ=šn shoe
    /c'ax̣íl=šn toenail
    ʔac/c'éˑt'=xan-m he
    balanced on his toes
    /c'əxʷúy'nwn'=šn little
    toe
    /c'íḱʷ=šn leg goes to
    sleep
    kaiˊlɛkcɛn ankle
    /ḱ'ál'=xn'-tn' trousers,
    pants
    /kʷupám=ap=šn palm
    of the hand
    /ɬawál'=xn– desert,
    leave
    ʔac/p'íX̣=šn flat feet
    /qaqáwls=šn hoof
    s/qíw=xn a track
    /qíw=xan– track an
    animal, smell a track
    */qʷúp=šn stockings,
    socks
    s/tál'=iq=šn instep; end
    of toe

*/táp=xn-mn spurs
s/t'alá=šn foot, instep
/wácxan- dance
s/xʷiyq̓ʷ=əšn ankle

*-ál=xan
variants: -ál'=xan-,
  -ál'=šn, -al=šn,
  -al=šin-
in: /ʔuɬ-ál'=šn barefoot
  /kan-ál'=xan- not know
    how, make mistakes
  s/X̓aláš-al=šn buckskin
    moccasins
  /taxʷ-ál'=šn buy shoes

*-ál-ɬ=xan
variants: -ál-ɬ=šn
in: /saʔ-ál-ɬ=šn make
    moccasins

*-áy=xan
variants: -áy=sxn,
  -áy=šn, -á·y'=šn
in: */lax̣-áy-s=xn toes
  /papáy=šn big toe,
    toenail, (sole of foot)
  /papá·y'=šn little toe,
    toes

*='xaw'ɬ row
variants: ='xaw'ɬ
in: /cám'=xaw'ɬ two rows
  /kan-áw'=xaw'ɬ three
    rows

/nak'-áw'=xaw'ɬ one
  row
/x̣əw̓ɬ, /x̣úwɬ road, row

*-ál'=xaw'ɬ
variants: -ál'=xaw'ɬ
in: /cilks-t-ál'=xaw'ɬ five
    rows
  /mus-ál'=xaw'ɬ four
    rows
  /t'x̣m-ál'=xaw'ɬ six
    rows

*=x̣ax house
variants: =x̣ax, =x̣x
in: *-áy'=x̣ax
variants: -áy'=x̣ax-,
  -áy'=x̣x, -ay'=x̣x,
  -i=x̣aš-
in: /ɬáʔkʷ-i=x̣aš-m'
    around the house
  /ɬákʷ-ay'=x̣x behind the
    house
  s/p'n-áy'=x̣x neighbor

*-úɬ=x̣ax-
variants: -úɬ=x̣ax-,
  -úɬ=x̣-
in: /saʔ-úɬ=x̣ax-n build a
    house

=yapí-
in: */ciqʷ=yapí-m'ɬ-n'
    hoe

Prefixes and proclitics vary little, and most occur in only one form. First the prefix or proclitic is given, then its meaning. Since many prefixes and proclitics occur freely with nearly any root, roots are listed only for those prefixes or proclitics which seem to occur under restricted circumstances. Because of limited data, the meanings of several prefixes are uncertain; several of these may be errors either of pronunciation or transcription. They are indicated by question marks. Numbers at the end of entries indicate the section of the grammatical sketch where more information on this affix may be found.

ʔa- your, sg. (*a proclitic*) 2.4.3.

ʔac- stative aspect (indicates a normal state or condition) 2.2.2.

ʔak- modal proclitic (translates 'might, should, could, evidently') (*sometimes a prefix, sometimes a proclitic*) 2.7.2.

ʔit cún kn ʔakwákstls I told him to leave.

ʔak ʔit ʔíkʷtqninumx ʔu They evidently stole it.

ʔaks- indefinite: which, what (*may be the same as the preceding, plus* s- imperfective; *only found preceding the interrogative predicate* ʔí *and* q̇ʷóʔc- *a little while*) 2.7.2.

ʔaksʔí xánʔx̣ What kind is it?

ʔit t'úl‡ wi ʔaksq̇ʷóʔc t swé·nax̣ He came but he didn't stay long.

ʔaks- color (*used with color terms*) 4.5.

ʔaksqʷúx̣ʷls tan He has gray hair now.

ʔa‡c- ??

tit qi ʔa‡ck̓ʷəpičəni the scales of a fish

ʔi- ?? (possibly 'if, when'; also occurs reduced to ʔə-) (*usually requires possessive affixes on the following predication*)

tl ʔacnám‡ ʔi nt'úlawanx It was done when I got here.

ʔə nqi ‡wáks ʔənca, qi ‡ t

303

wé·x̣ k na nə́wi qi
ⱡX̣aqʷséx̣n k tit
mé·l'm'x If I go now,
will you stay and take
care of the children?

ʔisu– ??
ʔisut'úlⱡ X̣ə́x̣ⱡ... if he
came earlier...

ʔnks + see nks +

c– stem formative 2.11.8.
(*see:* ʔíⱡani–, mús–,
p'áx̣a–)
cíⱡn food, meal
cmús face
ʔaⱡ cp'áx̣ in the sun

c– ?? (*reduced form of ʔac–*
?)
(*see:* ʔáy–, čə́nq'–, x̣ə́š–,
x̣úx̣ʷ–)
ʔnks + cʔáy'šitn č'ó·šm'
He's always trading.
ʔak + cx̣ášlx ʔu It tastes
spoiled.
ʔak + cx̣ʷúx̣ʷⱡ ʔu He
must be lost.

cxk– ??
ʔáy'tk cxkx̣ə́wⱡstuse xaⱡ
t síⱡn He grew crops.

či– ??
(*see:* ʔiləp–)
čiʔílp until, before
ⱡit cə́qstqn k čiʔílp nks +
ʔúpalaxʷ You cook it
first before you eat it.
míⱡta t ʔasx̣á·l'n, ⱡit
c'ə́x̣ʷn kn čiʔílp Don't

set the table until I've
washed the dishes.

čt– person from the place to
which this is prefixed
2.11.6.
čtX̣púlmx Cowlitz people
(X̣púlmix–)

kát– ?? (*?see* ká· where)
kátc'iq̇ʷim'ⱡtn' stirrups

kə–, ka–, kn–, kʷu– ??
(*attached to kin terms*
under unclear conditions)

ks– ??
kst'ə́q'tm underneath

la– ??
(*see:* wi–)
lawílatn You go on.

ⱡ– future (*indicates an event*
that has not yet occurred;
combines with ʔit as ⱡit)
2.6.2.1.
ⱡit wáks kn ʔaml ʔa +
ⱡwáks nə́wi I'll go
when you do.
q̇ʷó·can ⱡwáksinumx
They will be leaving
soon.

ⱡ– ??
ʔacq'ə́lp'cx tit ⱡsík'lxayuʔ
the snake is coiled up

ⱡc– ??
talíčinaʔ tit kə́waⱡmx xaⱡ
tit ⱡctíwt ʔaⱡ tit qál?
Help those women
across the creek!

n– my (*a proclitic*) 2.4.3.

nítl– going along, en route
2.11.4.
   nítli+n t'ix̣ swáksn He ate
     while he was going
     along.
nks +, ʔnks + (*once* nkʷs
   +) habitually, always (*a*
   proclitic; may co-occur
   with, and precede, ʔac–,
   tl, txʷ–) (*the variants are*
   in free variation, although
   ʔnks + *occurs primarily*
   in phrase-initial position
   by ENM) 2.2.3.
   nks + tl ʔacwé·x̣ xán?x̣
     He used to live there.
   ʔnks ʔacx̌aqʷséx̣nicx k
     You want to look out
     for that.
nkʷ– companion 2.11.7.
   nkʷyə́pi his companion,
     someone walking with
     him
ns– ??
   nsx̣ʷáli wi ʔə́x̣ʷ+ t stánawi
     his half-brother
nx– -tə́n–, nx– -tan–, nx–
   -tn, nx– -tn' plural of
   kinship terms 2.9.4.
   (*see*: ʔális–, ʔímac– (2),
     kayíʔ–, kʷa+á–,
     kʷúpaʔ–, mán–,
     maníʔ–, mátaxʷ–,
     náwa–, néʔsk–,
     núkʷi+–, pəsén'–,
     súc'us–, tán–, x̣ʷál–,

   yálxʷtak–)
qi subjunctive, dependent
   (derives adjuncts from
   predicates; 'for the
   purpose X, in order to';
   usually occurs with tit
   and ʔac–, and often with
   –tani–, –min–, or
   possessive affixes; takes
   non-imperfective endings)
   2.7.3.
   taw'ə́t qi q'alə́mn big
     camp
   tit qi x̣apánani ká· t qi
     sx̣apə́ts t sx̌aláš
     drying rack where he
     dries the deer meat
qi +– subjunctive + future
   (indicates future possibility)
   2.7.3.
   mí+ta t nqi +swé·x̣, ʔus
     nə́wi kn I wouldn't do
     that if I were you.
   qi + tit x̌áq̓ʷawm kn na, n
     qi +ʔúp+ Will I get well
     if I eat it?
qi s– subjunctive, dependent
   (less restricted than qi–
   alone; occurs with various
   affixes, although rarely
   with –n 3rd person
   imperfective) 2.7.3.
   mí+ta nqi sʔə́x̣inumx I
     can't see them.
   ʔacqínmn k na t qi
     sləpləpmit tit qál? Do

you want that water to
boil?

ʔáy'tk t qi sx̣ʷə́l'i He
sweats a lot.

qi tl s– past subjunctive
(same as **qi s–** with tl
past included) 2.7.3.

ní?x̣ t qi tl swé·x̣k+ We
used to live there.

qi t s– subjunctive,
dependent (same as qi,
but always has
imperfective endings;
always preceded by an
article) 2.7.3.

tit qi t syác'yəc'wn
taqál'pstn' swinging
door

tk ʔáy'tk t qi t skʷə́nyn tl
ʔá+ənca He gets more
than I do.

ql s– subjunctive (often
translated 'can, be
able,should'; commonly
occurs with mí+ta
negative, with the
meaning 'can't'; often has
possessive affixes) 2.7.3.

mí+ta t nql sʔé·tl' I can't
swim.

sʔáy'sumitanx ql sláx̣ʷm
kn I feel like throwing
up.

q'a+ + quality (*a proclitic*)
(probably irrealis
historically; co-coccurs

with –n'+) 2.7.1.
(see: ʔúšam–, č'áš–,
láx̣ʷa–, qát–, q̇ʷáx̣ʷ–)

q'a+ + č'ášn+ tit
nawí+m'x The man is
dangerous.

q'a+ + lá?x̣ʷn'+ funny

s– imperfective aspect
(indicates ongoing
activity, either present or
past) 2.2.1.

s– nominalizer 2.0.1.

sas– ??

sasí?+ani her cooking

sətn– *or* **tns–** *or* **ns–** ??

x̣áwqa+ nsətnswáks, wi c
npé·sn' t qi + t wáks I
can't go, but my sister
can go.

wáks kp ʔilápaʔ, mí+ta
nsətnswáks You folks
go, and I won't go.

sqas– so

ʔit q̇ʷí++ ʔaqa sqascíkn
kn It itched so I
scratched it.

t– ?? (*possibly part of the
stem*)

ʔit txʷíxʷk̇ʷc He waved at
me.

ta– back, again (may co-
occur with and precede
qi, s–) 2.11.3.

tawílaʔ Go away!, Go
back!

mí+ta t ʔataswítx̣ Never

do that again!

taswáksn tasX̣ə́qawn He's going back out.

ti– ?? (occurs only with t'úla– arrive)

tit'úl+ He came again.

tul– ??

ʔit cún'x̣ kn kánm kʷu tulswakə́si I told him where to go.

txʷ– get, become (may co-occur with and follow ʔac–, nks +, s–) 2.2.4.

ʔit txʷc'amə́k̓ʷstm Part of it came off.

ʔactxʷk̓ʷə́ctm It's calm.

txʷt– ??

x̣á+xʷms txʷtmə́kʷp firewood

t'at– ??

ʔacč'úyč'uyuk̓ʷ+ tit t'att'anémim'+tn' a crooked line

t'c– ??

ʔacc'úc'q̓ʷ t'cqit'éqlsmn' headband with feather

xʷ– ?? (*possibly a preposition*)

k'ə́+inaʔ xʷšéʔ Dump it here!

INFLECTIONAL AND DERIVATIONAL SUFFIXES

Suffixes often occur in many variant shapes. All variants are listed and referred to a main entry, where one or more sample paradigms are given showing actual usage, or indication is given as to what type of paradigm would apply to a particular suffix. A slash (/) is used to separate imperfective forms from perfective variants. For suffixes that appear not to be productive, or have been found with only a limited number of roots, all those roots (in the form given in the dictionary) with which the suffix has been found are listed following a colon. Numbers at the end of entries indicate the section of the grammatical sketch where more information on this affix may be found.

Paradigms have been selected to reflect stem variations that are not entirely predictable. The stems of the paradigms given were chosen so that most forms in the paradigm make sense semantically; it was not possible to elicit paradigms systematically, so many of the forms given here are not actually attested, but the inflectional endings given are. Because of this difficulty in eliciting appropriate forms, there are many gaps in the paradigms. Glottalization within suffixes is unpredictable, but usually absent. Examples of forms with third person plural objects have been omitted from the paradigms. Although such forms are possible, they are used very infrequently. My own data have them only in perfective aspect forms, where –áwmx or –i-mx is suffixed to a third person singular form. Paradigms are also given in **2.4**.

Pronominal affixes

	POSSESSIVE	SUBJECT	OBJECT
1 sg.	n–	–anx / kn	–cal–, –mal– / –c, –mx
2 sg.	ʔa–	–axʷ / k	–ci–, ? / –ci, –mi
3 sg.	–i, –s	–n / —	–t–, –y–, –∅– / –n, –x, –xʷ, –∅
1 pl.	–kɫ	–stawt / kɫ	–taw–, ? / –tawɫ, –mulɫ
2 pl.	–ilp	–alapt / kp	?, ? / –tawɫ, ?
3 pl.	–ɫ	–iɫt / –i-umx	3 sg. endings + –áwmx

sample paradigms

POSSESSIVE	
nstiqíw	my horse
ʔastiqíw	your (sg.) horse
stiqíwi	his horse
stiqíwkɫ	our horse
stiqíwilp	your (pl.) horse
stiqíwɫ	their horse

INTRANSITIVE

IMPERFECTIVE		PERFECTIVE	
sʔílan'anx	I am singing	ʔit ʔíln kn	I sang
sʔílan'axʷ	you (sg.) are singing	ʔit ʔíln k	you (sg.) sang
sʔílan'n	he/she is singing	ʔit ʔíln	he/she sang
sʔílan'stawt	we are singing	ʔit ʔíln kɫ	we sang
sʔílan'alapt	you (pl.) are singing	ʔit ʔíln kp	you (pl.) sang
sʔílan'iɫt	they are singing	ʔit ʔílinumx	they sang

TRANSITIVE
-t- Object Paradigm

IMPERFECTIVE		PERFECTIVE	
stal'íčicaln	he is helping me	ʔit tal'íčic	he helped me
stal'íčicin	he is helping you (sg.)	ʔit tal'íčici	he helped you (sg.)

stal'íčitn	he is helping him/her/it	ʔit tal'íčn	he helped him/her/it
stal'íčituln	he is helping the other one	ʔit tal'íčtwali	he helped the other one
stal'íčitawn	he is helping us		
??		ʔit tal'íčitaw⁴	he helped you (pl.)
stal'íčtwaln	they are helping each other	ʔit tal'íčitawəlx	they helped each other
stal'íčicšitn	he is helping himself	ʔit tal'íčicx	he helped himself
stal'íčictx	he is being helped	ʔit tal'íčitm	he was helped

Causative Object Paradigm

sáw'lamaln	he is asking me	ʔit sáw'lamx	he asked me
sáw'lamin	he is asking you (sg.)	ʔit sáw'lami	he asked you (sg.)
sáw'layn	he is asking him/her	ʔit sáw'lix	he asked him/her
sáw'lawaln	he is asking the other one	ʔit sáw'lawali	he asked the other one
??		ʔit sáw'lamul⁴	he asked us
??		ʔit sáw'lawəlx	they asked each other
??		ʔit sáw'licx	he asked himself
??		ʔit sáw'laym	he was asked

−∅− Object Paradigm

s⁴awálamaln	he is leaving me	ʔit ⁴awálamx	he left me
??		??	
s⁴awáln	he is leaving him/her	ʔit ⁴áw⁴	he left him/her
??		??	
??		??	
??		ʔit ⁴aw'ál'wəlx	they left each other
??		??	
??		ʔit ⁴awálm	he was left

−V˙−, −ʔ−, −V˙ʔ− diminutive
2.10.
sk̓ʷá˙ymtn he's nibbling
vs.
sk̓ʷáyatn he's chewing it
x̣áʔx small house *vs.* x̣áx house
kʷó˙m'⁴ little piece of wood *vs.* kʷúm⁴ piece

of wood
sčéʔtxʷaniʔ⁴ bear cub *vs.* sčətxʷn' black bear

−aʔ−, −a− multiple activity
(infrequent; follows the first consonant after the root vowel) 2.9.1.
(*see:* ʔí⁴ani−, c'úq̓ʷ−, ká⁴−, X̣áq−, múq̓ʷa−, náwa−,

q'áxʷa-, q̓ʷíx̣- (?),
t'úla-, wakəs-, wáq'-,
x̣ʷə́t'a-, x̣ʷíl-, yáƛa-,
yáp'a-)
ʔacwáq'aɬ They are open.
ʔit káɬaʔtumix He
distributed them.
ʔacc'úq̓ʷaʔɬ posts

-aʔ -a sg. imperative
(*transitive or intransitive*)
3.2.3.

-acx perfective reflexive (*see*
-cši-t-)

-ál-, -al-, -l- compound
(*links members of a
compound word*) **2.1.2.**
(*see*: čilks-t-, kan-, kás-,
kʷə́c-, ləq-, lílʔ-,
mús-, p'én'-)
ləqálkuwɬ buy a wife
(ləq-, kəwál-)
musalsq'íx̣ Thursday
(mús-, q'íx̣-)
p'énlxawɬ by the road
(p'én'-, x̣əwál-)

-alapt, -alp second person
plural subject,
imperfective aspect (*see*
intransitive paradigm)
2.4.1.

-aɬ, -yaɬ possessive of
predicative pronouns
2.4.3.4, 4.1.
(*see*: ʔə́nca-, ʔiním-, cə́ni-
(2), nə́wi-)
siníḿaɬ our, ours
səncáyaɬ my, mine

-amal-, -mal-, -mal'-,

**-aml-, -ml-, -m'l-,
-ml'- / -am'ɬ, -amɬ,
-m'ɬ, -mɬ** implied
transitive (*changes
transitives to
intransitives, but implies
an object that is not
stated*) **2.3.7, 2.4.2.**

Implied Transitive

IMPERFECTIVE

sk̓ʷə́nmlanx	I am counting
sk̓ʷə́nmlax̌ʷ	you (sg.) are counting
sk̓ʷə́nmln	he/she is counting
sk̓ʷə́nmlstawt	we are counting
sk̓ʷə́nmlalapt	you (pl.) are counting
sk̓ʷə́nmliɬt	they are counting

PERFECTIVE

ʔit k̓ʷə́nam'ɬ kn	I counted
ʔit k̓ʷə́nam'ɬ k	you (sg.) counted
ʔit k̓ʷə́nam'ɬ	he/she counted
ʔit k̓ʷə́nam'ɬ kɬ	we counted
ʔit k̓ʷə́nam'ɬ kp	you (pl.) counted
ʔit k̓ʷə́nam'iɬumx	they counted

-amn relational (*see* -mis-)

-anx, -nx first person
singular subject,
imperfective aspect (*see
intransitive paradigm*)
2.4.1.

-aw- kinterm extender before
possessive -*i*) **2.4.3.3.**

-aw-, -u- inchoative
(*followed by* -mit-/-m
middle) (indicates
something becoming
something else) **2.11.2.**
(*see*: ʔáy's-, ƛáq̓ʷ-)

ʔit ƛ̓áq̓ʷawm He got well.
sʔáy'sumitn He's getting
sick.
-awal-, -awl-, -awll-,
-wal- / -awlx, -aw'lx,
-awl'x, -wlx, -wl'x,
-swlx, -wlx, -w'lx
reciprocal (*see transitive
paradigms*) 2.4.6.
-áwmiš- / -awmix-,
-áwmx, -áwm'x,
-awm'x plural 2.9.2.
-aw'lx reciprocal (*see*
-awal-)
-axʷ, -xʷ second person
singular subject,
imperfective aspect (*see
intransitive paradigm*)
2.4.1.
-ayumx plural (*see* -umiš-)
-c first person singular
object, perfective aspect
(*see transitive paradigms*)
2.4.2.
-cal- first person singular
object, imperfective
aspect (*see transitive
paradigms*) 2.4.2.
-ci- second person singular
object, imperfective
aspect (*see transitive
paradigms*) 2.4.2.
-ci second person singular
object, perfective aspect
(*see transitive paradigms*)
2.4.2.
-cši-t-, -cš- / -cx, -acx,
-icx, -cxi- reflexive (*see*

transitive paradigms)
2.4.5.
-ctx, -ctix- / -m passive
2.5.2.1.
-cwlx reciprocal (*see*
-awal-)
-cx, -cxi- reflexive (*see*
-cši-t-)
-ell- developmental (*see*
-lt-)
-élx- developmental (*see*
-lt-)
-i third person singular
possessive (*see possessive
paradigm*) 2.4.3.1.
-icx reflexive (*see* -cši-t-)
-il-, -ili- developmental (*see*
-lt-)
-ila? plural imperative 3.2.3.
-ílax developmental (*see*
-lt-)
-ilix developmental (*see*
-lt-)
-ills- developmental (*see*
-lt-)
-ilp second person plural
possessive (*see possessive
paradigm*) 2.4.3.
-ílx developmental (*see* -lt-)
-iɬt third person plural
subject, imperfective
aspect (*see intransitive
paradigm*) 2.4.1.
-inumx plural (*see* -umiš-)
-i-umx third person plural
subject or object,
perfective aspect (*the* -i-
precedes the last

consonant of the stem)
2.4.1, 2.9.2.

-kⱡ first person plural
possessive (*see possessive
paradigm*) 2.4.3.

-kʷu non-control passive (*as
in 'I got rained on'*) 2.5.2.3.
(*see*: qʷíx̱-, x̱ʷúxʷa-,
x̱asíli?-)
?it qʷíx̱kʷu kn It got dark
on me.
?it qʷíx̱kʷuy'umx
Darkness came on
them.
sx̱asíl?kùstawt It's raining
on us., We're getting
rained on.

-l- developmental (*see* -lt-)
-l- compound (*see* -ál-)
-la? sg. imperative
(*intransitive*) 3.2.3.
-lix developmental (*see* -lt-)
-llt- developmental (*see*
-lt-)
-lm'x plural (*see* -umiš-)
**-lt-, -l't-, -llt-, -ills-, -éll-
/ -ili-, -ilix, -lix, -l'ix,
-ílax-, -ílx, -élx, -l'ix,
-lx, -l'x, -l's, -il-, -l-**
developmental 2.11.1.
(*see*: ?áwat-, ?áy-, ?íˑ-,
lé?q-, ⱡə́k'-, ⱡə́k'a-,
x̱'aqám'-, x̱'atə́x̱-,
x̱'ə́x̱ʷ-, x̱'íx- (3), níⱡi-
(2), qíxʷ-, qʷíx̱-,
síq̓ʷ-, tál'š-, taw-
ílax- (6), tə́q-, túkʷa-,
xasə́k̓ʷ-, x̱ə́m-, x̱ə́š-,

x̱ʷalá?- (2), x̱ʷél'-)
?it ?áylx He got well. (*see
?íˑ good, nice*)
?it léˑ?qilix He softened it.
(*see* lé?q soft)
sníⱡili his coming back to
life (*see* ?acníⱡⱡ he's
alive)
sqʷíx̱ltn night, darkness
(*see* sqʷíx̱ night)
stúkʷtukʷalltn He's
dreaming.

-lx developmental (*see* -lt-)
-l'ix, -l's, -l't-, -l'x
developmental (*see* -lt-)
-ⱡ intransitive, perfective
aspect (*see* -w-) 2.3.1.
-ⱡ third person plural
possessive (*see possessive
paradigm*) 2.4.3.
-ⱡ- compound (*links
members of a compound
word*) 2.1.2.
(*see*: ?áwat-, ?ilə́p-,
taw'ə́t-)
?áwtⱡnawi behind you
(nə́wi you, sg.)
?ílpⱡənca in front of me
(?ə́nca I, me)

-m middle voice (*see* -mit-)
-m passive (*see transitive
paradigms*, -mis-
relational, -stw- *and*
-tw- causatives, *and*
-tas-) 2.5.2.1.
-mal- first person singular
object, imperfective
aspect (*see transitive*

paradigms) 2.4.2.

-mal-, -mal'-, -ml-, -m'l-, -ml'- / -m'ɬ, mɬ
implied transitive (*see* -amal-)

-mi second person singular object, perfective aspect (*see transitive paradigms*) 2.4.2.

-mi- relational (*see* -mis-)

-min- relational (*see* -mis-)

-min-, -ə́min-, -ə́mn, -mn, -mn', -m'n
instrumental, implement, site 2.11.5.

(*see*: ʔáy-, ʔə́x̣-, c'əwə́k'-, c'ípxʷ-, c'íq̓ʷa-, c'íwi-, kálax-, kʷəná-, kʷə́s-, ləw-, ɬâ´mɛn, X̌aʔáwi-, X̌amə́mn, məkʷə́-, mə́q̓ʷa-, náwa- (2), pátaq-, patao´xɛmɛn, púti-, q'ayúq̓ʷ-, q'ét'a-, q'əlá- (2), qʷéx̣iʔxʷ-, q̓ʷax̣ʷə́-, sánti- (3), səc'ə́-, səxʷáy'-, šúkʷa-, tu–íl–ŭ–pa–min, táxʷayway- (2), tə́p-, tíwat-, t'ám-, t'ə́qi-, xay'álu-, xʷay'ús-, x̣áɬxʷa-, x̣asíliʔ-, x̣əX̌-, x̣ʷál'a-, yal-, yáx̣a-)

-mis-, -ms-, -mi-, -min-, -mn, -mn', -amn
relational 2.3.5, 2.4.2.

Relational
IMPERFECTIVE

sqínmicaln he is wanting me
sqínmicin he is wanting you (sg.)
sqínmisn he is wanting him/her
??
??
??
??
??
??

STATIVE

ʔacqínmic he wants me
ʔacqínmici he wants you (sg.)
ʔacqínmn he wants him/her
??
ʔacqínmitawɬ he wants us
ʔacqínminumx he wants them
ʔacqínmistawlx they want each other
??
ʔacqínmism he is wanted

-miš plural (*see* -umiš-)
-mit-, -mt- / -m middle voice 2.5.1.

Middle
IMPERFECTIVE

sX̌á·x̣nmitanx I am hunting
sX̌á·x̣nmitaxʷ you (sg.) are hunting
sX̌á·x̣nmitn he/she is hunting
sX̌á·x̣nmitstawt we are hunting
sX̌á·x̣nmitalapt you (pl.) are hunting
sX̌á·x̣nmitiɬt they are hunting

PERFECTIVE

ʔit X̌á·x̣anm kn I hunted
ʔit X̌á·x̣anm k you (sg.) hunted
ʔit X̌á·x̣anm he/she hunted
ʔit X̌á·x̣anm kɬ we hunted
ʔit X̌á·x̣anm kp you (pl.) hunted
ʔit X̌á·x̣animumx they hunted

-ml-, -ml'-, -mɫ implied transitive (*see* -amal-)

-mn, -mn' relational (*see* -mis-)

-ms- relational (*see* -mis-)

-mt- middle voice (*see* -mit-)

-mulɫ first plural object, perfective aspect (*see transitive paradigms*) 2.4.2.

-mx first person singular object, perfective aspect (*see transitive paradigms*) 2.4.2.

-mx plural (*see* -umiš-)

-m' locative (*see*: ʔímn-, č'úš-, káˑ-, lílʔ-, ɫáʔkʷ-, ɫákʷ-, ɫáX̣p-, X̣áq-, X̣ə́p-, X̣úkʷ- (4), pútmix-, p'aléˑč'-, p'étl-, tál'-, xašém', xʷáw'kʷ-, xʷúʔkʷ-, yaləm'-, yəlúx̣ʷ-)

  -l-m' (*see* páɫkʷu-)

  léˑlm' away (*see* lílʔ far)

  ɫáX̣pm' downwards, downstream (*see* ɫáX̣p below)

  póʔtmišm' towards the river (*see* pútmx downriver, down to the river)

-m'l-, -m'ɫ implied transitive (*see* -amal-)

-m'ɫ implied transitive (*see* -amal-)

-n third person singular subject, imperfective aspect (*see intransitive paradigm*) 2.4.1.

-n perfective transitive (*see transitive paradigms*) 2.3.2, 2.4.2.

-ni third person singular possessive (*see* -i) (*see*: ʔə́mx̣kʷu-, wi-)

  míɫta t swini ʔaccépɫ He's not proud.

  míɫta t swini q'íc'x̣ They aren't the same.

-ni- / -ni, -n applicative (*followed by* -t- *objects*) 2.3.6c. (*see*: ʔáyax-, ʔə́x̣-, kʷáy'us-, mə́k̓ʷ-, tál-, túɫi-, wə́n'-, yáy-)

  sʔéˑx̣nitn He's looking at it., He's watching him.

-ni- / -ni applicative (*followed by* -y- *objects*) 2.3.6d. (*see*: ʔíɫp-, kʷəná-, ʔúxʷa-, yáxa-, yáy-)

  ʔit yáxanix̣ He carried it on his back.

-ns third person singular possessive (*see* -s) (*see*: wi-)

  ʔanám' qi ɫwins kanémm' kʷu That's unusual., Just how can it be done?

  cámaqʷ ʔaqa l wins nawíɫm'x̣ He was born

two days ago.

-nx first person singular imperfective subject (*see* -anx)

-s, -ns third person singular possessive (*on transitive verbs*) 2.4.3.2.

pənká ɬmúx̣ʷics When will he pay you?

ʔit x̣aX̣én kn ʔakʔíɬans I forced him to eat (it).

caməšn tit swan'əts He folded it twice.

tit qi x̣ap-ánan-i ká· t qi s/x̣ap-ə́t-s t s/X̣aláš drying rack where he dries the deer meat.

-s- / -st applicative (*followed by* -t- *objects*) 2.3.6e. (*see*: kʷəná-, k̓ʷə́p-, q̇ʷəɬé-)

skʷə́nscaln He's grabbing it away from me.

ʔit q̇ʷaɬéʔsc He signed for me.

-staw-, -stw-, -stu-, -st- causative 2.3.4, 2.4.2.

Causative
IMPERFECTIVE

smúx̣ʷstumaln	he is punishing me
smúx̣ʷstumin	he is punishing you (sg.)
smúx̣ʷstawn	he is punishing him/her
??	
??	
??	

PERFECTIVE

ʔit múx̣ʷstmx	he punished me
ʔit múx̣ʷstumi	he punished you (sg)
ʔit múx̣ʷix	he punished him/her
ʔit múx̣ʷstwali	he punished the other one
ʔit múx̣ʷstumuɬ	he punished us
ʔit múx̣ʷstm	he was punished

-stawt first person plural subject, imperfective aspect (*see* intransitive paradigm) 2.4.1.

-ši- / -š- applicative 3.2.6a, 2.4.2.

Applicative
IMPERFECTIVE

sʔúx̣ʷšicaln	he is blaming me
sʔúx̣ʷšicin	he is blaming you (sg.)
sʔúx̣ʷšitn	he is blaming him/her
sʔúx̣ʷšituln	he is blaming the other one
sʔúx̣ʷšitawn	he is blaming us
sʔúx̣ʷšitawaln	they are blaming each other
sʔúx̣ʷšicšitn	he is blaming himself
sʔúx̣ʷšictx	he is being blamed

PERFECTIVE

ʔit ʔúx̣ʷšic	he blamed me
ʔit ʔúx̣ʷšici	he blamed you (sg.)
ʔit ʔúx̣ʷšn	he blamed him/her
ʔit ʔúx̣ʷštwali	he blamed the other one
ʔit ʔúx̣ʷšitawɬ	he blamed us
ʔit ʔúx̣ʷšitawəlx	they blamed each other
ʔit ʔúx̣ʷšicx	he blamed himself
ʔit ʔúx̣ʷšitm	he was blamed

-t, -ə́t, -it subordinate passive 2.5.2.2.

-t- imperfective transitive (*see transitive paradigms*)

2.3.2, 2.4.2.

–tan– plural of kinship terms
(*see* –tə́n–)

–tas–, –ts– transitive 2.3.3,
2.4.2. (*see*: kʷáta–,
kʷáxʷa–, q'íw'–, qʷán–,
q̇ʷól'–, wə́q'a–, xə́y'–,
x̣ʷə́qʷa–)

Transitive –tas–
IMPERFECTIVE

sq'íw'tsmaln he is calling me
sq'íw'tsmin   he is calling you (sg.)
sq'íw'tasn   he is calling him/her
sq'íw'tswaln he is calling the other one
??
??
??
??

PERFECTIVE

ʔit q'íw'tsmx   he called me
ʔit q'íw'tsmi   he called you (sg.)
ʔit q'íw'tas   he called him/her
ʔit q'íw'tswali he called the other one
ʔit q'íw'tsmulɫ he called us
ʔit q'íw'tswəlx they called each other
??   he called himself
ʔit q'íw'tasm   he was called

–taw– first person plural
object, imperfective
aspect (*see transitive
paradigms*) 2.4.2.

–taw–, –tw–, –tu–, –x
causative (*inflected just
like* –staw– *causative*)
2.3.4, 2.4.2.

–tawɫ first person plural
object, perfective aspect
(*see transitive paradigms*)

2.4.2.

–tawɫ second person plural
object, perfective aspect
(*see transitive paradigms*)
2.4.2.

–tə́n–, –tan–, –tn, –tn'
plural of kinship terms
(*only with* nx– *prefixed to
the root*) 2.9.4. (*see*: ʔális–,
ʔímac– (2), kayíʔ–,
kʷaɫá–, kʷúpaʔ–, mán–,
maníʔ–, mátaxʷ–,
náwa–, néʔsk–, núkʷiɫ–,
pəsén'–, súc'us–, tán–,
x̣ʷál–, yálxʷtak–)

**–tə́n–, –tan–, –tan'–, –tn,
–tn'** instrumental, abstract
2.11.5.

(*see*: ʔáx̣ʷ–, ʔáy's–, ʔə́x̣–
(6), ʔíʳ–, ʔíɫani–, ʔíɫp–,
ʔitám–, ʔitámaʔ–,
ʔiyə́q– (2), cána– (2),
cáqʷa–, caqʷə́l–,
cə́kʷa–, cə́q– (2),
cípɫ–, cɫqʷála–,
cópsqʷli–, c'ám'–,
c'ax̣–, c'ə́q'–,
c'əwə́k'–, c'ə́x̣ʷi–,
c'ípxʷ–, c'íq̇ʷa– (2),
c'íwi–, č'íxʷip–, č'íx̣i–,
kátyn–, k'ál'ax– (2),
kʷáx̣ʷ–, k̇ʷə́p–,
ləpə́x̣ʷa–, ɫánaʔ–,
ɫáx– (2), ɫə́mi–, ɫə́x̣–,
ƛ̓ax̣án'–, ƛ̓əmə́x– (2),
ƛ̓ə́p–, ƛ̓ə́x̣ʷ–, ƛ̓íp–,
ƛ̓íq'a–, ƛ̓íx–, tlu´ k.tEn,
ƛ̓úqʷi–, masəntə́n–,

máta– (2), nəka–,
níɬi–, pəl'ə́kʷa–,
qā´.tɛn, qalí–, q'áy'–,
q'ét'a–, q'ə́l–, q'íx̣–
(3), qʷálitn–, qʷə́na–,
qʷíx̣–, qʷóʔ–, q̇ʷalí–
(2), q̇ʷəɬé–, q̇ʷíc'i–,
satska´ustɛn, səc'ə́–
(3), sə́k'–, sə́q̇ʷɬtn,
síl–, súps–, talíči–,
tása– (2), tawílax̣–,
tə́m'š–, tə́q– (3),
təqʷə́či– (2), tíwat–,
t'anáw's–, t'aními–
(2), t'ələ́p–, t'ə́qi– (4),
t'íqi– (2), t'úyxʷ–,
wə́l–, wə́xa–, wiq'ə́s–,
wít'i–, x̣ə́lk– (2),
x̣ə́pa–, x̣əpayíʔ–,
xʷákʷa–, xʷə́l'p–,
xʷə́plq–, x̣ála–, x̣ə́m–,
x̣ə́pa– (2), x̣ə́š–,
x̣ʷaláʔ–, x̣ʷáq̇ʷa–,
yayús–, yə́q'–)
–tiʔ adjective plural **2.9.3.**
  (*see*: X̌áq– (3), X̌ə́p–,
    náwa–, nə́q–, tawə́'t–)
ʔacnáwaɬtiʔ old people *vs.*
  ʔacnáwɬ old person
X̌aqaɬtiʔ, X̌áʔqaʔɬtiʔ pl.
  long *vs.* X̌áqɬ long, tall
  X̌áʔqaʔɬtiʔ tit sx̣əykʷóʔsi
  She has long curls.
–tn, –tn' plural of kinship
  terms (*see* –tə́n–)
–ts– transitive (*see* –tas–)
–tu– causative (*see* –taw–)
–tuxʷt applicative (*see*
–txʷt–)
–tw– causative (*see* –taw–)
–txʷt– / –tuxʷt applicative
  2.3.6b, 2.4.2.

Applicative
IMPERFECTIVE

scíx̣txʷcaln he is showing it to me
scíx̣txʷcin he is showing it to you
  (sg.)
scíx̣txʷtn he is showing it to him

PERFECTIVE

ʔit cíx̣tuxʷc he showed it to me
ʔit cíx̣txʷci he showed it to you (sg.)
ʔit cíx̣tuxʷt he showed it to him

–u– inchoative (*see* –aw–)
–ul– / –uli, –wali topical
  object (*indicates that the
  topic of discourse is a
  direct object rather than a
  subject; see transitive
  paradigms*) **2.4.4.**
  ʔit tálaqapn, wi ʔit ʔə́x̣tuli
    He₁ called him₂, and he₂
    looked at him₁.
  ʔit caqíy'n tit qáx̣aʔ, wi ʔit
    t'ə́k̇ʷtuli ʔu He kicked
    the dog, but it bit him
    anyway.
–umiš–, –miš / –umx, –
  um'x, –mx, –ayumx, –
  yumx, –y'umx, –inumx,
  –lm'x plural **2.9.2.**
–umx third person plural
  subject or object,
  perfective aspect (*see*
  –i–umx)
–umx, –um'x plural (*see*

-umiš-)

-w- / **-ɬ** intransitive (CVC-
  or CVCR- roots only)
  2.3.1.

Intransitive
IMPERFECTIVE

sqə́ɬxawanx	I am getting angry
sqə́ɬxawaxʷ	you (sg.) are getting angry
sqə́ɬxawn	he/she is getting angry
sqə́ɬxawstawt	we are getting angry
sqə́ɬxawalapt	you (pl.) are getting angry
sqə́ɬxawiɬt	they are getting angry

STATIVE

ʔacqaɬə́x̣ɬ kn	I am angry
ʔacqaɬə́x̣ɬ k	you (sg.) are angry
ʔacqaɬə́x̣ɬ	he/she is angry
ʔacqaɬə́x̣ɬ kɬ	we are angry
ʔacqaɬə́x̣ɬ kp	you (pl.) are angry

-wal- reciprocal (*see*
  -awal-)

-wali topical object (*see*
  -ul-)

-wlx, -wl'x reciprocal (*see*
  -awal-)

-x, -xʷ, -ə́x causative, third
  person object (*see*
  transitive paradigms,
  -staw- and -taw-

causatives) **2.3.4, 2.4.2.**

-xʷ second person singular
  subject (*see* -axʷ)

-x̣, -'x̣ definite (*often causes
  glottalization of a
  preceding consonant or
  addition of ʔ*)
  (*see*: có·-, cún-, cút'x̣,
  níʔ- (2), paxʷán'x̣,
  q'íc'x̣, šixn'-, tá-,
  tíʔ-, tit-, t'íx̣, wé·-,
  wíʔx̣, wín-, wítx̣,
  xán̓-, xašém'-,
  xʷáw'kʷ-)
  **míɬta t nspútn
  xʷuxʷáw'kʷm'x̣** I don't
  know the way.
  ƛ̓áqɬanawx̣s wínwinnx̣
  This went on for a long
  time.

-y- third person object,
  imperfective aspect (*see
  transitive paradigms*)
  2.3.4, 2.4.2.

-yaɬ possessive of
predicative pronouns (*see*
  -aɬ)

-yumx, -y'umx plural (*see*
  -umiš-)

Endings and infixes listed here are possibly affixes, but cannot be clearly identified as such, and can be given no meanings. Most occur with only one root, and some may be errors (that is, misrecorded or misanalyzed). After each possible affix, the root or roots with which it occurs is given (in the form given in the dictionary) followed by the whole word in which it occurs if there are only a few instances (otherwise just the roots are given).

–ʔ– (*see*: cáq–, tá⁴–, máta–, pá⁴kʷu–, púti–, p'áqʷ–, nə́q–)
  cáʔqstqtn canoe-bailer
  ʔactáʔ⁴cx lie on the side
  máʔtam'⁴tn' a file
  pá⁴kʷulm' toward the outside
  póʔtlkmn lesson
  p'áʔqʷm'⁴ gray
  ʔacnéʔqm dark, black

–ʔs– (*see*: q̇ʷə⁴é–)
  ʔit q̇ʷa⁴éʔsc He signed for me.

–á– (replacing the stem vowel) (*see*: ʔə́x̣– (5), ʔíˑ–, c'əwə́k'–, c'ə́x̣ʷa–, k̇ʷə́p–, ləpə́x̣ʷa–, ⁴ə́k'a–, x̣'əmə́x̣–, x̣'ə́x̣ʷ–, pəl'ə́kʷ–, tə́q– (3), təqʷə́či– (2), wə́x̣a–, x̣ə́pa–, x̣ə́š– (2), yə́q'–)

–a– (*see*: ⁴ə́k'a–)
  mí⁴ta t s⁴ə́k'amcšas He's not sad.

–a (*see*: lílʔ–)

[tl] sléˑla ⁴ stə́q̇ʷ a foreign language

–áʔ (*see*: cə́q–)
  caqáʔn she roasted it on a stick

–akaʔ, –aka (*see*: č'úš–, pút–)
  č'úšaka ʔacyóˑx̣ʷcx He's a bully.
  pútakaʔ half-done

–al– (*see*: púti–)
  ʔacpútali her knowing

–ál⁴ (*see*: sáʔa–, tə́p–)
  saʔál⁴šn he's making moccasins
  tapál⁴ bump one's feet together

–alxʷ (*see*: wéˑ–x̣–)
  wàˑ´naxạ´lexʷ goodbye

–ám (*see*: x̣ə́n–)
  sxanám marry

–amn (*see*: x̣ʷóʔan–)
  x̣ʷóʔanamn tuberculosis

–an (*see*: kʷəná–, q̇ʷóʔc–)
  kʷə́nanxʷ he caught him
  q̇ʷóˑcan a little while, a

little bit, soon,well

-ánan- (*see*: x̣ə́pa-)

tit qi x̣apánani ká· t qi
sx̣apə́ts t sx̌aláš
drying rack where he
dries the deer-meat

-as (*see*: ʔitáma?-, k'ə́c'a-,
ták-)

ʔit č'íɫn tit ʔitáma?asi ʔaɫ
tit x̣áx He scattered his
clothes around the
house.

ʔit k'ə́c'cxas kn tit stiqíw
I rode a horse.

ʔactákcxas kn I'm leaning
against it.

-awam'ɫ, -awm'ɫ,
-wamiɫ-, -w'am'ɫ,
-w'ml- (*see*: k'ʷəná-,
k̓ʷə́p-, x̌íx-)

ʔack'ʷanáw'am'ɫ He's
hanging on.

sk'ʷənáw'mln He's hanging
on.

sámln sk̓ʷə́pawm'ɫ
making a choice

qi sx̌íšltawam'ɫ a fan

-awilm (*see*: č'íl'k-)

ʔit č'íl'kawilm widower

-áwmx (*see*: ʔíni-)

ʔit ʔináwmx k'ʷu What's
the matter with her?

-awn (*see*: wítx̣-)

swítawn'x doing

-c- (*see*: púti-)

k'ʷumay ʔí· t spútcs He's
smart.

-c (*see*: x̣ʷáq̓ʷa-)

qi sx̣ʷáq̓ʷac č'ípqs shave

-ccx̌ʷ (*see*: tamán-)

tamániccx̌ʷ tit sp'ə́x̌ʷ Pus
is coming out of the
boil.

-čak (*see*: ʔítl-)

ɫítlčak yás yesterday

-či (*see*: sá?a-)

sá?ayu?či used it for
medicine

-é·- (*see*: q'ʷan-)

ʔit q'ʷané·c He scared me.

-é?- (*see*: x̣ə́x̌-)

x̣ax̌é?k'ʷn someone who
wants to argue, mean
person

-ét- (*see*: ʔə́x̣-)

s?ax̣étpipa?n He's reading.

-ə́c- (*see*: p'ələ́q'ʷ-)

p'əlq'ʷə́ctm bring it out

-ə́mip (*see*: púx̣ʷi-)

ʔit pəx̣ʷə́mipn He smoked
a hide.

-ə́ni- (*see*: ɫə́mi-)

ɫamə́nitm it was tied up, it
was caught

-əs (*see*: ʔís-)

tl t sk'ʷumay s?íɫaniɫt
taqə́mɫ tat s?ə́x̣tus
?isəsstawt. They were
so busy eating that they
didn't see him coming.

-í- (*see*: q̓ʷə́la-, tə́q̓ʷa-,
x̣ʷúx̣ʷ-)

q̓ʷalín she baked it

taq̓ʷín he scolded him

x̣ʷux̣ʷín owe, be in debt

-i- (*see*: q'íx̣-)

sq'íx̣iwn It's daytime., It's getting daylight.

-i, -i? (*see*: k'é·c-, qas-, q'íc'x̣-, tan-)

k'é·ci little

qasi because

q'éc'i?x̣ that's the kind

tani now

-i?- (*see*: wə̣xa-)

wə̣xi?n he pulled it up

-íl-, -il- (*see*: ?acq^w-, ?átq^wil-, cáq^w-, cə́k^wa-, kác-, q^wóq^wstmi?ɬt-, sá?a-, x̣^walá?-)

?ácq^wiln baking potatoes

?átq^wɬili its fin

scaq^wíli his arrow

cak^wíliɬtn' cradle-basket, cradle

skáciln He's putting it down.

sq^wóq^wstmiɬtili its egg

sa?ák^wtiliɬt ɬ tit q^wéx̣i?x̣^w They're going to have a funeral this morning.

?aksc'íq ?aqa tit sx̣^walá?ili It's red-hot.

-ilɬ (*see*: x̌'aqám'-)

x̌'aqám'ilɬ spring

-iɬ (*see*: caq^wə́l-, tám-)

cáq^waɬiɬ potatoes

?actəmtám'iɬx beaded [moccasins?]

təmtám'iɬalič̓n beaded bag, beaded clothing

-iɬšn (*see*: tám-)

acc'úc'q̓^w ?aɬ tit ?actəmtámiɬšn qi

st'éqls feather with a beaded head-band

-im (*see*: ká·-)

kaním' k^wu what way, which way

kanémm' k^wu Which way is it?, How do you do it?

-in (*see*: wakə́s-)

swáksinanx I'm going.

-inum (*see*: t'ə́x^w-)

t'ə́x^winum thresh

-ís- (*see*: c'ələ́pa-)

tsEɬpe´s.ɬko eddy

-is (*see*: cún-)

?it cúnis kn ?akx̌él'cšs I told him to calm down.

-it (*see*: k^wəná-)

?astuɬk^wə́nnit what you'll be getting

-k (*see*: č'úš-)

č'ó·šm'k scə́mcaln He's always hugging me.

-kas (*see*: q^wúx̣^wa-)

?it q^wúx̣^wcxkas kn I barked back.

-k^wani-, -k^wan-, -k^wn, -k^wa-, -k^w- (*see*: pən-, qalí-, x̣ə́x̌-, yúpi-)

pəntípik^wn a warrior

pənyúpik^wn wartime

qalík^wn fight

x̣ax̌é?k^wn someone who wants to argue, mean person

yúpik^wn war, wartime

-k^waw- (*see*: ?úx^wa-)

s?úx^wnk^wawn ɬ t stə́q̓^w

interpreter

-kʷp (*see:* ʔíɬani-)

ɬit ʔíɬnkʷp xʷáʔkʷuʔ tl tat st'úl ʔaɬ tit sxam'álaxʷ be honored

-kʷu, -kʷuʔ (*see:* ʔá·x̣ʷa-, kál'kʷu-, láxʷkʷu-, məq̓ʷskʷu-, páɬkʷu-, təq-)

ʔacwəq' sʔá·x̣ʷkʷumitn It's galloping.

skál'kʷutn He's looking for lice.

ʔit kál'kun kn wi míɬta t nst'úqʷn I looked for lice, but didn't find any.

sláxʷkʷumitn He's breathing.

ʔit məq̓ʷskʷuən He liked him.

páɬkʷu outside

ʔactəqlixkʷuʔ air-tight

-kʷua (*see:* X̣áq̓ʷ-)

ʔúpaɬaʔ tit lakamín, kʷaɬ ta X̣áq̓ʷawmkʷua If you don't eat it, you won't get well.

-l-, -l'- (*see:* c'ax̣íl-, c'ík̓ʷ-, láxʷkʷu-, páɬkʷu-, q'íx̣-, qʷíx̣-, wəq'a-, xʷákʷa-, x̣áɬxʷa-)

c'ax̣ílkal'i his fingernail

ʔit c'é·k̓ʷlšn kn I made faces at him.

sláxʷləxʷkʷlmitn He's breathing.

páʔɬkʷulm' towards the

outside, go outside

.tsqế·.x̣EltEn light

qʷíx̣ltn night, darkness

ʔit wəq'ɬ tl ʔaɬ tit x̣áx̣, wəq'aln xaɬ tit stiqíwlwltxʷ It ran out of the house and into the barn.

x̣wa´kwolEmtEn sweep

ʔit kʷumay x̣áɬxʷlmx They played hard.

-lk- (*see:* púti-)

póʔtlkmn lesson

-lkʷ- (*see:* xʷákʷa-)

xʷáklkʷcšitn The clouds are travelling fast.

-lkʷukʷɬ (*see:* x̣əš-)

ɬit kʷumay x̣ášlkʷukʷɬ There's going to be a thunderstorm.

-lnm'- (*see:* ɬáx̣-)

ɬáx̣lnm'tn plant sp.

-ltam (*see:* xʷákʷa-)

xʷáklʷtm sweep

-luɬ, -l'uʔɬ (*see:* má·na-, púti-)

smá·nam'luɬ spawning

ʔit wáks póʔtpipal'uʔɬ He went to school.

-l's (*see:* náma-)

ʔacnáml's tan, snáml'stn ready

-ɬ (*see:* čílačš-, məx̣kán-, nám'u-, súlt-)

číl'ɬ half-dollar, fifty cents

məx̣kan'ɬ Lacamas Creek

nám'uɬ perhaps, might, maybe

súltɬ salt water

-ɬəq̀ənqs (*see*: q'íx̣-)
    q'íx̣ɬəq̀ənqs in the
    morning

-ɬikʷn (*see*: sáwla-)
    tákcani ʔit sáw'laɬikʷn he
    asked himself

-ɬstmɬəx (*see*: tó·lu-)
    ʔactó·lɬstmɬəx kn I heard
    about it.

-ɬx (*see*: yáy-)
    yáyɬx stingy with food

-m- (*see*: ʔís-, wakə́s-)
    sʔísmcaln It's coming at
    me.
    ʔit wákasimumx They
    kept on going.

-mi- (*see*: x̣áɬx̣ʷa-)
    ʔit x̣áɬx̣ʷamix kn I played
    with him.

-miɬ- (*see*: x̣ʷalá?-)
    x̣ʷalíɬkʷumiɬa? Heat the
    water!

-n (*see*: ʔíkʷtaq-, ʔúx̣ʷa-
    (3), ká·- (4), káɬ-, k̓ʷí-
    (3), láx̣ʷkʷu-, ƛ̓áq̓ʷ-,
    má·y-, məl'qsi-, níɬi-,
    q'ə́l-, q̓ʷəɬé-, q̓ʷáx̣-,
    sá?a-, tál-, yəlúx̣ʷ-)
    ʔak ʔit ʔíkʷtqninumx ʔu
    They evidently stole it.
    ʔit ʔúx̣ʷntuxʷc He taught
    me.
    sʔúx̣ʷnkʷawn interpreting,
    teaching
    nks + ʔúx̣ʷn'mal'n teacher
    ʔikán everywhere,
    somewhere

kánm kʷu to where?

kaním' kʷu what way,
    which way

kanémm' kʷu Which way
    is it?, How do you do
    it?

ʔit káɬcn ʔə́nca He forgave
    me.

ʔik̓ʷín few, a few

k̓ʷináwmx kʷu how
    many?, several others

k̓ʷínlšn how many times?

yáis míɬta t nsláx̣ʷkʷunm
    I can't breathe.

ʔit ƛ̓áq̓ʷnstumx He healed
    me.

ʔacmá·yusn tl ʔaɬ tit
    tə́mx It's sticking up
    out of the ground.

ʔit mə́l'qsn kn I dived.

sníɬntn He's becoming
    alive.

tit qi sq'alánn yəmyú the
    whole camp

ʔit q̓ʷaɬénn x̣ʔáɬənca She
    wrote it to me.

q'aɬ q̓ʷáx̣nɬnati his
    getting mad

ʔə́x̣ʷɬ qi ssá?nmli it's
    doing it strangely

tálaqpnina? Holler at him!

ʔit yalúx̣ʷakanm He
    doubled up his fist.

-ns (*see*: nə́q-)
    ʔaksnə́qns ʔaksqʷə́s
    ʔaksqʷúx̣ʷayaqn
    ʔaksqʷúx̣ʷi?ps
    chestnut sorrel with

white mane and white
tail

–nskst (*see*: q'áxʷ–)

sámlan k t sq'áxʷnskst
stó·l'šn t qalíʔi You're
making jelly.

–nx, –n'x (*see*: táln'x– (?),
x̣ə́pa–)

stáln'x over, across

x̣ə́pnxtn xaɬ tit stó·l'šn
drying-rack for berries

–n'ɬ, –nɬ (*see*: ʔúšam–,
č'áš–, k̓ʷpyáluci–,
láx̣ʷa–, qát–)

q'aɬ úšmn'ɬ poor

q'aɬ č'ášnɬ tit nawíɬm'x
He's dangerous.

míɬta t nsk̓ʷpyálcnɬ I
can't understand him.

q'aɬ láʔx̣ʷn'ɬ funny

q'aɬ qátnɬ He's nice, he's
kind.

–s (*see*: qín–, wi, qanóm'–)

ʔacqíns + inflected
predicate: want, do

míɬta t spútc wis cə́ni t
knmáʔi No, it's his
father.

míɬta t nspútn wis ʔit
ʔátamn I don't know
that he died.

ʔit qanóm's kn I
quarrelled with him.

–stal– (*see*: táxʷayway–)

stáx̣ʷiyustaln selling

–stn (*see*: múlukʷ–,
šak̓ʷíy'–)

txʷmulúkʷstn he fainted

ʔit txʷšak̓ʷíy'stn kn It
surprised me., It startled
me.

–stumx (*see*: cə́ni–,
q'əx̣áp–)

k̓ʷumay ʔaccə́nistumx
He's greedy.

k̓ʷac ʔacq'é·x̣pstumx
He's unfaithful.

–stus– (*see*: x̣ə́wali–)

ʔáy'tk cxkx̣ə́wɬstusi xaɬ t
síɬn He grew crops.

–šɬ– (*see*: kác–)

ʔit kácšɬšn ɬ t mə́kʷp
x̣̓úk̓ʷičn He put the fire
on top of it.

–t– (*see*: ʔə́x̣ʷ–, k̓ʷəná–,
nə́x̣ʷa–)

tit ʔə́x̣ʷtálmx strange
people

sə́x̣ʷtam'x foreign country

ʔit k̓ʷanátn He married her.

ʔilápaʔ nə́x̣ʷtilaʔ You folks
discuss it!

–t (*see*: có·–, cún–, káɬ–,
k̓ʷəná–)

có·t think, plan

ʔaccó·tumx He blamed
me.

cút say

káɬt give to

k̓ʷə́nst He grabbed it away
from him.

–ta (*see*: ʔíɬp–)

ʔíɬptanix He squirted him.

–taʔas (*see*: q̓ʷúx̣ʷ–)

qi sʔísi tit sq̓ʷúx̣ʷtaʔas tit
ʔacpal'ə́k̓ʷɬ smokehole

-tač (*see:* lə́k'-)
  ʔit lə́k'tač ɬ tit tálkni He
    has a bagful.
-tači- (*see:* kʷəná-)
  ʔit kʷəntáčic He led me by
    the hand., They shook
    hands.
-tam-, -tm (*see:* xʷə́l-)
  xʷə́ltm white man
-tawmln (*see:* ʔíɬani-)
  sʔíɬntawmln feast
-taw'íɬ (*see:* tə́p-)
  qalíkʷaniɬt tit sx̌aláš
    stapállustaw'iɬ tit
    məx̣kánɬ The deer
    fought and locked
    horns.
-tl- (*see:* ʔís-, wakə́s-)
  ʔit cún kn ʔakʔístls I
    invited him.
  ʔit cún kn ʔakwákstls I
    told him to leave.
-tm- (*see:* ʔíɬani-)
  sʔíɬntmšitn ʔaqa tit
    sčə́txʷn' ɬ tit stó·l'šn
    a bear eating berries
-tmɬ- (*see:* sə́k'-)
  sək'áytm'xtmɬtn a plow
-tmɬi- (*see:* kə́ɬ-, sáwla-,
    x̣íp'-)
  ʔit kə́ɬaʔtmɬix tit cíɬn He
    distributed the food.
  ʔit sáw'latmɬix He asked
    for it.
  ʔit x̣íp'tmɬix He forbade it.
-tn (*see:* qáx̣-, saqá·x̣-)
  ʔit qáx̣tnw'lxumx They
    met each other.

ʔit qáx̣tnx kn We met each
    other.
  ʔit saqá·x̣tnmn He made
    fun of him.
-tum (*see:* ʔə́x̣-)
  ʔacʔé·x̣nitum kɬ We're
    watching.
-tumi-, -tm- (*see:* kə́ɬ-)
  ʔit kə́ɬtumix kn I gave it
    away.
  skə́ɬtmstawanx I'm giving it
    away.
-uʔ (*see:* kʷaɬá-, qʷán-)
  kʷə́ɬuʔ aunt
  ʔacqʷánuʔ afraid, a coward
-uʔɬ (*see:* kəwáɬ-)
  ləqálkwaʔɬuʔɬ buy a
    woman, wedding
-uk̓ʷ (*see:* ʔáy-)
  ʔit ʔáyuk̓ʷ kn I traded it
    [for something else].
-ús (*see:* k̓ʷə́p-)
  k̓ʷapús tan better
-uws (*see:* c'ə́p'a-)
  sáli t sx̌íx tl c'ap'úws
    Two years ago it
    flooded.
-wamiɬ-, -w'am'ɬ, -w'ml-
    (*see* -awam'ɬ)
-wiwi (*see:* qə́x̣-)
  qə́x̣wiwi rich
-w'ən- (*see:* ʔíni-)
  sʔínw'əncals kʷu what he
    is doing to me
-x- (*see:* c'ax-, síl-, tíwat-,
    t'úla-, x̣əmím')
  ʔaccax̣íl'sxtani tit pípa
    sandpaper

ʔacsílxtani t wíɬ sailboat

tíwxtn crossing a little creek

st'óˑlxšitn He's bringing it to him.

t'úlx- bring to

xəmím'x mourning dove

-x (*see*: x̌'íp-, qáx̣-, t'úla-, wála?-)

ʔacx̌'ípx tan It's covered.

ʔit qáx̣tnx kn We met each other.

ʔit t'úlxci He brought it to you.

tx̌ʷlá?xšn He stared at him.

-xn (*see*: ɬəwála-)

ʔit ɬawál'xnmn kn xán'x̣ I left/deserted him there.

-xʷ- (*see*: t'ələp-)

ʔact'ə́lpxʷtani his shield

-xʷs (*see*: x̌'áq-)

tl t swáksn x̌'áqɬan'ɬxʷs titx̣t'íst This went on for a long time.

-yusm (*see*: q'ə́l-)

ʔalq'álm'yusm January, "a month the people don't camp out"

Few Cowlitz place names are available. No one now alive knows more than two or three, and earlier records are sketchy. Warbass (1858) sent Gibbs about two dozen names, about twenty of which he included on a very rough map of Cowlitz territory along the Cowlitz River. Curtis (1911) gives a list of nearly thirty "villages" (obtained from Esther Millett, mother of Emma Luscier), most of which were rechecked by Harrington (1942) with Emma Luscier at Bay Center (and a few with Joe Peter on the Yakima Reservation). Adamson (1926-27 and 1934) gives a few Cowlitz place names, but they are often poorly located; these names were provided by Joe Peter, a Mrs. Youckton, and a Mrs. Johnson. Jacobs (1934) includes two texts with a large number of place names; he obtained over 270 place names from Jim Yoke and about 70 from Lewy Costima (Castama). Most of the Costima names are included in the material from Yoke, and the vast majority from both men are Taidnapam, i.e. pertain to territory upriver from Mossy Rock and in Yakima County. A few of the names from Yoke which do pertain to (Lower) Cowlitz territory are apparently translations of Cowlitz names into Sahaptin. Nor are all the names provided in other sources true Cowlitz. Some of the sites identified by Curtis are Kiksht (Upper Chinook) (a few along the lower reaches of the Cowlitz River), and some of the names in Warbass may also be Taidnapam. The numbers of the following list are keyed to the accompanying map so that the actual location of the places can be seen. However, because of the difficulty of correlating names from the various sources and determining their actual locations, the locations of the numbers on the maps should be considered as only approximate in many cases.

1. káwlicq' Cowlitz River   Tawallish, Twallish,
   (qáwlicq FBb?;   Tawallitch, Cowlitz
   kauwilē´t_sk MJa,b-lc;   WFTolmie 1963;

q'αwwɪlíˑtsq' JH); the
Taidnapam name for the
Cowlitz River is ščíl (ctcíl
MJa,b-lc).

2. nu-che-lip UWa The
Cowlitz River downstream
from Toledo.

3. nawὐtsαn JHjp Mouth of
the Cowlitz River (now-
oo-tson UWa Monticello):
"river mouth" [a Cowlitz
name] (łakłep m TAa-ly
mouth of the Cowlitz
River).

4. qαwîˑmἀní JH Coweman
River (q'αwirˑmdnɪ,
q'αwímαn JHss;
q'αwímαn JHjp;
'aˑwíˑmαnɪ JH; Kawímni
EC a village at the mouth of
the Coweman River;
Cowee-men UWa;
qawíˑmən MJb-jy).

5. mαnsélu JH Monticello (an
early settlement about a
mile from the mouth of the
Cowlitz River on its west
bank; it washed away and
was abandoned; the Indian
name is a corruption of
Monticello) (mαnsél'o,
mαnsélo, mἀnsélo,
mἀnsél'o, mαnsélα,
mαnsélαw̥ JH; mansála
MJb-lc,jy, MJa-lc Kelso).

6. Tiáhanakŝhiħ EC "On
Rock", at the site of Kelso.

7. Wakóthmali EC

"Perpendicular", a mile
above Kelso on the east
side of the Cowlitz River
(possibly Rocky Point, two
miles upstream from
Kelso).

8. Sthwe EC "Marten", about
one half mile above #7 on
the east bank of the
Cowlitz River.

9. t'uˑˊs MJb-jy A creek
downriver from niłhwiˊ
(tosp UWa) (possibly
Ostrander Creek).

10. nἀˑyαq'otsɪx JH A
village about two miles
above #8 on the east bank
of the Cowlitz River
(Naíyakotˆsuiħ EC).

11. Silkén-stá'ħl'ⁿsħ EC
"Slave Town", about one
mile above #10 on the west
bank of the Cowlitz River
(*see* syəlqín? slave).

12. sâˑ'k.lἀmαx JH "Red-
Colored Dirt, Red Earth",
about a mile and a half
above #11 on the east bank
of the Cowlitz River
(Tsákalŭm'ħ EC; tsa-ka-
lump UWa name of a
rapids).

13. Kamá'lstn EC A village a
mile above #12 on the west
bank of the Cowlitz River
just below Arkansas Creek.

14. niłhwiˊ MJa,b-lc,jy A creek
name (possibly Arkansas

Creek or Whittle Creek; identified by jy as being six miles above Kelso and by lc as being opposite Castle Rock) (neth-wee UWa).

15. wa·ɬɑ̓x JH A village a mile and a half above #13 on the west bank the of Cowlitz River, "put fire in the brush and burn all" (Waḥlũ̓ḥ EC).

16. wɪyâ·mɑtɪx, wɪyâ·mɑtɪxw JH "Long Riffle", about two miles above #15 on the east bank of the Cowlitz River (Wíyamitiḥ EC; ne-yam-a-tikh UWa name of a rapids).

17. Waḥláḥetkũ̓k EC A village one mile above #16 and a quarter mile below the mouth of the Toutle River, on the east bank of the Cowlitz River.

18. ší·q̓ʷk Toutle River (c'e·´q'ᵘk MJa-lc; c'ei´q'ᵘk MJb-lc; c'e·´q̓ʷkᵘ MJb-jy; sɪ·´ʔq'w TAb; Se-a-kt UWa; síq̓ʷɬ MDK; seh-quu Pacific Railroad Reports 1855-60; River Seko or Lee Notices & Voyages 1956).

19. Tsiũ̓kḥlewala EC A village on the west bank of the Cowlitz River just above the mouth of the

Toutle River (Tse-qual-i-sen UWa forks of the Cowlitz River and a tributary; probably also wi´lapsas MJb-jy "sturgeon place") (see c'íwq sturgeon).

20. sk'wɑɬî·mɑx JH A site about a mile and a half above #19 on the west bank of the Cowlitz River (Tsqaḥlímĩ̓ḥl EC).

21. Tskelé'tn EC A village two miles above #20 on the east bank of the Cowlitz River.

22. Skatiĕḳá'tns EC "Crow's Sweat-Lodge", about a mile and a half above #21 on the west bank of the Cowlitz River (see sk'á·k'aʔ crow; qā´.tɛn FBa sweathouse).

23. k'a´matsi MJb-jy A prairie at Olequa (k'a´matsi MJa,b-lc Olequa River; k'â·mɑtsɪ JH a site at Olequa; k'ɑ́mɑtsɪ, k'ɑ́mɑts'ɪ JHss a slough on the west side of the Cowlitz River in the Olequa region; Ḱámatsiḥ EC a village two miles above #22 on west bank of the Cowlitz River at the site of Olequa; K'amatsi TAa-ly, Cow-mat-tsen UWa).

24. stɑm'tá·mɑnɬ JH A

village a mile above #23 on the west bank of the Cowlitz River (Stŭmtáma'nh̓l EC; Tunta-malk UWa Grand Rapids).

25. skwɑtí·xɑ' JH A village about two miles above #24 (Tsqatíh̓a EC) (*?see* qʷatíxaʔ body louse).

26. mɑ́x̣kɑn'tɬɑlutsɑn, mɑ́x̣kɑn'tɑ̓́lutsɑn JH "Elk's Horn, Deer's Slough", Olequa depot (Mock-kaults UWa Mill Creek; M&xkant, M xkant TAmd a prairie and creek the other side of Jackson near the Catholic church, mə́x̣kan'ɬ MDK Lacamas Creek; probably also 'n' ́n MJb-jy "horn, antler") (possibly Lacamas Creek) (see mə́x̣kn horn, antlers).

27. q'ápn'ɬ TAb "Blueberry Plant", Winlock (K'ap&nt TAa-ph) (*see* q'áʔp short huckleberry, blueberry).

28. kulu´ɬn MJb-mi Jackson Prairie.

29. náwaqʷm "Big Prairie", Newaukum (prairie) (náwaq'um JH Jackson Prairie?; na´waqum TAb; n wak m TAa-gs; Nawaq'vm TAa-mi; Nawaqum TAa-lh;

nawa´qum MJb-mi Newaukum Prairie, Forest) (*see* náwɬ old, big).

30. nə́xʷc'al'x̣ "Crawfish River", Newaukum River (nulk-tsulk UWa).

31. ts'í·x̣pɑn'ɬ JH A village two miles above #25 on the east bank of the Cowlitz River (Tsíŭh̓pŭnh̓l EC) (*see* *c'íxp root sp.).

32. ɬɑkwɑl JH A place a little above #30 (Hlaqŭl EC A village about three miles above #30 on the west bank of the Cowlitz River; Claquil UWa).

33. Klac-olks, klac-olts UWa Cowlitz Landing (the first white settlement at present-day Toledo).

34. 'ɑwí·lkɑ'n'ɬ JH "Red-Ochre Place", a village a half mile above #31 on the west bank of the Cowlitz River (Awélkĭnh̓l EC; owwell-kenkk UWa Paint-illahee [a prairie at Cowlitz Landing]; awelkanɬ TAa-ly) (*see* *ʔawílk Indian paint).

35. matə´p MJb-jy Salmon Creek (opposite Toledo) (matə´ ß̣ MJa,b-lc; mɑtɑ́p JH; Maṭŭp EC a village a mile above #33 on the east bank of the Cowlitz River opposite the site of Toledo; mat p TAa-ly; ma-tap-

pa–lw UWa; natə́p MDK;
macə́p MDK a creek that
flows into the Cowlitz at
the Toledo grange hall).

36. stɑ̀w'úm'ɑn'ɬ–xɑ̀w'ɬ JH
"Mowing-Place Road", a
village at the site of Toledo
(Tawámilŭháwĭh̄l EC) (*see*
*st'awə́m' cut grass, xə́wɬ
road).

37. nâ·w·qw̥, nɑ̀wq',
nɑ̀wq'w̥, nɑrwq' JH "big
prairie", Cowlitz Prairie,
the site of the Catholic
mission and the Puget
Sound Agricultural
Company farm [a branch of
the Hudson's Bay
Company] founded in the
late 1830's (náwk' JHjp;
Now-ok UWa; na´wq MJb-
mi) (*see* náwɬ old, big).

38. nɪxk'wâ·nɑxt'ɑn JHlj
"stretching a hide",
Lacamas Prairie
(nɑʃk'wâ·naxt JHgs).

39. lɑkɑmɑ̀s 'ílɪ'ɪ,
lɑkɑmá·s 'ɪlɪ'ɪ JHmc A
prairie close to Cowlitz
(lakamasili TAa-ly a creek
about a half mile from
Cowlitz Prairie) (possibly
the Chinook Jargon name
for #37).

40. ɬá·kdlútsɑn JH A village
about two miles above #35
on the east bank of the
Cowlitz River

(H̄atlákaluŭ't͡sn EC).

41. sq'wɪ̀·ɬp–ɑn'ɬ xɑwɬ JH
"stumpy road", a village a
mile above #39 on the west
bank of the Cowlitz River
(Sqéh̄lapilŭh̄awih̄l EC)
(*see* q̓ʷíɬp roots, xə́wɬ
road).

42. t'ɑkwɑ̀p JH "Spotted
Buttock", a village two
miles above #40 on the east
bank of the Cowlitz River
(Taqŭp EC; t' kwap TAa-ly
a place at Cowlitz where a
fish-trap was made).

43. t'ɑkwɑ̀pɑn'ɬ JH A
Cowlitz village (possibly
the same as #41).

44. skwɑyừx JH "River
Bend", a village two miles
above #41 on the east bank
of the Cowlitz River
(Tskaiyúw EC).

45. Qĕ'lt EC A village three
miles above #43 on the east
bank of the Cowlitz River
(Quailt UWa; kw'ᴇ·´lt MJb-
jy the prairie at Mossy
Rock; qw'ᴇ·´lt MJb-lc).

46. ʃí·lɑlɑlx JH A village
four miles above #44 on
the east bank of the
Cowlitz River ('ɴsh̄ĭlalál'h̄
EC).

47. Lala moxᵘ TAa-ph A place
at the border between the
Cowlitz and the Taidnapam
(L'alam xᵘ, L'alamxu TAa-

ph people who lived between the Cowlitz and the wánəkʷt; Laɬa nɬ TAa-ph people of Lalamoxᵘ; ɬaɬaˊmu'x, ɬE'lêˊmEx̱ MJb Interior tribes, Klickitat, Taidnapam [?]) (probably a people rather than a place name).

48. Ti–tin–a–pam UWa,b Cowlitz River above Cowlitz Landing (probably refers rather to the Taidnapam people).

49. laˑlɑ́lx̱, lɑláˑlx̱ JHjp Tilton River (lalaˊlx̱ MJb-jy,lc).

50. ɬɑ́qɑtɑt JH Klickitat.

51. ɬɑqˈɑtɑt ílɪ'ɪ JHss Big Bottom (a place up the Cowlitz River) (apparently a Chinook Jargon name).

52. sáˑk̓ʷ, nšsáˑk̓ʷ MDK (from Silas Heck) Mount St. Helens (the Taidnapam name is apparently lɑwíˑlɑt ɬɑ́ JHjp; lawe ́latə TAb-mc; lawe ́latɬa TAb-mi; law'E'ˑlatˑɬaˊ MJb-lc).

53. lawe ́latə TAb-mc Mount St. Helens; TAb-mi lawe ́latɬa (a Sahaptin name: lawilayt–ɬá "the smoker").

54. təx̣oˊma TAb-mc; tax̣oˊma TAb-mi; taqoˊmən TAb-jc Mt.

Rainier.

55. c'ilíləɬ MDK Mt. Adams (tc'iliˊ ɪɬ TAb-mc; the Sahaptin name is patuˊ? TAb-mi; paˊtu MJb-lc).

The following names either cannot be located with any degree of certainty or are upstream from the above, proceeding into Taidnapam territory, which began somewhere near Mossy Rock. Most of these upriver names are from Jacobs (1934), and are probably Sahaptin, although some look possibly Cowlitz. Few of the numbers from this list appear on the accompanying map.

56. Tsalkh UWa A lake at the head of a creek with no name flowing into the Cowlitz River from the west between Coweman River and Ostrander Creek; current maps show no such lake (note that Cowlitz for lake is célˈɬ, and that may be all that is meant by this name).

57. cayles UWa This word occurs on Warbass's map, on the east side of the Cowlitz River above what is probably Arkansas Creek; the correct reading may be 'eagles'.

58. qɑ́wɑt'ɑ́lᵃqɑn JH A big rock on the west side of the Cowlitz River (somewhere on the lower reaches of the river, south of Olequa).

59. wálɪkwayʊs JHjp Either Olequa or a man's name (Harrington's notes are unclear).

60. tcawap' TAa-ly Name of a creek where camas was dug (che-wap-pow-lik UWa a creek between Toledo and Salkum on the north side of the Cowlitz River).

61. tsali´tsali+ən MJb-lc A creek upstream from Toledo.

62. k'walsa´lyals MJb-jy A creek five miles above Toledo (*?see* q̓ʷá·l's raccoon).

63. pcwa´pcwa MJb-jy A creek upstream from Toledo.

64. +əq'a´tcən MJb-jy "white fir", a creek upstream from Toledo (+ə´k'atcən MJb-lc).

65. suspa´nas MJb-jy,lc "strawberry place", two or three miles below Salkum.

66. sa´lkum MJb-jy,lc A creek at Salkum (Mill Creek) (Sol-cum UWa).

67. t'ca´lt'calc MJb-jy Winston Creek (below Mayfield) (t'calt'ca´lc MJb-lc).

68. tsi´qls MJb-lc A river name.

69. tsiˑ´x̣iwun MJb-lc Silver Creek.

70. cqw'eˑ´litam MJb-jy Klickitat Creek (cqw'e´latəm MJb-lc).

71. t'cqa´+ən+ MJb-jy A falls above the Ike farm.

72. ala´layac MJb-jy "place of nettles", a prairie opposite Mossy Rock.

73. tca´luwaik MJb-jy A valley near the following.

74. iya´nc MJb-jy "driftwood, jam", a narrow place in the river.

75. nu´cnu MJb-jy,lc "nose", a creek.

76. sqa´litcəm MJb-lc A creek near Mossy Rock.

77. cq'ilq'i´lt MJb-jy "skunk cabbages", a creek one mile west of Riffe (cqilqi´lt MJb-lc).

78. cxu´mtani MJb-jy An eddy and fishing site below Riffe (cxu´mtani MJb-lc).

79. sa´lk MJb-mi [Unidentified site.]

80. q'wa´ya MJb-mi [Unidentified site.]

81. waxa´lat MJb-mi [Unidentified site.]

82. lapa´ləm MJb-mi [Unidentified site.]

83. kawaˊswai MJb-mi
[Unidentified site; a place
for gathering hazelnuts and
salalberries.]

84. tsalaˊɬiˑqɬ MJb-mi A lake
near Cinnabar Mountain at
head of the Chehalis River.

85. scow-wow-woulk UWa
A stream entering the
Cowlitz from the south
upstream of Salkum.

86. cha-chin UWa A tributary
to #78.

87. tɬ'αpαy'ǽˑn'p JH A
village up the Cowlitz
River.

88. X̱wαnaˊye TA Name of a
river and Coyote's
daughter.

89. lalaˑˊx̱um TAb-mi A place
where camas grows.

90. t'aˊɩxˑ TAb-ss Name of a
creek.

91. tapaˊɬ TAb-mc A creek
adjoining Dip Creek.

92. ʔacx̱ʷíx̱ʷiʔɬkl MDK Windy
Point.

The following sites are all
outside Cowlitz territory, but
were given by Cowlitz
speakers, and represent
Cowlitz pronunciations of
these places.

93. ɬíˑkwáto' JHjp A prairie
between Jackson Prairie
and Chehalis Prairie
(Claquato, just west of
Chehalis) (Upper Chehalis
ɬakʷítu).

94. taˊɬɩnk'ən TAb-mc Ford's
Prairie (northwest of
Centralia) (Upper Chehalis
táˑɬn'čšn').

95. L'aqaˊyαqɬ TAb-mc
Grand Mound Prairie
(Upper Chehalis X̱'aqáyqɬ).

96. waɬaˊlən TAb-jc,mc
Scatter Creek (Upper
Chehalis waɬáˑln).

97. ɩɬtaˊls TAb-mc Little
Rochester Prairie (at
Rochester) (Upper
Chehalis ʔiɬtál's).

98. manɩˊk'oɬ TAb-mc Across
the river from Gate City
(between Rochester and
Oakville) (Upper Chehalis
manáč'uw'ɬ).

99. t'əaˊwən TAb-mc Oakville
Reservation Prairie (at the
eastern end of the Chehalis
Reservation) (Upper
Chehalis t'áwn).

100. saˊts'αɬ TAb-mc Black
River (Upper Chehalis
sácəl'ɬ).

101. wɩlíˑmpya JHjp Olympia.

102. swǔˑl, swâˑl JHlj
Kwalhioqua at Pe Ell
(swáˑl JH).

103. ɬâˑkulutsαn JH "the
way-down water", the
Columbia River or
Shoalwater Bay.

104. wíɬtk JHjp "smoking",
    Lewis River (between
    Kelso and Portland).
105. pûˑtɬɑn JH Portland.

106. luˑˊniya TAb-mi Rainier
    (a town in Oregon)
    (luˑˊníyɑ̀, lî ˑnɪyɑ JH).

Appendix C. Personal Names

In addition to the personal names listed below, a number of
Cowlitz names can be found in Warner and Munnick (1972).
This volume reproduces Catholic church records from the
Northwest from 1838-1860. Included are the names of a
number of Cowlitz Indians married, baptized, or buried at the
mission at Cowlitz Prairie.

ʔaɬímx̣ A cousin of Frances
    Northover.
ʔašél Aunt of Frances
    Northover.
'ɑtwén JH Antoine, uncle of
    Emma Luscier (also
    known as stɑˑx̣ɑm').
'ɑyâˑl, 'ɑyyáˑl JH Younger
    half-brother of Emma
    Luscier's mother.
'îˑmtɑtʃ JH Emma Luscier's
    mother's mother's brother;
    David Frank, Jr.
Ow–hve, Ow–hva (Treaty
    Records 1855) A Cowlitz
    man.
scayídut Lucy James.
čǝx̣ʷúɬ Cheholts; TAb
    tciho´ɬ; JH ts'ɪx̣ùˑɬ,
    ts'ɪ'x̣uˑɬ, ts'ɪxx̣ùˑɬ
    Henry Cheholts; JHjp
    ts'ex̣óɬ Cheholts.
Hoh–hoh UWa A Cowlitz
    Indian (one of Warbass'

    sources).
How–How (Ross 1855) A
    Cowlitz chief.
k'aɬx̣áɪm JHjp, k'aɬx̣aˊyim
    MJb-mi Mother of Minnie
    Case.
Caw–wacham (Kane 1859)
    A Cowlitz woman.
Kiscox (Kane 1859), Kish-
    kok (Treaty Records 1855)
    A Cowlitz chief.
kiyaˊitani MJb-mi Mary Iley.
ktá George ktá, father of
    Frances Northover.
k'apú LY Lillian Young's
    father's mother's father.
k'âˑktsɑmɑ, k'ɑ̂k'tsɑmɑ
    JH Esther Millet (mother of
    Emma Luscier); VR
    qaˑˊktsǝm'.
Kwon–esappa (Treaty
    Records 1855) A Cowlitz
    sub-chief.
k'wɑˑnɑsâˑppɑm JH [Man's

name].

ɬámɑyɑ' JHss [Woman's name] (possibly a Chinook).

məsímx Emma Mesplie; Emma Mesplie's nephew's daughter.

pílikʷàya Aunt of Frances Northover; granddaughter of Emma Mesplie.

sáˑt.wɑnux JH Maternal grandfather of Emma Luscier (also known as wɑ̀hɑwɑ).

səpéʔl [Woman's name].

Schannaway (Simpson 1830), Schachanaway (Douglas 1914) A Cowlitz chief.

táwni A cousin of Frances Northover; Lucy James' youngest daughter.

stâˑxɑm' JH Antoine, uncle of Emma Luscier (also known as 'ɑtwén).

t' 'ɔm t' 'ɔmáˑ JHjp [Man's name].

txʷst'ílib Paternal grandmother of Lucy James and Emma Mesplie.

wɑ̀hɑwɑ, wɑ̀hhɑwɑ JH Maternal grandfather of Emma Luscier (also known as sáˑt.wɑnux); VR waˊxawa.

wátpili [Woman's name].

wɑyáˑnɑʃɑt JHjp Captain Peter; father of Captain

Peter.

wəɬxə́n Lillian Young.

hwʊnhwâˑnɑtʃ' JH Wife of k'wɑˑnɑsâˑppɑm.

sx̣aˑnîˑwɑ JH [Man's name].

x̣imálcɬ Half-brother of George ktá.

Yack–kannan (Treaty Records 1855) An old Cowlitz chief.

yáɬlaʔ A cousin of Frances Northover.

yúyəx̣nut Emma Mesplie's father's aunt.

yûˑy'yʊ̣x̣tɑn' JH Jim, son of Henry Cheholts.

Names from Cowlitz speakers found in TAa:

Kemol&mx[†] TAa-ly Queen Susan (a Chehalis?).

sqsaⁿn TAa-jp Joe Peters' father's third wife (a Taidnapam).

ɬc&l–inai TAa-jp Joe Peters' older sister's mother (a Taidnapam).

Wak'e TAa-ly A man's name.

Kaɬ TAa-ly Lucy Youckton's uncle (a Cowlitz).

[†] Cowlitz personal names from Adamson are reproduced exactly as they appear in Adamson's typescript of her original fieldnotes, which have never been located. No attempt has been made to interpret such symbols as "&" and "v".

wvk' m nos TAa-ly Lucy
Youckton's uncle (same as
Ka⁴).

yap tn TAa-mi A woman's
name.

olakwas, lakwa's, lakwas
TAa-mi A man's name.

Qw qweo⁴ TAa-mi A woman's
name.

ts'a⁴ TAa-mi Lena Heck:
"laké".

Qa os TAa-mi A female slave's
name.

Mo o⁴ TAa-mi A woman's
name (?).

M&x&si TAa-mi A woman's
name (?).

Watatanx TAa-mi A man's
name.

APPENDIX D: LOANWORDS

A number of loanwords are found in Cowlitz, mostly to
account for new animals and objects brought in with
Euroamerican traders, missionaries, and settlers. The largest
number of these loanwords come from Chinook Jargon, the
trade language of the area, and these in turn come mostly from
French and English. Some words come directly from English.
A small number can be identified as coming from neighboring
native languages, such as Chinook and Sahaptin.

/ʔalútq deep, long canoe
(*see* Quileute *ʔà·ʔlútqat*
'sealing canoe').

/ʔápls apple, apples (*see*
English *apples*).

ʔáqa now (*see* Kathlamet
Chinook *aqa* 'then').

/ʔayayáš dumb, stupid,
clumsy, stubborn (*see*
Sahaptin *ʔayayaš* 'stupid,
clumsy, dumb').

/ʔíka acre (*see* English
acre).

bo´Ets FBa boots (*see*
English *boots*).

/čáyni Chinese (*see*

Chinook Jargon *chaynee*
'Chinese', taken in turn
from colloquial English
[čayní], a back formation
from English *Chinese*).

/č'amúyq'aʔ snail, snails
(*see* Lower Chinook
c'əmó·ikxan 'snail').

/háps hops (*see* English
hops).

/hə́ndəd hundred (*see*
English *hundred*).

hùlhùl JHjp wood rat (*see*
Chinook Jargon *hóol-hool*
'mouse', taken in turn from
Lower Chinook -*kólxul*

'mouse').

/kapú coat (*see* Chinook Jargon *ca-pó* 'coat', taken in turn from Canadian French *capot*).

kā´.s FBa train (*prob.* /kás; *see* English *cars*).

kaukou´lac FBa drum (*poss.* kawkáwlaš; *see* Sahaptin *kiwkíwlas* 'drum') (*here* c = š).

/kíkʷəlikʷut skirt (*see* Chinook Jargon *keé-kwil-lie* 'low, under, beneath', taken in turn from Lower Chinook *kikʷili* (?) 'below, under'; and Chinook Jargon *coat* 'dress, gown', taken in turn from English *coat*).

/kʷáqkʷaq duck (*see* English *quack quack*).

/kʷáta quarter, twenty-five cents (*see* Chinook Jargon *kwáta* 'quarter of a dollar', taken in turn from English *quarter*).

/kʷílt quilt (*see* English *quilt*, perhaps via Chinook Jargon *kwilt* 'quilt').

/kʷúkʷ– cook (*see* English *cook*).

/kʷušú pig, hog (*see* Chinook Jargon *co´-sho* 'pig', taken in turn from French *cochon* 'pig').

/lakamín soup, gravy (*see* Chinook Jargon *lakamin*

'stew, dumplings', taken in turn from French *le commun* 'the common pot').

/lakláš barn (*see* Chinook Jargon *lekalash* 'garage', taken in turn from French *le garage* 'garage').

/lalupá ribbon, ribbons (*see* Chinook Jargon *lalopa* 'ribbon', taken in turn from French *la ruban* 'ribbon').

/lám whiskey (*see* Chinook Jargon *lum* 'rum, whiskey', taken in turn from English *rum*, or possibly from French *le rhum* 'rum').

/lapíp pipe (*see* Chinook Jargon *la-peep* 'pipe', taken in turn from French *la pipe* 'pipe').

/lapišmú saddle blanket (*see* Chinook Jargon *le-pish-e-mo* 'saddle blanket', taken in turn from Ojibwa *appiššimo·n* 'something to lie or sit on', with a French article attached).

/laplít bridle, bit (*see* Chinook Jargon *lableed´* 'bridle', taken in turn from French *le bride* 'bridle').

/lapuén pan (*see* Chinook Jargon *la-po-el´* 'frying pan', taken in turn from French *la poele* 'frying pan').

/**lapyó·š** hoe (*see* Chinook Jargon *la-pe-osh´* 'hoe, mattock', taken in turn from French *la pioche* 'pickaxe, mattock').

/**lasúp** soup, stew (*see* Chinook Jargon *lasup* 'soup', taken in turn from French *la soupe* 'soup').

/**lá·š–** clear forest (possibly a loanword: *see* English *slash*).

/**lašəmní** chimney (*see* Chinook Jargon *lashimney*, *la-shum-ma-na* 'chimney', taken in turn from French *la cheminée* 'chimney').

/**latám** table (*see* Chinook Jargon *latáhb*, *la-tem* 'table', taken in turn from French *la table* 'table').

/**lawé·n** oats (*see* Chinook Jargon *la-wen´* 'oats', taken in turn from French *l'avoine* 'oats').

/**ləmitén** gloves (*see* Chinook Jargon *lemitten* 'mitten', taken in turn from French *la mitaine* 'mitten, mitt').

/**liǰúb** devil (*see* Chinook Jargon *le-jaub* 'devil', taken in turn from French *le diable* 'devil').

/**likát** cards (*see* French *les cartes* 'cards').

/**likáy** spotted horse (black and white) (*see* Chinook Jargon *leky´e* 'piebald horse, spotted, speckled', taken in turn from French *le caille* 'piebald horse').

/**likʷó·k** rooster (*see* Chinook Jargon *le-cock´* 'rooster', taken in turn from French *le coq* 'rooster').

/**limitú** sheep (*see* Chinook Jargon *lamuto*, *le-mo-to* 'sheep', taken in turn from French *le mouton* 'sheep').

lʋ·´niya TAb-mi Rainier, Oregon (*see* English *Rainier*).

/**liplét** priest (*see* Chinook Jargon *le-plét* 'priest', taken in turn from French *le prêtre* 'priest').

/**lipuá** peas (*see* Chinook Jargon *le-pwau´*, *lepoah* 'peas', taken in turn from French *les pois* 'peas').

/**lipúm** apple (*see* Chinook Jargon *lapóme* 'apple', taken in turn from French *le pomme* 'apple').

/**lisák** sack, bag, pocket (*see* Chinook Jargon *le-sák* 'sack, bag', taken in turn from French *le sac* 'sack, bag').

/**lišál** shawl (*see* Chinook Jargon *leshawl* 'shawl', taken in turn from French *le chale* 'shawl').

/máʔksns moccasin (*see* English *moccasins*).

/máli Virgin Mary (*see* English *Mary*).

/malyí marry (*see* Chinook Jargon *mal-i-éh* 'marry', taken in turn from French *marier* 'marry').

/məšín car, automobile, machine (*see* English *machine*).

/mətá·s leggings, Indian stockings (*see* Chinook Jargon *mit-áss* 'leggings', taken in turn from Ojibwa *mita·ss* 'leggings').

/mín– be mean (*see* English *mean*).

/ninəmú LNJ, /niminú turnip (*see* Chinook Jargon *lenawo* 'turnips', taken in turn from Acadian French *le navot* 'turnip').

/pástn– White man (*see* Chinook Jargon *boston*, *pos-ton* 'white man, American', taken in turn from English *Boston*).

patu´ʔ TAb-mi Mt. Adams (Sahaptin name, *pátu* 'snowcap peak').

pai´cîp FBa steamboat (*see* Chinook Jargon *piah-ship* 'steamer', taken in turn from English *fire* and *ship*).

/pípa paper (*see* Chinook Jargon *peh´-pa* 'paper, letter, writing, book', taken in turn from English *paper*).

/píšpiš cat (*see* Chinook Jargon *pish-pish* 'cat').

/pləms– plum (*see* English *plums*).

/pyəx̣í, /pyax̣í bitterroots (*see* Sahaptin *pyax̣í* 'bitterroot').

/qašqáš strawberry roan (*see* Sahaptin *qa·šqá·š* 'strawberry roan').

ki´pixLE⁺ FBa hair seal, fur seal, or harbor seal (loanword; *see* Chinook *-gé·pixL* 'sea lion').

/sálti salty (*see* English *salty*).

/sámn, /sémn fish (*see* English *salmon*).

/sánti Sunday, week (*see* Chinook Jargon *sun´-day* 'Sunday, week, flag', taken in turn from English *Sunday*).

/saplə́l bread (*see* Chinook Jargon *sap´-o-lill* 'wheat, flour, bread'; further derivation is unclear).

/sása saucer (*see* English *saucer*).

sánux̣ JHjp silverside, silver salmon (prob. sə́nxʷ; *see* Sahaptin *sɨnx̣ʷ*, *sínux̣* 'coho or silver salmon'.

/síl cloth (*see* Chinook Jargon *sail* 'cloth, cotton', taken in turn from English *sail*).

/**sil/háws** tent (*see* Chinook Jargon *selhaus* tent, taken in turn from English *sail* plus *house*).

/**skáw** ferryboat (*see* English *scow*).

sku´lhau´s FBa schoolhouse (prob. /sk^{w}ulháws; *see* English *schoolhouse*).

/**spalyán** Spaniard; cayuse (horse) (*see* Spanish *español* 'Spanish').

/**spún** spoon (*see* Chinook Jargon *spoon* 'spoon', taken in turn from English *spoon*).

/**stákn** stockings (*see* Chinook Jargon *stock-en´* 'stocking', taken in turn from English *stocking*).

/**súlt–** salt (*see* Chinook Jargon *salt*, *solt* 'salt', taken in turn from English *salt*).

/**šíp–** (*see* English *sheep*).

/**šúk^{w}a–** (sū´ga FBa) sugar (*see* Chinook Jargon *shu´-kwa* 'sugar, honey', taken in turn from English *sugar*).

/**šúšukli** God, angel, heaven (*see* Chinook Jargon *Sesu Kli* 'Jesus Christ', taken in turn from French *Jésus Christ* 'Jesus Christ').

/**tála** money (*see* Chinook Jargon *táh-la* 'money, dollar', taken in turn from English *dollar*).

/**táytnapam** Taitnapam, Upper Cowlitz (*a Sahaptin name*).

/**tíntin–** music, ring (*see* Chinook Jargon *tin´-tin* 'bell, music'; imitative).

/**wáč** clock, watch (*see* English *watch*).

/**wá·či–** watch (possibly a loanword; *see* English *to watch*).

/**wáylšip** mountain goat (*see* English *wild sheep*).

/**wəmúsmuski,** /**wəmúsəski** cow (*see* Chinook Jargon *moos´-moos* 'cow, cattle'; source unclear).

/**x^{w}ít** wheat (*see* English *wheat*).

/**x̣áwqa⁴** can't (*see* Chinook Jargon *how´-kwutl* 'cannot, stubborn', taken in turn from Lower Chinook *xáoxaʟ* 'cannot').

/**x̣áwš** cous, biscuitroot (*see* Sahaptin *x̣áwš* 'cous, biscuitroot').

/**yá·n** yarn (*see* English *yarn*).